GW01276056

THE MEMORY OF BONES

*Joe R. and Teresa Lozano Long Series in
Latin American and Latino Art and Culture*

UNIVERSITY OF TEXAS PRESS, AUSTIN

THE MEMORY OF BONES

Body, Being, and Experience among the Classic Maya

STEPHEN HOUSTON ◆▶ DAVID STUART ◆▶ KARL TAUBE

Copyright © 2006 by the University of Texas Press
All rights reserved
Printed in the United States of America
First edition, 2006

Requests for permission to reproduce material from this work should be sent to:
Permissions
University of Texas Press
P.O. Box 7819
Austin, TX 78713-7819
www.utexas.edu/utpress/about/bpermission.html

♾ The paper used in this book meets the minimum requirements
of ANSI/NISO Z39.48-1992 (R1997) (Permanence of Paper).

LIBRARY OF CONGRESS CATALOGING-IN-PUBLICATION DATA

Houston, Stephen D.
  The memory of bones : body, being, and experience among the classic Maya / Stephen Houston, David Stuart, and Karl Taube. — 1st ed.
      p.   cm.
  Includes bibliographical references and index.
  ISBN 13: 978-0-292-71294-2 (hardcover : alk. paper)
  ISBN 10: 0-292-71294-4
  1. Maya art. 2. Maya sculpture. 3. Inscriptions, Mayan. 4. Maya philosophy.
5. Body, Human—Social aspects. 6. Body, Human—Symbolic aspects. 7. Human figure in art. 8. Figure sculpture. I. Stuart, David, 1965– II. Taube, Karl A. III. Title.
    F1435.3.A7H68   2006
    972'.01—dc22
                                                              2005025942

For our mothers, Maj-Britt, Gene, and Mary

Contents

Preamble **1**

CHAPTER ONE The Classic Maya Body **11**

CHAPTER TWO Bodies and Portraits **57**

CHAPTER THREE Ingestion **102**

CHAPTER FOUR Senses **134**

CHAPTER FIVE Emotions **180**

CHAPTER SIX Dishonor **202**

CHAPTER SEVEN Words on Wings **227**

CHAPTER EIGHT Dance, Music, Masking **252**

EPILOGUE Body, Being, and Experience among the Classic Maya **277**

Bibliography **281**

Index **315**

THE MEMORY OF BONES

Preamble

El ojo piensa,	The eye thinks,
el pensamiento ve,	the thought sees,
la mirada toca,	the gaze touches,
las palabras arden . . .	the words burn . . .

Octavio Paz dedicated this verse to the photographer Manuel Álvarez Bravo (Paz 1991:393). A poet thus found power in words to praise the captor of raw, vital images. For many years we have been fascinated, as archaeologists, by whether the dead can truly speak to us, the dead who fathered and mothered people far distant from our own roots in Europe and North America. Can the eye that scans images and texts today find past thought; can it see and touch as others did; is there still within reach the ardor, joy, and despair of departed life? Hence the subtitle of this volume: "Body, Being, and Experience among the Classic Maya." The main title, too, comes in part from Paz, who spoke of his own bones as the repository of memory and inextinguishable desire. More than most poets, he discovered the words to express loss and eternal return.

The Classic Maya, who lived within distinct societies conjoined by many beliefs and practices, left many tracks, many bones. Through those vestiges, they can return, or so we assert. From about AD 250 to 850, the Classic Maya of southeastern Mexico and northern Central America created many thousands of glyphic texts and rich, codified images that, with careful study, reveal unsuspected clues to body concepts and to the nature of what the Maya regarded as life and experience. For some scholars, approaching such matters is laden with methodological obstacles. Here are the problems. (1) *Using evidence from historic or ethnographic Maya:* These people utterly differ from those of the Classic period. They are too altered by change to reveal patterns of centuries before. (2) *Using what Classic elites say:* Such statements, whether in text or imagery, are mere (mis)representations and self-serving bombast, disconnected from everyday life and even from what the elites themselves believed. (3) *Using information, past and present, from other parts of Mexico and northern Central America:* Context disappears and, through such evidence, tangible differences blur in favor of consistent similarity. This creates artificial designs that exist only in the minds of interpreters. (4) *Using comparative anthropology:* Humans are made radically different and incommensurable by culture and history. (5) *Using data from one Maya site to explain another:* All sites possess divergent local meanings attached to text and imagery. There should not be an assumption that icons at different sites refer to the same things. (6) *Using glyphs and imagery at all:* Recent research rests on weak foundations. There are no standards of proof or disproof, no real means of testing proposals.

All of these claims are both true and false. Comparisons *do* require considerable thought and marshaling of evidence; arguments need to be carefully assembled; comparisons between sites need to establish clearly that they draw on the same concepts, something to be discerned from consistent patterns of use; ideas and ways of framing and showing them modulate historically; the systematic images and texts left to us (many more remain to be found) exist as culturally encoded representations, not direct pathways into the brain. An elusive scent, sweet and intense, or the spasm of desolate fear—these have disappeared forever, as scattered feelings and sprays of pheromones. We cannot savor a Maya version of Marcel Proust's madeleine. But, at the same time, the claims are false, systemically so. A priori statements about what can and cannot be done deserve considerable suspicion, based on past experience in scholarship. At core, a claim is eternally ad hoc. It is only as valid as its intrinsic worth. Does it gather enough evidence; is that evidence consistent; are counterclaims, if they exist, successfully refuted; do successive arguments integrate past results in mutually confirming ways?

A final problem, indulging in "grand narratives" that attribute mentalities or attitudes to certain periods and not to others, has been noted in historical scholarship, particularly by those who criticize the tendency to see "the Middle Ages . . . as a convenient foil for modernity" (Rosenwein 2002:828). One such narrative would be the growing restriction and control of emotions in the history of the West: from the Middle Ages, a time of childlike and public, even fierce emotion, arose a later emotional regime of "self-discipline, control, and suppression" (Rosenwein 2002:827), an idea that came to the fore in the work of the historical sociologists Lucien Febvre and Norbert Elias (Burguière 1982:435). As academic reconstructions, grand narratives or claims for widespread meaning can seem schematic or glib. The same can be said more broadly for any attempt to understand the history of *mentalités,* an enterprise that focuses on joint representations and the assertion of consistent, underlying logic (Burguière 1982:436; cf. Kobialka 2003:2, 6, 38). Yet these formulations are not always wrong either. Conventional attitudes clearly exist in most parts of the world, and at different times, in varying configurations. Our book builds on the conviction that conventionalized representations expressed conventionalized ideas among the Classic Maya.

Focusing on the body is necessary. In the first place, it is part of a cross-disciplinary dialogue of exhilarating scope and, at times, insight (Abbott 1999; Barasch 2001; Braziel and LeBesco 2001; Classen 1993b; Counihan 1999; Falk 1994; Friedman 2001; Shilling 1993; Yalom 1997). The topic is also, to us, a central means of organizing hitherto unintegrated evidence about the Classic Maya, and the very theme that makes Maya imagery of the time so innately appealing: it corresponds to our own rooting in Greco-Roman naturalism and the bodily preoccupations of that tradition (Khristaan Villela, personal communication, 2003). Finally, the body is unavoidable. Without bodies, there would be no Classic Maya, no *us* to interpret these ancient peoples. The body is for that very reason a shared legacy, inherited from long before Beringia. It allows a fundamental reach toward empathy and an entrée into past experience.

Our approach is inspired by Alfredo López Austin's *Cuerpo humano e ideología: Las concepciones de los antiguos nahuas* (1980), a pioneering study of Nahuatl body concepts, now also in English (1988). This work, so good that it arouses both admiration and envy, provides insights almost too numerous to mention, including ideas about the intersection of body and cosmos, being, spirit, and vitality. Another inspiration is Jill Furst's *Natural History of the Soul in Ancient Mexico* (1995). Furst's book, which follows Edward Tylor's view that religions arise to explain natural phenomena (Houston 1997), fits comfortably within other "naturalist" models of human religious sentiment (Boyer 2001; Guthrie 1995) and dazzles the reader with audacious and lively exposition. A volume by Constance Classen (1993a) that explores the relation between Inka body concepts and cosmos was equally stimulating, if not exactly the model followed here.

The content, network, and texture of body concepts among the Classic Maya form the subject of this book. We believe such ideas can be studied according to the "realist" program of research: that is, there can be progress as determined by data, there is inherent, recoverable structure in the world, and, once achieved, findings prove relatively stable (Hacking 1999:33, 68–92). Take, for instance, our use of later lexical sources, often at the beginning of each chapter. The historical connections between Mayan languages explain in large measure why there is coherence between glosses. The greater the consistency, the better the chance that meanings go back in time, to the Classic Maya and before. The finding that the majority of inscriptions record some version of the Ch'olti'an branch (Houston et al. 2000) of Mayan languages makes this task easier by suggesting a scale of reliability that radiates outward. If a gloss occurs in Ch'olti' or Ch'orti', the more likely it is to be relevant and to carry the same meaning back to the Classic period. And, despite their semantic treasures and sheer abundance, the sources in Yukatek Mayan must be seen to lie farther away in relevance, as do those from highland languages, which are often widely divergent from what is seen in lowland hieroglyphs. (Highland hieroglyphs number in the handful and are of uncertain linguistic affiliation.) Conversely, an isolated gloss without clear cognates constitutes weak evidence. There is also a hierarchy of proof. Independent lines of information that converge to shared shadings of meaning indicate that an argument is sound. Information coming only from general, comparative sources (i.e., "what humans are like") defer to multiple Mesoamerican sources, and Mesoamerican sources to Maya ones. There is no foolproof method, only reasoned argument and serendipitous insight. Moreover, the notion that Classic data must take primacy is one we endorse, for that time and its remains continue to be our destination. We think it mistaken, however, to suggest that later evidence must be ignored at some early stage of interpretation or that Colonial information can only be adduced at the end of an argument because "a historicized reading . . . [must proceed] from the earlier state to the later" (R. Joyce 2000b:281). That is not how most of us come to know the Maya through the key portals of, say, Bishop Diego de Landa's *Relación*. Those later clusters of meaning, often more clearly stated than clues from the Classic, allow us to frame hypotheses and hone particular lines of reasoning, which can then be evaluated against the earlier sources at no jeopardy to strength of argument.

Broader intellectual models for our book are not hard to find. One could argue that the only valid approach to ancient experience is replication. How is one to understand the flintknapper without taking hammerstone to nodule? Or, as in Maya heart extraction, without using flint or obsidian on cadavers (Robicsek and Hales 1984)? For us, Maya cities are, from an olfactory perspective, best imagined by walking through a market in Tabasco, Mexico, on a hot day, the reek and rotting interspersed with smoke, shouts, clucks, food smells, music, song, and squeals: Maya cities were cooked by the same sun and swept clean by comparable sheets of rain. The frequent display in Classic art of nobles sniffing flowers may have been part of a new olfactory regime during the Late Classic period (ca. AD 600–850), perhaps in response to heightened smells in increasingly congested settlements (see Corbin 1986:72–77, for the shift from musk to vegetal perfumes in *ancien-régime* France). Acoustical properties of Maya buildings, and attempting to understand them as elaborate sounding boards, are not yet on our collective research agenda, although they should be (see A. Watson and Keating 1999). Isolated, unpublished studies of Pre-Columbian instruments in Guatemala have simulated the complex, concurrent tonalities of Maya flutes, whistles, and other sound-making devices. It is likely that some of those instruments, such as a peculiar device for reproducing jaguar calls (Schele and Mathews 1998:pl. 11), have now disappeared or nearly so, much as the bagpipe, once common throughout Europe, now exists only on the Celtic margins of Scotland, Ireland, and Galicia.

Also of great value are comparative studies of the body in a variety of cultural settings, including an insightful but relatively brief work, published after this manuscript was prepared, by Lynn Meskell and Rosemary Joyce (2003; see also a recent doctoral thesis by Pamela Geller [2004]). The benefit of such analyses is that they stimulate thoughts from unexpected directions. This volume strives for an aesthetic and analytical balance between theory and information. The relevant literature on body theory belongs to two categories: one that approaches the body in general and another that studies kingly bodies, of the sort commonly depicted by the Classic Maya.

BODY THEORY

For the purposes of this discussion, the human body has four principal properties. Most importantly, it is an organism. It also thinks and acts (Scheper-Hughes and Lock 1987:7), defines itself through social existence and interaction, and displays attributes that inform the way we comprehend other matters. The body performs a pivotal role in human existence precisely because of these properties, which merge physicality and concept, image and action. The body is the right place to look at the connection between naturalism, which stresses physical features, and constructionism, which looks at self-concepts and collective ones (M. Weiss 2002:11). Such properties help us understand *all* bodies, whether royal or nonroyal. They deserve separate treatment.

The first two properties are, respectively, phenomenological, having to do with the experience of life, and interactional, concerning the body in society. The body literally makes action and thought possible through physical motion and the firing of synapses. Scholars may refer to disembodied, generalized entities like "society," "culture," or "state," sometimes imputing intention and agency to them. But it is the body, and the body alone, that truly hosts intellect and enables humans to act. More deeply still, the body combines sensation, cognition, meaning, and identity. Jacques Lacan would have us believe that this combination occurs when the body and its mind assemble a self-image from countless tactile and kinesthetic experiences. By looking at other beings, by internalizing a "specular image" of other people, the body distills such encounters into a conception of itself as a complete entity, a body with boundaries and a minimal set of features (Grosz 1995:86; Lacan 1977:19). In this, Lacan follows far clearer writers, such as George Herbert Mead, who believed "[we] must be others if we are to be ourselves . . . [so that a]ny self is a social self[, although] it is restricted to the group whose roles it assumes" (1964:292; see also Cooley 1964 and his concept of the "looking-glass self"). As a concept and as a physical thing, the body can only be understood in relation to other bodies, a point particularly relevant to royalty. At the same time, the body is always confronted with the problem of being different, since it manifestly fails to conform fully to collectively held ideal shapes and behaviors (Falk 1994:137).

Still, assertions about "complete beings" deserve some caution, since they presuppose a gestalt model of human identity. Recent studies suggest strongly that, within a person, there can cohabit multiple "narrative selves" that "constitute the subject of the person's experience at some point in time" (Lock 1993:146; see also Young 1990). Leaving to the side the problem of how such selves articulate with one another—can it only be because of a shared body?—there are parallels in Pre-Columbian data. In the formal rhetoric of Maya inscriptions, distinct "narrative selves," usually linked to mythic identities and their tropes, can be attached to the person of Maya lords through dance (inspiriting action) and ritual impersonation (inspiriting ornament; Houston and D. Stuart 1996:306).

Along with body images come notions of space and time, either with respect to individuals—the "egocentric" frame of reference that situates the individual as a participant—or to an "absolute" view that involves the mind as a kind of "disengaged theorist" viewing space and time comprehensively, without individual vantage point (J. Campbell 1994:5–6; a close parallel is that of the body as feeling subject and object to be seen and manipulated [Falk 1994:2; Merleau-Ponty 1964]). Egocentric space exists in relation to parts of the body, right, left, up, down. The body as an active force resides in the center. In contrast, absolute space corresponds to coordinates that have no central point. So, too, with time. A body moving through time senses the potential of the future and retains memory of the past. Yet, according to one phenomenological interpretation, it can be said to exist only in its present phase of existence, shuttling from experience to experience (Luckmann 1991:154). The body is never static; it is always in the process of becoming and doing (Shilling 1993); indeed, this is the very problem of going from static images, as are scrutinized in this book, to any authentic sense of passing experience and the body as it develops continuously through time. That same body, however, also exists within absolute time, time without end, time that does not depend on individual experience. Patently, space and time are causally connected. A self-conscious human relies on them to act or perform as an agent, since the full use of instruments to achieve desired ends requires spatial sense as well as temporal calculation (J. Campbell 1994:38–41). The example of the royal body accentuates egocentric and absolute perspectives. A prime mover of social action and a privileged receptor of perception, the royal body also serves conceptually as a central axis of cosmic order.

Another element of embodiment is that shared images of the body permit our very existence as social beings. Through the medium of the body, philosophical subjects (our conscious selves) relate to objects (all that is external to those selves), an existential task of the body emphasized by both Lacan and Mead. A result of this interaction is that the body learns that it is not alone, that it coexists, not with projected phantasms of the mind, but with fellow subjects that are equally capable of thought and activity. The result is a capacity to live in human society (Holbrook 1988:121–122). The body image permits us to confide in "a stable external world and a coherent sense of self-identity" (Giddens 1991:51) and to synchronize our experiences and actions with those of other bodies (Luckmann 1991:156).

The body is central in another way, too. It possesses attributes that form a natural, forceful, and readily structured model for categorizing other aspects of the world. As such, the body, its symmetries, and its asymmetries are, in Robert Hertz's words, "the essential articles of our intellectual equipment" (Hertz 1973:21; see also Coren 1993). Indeed, the body as experiential filter unavoidably imprints its properties on the world around it. At once physical entity and cognized image, the body endlessly generates metaphors for ordering thoughts and actions about everything from society to morality, buildings to geography, often linking body space with cosmic and social space (Bourdieu 1990:77; Eliade 1959:168, 172–173; Flynn 1998:46; Lock 1993:135). To some, it is doubtful that the body can truly exist in a "natural" or preconceptual state. After all, it is the mind that necessarily organizes perception of the body (Lock 1993:136). Mark Johnson would put this differently. The meanings of the body arise from the experience of physical acts; abstract concepts (such as institutions or morality) acquire meaning by being likened to recurrent physical actions or entities (Johnson 1987:98). This metaphorical structuring allows us to comprehend experience. Nonetheless, the use of terms like *metaphor* may be misleading. Conceptually, things presumed to be similar may share essences: that is, they do not so much resemble, as form part of, each other (Scheper-Hughes and Lock 1987:20–21). Such beliefs closely recall doctrines of monism that acknowledge only one principle or being and that discount Cartesian dualisms between mind and matter.

The body is also a vehicle for meaningful gesture, movement, and ornament. Marcel Mauss noted that "the body is the first and most natural instrument of humanity" (1950:372). What interested Mauss were not so much internal images as the "techniques of the body," how the body was manipulated according to age, sex, prestige, and form of activity. In Mauss's personal experience, these "techniques" varied by society and changed dramatically through time. The body has a "history"; it is not so much "a constant amidst flux but . . . an epitome of that flux" (Csordas 1994:2; see also Dreyfus and Rabinow 1982:128–129). Body practices, which Mauss included within his notion of "habitus," were acquired socially as repetitious acts, often learned from childhood, and under the authority of prestigious individuals whose example others tended to follow (Mauss 1950:368–369). Through habitus, the body became a workable paradox, functioning as "tool, agent, and object" (Csordas 1994:5). Michel Foucault developed similar ideas, albeit within a history of Western prisons, by showing how bodies undergo "surveillance" from more powerful bodies that, in Foucault's words, "invest it, train it, torture it, force it to carry out tasks, to perform ceremonies, to emit signs" (1995:25; see also Bourdieu 1990:54–56; Gell 1993:3–4). Foucault's views, however, have a tendency to reduce all interaction to an elastic concept of "power" that seems largely blind to gender (Meskell 1996:8–9). They also treat humans like weirdly passive automata or fleshy but inert pawns on a chess board.

Mauss focused on movement and interactions with objects, but one can scarcely avoid another "technique of the body": its ornamentation, whether by dress, paint, tattooing, or physical deformation. Such surface modifications are focal because they involve the "social skin," the "frontier of the social self" that serves as a "symbolic stage upon which the drama of socialization is enacted" (T. Turner 1980:112). Some of these modifications or body disciplines are more or less permanent or accretional, others are fleeting and discontinuous, yet all advertise something that a particular body wishes to communicate (R. Joyce 1998:157, 159). The social skin inverts Hertz's metaphoric extensions by both projecting and receiving signs from other semantic domains; bodily metaphors help structure the world, and the world semantically structures the body. This complex interplay of meanings results in widespread notions of multiple bodies (Csordas 1994:5), including social and physical bodies (Douglas 1973:93–112); bodies that experience, that regulate or represent symbols (Scheper-Hughes and Lock 1987:18–23); and medical and consumer bodies (O'Neill 1985: 91–147), each connected to its own realm of thought and behavior but linked physically and compellingly in the flesh. As much signboard as mirror, the social skin can equally express inner qualities and conditions (Gell 1993:3–31; Strathern 1979). Its symbolic density makes it central to understanding meanings that converge on the body.

ROYAL BODIES

If the body records core concepts of societies, it must also generate social difference and hierarchy, whether of the sexes or of unequals within society (Laqueur 1990:11). The problem of the royal body assumes primary importance here. What symbolic domains intersect uniquely in the royal body? What is its relation to time, space, and action? How do people establish and mark its singularity? How, in short, are transcendent beings created out of human flesh, and "stranger kings" devised out of kin (Feeley-Harnik 1985:281)? Along with James Frazer (1959), whose work on divine kings remains topical if controversial, Ernst Kantorowicz (1957) showed the way in a study that has influenced historical disciplines as diverse as Egyptology and Classical studies (L. Bell 1985; Dupont 1989).

According to Kantorowicz, in late Medieval kingship the royal body conflated the physical presence with corporate symbols. Although it might wither and die, the body attained immortality and ceaseless vitality when conceived as the corporeal representation of high office (Kantorowicz 1957:23, 506). Such concepts—which in Europe descended principally, but not solely, from Pauline concepts of the body of Christ—come to the fore in rituals and regalia of accession and burial. At accession, these rituals merged and then, at burial, disentangled distinct meanings of the body, thus sustaining the seamless dignity of office in the face of physical corruption and the disturbance of office entailed in royal succession; images or immediate inheritance ensured that seamless quality (Flynn 1998:17; but see Elizabeth Brown [1981:266], who questions the supposed unimportance to kingship of the interred corpse). The royal spouse shared in this ritual processing, but incompletely. Royal couples are necessary for propagation yet symbolically violate the integrity of the monad that should, ideally, encompass only the ruler. The Egyptian and Andean cases bring two royal bodies together by the expedient of incest, which concentrates wealth and regal essence. Incest provides another mark of distinction. It differentiates royal practice from that of other people and establishes parallels with the behavior of gods (Gillespie 1989:52–55).

Of key importance in Medieval mortuary effigies and Roman antecedents were images (imagoes) that housed—indeed constituted—the body incorruptible, to be fed and paid court to as the successor prepared himself for ritual "estrangement" from other mortals (Dupont 1989: 407–409; Flynn 1998:16–17). Among the Romans, the rights to such images (*ius imaginum*) correlated tightly with claims to nobility (Dupont 1989:410). As we shall see in Chapter 2, such images abounded in Classic Maya art as well, and they accorded with pan-Mesoamerican beliefs in the extension of an individual's essence to other images or objects—for example, the royal "skin" could also wrap over stelae and altars, multiplying its presence (Chapter 2; López Austin 1997:42). Body and alter image used clothing and ornament to create a social skin that marked them uniquely. As immortal bodies, they neutralized time by appearing forever fresh and regal, in flagrant disregard of decay. And as bodies of centrality, they could, as in Southeast Asian models of kingship, exist at a pivotal place from which a gradient descends to other beings. They then "giv[e] way at the periphery to realms of equal but opposite kinds of power" that exhibit disorder and decentered excess (Feeley-Harnik 1985:25).

For this reason, spaces distant from the ruler's body tend to be morally ambiguous and dangerous. The ruler's space is egocentric, focused on his body and its perception, and absolute, in that royal space cannot inherently assign equivalence to other bodies in the regions it occupies. In kingly models that center the ruler cosmically, the royal body can be imagined in two ways: as a central, static point around which the world revolves; and as a restless, heroic, and primary force of agency from which other human activities ripple (Tambiah 1976: 112–113, 118–119). Better than anything else, these properties exemplify the body as a paradoxical mixture of tool, agent, and subject.

Conceptually, bodily practices of the ruler take place in "monumental time," which is "reductive and generic" and "reduces social experience to collective predictability" (Herzfeld 1991:10; see also R. Joyce 1998:159). This is simply a fancy way of saying that activities are formulaic and repeated from earlier ones—or so traditions allege. Nonetheless, these practices often originate in common acts, appropriating the form and logic of everyday activities, such as bathing, eating, or planting; these are then modified to the extent that they attain a different order of meaning among rulers (Bloch 1985:272). From the pull of the familiar and its transformation into actions of striking dissimilarity come the emotional force of these rituals for all who witness them. They generalize and exalt the mundane within an idiom shared by the ruler and the ruled, presenting "complements and counterfoils to commoner traditions" (Blier 1995:346).

Perhaps the most telling example is the royal feast, which historians and anthropologists typically see largely in terms of payment and reciprocity or studied ostentation (e.g., Murray 1996:19; see also Chapter 3). Feasts can certainly be seen in such ways, but the superabundance of food offered to rulers at Hellenistic, Aztec, and Bourbon courts captures more of the prodigious appetites expected of the royal body, which summons foodstuffs that no mortal could consume at one sitting. The royal body could also crave, and pretend to satisfy, other pleasures in superhuman quantity, as suggested by the 450 women in the Ottoman harem just after the fall of Constantinople (Necipoglu 1991:160). These patterns remind us that royal bodies function in a supercharged symbolic realm, culturally and locally idiosyncratic but essential to understanding the ruler in time and space.

A BOOK'S BACKBONE

The foregoing suggests that our main goal in writing this book is to contribute a few lines toward a general and rather abstract theory of the body. That is not the case. The question for us is always (and it is a suitable view in this age of historical contextualism), how does theory illuminate what we see in evidence? Is theory—a prestigious niche within present-day hierarchies of knowledge—truly doing its work? Readers will judge for themselves. As Gail Weiss points out, there may be conventional images or notions of "the body," but every body is, of course, unique, with multiple self-images (1999:1–2). Simply put, the body as concept and object is an untidy thing, but the Classic Maya looked at it in a highly stylized, formulaic fashion. Even the much-touted attention to detail in Dutch painting of the seventeenth century is now understood to pass through similar, distorting filters (de Vries 1991:221). Our assumption is that those images from the Classic period channel ideas about what should be or what is being seen. They are as composed and carefully selected as the artful photographs of Manuel Álvarez Bravo. At the same time, the abundant imagery of the Classic Maya did not only reflect or stereotype. It provided ample models for how people should behave. In part, such models must have been followed. Even the scrutiny of images would recall and mold memories of earlier events.

The following chapters are the vertebrae of this book. They appear in an order that seems logical to us, yet rely on each other for support. Chapter 1 outlines a cartography of the Maya body, its parts and meanings as understood from imagery and texts. Chapter 2 addresses the key question of the Maya body and its replication in "portraiture." The next three chapters, "Ingestion" (Chapter 3), "Senses" (Chapter 4), and "Emotions" (Chapter 5), consider Classic Maya representations of experience. Parts of these chapters will find an empathetic response in readers; others will repel and mystify. Chapter 6 looks at a key component of Maya being and experience: that related to war captives and other sacrificial victims. The meanings of pain and sexuality find a place here. The final chapters, on oracular words and masking (Chapters 7 and 8, respectively), look at embodied words, often heaven sent, and the blurring of bodies by spirit possession. If the ruler can replicate his body through "portraiture," then he (and nobles) can also condense multiple identities into one physical frame. A final section, an epilogue or a closing exhalation as it were, summarizes key points, leaving openings, however, for work to come. The more we toil on this project, the clearer it becomes that Maya body concepts are barely probed.

Authorship: much of the prose was written by Houston during his sabbatical year, with emendations and suggestions by Stuart and Taube. Ideas come from all three authors. We believe our skills at epigraphy and iconography work nicely in unison. Parts of the book have appeared, often shaped differently, in a number of places and conferences or symposia: Preamble (Houston and Cummins 1998); Chapter 2, "Bodies and Portraits" (Houston and D. Stuart 1998; D. Stuart 1996); Chapter 3, "Ingestion" (Houston 2001b); Chapter 4, "Senses" (Houston and Taube 2000); Chapter 5, "Emotions" (Houston 2001a); Chapter 7, "Words on Wings" (Houston 2001c); and Chapter 8, "Dance, Music, Masking" (Houston 2002b). All those published before (Chapters 2, 4, and 5) are used with permission here, with gratitude to the editors and presses. Dr. Francesco Pellizzi and his journal, *RES: Anthropology and Aesthetics*, along with the Peabody Museum Press, Donna Dickerson, manager, permitted publication of a heavily reworked version of Chapter 2. Dr. Chris Scarre of the *Cambridge Archaeological Journal* did the same for Chapter 4. Prof. Tom Cummins saw no objection to our use of some parts of his joint paper with Houston (the lifted prose was Houston's, however). Dr. Peter Rowley-Conwy, editor of *World Archaeology*, the publisher, Routledge, and its permissions administrator, Sarah Wilkins, granted permission to include Chapter 5, which first appeared in different form within the pages of that journal (see also its Web site, at www.tandf.co.uk). For comments on those pieces, and for much other kindness, encouragement, and advice during the preparation of this manuscript, we thank the following friends and colleagues: Elizabeth Boone, Una Canger, Mark Child, José Miguel García Campillo, Arlen and Diane Chase, Andrés Ciudad Ruiz, John Clark, Michael Coe, Connie and Charlie Dayton, Michael ("Mickey") Dietler, Héctor Escobedo, Susan Evans, Gelya Frank, Elizabeth ("Liz") Graham, Ian Graham, John Hawkins, Ingrid Herbich, Josefa ("Pepa") Iglesias Ponce de León, Spence and Kristin Kirk, Cecelia Klein, Alfonso Lacadena, Richard Leventhal, Nancy Owen Lewis, Alan Maca, Patricia McAnany, Lynn Meskell, Mary Miller, Jesper Nielsen, Johan Normark, Joanne Pillsbury, Shannon Plank, Jeffrey Quilter, John Robertson, Marshall Sahlins, Robert ("Bob") Sharer, David Webster, Kathy Whittaker, Ken and Athelia Woolley, and Norm Yoffee. Stouthearted Allen Christenson, Simon Martin, and Khristaan Villela read drafts of chapters with much wisdom and greatly to our benefit. Their deep knowledge improved all that they read, as did comments from Patricia McAnany and another, anonymous reviewer for the University of Texas Press. At the Press, Theresa May was, as ever, a pillar of support, along with her very capable staff, including Alison Faust and Leslie Doyle Tingle. Cassandra Mesick, loyal and helpful graduate student at Brown University, gave great help in the final preparation of the manuscript, a task supported by Houston's professorial funds. Oswaldo Chinchilla permitted the use of his fine drawings of monuments from the piedmont of Guatemala; other drawings and photographs are used here with the permission of: Mark Child of Yale University; Mary Miller and Michael Coe, also of Yale; Ian Graham and, separately, Marc Zender of the Peabody Museum at Harvard; Arlen and Diane Chase of the University of Central Florida; Justin and Barbara Kerr of Kerr Associates; Sharon Misdea of the University of Pennsylvania Museum; William Saturno and Heather Hurst of the San Bartolo Project and, respectively, the University of New Hampshire and Yale University; and Tara Zapp of George Braziller, Inc. John Robertson (n.d.) supplied us with a version of his exhaustive scanned database of Mayan dictionaries, including many gems from the Gates Collection at Brigham Young University. Without it, our job would have been much harder.

Those with more technical interests in Mayan languages should note that we have preserved, where possible, the original spellings from various Colonial dictionaries, a practice that respects those sources. In general, we have avoided the use of /b'/ for the glottalized bilabial, preferring /b/ in all cases: John Robertson convinces us that the /'/, an inevitable component of /b/, does not need an extra, noncontrastive diacritic. We have also simplified the customary epigraphic practice of using eye-popping boldface to distinguish glyphs from the transcription of the word(s) they spell. It seems easier on the reader to use square brackets [*] for the first and paired forward slashes /*/ for the second. Additionally, full caps denote a logograph, or word sign, and lowercase is used for a syllable. An asterisk represents a reconstructed form or "Fill in word here," and hyphens are used as dividers between glyphs, whether word signs or syllables. In some instances following a Mayan term, we have added in parentheses a phonologically more accurate or correct version of a spelling from a Colonial dictionary, as in *keuel* (*k'ewel*).

Justin Kerr's extraordinary collection of rollout photographs from Maya ceramics, cited throughout this book by their "K" or "Kerr" number (e.g., K4682), has, without overstatement, revolutionized the study of the Classic Maya. To Justin and Barbara, his wife, our warm thanks for their many acts of liberality in the use and presentation of these images. Readers may consult the Kerr archive readily by going to www.famsi.org on the Web.

Institutional support came, as always, from the generous coffers of Brigham Young University, with particular help from Vice Presidents Alan Wilkins, Gary Hooper, and Noel Reynolds and Deans Clayne Pope and David Magleby. A grant from the National Endowment for the Humanities (NEH Grant RO-22648-93) supported earlier research by Houston and Stuart. During the 2002–2003 academic year, Houston received a leave from Brigham Young University and supported himself with fellowships kindly bestowed by and gratefully received from the John Simon

Guggenheim Memorial Foundation and the School of American Research, National Endowment for the Humanities Fellowship. The School and its staff, particularly Richard Leventhal, Nancy Owen Lewis, and Leslie Shipman, helped greatly in expediting the work. Finds from Piedras Negras, Guatemala, were recovered courtesy of a permit from Guatemala's Institute of Anthropology and History, and because of generous benefactions from the Foundation for the Advancement of Mesoamerican Studies, Inc., Mr. Lewis Ranieri, President; the National Geographic Society; the National Science Foundation; the Ahau Foundation, Dr. Peter Harrison, President; and our mainstay, Brigham Young University. Houston's departmental chairs, John Hawkins and Joel Janetski, and, at Brown, David Kertzer and Phil Leis, were always there to help, as was Stuart's, William Fash, and Taube's, Tom Patterson. The Bartlett Curatorship at the Peabody Museum, Harvard, assisted Stuart in his research. Our spouses, Nancy, Bridget, and Rhonda, put up with us and kept us sane. Our children, Anders and Hannah (Houston) and Peter and Richard (Stuart), did the same, reminding us that academic work is far, far less interesting than a good DVD or video game.

But how could we write a book without the mothers who gave us minds, bodies, and, above all, hearts? Maj-Britt Nilsson Houston and Gene Stuart, now passed on, give us daily memories of love; Mary Taube, very much with us, sends her best, too. To them we dedicate this book.

◂▸ CHAPTER ONE

The Classic Maya Body

A human body is unique yet, at the same time, like any other body. Regardless of setting, it will have, in the absence of deformities, a common array of attributes: a head, limbs, facial features, and so forth. But the body is also perceived, labeled, and interpreted in ways distinctive to its time and place. As a chart or map of the basic body parts and their terminology, this chapter begins by examining the concept of "a person" and "a body," categories that seem deceptively simple at first. We will chart the Classic Maya body from all available sources, those that look back from a more richly documented time in the Colonial and modern periods, and those that draw directly on what the Classic Maya left by way of images and texts. The leavings are varied, some surprisingly rich and others nothing but blanks that hold little promise of being filled. These pose queries for future work, should scholars be lucky enough to acquire relevant evidence to complete those gaps. The body parts and concepts related here serve as a necessary preface to the chapters that follow. This is where those bits of flesh and the ideas attached to them "move," interact, and release yet other meanings. Ensuing sections explore the skin and surface; head, torso, and extremities; fluids, energies, and internal parts; they also scrutinize the extension of vitality beyond the body, and the sex, sexuality, and gender of the Classic Maya as channeled by available information. These sections form the framework for what follows, a lexicon for later chapters. A final segment discusses a fundamental restriction in the otherwise enlightening sources, namely, that the ancient eye through which we look is strongly masculine: whatever gender narratives these data offer are incomplete by lacking a clear female perspective. This point of view will likely prove controversial, yet it is forced on us by the evidence.

THE OVERALL BODY

The Classic Maya labeled distinct beings with the word *winik*, "person," but it perhaps carries the more nuanced sense of "animate, sentient being." There were many varieties of *winik*, even supernatural ones: each seems to have involved roles and attributes that were distinctive to a particular *winik* (Fig. 1.1). The term had numerological connotations in that the same term was used in Classic times to identify a unit of twenty days, obviously because the principal digits of counting, the toes and fingers, number twenty among human beings. (The Maya made this clear with a variant sign for the number one, a single finger.) In addition, as will be explained in Chapter 2, there was a corporeal "self" or "entity" called *baah,* perhaps originally derived from the word for "forehead" or "head" and then extended to other parts of the body and even to depictions of it (see Fig. 2.2). In this way the Classic Maya explicitly identified flesh with its representations in stone, wood, and other media.

As one might expect, the dictionaries of Colonial and more modern times present a complex assortment of words from different Mayan languages, some directly related to the terminology we find in Classic sources. Terms for "body" include *takupalil,* an unanalyzable word from Colonial Tzotzil (Laughlin 1988, 1:307)—perhaps a partial loan from some other language, such as Nahuatl (*tlactli,* "torso" [Louise Burkhart, personal communication, 2004])—**bak'et,* "flesh, body," from Common Ch'olan (Kaufman and Norman 1984:116); and from Common Tzeltal-Tzotzil, **bak'et,* **kuket-al,* and **lew,* the last specifically for "body, muscle, fat" (Kaufman 1972:95, 106, 108; see also Colonial Tzeltal for *baquetal,* "body, fleshy thing," and *cuquet,* "body" [J. Robertson n.d.]).

Fig. 1.1. *Winik,* "person" (drawing by David Stuart of unprovenanced vessel).

Colonial Yukatek has the related term *kukut* for corporeal thing and, interestingly, employs the same word as a root for "skin" or even "bodily senses" (*kukutil u'bah;* Barrera Vásquez 1980: 347–348). Someone who substitutes for another is that person's *kukutila'n,* as in *u kukutila'n Kristo,* "vicar of Christ who is the pope," or *kukutila'n k'oh,* "substitute for another, as the viceroy is of the king," *k'oh* being used both in the sense of "substitute" and "mask" (Chapter 8; Barrera Vásquez 1980:409). Thus, "skin" and "body" appear to have been closely interchangeable concepts, and the adoption of that surface by another led to the transfer or delegation of authority. Not a few of these languages, from Colonial Tzendal to Yukatek, used *winik* as a root for "body" or, in Tzendal, *vinquilel,* "part of the whole" (Barrera Vásquez 1980:924; J. Robertson n.d.). Aside from *winik,* however, not a single one of these terms makes an appearance in the Classic inscriptions, and *winik* seems not to have been used to mean "body."

The key underlying concept, as worked out by John Robertson, is expressed grammatically through a suffix, -*Vl,* that is attached to glyphic nouns and adjectives (Houston et al. 2001). It has a vowel (*V*) that varies in complex and not yet predictable ways (Fig. 1.2). Robertson suggests that, in meaning, this suffix creates an abstraction, such as English "whiteness," and then requires that this quality and whatever it is attached to be imagined as a single thing. That is the general explanation. More precisely, the suffix can be used in longer phrases to mark qualitative relations with otherworldly or supernatural beings, such as gods or the deceased (the usual form is -*il*); to link one thing to a whole, as in *u pasil yotoot,* "it is the opening [doorway] of his home" (here also the form is usually -*il;* Fig. 1.2b), the opening not being possible without the structure around it; or to create abstractions, as in *ajawil,* "king-ness"; to attribute abstract, generalized qualities to things, as in "earthly gods," or *kabal k'uh* (the vowel in the suffix -*Vl* varies according to the first word, in this case *kab*).

In Mayan writing, the "part forming part of a whole" plays a strong role in describing the body and its components. Yet there is a grammatical contrast with, say, the relationship between parts of buildings. In bodies, the *-Vl* always takes the form *-el*, so that *u-bakel bahlam* means "the bone of the jaguar" (Fig. 1.2c). One can think of this as a bone *from* the jaguar's body rather than something that happens to belong to an acquisitive jaguar. Neither the jaguar's bone nor the jaguar itself can be understood apart from the other. For this reason, Yukatek Mayan uses *bayel* to refer to "part of the body" (Michelon 1976:24). The slippery problem for linguists and Mayanists is seeing these forms of *-Vl* both as distinct elements (they seem to have slightly different vowels, according to the concept at hand) and as expressions that ultimately relate to a shared concept of qualitative abstraction.

The emphasis placed by the Classic Maya on part/whole relations, on things that necessarily require a bodily context, helps explain a good deal of glyphic detail. (Parenthetically, such part/whole relations of severed body parts are also described in a key Nahuatl source, the Florentine Codex [Sahagún 1950–1982, bk. 10:149–153]). Most Maya glyphs for body parts, whether of the lower torso, a hand, a finger, or a head, show a circle within a circle always at the point where that body part articulates with the rest of the body (Fig. 1.3). A hand, for example, has such circles where there should have been a wrist; the glyph exists on its own, and has a variety of sounds, especially /chi/, but the scribe could only contemplate it as having been, at one time, part of a body. The outer circle is probably the fleshy layer, the inner one of bone. Animal heads probably show a superficially similar but unrelated feature: two marks like the "darkness" sign that probably show them to be nocturnal animals (Fig. 1.3e; Marc Zender, personal communication, 2004). For unknown reasons, hair does not display part/whole markings either, despite being something cut from the body; in all likelihood, locks were treated differently from other body parts because they could be clipped without any real violence. The "circles of severance," to coin a phrase, also mark buildings, by analogy with the human body. A platform is not on its own, but must relate to other structures; it, too, then, has such circles, much like those on a human

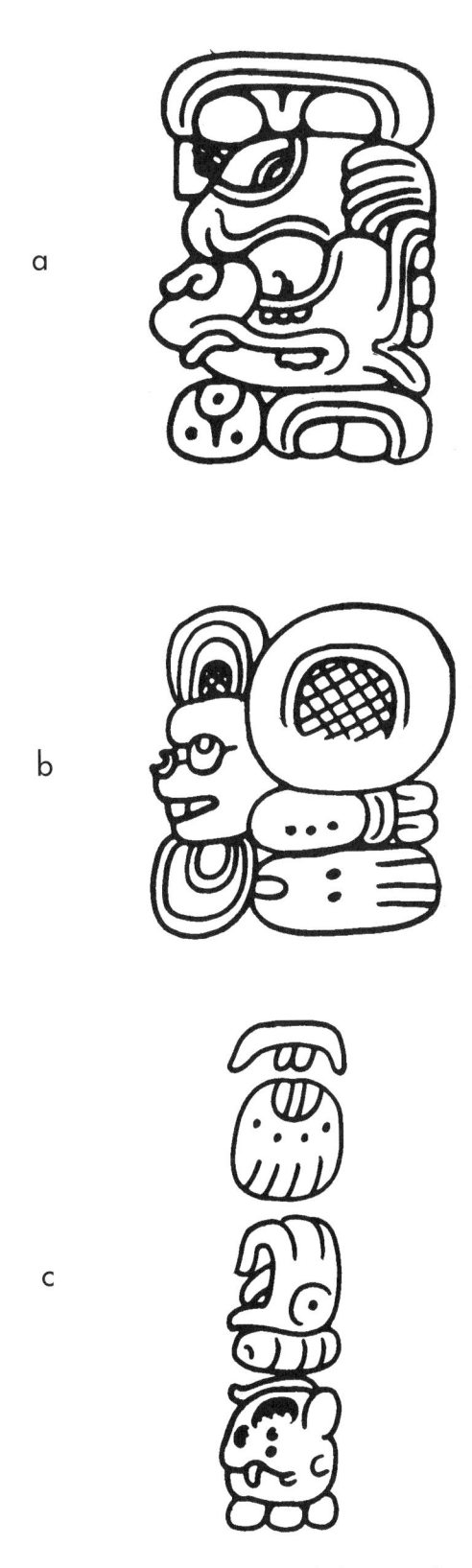

Fig. 1.2. "Part of a whole" and its glyphic expression: (a) *u k'awiilil*, Yaxchilan Lintel 25:B1 (I. Graham and von Euw 1977:56); (b) *u pasil*, Yaxchilan Lintel 23:B2 (I. Graham 1982:135); and (c) *u bakel bahlam* (drawing by Stephen Houston).

hand. For that reason, the Classic Maya may well have envisioned the articulation of buildings as comparable, perhaps even equivalent to, that of the human body. The slathering of such buildings with red pigment, a frequent occurrence in Maya cities, would have lent a fleshy, blood-enveloping quality to structures.

A short comment needs to be made about body proportion in the Classic period, and whether it ever conformed to anything as rigid as the system of human representation in ancient Egypt, where size of representation correlated to variables such as status and gender (Robins 1994; Spinden 1913:23). The matter is not new to Mesoamerica, as other scholars have written about proportion in Olmec imagery, which makes the head unusually large in relation to the rest of the body (e.g., de la Fuente 1996). Generally, the length of the limbs in depictions of Classic bodies followed a set of rough and rather conventionalized multiples, the lower limb, for example, being the same as the entire arm from shoulder to wrist (Clancy 1999:64–141). The torso was about the same length as the arm from shoulder to end of finger, and the head approximated the length of the lower leg from knee to ankle. Body thickness accorded with a scheme in which the arms were treated as an acute triangle, the wrist half the width of the shoulder joint. With few exceptions, the upper thigh was as thick as the torso. Hands tended to be more elongated and expressive than the feet. Body contours were, aside from representations of the weak, deformed, and aged, heavily rounded. A historical study of such canons still needs to be done.

SKIN AND SURFACE

Mayan terms for "skin" are quite diverse, depending on the body location. In Ch'olti', the "skin of the face" is *tzumal,* probably related to

Fig. 1.3. "Circles of severance" and "nocturnal" markings: (a) hand, [ye] syllable, Tikal Miscellaneous Text 9, Burial 48; (b) hand, part of [K'AL] logograph, Tikal Stela 31:D18 (after C. Jones and Satterthwaite 1982:fig. 52b); (c) hand, [chi] syllable, Aguateca Stela 1:D6 (after I. Graham 1967:fig. 3); (d) human legs and pelvis, Dos Pilas Stela 14:E2 (after drawing by Stephen Houston); (e) jaguar head, Palenque stucco, area of the Temple of the Cross; and (f) woman's breasts, [chu] syllable, Piedras Negras Throne 1:F4 (after drawing by John Montgomery).

tzuhum, "leather, whip" (related to Common Tzeltal-Tzotzil *uh, "hard gourd"; Kaufman 1972:97), and the verb "to skin" something or someone is *zulpael* (Ringle n.d.). Colonial Tzotzil refers to "skin" as *cho'* or *nukulal*, the former from a word for "cheek," Common Ch'olan *choh, and the latter with the sense of "animal skin" (Kaufman and Norman 1984:118; Laughlin 1988, 1:455). The same word in Tzendal (Colonial Tzeltal) is *nucul*, with the added meaning of "wrinkled" when used in *nucultic* (J. Robertson n.d.). This description may allude to the pliable nature of skin. In Colonial Yukatek, a "thin, human skin" is *oth* (*ot'*), and *keuel* (*k'ewel*) specifies the cut, processed skin of an animal, including the vellum used by scribes (Acuña 1984, 2:352v; Michelon 1976:276). The San Francisco dictionary of Yukatek refers to the second term in a peculiar expression, *ah koh keuel*, "he that covers the face and hands with feline hide [a mask] in order to rob" (Michelon 1976:4). In Ch'orti', animals, trees, and humans may shed skin, *hihn*, or be chapped or have roughened epidermis, *insak' u k'eweer*, just like Yukatek *keuel*. Or, as a flayed creature, that very same skin may be scraped or peeled off, *kohr* or *tz'uhri* (Wisdom n.d.).

The fleshy, round, skin-covered part of the body is, in Ch'orti', the *k'eweerar*, which can be used to describe epidermis on different areas of the body: *k'eweerar uhor*, "scalp" or "skin of the head"; *k'eweerar ukur*, "foreskin of the penis"; *k'eweerar uti'*, "lips" or "cheek"; and the "dry skin," *ta'*, that is picked off the body (Wisdom n.d.). This last word applies to anything left behind by the body, from a footprint to excrement. There is also, in Colonial Yukatek, a rare expression for "work oneself as the Indians did anciently," *hots ich*, either as tattooing or branding; this action, a marking of the face and thus an enduring, visible shame, pertained to slaves and chattel (Barrera Vásquez 1980:234). Body paint may have involved a common term for "pigment," *bon* in Yukatek, or, for the clever craftsman, the ingenuity of making something look alive, *winkilis*, as though imparting "humanity," or *winikil*, to it (Barrera Vásquez 1980:924). Colonial Tzotzil is far more explicit, however, providing a term, *naban*, meaning "to paint oneself with dye or red ochre" (Laughlin 1988, 2:431). The same root occurs in Ch'olti', with *nabi*, "stain"; in Yukatek as *nab*, "anoint, smear, spot"; and in Tzendal as *nabel*, "makeup," or *nabantezon*, "make up, beautify with colors and daub with ochre" (J. Robertson n.d.).

Ch'orti' dictionaries supply many terms for afflictions of the skin. Some labels refer to white discolorations (*ak'ax*), along with white skin and blond hair (*sak u'ut*, "white face"), not, apparently, an attractive condition. There are also "pimples" (*k'u'x*, from Common Ch'olan for "pain," **k'ux*), including those that cover the entire body (*k'u'x tunor ubah*) or face (*k'u'x u'ut*), "moles" (*mam*), "wens" (*ut u k'eweerar*), "warts" (*sak' k'u'x*), "mange" (*sar*), "itch" (*saran*), "dandruff" (*sar uhol*), "spotted body," usually from measles (*sarin ubah*), "eczema that covers the body" (*sar ubah*), and a "fiery dermatitis" (*k'ahk'ir sarar*) or mere "redness" (*k'ahk' uk'ewe'erar*). This root, *sar*, "mange," which goes back to Common Ch'olan *sal (Kaufman and Norman 1984:130), also refers to "spotted paper," *sarin hun*, a material employed by the Ch'orti' in the 1930s to decorate ritual objects. Similar kinds of spotted paper, usually daubed with blood, occur in Classic imagery, and it seems reasonable to suppose that the same term or something much like it was applied at that time. Another word for "spot," *pat ax*, comes from an expression *pa't*, as in "foreskin of penis," *upa't e qur* (Wisdom n.d.), and a frequent term for "wart" or "skin blemish," *ax* (Yukatek; Barrera Vásquez 1980:19).

As yet, none of these terms for skin or its features makes a clear appearance in hieroglyphs. There are some supernaturals, *way*, or "co-essences," that have either freckles or pimples (M. Coe 1978:pl. 3), perhaps as a mark of disease or adolescence. The wrinkles of aged gods and goddesses serve as secure markers of the elderly, along with loss of teeth (Fig. 1.4). In other cases, we can categorize skin markings in three ways: (1) those that reflect some surficial or inner quality of a generalized sort, such as age, privation, godliness, or quality of skin; (2) others that are permanent, including scarification, cicatrization, branding, piercing, stretching, and tattooing; and (3) skin markings of paint that appear to have been impermanent. The differences between these three are obvious: the first two are more or less permanent conditions, and the third is intrinsically mutable. The latter uses the skin as a painting surface like any other, to be wiped clean for other, future displays. In both the permanent and impermanent processes, the intent is to create a personal display that distinguishes one body from another or establishes similarities between them. The modified skin becomes, according to Alfred Gell (1993:29–30; see also T. Turner 1980:140), a surface that protects what is inside yet also projects that interior to the outside world. It is both a physiological layer and a surface that conveys meaning (Benthien 2004:235).

The first category, an almost adjectival label of some personal or surficial quality, appears in a variety of ways. As just mentioned, age is consistently shown in Classic imagery by wrinkled, spotted, and sagging skin, especially in folds on the chest, along with a hunched back, toothless gums, prominent outward-jutting shoulders and jaw, and a prominent belly (Naranjo Stela 22, I. Graham and von Euw 1975:55; K1404, K2068; Yadeun 1993:120).

The mark for "rough texture" or "wrinkle," an oval with spots inside, also appears on the depictions of crocodiles, turkey skin, eggs, cacao pods, leaves, and some trees, which, in the tropics, can display a corrugated bark that resembles skin (Fig. 1.5; e.g., K2041, K2797, K3007). On one ceramic vase, a monkey with a single rough spot scratches it as though it were some skin condition, perhaps mange or a bald spot (K1211). In addition, a glyphic syllable, [bo], may consist of wrinkled testicles cut from the body and penis. It is clear that the elderly are not accorded any special beauty but are rather seen as figures of authority and, in the case of aged women, danger and transition (Taube 1994a:657–658). Youthful skin is in many respects the "unmarked" condition, with no visible signs to distinguish the skin of mature, not-yet-aged adults from that of infants.

Another important type of visual symbol found on skin are "god markings," first mentioned and so named by Michael Coe (1973:54) for the reason that they never occur on depictions of humans (Fig. 1.6). When they occur—and this is not always routine—they generally emboss the upper arms and legs, possibly because celts were tied to those parts of the body in Olmec and later times (Taube 1996:

Fig. 1.4. Aged god (after K5164).

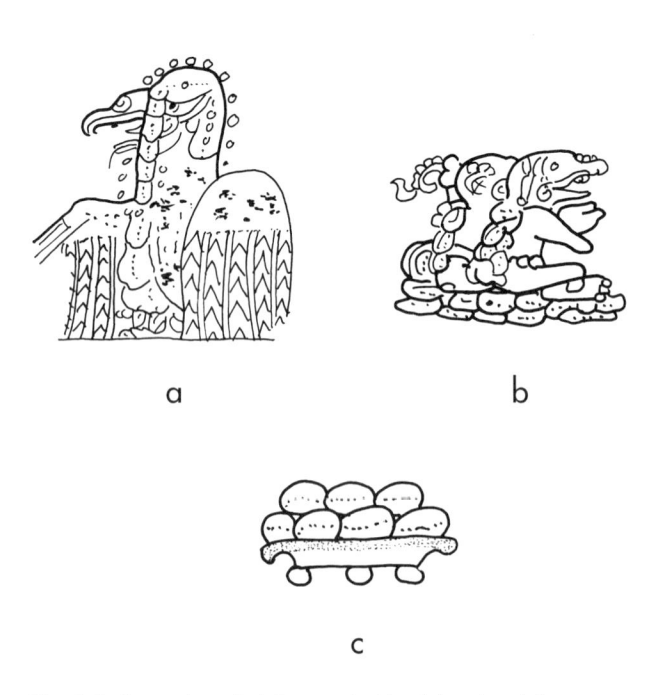

Fig. 1.5. Spotted symbol for rough skin: (a) turkey (after K2041); (b) crocodile pair (after M. Coe 1973:82); and (c) whole eggs (?) in bowl (after K2797).

figs. 10–11). The god markings reveal some quality of the surface of the god. Celtlike designs show hardness and sheen; watery swirls and scutes indicate a fishlike surface of rasping scales. The *ak'bal,* or "night," sign indicates a black finish or, as on animals, a condition of frequent activity in darkness. The hard or shiny deities would include the Maize God, God D, God N, God K, winged emissaries, monkey scribes, the Jaguar God of the Underworld, the Hero Twins, and the Death Gods (M. Coe 1973:55, 79, 82, 92, 133; K1183, K1524, K4020, K4926, K4962, K5610, K5978, K6298, K7190, K7287). Scaly or fishy features mark the G1 god of the Palenque Triad, God B (Chaak), and God K (K504, K521, K5164); at times Chaak can display water swirls as god markings on his body (M. Coe 1978:vase 4). A few entities, such as mosquito beings and gods of drunkenness, exhibit the "night" or "darkness" sign, perhaps to indicate a black, carapace-like surface (M. Coe 1973:124; K2286, K2993, K8007). The Sun God displays the *k'in,* or "sun, day," sign on his skin, probably to show that his skin is hot and bright, a dispenser rather than an absorber or reflector of light (K1398). Other supernatural beings, God N in particular, bear the sign for "stone," *tuun,* to denote their rocky substance (K1485) or, as in the Cacao God, a "wood" sign to indicate the vegetative pith of the tree (K4331). Another personage has a forehead with a smoking torch that duplicates the Classic verb "to burn," *puluyi* (K4013). Strangely, almost no women have god markings, not even goddesses, nor are there many co-essences, or *way,* with surficial marks of this sort (we suspect that the one or two exceptions come from the hand of present-day restorers). What does this mean? Did it mirror some qualitative difference between gods and goddesses, deities and *way,* with the former "hard" and the latter "soft"? Or was this an aesthetic decision, made to avoid any disfiguring blemishes on womanly flesh? Presumably, the Classic Maya could readily see in the hard surfaces of god effigies the adamantine density of the gods themselves as well as a connection between "preciousness" or "high value" and polished, exotic objects that required enormous investments of labor.

At an intermediate stage between qualitative signs and actual body markings is a loosely defined set of spots and other symbols. Good examples are the broad dots that characterize the body of 1 Ajaw, the dominant Hero Twin of Classic Maya belief (Fig. 1.7; M. Coe 1989:167–168; Taube 1992b). These spots have some association with death, especially the blotches left by pooled blood in cadavers, or with "filth" and "dirt," as can be seen by several scenes where this being "speaks" and "breathes" excrement (e.g., K511); in addition, the recently dead may continue to have bowel movements. Yet a fair number of dynastic images show that some lords adopted these singular markings, including lords of Aguateca, Arroyo de Piedra, Tamarindito, and Tikal, Guatemala (Houston 1993:figs. 3-4, 3-5; Taube 1992b:119). In other contexts, as at Tonina and Yaxchilan, Mexico, the people with such spots are captives who may be impersonating 1 Ajaw (I. Graham 1982:166; I. Graham and Mathews 1996:80). The explanation for these diverse expressions may be that such blemishes, whether applied to the body or qualitatively intrinsic, bespeak a state of death and rejuvenation, a trope that well suits 1 Ajaw and his impersonators. The other marking of this sort is the enigmatic so-called IL mark that appears on the faces of glyphs recording [na] or [IXIK], "female,

Fig. 1.6. God markings, here a deity grasping a depiction of sky, Yaxchilan bench (after drawing by Ian Graham).

Fig. 1.7. Spots on 1 Ajaw (after K732).

woman." This may refer to the Maize God, maize flesh, or to a generalized quality of great beauty, such as may be seen in the Wind God, which is associated with music, flowers, and the breath of life (Houston and Taube 2000:fig. 4e; Taube 2004a:fig. 2).

Alfred Gell, whose work was mentioned before, has produced the most comprehensive study to date of ethnographic tattooing. His analysis seeks to correlate societal types with traditions of tattooing in Polynesia. Gell (1993:18) proposes that, with few exceptions, tattooing—which can serve here as a proxy for other kinds of skin marking—characterizes marginal groups in state societies, from Russian prisoners to punk musicians (Schrader 2000:189–192; see also Schildkrout 2004). These markings are "oppositional" in that they transgress social norms and seek some connection with "pure" or "authentic" conditions of existence. At the same time, they broadcast an identification with other like-minded people (S. Benson 2000:242). The other context in which tattooing occurs is in "preliterate tribal societies," where people use tattooing to enhance personal identity (Gell 1993:18, 296).

Tattooing diminishes in importance when political life becomes bureaucratized, or, conversely, it may play a diminished role when relationships are *too* close. Tattoos offer little benefit in hierarchical, highly populated societies like pre- to early-contact Hawaii; the relative anonymity of social interaction detracts from their usefulness (Gell 1993:298, 301). By the same token, mutual recognition on a tiny, isolated atoll is such that no overt, indelible markers are needed. Personal histories and qualities are known to all. Gell recognizes that tattooing and its "close sister" scarification have a wide variety of functions in other parts of world, especially Africa and Asia. These marks highlight ethnic identity, project moral exhortations, beautify, and accent rites of passage—a pattern also seen in the initiatory practices of youths in traditional Samoa; in Africa and Southeast Asia, scars and tattoos also insulate the body from evil (Blier 1995:42, 145, 284, 392; 1998:53; Faris 1972; Gell 1993:302; Tannenbaum 1987:693). To Gell, all such tattooing arises in societies that emphasize "hierarchy and domination" and exists in relation to "parallel institutions" such as warfare and lordship (Gell 1993:4).

Gell himself notes that a good deal of evidence counters his "marginalist" or "tribalist" theories of permanent body markings. For example, Khmer or Burmese script occurs in protective tattoos of mainland Southeast Asia. Contrary to Gell's proposals, these settings are neither "preliterate" nor consistently "tribal" (Gell 1993:18; Tannenbaum 1987:695; Terwiel 1979). The Classic Maya, too, are a case in point. They understood that flesh could be sculpted, allowed to heal, and left with raised welts. As in many societies, this was probably done to fairly mature bodies so as to avoid distortions of design that might result from further physical growth. Much like the Maori of New Zealand, who practiced a form of "face carving," the sculpting of flesh was done either with "combs" or with chisels (Gell 1993:51). Of course, the Classic Maya were literate and more courtly than "tribal" in their cultural emphases. According to Diego de Landa, such body practices continued into the time of the Spanish Conquest. The people most likely to have tattoos or scars were warriors, a component of society "marginalized" or distinguished by their ability to kill, maim, and "hunt" in the wilds. During the Colonial period, they expressed pride at the pain implicit in painting the skin, pricking it, and then kneading the pigment into the epidermis (Thompson 1946:18; Tozzer 1941:91). The pain was so great that, as much among the Maya as the Maori, tattooing was probably done one sector at a time, often beginning at puberty and in preparation for marriage (Gell 1993:246). The agony of tattooing and other modifications of the body recorded itself deeply in memory, along with other meanings that were inculcated at the time (Clastres 1974). Among the Maya, designs on women appear to have been "more delicate and beautiful" and were only from the waist up (Thompson 1946:19). Colonial visitors to the southern lowlands of the Maya region also reported, as did Agustín Cano, seeing men with "breast, stomach, and thighs" tattooed, and penises "with very large ears or horns made by hand" (see Chapter 6; Thompson 1946:21). Some of the designs corresponded to the *way*, or co-essence, of the marked individual, a clear instance in which an internal attribute played across the surface of the body (Thompson 1946:21).

The very act of tattooing was an aesthetic transformation that made the bodies into "flowers" (Thompson 1946:22). A couple shown on the back of a throne in the Museo Amparo in Mexico show one day sign, Ajaw, "lord, flower," repeated on their foreheads; these appear to mark intervals of two *k'atun*s (one *k'atun* = twenty years), or forty years (Fig. 1.8). Nonetheless, at a later time, tattooing appears to have also been a punishment for thieves of high birth; inadvertently, it prevented a tattooed Spaniard, Gonzalo Guerrero, from returning to his people, as he felt too altered physically for such reintegration (Thompson 1946:19, 20). Yet in no Maya example is there information pointing to the idea of using bodily modification to "pass" for someone more beautiful or more socially acceptable, as seems to have been true in the history of Western aesthetic surgery (Gilman 1999:330). There was no "deceit,"

"intent to happiness" or concealment, only accentuation of intrinsic properties. Although relatively late and probably introduced from outside the Maya region, the practice of piercing the nasal septum as a marker of royalty occurs at sites such as Seibal, Guatemala, and Uxmal, Mexico (Fig. 1.9; I. Graham 1992:108; 1996:17, 32, 37).

The most abundant evidence of Classic Maya scarification and tattooing occurs on figurines.

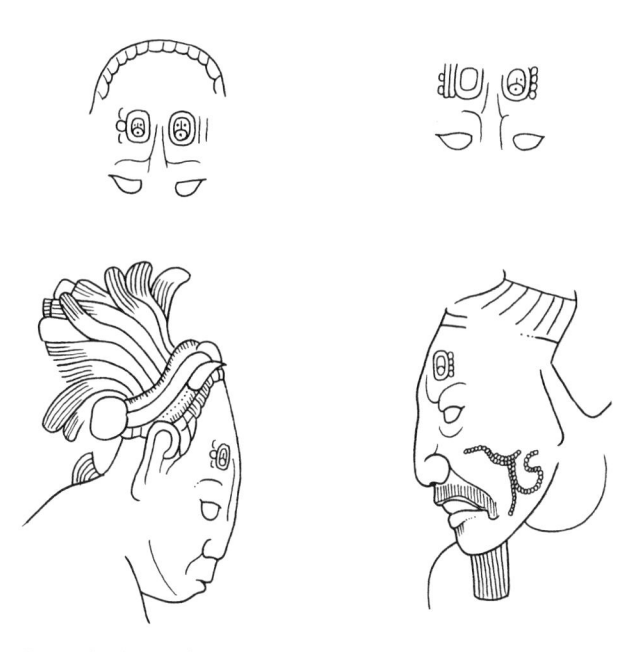

Fig. 1.8. Tattooed markings: day signs on forehead of lady and lord on Sáenz Throne, Museo Amparo, Mexico City (after field drawing by Ian Graham).

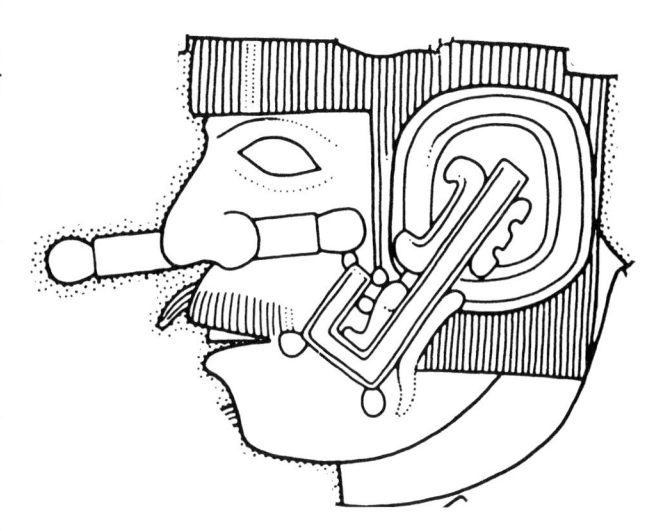

Fig. 1.9. The pierced septum of royalty, Seibal Stela 10 (I. Graham 1996:32).

There are secure indications that these practices build on a deep foundation, in that scars or tattoos, albeit of very different design, go back to the Preclassic period (Fig. 1.10a; Laporte and Valdés 1993:fig. 8). In Classic figurines, females emanate "breath" from their mouths, but visibly so through permanent scars (Fig. 1.10b; Schele 1997:pl. 3). The breath may also appear as slits extending from the corners of the mouth or as raised dots (Fig. 1.10c; Corson 1976:figs. 2a, b, c, 3b, 18b; Schele 1997:pls. 5, 10). Other figurines show mock beards (Schele 1997:pl. 28) or dots above the nose (Fig. 1.10d; Becquelin and Baudez 1982:figs. 265h, 270j). Men may have facial ornaments suspended over the mouth and below the nose, probably as objects to be worn during impersonation dances (Schele 1997:pls. 9, 10). Some figurines represent people who have human skin attached to

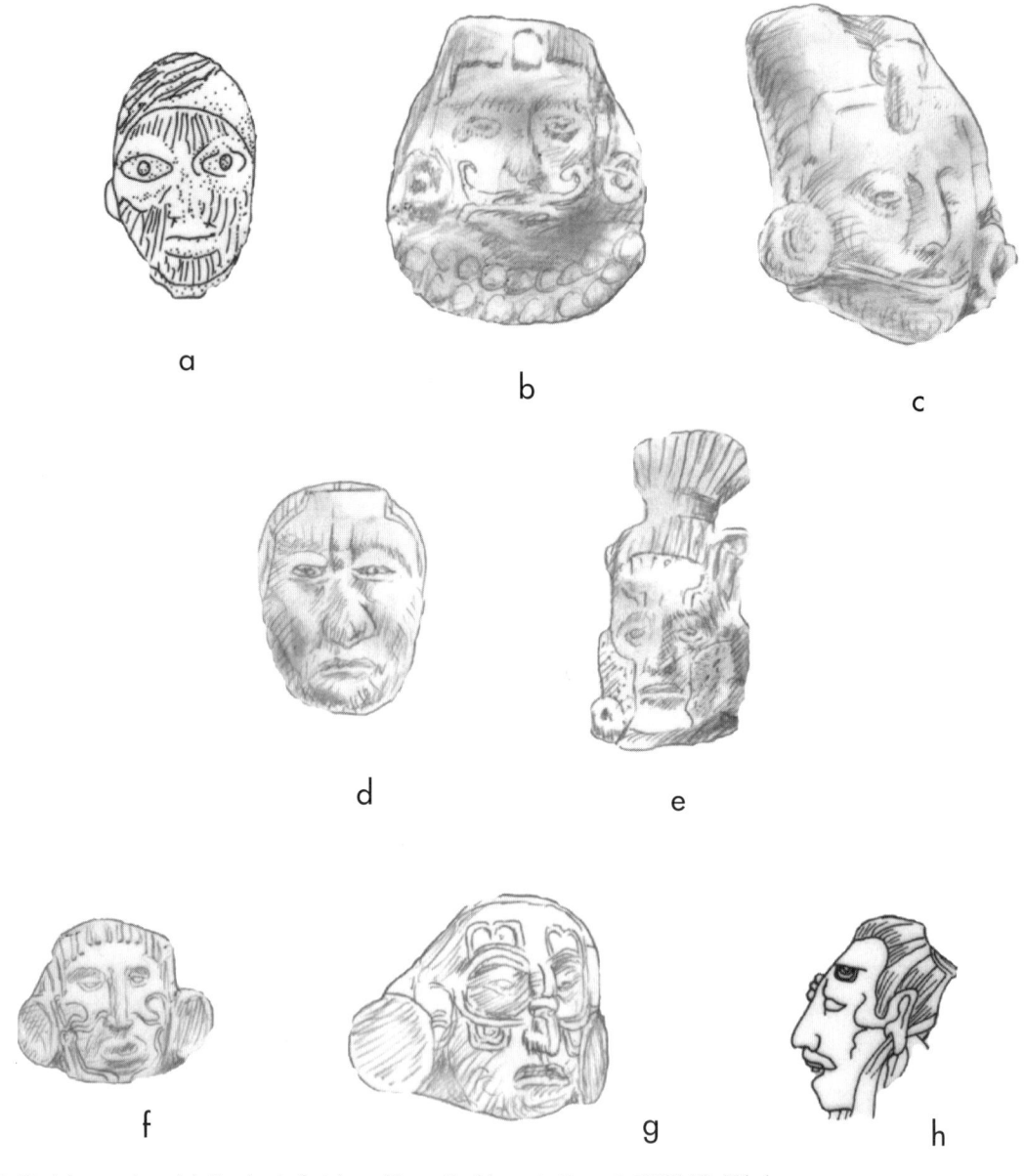

Fig. 1.10. Facial tattooing: (a) Preclassic facial markings, Problematic Deposit PNT-12, Tikal (after Laporte and Valdés 1993:fig. 8); (b) female with breath mark (after Schele 1997:21); (c) female with slit lines near mouth (after Schele 1997:28); (d) male with beads above nose (after Becquelin and Baudez 1982:fig. 270j); (e) male with attached skin (after Schele 1997:71); (f) male with centipede jaw tattoo (after Schele 1997:78); (g) male with god markings (after Schele 1997:76); and (h) Palenque Table of the Scribe (after Schele and Mathews 1979:142).

their face, perhaps as part of war trophies (Fig. 1.10e; Schele 1997:pls. 12, 13, 14, 16). The pitted surface of this skin may denote decomposition or desiccation. Facial skin was sometimes used in protective kneepads for ballplayers, presumably for the purpose of mashing despised visages (Schele and M. Miller 1986:pl. 104; Taube 1992b:fig. 55).

A few men—or at least the depictions of them in clay—possess highly complicated scars or tattoos (it is hard to tell which) that blazon centipede jaws over the jawbone or trace the facial characteristics of gods, perhaps the namesakes of the person so depicted (Fig. 1.10f; Schele 1997:pls. 17, 19, 21, 22). Other figurines have full, almost Maori-style chiseling (Fig. 1.10g; Schele 1997:76) as well as both asymmetrical and symmetrical designs (Schele 1997:pl. 12). Citing a wide variety of sources, Alfred Tozzer suggests that such marks were intended for beautification but also to frighten enemies with fearsome faces (Tozzer 1941:88). A captive at Palenque, Mexico, has additional "god" eyes on the forehead and emanations from the ears, as though stressing the perceptual acuity of the body, creating an entity that sees far and hears widely (Fig. 1.10h; Schele and Mathews 1979:142). An indication of what such tattooing might have looked like in the round comes from an engraved Early Classic skull from Kaminaljuyu Tomb B-IV (Kidder et al. 1946:fig. 165). Some of the facial or body markings may have been imposed after a person's capture, perhaps as a sign of "otherness." The Classic Maya depicted captives with distinctive, ripped clothing (Chapter 6) and, likewise, would portray the countenance of a captive so that it resembled a flayed face, such as those used to cover shields (Fig. 1.11; Schele and Mathews 1979:71); in Figure 1.11a, note especially the line around the lips, revealing another mouth beneath, and the pitted marks near the face, which hint at decomposition or a single red handprint, as in the Bonampak murals. (Not a few Maya walls have red handprints, and the allusion may have been to faces [Trik and Kampen 1983:figs. 14, 97, 104].) The extraction of body parts from dishonored people stresses the profound lack of control they had over their own bodies. In the *pars pro toto* ("part for the whole") principle, these parts connote the entire body, much as fragmentary bodies of ancestors imply the whole (Chapter 6, and above). Two stelae at Xultun show such faces oriented toward the ruler as though already detached and tanned into stiff, expressionless masks (Fig. 1.11b, c; von Euw 1978:19, 23).

Another kind of "anticipatory" presentation, in which war captives reveal their vanquished status on the very field of battle, can be seen in the beaded scars that fleck their jaws and run up their noses and foreheads. Such scars are widely depicted on captives at Yaxchilan, Mexico (I. Graham 1979:99; I. Graham and von Euw 1977:33, 41, 57), and Tonina, Mexico (I. Graham and Mathews 1996:71, 113). One image at Tonina even shows captives with "flinty" earspools, perhaps less a clue to their substance than an indication of warlike speech entering the ears (Chapter 4; Becquelin and Taladoire 1990:fig. 142a). A more benign form of tattooing from Tonina shows "flowery breath" that has been scarred or tattooed around the mouth (Yadeun 1993a:98), a mark that occurs on Yaxchilan Lintels 24 and 26. These are interpreted as "blood scrolls" by David Stuart (1984) and as enduring marks of fragrant breath by Stephen

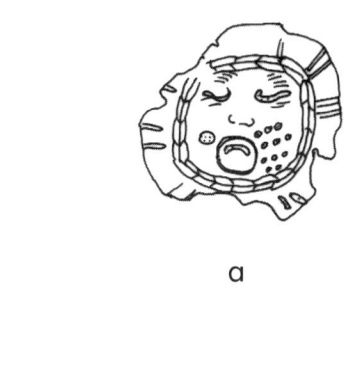

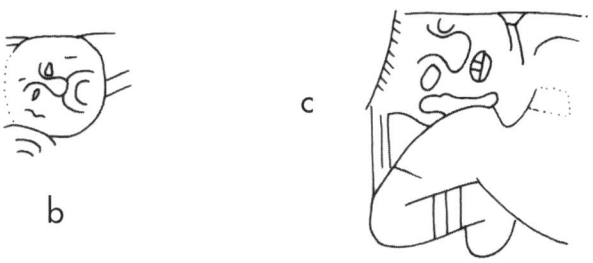

Fig. 1.11. Flayed face and frontally disposed faces: (a) stucco shield (after Schele and Mathews 1979:71); (b) Xultun Stela 4 (after von Euw 1978:19); and (c) Xultun Stela 5 (after von Euw 1978:23).

Houston and Karl Taube (Fig. 1.12; I. Graham and von Euw 1977:53, 57; Houston and Taube 2000). At other sites, such as Naranjo, Guatemala, the beaded scars are displayed by victorious lords and are located over the nose (I. Graham and von Euw 1979:25) or pass over the front of the face (K4412). Naranjo is also noteworthy because of the consistency of scars from image to image of the same lord, as of the welts across the chin on Stelae 6, 13, and 19 (I. Graham and von Euw 1975:23, 37, 49). The mutilated body of a captive is further documented in three ways: a decapitated body with an angular, jagged edge where the head used to be (Fig. 1.13a); S-shaped cuts into the flesh, as in the Bonampak murals (Fig. 1.13b); and the so-called *tuerto*, or head with a closed or damaged eye, in some cases still hanging from its tenuous optical stalk and exuding fluids (Fig. 1.13c, d; D. Stuart 1989a). The *tuerto*, known elsewhere in Mesoamerica, especially in Classic Veracruz, Mexico (M. Miller 1989:figs. 11–12, 14), may be a personage injured in boxing or ballplay, the orbit so crushed that it can no longer hold an eye.

Body paint is widely attested in Classic Maya imagery, but, like the schematic and abstract patterns on textiles, it is nearly impossible to understand semantically; available contexts are too vague to pinpoint meaning, although this may be remedied by further research. (The great diversity of meaning in body paint among North American peoples points to the imposing interpretive problems before us [Anton 1997:38].) A few pots showing body-painted hunters or warriors imply that paint was a form of camouflage for those desiring stealth. The human body could thereby not be easily distinguished from the mottled light and

Fig. 1.12. Supposed "blood scrolls" that are in fact tattooing of "breath," Yaxchilan Lintel 26 (I. Graham and von Euw 1977:57).

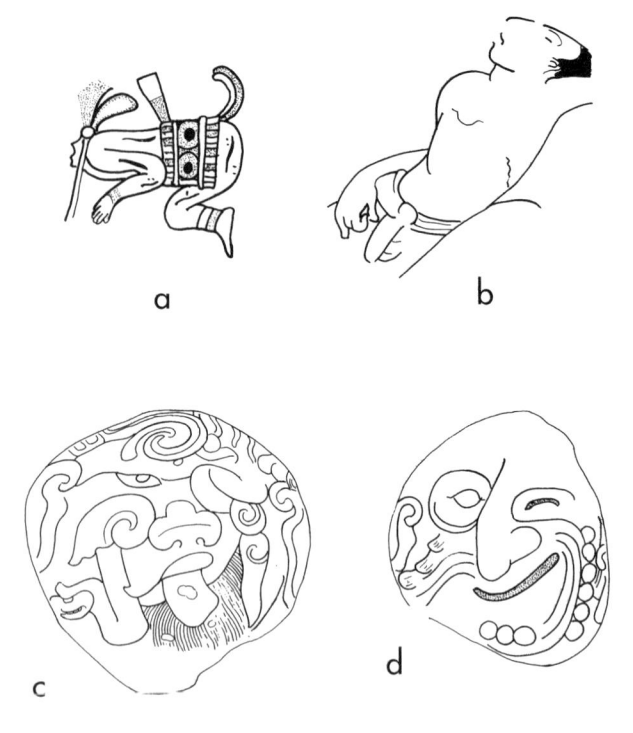

Fig. 1.13. Wounds and *tuertos* in Maya imagery: (a) decapitated head (photograph by David Stuart of unprovenanced vessel); (b) cut captive, Room 2, Bonampak murals (reconstruction by Heather Hurst [and in some cases, "with Leonard Ashby"], copyright the Bonampak Documentation Project); (c) Early Classic *tuerto*, Princeton Art Museum (after D. Stuart 1989a); and (d) Maya *tuerto* in shell (after Westheim et al. 1969:fig. 115).

color under the jungle canopy (Fig. 1.14; K1373). Face paint on some females may have been seen as alluring, such as an example in which a woman exhibits what is almost a moon sign on her face, daubed over a white undercoating (K4996). Other women and some men have red on their neck or upper shoulders as though to highlight the neck and the separation of the head from the chest (M. Coe and J. Kerr 1997:pls. 8, 10; Reents-Budet 1994:fig. 6.27; Taube 1994a:650–651). Most likely, the pigment was an organic material like annatto, which could be removed with water yet, when mixed with resins, stayed put on a sweaty body (e.g., Reents-Budet 1994:figs. 3.23, 5.2).

In many such cases there may be no direct meaning attached. Rather, the intent was to beautify, even to eroticize the body. A vessel from the general region of Oxkintok, Mexico, shows a male deity (1 Ajaw) or his impersonator daubing paint on the face of a female who is already covered with cloud swirls (Fig. 1.15; K4022). She holds a receptacle for the pigment in a nice gesture of intimacy, and the instrument for applying the paint is spelled *chehb* (M. Coe and J. Kerr 1997:149). Note also that such painting might have explained in folkloric terms the origins of particular markings, whether of deity or of beast; one such painting on an early Late Classic vessel from the area of Naranjo, Guatemala,

Fig. 1.14. Body paint as hunting camouflage (K1373, copyright Justin Kerr).

shows "how the jaguar got his spots": for unknown reasons, a rat daubs paint on a seated jaguar (Robicsek and Hales 1981:fig. 32). A culture of intense vanity and self-regard permeated Classic Maya courts, and several pots show lords or gods appraising their looks in a mirror (K5764; Reents-Budet 1994:figs. 3.17, 4.35). One kind of artifact, a small dwarf carved out of wood, is now known in three examples. These served as supports for mirrors, an apparent role of dwarfs in royal courts and a sly allusion to their ugliness in comparison to the comeliness of the king (Campaña and Boucher 2002; G. Ekholm 1964; K1453). Rapid designs could have been imprinted with clay stamps such as those found in a royal tomb at Calakmul, Mexico, although these might also have been applied to textiles (Fig. 1.16; Carrasco 1999:31). Unfortunately, we cannot know whether body paint was used on a daily basis or whether it helped define special moments. Nor does there seem to have been a clear relationship between the pigments emblazoned on pots and those that, when preserved, cover stone sculptures (Schele 1985). On sculptures, red is the dominant color, possibly because it was the least difficult or expensive to produce. When contrasted with other pigments (the palette on such sculptures tends to be quite limited), human skin is red or yellow; the hair and lips are red; and blue is reserved for jewelry, feathers, or deity heads (M. Coe and J. Kerr 1997:pl. 91; Yadeun 1993:121, 123, 127). On a panel from the area of La Pasadita, Guatemala, the glyphs are rendered with the same color as human skin. Perhaps this was simply for visual emphasis, possibly to feature a body pulsing with blood and life (M. Coe and J. Kerr 1997:pl. 91). Linda Schele and Peter Mathews (1979:

pl. 404) note that at Palenque, Mexico, "the only element in the entire Temple XVIII stucco inscription that was painted red" happened to be a glyph for a stingray spine. Color itself has yet to be studied systematically in all the evidence from the Classic Maya: some colors, earthen ones, appear to be basic, only to be embellished when the surface is "touched up" at a secondary level of refinement with greens and blues.

Other questions remain unanswered and unaddressed: Did the Maya have a concept of color systems or focal colors of a particular intensity (J. Gage 1999:21–23)? Why did certain schemes, such as those on "codex-style" pots, restrict themselves so rigorously to a two-toned palette—that is, did certain regions have a stronger "colorist" tradition than others? Were certain colors favored by women, others by men (J. Gage 1999:90; Pastoureau 2001:8–9)? What moods or emotions were thought to be elicited by color? Was there an implicit theory of "harmony" and decorum in the play of color? How, precisely, did colors correlate with space and direction (Jameson and D'Andrade

Fig. 1.15. Applying paint with a brush or quill (K4022, copyright Justin Kerr).

Fig. 1.16. Body or textile stamps, Calakmul (after R. Carrasco 1999:31).

1997:315–316; Kelley 1976:55–57)? Were some colors, such as blue, valued more highly than others, as was the case in later European tradition and as seems likely among the Maya (Pastoureau 2001:49)? Did those values and the use of colors change through time (Baines 1985)? What role did cross-sensory stimulation, or synesthesia (Chapter 4), perform in triggering senses beyond the reception of color (J. Gage 1999:262–265). In all likelihood, "blue" or "green" was associated in Maya thought with something fluid, and yet, in the case of jades, these two colors indicate hard-stone luster and preciousness (Saunders 2001:210–212). The relatively common opposition in Maya images and text of "1 Yax (blue, green) and 1 K'an (yellow)" may relate to agricultural tropes having to do with verdant, new growth ("unripe") and the dry ("ripe") growth required for swidden burning, a totality that comes together into a whole of human practice. This expression is doubtless related to the phrase in modern K'ek'chi, *raxal k'anal,* "unripe/ripe" or "abundance" (Haeserijn V. 1979:282).

Hair is another feature of the body surface. Yet it is a paradoxical element, extending beyond the body, attached but without feeling. In Common Ch'olan, the term for "hair" in general is *tzutz,* a word also used for "eyelid" in Ch'olti', along with the term *matzab* (Kaufman and Norman 1984:134; Ringle n.d.). In Colonial Tzotzil, the relevant term, obviously cognate with Ch'olan, is *tzotz,* but the idea of "clipping hair," as of criminals, also involves the idea of "pulling the head," *tulbey jol,* suggesting a rather rough, painful process (Laughlin 1988, 1:321, 2:403–404). In Ch'orti', the pubic hair, especially of women, was *mah chir,* "false netting," using a root *mah* with the meaning of "false, evil" (Wisdom n.d.). The hair on the head could be "arranged," *lapi u tzutz;* "braided," *harbir utzutz;* or, as in Ch'olti' and Yukatek, wrapped into a ponytail, *cuc* (*kuk*), a measurement of an elbow's length and perhaps a reference to a "squirrel [tail]," *ku'uk* in Yukatek (Barrera Vásquez 1980:346; Ringle n.d.; Wisdom n.d.). The term for "fingernail" or "toenail" in Colonial Yukatek is *ich'ak* (Michelon 1976:163). An entire study could

be done to good effect on women's hairstyles in Classic Maya imagery, much along the lines of Joyce Marcus's investigation of hair treatment among the ancient Zapotec (1998:31–38, 312–313).

Aside from the hair on the head, face, armpit, and pubis, body hair seldom appears in Classic Maya imagery, and that of the last three locations is faint when present at all (Fig. 1.17). One noteworthy exception is the set of wispy chest hairs on a "full-figure" glyph from the Palace Tablet at Palenque (Fig. 1.18; M. G. Robertson 1985b:fig. 265). Hair itself was usually cut in bangs across the forehead. This may have assisted those wearing diadems and headdresses. The hair was then pulled tightly back into a ponytail, the *cuc* in Ch'olti' and Yukatek. Anything longer than this may have prompted a haircut. Other cuts were shorter in back, with the same angular shape as the bangs, although a counterexample may be found on Calakmul Stela 51, which shows hair that rolls flamboyantly. During the Terminal Classic period (AD 800–900), especially at Seibal, Guatemala, hair began to appear in a more splayed, wild state, in part to reflect an aesthetic sensibility that likened luxurious, long hair to feathers, as on Seibal Stela 3 (I. Graham 1996:17, 37, 45). The other kind of wild hair appeared on captives and decapitated heads or death gods such as those on Uxmal Monument 3, Yaxchilan Lintel 9, or the stucco skull rack at Tonina (Fig. 1.19; I. Graham 1992:127; I. Graham and von Euw 1977:29; Yadeun 1993:113). This stiff, wiry hair may come from a lack of combing—the dead do not ordinarily tend to their toilet—or a matting from preservative fluids, tanning, or exposure to the sun. In most Classic Maya painting, fingernails and toenails are shown to be quite long. This may have signaled the absence of hard, manual labor among elites (K1453).

The adornment of bodies with clothing, *buhk* in Classic Ch'olti', is a final level of "skin" that requires its own book-length project. Sprinkled throughout this and later chapters are references to particular items of clothing or headdresses. Suffice it to say that the clothing for everyday use, and as

Fig. 1.17. Slight beard on aged man, panel from area of Bonampak, Mexico.

Fig. 1.18. Chest hair on figure, Palenque Palace Tablet.

Fig. 1.19. Hair of shrunken (?) bodies, Yaxchilan Lintel 9 (I. Graham and von Euw 1977:29).

documented in images from the Classic period, was a highly practical form of covering: it consisted of lightweight confections that allowed ample circulation of air around the chest and legs; yet it also preserved a modicum of dignity by concealing the privates (Fig. 1.20). There appear to have been two layers, especially when elaborate dance costumes were placed on the body. First came "underclothing," worn at all times; second was an array of straps, jewelry, shells, capes, and belts that took the meaning of clothing to a different level. Most ponderous of all would have been the carved and feathered headdresses that must have presented great difficulties. A graffito from Caracol, Belize, shows a person balancing a headdress consisting of stacked masks; an assistant stands behind to provide a helpful hand (Fig. 1.21; A. Chase and D. Chase 2001:fig. 4.12). Balancing the headdress during vigorous movement demanded special skill. Objects of this weight and symbolic importance, such as representations of *witz*, "hills," or cosmic models with sky and stone (e.g., M. Coe 1978:pl. 14), represented the *kuch*, the "burden" of office expected of all high-ranking people in Maya society. To carry something heavy was to embody graphically the duties of high rank. This also extended to godly obligations: a well-known series of vessels from the northeast Peten, Guatemala, shows the

Maize God "supporting" the locations and tutelary deities of particular cities (Fig. 1.22).

The skin in all of its manifestations is most keenly noticed when it is cut and violated. Unlike modern medical students, who frequently experience emotional trauma when dissecting humans (Finkelstein and Mathers 1990), the Classic Maya probably took these sights in stride, since they witnessed such practices from childhood on. Any repulsion was further numbed by seeing or participating in the butchery of animals or gutting of fish. In current medical training, "dissection" is the sanctioned dismemberment and evisceration of human beings and other creatures. During the Renaissance and later, most cadavers came from the condemned, who had, through criminal action, legally "transferred" their bodies to the state; in the process, executed criminals lost the right to have their postmortem bodies treated as integral wholes (Carlino 1999:93–98). However, pollution of a physical and spiritual sort was a serious risk. The physician often stood behind a lectern, reading from a book while a low-status individual known as a *sector* did the actual cutting; other assistants pointed to the relevant body part (Carlino 1999:12–14). In much the same way, the striking feature of Classic Maya bloodletting is the absence of direct royal participation. When captives were

Fig. 1.20. Informal clothing worn by male (M. Coe 1973:70).

Fig. 1.21. A graffito from Structure B-20, Caracol, Belize (after drawing supplied by Arlen Chase).

Fig. 1.22. Backrack on Maize God (after M. Coe 1978:pl. 14).

sliced ritually, it was the work not of kings but of other figures, including someone in the Bonampak murals known as *ba-*a-took'*, "first person of the flint" (Fig. 1.23; M. Miller 1986:56; see Tonina monument, Yadeun 1993:73). The violation of a royal body was most likely by the ruler himself or, in the case of royal youths, by high-ranking members of the court, a pattern exemplified by the scene on Panel 19, Dos Pilas, Guatemala (Chapter 3).

HEAD, TORSO, AND EXTREMITIES

The surface of the Classic Maya body was divided into parts. First came the head, known in Common Ch'olan, Ch'olti', and, indeed, Classic Ch'olti', as *hol* or *jol* (Kaufman and Norman 1984:122). Strangely, Classic Maya glyphs depicted this not as a full head, with hair and skin, but as a skull stripped of its jaw (Fig. 1.24a). Common terms for "face," such as *ut* or *hut/wut*, either of a human being or a fruit, both markers of identity, may be present in Classic sources as *u wuut* (Fig. 1.24b; Laughlin 1988, 1:296; Ringle n.d.; Wisdom n.d.). In the head are "eyes," rounded objects known as *nak'* (Ch'orti'), and their "pupils," *yalteil ut* (Ch'olti'), with their "eyelids," *chuch* (Ch'olti'), and optical stalk (Chapter 4), and the

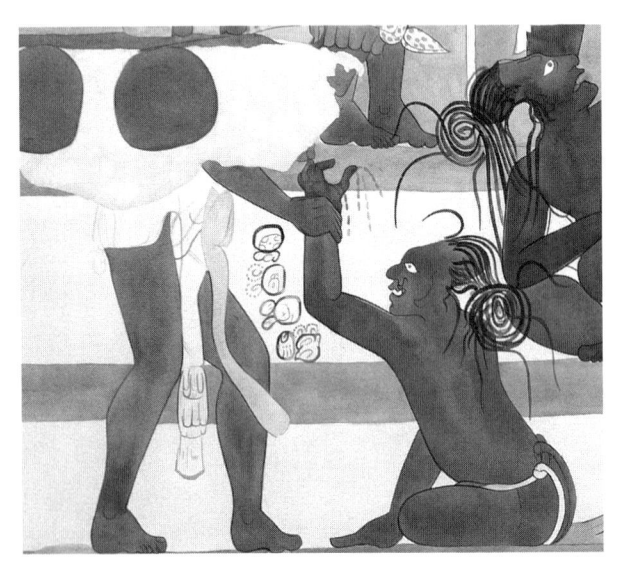

Fig. 1.23. Bloodletting of captive done by subordinate, Room 2, Bonampak murals (reconstruction by Heather Hurst [and in some cases, "with Leonard Ashby"], copyright the Bonampak Documentation Project).

"mouth," *ti'* (Ch'olan languages; Fig. 1.24c), including its corner; the "tongue," **ak'* (Common Ch'olan and Yukatek; Kaufman and Norman 1984:115; Michelon 1976:6); and the "upper lip," *u yemal ca ti*, "descent of the mouth," or *u hol ca ti* for "upper lip" or "head of the mouth" (Ringle n.d.). In the mouth are "teeth," *eh* in Common Ch'olan, *e* in Ch'olti'; in Ch'olti', too, we have *caan* for "molars," and the "cleaning of teeth" as *pichi*, a rather energetic motion that could also apply to "carving stone"; without such cleaning one would lose the teeth to "pustules," *sobil* (Ringle n.d.). The "cheek" might have been **choh* in Common Ch'olan, *cho* in Colonial Tzotzil, or *puc* (*puk*) in Ch'olti' (Kaufman and Norman 1984:118; Laughlin 1988, 2:372; Ringle n.d.).

Of the terms for "teeth," only *eh* is evidently documented from the Classic period, at Comalcalco, Tabasco (Fig. 1.24d; Marc Zender, personal communication, 2003), along with a term for "teeth," *ko*, that, to Yukatek Maya, resembled "grains" (Fig. 1.24e; Barrera Vásquez 1980:323), perhaps because of ancient myths that linked the two (Christenson 2000:60). *E(h)* may also have been extended to mean "sharp edge" or "point [of instrument]," as in a parentage statement at Palenque that employs the phrase /yeh-SPINE/, "point of the spine." Nearby were the "nose," *ni* in many Mayan languages, and "ears," **chikin* in Common Ch'olan (Kaufman and Norman 1984:118), perhaps spelled on a pot in an Australian collection, or "things for hearing," *ubianib* in Ch'olti' (Ringle n.d.). *Ni* makes an appearance in a glyph that emphasizes a lush crop of nose hairs (Fig. 1.24f). Finally, the "forehead" was the *tab*, probably because that is just below where the "tumpline," the *tab*, rested or vice versa (Barrera Vásquez 1980:748); the "neck" was *nuc* (*nuk*) in Ch'olti', the "place where sound issued" (Ringle n.d.); and, in Ch'olti', the "crown of the head" was *u tzutut ca hol* (*u tzutzut ca hol*?), "hairy face of head(?)" (Ringle n.d.). Underneath was the "jaw" or "chin," the **kahlam* in Common Ch'olan (Kaufman and Norman 1984:122).

Below the head, the locus of identity (Chapter 2), is the "torso," **kuktal* in Common Ch'olan and an alternative term for "body" (see above; Kaufman and Norman 1984:123). The "back" of the torso occurs in Classic Ch'olti'an as *paat*, certainly related to the Yukatek term *pach* (Barrera Vásquez 1980:615). The "stomach" in Ch'olti' was *nac* (*nak'*), the "navel" was *chumuc* or *muc* (*muhk*), the "waist" was *com* (*kohm*)—the same as "short"—or *yitnac* (*yitnak'*), the "buttocks-belly" (Ringle n.d.). The "shoulders" were the *queleb* (*kehleb*); the "right arm" was the "big hand," *u no cab* (*u noh k'ab*); the "left arm," the *u tzitic cab* (*u tz'itik k'ab*), or "small hand," and, like anything on the left, it was "small and weak," *chuchu'* in Ch'orti' (Wisdom n.d.). For this reason, most objects to the viewer's left in Classic imagery are invariably of lower status than those to the right;

Fig. 1.24. Glyphs for body parts: (a) *u jolil*, Comalcalco Urn 26, Spine 6 (after drawing by Marc Zender); (b) *u wuut*(?), Copan Stela 11:B3 (after drawing by Barbara Fash); (c) *u pakab ti'il*, "its lintel-door/mouth," Chichen Itza Las Monjas Lintel 3a:A2 (after drawing by Ian Graham); (d) *ti 1 yeh xook*, Comalcalco Urn 26, Pendant 17a (after drawing by Marc Zender); (e) full-body name glyph, showing [ko] where teeth should be, Naranjo Stela 43; and (f) [ni] or "nose" sign, Copan Stela A:B12 (after drawing by Barbara Fash).

not surprisingly, things that are high outrank those that are low (Houston 1998). And the "armpit" is *chitam mez,* "peccary broom(?)," producing, like its namesake, a thoroughly bad smell. Further down is the "elbow," *chuc,* or *-amas* in Ch'orti'; that was "a bony place" in Ch'orti' (*bahk*), but also, according to some Classic Maya iconography, as in sculptures at Piedras Negras, "a place of water," to judge from the aquatic swirls at such locations on supernatural bodies.

The hands come next. As central tools of the human body, they merited close attention. The "hand" itself was *k'ab* in most Mayan languages, including Common Ch'olan (Kaufman and Norman 1984:123). The "wrist" was the "neck" of the hand, as in Ch'orti' *nuk uk'ab,* just as "knuckle" and "ankle" were respectively the "neck of the head of the hand" (*nuk u-or uk'ab*) and the "neck of the foot or leg" (*nuk u-ok;* Wisdom n.d.). Ch'orti' had *u tun ca cab,* the "egg/stone of the hand," for the fleshy part of the hand, on which one could find "lines" or "roads," as in Yukatek *u beel kab* (Andrews Heath de Zapata 1978:78). Consistently, the right hand is "straight, correct, large" (*no* or *to* in Ch'olti'), or "fine, pure" (*batz'i k'ob* in Colonial Tzotzil; Laughlin 1988, 2:404) and *wikiaq'ab,* "decorated, adorned" in K'iche' (Allen Christenson, personal communication, 2003), while the left hand is not quite obedient and thus, as in Colonial Yukatek, "ill behaved, graceless" (*tz'ik*) or "clumsy like a cloven hoof" (*tz'itz';* Barrera Vásquez 1980:883, 887), and, in K'iche', *moxq'ab,* "crazy hand" (Allen Christenson, personal communication, 2003).

The Ch'olti' arrangement of fingers is logical in its use of metaphor: "fingers" in general or the "fleshy tips of fingers" are *u ni ca cab* (*u ni ka k'ab*), the "nose of the hand"; the "little finger" is the "child of the hand," *v-y-al ca cab* (*yal ka k'ab*); the "ring finger" is *v-yaxin ca cab* (*u yaxin ka k'ab*), or the "greening" of the hand (a reference to a greenstone ring? or *mak u k'ab,* "covering of the hand" in Ch'orti'); the "middle finger" is *u cha te,* the "second" (Ringle n.d.; *noxi',* "tall" in Ch'orti'); and, in Ch'orti', the "index finger" is *noh hor uk'ab,* "great, the head of the hand," and any area between the fingers is a "groin" or "crotch," *xahr* (Wisdom n.d.). Among the Ch'orti', the thumb "creates" and guides the rest as the "mother of the hand," *u tu' uk'ab* (Wisdom n.d.).

Other extremities are the feet and legs. Here, as elsewhere, the Common Ch'olan word for "muscle" was **a'* (Kaufman and Norman 1984:115). The leg itself was conceived fundamentally as "standing," thus we have terms in Ch'olti' like *patva,* "back of [standing] leg," and *uutva,* "face of [standing] leg" (Ringle n.d.). Alternatively, these terms were *patya* or *uutya,* referring to "back of muscle" or "face of muscle"—the Ch'olti' source by Francisco Morán is notoriously difficult to interpret in some of its spellings. The "lower leg" was *pix* in both Ch'olti' and Ch'orti', making the "knee" the "head of the lower leg," *holpix* in Ch'olti' (Ringle n.d.), or the "crest of the fowl, crested ridge, tibia," *tzelek* (Ch'olti') or *tzerek* (Ch'orti'; Ringle n.d.; Wisdom n.d.). The "foot" itself was *-ok* but had many components: the "heel bone" or "heel" was the "stone of the foot," *tun oc* in Ch'olti'; the instep, the "back of the foot," *pat oc;* the sole, *tan va,* the "chest of the muscle(?)/standing(?)"; and the "crack of the foot," *cazcaz* (*k'as-k'as*(?)), the "break-break(?)" (Ringle n.d.). As for the "toes," they are the "children of the foot," *y-al oc* (*y-al ok*), just like the "fingers of the hand," and in logical sequence among Ch'orti' speakers follow: "toe near big toe," *cha' uhor uyok,* "second the head of his foot"; the "small toe," *ukumixir wor uyok,* "its smallest the head of the foot"; and all toes but the big toe, *bikit,* "small and collective object" (Wisdom n.d.). The Ch'orti' Maya distinguished between the properties of the thumb and big toe, and all other fingers and toes.

A few of these terms or images of them make an appearance in the Classic period. *Paat* is relatively common in the Classic texts, and so is an undeciphered glyph that appears to represent the lower body and legs, with an affix that transformed visual punning into two dots of excrement (Fig. 1.25). Other glyphs show the decapitated bodies of dwarfs or a glyph that may be the logograph, or word sign, for *paat,* "back," a body leaning over to expose the back (Fig. 1.26). Navels are shown either with depressions or, in the case of old, herniated men, with extruded belly buttons, a relatively common sight in Classic iconography (Fig. 1.27). There are several examples in which, just as we would expect, "hand" is spelled phonetically as *k'ab*, and there is also a systematic contrast between the "right" and "left" hands, especially in sources from the Early Classic period (Fig. 1.28; D. Stuart 2002). These hands are often disposed into an elaborate gestural language that is extremely enigmatic (Ancona-Ha et al. 2000). One gesture, that of a hand over the shoulder, is certainly one of submission, as is what may be a "dirt-eating" gesture of one hand brought up to the mouth (Fig. 1.29). Hands are also shown as isolated body parts (see above), but glyphic terms as such do not appear in the Classic corpus. "Foot," *-ook*, is well attested, however, and may be used in expressions like "step on," *tehk'aj yook tuwitzil*, "his foot is stepping on his hill" (Fig. 1.30).

BONE, FLUIDS, INTERNAL ORGANS, AND EXCRETA

"Bone," *baak* in Classic Ch'olti'an, has been detected in inscriptions since the 1980s (Fig. 1.31a, b; J. A. Fox and Justeson 1984:42; D. Stuart 1985). Other terms, such as Ch'olti' *chechec*, "ribs," and *chibal*, "spine," have no secure references in the hieroglyphs other than an occasional word sign (Fig. 1.31c). Around such bone or near it, the Ch'orti' see *chich*, "cartilage," and a flow of "blood," *ch'ich'*, coursing through veins, making the person "happy," as in Ch'olti' *ch'ich'ael*. The veins were "small *chich*," or cartilage, the arteries "large" ones, *noh chich*; even the "nerves" went by this all-purpose descriptive (Wisdom n.d.; also in Ch'olti', Ringle n.d.). The cramping or sharp contraction of muscles was understood in Ch'olti' as a form of "death," *cham en chich* (Ringle n.d.).

The bone protected organs, such as the "lungs," *tzem* in Ch'orti'; the "marrow" or "brain," *ulul* in Ch'olti' and *chinamil* in Colonial Tzotzil; the "physical heart," *tum* or *puczical* in Ch'olti'; and the "liver," *tahnal*, or "thing of the chest" and the seat of guilt and sin to Ch'olti' speakers, perhaps due to the influence of the friars. The intestine was "snake," *chan* in Ch'orti', because of its winding appearance, and a "place known to store excrement," *ta'* (Wisdom n.d.). The Postclassic Tancah murals show explicitly the connection between entrails and snakes (A. Miller 1982:pl. 6). In Colonial Yukatek the stomach was a "belly" or "rounded thing," *nak'* or *chochel* (Barrera Vásquez 1980:103; Michelon 1976:94). Naturally, the body emitted fluids as the product of these soft innards. In the main, these were all a form of "excrement," *ta'*, as in "earwax," *tachiquin* in Ch'olti', but there was also "sweat," **bulich* in Common Ch'olan; "urine," widely known as *abich*; "saliva," or *tub*; "snot" or "bodily mucous," *zihm*; "vomit," or *xeh* (with a hint of bulimia, *poc nuc* in Ch'olti'); "flatulence," or *tis*; "belch" as **keb*; "tears" as in *uyarar una'k' uut*, meaning "its watering of the eyeballs"; and "drool," *uyarar u yak'*, "its watering of the tongue" (Ringle n.d.). Of these terms, only a few are known from Classic texts, principally *tis*, "flatulence." Nonetheless, urine and vomit are shown iconographically, as is excrement. Intestines appear as a bubbly, almost shapeless mass with an irregular outline (Fig. 1.32). Blood will be discussed in Chapter 2.

ACTION

The human body during the Classic period undertook a wide variety of actions (Fig. 1.33). The body left (*bix-n-i*); returned (*pak-x-i*); arrived

Fig. 1.25. Buttocks with affix [la] as "excrement," Dos Pilas Hieroglyphic Stairway 4, Step 1:K2.

Fig. 1.26. Possible *paat* logograph, unnumbered Tonina panel, position B2 (after drawing by Simon Martin, in Martin and Grube 2000:188).

Fig. 1.27. Extruding belly button on old deity (after Robicsek and Hales 1981:21).

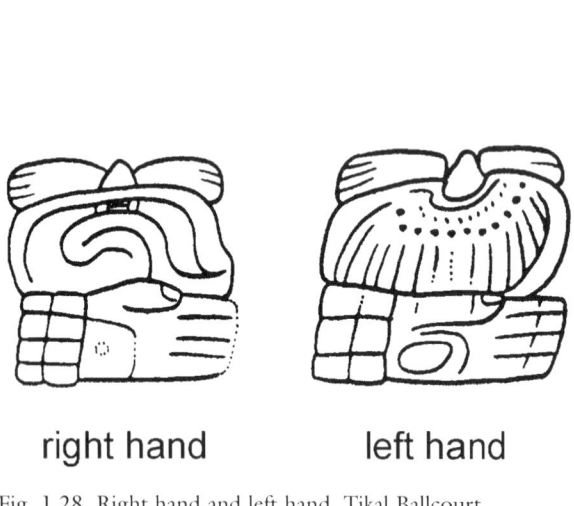

Fig. 1.28. Right hand and left hand, Tikal Ballcourt Marker:D3–C4.

Fig. 1.29. Dirt-eating gesture, Yaxchilan Lintel 16 (I. Graham and von Euw 1977:41).

THE CLASSIC MAYA BODY

tehk'aj   yook   tuwitzil

Fig. 1.30. Glyphs using *-ook,* "foot," Dumbarton Oaks Palenque-style panel:C3–C4 (after drawing by Linda Schele).

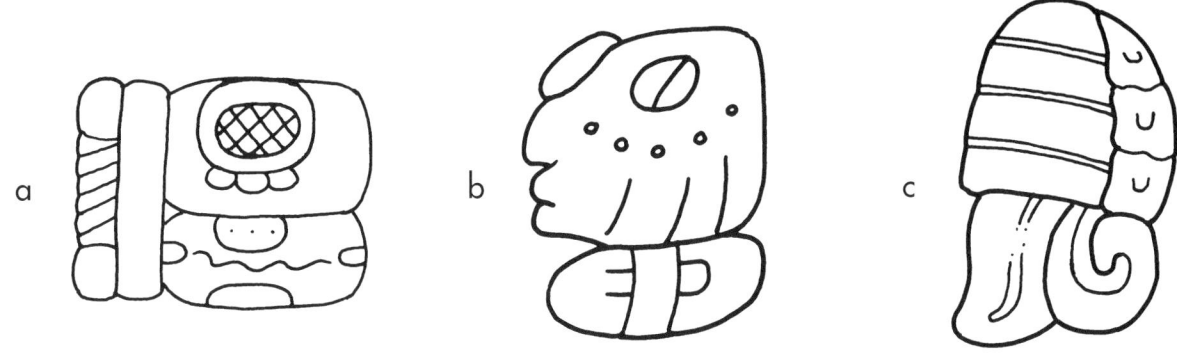

a   b   c

Fig. 1.31. Bone glyphs and rib cage with spine: (a) *aj 20 baak,* "he of 20 captives," Yaxchilan Lintel 3:E2 (after I. Graham and von Euw 1977:17); (b) spelling of "bone," *baak,*" on Tikal bone (after M. Coe and van Stone 2001:pl. 12); and (c) Tikal Miscellaneous Text 9, Burial 48.

(*hul-i*); threw (*yal*); was born (*sih-y-aj*); died (*cham-i?*); was buried (*muk*); received (*ch'am*); sat, usually in office (*chum*); danced and prayed (*ak'ot-aj*); carried (*kuch*); bound (*kach*); seized (*chuk*); ate (*we'*); drank (*uk'*); cut (*sus*); drilled (*joch'*); slept (*way*); spoke (*-al*); and did a limited number of other activities, including some not yet deciphered. A vigorous commitment to "sports," highly controlled yet bellicose activities such as ballplay, boxing, and even gladiatorial contests, figured strongly in the strengthening of warriors' bodies and the expression of their prowess (Fig. 1.34). What is always a matter of surprise to Mayanists is how few actions are recorded out of the great variety listed in Colonial dictionaries and ethnographic lists. Reproducing a set of such unmentioned activities is fruitless, as it would extend into the many hundreds and underscore only the poverty of events thought worthy of record in Classic times.

VITALITY, BODY PARTS, METAPHOR, AND MEASUREMENT

The nature of "being alive" in Common Ch'olan and Yukatek was **kux,* a word that found its way into all descendant languages, as in Ch'olti' *cuxtal,* "life," or Colonial Yukatek *cuxtal,* "to live" (Kaufman and Norman 1984:123; Michelon 1976:76). Colonial Tzotzil confirms the widespread appearance of the expression in *kuxul,* "alive," but also *kux,* "to come back to life, to revive (a plant, person, tree)" (Laughlin 1988,

1:225–226). The shading of related terms in Tzotzil suggests a concept of being free, as in *kuxul vinik,* "freedman," that is, someone capable of doing as he or she wills (Laughlin 1988, 1:226). The motivating forces behind such energies are highly varied, from Ch'olti' *music* [*musik'*, "wind"), or "soul, spirit," to Colonial Tzotzil *ch'ulelil* and *pixanil* or *'ik,* "wind," and *pixan,* "soul," perhaps from a term for "wrapped thing," a thing that covers or protects (Laughlin 1988, 2:458; Ringle n.d.; Stuart 1995). Even "memory" is connected with "wind" or, probably by extension, "breath-soul," as in Colonial Yukatek *ah tub ik* or *ah tubul ik,* "person of the forgotten wind" (Andrews Heath de Zapata 1978:53). Other terms for "memory" in that language, *k'ahlay* or *puksík'al* (also "heart"), relate explicitly to potentialities, graven records, and the seat of the soul (Barrera Vásquez 1980:363).

The terms attested in hieroglyphs are *ch'uh*, or more likely *k'uh,* for "god," and *ik'* for "wind" (Fig. 1.35; Chapter 4; Ringle 1988). When functioning as an adjective, the first sign reads *k'uhul,* "holy, sacred," and has a clear iconographic link to "fluids" or "beaded shapes" gushing from the

Fig. 1.32. Bowels torn out of man by jaguar (after Robicsek and Hales 1981:25).

a

b

c

d

e

f

Fig. 1.33. Classic Maya actions: (a) *bixniiy*, [bi-BIX-ni-ya], "went away," panel from La Corona:K3 (after field drawing by David Stuart); (b) *pakax*, [pa-ka-xi], "returns," Naj Tunich Drawing 65:B2 (after A. Stone 1995a:fig. 8.65b); (c) *huli*, [HUL-li], "arrives," Naj Tunich Drawing 34:A3 (after A. Stone 1995a:fig. 8.34); (d) *yahlaj,* [ya-la-AJ], "is thrown," La Amelia Panel 2:A3 (after Houston 1993:fig. 3.21); (e) *chumwani,* [CHUM-mu-wa-ni], "he sits," Dos Pilas Stela 8:F14 (after drawing by Ian Graham, in Houston 1993:fig.4.14); and (f) *chuhkaj,* [chu-ka-AJ], "is grabbed," Yaxchilan Lintel 44:A3 (after I. Graham 1977:97).

hands of lords (D. Stuart 1984, 1988a). This suggests that "holiness" emanated from the body of kings, perhaps through acts of bloodletting or its symbolic proxies. The identification of sacred and vitalizing essence with the blood is fully consistent with what is known of the ethnographic Tzotzil, among other people, for whom *ch'ulel*, cognate with *k'u*, means "indestructible soul," and damage to it, *ch'ulelal*, an unhappy state when it leaves the corporal body (Guiteras Holmes 1965:229, 262). A separate feature of the soul is a co-essence, or *way*, an aspect of the soul that may leave the body at night (Grube and Nahm 1994; Houston and D. Stuart 1989). The problem in relating ethnographic concepts such as these to the Classic evidence is that not everything fits: *ch'ulel* in Tzotzil is an abstracted form of *ch'u*, but, as a generalized property of all and sundry, it is not clearly the same thing; in Classic sources, *k'uhul*, the adjective, is only ascribed to very few people, those of the highest rank; and the *way* known from the Classic period seem strangely impersonal and even disease-related or altogether dangerous (Chapter 3). The *way* are heavily masculine, a possible indication that the gender of grim, disease-bearing beings or death itself was male, not female as in parts of Europe (Guthke 1999:pls. 9, 18–20). As demonstrated in Chapter 4, "wind," or *ik'*, is far closer to ethnographic concepts in both its foul and fragrant form.

Undeniably, however, the Classic Maya saw bodies as "alive." They acknowledged this by using those same body parts to impart vitality to glyphic signs. This underscored the energized quality of words by means of "animation," in which signs would sprout body parts, starting with the outline of a human face, then eyes and other facial features, and eventually a torso and limbs (Chapter 2; e.g., Schele and Mathews 1979:fig. 397). One syllable on Xcalumkin Panel 2 is a head that, although completely phonetic, drops tears from the eyes as a living face might (Fig. 1.36a; I. Graham and von Euw 1992:180, position A9). Another uses a [ko], "tooth," sign in a place where one would expect such a body part, at the front of the "face" (Fig. 1.24e). The [jo] sign has been made to look like a dotted (wrinkled) ear—perhaps the iconic origin of

Fig. 1.34. Boxing by ballplayers, panel on Structure K-6b, K-6 Ballcourt, Piedras Negras (after drawing by Tatiana Proskouriakoff, in Satterthwaite 1944:fig. 22).

Fig. 1.35. "God," "holy," and "wind": (a) [K'UH], *k'uh*, "god" (after K1398); (b) [k'u-hu], *k'uh*, "god" (from unprovenanced jade); and (c) [IK'], *ik'*, "wind," Dos Pilas Stela 8:I10 (after drawing by Ian Graham, in Houston 1993:fig. 4.14).

the syllabic sign?—and positioned where just such an element should be (Fig. 1.36b; MacLeod and A. Stone 1995:fig. 7-25). For this reason, too, depictions of caves, including very early ones discovered by William Saturno at San Bartolo, Guatemala, contain open mouths and, instead of teeth, stalactites. The proposal that caves are the mouths of animated hills, or *witz*, is now commonplace in Maya studies. What is relevant here is that the means of showing vitality was to give such things faces and, more rarely, body parts. Immovable objects such as hills lacked legs for the obvious reason that they were unlikely to shift, although they might show foliage in the form of the Maize God (Fig. 1.36c). The "shifting earth" is for that reason represented as a crocodile or a turtle, both of which are mobile. A related idea is that of imparting human attributes, especially the wearing of clothing and the practice of bipedalism, to animals. This may have indicated sentient will in such creatures, as one might expect of supernatural beings.

The centrality of the human body in fixing things in space is amply documented (Fig. 1.37). The glyph for *tahn*, "within," but also "chest," is shown in later examples by the arch of the solar plexus, two nipples, and a belly button. Earlier examples with quincunx signs probably indicated "centrality," the center of the body. "Inside," *yohl*, is recorded with a sign that resembles a tamale and is perhaps a symbolic form of the human heart (Chapter 3). Something that is "straight" and even "good" is linked to the word for "right," clearly in reference to a dominant hand orientation (Palka 2002). The "top" lord, *baah ajaw*, is the one on the "forehead" (Chapter 2). One could look on these as mere metaphors or as a literal transference of the human body to other features around it, all the way up to cosmic scales or frameworks (Benthien 2004:25; Danziger 1996). For example, in most Mayan languages today, and in those of the Colonial period, the doorway is the "mouth of a house," the post its "foot," and the ridgepole its "head" (Wauchope 1938:34, 101). Similarly, as in Ch'olti, the crossbeam of a structure is its "spine," *u pat solera*, and the "corner," *ni xuc*, is the "nose of the side" (Ringle n.d.). The same holds true in the Classic inscriptions: *ti'*, "mouth," refers widely to "doorway," and sometimes the opening of a building is literally depicted as a maw (Fig. 4.8a–f). In Classic iconography there is also a visual overlap between human fingers and tree roots, with an overt nod to the relation between the human body and World Trees or World Pillars (Schele and Freidel 1990:90–91). The use of resin as incense may have been a literal replacement for "blood" in such offerings, as most Mayan languages apply the same word to both. Several early chocolate pots, so labeled with glyphs, have on their lids the head of the Cacao God, his hair festooned with beads. By extension, the actual "body" of the god—the vessel—contained the liquid made from his pulp and seed (Fig. 1.38).

Fig. 1.36. Signs with markers of intrinsic vitality: (a) "weeping" [na] syllable, Xcalumkin Panel 2:A9 (after I. Graham and von Euw 1992:180); (b) [jo] syllable in shape of ear, Naj Tunich Drawing 49:A2 (after A. Stone 1995a:fig. 8.49); and (c) base of Bonampak Stela 1 (after Mathews 1990:fig. 3).

The measurement of space by means of the body is nearly a human universal: witness the "foot" in English. Ch'olti', for example, has *zapin* for "to measure by arm span," *hun-te zap* for "armful," and *u halabteil ca cab* for "distance from the elbow to the hand" (Ringle n.d.); Yukatek has a wide variety of terms, including *sap* for "arm width," *betan* for "yard," *lata* for "to carry in hands," and a sinister term for "measuring a man's life," *ah nab cuc*, which involves a label for the width from the extended forefinger to the extended thumb (Andrews Heath de Zapata 1978:79). There is some evidence that the Classic Maya regarded an old goddess almost as a Greek "Fate" or a Scandinavian Norn; as archetypical midwives and world-destroyers, their heads sport spindles with cotton, the thread of a life (Taube 1994a: 662–663). The *nab* is one of the very few measurement terms attested in glyphs, with a sign, [na-ba], that shows a hand in open position alternating with a syllabic spelling of the same (Fig. 1.39; Kevin Johnston, personal communication, 1985; Barrera Vásquez 1980:546; see also a more recent study, Eberl and Bricker 2004). This unit was chiefly used to measure rubber balls, in itself a suggestion of massive objects, or, as another possibility, a unit used in scoring points. It may be, as Michael Coe (2003:200) argues, that Maya balls were rather like the "bladder-balls" still used at Yale University; these are hollow on the interior, prodigiously large, and somewhat unpredictable in bounce. The size of Classic Maya balls in comparison to players nearby supports this comparison.

A final aspect of space needs to be mentioned. This is the inviolate space around human beings. Excepting captives and a few other figures, humans seldom touch one another in Classic Maya imagery. This is still common today in highland Maya communities (Allen Christenson, personal communication, 2003). Social distance may have been close among Classic Maya courtiers, but it expanded greatly with rulers and high-ranking lords, who

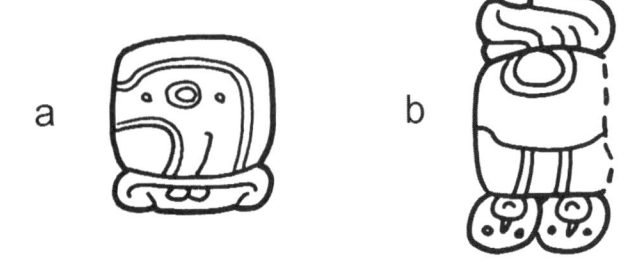

Fig. 1.37. Body parts: (a) *tahn*, "within, chest," Tikal Temple IV, Lintel 3:H5 (after C. Jones and Satterthwaite 1982:fig. 74); and (b) *yohl*, "inside, heart," Palenque Palace Tablet:D4 (after M. G. Robertson 1985b:fig. 258).

Fig. 1.38. "Body" of Cacao God as vessel container (photograph by David Stuart of unprovenanced Early Classic cylinder tripod).

often sit apart, well displaced from any cluster of bodies. Some of the parasols (*boch' k'in*, "covering-sun" in Yukatek) that occur in Maya imagery, such as those in the Bonampak murals, offered protection against the intense tropical sun, especially at midday, but they may also have framed, as they do in West Africa, the sanctified space around rulers (Fig. 1.40; Blier 1998:98, 140). A few deictic (spatial and temporal) markers are known in Classic Maya texts—*ha-i*, "this relatively near to speaker(?)"; *hin-a* (or *hiin*), "that further away from the speaker(?)"; and *waj-i*,—"there" (see Ch'orti' *vai* for "here"; Ringle n.d.)—but they tend only to refer to actions or conditions (Fig. 1.41; see Knowles 1984:206). The best-known spatial locator, connected with the notion of peripheral, ego-centered vision, is *-ichnal*, discussed in Chapter 4.

SEX AND SEXUALITY

If gender is a series of roles, practices, and attitudes engineered within a certain cultural and historical setting, then sex relates to biological identities and the physical, erotic stimulation of bodies (Houston and McAnany 2003:32–34). Chapter 6 presents evidence that sexual activity among the Classic Maya was an ambivalently charged activity, a matter of merriment or reproof, or seen, in the context of captives, as potentially degrading. In Colonial and modern Mayan languages, the state of being "male" or "female" is conveyed by a wide variety of terms. For "female" of any species, Tzendal uses *antz* and extends that term to a label for the "vagina," *antzilel*, or for a "beardless person," *antzil*

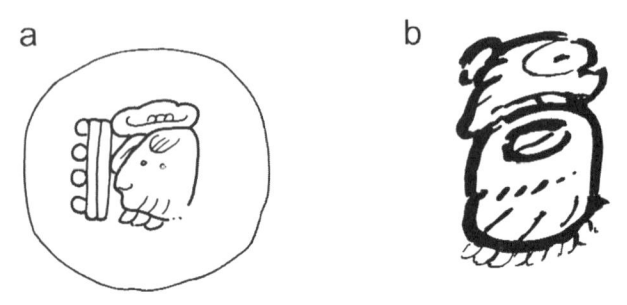

Fig. 1.39. *Nab* as measurement of balls: (a) "14 *nab*" within ball (after Schele and M. Miller 1986:pl. 101); and (b) [NAB-ba], *nab*, showing extended hand (after K1383, vessel from area of Río Azul, Guatemala).

vinic (J. Robertson n.d.). Colonial Tzotzil uses *'antz* in precisely the same way, along with words for "hermaphrodite" or "barren female," *'antzil xinch'ok*, "female-male" (Laughlin 1988, 1:136, 302, 2:393). In Ch'olan languages, *ixik* means "woman" or even "wife" (Kaufman and Norman 1984:121; Smailus 1975:147), cognate with Colonial Kaqchikel *ixok* (Coto 1983:362), while Yukatek employs *ch'up*, a term that could also be applied to "female-hearts," or effeminate, cowardly men (Barrera Vásquez 1980:144). Another term refers to "ladies of high rank," *kolel*, including the Virgin Mary and the Moon Goddess. But the word must be related distantly to the morally dubious category of *ko'*, "false woman of a certain type . . . prostitute" (Barrera Vásquez 1980:333).

The terms for "man" or "male" are somewhat more limited. Colonial Tzotzil has *xinch'ok* or "old man," *mool*, a counterpart to "old woman," *me'el*, in the same language (Laughlin 1988, 2:420, 480). In Yukatek, "male" is either *ton*, a reference to testicles, or *xib* (Barrera Vásquez 1980:806, 941); "man" is usually the marked form of *winik*, although there were many terms that linked "men" to "polish" and "elegance," especially in acts of dance (Barrera Vásquez 1980:865). In the same manner, Common Ch'olan referred to "man" as **winik* and "male" as **tat*, "father, male," or **xib* (Kaufman and Norman 1984:132, 136). The latter term, *xib*, is known in Classic texts, but with a distinctive "helmet" and no hair on the head (Mayer 1995:pl. 148). "Facial hair," which does not grow so readily among the Maya, was known in reconstructed form as **tzuk ti'* in Common Ch'olan (Kaufman and Norman 1984:134); *'isim* in Colonial Tzotzil (Laughlin 1988, 2:363); and *keb*, *me'ex*, *no'ch*, or *tuy* in Colonial Yukatek (Barrera Vásquez 1980:308, 522, 572, 829). Very wispy beards or moustaches are seen in Maya imagery, but the impression is that shaving took place rarely. Among contemporary highland Maya, women pluck their husband's facial hair as a form of sexual foreplay (Allen Christenson, personal communication, 2003).

The sexual and erotic equipment of the Maya body is well documented, perhaps because the Spanish clerics who compiled early Mayan dictionaries were so very vexed (and fascinated) by it when thinking about problems of personal salvation

Fig. 1.40. Parasols in Room 2, Bonampak murals, Mexico (reconstruction by Heather Hurst [and in some cases, "with Leonard Ashby"], copyright the Bonampak Documentation Project).

Fig. 1.41. Deictic expressions in Maya glyphs: (a) [ha-i], *ha-i*, "this," Copan 18:D3 (after drawing by Barbara Fash); (b) [HA-i], *ha-i*, "this," Pomona Panel 8:Bp2 (after drawing by Peter Mathews); (c) [hi-na], *hin-a* or *hiin*, "that" (after K1398); and (d) [wa-ja-i], *waj-i*, "there," Comalcalco Urn 26, Spine 3 (after drawing by Marc Zender).

(Restall 1997:145–147). In lowland Mayan languages, the "penis" is either *ach* or *at* (Fig. 1.42a; Kaufman and Norman 1984:116), and either word might be applied to any darting thing leaving an effect, such as Colonial Tzotzil *'at k'ok'*, "penis-fire" or "flame" that might burn wood (Laughlin 1988, 1:137) or, in Colonial Yukatek, might be the sting of a bee, wasp, or scorpion that resulted in welts or worse (Barrera Vásquez 1980:2). Perhaps this is why the penis of some Classic deities, such as the Storm God, is often depicted as a snake (Freidel et al. 1993:fig. 2:27). The Kaqchikel term for "man," *achi* or *achih*, is probably related (Coto 1983:276; J. Robertson, personal communication, 2003). Colonial Tzotzil also stresses the use of "penis" in expressions for "friendliness," "frankness," and a "generous, noble person" (*'atil vinik*; Laughlin 1988, 1:137). Is this because a nobleman disseminates largesse, just as the penis helps to create life? Yukatek has yet other words, *kep* and *mah* or *ma'ah*, the latter meaning "groin" and equally applicable to male and female privates, along with a word for "scrotum" that likens it to a small "bag," *boon* or *chim* (Barrera Vásquez 1980:311, 475, 806); today, in Quintana Roo, Mexico, deer scrota are used in exactly this way. In some Mayan languages, such as modern Tzotzil, the penis of a young man is jokingly referred to as a "bird." This may explain why some wedding breads took an avian shape, since the "bird" would be brought into service soon after the festivities (Coto 1983:348; Laughlin 1975:245). In contrast, Ch'olti' uses *cul* to mean "penis," a word that could also be deployed in counting "eggs," again in relation to testicles (Ringle n.d.). The sign for "nest," the syllable [k'u], may also have alluded to two testicles (metaphorical eggs) surrounded, not by twigs, but by pubic hair (Fig. 1.42b).

The closely related language of Ch'orti' has an astonishingly wide array of terms for parts of the penis. This organ has a "head" (*p'it, hor*) or "tip" (*chakar*); a short, flat "top" (*pek*); a "cave" or

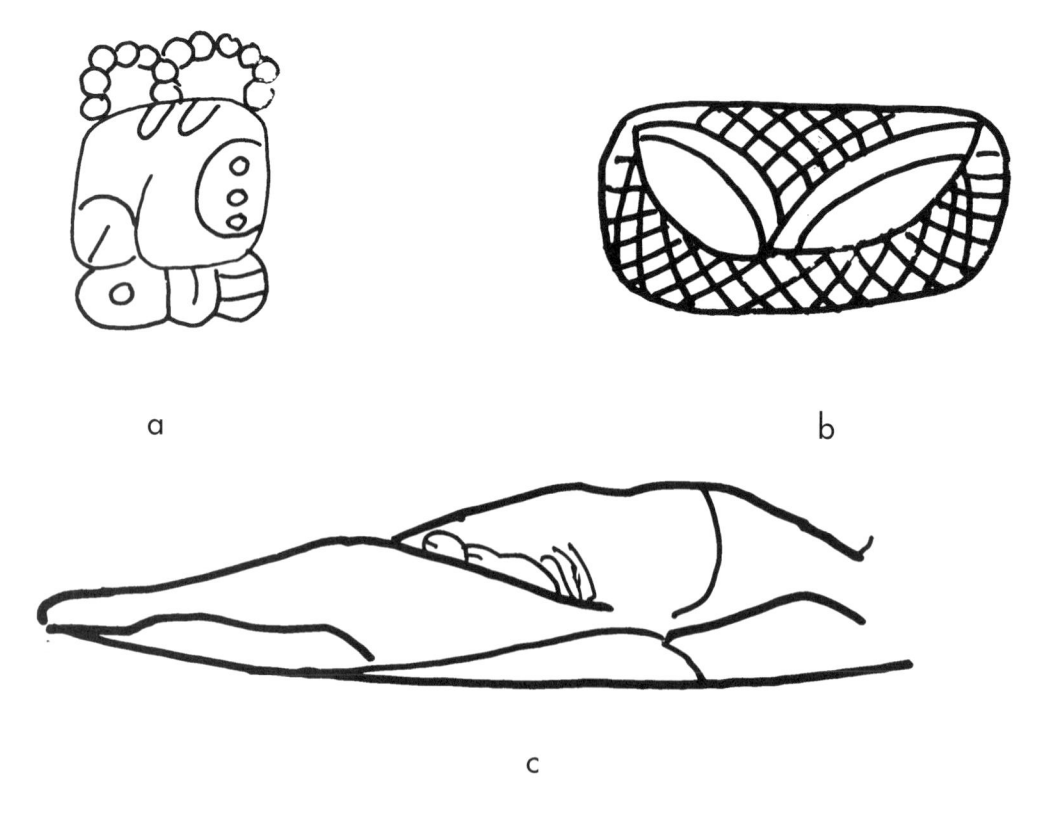

Fig. 1.42. "Penis," *aat:* (a) name of deity, part of royal epithet, Quirigua Structure 1B-1 (after Martin and Grube 2000:225); (b) "eggs" (testicles?) in "nest," Tikal Hombre de Tikal:E2 (after Fahsen 1988:fig. 4); and (c) man with penis and pubic hair (after photograph by David Stuart of unprovenanced vessel).

groove around its head (*ch'en*); a "fleshy" foreskin or "husk" (*k'eweerar, pat*); and a vein or "passage" (*numib*) leading to an "eye" or "opening" (*ut, wa'arib*), plus it can be seen overall as a "stalk" (*ox*) or "whiskbroom" (*sarak;* Wisdom n.d.). The penis could "die" (*chamay*) when it lost its erection or be likened to a "hanging flap" (*buch*). It might "dangle" like hair (*chuur*), "stand up" (*wa'waan*) or "rise" like steam or an excited woman's nipple (*hachbah awa'wan*). And the penis could "burn with venereal disease" (*ik'ar, k'ux, yah*), "swell" (*sanba'ar*), or "excrete pus" (*pohowiaar*). The worst of all was to suffer impotence, to be hopelessly "soft and tender" (*ink'un;* Wisdom n.d.). The penis could have the "foreskin pulled back" (*kori*), for whatever reason, or "be gripped or stroked during masturbation" (*kor-ox,* "fist-stalk," or, in Colonial Tzotzil, *ch'oj te',* "pierce-stick"), at which time "semen" (*arar,* "sap, juice") would "disgorge" or "vomit" forth (*xuu*). The penis would then "weaken" (*ak'unbu*) like an "old woman's breast" (*chu';* Wisdom n.d.). A few unfortunates might even be "castrated," as in Ch'olti' *puch tun* (*p'uch-tun*(?)), perhaps "squash-testicles" (Ringle n.d.). It would not be surprising if courtly societies among the Maya used such people, who could not, by their nature, create offspring. Theoretically at least, these servants would reserve loyalty for their masters (Abbott 1999:321; Scholz 2001:125–157, 193–234).

Ch'orti' is equally explicit about female genitalia. (One can only imagine Charles Wisdom, who compiled the list, eliciting such terms in the 1930s.) The principal word is *tux,* "vulva," which goes back to Common Ch'olan **tux* and even beyond, to Common Mayan, along with "vagina," *kuhr,* probably linked in some way to the word for "penis" (Kaufman and Norman 1984:133). The "womb" is something that "holds" a child and is thus *kuch,* for "carrying." The "vaginal lips" are *ti' ukuch,* "mouth of the womb"; *we'erar,* "lips"; or *num,* "passages," and the stiff "pubic hair" is *tzu'n,* like "spines." Typically, it is the head and its parts that supply terms for other parts of the body. Ch'orti', at least in Wisdom's list, appears to have words for "douching," including *poki,* "wash out," and *bu'ht',* "stuff, fill," perhaps in response to worrisome excretions, or *ta'* (Wisdom n.d.). In Colonial Yukatek, the female genitalia were a place of "ugliness" and "pollution" (*k'asal*), qualities also attributed to semen (Barrera Vásquez 1980:381). It is perhaps for that reason that these features are seldom shown in Maya imagery (A. Stone 1995a:fig. 6-14).

The female body issues fluids, a point carefully noted in Mayan languages. For Yukatek speakers, menstruation involves an "arrival" (*hula,* also a word for "guest"), a "seeing" and a "moon" (*ilmah ú*), "blood" (*k'ik'*), or even a "weaving woman" (*sakal ixik;* Barrera Vásquez 1980:242, 268, 399, 710, 896), perhaps in allusion to the Moon Goddess, whose movements, like menses, fluctuated every month. In a peculiar coincidence, royal or aristocratic ladies in France and England referred to menses in a personalized fashion, as "the French Lady" or "the General's Wife" (Fraser 2002:112n). Colonial Tzotzil identifies menstruation principally as an act of "seeing" (*'ilomajel*), probably of blood, or, inexplicably, as a "soft beard" (*k'un 'isim;* Laughlin 1988, 2:422). In most Mayan languages, "milk" is indicated by the same word as "breast," *chu',* or its derivative, *chu'il,* to be distinguished, as in Ch'olti', from "sap," *itz* (Kaufman and Norman 1984:118; Laughlin 1988, 2:423). In contrast, Yukatek appears to use *its* or *k'ab,* "juice," for this term, especially *k'ab im,* "juice of the teat" (Barrera Vásquez 1980:361). In Classic times, female pubic hair was rarely exhibited, and then only as a slight spray of lines irradiating from the groin, as was also true for hair under the armpits (Fig. 1.43; I. Graham and Mathews 1996:80; K1339; A. Stone 1995a:figs. 8-18, 8-20).

In describing the sex act, Ch'orti' records *bu't'mah,* "to stuff, fill" when referring to animals but *kuruh* for humans; "to abstain" is *ak'ta e ixik,* "to drop or leave woman" (Wisdom n.d.; note, however, that "pregnant woman" in Ch'olti' is *butul ixic* [*but'ul ixik*], "stuffed woman"). Yukatek and Common Ch'olan use *p'en* for "human copulation" and *p'enel* for "sperm" or "offspring of man" (Kaufman and Norman 1984:129). Yukatek goes on to identify a "gluey joining" as *tsay,* a "taking and use of concubines" as *tsub,* and a "bordello" as *tsuk achil na,* which combines words for

Fig. 1.43. Female genitalia: (a) woman with pubic hair (after K1339); and (b) vulva, Drawing 11, Dzibilchen, Yucatan (after A. Stone 1995a:fig. 4.70).

"penis" and "structure" (Barrera Vásquez 1980:853, 866). Colonial Tzotzil describes male-female relations as *kob* yet employs the same word in a term for "active homosexuals" or penetrators, *jkob-xinch'ok,* and "passive" ones or those who are penetrated, *jkobel-xinch'ok* (Laughlin 1988, 1:221).

In Classic sources, there are only a few words or depictions of male or female sex organs, and female genitalia are exceptionally rare (Fig. 1.43). In contrast, there is a glyph that represents the penis and scrotum, with slashes from bloodletting and wrinkled skin, but the referent may be to a particular deity, not to a body part per se (see R. Joyce 2000b:273). Nonetheless, in one image, this god, a variant of Chaak, does appear to be especially well endowed, so the glyph may refer to his member (K4835). Other examples of an erect penis appear to be almost comical, as though flaunted for the purposes of clowning (Trik and Kampen 1983:fig. 83g). No glyph shows the vulva or womb. When naked females are shown, the privates are coyly concealed by a thigh or they are barely sketched, almost always without pubic hair. Exceptions appear to be a female captive (Schele 1997:pl. 15) and various crude and stylized graffito (A. Stone 1995a:figs. 4-10b, c, 4-68; Trik and Kampen 1983:fig. 78b). In the masculine gaze of the Maya artisan, we see an erotic emphasis on the breasts, which do occur, infrequently, as a glyph [chu] with a circle of severance just where the neck should be. Old gods paw the breasts, and highly asexual beings, old goddesses associated with midwifery, contrast with their male counterparts by revealing sagging, nearly conical breasts that extend to the waist (K1339, K1981). The aesthetic impulse is to emphasize a rounded, almost fatty form in the body and breasts, with great attention to the nipple and areola. The modest female, especially in highly public settings such as stelae, does not display her chest; rather, a show of breasts suggests a domestic setting among close kin or, especially when females are stripped below the waist, a scene charged with eroticism (e.g., K2914). The female who inclines backward advertises that she is sexually receptive (e.g., K5164, K8076; see also Robicsek and Hales 1981:vessels 8 to 13).

Actual scenes of coitus or other forms of sexual stimulation are extremely rare in Classic Maya imagery, although they are more common in Postclassic documents such as the Dresden Codex (Chapter 6). The notable exceptions are the Naj Tunich cave, where a man is shown masturbating and an older man and younger male engage in what appears to be intercrural or between-the-thighs sex, and a graffito at Kinal, Guatemala, where anal penetration or erotic fisting is depicted (A. Stone 1995a:figs. 8-18, 8-20; Chapter 6). A pecked graffito from Tikal, Guatemala, features a stylized penis entering a vulva, and one scene of anal penetration may occur in another graffito at Tikal (Fig. 1.44; Trik and Kampen 1983:figs. 21a, 78b). Interspecies lovemaking also occurs and tends to involve a voluptuous young woman with a monkey or even an insect (Fig. 1.45). In another setting, there is a female in the process of being "carried" (*kuhchaj*) by a deer (e.g., the Actun Balam vase [Pendergast 1966]). A large number of Classic Maya pots stress the oversexed nature of the deer (K1339), perhaps as a creature involved in mythic cuckoldry; occasionally, the elderly Zip, god of wild animals (the husband?), sleeps or is in the midst of dying while the female flees or is stolen (K1182; Robicsek and Hales 1981:vessels 14 to 16). A more decorous pairing is indicated by the expression *-atan*, "wife," which is rarely employed. It remains a puzzle why marriages are not accorded more formal treatment in the inscriptions. The term for "marriage," *nup*, is attested with equal rarity, one example being on Bonampak Stela 2, where it is connected with the binding of a stela and bloodletting rites (Mathews 1980:fig. 2). The notion of marriage is probably implicit in the "arrivals" that celebrated the entrance of ladies to the cities that would embrace them as royal spouses (Naranjo

Fig. 1.44. Schematic copulation, Tikal graffito (Trik and Kampen 1983:fig. 78b, used with permission of Sharon Misdea, Tikal Project, University of Pennsylvania Museum).

Fig. 1.45. Interspecies lovemaking (after K1339).

a   b

Fig. 1.46. Arrival of wives by tumpline transport: (a) with "matchmaking" figure (after image in Hellmuth Slide Archive, Dumbarton Oaks); and (b) wedding scene from Colonial Aztec source (after the Codex Mendoza, folio 61r).

Stela 24:C7, I. Graham and von Euw 1975:64). One unique image from the Late Classic period exhibits what may be a matchmaking or marriage ceremony, in which an opossum (*mam*, a "matchmaker" rather than an "ancestor"?) carries a couple in a tumpline (Fig. 1.46). This is consistent with Nahuatl accounts in which the bride was carried to the groom's house on someone's back (Sahagún 1950–1982, bk. 6:131). Note, too, that in both cases the bride has red pigment smeared over her mouth. Another vessel shows the arrival of ladies, perhaps as spouses of a god; to the side may be a bundle containing bride wealth (Fig. 1.47; K5847).

Fig. 1.47. Arrival of brides (K5847, copyright Justin Kerr).

THE BEAUTIFUL AND THE UGLY

Extracting an aesthetic of the body from images is never an easy thing. Nonetheless, it is evident that the Classic Maya focused on the lithe and unblemished body of the Maize God as an exemplar of beauty (Taube 1985). The Maize God, much like the plant he represents, embodies graceful if rooted movement, his long hair swinging in a contained fashion; this is further buttressed by his role as a contortionist, in which he appears, in the free motion of his body, almost to lack joints (Fig. 1.48). For the Classic Maya, such stunts were a source of amusement, too; several vessels show images of balancing acts (K413) or pole climbing during dances (Fig. 1.49; K2356). Colonial Yukatek had a wide variety of terms for such people, *ah kax muan,* a kind of "forest bird," and *ah 'pitil'pit,* "jumper, climber," being two of them (Andrews Heath de Zapata 1978:44, 51).

The Maize God's head is nearly conical, thus simulating the corn cob. In the same way, and probably to evoke that forehead, the Classic Maya practiced cranial deformation to approximate the shape of the Maize God's skull: as humans consisted of maize flesh, so did they reflect that origin in the very form of their heads, the principal locus of Maya identity (Chapter 2). The harvesting of that cob would, of course, have constituted an act of decapitation.

In Mayan languages, the notion of being "handsome" tends to focus on supple youth, as in Yukatek *kichkelem,* "good/saintly youth," with the connotation of inner goodness, *'utz,* as well (Barrera Vásquez 1980:314). In Colonial Tzotzil, *lek* has the meaning of "handsome" but also of "something polished and subtle" (Laughlin 1988, 1:242). These terms applied to women also, implying that "beauty" was behavioral and internal as well as an attribute gracing the external surface of skin and body.

The problem of royal aesthetics is this: Should the ruler be more "beautiful" than others, both in appearance and actions, if only for the purposes of currying admiration and support? A crude answer to this question would be that "the ruler is beautiful and elegant, so let us obey him." Such a response does not seem credible, or is only faintly so. Many other calculations, both conscious and unconscious, must have been at stake in thoughts

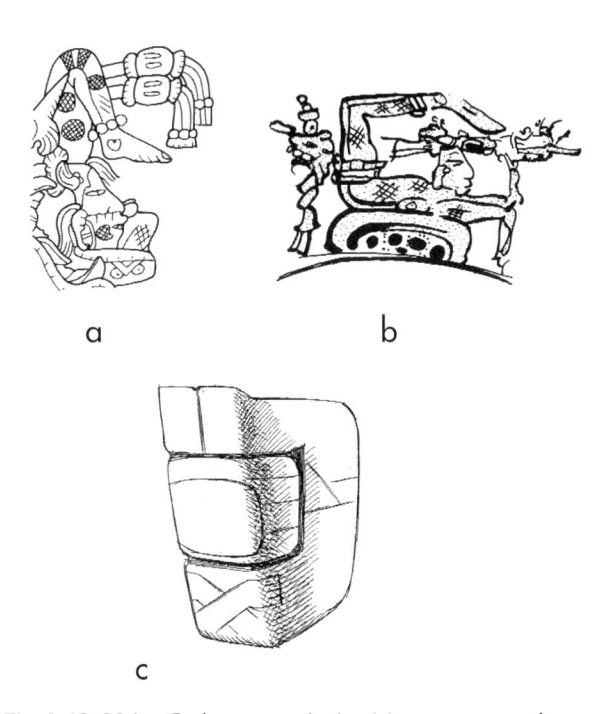

Fig. 1.48. Maize God as contortionist: (a) unprovenanced vessel (after Hellmuth 1988:4.2); (b) unprovenanced vessel (after M. Coe 1977:fig. 7); and (c) Olmec jade (unpublished drawing by Miguel Covarrubias).

Fig. 1.49. Pole climbing and acrobatics (K2356; copyright Justin Kerr).

about legitimacy or, less abstractly, the problem of obeying or disobeying figures of authority and to what degree. A more subtle answer might be that the ruler and his court accord with decorous and appropriate conduct, with polished movement in dance and gracious gestures while seated at court. The great knowledge required of all participants in courtly activity necessarily sets them apart from those who are untrained in such matters. At the same time, there is, most notably in images from Palenque and along the western edge of Lake Peten Itza, Guatemala, an intrusion of idiosyncratic portraiture. At Palenque, the tradition was to highlight the features of individual bodies and to "offer a profound move toward naturalism": the presence of particular people, not generic categories of personage, is acute and powerful (M. Miller and Martin 2004:205). From the Peten Itza region, there are fat, even immense bodies with bellies hanging over the belt (Fig. 1.50; e.g., K680,

Fig. 1.50. A fat lord (K1463, copyright Justin Kerr).

K1050, K1399, K1453, K1463, K3464, K3984; M. Coe 1978:pl. 20). In the main, these images were produced over a very short time, perhaps no more than a single generation, and in connection with the reign of someone named Yajawte' K'inich and his immediate relatives. Most images of Maya lords and ladies have a highly stylized or conventionalized quality. But these images reflect either a different aesthetic of the plump, vibrant body, such as occurs in parts of Oceania and Africa (Gell 1993:223), or a close detailing of an individual body's proportions. This attention to what is seen before the sculptor or painter and what is merely projected may also account for the supposedly "non-Maya" appearance of late depictions at Seibal, Guatemala, where the noses are aquiline, jaws jut out, and faint beards and moustaches mark the face (e.g., I. Graham 1996:13, 32, 34). These faces may not be non-Maya so much as meticulous presentations of actual faces.

The beautiful must exist in relation to the ugly, the good be shown against the bad, and in the Classic Maya context, the ugly and bad were represented by the various kinds of deformed beings. Mayan languages have many terms for them: in Ch'olti', "the crippled" (*huc*), "the skinny" (*bac* or *sem*, the last word relating to the term for the cooking *comal*, a flat plate), "the pustulant and poxy" (*tzobil, pulel,* or *xox*), and "the hunch-backed" (*puzpat*, "crooked-back," or *xucul chinil*); other words come from Colonial Yukatek and include "the noseless" (*ah cul nii*, "person of the cut nose"), "the bucktoothed" (*ah noth* or *ah ni'ch-ni'ch co*), "the one-eyed" (*ah 'chop*), and "near-sighted" (*ah zaz*, "person of the light, clarity [and with eyeglasses]"; all entries from Barrera Vásquez 1980 and Ringle n.d.). On some Late Classic vessels, the Maize God is accompanied by misshapen dwarfs or midgets (Fig. 1.51; M. Coe 1978:pl. 14), and the thought comes to mind that these are deliberate contrasts between the very beautiful and the very ugly. The occurrence of dwarfs in royal images may reflect their role at royal courts as counterpoints to royal beauty and polish (Houston 1992; V. Miller 1985; Otto 2001:23). There were features the Classic Maya regarded as ugly and even comical, as on the display of grotesques on one vessel (K5093): some are fat, others hunchbacked; on others the lips stick out, the nose is flattened, and the forehead is deeply ridged. One figurine, the fat scribe, his chest drooping like breasts, suggests a disapproving comment on the indolence of literate courtiers (Reents-Budet 1994:pl. 3).

YOUTH AND AGE

Classic Maya societies present a paradox: they stress an aesthetic of youth yet value accumulated wisdom and ancestors. Words for "age" and "youth" abound in Mayan languages. Colonial Yukatek refers to "adults" as those for whom the "heart" is "alive" and "prudent" (*kux ol*), while old people, including those who do not yet have white hair (*ek'bate*), are "used up, rotten" (*lab*), "hard" (*y'ih*), or "dried up" (*chuchul*), and, more positively, "rich with wealth and family" (*k'ilis;* Barrera Vásquez 1980:15, 108, 356, 400, 429, 976; see

Fig. 1.51. Dwarf (photograph by David Stuart of unprovenanced vessel).

Colonial Tzotzil *yijil vinik*, "old person," or *poko'*, "ancient, stale," in Laughlin 1988, 2:287, 429). In the same language, terms for "youth," such as *mun*, often refer to "tender, green" things, but also to servants or slaves (Barrera Vásquez 1980:540). In Common Ch'olan, the "old man" or "husband" is a "big man," **no-xib*, and a "young child" is *ch'ok*, an "unripe thing" along the lines of the vegetative metaphors mentioned above (Kaufman and Norman 1984:127). In Ch'olti', there is a decidedly ambivalent tone toward an "old woman," *yx-calel*, who has a sinister, dangerous quality (Ringle n.d.), and the word for "rotten," *noh-xib*, is the same as the Common Ch'olan term for "old" or "big man."

Classic Maya images of the aged are those in which the legs are skinny and knobby, the belly distended, the chest fallen (Fig. 1.52; K2068). Few living lords were shown in this fashion, and the depictions we have of the aged are almost always of deities. There is a strong impression that any display of protruding bone, such as from a thin torso, was regarded negatively. Not surprisingly, the aged often have few to no teeth, and their faces are covered with wrinkles; if female, their breasts have lost all tone and hang far down the chest, with hard, angular outlines (Taube 1994a:657–658). The ancestors, identified by the *mam* glyph, display an abundance of rather wild hair (a sign of uncontrollability or unpredictable behavior?), beards, and an evident loss of teeth.

Youth is shown in two ways, either as miniature adults or as creatures that look far different, with distinctive haircuts that exhibit only a few patches of hair (Fig. 1.53; K7727). If very young, even newborn, they sprawl on their back or squirm in the arm, a property that extends also to newborn gods (Xultun Stela 5, von Euw 1978:23; see also K521, K1890). This state was known to the Classic Maya as *une,* meaning simply "baby," a hieroglyphic description that is worked out explicitly in some texts (Simon Martin, personal communication, 2000). The Classic Maya entertained what appear to have been paradoxical notions, in that certain gods who were, one presumes, timeless or static, such as the Storm God, could be shown as a baby (Chaak, Xultun Stela 5, von Euw 1978:23) and as an aged and withered version of the same deity (K2068). Other gods were born "old" and, it seems, in pairs, from different placentas (Taube 1994a:663, Sides II, III). Evidently, "old" did not mean "lacking in vitality." Age implied not decrepitude but an inherent authority and strength (Taube 1992b:126).

Sources from Colonial and modern Yucatan refer to an important age-grade ritual called the *hetzmek',* when a child was placed astride the hip

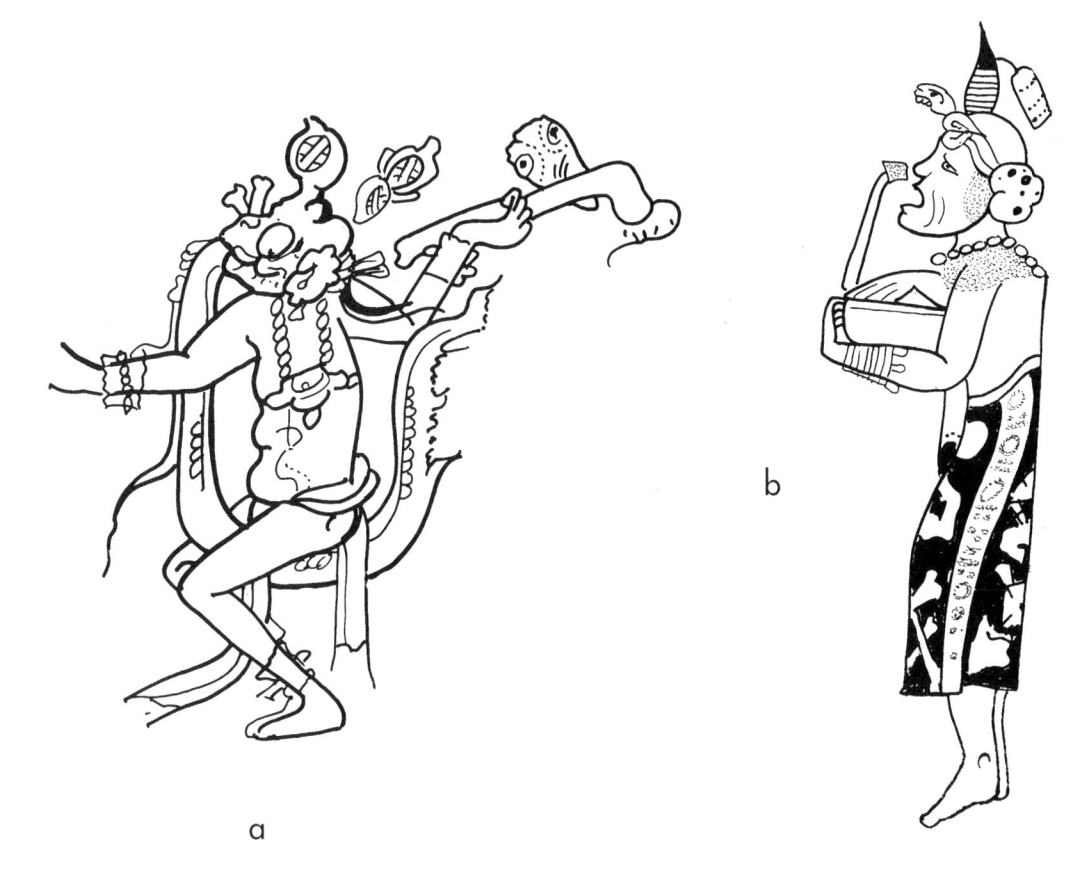

Fig. 1.52. The elderly: (a) an old Chaak (after K2068); and (b) a midwife goddess with drooping breasts (after K5113).

for the first time (Redfield and Villa Rojas 1934:188–190; Tozzer 1941:88). Finally, most youths, or at least those not yet married, went by the *ch'ok* title in Classic Maya texts. Our suspicion is that, as in Classical Greece, the passage to adulthood among the Classic Maya varied between genders, and that a difference existed between the recognition of "biological maturity (the pubertal state)" and "social maturity (the unmarried state)" (Beaumont 2000:47). Young people sometimes participated in important ceremonies, including ones where "gifts" or "sacrifices" (*mayij*) were involved, perhaps concerning acts of bloodletting and the use of stingray spines, and, at Piedras Negras, in the "covering" (*mak*) of young females. This last ritual confirms some sensitivity about open presentation of the privates.

Fig. 1.53. Mother with partly shorn infant (after K7727).

One final age category cannot be avoided, although, strictly speaking, it does not involve living beings: these are the ancestors, the beings that went before and established the pattern for what was to come (McAnany 1995, 1998). Explicit marking of ancestors involves, as indicated before, the [MAM] glyph of an aged male without teeth and with a long forelock. The use of this sign is relatively uncommon, perhaps even more so as the Classic period proceeds, but it seems largely to occur on objects that might be described as "the ornament of the ancestor" (Fig. 1.54; M. Coe and J. Kerr 1997:pl. 39). These artifacts, again mostly of early date, attach the names of deceased kings to precious objects to be worn by descendants. Images, too, might be described as the "ancestor's corporal body" (*u-baah* [of the] *mam . . .*), as on Tikal Stela 31 (C. Jones and Satterthwaite 1982:figs. 51a, 52a, positions I1–J1, M1–N1; see also Chapter 2). However, the more usual pattern is not to stress the full body of the ancestor but to use an abbreviated version of it: one arm, a head, and little else, with what remains wreathed in smoke and flame. The ancestors possess not only objects: on one stela, a god is also described as belonging to the "ancestors," perhaps in the sense of being accorded special dynastic devotion (see Fig. 2.15). Other ancestors were likened to K'awiil, the concrete form of divinity and perhaps of ancestral authority, as at Copan, Honduras, and La Amelia, Guatemala (Chapter 2). In all cases, incontrovertibly, the Classic Maya saw a witnessing, participatory role for ancestors. Much like the waxen, fleshy-looking *imagines* deployed as ancestral presences among the Romans, effigies of Maya ancestors were brought together with the living in ways that reflected mutual relationships and responsibilities. There is a possibility that the especially large figurines, modeled freely and found at sites like Aguateca and Piedras Negras, Guatemala, represent precisely such presences. At Piedras Negras, most have been violently destroyed, pointing to a neutralization of such beings, if they are indeed embodied in such objects of fired clay. One of the puzzling features of Classic references to *mam* ancestors is that, in our experience, none refer to women, although deceased female members of

THE CLASSIC MAYA BODY

royal families were regarded with all due reverence (McAnany 1995:43–49). Was the collective group of ancestors regarded by the Classic Maya as "male"? This would differ from most ethnographic Maya, who freely acknowledge male and female beings among the ancestors (e.g., Guiteras Holmes 1965:271).

A MASCULINE GAZE

It has been suggested that genders or even sexual distinctions among the Classic Maya were fluid and, in the jargon of present-day academic language, "performed" or "inscribed," as though physical attributes could be reconfigured by force of will or caprice of thought (e.g., R. Joyce 2000a:6–10, 64–66, 78–79, 178). The distinction here between gender, a series of learned habits and attitudes linked with sex, and sex itself, a biological property, is basic, although a number of scholars have begun to assert that the latter, too, is culturally conditioned (Gosden 1999:146–150; cf. Astuti 1998:46–47; Stein 1992:340–350). The premises that underlie these suggestions about the Classic Maya—that sexuality and gender were flexible and only intermittently marked, that female characteristics were reduced or overlooked in favor of male ones, that women's status became eroded in dynastic settings—are questionable (Houston and McAnany 2003:32–34). In all known cases of hieroglyphic captions for women, they are named by a distinctive marker, *ix-*; when stripped of clothing, women are shown with breasts, a lack of male genitalia, and, it must be admitted, a certain degree of avoirdupois that is not currently fashionable in aesthetics of the female body. Finally, the supposed claims for "cross-dressing" or "third-gender" portrayals have no support, because they misinterpret

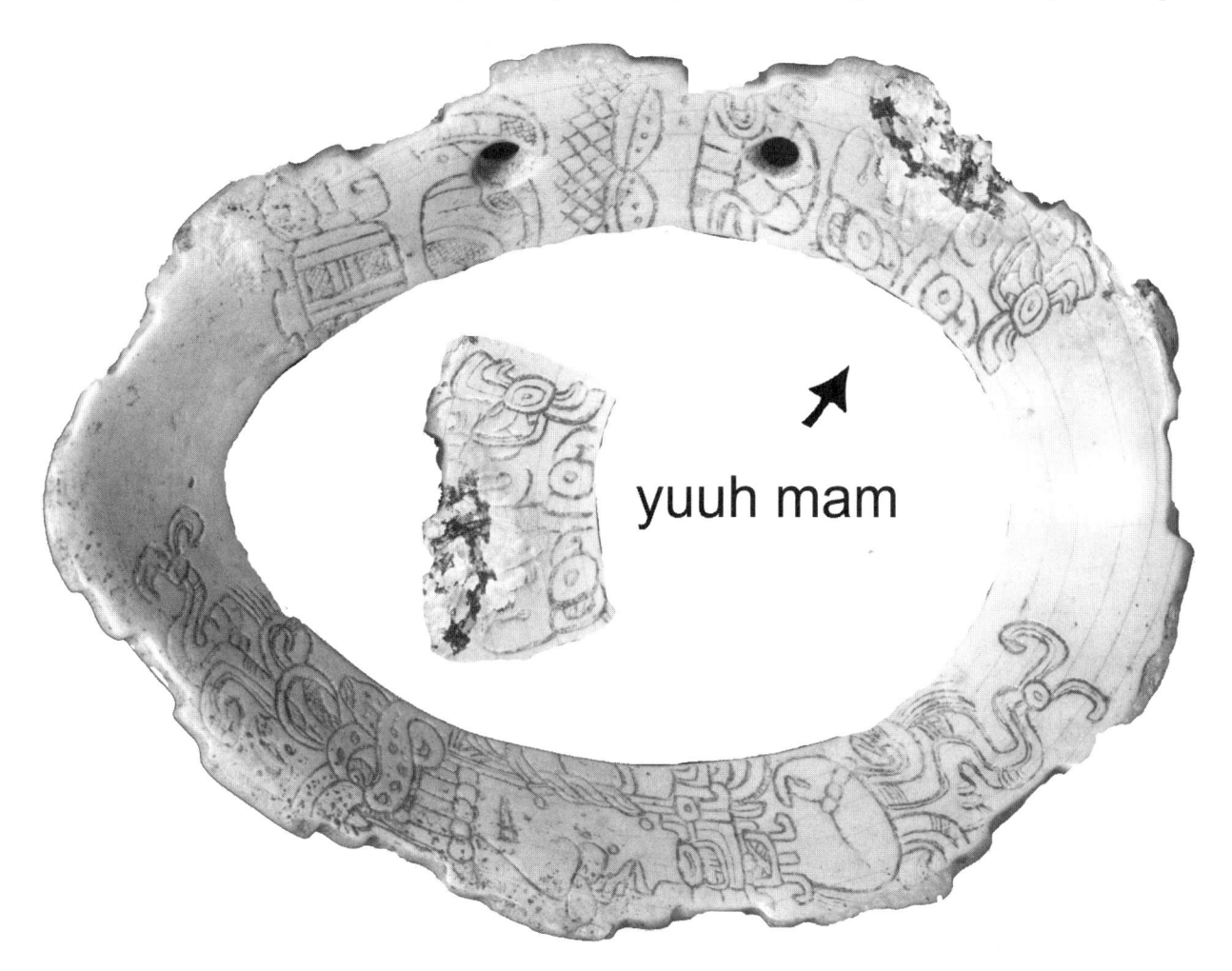

Fig. 1.54. An heirloom of the ancestors (M. Coe and J. Kerr 1997:pl. 39, copyright Justin Kerr).

the garb of the maize deity as being intrinsically female; in fact, these costumes relate to a particular category of deity, not to a blurring of genders (cf. Looper 2002:173–177). A rare exception forms part of a clowning dance in which a man seems to dress as a woman (K1549). Rosemary Joyce has mentioned the "erosion" of female status in elite contexts, yet we do not know what that status might have been prior to the creation of dynastic societies among the Classic Maya, nor can we assume a precondition of matriarchy, female empowerment, or, during the Late Classic period, "a higher status for women in nonruling noble house compounds, where they could claim credit for the products of their labor" (R. Joyce 2000a:89). In fact, women make their greatest appearance in texts and images during the Late Classic, when they are alleged to have had the least power (Fig. 1.55).

Yet Joyce, the most ardent advocate of "performative" and "fluid" categories of gender and sex among the Maya, is certainly correct in one thing, although she does not state it openly: that women did not control image or text making during the Classic period (R. Joyce 2000a:89; 2000b:278; but cf. Vail and A. Stone 2002:203). Every identifiable sculptor (there are many dozens) is male. Every named calligrapher (there are more than a dozen) is male (Houston 2000:fig. 4), although, to be sure, there is one Jaina figurine of a woman posed with a codex. The odds are high, then, that the perspective in Classic Maya texts and images reflects an "androcentric vision" or a "masculine order . . . of perception and appreciation" (Bourdieu 2001:5, 9, but cf. 49–53; I. Winter 1996:11) that might be contrasted with the feminine vision studied by Regina Stefaniak (1993) in Renaissance Italy. The trove of available inscriptions and depictions portrays anything but unbiased snapshots of Classic Maya life. They are selected from a certain vantage, that of male painters and sculptors under close supervision by royalty and other elites. Women could own objects commissioned from such masters, including drinking bowls and weaving pins (Houston and D. Stuart 2001:fig. 3.2). They might even have provided commentary and criticism on such works. But their voices are nowhere

Fig. 1.55. A royal lady from the Late Classic period, Piedras Negras Stela 1, front (drawing by David Stuart).

front and center. To assert the opposite involves a clear challenge to scholars—that they find the names of women who served as scribes and artists. To our knowledge, no such clear evidence exists.

Claims of this sort from three male authors may occasion skepticism. But the trend of the data is clear, to the extent that there is even one scene from the Classic period that records a charter for gendered activity, including the practice of writing (Fig. 1.56). The image comes from a pot that has been repainted in modern times but was documented prior to retouching; for that reason, we can rely on most of its details. The pot shows an act of emergence from some underworld aperture that resembles a stony altar (M. Coe 1978:pl. 16). A male and female pair climb out of this hole. The male is a traveler, as indicated by his broad straw hat. He probably plays a role in the emergence of the first humans from caves, a theme that occurs throughout Mesoamerica and the American Southwest. This vessel scene also assigns activities according to sex, thus helping to shape gender roles. An elderly deity, perhaps one half of a creator pair—another common theme in Mesoamerica—offers an inkwell to the male. Off to the same side are two deities associated with writing and accounting. In contrast, the side with the emerging female exhibits a creator goddess who carries, not a child, as might be presumed from the band around her waist, but a censer burner, perhaps to indicate the duty of tending domestic and ritual fires. If correctly interpreted, the pot attests to an explicit understanding from the Classic period that gendered activities came into existence at some mythic time of emergence.

In her book *Between Men,* Eve Sedgwick (1985:1–2) explores what she calls "homosocial desire," the need for men (or women) to form social bonds with their own sex. Sedgwick writes from the point of view of a social critic who beholds homosexuality as a necessary prelude to the destruction of "patriarchy" or the unjust dominion of women by men. Still, as a term, *homosocial* can be used apart from Sedgwick's particular disposition: the word expresses the need that males or females have, for whatever motivation, to meet or commune in same-sex gatherings. Classic Maya imagery tends to be homosocial (taking place among the same sex) and androsocial (taking place among men); when women appear, they are usually alone or in small clusters—the free interspersion of females and males, as on several mythic scenes from polychrome ceramics, is probably a sign of eroticism, not of everyday interaction between the

Fig. 1.56. Mythic charter for gendered activities (M. Coe 1978:pl. 16, copyright Justin Kerr).

sexes (M. Coe 1978:pl. 11). This is accentuated when the males are elderly, and the females young. A vessel from Tonina, Chiapas, exemplifies androsociality. Two youths speak to one another in a courtly setting, with hints that one, the *ch'ok bakab*, is ranked over the other (Becquelin and Baudez 1979:fig. 183). Later chapters in this book address at greater length the evidence for age-grade associations and even sexual relations between older and younger men. Those rare images that feature only women usually appear next to sculptures showing men, as in the series of stelae at Calakmul or on Piedras Negras Stelae 1 and 3; the latter may even have a male on the other, highly eroded side, although its legible face highlights a queen and a princess on a throne.

The question remains, if Classic Maya scenes are funneled through a masculine sensibility—we have no clear Jane Austen or Madame Vigée–Le Brun—where can we see a distinctively female perspective? Two possibilities come to mind. One might be the ceramic figurines that are quickly made, widely distributed, and, on occasion, thematically incongruent with monumental imagery (e.g., Schlosser 1978; Willey 1972). Nonetheless, these are not securely the products of women, and,

Fig. 1.57. Woman's costume (after photograph by David Stuart of unprovenanced vessel).

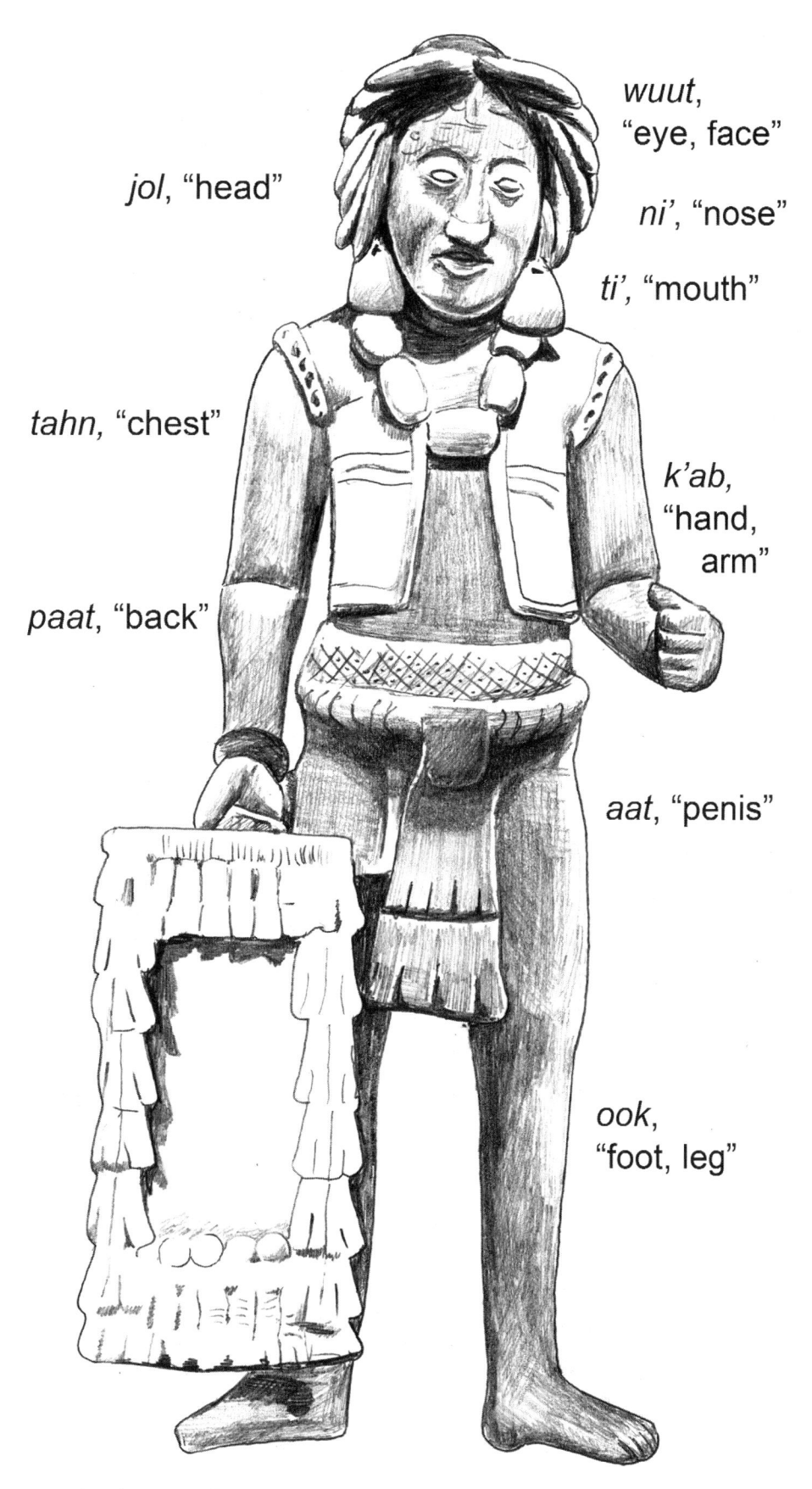

Fig. 1.58. Classic Maya body parts (male figure after Schele 1997:72).

in any case, many are made from a limited number of molds. Another, more persuasive domain of female vision consists of textiles, which most scholars feel were fashioned by women (Taylor 1983). The vast majority consisted of one or two pieces of large cloth. On men they were draped around the midsection several times, with loose ends coming down the front and hanging between the legs. (There was probably some intent both to cover and to evoke the phallus.) The two pieces of cloth were necessary to create a colorful and textural contrast between the waist and the skirt or kilt (e.g., K5176). Even a simple cotton kilt could be distinguished by an elaborate selvage to mark its edges and give greater definition to the shape of the clothing (K625). In general, the amount of cloth worn by males and females was about the same, with the females perhaps having a bit more: the males bunched up cloth around the midsection; females stretched such cloth (*pik* in Colonial Yukatek) to cover the body yet, at the same time, reveal underlying contours (Fig. 1.57).

A few garments represented elaborate productions that involved a variety of materials, including the jaguar pelt linked to lords. Some show what may be the heads of deities (K6316), depictions of sweet exhalations and flowers (K2695, K5456, K6059, K6552), open snake mouths with faces inside (K5037), crossed long bones and eyeballs (K1440), embroidered day signs (K2572), and the very rare glyphic text, as on dedicatory phrases at Bonampak, Calakmul, and Chinikiha (M. Miller and D. Stuart 1981; see also K764, K1599). The surfaces of many vessels play with cross-media transfers by showing images that reproduce cloth or pelt as markers of opulence (e.g., K679, K772, K4617, K5606; Reents-Budet 1994:pls. 1.15, 1.16, 3.43). Nonetheless, these figural designs cannot be securely assigned to women. The one relatively complete nametag on a textile, from Calakmul Stela 9, appears to record a man's name, perhaps the person offering the garment rather than the maker. Those in the Bonampak murals are incomplete and stop, perhaps not coincidentally, just when the name should appear in the dedicatory phrase. With caution, one can infer that the "female gaze" and its expression may have been directed systematically toward less figural modes of display, as was true prior to the late nineteenth century among many indigenous groups on the North American plains (Gugel 2000:194, 212; Khristaan Villela, personal communication, 2003). Still, the broader implication of the masculine gaze in Classic Maya imagery is disquieting. As a massively skewed sample, it creates some difficulty in allowing us to speak conclusively about gender polarities, fusions, and relations during the Classic period, since fully one-half of the system, that involving women, is hazy at best, invisible at worst. More to the point, the interpretive challenge is not for want of theory or scholarly will but arises from inherent limitations of data. The same might be said of the "invisibility" of children, a recent theme in archaeological and anthropological research (Grimm 2000:53–54; Kamp 2002:73; Scheper-Hughes and Sargent 1998:13–15).

EXPLORING THE CLASSIC BODY

The Maya body had many features, of which only a few were noted by the scribes and sculptors of the Classic Maya world (Fig. 1.58; compare with a Zapotec example in Marcus 1998:frontispiece). Here we have examined some of its fundamental attributes, hinted at vaguely in later sources but emphatically declared in Classic materials, and sketched its various contrasts, such as between young and old, the beautiful and the ugly. Any Mayanist should wish to know something of these terms and concepts. It is the Classic body that archaeologists exhume, and its works, the muscular labor of centuries, created the sites scholars dig and the landscapes they survey. Nonetheless, as many have commented before, the images and texts that form the substance of this volume reveal a thin view, one concerned above all with elites and imbued strongly with the gaze and interests of men.

CHAPTER TWO

Bodies and Portraits

Anthropological literature from the last several decades testifies to the complex ways in which the human "body," "person," and "self" can be perceived across cultures (Carrithers et al. 1985; Cohen 1994; Goffman 1959; G. Harris 1989). Studies of personal identity and individuality, and how these are constructed within particular social settings, now occupy a central place in the ethnographic study of human interaction. Indeed, the study of the self, person, and body in culture goes far beyond the analysis of the individual to encompass myriad facets of social life. It also touches on political representation, kinship, and ritual, among other important themes.

In this chapter, we investigate the concepts of "self" and "person" in ancient Maya society, especially as they are linked to physical presence. Any consideration of the self as perceived in antiquity is fraught with difficulties, since archaeological and epigraphic techniques fall far short of direct ethnographic experience and observation. An added difficulty comes from the fact that much of the anthropological literature on "self" and "person" derives from a brilliant but, in some respects, misguided study by Marcel Mauss (1985), an insightful pioneer in anthropological theory but also among the least traveled of ethnographers: Mauss followed more in the tradition of earlier armchair specialists like Sir James Frazer than fieldworkers like Bronislaw Malinowski (Fournier 1994:702–707).

For Mauss, the problem of identity was best understood in a Western framework, in which rather anonymous, group-oriented categories evolved into the exalted Western individual, a "great possession" of "sacred character" that he felt would disappear with the rise of fascism in the 1930s. It is well to remember that his essay on the "self" and "person," among his last works, was presented in that gloomy year 1938, a time of increasing desperation among Mauss's fellow Jews in Germany (Mauss 1985:22; see also Falasca-Zamponi 1997:187; Houston and McAnany 2003; cf. Gillespie 2001). Mauss thus presented an idea with more than a tinge of "teleology," the belief that processes move toward some final purpose or design. And he did so as a topical comment on distressing developments around him. At the same time, "individuation" as a strong sense of individual difference and identity is also found among tribal or non-Western peoples (Kray 1997:32), just as twenty-first-century Westerners can imagine their identity in constant relation to others and the roles they play (Shweder and Bourne 1984). A total and absolute divide between being a monad and forming part of something larger is, we believe, implausible in any society, although this has not stopped anthropologists and psychoanalysts from trying to establish such a distinction: consider the supposed contrast between "sociocentric" and "egocentric" societies, the first stressing, in Marilyn Strathern's terminology, an unstable "dividual person," and the second, a more stable, independent "individual" (Corin 1998:83; Strathern 1988). Alan Roland, too, distinguishes between a "familial self" in Japan and India and an "individualized self" in the United States (1988:7–8). Of late, and in a measured response to such stereotypes, some anthropologists have stressed the subjective experience of being "someone," regardless of cultural setting (Battaglia 1995; Mageo 1998; Spiro 1993), and others, the group relationships that reach beyond individual bodies (A. Becker 1995:4).

Fortunately, as Mayanists, we have at our disposal numerous written sources that reveal underlying concepts of the body and its extendible meanings in Maya society during the Classic period. Quite plainly, Mauss's use of Northwest Coast or Roman examples is unnecessary when Maya ones are available. Our discussion hinges on two key expressions in the ancient texts, *winik* and *baah*, that have received some scholarly attention in the past. These terms reveal core details of Classic Maya perceptions of personhood and the body, as does, according to John Monaghan and Allen Christenson, the related highland Mayan (K'iche') concept of *wach*, which translates as "face," "image," "visage," and "self" (Allen Christenson, personal communication, 2003; Monaghan 1998). For the purposes of this chapter, we are less concerned with teleology or Western-oriented, categorical notions of the "person" or "self" than with the following questions: How did the Maya distinguish between themselves? How did they understand the body as a thing? And how did that concept of the body influence the depiction and glyphic mention of people and their relation to time?

For our purposes, the "person" is a set of roles and attributes that uniquely intersect in one human (or supernatural) and distinguish him or her from others. At the same time, it intrinsically exists in relation to other, complementary clusters of roles and attributes, that is, other "persons." A "self" is that person in relation to others, a being that ponders, when it cares to, the nature of its existence and its relative autonomy from others. Here is a strong sense, an internal, subjective one, of "I" and "me," as spoofed in *Tristram Shandy* by Laurence Sterne, "And who are you, said he? Don't puzzle me, said I" (R. Porter 1997:1). Always present, a thing that cannot be ignored, is the "body." It is a physical object, although, naturally, people will think about what it means and how it should be defined. For Mayanists, the contemplative, introspective features of the Classic "person," "self," and "body" lie beyond reach, the internal queries and doubts about the nature of a single life unavailable to us, as synapses fired over a millennium ago have spent their electrical charge. What we *can* study are the ways in which these concepts were categorized. For the Classic Maya, the "person" and "body" are the closest to the surface; the "self" remains a more distant, almost conjectural notion, sketched by comparative anthropology but elusive to the epigrapher and iconographer. Whether it can even be studied with available evidence is highly debatable.

WINIK, BAAH, AND THEIR MEANINGS

Classic Maya inscriptions have a term for the concept of "entity," a distinct being with certain features and behaviors. This is *winik*, a word that, in various cognate forms, occurs in all Mayan languages, from Common Ch'olan *winik, "man" (Kaufman and Norman 1984:136) to Colonial Tzotzil *winik*, "human, person" (Laughlin 1988, 1:328), generally with the sense of "person" but often, and rather more specifically, of "man" (Michelon 1976:385; Smailus 1975:176). Many kinds of *winik* exist in the inscriptions. They are usually preceded by a descriptive term that specifies what sort of *winik* this might be, such as *k'uhul winik,* "holy person, holy man" (Fig. 2.1). The inscriptions suggest that this category is only *recorded* for men, although, perhaps, it also applied to women. The use of *winik* by women, especially by a single figure at Yaxchilan, seems to be part of an elaborate sequence of titles rather than a descriptive of personhood (e.g., Yaxchilan Lintel 1:G2, I. Graham and von Euw 1977:13). A few texts, such as those found on Yaxchilan Lintel 21, position A3 (I. Graham and von Euw 1977:49), confirm that precisely the same word applies to the Maya unit of "twenty days" as well as to "person." This is completely logical, since a unit has twenty days, and a person has twenty digits. It seems likely that the older term, "person," came to be used for a later calendrical expression.

Another term relates less to a general meaning of "being" or "person" than with the material form of the person. Such a term involves one of the most common hieroglyphs in the Mayan script. It reads [U-ba-hi] (*u-baah*) and can assume one of a few equivalent forms (Fig. 2.2). With her customary insight, Tatiana Proskouriakoff (1968) was the first to define the basic environment of this glyph in Maya texts, even though she was not at the time aware of its phonetic reading. Her discussion of the expression is worth repeating: "The precise meaning of the opening glyph (T1.757 or T1.788) [these numbers designate particular signs] is unknown, but because it is used in a wide range of contexts, almost always occurs at the beginning of a passage, and often appears in direct association with individual figures, it must stand for some widely applicable expression, such as for example: 'Here is portrayed (or recorded)' . . ." (Proskouriakoff 1968:247). Barbara MacLeod (1987:105) and Victoria Bricker (1986:112–113)

Fig. 2.1. *Winik* glyphs: (a) *k'uhul winik,* from a Late Classic vessel; (b) Naj Tunich Drawing 65 (after A. Stone 1995a:fig. 8.65); and (c) *k'uhul chatahn winik,* from unprovenanced Late Classic vessel.

later pointed the way to a more complete interpretation of the sign by suggesting a connection between it and a reflexive suffix *-ba*, which, when attached to verb roots, indicates reflexive or self-directed action. This same root may appear with a pronoun such as *u-* for "himself, herself, itself" (first- and second-person pronouns are equally possible; Attinasi 1973, Knowles 1984:404). A few examples show the widespread use of this morpheme, ranging from Yukatek Mayan *hats'ba*, "scourge-self" to Colonial Tzotzil *ta j-maj j-ba*, "I hit myself" (Barrera Vásquez 1980:21; J. Haviland 1988:95); Tzendal has *ba*, "head, point or principal, first"; *bail*, "face"; and *itbahil, quitba*, "front, forehead," and modern Tzotzil has *bail*, "myself, yourself [etc.]" or "top . . . visage" (Laughlin 1975:75–76; J. Robertson n.d.). In Ch'orti', the noun *p'ah* means "self, body, person, spirit" (Wisdom n.d.). The semantic complex "head, face, top" is also linked with "self" in Tzeltal and Tzotzil.

Current readings of hieroglyphs make it clear that the expression appears in two ways, as a syllabic spelling that shows all of its sounds, *baah,* and as a word sign, or "logograph," that uses a homophone, such as the head of a pocket gopher, to spell the same word, *baah*. In Maya texts from the Late Classic period and later, the rodent head comes to be used as a syllable itself, probably because the underlying word had begun to change from one with long vowel and final /h/ to one without those features. The primary sense of *baah* is "body." This was the actual object of reciprocal or reflexive action; during Classic times, the concept seems to have been visible semantically, unlike later reflexive expressions in which it has only a ghostly presence. "Head" and "face" are closely related meanings. The bridge between the notions of "body" and "head" is crucial. It is the front surface or top of the head that facilitates individual recognition and receives reflexive acts. As the locus of identity, the face or head establishes individual difference and serves logically as the recipient of reflexive action. Mayan languages spoken today or recorded in the Colonial period establish that other meanings flow from the basic concepts of "self" or "person" and "face" or "head." One set is metaphoric, hence the

Fig. 2.2. Sample of *u-baah* expressions: (a) Tikal Stela 5:D4 (after C. Jones and Satterthwaite 1982:fig. 8a); (b) unprovenanced jade (after Covarrubias 1957:fig. 94); (c) unprovenanced vessel, K2914 (after J. Kerr 1990:297); and (d) slate mirror back from Bagaces, Costa Rica, A4 (after D. Stone 1977:fig. 84).

references to the "top" of a cave or a "top-ranking worker." English, too, uses "head" as an adjectival descriptive for the leader of a particular group, such as the "head chef" or "head of state." Being immediately obvious—and close at hand—bodily metaphors in Mayan and other Mesoamerican languages organize one semantic domain by referring to another (Danziger 1996:72; see also Chapter 1).

Another set of meanings reveals Maya beliefs about the head or face and their relation to individual identity. The entries from Tzotzil and Yukatek Mayan define *baah* and its various forms as aspects of appearance, a recognizable "visage" or overall mien, if always in a corporal, embodied sense. That visage is transferable to an "image" or "portrait," a "thing similar to another thing," as in *bail* (Barrera Vásquez 1980:26). A deeper notion operates as well. The body extends visibly to other representations, yet essence transfers along with resemblance: the surface, the "face," does not so much mimic aspects of identity as realize them. In terms of being, an image embodies more than a clever artifice that simulates identity; it both resembles and *is* the entity it reproduces (D. Stuart 1996).

BODY PART, METAPHOR, AND ESSENTIAL IDENTITY

In Classic examples, "body" is a productive translation of [BAAH] glyphs in many contexts, and the more concrete meaning of "head" (attested in Greater Tzeltalan languages) was applied in Classic times as well. We find this in the name glyph of a deity of inebriation, Akan, "groan," who served as a *way,* or "companion spirit" (Fig. 2.3; Grube 2001a; Grube and Nahm 1994:708). His name consists of an "axe" sign, probably meaning "chop," followed by *baah* and Akan (Orejel 1990:4). "Body-" or "Head-chopping," indeed! The supernatural hacks his head off with an axe. But is *baah* used with general reflexivity in mind, or does it describe a particular form of bodily mutilation? In all instances, the chopping cuts the neck and head, so the answer must be the second—that the term refers to self-decapitation. The mythological references on Hieroglyphic Stairway 3 at Yaxchilan and in the K'iche' *Popol Vuh* suggest that this action has supernatural overtones (Christenson 2000:195). Parallel scenes occur in some later Mexican sources, such as the Codex Laud, p. 24 (Moser 1973:fig. 25).

Another literal use of *baah* as "face" or "head" occurs in the phrase, *t-u-baah,* where Victoria Bricker first detected reflexivity in Classic inscriptions. This is most frequently a prepositional phrase in certain verbal statements for royal accession, read by Bricker as "the ruler entered office 'by himself'" (1986:113). The two examples assembled in Figure 2.4 (a and b) show the following sequence, reading from left to right: first, verbs referring to "fastening" or "enclosing" in the sense of "wrapping"

Fig. 2.3. Depiction of the god of drink on an unprovenanced vessel (after Robicsek and Hales 1981:28).

(*k'a(h)l-aj;* D. Stuart 1996)—that is, something (or someone) is "fastened"; second, the name of an object that is partly made of paper (*huun*), probably referring to a specific headdress wrapped around the foreheads of Maya lords (Schele and Grube 1995:37–38); third, *t-u-baah;* and fourth and last, the name of the person achieving high office at this time. These passages refer to the "fastening" of a forehead diadem, long recognized to be a badge of royal rank, "on the head/face" of a lord. Many depictions exist of lords wearing such diadems on the top of their foreheads. Nowhere do the corresponding texts unambiguously indicate agency or self-directed action. Yet this pattern may also be consistent with a process common in language, in which semantically motivated expressions are later, or even concurrently, construed as grammatical particles (John Robertson, personal communication, 1996).

Mayan script and language also make metaphoric use of "head" as a means of exaltation, of designating someone as the principal member of a particular category of person. Several examples appear in Classic sources (Fig. 2.5). For example, *ba-al* probably refers to the firstborn child of a woman (from *al,* "child of woman"); *ba-sajal* is a title for the "principal *sajal,*" based on the title commonly associated with subordinate lords; the *baah-ch'ok* is a position that translates as "top youth" (or the abstractive *baah-ch'ok-l-el,* the rather awkward "first youthship-ness"); the *baah-ajaw,* "first lord"; and the *ba-* "sculptor," or the "top sculptor." (In some of these examples, the Maya had begun to shorten the earlier *baah* to *ba* because of changes in their scribal language. All, however, refer to the same word.) One reasonable interpretation of these signs would view them as indications of ordinal rank within a certain class of people, signifying "first" rather than "top." But, strictly speaking, these are not ordinal number constructions, which are otherwise well attested in the Mayan script. Rather, they represent unique categorizations, a setting apart from others.

One of the most important titles of Maya lords, and high-ranking ones at that, is the *bakab* title (Fig. 2.6a). It usually appears at the end of long strings of titles and has some relation to mythological figures known as the *bakab,* who played a role in Postclassic Yucatan as supporters of heaven "so that it should not fall" (Tozzer 1941:13). During the Classic period, however, the term applied exclusively to human beings, including some women known as Ixbakab. It is now evident that the title can be disassembled into meaningful parts. This is made possible in the first place by a clue from later uses of the title, found on incised vessels from the Puuc area of Yucatan, Mexico (Grube 1990b:fig. 7). The final elements spell out [ka-KAB], the expression for "earth," especially in the sense of agricultural soil with fertilizer (a key element within is the sign for "excrement"; Fig. 2.6b). The first element is usually the syllable [ba], but early examples from areas to the south, in Guatemala, show that this element began as the word sign [BAAH], the sign for "head" or "top" (Houston 1986:fig. 9). The problem is determin-

Fig. 2.4. Fastening of royal headbands: (a) Yaxchilan Hieroglyphic Stairway 3, Step III:D11–D13 (I. Graham 1982:169); and (b) Quirigua Stela J:H4–H7 (Maudslay 1889–1902, 2:pl. 46).

ing what this might mean. Was the title "top of the earth" or, as with other words, did it contain a hidden particle, *a(j)*, meaning "person of," as in *aj baak*, "person of captive," "captor" or "warrior"? In either case, the term assigned a key geographical role to high-status figures at Maya courts, a metaphorical and perhaps literal "hilltop" that supported the sky (a reference to elevated palace dwellings and temples controlled by lords?) or someone in charge, ultimately, of agricultural terrain.

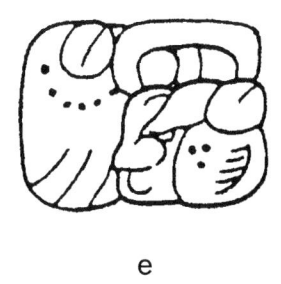

Fig. 2.5. The term *ba/BAAH,* meaning "head/top": (a) [ba-AL], Tonina Monument 69:F1 (after I. Graham and Mathews 1996:103); (b) [ba-sa-ja-la], Piedras Negras Panel 3:D'1 (after field drawing by Stephen Houston); (c) [BAAH-hi/ch'o-ko-le-le], Palenque Palace Tablet:L12–K13 (after drawing by Linda Schele); (d) [BAAH-AJAW], Palenque Tablet of the Slaves:D2 (after drawing by Merle Greene Robertson); and (e) [ba-u-lu-?], Piedras Negras Lintel 3:R'2 (after drawing by John Montgomery).

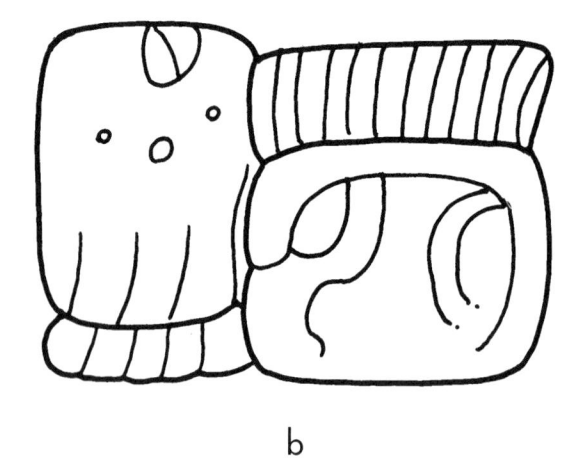

Fig. 2.6. *Bakab* title: (a) spelling from Naranjo Stela 24:A9 (after I. Graham and von Euw 1975:63); and (b) example from Yucatan, Mexico (after K2774).

As noted, the most frequent application of *baah* is in the contexts first described by Proskouriakoff. With only a few exceptions, these follow the pronoun *u-*, "his, hers, its." We have determined already that *u-baah* takes suffixes peculiar to nouns. There is no cogent epigraphic reason to distinguish them from the literal and metaphoric uses of the term. We may then go forward in assessing a new decipherment of the term as "his body, Juan," or "Juan's body." (In usual Mayan syntax, regardless of the particular language within that family, the possessed thing or person precedes the possessor, so that "*u-baak*/Juan" means "his bone/captive, Juan" or "Juan's bone/captive.") Through remarkable insight, Proskouriakoff may have come close to the correct understanding of *u-baah*. The glyphs record that a particular "body" belongs to an individual, an explicit if culturally bound reference to portraiture.

A few examples will illustrate this point. Stela 22 from Naranjo (Fig. 2.7) displays a portrait of the contemporary ruler, K'ahk' Tiliw Kan Chaak, whose long regnal name probably meant something like "Storm God, Fire-Kindles [in] the Sky," among several possible interpretations of these extended names, many of which can be exceedingly difficult to translate. He sits on a pillow throne, holding a long bar, and in the scene is clearly identified by the name glyph in his headdress. The accompanying text begins with a date, followed by *u-baah* and the ruler's name and title. A full translation is: "On 7 Ajaw 3 Cumku, (it is) the 'body' of K'ahk' Tiliw Kan Chaak." Here the textual reference to "body" has been supplemented by the portrait of the lord in glorious panoply appropriate to his role and status. Many examples of this most basic use of *u-baah* can be cited. Whereas the Naranjo example just cited includes a date before the *u-baah* noun, most do not. Typically, a portrait of a god or a person simply takes a name caption introduced by "the 'body' of." Name captions with portraits may appear with no such introductory phrasing, but the inclusion of *u-baah* serves as a possessed descriptive of the image. It is also a good example in which the Maya extended the key reference, the head as a mark of individuality, to the entire body and beyond, to its image hewn from stone. It takes a small part of the person and makes it stand for the whole, a common practice in Classic Maya culture and its Mesoamerican precursors (Chapter 1).

Another context links those "heads" and the bodies attached to them to actions, often in the form of "dance" (Fig. 2.8; Grube 1992:fig. 4; Josserand et al. 1985). All such references accompany scenes or portraits with texts recording *u-baah ti-ak'ta* or *ak'oot*, "his body in [the act of] dance." Other examples include *u-baah ti-chum*, "his body in [the act of] sitting"; *u-baah ti-chok*(?), "his body in [the act of] throwing"; and *u-baah/*

BODIES AND PORTRAITS 65

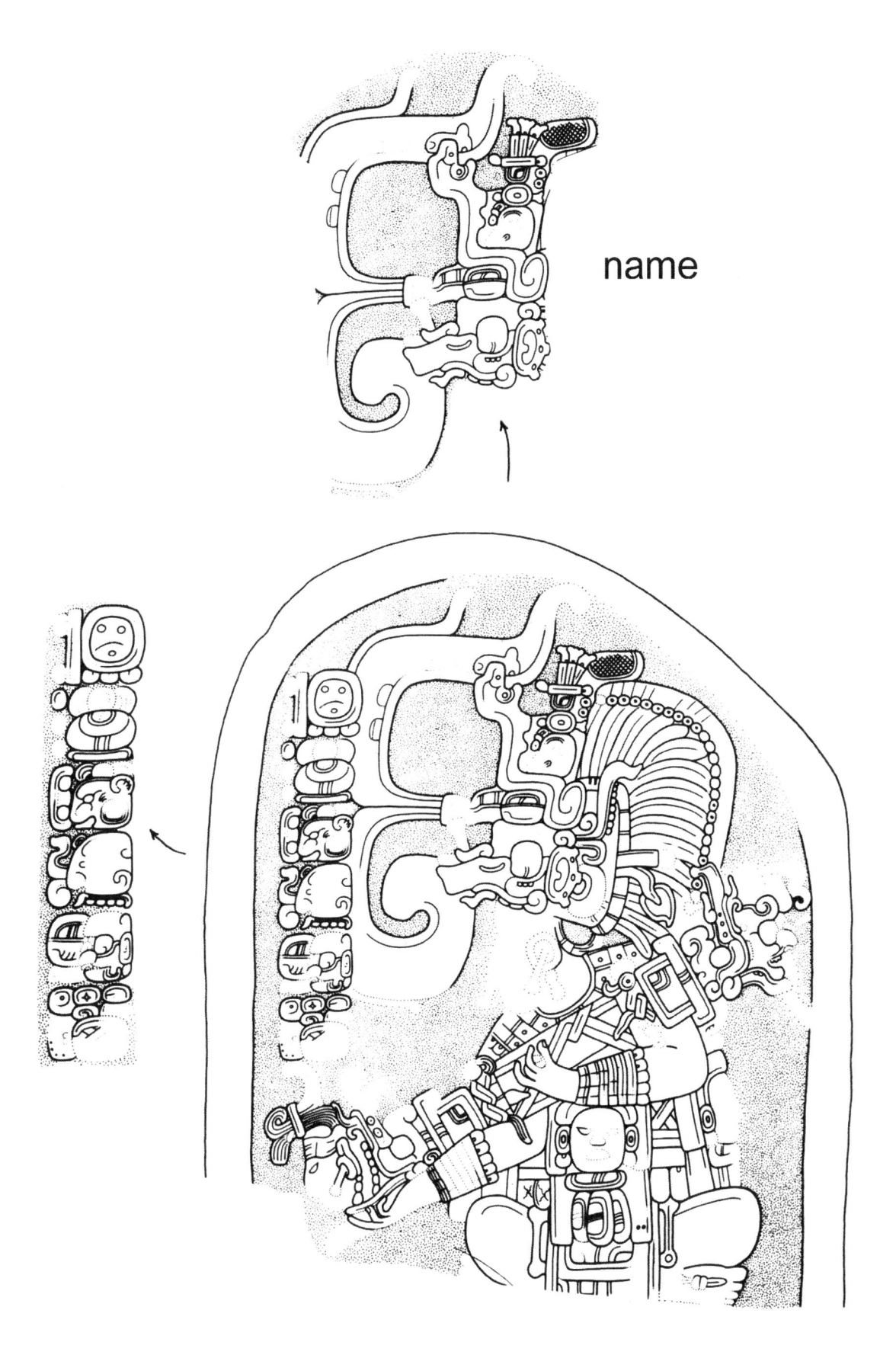

name

Fig. 2.7. Top front of Naranjo Stela 22 (I. Graham and von Euw 1975:55).

ti-way, "his body in [the act of] sleep." Another context, discussed more fully in Chapter 8, employs *u-baah* in a special phrase for god "impersonations" by rulers. Here *u-baah-il* initiates a sequence of signs that begins with an enigmatic term [a-nu] and then the name of a deity. The name and titles of the lord who adopted this supernatural identity follow thereafter (Houston and D. Stuart 1996:figs. 6–7). More than mummery or costumed drama, royal performances in deity costume permitted rulers and certain nonregnal figures to perform and relive mythic pasts, much as they do today in highland Chiapas and Guatemala (Christenson 2001:24; Vogt 1993:161). Of course, they also allowed Maya kings to share in the divinity of gods, in what we will call later, in Chapter 8, the practice of "concurrence," of essences that can inhabit the same space at the same time (Houston and D. Stuart 1996:297–300; see also A. Stone 1991). Textual allusions to the "body," *baah,* as part of this impersonation point directly to the transcendent merger of supernatural and human identity, to say nothing of further linkages with community deities (Calnek 1988b:47–48; Houston and D. Stuart 1996:302). In this, Classic Maya practice resembles those of Central Mexico, where rulers proposed their "likeness" to a particular god by means of performance and clothing (Klein 1986:153).

Some select cases of the *u-baah* expression appear embedded within long texts, where the labeling of a particular image cannot be its function. The inscription on the Tablet of the 96 Glyphs from Palenque is a case in point. The stone bears no portrait image at all, although at one time it was attached to other pieces, now scattered. Yet

u baah

Fig. 2.8. Dance verb from Yaxchilan, Mexico, Lintel 2:F1–H1 (I. Graham 1979:15).

u baah   u 1 tahn

Fig. 2.9. References to "body" in a parentage expression, Palenque Tablet of the 96 Glyphs:J7–I8 (after drawing by Linda Schele).

the [U-BAAH] glyph appears in the middle of the ornate inscription (Fig. 2.9). Here, *u-baah* clarifies ambiguous points of reference, often in so-called parentage statements. In many inscriptions of the Classic period, royal subjects include among their titles extended references to their mothers and fathers. These are structured so that the subject is named first, followed by a relationship glyph ("the son of Juan"), which is in turn followed by a second statement of relation to the other parent ("the son of Juan"; kinship terms expressing the relations between offspring and each parent varied according to the gender of the parent, as is true in Mayan languages today). The *u-baah* expression sometimes appears before mention of the second relationship, immediately before the kin term. In lengthy citations of one's parentage, with relationships expressed one after the other, a reader might lose sight of the child. In such passages, *u-baah* respecifies the referent in an explicit way. This means that *u-baah* may precede the phrase *u-juuntahn*, "the cared one of . . . ," which then introduces the name of the mother. Thus, "his body is the cared one of (her)," where the "body" in effect restates the subject commemorated by the text.

Several compound nouns with *baah* refer to types of objects, probably in the sense of "images" (Fig. 2.10). One such expression is *winba*, a Yukatek term meaning "image, figure, portrait in general" (Barrera Vásquez 1980:923). The hieroglyphic form is [U-wi-ni-BAAH], which occurs in possessed form among the fallen stucco glyphs of Temple XVIII at Palenque (Fig. 2.10a; Houston and D. Stuart 1996:302–303). Unfortunately, the displacement of this glyph from the wall that held it obscures its original setting. The other examples pose equal challenges, for the reason that their adjectival descriptives are not yet deciphered. Dos Pilas Stela 15 records the "so-and-so"-*baah* of a deity (Fig. 2.10b). This may refer to the effigies attested in Mayan script and iconography (Houston and D. Stuart 1996:302–306). More readable is a passage on Stela 4, from Copan, Honduras, which names the stela as the "polished-stone"-*baah-il* of the god who is presumably impersonated by the ruler portrayed on the face of the monument (Fig. 2.10c). The same expression is also found on Throne 1 at Piedras Negras, Guatemala, where it refers in enigmatic fashion to an object, perhaps a sacred object of polished stone (a mask or type of "body"?), that "arrives" and then "rests" for the first time (*ba-hil-i*) before coming to a halt. These rituals prepared for the accession of a new king, who may have needed these ceremonial processions to succeed a ruler who had evidently departed the throne, perhaps unwillingly (Martin and Grube 2000:151). The "polished stone" element is the key to meaning, although we lack a firm decipherment of the sign. It is known to refer to celts, masks, and stelae, recalling James Porter's (1996) demonstration of ancient Olmec-period conceptual ties between celts and stone monuments. This point is developed further by Taube (1995), who finds their origin in primordial ritual fetishes. What seems certain is that the idea of "image" often hinges on terms that are based on *baah*.

One final matter deserves thought. There are suggestions that a Classic Maya deity known as K'awiil represents a pivotal distinction in Maya thought, one between visible, material godhood and a more elusive, immanent version of the same spiritual force (Fig. 2.11). K'awiil has long presented problems for scholars, in that he seems to represent a generic deity, seldom involved in the independent actions that characterize other Classic gods. He is held as an axe that is sometimes in the process of transformation into a snake. But the point is: he is used as someone else's equipment, often by people in dance. In some highland Mayan languages, *kauil* means "idol, false god," as in Poqom (J. Robertson n.d.) and Kaqchikel (Coto 1983:289). The possibility exists that such a word and its related meaning of "effigy" describe palpable or material expressions of godhood. The Yukatek meanings of *k'awil* include a peculiarly diverse range of concepts, from "food" to "supplicant" (Barrera Vásquez 1980:387)—are these the physical expressions of "godhood," as exemplified by god-endowed sustenance and spiritual intercession (Chapter 3)? In this, K'awiil, whose properties seem closely linked to lineage and royal succession, contrasts with the enigmatic God C, read *k'uh*, or "god." Equally generic, God C may express the

Fig. 2.10. Terms using *ba:* (a) [U-wi-ni-BAAH], Palenque Temple XVIII (after drawing by Linda Schele); (b) Dos Pilas Stela 15:C2–C3; (c) Copan Stela 4:A15–B18 (after Maudslay 1889–1902, 1:pl. 104).

invisible, immanent quality of "godhood." In Classic imagery, he is never depicted in independent action. A scene from the Postclassic Dresden Codex is revealing, for God C looks out from a mirror while another deity gazes in; he reflects godliness that can be sensed but not grasped (Fig. 2.11c). This peculiar lack of an embodied state also occurs in the Postclassic Madrid Codex, where God C is a qualitative epithet for other deities.

THE HEAD AS INDIVIDUAL SIGNIFIER

As we have seen, linguistic and epigraphic evidence suggests that *baah* refers to the head or face, in addition to the more generalized body, of an individual. This association may reflect a fundamental conception in Maya and Mesoamerican thought (if not beyond), in which the head or face is seen as the essential manifestation of the body, as in the far earlier Olmec heads. This connection may elucidate several features of Maya iconography. For example, in Maya imagery, name glyphs frequently occur in the headdresses of lords (or indeed, as the headdresses themselves). David Kelley (1982) has observed this to be a pan-Mesoamerican phenomenon, which goes back into the Olmec period (Houston 2004). One of the first examples known for the Maya is the Late Preclassic Monument 65 from Kaminaljuyu, a sculpture that portrays rulers and captives alike with personal names in headdresses (Kaplan 2000). Other cases abound in Early Classic carvings. The Late Classic murals of Bonampak are unusually full of such correspondences between headdresses and personal names (Fig. 2.12). This pattern also occurs with war

Fig. 2.11. God C and K'awiil: (a) Copan Altar of Stela I:K1 (courtesy of Peabody Museum, Harvard University); (b) vessel (K5071, copyright Justin Kerr); (c) Dresden Codex, p. D42a; and (d) effigy from Tikal Burial 195 (after W. Coe 1967:57).

captives, but they often display their names on the thigh, as though in a form of metaphorical branding. The lower the captive's rank, as on Piedras Negras Stela 12, the more likely the body would be marked in this fashion; higher-ranking captives carried name glyphs in separate captions. Through such emblematic devices, the Maya and other Mesoamerican peoples displayed in tangible, concrete form an aspect of individuation, an advertisement of their personhood, of how this or that image corresponded to one being and that being alone. Postclassic Mexican sources also show a special connection between hieroglyphs and individual identity as expressed hieroglyphically. Aztec warrior suits, especially the *tlahuiztli* costume, included helmets that, in the Codex Mendoza, show what may be personal names, although these symbols are often interpreted purely as badges of rank or membership in warrior orders (Hassig 1988:fig. 15). Similar customs are well documented among the Mixtec, who placed personal names in the headdress, "helmet," or necklace (M. Smith 1973:27).

A comprehensive study of Classic personal names is still in its infancy (Colas 2003, 2004; Grube 2001b), but enough is known to affirm that such names reveal indigenous beliefs about personhood and individuation. The fact that some appellatives change with shifts in status, such as elevation to rulership, suggests the importance of this line of inquiry, as does the fact that some rulers, especially in parts of northern Guatemala, may even have multiple formal names, each referring to different facets of a deity. This pattern recalls Jon Crocker's discussion of naming practices among the Bororo of the Amazon, who use names to accentuate the "'spiritual' aspects of corporate membership" (1979:257). In his study of the people of New Caledonia, Maurice Leenhardt makes the point that "[n]o single name includes him [a person] entirely. Each name represents him in one of his kinship or mythic relationships" (1979:154). This brings to mind Classic Maya practice, in which multiple names represent different relationships between humans and the supernatural, each investing the self with a complex identity from different vantage points, an intersection of selfhood that exists at the confluence of many different potential identities. Again, Leenhardt (1979:157): "A personality is the result of intellection about the former personage in certain of its characteristics, retaining various angles and aspects." "Sociomythic domains," those areas where social life touches myth, blend two or more personages into shared realities by the sharing of certain names, just as, among Classic rulers, grandsons often took the names of their grandfathers or other pivotal ancestors. Individuality, however, is partly achieved by connection to the body, which creates a disengagement from such sociomythic domains. At this point any one New Caledonian becomes "a true person," a unique meeting of identities and flesh (Leenhardt 1979:163, 165).

Heads play a distinctive role in Maya iconography. Avid practitioners of decapitation, the Maya often wore inverted shrunken heads about their belts or collars (Figs. 1.19, 2.13b). The same was true of the Aztec (Klein 1986:142; Motolinía 1950:76), who, like the Classic Maya, flayed, tanned, and exhibited the faces and hair of slain enemies. Superficially, such body tokens proclaimed proficiency in battle, but their use, care, and display conveyed much more: "The captor himself never personally wore the skin of his prisoner, no doubt because the latter's flesh was considered 'one' with his own . . . his captive [served] as

Fig. 2.12. Headdress and name hieroglyph, Bonampak Room 2 (reconstruction by Heather Hurst [and in some cases, "with Leonard Ashby"], copyright the Bonampak Documentation Project).

BODIES AND PORTRAITS

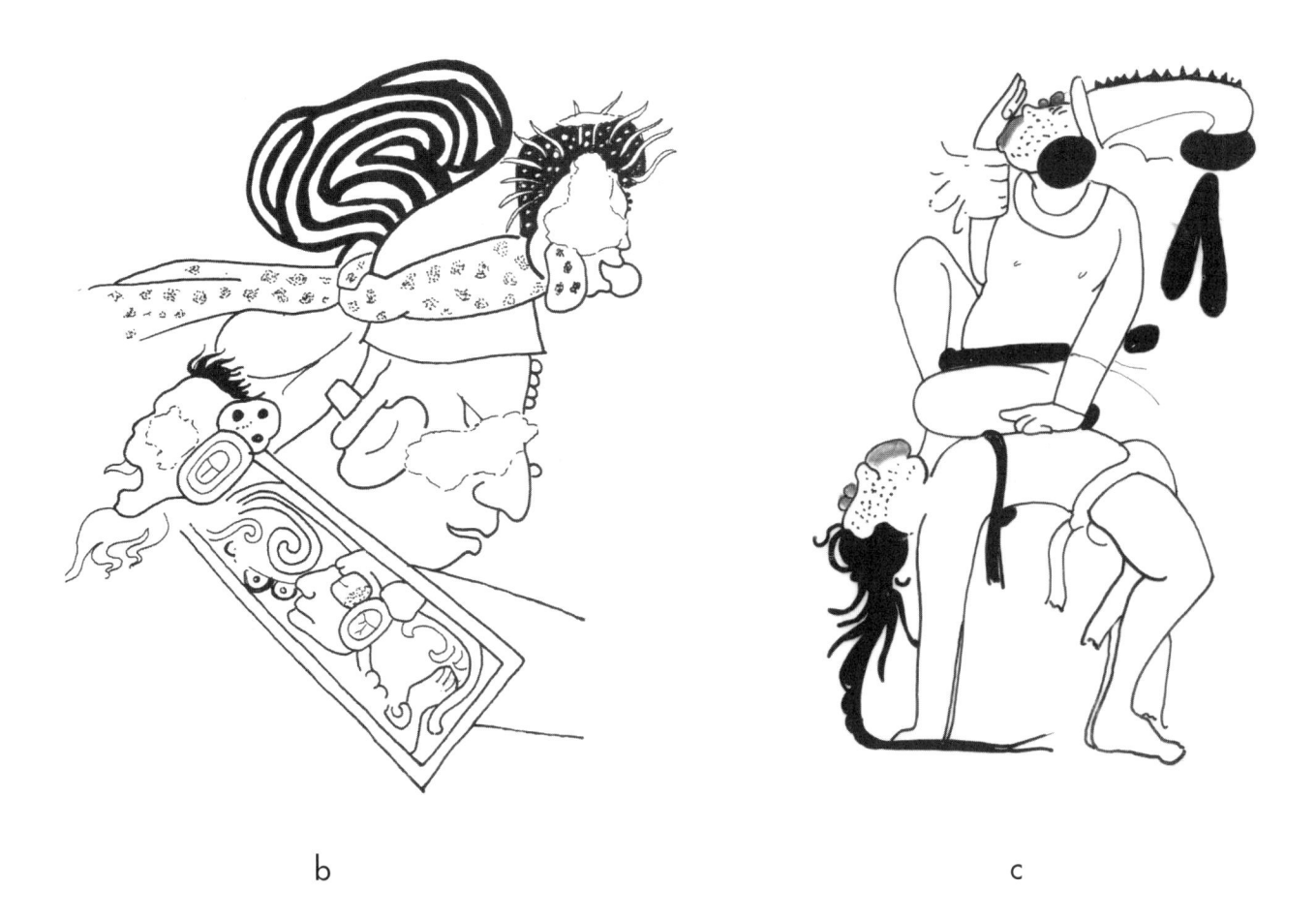

Fig. 2.13. Trophy heads: (a) Tonina stucco façade; (b) stuffed, shrunken heads in Bonampak murals (field drawing by Karl Taube); and (c) dance of decapitated heads (after K2025).

surrogate" (Klein 1986:143–144). Through preservation of a head, the captor participated in or absorbed the identity of someone else, and it is through the prism of personhood and its signifiers that Classic decapitation may best be understood. Rosemary Joyce (1993), working with much less promising evidence, notes similar bonds between the head and "individual distinction" in the stylized images of ancient Costa Rica. Writing of the early Colonial Zapotec, Fray Juan de Córdova documents the flaying of heads and their preservation for display in dances (Moser 1973:6). Similarly, the assembly of Classic Maya captives in Room 2 of Bonampak, Chiapas, includes supplicant (and supine) captives as well as a severed head resting on leaves; presumably this showed the "head's" participation, far more than would other pieces of the body. Epigraphic references to "heaped" (*witz-aj*) skulls, probably in combination with "pools" (*nab*) of blood, may be found in a number of contexts, as at Dos Pilas and Naranjo, Guatemala.

In much the same way, the Maya and Aztec devised *tzompantli* or "skull racks" of the rotting heads of enemies. (The hanging hair of such heads recalls the Nahuatl roots of *tzompantli*, "hair" and "wall" or "banner" [Karttunen 1992:186, 316].) Aside from a well-known Terminal Classic example from Chichen Itza, Yucatan, portrayals of skull racks covered with leaves occur in Late Classic Maya vessel scenes (Taube 2003a). Another representation of a skull rack with leaves has been uncovered at Tonina, Chiapas, in the form of a leafy arbor emblazoned with the upside-down heads of captives (Fig. 2.13a). Postholes in front of this display could have supported a three-dimensional extension of this skull rack. Severed heads could not only come "alive," and be featured as dancers (Fig. 2.13c), but contained the cavorting essences of the *way*, or companion spirits.

The significance of the head did not only involve war captives. Diego de Landa notes the custom of drying and remodeling the heads of venerable lords for storage in "oratories of their houses with their idols"; the ashes of cremated nobles were gathered and inserted in "wooden statues of which the back of the head was left hollow" for this purpose (Tozzer 1941:131; see also Calnek 1988b:48, on the veneration of ancestral bones among the Postclassic Tzeltal). Early Classic imagery in particular records a strong preoccupation with heads costumed in elaborate headdresses and framing devices, such as knots or collar ornaments. Such themes abound in facial representations on cache vessels or censer burners, both noted for their emphasis on their contents (jade, shell, incense, and other materials) as well as surface modeling in the form of faces (e.g., A. Chase 1994:figs. 13.2, 13.6, 13.7). Ancestral figures, often with name glyphs above their foreheads, appear in belt ornaments around the waists of Classic rulers (Fig. 2.14; M. Miller and Martin 2004:pl. 133). A stela fragment from the middle years of the Classic period portrays a supernatural figure holding such a belt-celt assemblage (Fig. 1.24e). Presumably, the clinking of the celts represented ancestral speech. The "belt heads" are more likely to be of jade or some other material than to be the actual preserved heads of ancestral figures—see an example taken in antiquity from the site of Piedras Negras, Guatemala (Proskouriakoff 1974:color pl. 1a, pl. 60.1, fig. 12.3). However, they do emphasize a perception of the head that goes beyond a feeling of contempt for, and physical mutilation of, captives. The accent on heads as signifiers of identity and implicit evocations of the whole body brings to mind the heads commonly employed in Maya writing. Full-figure variants also occur, but it is the head that communicates sound and meaning. (This may also explain the many verbal glyphs in the form of hands.) The reader's eye scans the glyphs as though in direct conversation with them. The glyph's face confronts the direction of reading, meeting it, and the eye of the reader, in a distinct form of social interaction.

THE VITAL IMAGE

So far, we have documented three uses of the term *baah*: as literal references to the "body" or "head," all things related at a basic level; as metaphoric characterizations of a "head" or "top" individual within a class organized by title, age grade, role, or descent; and as allusions to "images" that extend aspects of the "body." Of the three, the

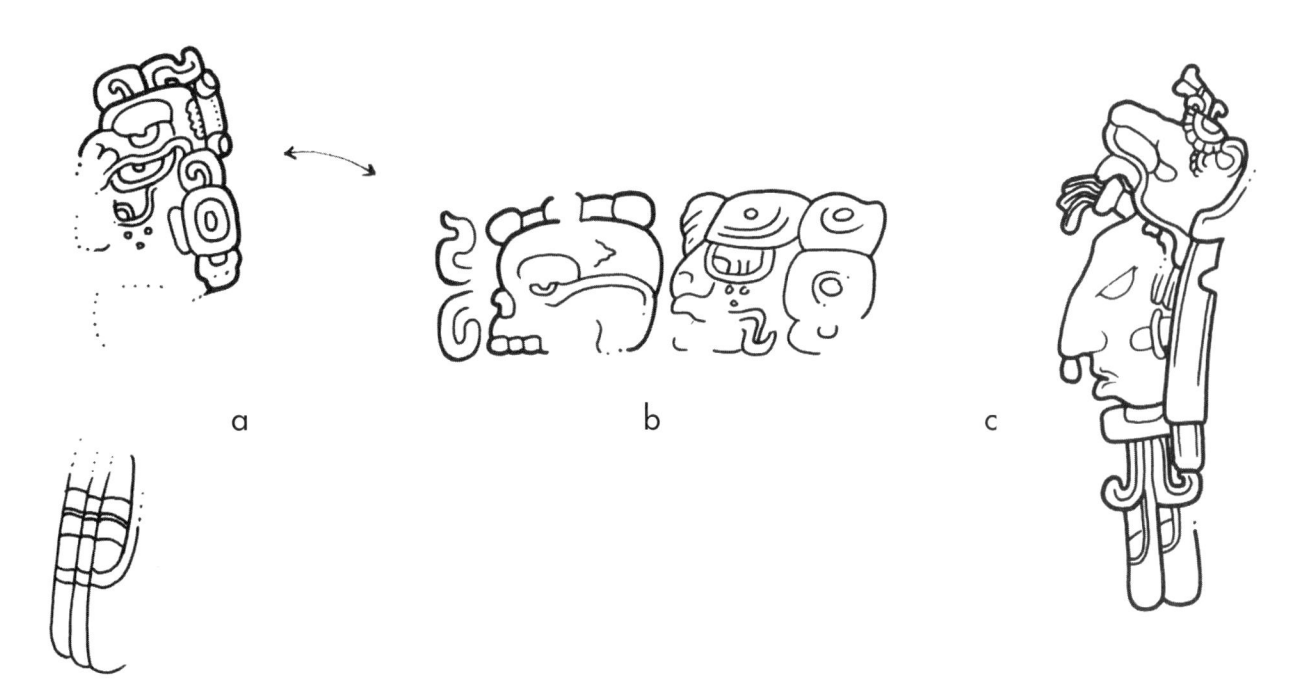

Fig. 2.14. Ancestral heads depicted on belt ornaments: (a) Caracol Stela 6, back (after Beetz and Satterthwaite 1981:fig. 8); (b) comparison with name glyph, Caracol Stela 16:C11–D11 (after Beetz and Satterthwaite 1981:fig. 15); and (c) La Pasadita Lintel 2 (after drawing by Ian Graham).

last penetrates deeply into Classic Maya notions of portraiture and being.

In Western thought, a representation—or, more precisely, an icon—recalls an original through an evocative imitation. Nonetheless, the relationship between the icon and its original is unstable, involving moral and aesthetic paradoxes that have troubled philosophers since Plato, who elevated the icon above other images because it approximated more closely the "internal essence" of the original (Deleuze 1990:257). To Plato, the image should not be a "false claimant to being," the "phantasm" or simulacrum that tricks the viewer into moral confusion and inattention (Camille 1996:32). Today, there exists a Western premise that copies cannot be confused with the reality that inspired them: such is the message of René Magritte's famous painting, *Ceci n'est pas une pipe*, which depicts a pipe and then coyly implies that the viewer is merely looking at canvass covered with paint (Steiner 1995:76). The special experience offered by this imagery comes from its paradoxical quality, its similarity to but virtual existence apart from reality, its capacity to allow us "to understand without assenting, to go over to the other side and still stay home" (Steiner 1995:211–212).

But this was not always the case. Two recent studies of the history of images in Western art emphasize the notion of transcendence between the image and the entity it represents (Belting 1994; Freedberg 1989). For most of European history, and indeed throughout Classical antiquity, images could readily embody the power and identity of their subjects. There existed, in David Freedberg's (1989:30) words, a "fusion between image and prototype." And, as Hans Belting (1994:6) claims, "authentic images seemed capable of action, seemed to possess dynamis, or supernatural power" (see also Barasch 1995:36–39). This has been termed "effigy magic," an act of artistic creation, potentially dangerous and impious, that establishes a special bond between "art and theurgy" (Kris and Kurz 1979:73, 79).

Yet there needs to be some caution in discussing such matters. Moshe Barasch points out that there was no uniformity of belief in Greece or Rome; in fact, ample skepticism about religious practices and their expressions appears among a "thin layer of intellectuals" (1995:60). A similar aniconic or "anti-image" reaction also developed in India, where liturgy focused centrally on the worship of images, sometimes to the distress of those wishing to exalt direct experience of divinity (Davis 1997:44–49). The same held true for Islam. Apparently voicing iconoclastic anxieties, Jean Baudrillard suggests that icons inherently endanger belief, since "a visible machinery of icons . . . [substitutes] for the pure and intelligible Idea of God" (1988:169). Possibly, the worshiper will draw the conclusion that such images are not true representations, but self-contained simulations that reflect "nothing at all" (ibid.). Nonetheless, Baudrillard makes the mistake of assuming the general applicability of Platonic distinctions between essence and material substance.

In fact, evidence suggests a Maya (and probably Mesoamerican) understanding of representation that makes use of an extendible essence shared between images and that which is portrayed (D. Stuart 1996). The act of carving, modeling, or painting creates a surface that resembles the original and yet transfers a vital charge, a living spark, of that original. This has long been a theme in regional research, especially for Postclassic Mexico (Houston and D. Stuart 1996:297–298; also A. Stone 1991:194), where *teōtl*, a divine energy manifested in the *teixiptla*, "the physical representation or incarnation of the teotl . . . is called forth by the creation of a *teixiptla*" (Boone 1989:4; also Hvidtfeldt 1958:76–100). There "is such a resemblance between image and god that . . . visible forms charged with sacred power are considered to be gods themselves" (López Austin 1993:137, 138).

The essential sameness between image and subject in Maya belief is well illustrated by the Early Classic Stela 1 from El Zapote, Guatemala (Houston and D. Stuart 1996:304; D. Stuart 1997). The front image shows Chaak, the Storm God, or at least one of his many manifestations, as the "god of" (*u-k'uh-il*) a local lord (Fig. 2.15a). The text records two relevant passages, one stating that the deity's "big stone" (*lakam-tuun*) is "heaped" or "set into the ground" (*ts'ahp-aj*) on a particular date (Fig. 2.15b). Yet the final passage hints at an equivalence between god and depiction of god. In a restatement of the monument's placement and dedication, the name glyph for the deity occurs in place of the "big stone" glyph used earlier in the same inscription (Fig. 2.15c). That is, now it is the supernatural who is "heaped" or "set into the ground." This fusion of identities—identities that can be transposed or shared—accords with glyphic expressions of *baah* as "body." It is worth recalling, moreover, that *baah* was the basis of a somewhat enigmatic glyph on Stela 4 at Copan that referred to the monument's image. Surely there is a connection between the references to monuments at El Zapote and Copan.

The contention that such images are more than inert, inanimate objects fits with the interactive properties of some Maya sculptures, which exhibit a capacity for carefully staged interaction, even conversation, with flesh-and-blood actors. The sculptural ensemble around Palenque's Tablet of the 96 Glyphs, possibly a throne composed of several parts (J. Porter 1994), incorporates two panels on sloping balustrades to either side of the throne (Fig. 2.16). These are the so-called Tablets of the Orator and the Scribe, named for the Orator's speech scroll and the supposed stylus held by the Scribe (Schele and Mathews 1979:figs. 141–142). They exhibit kneeling figures that, when in place, would have looked across the throne, presumably at its occupant. To a notable extent, they appear to be the same size as human participants. Comparable care with the scaling of twinned figures in interactive sculpture characterizes ballplayer images at places like La Amelia (Houston 1993:fig. 3-21). Similar scaling marks the two ritual clowns in the Reviewing Stand of Temple 11 and the Jaguar Stairway of Copan. What is relevant, however, is the glyphic phrasing accompanying the figures, for in each case they employ the rare second-person pronoun *a-*, "your." Not all of these phrases can be deciphered, but one section spells: [ILA-ji/a-ba/ma-ta-wi-AJAW/u-si-?-na/a^2-CH'AHB-AK'AB-li], or *ila-j-i a-baah matawi*l-ajaw/u-si-?-Vn/a-ch'ahb a-*w-ak'ab-il*, "(it is) seen, your body, Matawil Lord, his ?, (he is) your creation/fasting/penance, your darkness" (Chapter 3). That the figures are addressing someone on the throne or the

BODIES AND PORTRAITS 75

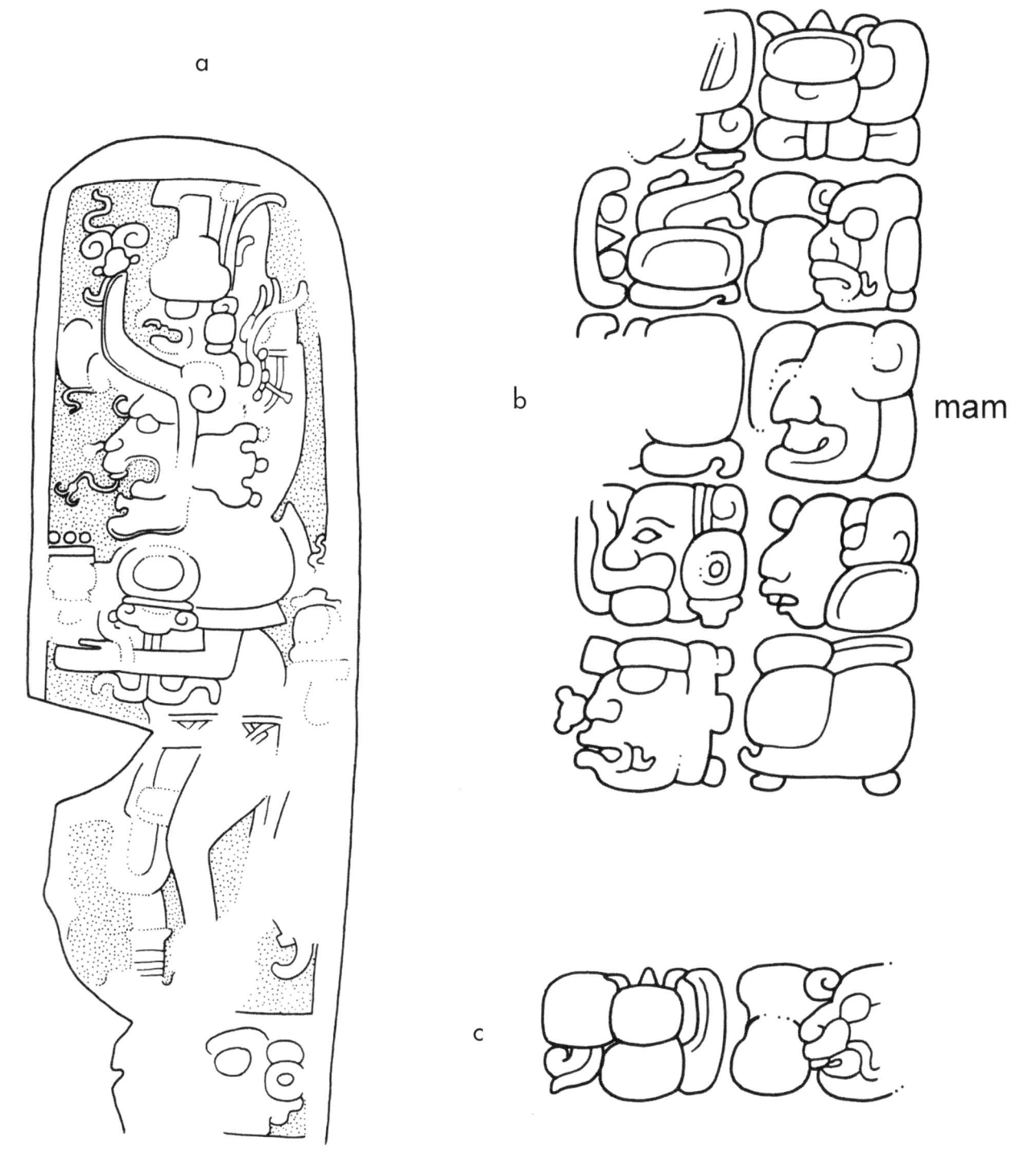

Fig. 2.15. Texts from El Zapote Stela 2: (a) front of monument, showing deity with name glyphs in headdress (after field drawing by Ian Graham); (b) reference to "heaping" or "driving into ground" of monument belonging to the deity (after field drawing by Ian Graham); and (c) deity itself is "heaped" or "driven into ground" (after field drawing by Ian Graham).

stairway on which it rests is implied by their kneeling position and symmetrical arrangement; the perforated clothing and submissive gestures underscore their subordinate status (Chapter 6). The speech scroll on the Tablet of the Orator accords with the second-person references and accentuates the intimate oration directed to living actor by sculpted image. A very similar concept underlies the use of captives showing earspools: they face the head of the wearer, in a position of continual entreaty (Chapter 6).

To an equal extent such stylized forms of address shape the La Amelia Hieroglyphic Stairway (Fig. 2.17). It comprises two side panels depicting players about to strike a ball. Hieroglyphic texts on the panels and the stairway blocks firmly establish a conceptual merger of "ball" and "captive," a rhetorical device recalling images at Yaxchilan, where a ballplayer poises to strike a ball encircling the cramped body of a lordly captive (I. Graham 1982:160). Stairways have many functions in Maya ritual, among them the display of captives (M. Miller and Houston 1987). Presumably the individuals periodically stationed on the La Amelia stairway fulfilled the role of metaphorical ball, in perpetual threat of being struck by the ballplayers to either side. Yet the essential point is that these images communicated with human participants. This took place not so much through a theology of transubstantiation, which converts one substance into another. Instead, the connection results from shared ontological properties, in which sculpted stone attains a vitality like that of living actors.

It is perhaps for this reason that facial mutilations, or lacerations of carved eyes, are so common in Maya sculpture, as we have personally seen at numerous Maya sites. Being so systematic—most Classic Maya figural images, including those in the Bonampak murals, show such scarring—this scarcely represents a casual form of destruction, but instead reveals an attitude about the vital nature of Maya portraiture and the seat of identity in the face. By pecking out eyes, the vandal or iconoclast destroys the field of view of a person and the vigilant gaze of a god-king, not an inert thing (see Freedberg 1989 for a fascinating discussion of comparable vandalism in Western art). In much the same way, in stucco façades from Acanceh, Yucatan, both the face *and* the earspools were pecked out, thereby neutralizing both channels of perception by this act (Fig. 2.18). Yet another example of destroyed "ears" can be found on Censer Altar C from Altar de Sacrificios, Guatemala (not visible in the published photograph [J. Graham 1972:fig. 56], but the original is now on display in the National Museum of Guatemala). Still, the "interaction" between image and human can only be taken so far. Of course, imagery and glyphs cannot communicate with people in a sustained, reciprocal fashion. Instead, they choreograph settings that happen to exploit humans as props. The intended audience is the one viewing such compositions, although "audience" cannot be smoothly distinguished from "participant." Viewers could have functioned as components of an overall scene, to be appreciated in turn by some hypothetical "meta-audience," yet another group of people looking on and commenting on the image before them.

That stone "lives" or contains vital essence—that it contains the "body" of something else—helps explain the "animation" of Maya hieroglyphic elements (Chapter 1). Signs of the script frequently convey a certain vitality, ranging from basic signs with a facial profile to "full-figure" forms that interact vibrantly and kinetically with other signs around them (Fig. 2.19). To some extent, glyphic animation follows a few well-established patterns. Generally, animated glyphs occur in less public settings, by which we mean inscriptions within structures. Those in some buildings, such as the stuccos of Temple XVIII at Palenque, teem with examples of facial animation, with glyphs contoured by human profiles. Usually, full-figure animation accompanies other examples of the same; full and partial animation rarely, if ever, coexist within the same text. Yet it would be a mistake to see animation as evidence of blurring between categories of text and image. Unlike iconography, the glyphs still obey a linear sequencing determined by the language it records. What is different is that they have adopted the characteristics of living beings, enjoying a vitality attested in the ensembles at Palenque and La Amelia.

IMAGES AND MAYA "SELF"

The evidence presented so far has several implications. If the representation of a person shares his or her essential identity, then the person, the body, and the self must exceed the boundaries of the human body—biological and cultural entities no longer occupy exactly the same space (Csordas

BODIES AND PORTRAITS 77

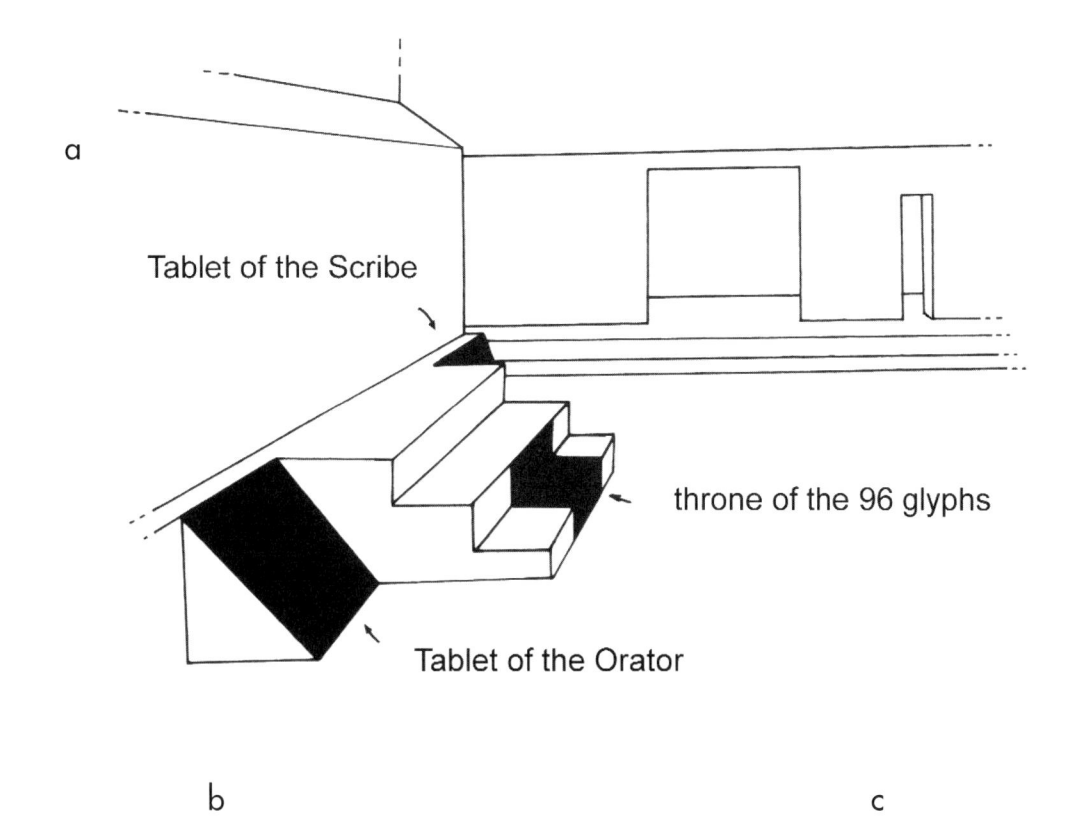

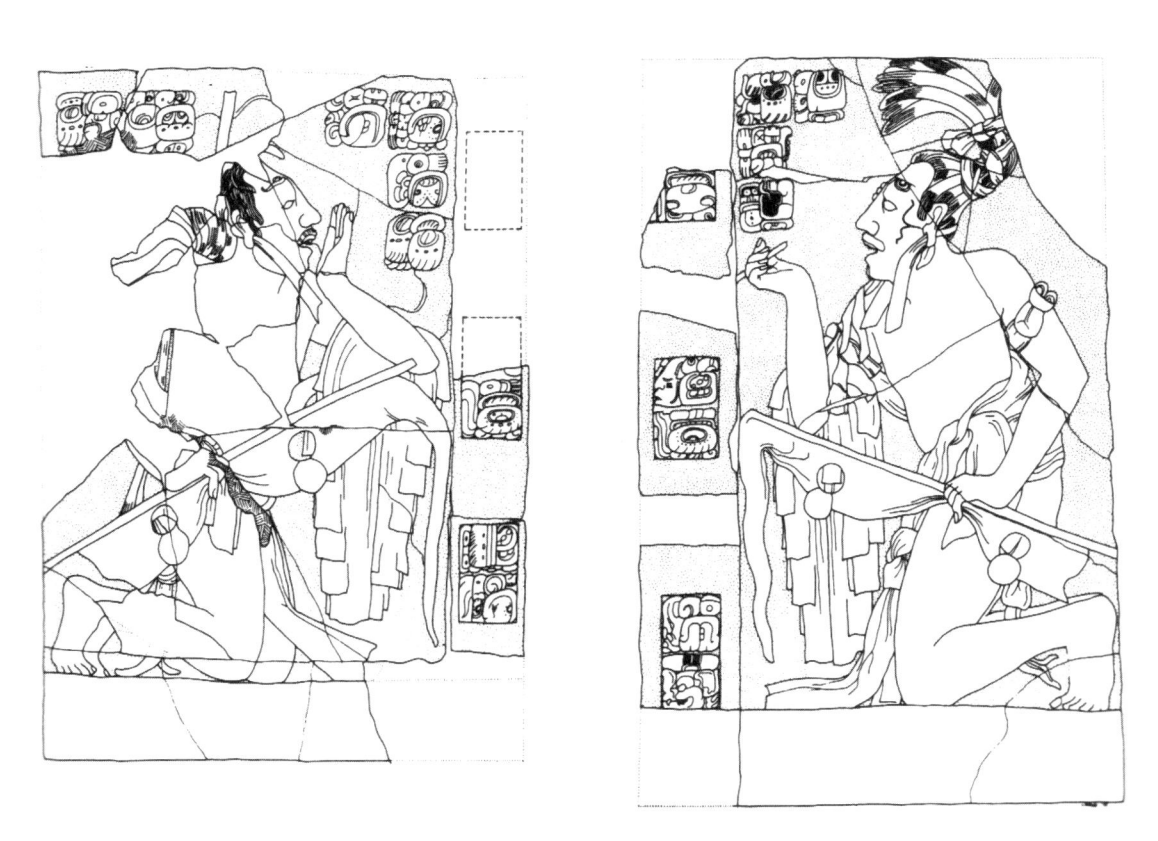

Fig. 2.16. Ensemble of monuments in Palenque, Mexico: (a) location of panels with respect to tower; (b) Tablet of the Orator, with glyphic details (Schele and Mathews 1979:141); and (c) Tablet of the Scribe, with glyphic details (Schele and Mathews 1979:142).

1994:4). Through this device, the Maya replicated both the image and the substance of body and began a grandiose enterprise on behalf of their lords. By reproduction in stone, such images achieved an enduring permanence that would be impossible in the physical body, which must die and rot. Such representations operated not only as memorials of matters of record and of participants in them but as overt embodiments or presences of the ruler, who thereby accomplished the extraordinary trick of being in several places at the same time. The depictions could be approached, supplicated, and venerated when it was not physically (or temporally) possible to do so in front of the physical person of the ruler. Through royal representation, the lord transcended the strictures of time and space and instituted a fixed, desirable state of being (D. Stuart 1996). So, too, for antagonists: by their very depiction, captives groveling in abject misery would remain forever in that unhappy state, even when decapitated, as in sculptures from El Jobo and Kaminaljuyu, Guatemala (Fig. 2.20). Far more than an expression of scorn, the compulsion to destroy images would subvert this intended long-term program. Also, the extension of personal identity into spaces beyond the body introduces a novel spin to William Hank's (1990:131–134) discussion of corporeal fields, the embodied frames

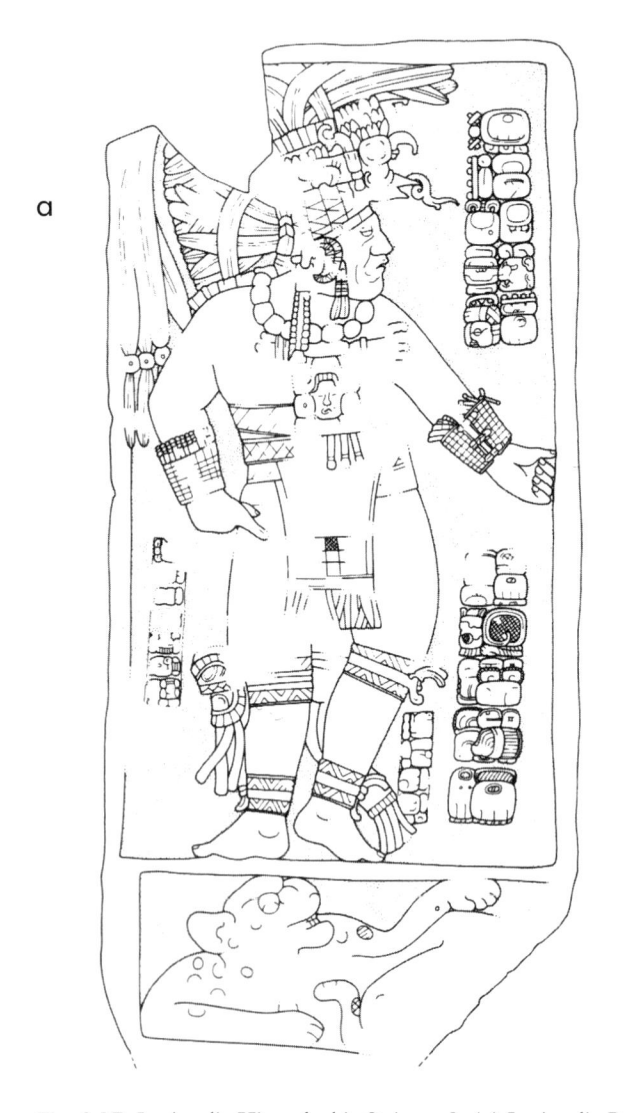

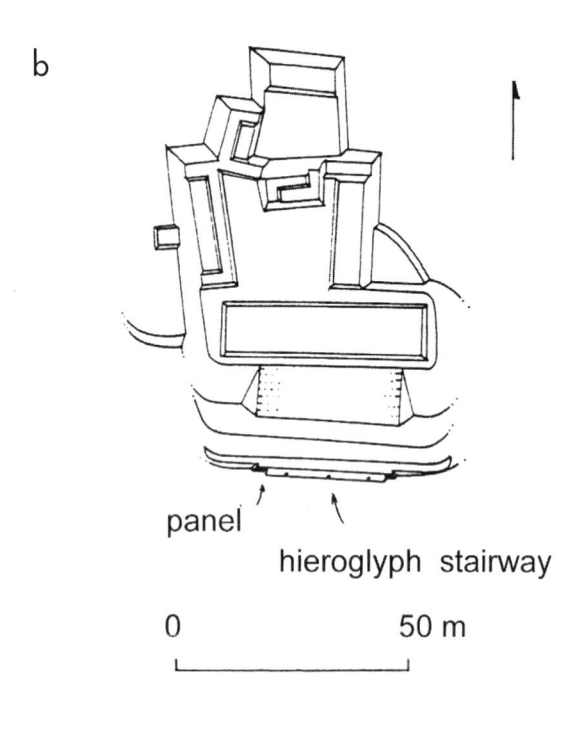

Fig. 2.17. La Amelia Hieroglyphic Stairway 1: (a) La Amelia Panel 1; and (b) plan showing position of panels and inscribed stairway blocks (mapped and drawn by Stephen Houston).

BODIES AND PORTRAITS

of reference that situate Maya interaction in time and space (Chapter 4). The extendible self enlarges and complicates the range of such fields.

But the extension of body raises other questions: What is the Maya person or self as an intersection of different roles and identities, all converging on a single body? What establishes its singularity, and how does this relate to the notion of *baah*? Alfredo López Austin (1988) and Jill Furst (1995) have written extensively on the Central Mexican soul and have demonstrated that it was thought to contain many parts. There was a *yōlia* that helped animate and define personal identity; this could survive death, and it tended to correspond to the senses. An *ihīyōtl*, a vaporous spirit, and the *tōnalli*, a destiny linked at or near birth to an individual, completed this package of essences. Of the three, the *tōnalli* was lodged in the head, associated specifically with "name or reputation" (J. Furst 1995:110). It could become detached from the body and might even be shared by twins. Most important for this discussion, the *tōnalli* could be evaluated, so Hernando Ruiz de Alarcón tells us, by holding someone over a reflective surface. Even the "image of gods and nobles on stone monuments in screenfold manuscripts . . . [were thought to] . . . present shadowy, insubstantial doubles of deities or ancestors" (J. Furst 1995:95).

Increasingly, we know more about Classic concepts of vitalizing energies, including the well-documented belief in the *way*, or companion spirits—aspects of the person that could move independently of the body but with which it shared bonds only breakable at death (Grube and Nahm 1994; Houston and D. Stuart 1989). Some evidence points to slight variance from later ethnographic beliefs, principally in their almost impersonal bonds with certain titles and places, and in wild and sinister disease-bearing properties (Chapter 3). We can also attest to the concept of *k'uh*, roughly analogous to the Central Mexican notion of *teōtl* mentioned before, a monist belief about a divine principle that appears in multiple forms.

Striking displays of *k'uh* appear in Maya tributary ritual. Several monuments from Yaxchilan, Mexico, show the ruler pouring a fluid substance

a

b

Fig. 2.18. Defacement: (a) Tikal Stela 9 (C. Jones and Satterthwaite 1982:fig. 88b); and (b) Mask 4, Structure 1, Acanceh Yucatan (after Quintal Suaste 1999:16).

over one of two things: one is a wrapped offering, perhaps a bundle of tributary mantles or a small stone altar (D. Stuart 1996:157); the other is the tributary lord himself (Tate 1992:191–194, 226). From other evidence, this liquid securely reads *k'uh*. It emanates from royal hands, perhaps within blood, where this essence dwells, according to ethnographic Maya, and embraces gifted objects

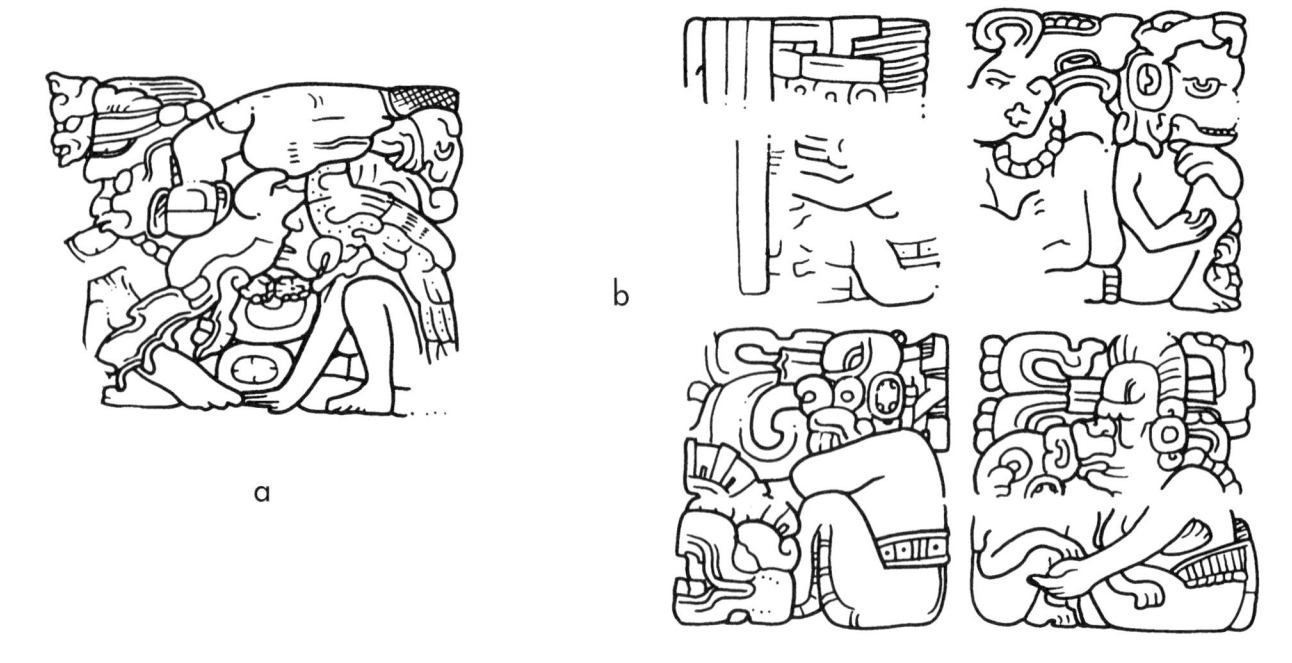

Fig. 2.19. Two examples of "full-figure" glyphs: (a) [4-K'ATUN- ch'a-CH'AJOOM], Yaxchilan Throne 1 (after field drawing by Ian Graham); and (b) [18-BAAH-K'AWIIL], summit temple, Copan Temple 26 (after field drawing by David Stuart).

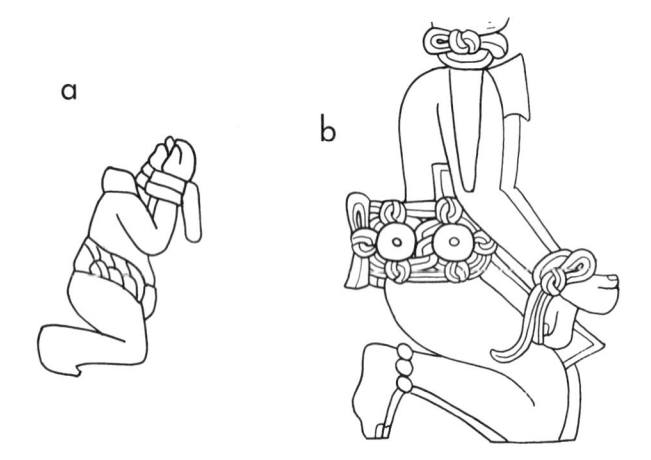

Fig. 2.20. Decapitated figures: (a) El Jobo Stela 1 (after Miles 1965:fig. 15b); and (b) Kaminaljuyu, unnumbered stela fragment.

and tributary lords with a florescence of royal soul. Although Classic evidence links *k'uh* exclusively with royal persons, it is more likely in reflection of their intense and singular concentration of such essences. This ritual may have demonstrated both reciprocity and the ultimate expression of ownership as part of the body politic. But what of the *baah* notion of "body"? Its emphasis on the head, surfaces, and persons that can be divided and extended points suggestively to a belief that parallels the Central Mexican *tōnalli*. This can be no more than an imperfect parallel, however, for we know next to nothing about comparable nuances of meaning for the *baah*, and its sheer physicality in Classic Maya references occludes other theological shadings.

TIME AND BODIES

Time and royal bodies were processed by similar rituals: the tying of headdresses, the wrapping of bundles, and the binding of mummy bundles. Even the sacrifice of the body had temporal consequences, and the units of time lived and experienced by the human body equated to those of twenty-year spans. To begin: *k'atun* was the name given in the sources from Colonial Yucatan for the period of 7,200 days (twenty *tun*). The ancient hieroglyph for this same time period, however, was probably never read as *k'atun* in Classic times. Syllabic clues at Dos Pilas, Guatemala, suggest a value beginning with *wi-*, possibly for *winik* or *winak*, both common words for "twenty" and "person" in Mayan languages; in temporal contexts, the signs probably read *winik-haab*, "twenty units of 360 days." It has long been assumed that *k'altun* meant "twenty *tun*," as *k'al* is the word for "score" in Ch'olan and Yukatekan languages, but the etymology is somewhat more complex. *K'al* also carries the meaning of "to fasten, enclose." A parallel case exists in Tzeltalan languages, where the word for "twenty," *tab*, signifies "knot, tie." This connection may have its origin in the tying or bundling of things counted in units of twenty, perhaps for purposes of trade. Whatever the case, the entry for *k'atun* in the *Diccionario Cordemex* of Yukatek Mayan suggests that the name of the time period originated not simply as a numerical term, but more precisely as *piedra que cierra* or "closing stone" (Barrera Vásquez 1980:386). According to this clue, the term or glyphic expression *k'altuun* can also be translated as "stone binding"—a term that came to be used as the later Yukatek name for the period of 7,200 days. It is important to emphasize that Mayanist scholars routinely use terms, such as "*baktun*," that are bogus, without independent evidence for such readings from Classic sources (e.g., Thompson 1950:147). This leads to a morass of terminological confusion, the choice being between the terms used by the Classic Maya and those that are, by now, firmly embedded in the scholarly literature.

The hieroglyph read as *k'altuun*, "stone binding," describes a special calendar ritual associated with stelae and other monuments. If "stone-binding" is the correct interpretation, what does it signify, precisely, in regard to the ritual event? A probable representation of the ritual appears on the famous Peccary Skull unearthed in Tomb 1 of Copan, Honduras (Fig. 2.21). In the central cartouche engraved on the Peccary Skull, two figures are shown flanking a large upright object marked with "stone" elements—the distinctive marks of the [TUUN] or "stone" sign. The shape and size of the large central object in the scene strongly suggest that it is a stela, and, most significant to our inquiry, it appears to be wrapped with bands of tied cloth. Shown before the upright stone is a zoomorphic "altar" in the tradition of some of the altars visible in Copan's main plaza. The hieroglyphic caption that accompanies this scene reads, applying the new interpretation of the event glyph: "1 Ajaw 8 Ch'een (is) the stone-binding (of) [ROYAL NAME]." The initial date corresponds to the period ending on 8.17.0.0.0 (October 21, AD 376). Thus, the peccary-skull image depicts the *k'altuun* ritual overseen by two nobles, demonstrating that the rite refers to the fastening of cloth around the stone monument. The ritual relates in some manner to the more general religious practice of wrapping or bundling sacred objects with cloth.

Appropriately, the Classic-period records of this *k'altuun* ritual are strongly associated with records of *k'atun* endings. At the great lowland site

Fig. 2.21. Peccary Skull from Tomb 1, Copan, Honduras (drawing by Barbara Fash).

of Tikal, the stelae erected in the so-called twin-pyramid groups—each built and dedicated on a particular *k'atun* ending (C. Jones 1969)—bear inscriptions that feature the [*k'altuun*] glyph (Fig. 2.22). In each twin-pyramid group, a dominant pair of pyramidal platforms defines the eastern and western sides of a large plaza. To the south of each plaza was built a vaulted range structure with nine doorways, and to the north, a large walled enclosure in which one carved stela with an associated altar was erected. Each stela bears a portrait of the current Tikal ruler engaged in the act of scattering incense, and each makes prominent use in its inscriptions of the [*k'altuun*] glyphs under consideration. The imposing walls built around these stelae may refer to their "enclosing" (an attested meaning of *k'al*, as well)—perhaps a sort of architectonic "bundling" or "binding." Stela 31 of Tikal, with its much earlier text, also shows the prominent use of the [*k'altuun*] glyph in its retrospective historical account of a series of *k'atun*-ending dates. The pattern is very similar to that found with "stone seating" glyphs, also featured in association with *k'atun*-ending dates. It cannot be coincidence that the "seating" and "binding" of stones recall the terminology of royal office-taking.

As noted above, "binding" is a concept that has considerable religious importance in Mesoamerica. The use of cloth or paper, especially, as a wrapping material for sacred objects and bundles is well attested both in ancient and modern custom. The intent may be to protect a holy object or substance, or to contain some sacred essence held within (Stenzel 1968). The metaphor of "bundling" a ruler at his accession is also thoroughly documented among the Classic Maya (Stross 1988), and this may have given rise to the use of the headband to "wrap" the divine king in office (Fig. 2.23). Not a few early stelae show that sculptures, too, could display carved headdresses as though standing in place of the royal body (Fig. 8.27).

Similarly, binding was associated with mortuary acts among the Aztec and Mixtec in which rulers were lashed and compressed into mummy bundles. The same general idea is arguably at work with regard to stones that are "wrapped" on or near period-ending dates. From what we know of the

Fig. 2.22. Tikal Stela 22:A1–A4 (C. Jones and Satterthwaite 1982:fig. 33, used with permission of Sharon Misdea, Tikal Project, University of Pennsylvania Museum).

importance of cloth wrappings and bundles in Mesoamerican ritual (Fig. 2.24; E. Benson 1976; Stenzel 1968; Stross 1988), it is reasonable to suppose that the purpose of the *k'altuun* ritual was to protect and contain the divine essence held within the stones that embodied time and its movement, and possibly to recall acts of biographical termination. Stelae, like rulers, possessed this divine soul-like quality (what Tzotzil Maya today call *ch'ulel*) and were in some way considered living things

Fig. 2.23. Royal diadems: (a) Izapa Stela 12 (after Norman 1973:pl. 24); (b) greenstone mask, Tikal (after W. Coe 1967:43); and (c) Dumbarton Oaks Plaque (after M. Coe 1966:fig. 7).

invested with *k'uh*. This is indicated by the occasional labeling of monuments as *k'uhul lakamtuun*, "holy banner stones." The possibility exists as well that the idea of wrapping or enclosing a sacred monumental stone derives from a far older "shamanistic" tradition of containing small divining stones or crystals in bundles, what the modern K'iche' call *baraj* (Freidel et al. 1993:226; B. Tedlock 1992:65). At the very least, both ancient stelae and stones of divination are intimately tied to the practice of timekeeping. It seems possible, too, that the so-called plain stela at Classic Maya sites were in fact covered by textiles or rope as a part of these ceremonies.

The "death" and mortuary wrapping of time itself is a common theme in Mesoamerica. Among the Aztec this is the *xiuhmohpilli* ("Binding of the Years") ceremony that was among the more significant rites performed by this people at the time of the Spanish Conquest (Fig. 2.25; Caso 1967:129–140). As noted, Nahuatl *xihuitl* and Mayan *tuun* seem to be related in their common meanings of both "precious stone" and "year." *Xiuhmohpilli*, equally translatable as the "binding of precious stones," referred to the rite of cosmic renewal performed at close of the fifty-two-year cycle, when the "new fire" was drilled at midnight atop the hill of Citlaltepec. The event was

Fig. 2.24. Bundles: (a) Vase of the Seven Gods (after M. Coe 1973:pl. 49); (b) Quirigua Stela C (after Maudslay 1889–1902, 2:pl. 19); and (c) *ikaatz* bundle (after K7750).

celebrated by the burning of ritual bundles consisting of fifty-two reeds lashed together with rope (Pasztory 1983:165). Similar bundling rites, often linked to the finishing of "days," or *k'in*, as well as hills for the drilling of fire, exist in Classic Maya imagery (Fig. 2.26), and it was probably in such locations that the Jaguar God of the Underworld was linked to "new fire" (Fig. 2.27; Newsome 2003:2). If there exists a connection to the Maya *k'altuun* rite, it would have to be a distant one, for the Aztec or Mexica ceremony was centered on the fifty-two-year cycle of the Calendar Round, and not the Maya concept of the twenty-year *k'atun*, and the two cultures were separate in both time and space. However, there is enough ideological continuity in Mesoamerican culture to make the connection plausible. The Aztec bundle was represented as though it were a mortuary bundle, wrapped with sacrificial paper (Codex Borbonicus, p. 36) and then buried within an altar emblazoned with skulls (Caso 1967:figs. 6–8). Almost exactly the same pattern occurs on a series of altars from Uxmal, Yucatan, that have not, to our knowledge, ever been excavated (Fig. 2.28; I. Graham 1992:121–133). Four such altars occur at Uxmal: Were these a form of *tzompantli*, or "skull altar"? Or did each represent the completion of some momentous unit of time? If they represented twenty-year units, then that would more or less approximate the fairly brief occupation at the site.

Central to understanding the connection between *tuun* and the body is the belief that rulers

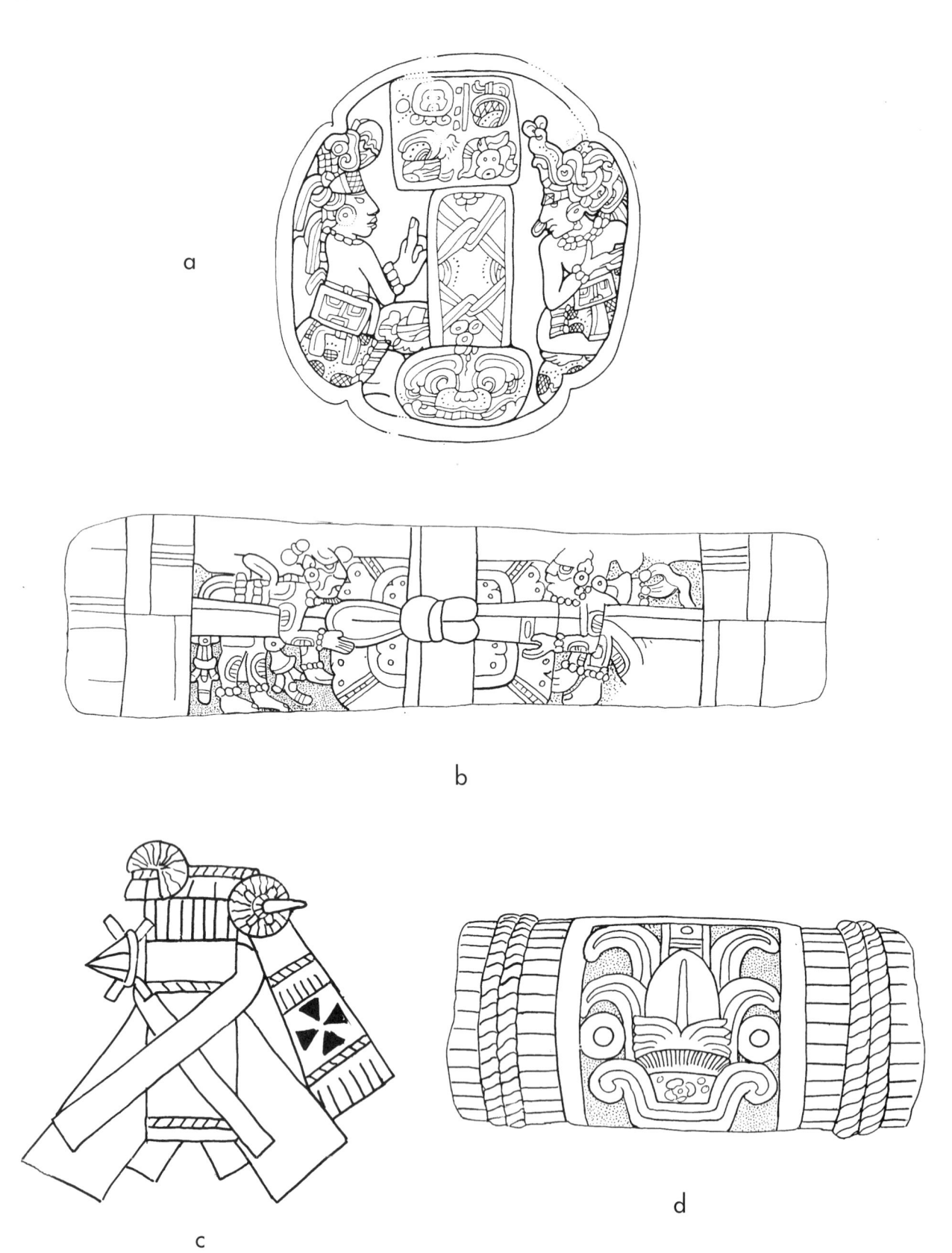

Fig. 2.25. Year bundles: (a) Copan Peccary Skull (drawing by Barbara Fash); (b) Copan Altar X (after drawing by Linda Schele); (c) as dead person, Codex Borbonicus, p. 36 (after Caso 1967:fig. 2); and (d) Xiuhmolpilli (Caso 1967:fig. 11).

Fig. 2.26. Hill where fire is drilled (after D. Stuart and Houston 1994:fig. 93).

were themselves embodiments of time and its passage—a role that was fundamental to the cosmological underpinnings of divine kingship. We find this expressed most directly by the overt solar symbolism that surrounded the office of Maya kingship. Individual rulers were closely identified with the sun and its personified manifestation as the god K'inich Ajaw, "Sunlike Lord." A shortened form of this honorific, *k'inich,* is often applied to Maya rulers at Palenque and several other sites. At Yaxchilan, Mexico, deceased rulers are depicted within the distinctive solar cartouche, and their consorts, within that of the moon (Tate 1992). In mythical representations and iconographic settings, the Maya Sun God himself often wears the accoutrements of rulership, including the cloth headband, suggesting that he was considered the ruler of the heavens.

The word *k'in* is customarily translated as "sun" or "day," but its meanings can be much more general and abstract. "Time" and "divination" are equally applicable glosses, depending on the context of use. For our purposes, however, one of the more important aspects of the Mesoamerican concept of the "day" as a time period is its animate quality (Thompson 1950:96). Individual days held personal attributes, and the names for days were the names of entities that exerted certain influences

Fig. 2.27. Jaguar God of the Underworld as "new fire" (El Peru stela after field drawing by Ian Graham).

Fig. 2.28. Base of possible year-bundle burial or skull rack, Monument 1, Uxmal, Yucatan (I. Graham 1992:121).

on daily life. Among the present-day K'iche' Maya, each day has its own "face" or identity, and they are commonly addressed directly by diviners with the honorific title *ajaw,* "lord," as in "Greetings sir. Lord 8 Batz" (B. Tedlock 1992). These days were also linked closely with the destiny of those born on them. Concepts of divine days are well documented among the communities where the 260-day calendar has survived, especially in the Guatemalan highlands, but the idea of animated time is hardly restricted to this region and period. As embodiments of *k'in,* rulers in their calendrical duties may have been considered "faces" of the sun and of time in a more general way: it is probably no coincidence that, in Kaqchikel, the term for "face" is the same as that for "destiny" or "fate," and that the movement of the sun helps integrate space, time, and being by situating all movement within its daily transit (Monaghan 1998:138–139). The practice of taking personal names from days is exceedingly rare, however well documented from later periods, and only a handful of examples are known from Classic Maya evidence, usually in association with scribes.

In the Classic Maya calendrical scheme, the twentieth day Ajaw stands out in importance. All period-ending dates of the Long Count calendar—when *tuuns* were dedicated—fell on the twentieth day Ajaw, "Lord." The day Ajaw was thus the "face" or "lord" of the period ending, an association that may go far toward explaining why the day name "Lord" appears only in the Maya area; elsewhere in Mesoamerica, where the Long Count calendar was not used, the corresponding day name is usually "Flower." That is, the twentieth day is named "Lord" only when it could "rule" over a period ending. In the iconography of Maya calendrics, we find a clear identification of the day sign Ajaw with portraits of political rulers (Fig. 2.29). In several examples, portraits of kings appear within day cartouches as full-figure Ajaw hieroglyphs, explicitly linking the person of the king with the current "lord" of time. The cyclical reappearance of the Ajaw day at each period ending in the Long Count calendar was a renewal not only of cosmological time but also in effect of the institution of kingship—an elaboration of the conceptual equation of ruler with the sun, as already touched upon. Throughout ancient Mesoamerica, certain time periods were believed to "reign" over the cosmos, and in Postclassic Yucatan the chronicles explicitly state this with regard to Ajaw dates and *k'atun*s. The *Book of Chilam Balam of Chumayel*, to cite one of many examples, notes that "Katun 11 Ajaw is set upon the mat, set upon the throne, when their ruler is set up . . ." (Roys 1933:79). The same metaphor is implicit in Classic iconography, where the calendrical rulers (the day bearing the name and face of Ajaw) and the political *ajaw* could be fused under a common identity.

This might seem an interpretive leap, were it not for explicit textual statements that establish a common identity between time and the rulers. On Stela 9 of Calakmul, the inscription above a portrait of a royal woman begins "*u-baah* 11 Ajaw 18 Ch'een . . ." Here the date seems to replace the customary royal name, labeling the portrait as "the 'body' of 11 Ajaw 18 Ch'een." If this particular reading is correct, it appears that consorts of the king (also worthy of the *ajaw* title) shared some of the fundamental connections with period-ending rituals. This is reiterated by a Maya vase that bears two day-cartouche portraits, one male, the other female (Fig. 2.30). We can presume that they are Ajaw days, based on numerous parallel examples. The captions both begin with *u-baah* and include references to the period-ending date 10 Ajaw 8 Yaxk'in (the *k'atun*-ending 9.12.0.0.0). The woman's caption reads, "*U-baah ti* 10 Ajaw [NAME]," or "her 'body' as 10 Ajaw."

SELF-SACRIFICE, CREATION, FOUNDING

There is still something left undiscussed: the evidence that time itself and the space in which it occurs could not exist without acts of bodily sacrifice. Here, what had been dynastic or narrowly temporal impinges on the cosmological, the shape of the universe and the communion of time and space. Central Mexican myth has many stories about the creation of the world through an act in which the earth was torn in two by the deities Quetzalcoatl and Tezcatlipoca, each operating as a monstrous serpent or as beings perched in trees growing to the sky (Taube 1992b:128–131; see also Garibay 1979:26, 32, 108). There seems to have been no absolute consistency in such myths, which may indeed have been acceptable alternatives of the same concepts. Similar imagery appears in the Postclassic Maya sites of Mayapan and Tulum, with additional information from later Colonial sources that the sacrificial animal was none other than a primordial crocodile (Taube 1992b:131).

A version of this myth, or at least a Central Mexican account of it, is illustrated on a crucial page in the Codex Féjerváry-Mayer (Anders et al. 1994:1). The body parts of Tezcatlipoca are shown ripped apart, each spurting blood from head, rib cage, leg, and arm. Was this a four-part classification of major portions of the human body (see Gillespie 1991:fig. 16.6)? These gory objects appear at the corners of the universe. World Trees, each with its bird; the deities presiding over them; and all the day signs integrate the scene and establish a comprehensive model of time and space. A tableau that is strikingly similar comes from murals at the Postclassic Maya site of Mayapan, Yucatan, on the bench of Structure Q. 95 (Fig. 2.31; Barrera Rubio and Peraza Lope 2001:fig. 31). The aquatic

Fig. 2.29. Ruler portrait as Ajaw day sign, Machaquila Stela 13 (I. Graham 1967:fig. 67).

BODIES AND PORTRAITS   91

Fig. 2.30. Female figure as Ajaw day sign (drawing by David Stuart of unprovenanced Late Classic vessel).

background is emphasized by the fishes floating about, including some that have been speared. A version of Quetzalcoatl, in this case Ehecatl, the Wind God (cf. Codex Borgia, pp. 22, 23, 510 [Anders, Jansen, and Reyes 1993]), the deity mentioned in the Aztec sources, swims or floats in front of a crocodile that is bound like a sacrificial captive. Together these fragments hint at the same origin myth that occurs in Central Mexico.

But to what extent did this model of creation exist among the Classic Maya? The south side of the bench text from Temple XIX, Palenque, Mexico, clearly relates to such narratives (Fig.

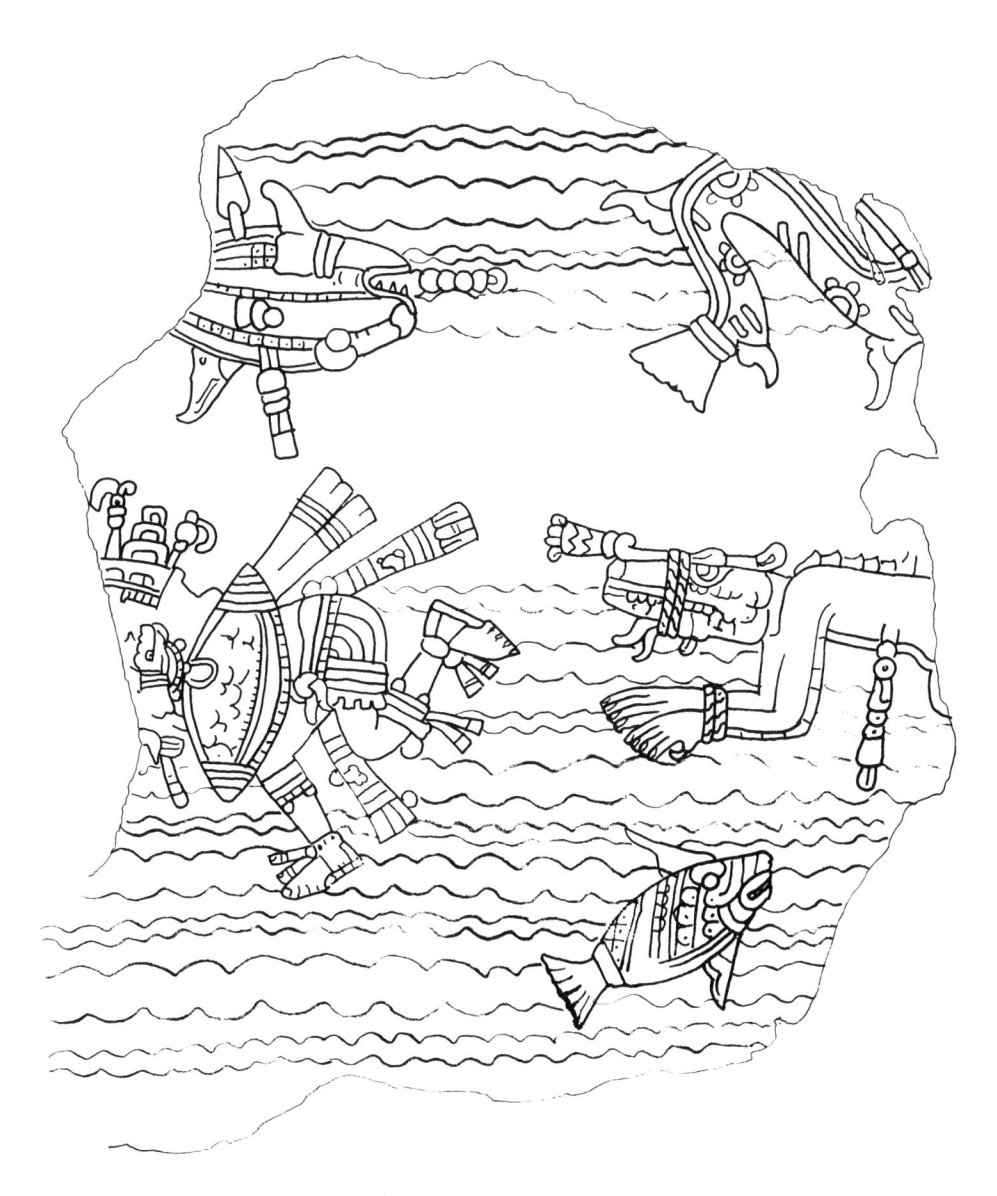

Fig. 2.31. Mural from Structure Q. 95, Mayapan, Yucatan (after Barrera Rubio and Peraza Lope 2001:fig. 31).

2.32). The events take place in the mythic past, well before any possibility of an actual historical record. A god known as G1 is enthroned in lordship (*ajawel*) under the supervision of Itzamnaaj, probably the overlord of all Maya gods. A few years later, a crocodile (*ahiin*) has his back (*paat?*) chopped; the back is described in a "coupletted" form, meaning that it is qualified by two separate adjectives that reveal its properties: a back with a "hole" in it and a back with "painting" or "writing." (A crocodile in the Dresden Codex, pp. 4b–5b, also shows a back with hieroglyphs, as does an earth crocodile from a Postclassic building at Coba; Taube 1989a:figs. 1a, 5a). An action that involves "fluid" in some way is then said to have taken place three times, and the object affected by this action is very likely to be the Maya sign for "blood," *k'ik'el* or *ch'ich'el* (the *-el* suffix often pertains to body parts in the language of the inscriptions [Chapter 1; D. Stuart 2003]). As part of the same ritual sequence, fire is drilled (*joch'-k'ahk'-a*) and an object is placed (*'i-pat-laj*).

These events in mythic time clearly represent a Classic Maya version of the creation myths attested in Central Mexico. A crocodile has its body or *baah* chopped, from which blood flows thrice and fire is

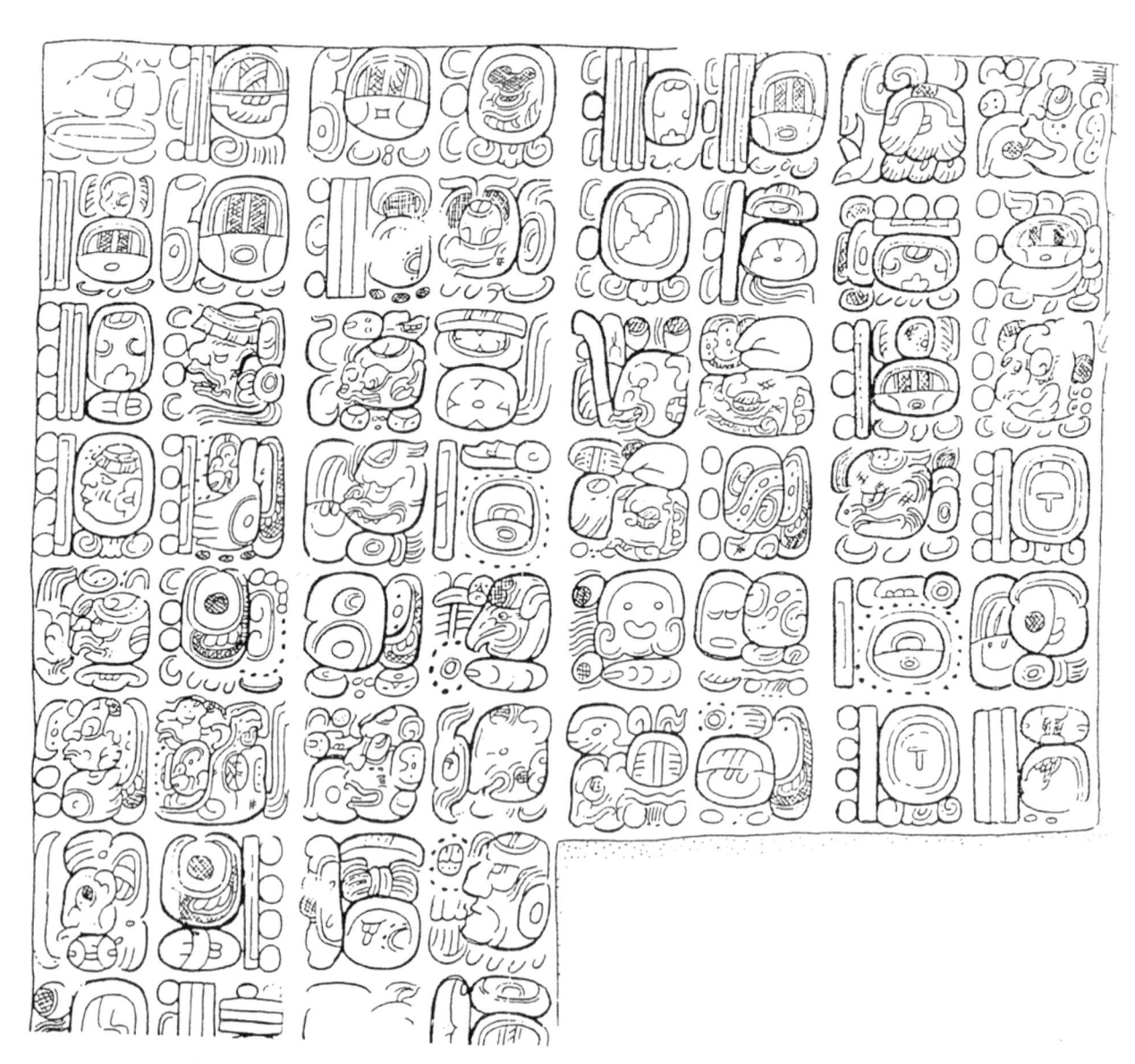

Fig. 2.32. South side of bench, Temple XIX, Palenque, Mexico (field drawing by David Stuart).

then kindled. These themes find other parallels in Classic Maya evidence. First, a crocodile is found within a three-pronged censer from Copan (Orefici 1997:no. 266)—the connection of new fire with a crocodile recalls the events mentioned at Palenque (Fig. 2.33). Second, in a divergent play on the same myth, a ballplaying scene on Step VII, Hieroglyphic Stairway 2, Yaxchilan, Mexico, refers to "body chopping" on three separate occasions, possibly as acts of "creation" or "awakening" (*ah;* Fig. 2.34; Barrera Vásquez 1980:3; cf. Freidel et al. [1993:353–354], who see these as "conquest" stairways with some features of creation mythology; Schele and Freidel 1991). Note that, in contrast to Palenque, these appear to be successive acts spread over many hundreds of years, all in mythic time. The text at Yaxchilan also refers to "death" or at least "road entering" as its metaphor, as well as two counterpoised mythic locals, a "black hole" and a "6-sky place," presumably one underworld, the other celestial. Susan Gillespie (1991:317–333) notes that, throughout the ancient Americas, ballplaying involves primordial struggles, seasonal change or transformation, and, above all, corporeal sacrifice, usually by decapitation or other forms of dismemberment. These allowed rejuvenation to take place: death was not the end but a continuation of life. Gillespie shows that some of the dismemberment within the ballcourt involves a crocodile that has been torn apart, as in a scene from the Codex Borgia (Fig. 2.35; Gillespie 1991:fig. 16.7). There is also increasing support for the idea that, in their earliest manifestations, Maya day signs represent bloody objects ripped primordially from a sacrificial body. Many day-sign cartouches, even from the Late Classic period, are red as though smeared with blood (Fig. 2.36). Moreover, the earliest day signs known—from Izapa and Jaina in Mexico, Kaminaljuyu in Guatemala, and San Bartolo in Guatemala, where the red-painted day signs are found—drip gore, just like a sacrificial head of about the same date from Chocola, Guatemala (Fig. 2.37, 2.38b). Later examples from Copan accentuate the connection with blood by highlighting the irregular outlines of the dripping blood; compare the blood scrolls under the massive Tlaloc face from Stair Block 1, Temple 16, and a day sign on the Early Classic Stela 37:A8 (Fig. 2.38; Fash 1991:fig. 37; Taube 2004b:fig. 13.12). Thus, the very day signs used by the Maya point to their sacrificial origin. Time itself issues from a dismembered body, in most cases from a crocodile. From these acts of sacrifice come a three-part flow of blood and the kindling of new fire.

Such origins generate a related model, that of the founding of Classic Maya dynasties. If time and, indeed, space come from sacrifice, then so did the beginnings of royal families. The so-called Hauberg "stela," in fact a carved slab that has archaic imagery far predating its actual time of carving, shows G1, the same deity mentioned at Palenque (Fig. 2.39). The sculpture is unusually small, perhaps because it involved a rite for a child, the "first penance/bloodletting" rite, *yax ch'ahb*. From the figure's upper torso gush three lacerated bodies, of which only the torso remains. Each of the bodies contains a headdress ornament that mentions the figure, including one who appears to be a ruler depicted on a sculpture from Kaminaljuyu, which shows three kings on thrones (L. Parsons 1986:fig. 149). The text itself says that this is the "first penance," "first creation," or *yax ch'ahb*, "for his god," *tu-k'uh-il* (Chapter 3). The imagery would be utterly enigmatic but for an altar of unknown provenance now stored at Tikal National Park (Fig. 2.40). This also shows three, perhaps four, figures with bodies cut in two, all in descending positions,

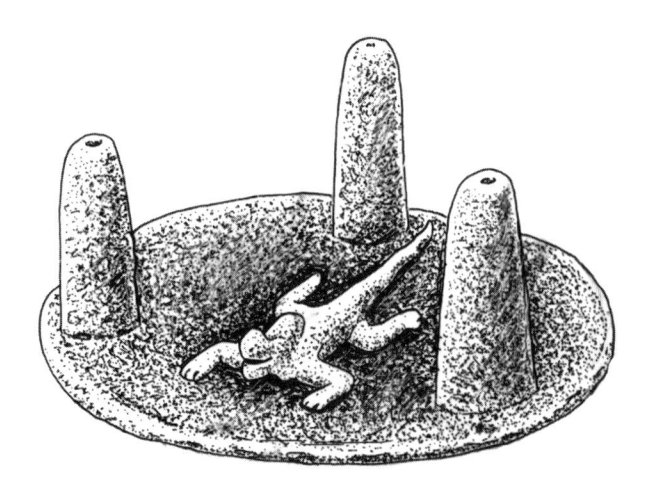

Fig. 2.33. Crocodile in incense burner, Copan, Honduras (Orefici 1997:no. 266).

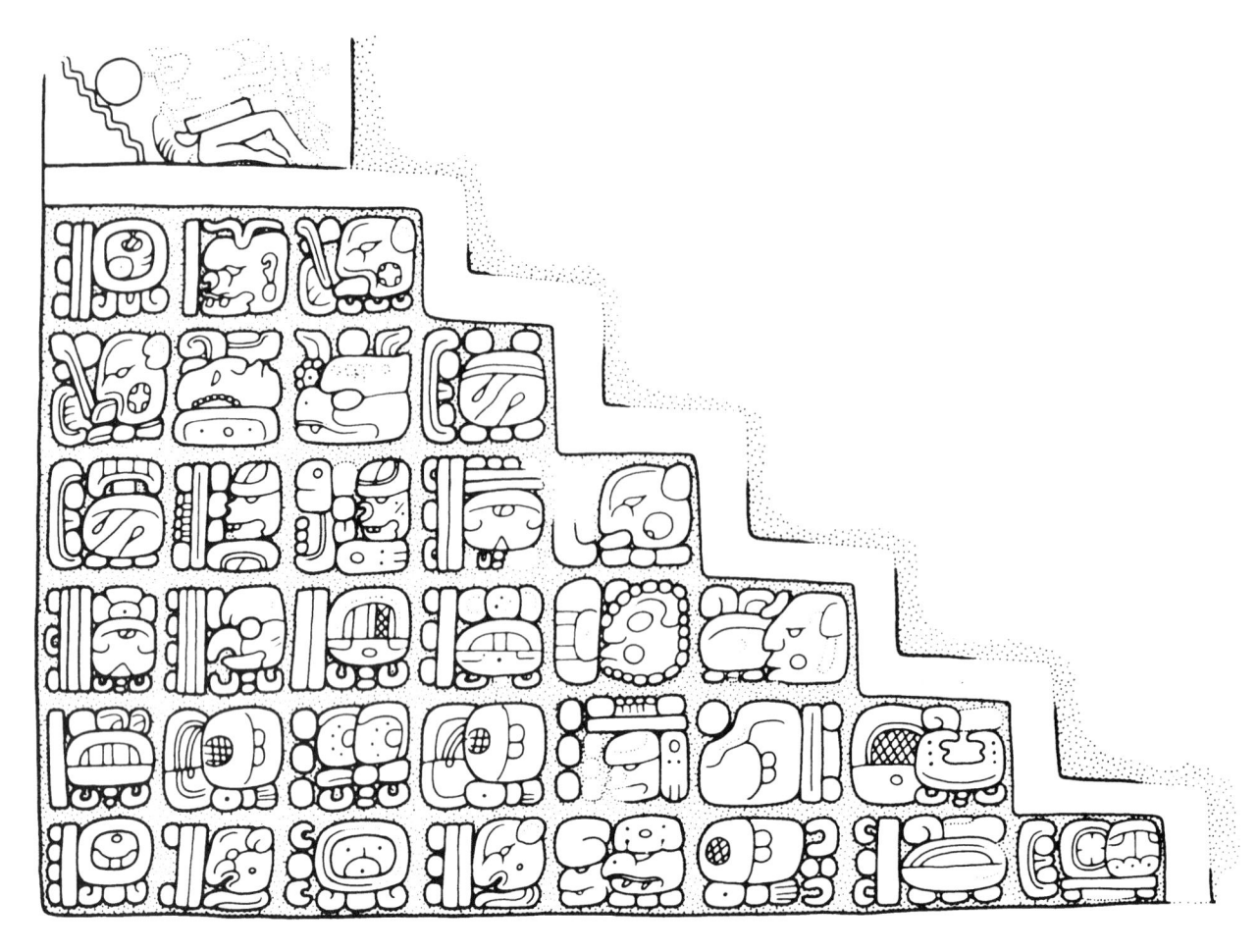

Fig. 2.34. Creation texts from Step VII, Hieroglyphic Stairway 2, Yaxchilan, Mexico (I. Graham 1982:160).

Fig. 2.36. Maya day sign painted red (photograph by David Stuart of unprovenanced Late Classic vessel).

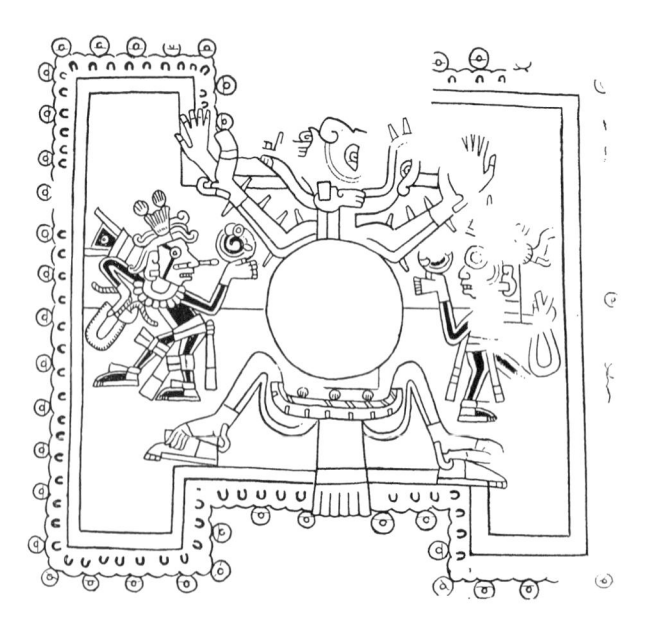

Fig. 2.35. Creation scene in ballcourt, Codex Borgia, p. 35.

Fig. 2.37. Sacrificial heads as day signs: (a) Miscellaneous Monument 60, Izapa, Mexico (after Norman 1976:fig. 5.83); (b) Jaina Panel 3 (after Benavides and Grube 2002: fig. 2); (c) Kaminaljuyu Stela 10; and (d) detail of Chocola Monument 1 (after drawing by Carl Beetz).

Fig. 2.38. Comparison of blood scrolls: (a) severed head from Mound J, Monte Albán, Oaxaca (Houston and Taube 2000: fig. 2e); (b) detail of Chocola Monument 1 (after drawing by Carl Beetz); and (c) Copan Stela 63:A8 (after drawing by Barbara Fash; Taube 2004b:fig. 13.12).

their intestines streaming out from the ragged tear along each body. One of these persons has precisely the same name as the dynastic founder of Tikal (Martin and Grube 2000:26). Finally, a recently discovered painting on the lid of a dish from Becan, Mexico, shows three figures of exactly the same shape, eyes closed in death and with an individual name dropping away from a crocodilian iguana, almost certainly the Itzam Kab Ain, "Iguana Earth Crocodile," mentioned in historic sources (Fig. 2.41; Taube 1989a:2). These three images indicate a shared trope between time and dynastic founding, in which apical ancestors were seen as *sacrifices* that allowed the royal dynasty to come into existence. The involvement of an iguana/crocodile at Becan points directly to a connection with primeval acts of sacrifice.

The likening of dynastic figures to units of time brings us to a remarkable find made recently at Altar de los Reyes, Campeche (Fig. 2.42; Šprajc 2003). Around its circumference an altar has a set of thirteen Emblem glyphs, or titles used by "holy lords" governing the most important Maya cities. This would appear to be a model of both space and dynastic sovereignty, representing the disposition of kings across the Late Classic Maya world. But there is time as well: the arrangement is identical to the positioning of thirteen Ajaw day signs around terrestrial turtles from the Maya Postclassic period (Fig. 2.43; Taube 1988a:fig. 2a). These embody models of the world, a gigantic turtle floating on the primordial sea, but also, around its carapace, an image of completed, cyclical time. It would seem that the Classic Maya were closely aware of, and strongly interested in, linking their models of political reality with the order of time itself, the inevitability of temporal sequence buttressing the succession of kingship.

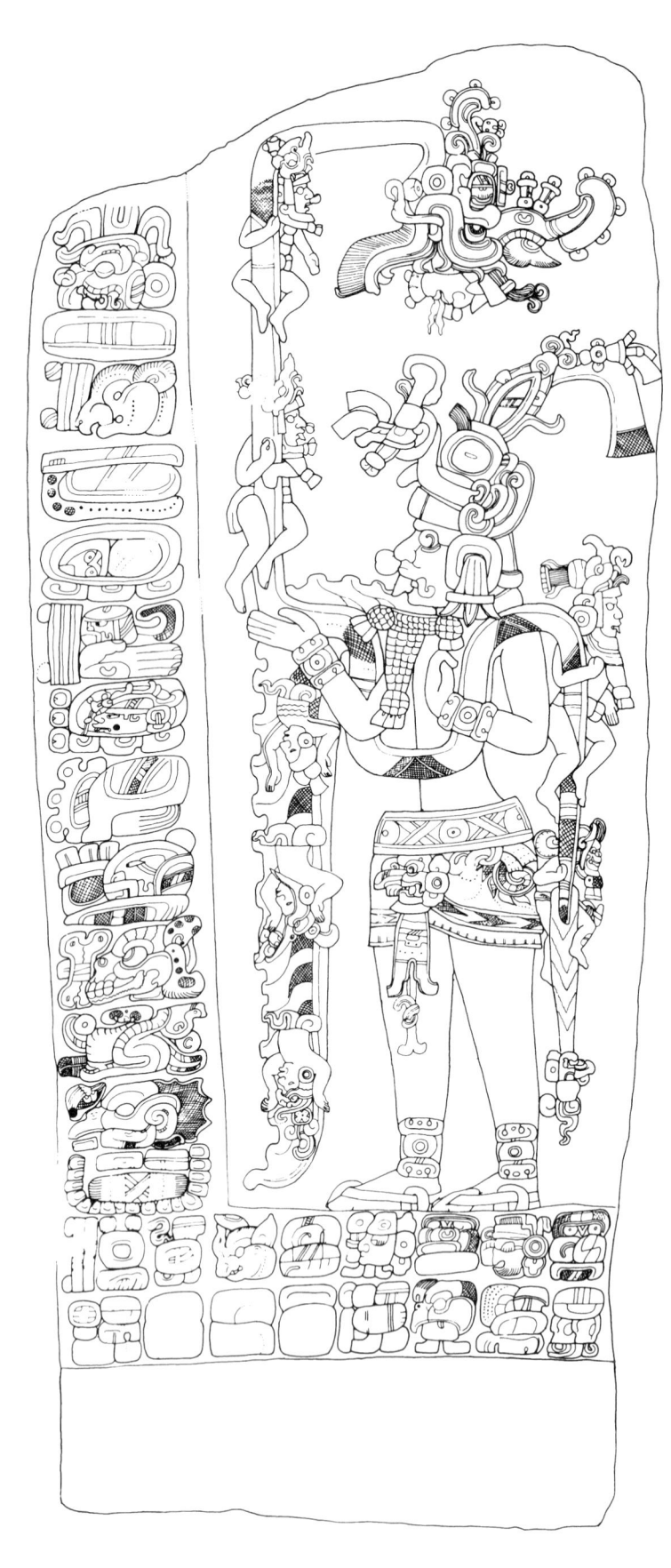

Fig. 2.39. Hauberg stela (drawing by Linda Schele).

BODIES AND PORTRAITS 97

Fig. 2.40. Altar in Tikal National Park (photograph by Stephen Houston). above.

Fig. 2.41. Lid of bowl from Becan, Mexico (drawing by Karl Taube after Campaña and Boucher 2002:65), right.

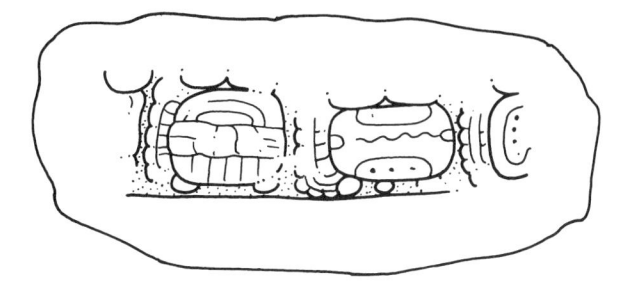

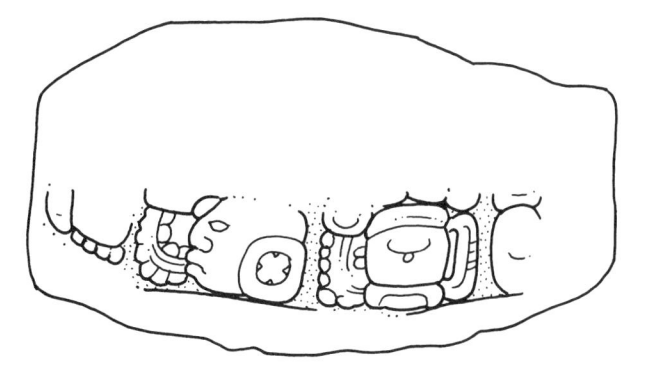

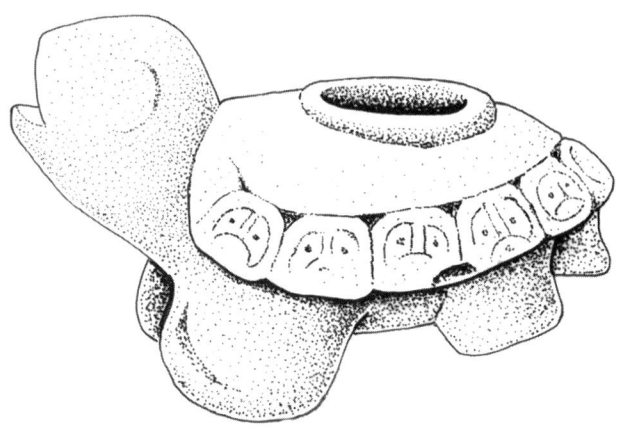

Fig. 2.42. Altar de los Reyes, two views of Emblem glyphs (after Šprajc 2003), left.

Fig. 2.43. Mayapan turtle (Taube 1988a:fig. 2a). above.

CLASSIC MAYA PERSONS AND PORTRAITS

We have presented a number of observations about Maya perceptions of images as possessors of vitalizing essence, and as indirect indices of Maya concepts of the "person," "body," and even "self," particularly as these were perceived and reproduced by the elite. Anthropological comparisons enrich this discussion by highlighting patterns not otherwise apparent. Humans everywhere ask certain questions: What is a person, a body, a self? What distinguishes it from others of the same class? What are its boundaries? The answers to these questions entail yet other subtleties. Do societies observe a distinction between a social person, a mask devised to perform expected roles, and an interior self that follows an individual destiny—an intimate self that puzzles, in a philosophical sense, over the existence of an exterior world and the self's conduct with respect to it (M. Rosaldo 1984:145–146)?

In either case, as Ludwig Wittgenstein (1953) writes, it is language that bridges self-consciousness and awareness of others. The result is an "intersubjectivity," an empathy of mutual understanding and feeling, that allows the self to exist with others in an atmosphere of "ontological security," the reassurance that we all know the same basic rules. Tantamount to "trust," such security allows humans to confide in "a stable external world and a coherent sense of self-identity" (Giddens 1991:51). Classic Maya image making confirms that coherent vision by displaying repeated examples of extended and extendible persons. The receivers of such images would correspond to what Stanley Fish has called "interpretive communities," members of which share "a point of view or way of organizing experience" that assumes similar "distinctions, categories of understanding, and stipulations of relevance and irrelevance" (1989:141). The process of interpretation, of constructing meaning from external catalysts, would itself lead to change in that interpretive framework (Fish 1989:150). This means that every attempt to fix an idea in an image would, through its reception, result in slightly different concepts. What prevents the construction of some cultural Tower of Babel is the need for humans to talk and share ideas—in ways that necessitate common frameworks.

The history of these ideas parallels closely the development of sociology, anthropology, and philosophy. Let us consider the "self." Earlier comparative treatments of the self distinguished between a sensory, self-concerned, self-satisfying ego and a social self "involved with conceptual and moral ideas" (Fogelson 1982:69). George Herbert Mead linked the two in his discussion of philosophical objects and subjects, emphasizing that the self originated fundamentally in interaction with other people: "[We] must be others if we are to be ourselves . . . [so that a]ny self is a social self, but it is restricted to the group whose roles it assumes" (1964:292; but see Doepke 1996:239–240 for a perspective of self-persistence, and in contrast to the proposition of discrete, successive selves). An evolutionary flavor suffused much of this discussion. In many societies, individuality existed—so scholars said—in a relatively undifferentiated state, under the firm control of group needs and expectations. Ironically, Marcel Mauss played to both ideas. He stressed the historical and cultural variety in ideas about "persons," but, as mentioned before, also reduced these to a peculiar evolutionary scheme that placed "primitives" on rungs of the ladder to the Western individual.

In much of this discussion, "personhood" involved concepts of the soul that could extend beyond the skin and include name, shadows, totems, and clans as extracorporeal expansions of the self (Fogelson 1982:71; Lévy-Bruhl 1966:114–115, 121, 127). We have seen some of those concepts at work in Classic Maya imagery. In contrast, Western thought concerned itself, particularly after the seventeenth century (R. Smith 1997:57), with an "individual" that could be isolated from social role and its attendant duties, an entity that had consequence precisely because of its individuality (Shweder and Bourne 1984:168) and thus became a "social concept [expressive] of a unique and indivisible unity" (La Fontaine 1985:124). Logically, such thinking would find greater meaning in terms like "privacy" or Erving Goffman's perception of a gap between inner, self-involved calculation and a social presentation of "face" that brought such calculations to realization through "impression management," whatever the sincerity or real intent of the performer (1959:18–19).

But to what extent were these reflections based on detailed knowledge of ethnography or on concepts specific to particular cultures? Paul Radin detected equally sophisticated deliberations about the self in the non-Western world, where people could represent a complex intersection of body and a variety of essences in dynamic flux (Cohen 1994:52; Fogelson 1982:82; Radin 1957:259). Similarly, in his pioneering studies of psychological anthropology, Irving Hallowell asserted that self-awareness was a cultural universal, but that scholars still needed to pay close attention to the "behavioral environment," through which participants experienced and interpreted the world (1976:358). The "person" may not be a human being, nor is a human being always a person (Leenhardt 1979:153): for example, among K'iche' speakers today, a North American is "not *qas winaq* ["true person"] because they do not share the same flesh as the Maya nor bear the same blood of their ancestors" (Allen Christenson, personal communication, 2003). Among many groups these concepts reside within "a coherent moral universe" expressed in grammar, "name usage, ideals about power, mythological beliefs, conceptions of dreams, metamorphoses, and 'souls'" (Fogelson 1982:83)—all of which form the basis for an understanding of metaphysics that lies outside the impositions of Western thought (Hallowell 1976:359). Even possession of things can be considered usefully as an expression and extension of the body (Crapanzano 1982:200, citing William James). In describing Kwakiutl endowment of things with the persona of the owner, Mauss (1985:10) offered an intriguing parallel to Classic Maya practice, in which hundreds of texts denote possession by the elite of bones, vessels, boxes, shell, and a wide variety of other items. Indeed, linkages of things with people are one of the central preoccupations of Maya writing (D. Stuart 1995).

The acknowledgment that personhood, the body, and the self exist—indeed, can only be understood—within distinct cultural and historically configured settings has several implications. For one, dramaturgical theories of selfhood, principally devised by Goffman, can be seen as existing unconsciously within a Western framework, where a superimposed identity, fashioned for purposes of social utility, becomes disconnected from underlying identity and egocentric motivation. The presentation of self occurs within an overriding social context of anxiety and distrust and attempts to save "face" (Hare and Blumberg 1988:35), all in all expressing the neuroticism of the modern age. But the supposed separability of these layers, of mask and self, is debatable. For example, as Raymond Fogelson points out for masking traditions among the Cherokee and the Iroquois, masks do not so much fulfill "role-playing or play-acting" as represent "temporary incarnation[s] of cosmic reality" (1982:76). "[T]he self, by way of the mask, can directly experience the properties of its most significant other," and vice versa, in a reciprocal transposition of attributes (Fogelson and Walker 1980:99). Henry Pernet justifiably questions whether any masking tradition truly removes the identity of the impersonator from the joint identity of the mask/masked dancer (Pernet 1992:117–135; yet he probably goes too far in viewing the transformative aspect of masking as little more than "the heart of the white man's mythic discourse about the 'primitive' and his masks" [ibid.:162]). One of the most cited criticisms of Goffman's views is that he posits the existence of actors motivated largely by self-advantage, who perceive roles and norms as instruments to their selfish purpose (Hollis 1985:226–227). Though central to his scheme, the self is left as a mysterious "we-know-not-what" that somehow "organises the repertoire, supplies continuity of motive or establishes the code" of human behaviors in an unspecified manner (ibid.:227).

At the same time, Classic Maya depictions of a king or noble unquestionably represent, in Goffman's phrasing, "presentations of self" or, more to the point for this chapter, "presentations of person and body," where many different roles and attributes converge. Insofar as they are molded to public expectation and individual need, they can be said to relate to social roles and "claimed" identities, which an individual displays to others as a way of influencing their perception of a particular self-presentation (Fogelson 1982:79; Norbert Schneider [1994:12–18] makes the same point about the "imago" of the Medieval ruler). As Leenhardt notes, the self exists in relation to others: interaction leads to self-affirmation, to an existence as a "recognizable personage" (1979:154). Among Pacific societies this collective, social aspect of the self achieves a singular prominence, so that, above all, the self represents shared relationships with others; potentially it exceeds the boundaries of the human body (A. Becker 1995:4). Other dramaturgic analogies apply, too, including "audience segregation," in which self-presentations may vary by intended audience; a performance dedicated to one group plays well to one but not to another (Goffman 1959:49). Many people could see a stela, but few could see a carved lintel visible only in cramped quarters. To our perspective, these distinct understandings of personhood do not have to be incompatible. In Clifford Geertz's studies of

Indonesia, his dramaturgic interpretations are persuasive because they focus on occasional unities of identity, such as those between the mask and the person wearing it; "drama" may work best when it moves to a connection between self and the role it plays (1973:367, 370). Another approach, that focusing on semiotic communication, skirts the issue altogether by conceiving of the self as a participant in a dialogue that extends well beyond role-playing. The self makes a statement about itself in relation to other selves through the combination of, say, a portrait (an iconic sign) and a name (an indexical sign; Singer 1980:491, 494). In such communication, personal identity might extend beyond the physical organism to other entities, as we have seen for Classic Maya portraits.

Regrettably, our data on Classic Maya personhood are not up to ethnographic standards. We cannot ask informants for clarification about intended audience, concepts of individual versus collective self, and the nature of expected roles and their public projection through monumental sculpture. But with textual sources in hand we can grope toward an understanding of person, self, and body within a distinctive "behavioral environment" that fully embraces physicality. As mentioned before, the Classic Maya self existed within a complex "bodily matrix" in which different essences, or "souls," were connected to different parts of the body, a feature found in many other parts of the world, albeit with subtle variations (Cohen 1994:52). What is far more unusual is Maya ritual practice with respect to such images. We can think of two ways, both drawn from other cultures, to model such practice, with the proviso that comparisons raise interesting possibilities but potentially ignore differences in the very "behavioral environment" we have just emphasized.

The first rests on the striking similarity between Classic Maya beliefs and those of ancient Egypt. The key concept is that of the royal *ka*, a part of Egyptian royal essence that represents "the divine aspect of the king, linking him both with the gods and all his royal predecessors" (Bell 1985:256). Depiction of the *ka* often takes the form of a *double*—that is, an image of the immortal, validating kingliness of the pharaoh. When that validity is questioned, as in the case of Hatshepsut after her death, the *ka* images of the pharaoh suffer systematic defacement (Bell 1985:257). Royal depictions reinforced the body politic, an embodiment of divine kingship that endured beyond the inexorable mortality of the king. Such images could be approached in supplication or as recipients of requests for oracular judgment. More to the point, they had to be periodically involved in royal ritual as reconfirmations of the pharaoh's divine soulfulness and hence his legitimacy (Bell 1985:258, 271, 293–294). As among the Maya, these images in stone were quite literally parts, albeit divine parts, of the ruler's "body." The only way to negate that claim was through mutilation; the way to confirm it was through constant ritual encounters with the image. Unlike Egypt, however, Maya defacement attacked not texts—perhaps an indication of illiteracy among vandals?—but the eyes and faces of lords, the apparent locus of their personal identity. Similar practices occur with Hindu religious images, where statuary can serve both as theophanies, translucent icons through which the devout could "glimpse . . . [the] more all-encompassing nature" of certain gods, and as politicized images that could become trophies of war whose identities were never "fixed or permanent" (Davis 1997:23, 261).

But the Egyptian parallel does not explain one important feature of Classic Maya ritual practice. Unlike ancient Egypt, the Maya political landscape consisted of many competing divine rulers. Another, equally distant parallel leads us to speculate about the competitive aspects of Maya image making. The large number of stelae at some Maya sites, such as those in competing centers of the Pasión region, Guatemala, are, in one common view, "propaganda"; in our perspective they are also interpretable as ancient displays of personhood that extend beyond the physical organism of the ruler, a point buttressed by documented understandings of an extendible, extrasomatic soul. In his study of the Naven ceremony celebrated by the Iatmul of New Guinea, Gregory Bateson described the incremental workings of "symmetrical schismogenesis," with "schismogenesis" meaning that norms of individual behavior began to differ as a result of interaction between individuals, and "symmetrical" indicating that this change might be highly competitive, as in boasting by one group leading to more boasting by another (Bateson 1958:176–177). Displays of "spirit," including those within a single village, could lead to escalating displays by those in symmetrical distribution. Similarly, Maya lords may have found that displays of the royal self by rulers in neighboring polities, or by earlier lords within their own sites, necessitated repeated self-presentations in the form of monumental portraiture. Such competitive image making for esoteric spiritual ends may have functioned as one of the driving forces behind the system of Maya royal representation. This pattern was especially marked during the Late Classic period, when the number of stelae increased greatly, as did evidence for increased competition in war; alliance building and royal visits, too, apparently gained in importance and frequency.

References in hieroglyphic texts reveal an essential unity between ruler and representation. More than mere likenesses, portraits contained part of the royal essence in ways that multiplied his presence, that made possible more than one simultaneous appeal by supplicants, perhaps in competition with other rulers. Underlying concepts show that such personal identity was embodied, perhaps like the Central Mexican *tōnalli*, in the face or top or forehead of the cranium, a key location that also was salient in references to people of different rank. It was the head or face that received royal diadems as marks of accession; it was the head or face that, through such usage, entered grammar as a reflexive element. Yet in extending the body to monuments, rulers also made themselves more vulnerable, in that images could be, and often were, hacked in places where such "living" representations might "perceive" the external world. Today, visitors to Maya sites will find few untouched faces in such portraits. From an indigenous perspective, the enterprise of glorifying and replicating the royal presence proved as unsuccessful in perpetuating personhood as the rulers did in preventing the eventual collapse of their kingdoms.

The question of whether Maya rulers were true "individuals" or whether they fit within some evolutionary scheme of "personhood" is ultimately trivial and misleading: trivial because the Classic Maya provide abundant evidence of how such kings embodied time, and how their essences shifted into other materials, many enduring well beyond the decay of flesh and the cities such kings occupied; and misleading because it is hard to imagine beings who were more singular in their identities, which combined individual birth names, regnal titles invoking various gods, and particular events that were recorded with great attention to unique confluences of calendrical and astronomical cycles and to expressions of individual agency that made them, perhaps, *the* individuals of their time, kings of stone and embodied time, but with distinct personalities that shine through the past darkly.

CHAPTER THREE ◂▸

Ingestion

Food, drink, and other ingestibles can be understood from many perspectives. They serve as caloric intake, pleasing, aesthetically evaluated input on the taste buds, and instruments of satiation and psychoactive mind alteration. Such alteration can range from mild stimulation to near coma. To anthropologists and specialists in the history of food, they are also substances freighted with categorical meaning. This is true intrinsically of the foods themselves, in what they signify to preparers and consumers, and as the centerpieces of "meals" (small-scale and domestic repasts), "feasts" (lavish, dramatic, reciprocal, and often competitive gestures of hospitality and communal consumption), and "banquets" (equally opulent repasts that highlight social difference and exclusive patterns of consumption). Unlike meals, feasts are usually about something more than bringing food and drink to a generous trough—although few of us, particularly those of Swedish descent, can deny the simple and direct pleasures of an abundant and varied spread. Feasts also involve acts of offering, receiving, and offering again, not only of ingestibles but of things, people, labor, and tokens of esteem and alliance (Dietler and Hayden 2001:3–4; Dietler and Herbich 2001:fig. 9.1). The degree to which such meals socially homogenize (construct intimacy and equality) or heterogenize (devise rank and segmentation) depends on the setting, with results that can be tense and inconclusive (Appadurai 1981:507). Michael Dietler (2001:86) would describe "banquets" as "diacritical feasts" because they mark or accentuate social inequalities through the use of different foods and styles of consumption. Typically, those foods and styles would cycle down through other groups of lower status or rank, requiring yet other refinements at higher levels.

The sharing of ingestibles writes large the affinity of family and kin, along with its tensions, hierarchies, and gender divisions. Regardless of time or place, this is how a sense of social bond and community coalesces. Conversely, a disinclination to eat together signals a serious breach in relations (Visser 1992:81). It is well to remember that odium, antagonism, and other caustic emotions exist within such units along with love and admiration (Dietler 2001:73). Moreover, among the Maya, those preparing and serving such meals and feasts tend to be women, who do not appear to consume the products of their labor, although, of course, meat may be provided by male hunters (Dietler and Hayden 2001:10). The role of host and gift giver invokes, to some, domestic images of authority, whether male or female, and clearly identifies the host's subordinates. It extends those models to broader asymmetries in society, thus "naturalizing" them and reciprocally remolding the domestic head into an exemplification of rule—most metaphors, after all, work both ways, for this is what gives them density and the ability to stir emotion and sentiment. At the same time, there is a functional divide between meals and feasts. In parts of Mesoamerica, as among the Mixtec of Oaxaca, feasts are more socially comprehensive than simple suppers. By involving calculations of quantity and content, by exceeding any expectation of what might appear in an ordinary repast, feasts invoke obligations beyond the mutual duties of intimate kin (Monaghan 1995:93).

Many social transactions thus condense into the preparation and consumption of ingestibles. Most such transactions are ephemeral or difficult to access, but their material residue and representations in texts and imagery are not. This is why there is cross-cultural interest among archaeologists in the manifold uses and meanings of ingestion. The relevance of eating and drinking to a book on Classic Maya physicality should be just as clear. Acts of ingestion sustain the body yet go beyond physical needs to create subtle markers of corporal vulnerability, intimacy, and control. These properties can be understood individually. *Vulnerability:* As external things, ingestibles pass through the mouth or anus and receive processing in the gut or colon; they then issue as feces or fluid from the anus and urine from the urethra. This consumption requires an act of faith that the ingestibles will not make the consumer ill or stone dead. *Intimacy:* Ingestion is intrusive in another way, in that, like sex, with which eating has often been compared in ethnographic sources (Counihan 1999:9–10; Siskind 1973:9), ingestibles satisfy carnal appetites and pass through human orifices in the most intimate, intrusive manner (Falk 1994:212; for Maya evidence, see Tarn and Prechtel 1990). By definition, consensual sex involves a bestowal of trust, with the promise that each partner will be contented, that neither will be abused beyond the bounds of pleasure, however extreme. The same holds true for the offering and consumption of ingestibles. *Control:* When to eat, when to drink, and in what quantity are hedged by proscriptions. The elaboration of those rules and styles of consumption in itself helps create social orders, groupings, and divisions (Sherratt 1995a:12) and activates concepts of what is edible (unambiguous symbolically, controllable, "safe") and what is not (ambiguous symbolically, uncontrollable, dangerous [Falk 1994: 71–76]). Here is where "banquets" or "diacritical feasts" play a role. For example, when dining in state, some early modern European monarchs ate alone. Nonetheless, the messages being disseminated—of the rarity and exquisite preparation of certain foods, their variety, the royal gifting of selected morsels as marks of favor, and even the eucharistic overtones appropriate to sacred kings—made them "diacritical" in that they had few consumers but many observers (Adamson 1999:30; Ikram 1995:215–216).

INGESTIBLES AND INGESTION: ETHNOGRAPHIC AND HISTORIC EVIDENCE

In the later lexical sources, a rich array of Maya terms helps illustrate indigenous notions of eating, drinking, smoking, douching, and the diversity of drinks and foodstuffs—none are obviously gendered, however, but rather apply to all human beings. In modern Ch'orti', the term for "food" involves the same root as that for "eat," *we'* or *we'eh/we'h* (Wisdom n.d.), an expression that goes back to Common Ch'olan (Kaufman and Norman 1984:135). The actual process of biting and, presumably, masticating, is *k'ux we'* (Wisdom n.d.), just as the same language speaks of *mak'i*, "eat, munch," especially soft things (Kaufman and Norman 1984:125). "Large bites" are *noh kahr*, which indicated more than enough to fill the mouth, but, before doing so, the food was best "picked up and crushed by the fingers" (*chik'i tuuor uk'ab*; Wisdom n.d.), in much the same way that a "mano," or grinding stone, *uk'ab cha'*, pulverized raw corn into meal. There is no evidence that the Maya developed hand tools for dining, these being "Ladino" things, such as the "spoon," or *lup,* a word that began as the description for a small bowl used to extract water from larger vessels. In Ch'orti', one can consume heartily or gingerly, in small bites or in sips (*we'hta,* "taste food," or *ha'hta,* "sip water"; Wisdom n.d.). Those who crave "strong" foods and those who "lust" in general—apparently, following Jean-Anthelme Brillat-Savarin's nineteenth-century maxim, "You are what you eat" (1971)—are *ah t'unir,* "lustful person[s], [those] who eat . . . only meat" (Wisdom n.d.), possibly a somewhat rare delicacy for most Maya, although the evidence for this assumption remains somewhat weak. Colonial Tzendal of Chiapas, Mexico, makes the same point by referring to "fortifying food," *ipaghib* (J. Robertson n.d.), which employs *ip,* a root for "strength, firmness."

Much like Ch'orti', to which it is closely related, Colonial Ch'olti' employs *cuxu,* meaning "bite" or "to eat meat, maize or cacao" (Ringle n.d.), along with *veel,* with what appears to have involved the concept of "eat [maize bread]," the Maya food par excellence and, by legend, the primordial substance of all human flesh (Taube 1985). (The *Popol Vuh* credits human fat to white ears of maize, ground fine and mixed with yellow ears [Christenson 2000:153–154].) In Colonial Tzotzil, there occur terms for "feast" (*ve'el*) and "eat . . . fresh corn, greens" (*k'ux*), both obviously cognate with Ch'olti' and Ch'orti' forms (Laughlin 1988, 2:619, 622), such as Ch'orti' *noh weaar,* "important meal" (Wisdom n.d.). The primary bread of the Maya was the *tamal* (tamale), a steamed corn bread with various flavorings that is known as *vagh* in Colonial Tzendal and **waaj* in Common Ch'olan (Kaufman and Norman 1984:135, an entry corrected for probable vowel length). Tortillas, a foodstuff easily compacted and dried for long-distance movement, were probably a relatively late introduction (Taube 1989b). It may be that the tortilla came with Teotihuacan influence in the Maya region, sometime during the middle of the first millennium AD. At that time, flat ceramic plates known as *comales* begin to appear with increasing frequency in the archaeological record. Nonetheless, Sophie Coe mentions that some tortillas could be baked by being placed directly on ash and hot stone, without detracting in the slightest from their edibility (1994:146).

Many places and times of refinement, especially in bourgeois France after the publication of *Physiologie du goût* (*The Physiology of Taste*) by Jean-Anthelme Brillat-Savarin (1971), experimented with new foods. They highlighted, not huge portions, but small bursts of flavor in a multiplicity of courses (Camporesi 1990:5–7). The task of the gastronome, always exploring new forms of pleasure, was to accept novel flavors into the mouth and deliver crushing opinions of them (Falk 1994:89–90; MacDonogh 1987:187). In haute cuisine, those foods or ingestibles should, ideally, be hard to find or secure (out-of-season fruit or sturgeon eggs), be difficult to prepare (the perfect crème brûlée), demand skilled labor (prodigious Lucullian roasts), and involve unique, nonsubstitutable ingredients (wild salmon, not farm-bred fish [Mintz 1996:101]). Nonetheless, alimentary courage and criticism left no obvious mark in the Classic evidence. The impulse of Brillat-Savarin and his followers was so thoroughly individual, even eccentric and dandified, in its quest for refinement that it must be seen to reflect the beginnings of modernity. Dining at royal courts of the Classic Maya was probably far more about abundance and variety of foods than about an avid, private savoring of taste. There is thus an almost transitional quality to what we know about Classic cuisine. It seemed to emphasize quantity over the presence of especially rare preparations (a feature of the reciprocal celebrations that Dietler terms "patron-role" feasts) yet made use of serving styles that stressed the hierarchical nature of "diacritical" gatherings (2001:82–83, 85).

Words for "drink" in the relevant lowland Mayan languages are largely the same, based on the root *uch'* (Wisdom n.d.). In Ch'orti', people could consume water (*ha' tua' uyuch'i*); *chicha,* a maize brew (*uch'in e chicha,* but *boj* in Q'eqchi'; Sapper 2000:20); or a decoction of cacao (*uha'ir e kakaw*), *cacao* being a word that appears early in the corpus of Classic Maya texts as well (D. Stuart 1989a). There are also many references to what can only be fermented agave, or pulque, *chih* in Colonial Tzendal, a term that was extended to mean "string," another product of agave, and sundry words for "sweet" and "wine," as in Yukatek *ci* or *ixmal haalil ci,* the "pure [unwatered] wine" (Michelon 1976:168; J. Robertson n.d.). It seems implicit, though, that the basic liquid is universally regarded as "water," a nuance suggested by related entries from Colonial Tzendal (*gh-uch ha,* "drinker," literally, "he who drinks water"; J. Robertson n.d.). Water quality was, and is, an issue, to the extent that porous stones were used for filtration (*chahrnib tun;* Wisdom n.d.). The Ch'orti' could gulp drinks but also sip them carefully (*kum*), perhaps as part of medical remedies (*uch'i,* "take a remedy"; Wisdom n.d.).

Another kind of treatment involved tobacco (*Nicotiana* sp.), a powerful ingestible throughout the Maya world (de Smet 1985:39–41, 92–93; Robicsek 1978). Ch'orti' contains many words related to smoking: *cha mar,* "tobacco smoking"; *ah chamar,* "tobacco smoker"; *kahp,* "anything held in the mouth, tobacco paper"; "cigar making," *tz'ot k'uhtz',* which involved "rolling" (*tz'ot*). Among the Ch'orti', tobacco is consumed in a variety of ways, from "smoking" (*but k'uhtz'*) to the use of snuffs and powdered or ground tobacco (*muxurbir k'uhtz'*). Snuff was known as *may* in the Ara dictionary of Colonial Tzendal ("a powder that comes from the pepper or chile and of tobacco when it is used with the hands"; J. Robertson n.d.). This Tzendal word was probably cognate with the Colonial Yukatek term *maay,* "ash of stick when it is burned," both being vegetal powders (Michelon 1976:224). The practice of habitual consumption of tobacco powder mixed with lime, a combination that, as a chewed quid, activates nicotine even more powerfully, is attested throughout Mesoamerica and South America (Starr 1902:71; Thompson 1970:110–112; Wilbert 1987:48–64; J. Winter 2000:54), including Tzeltal Maya communities such as Oxchuc, Chiapas, Mexico (Redfield and Villa Rojas 1939:111). Ch'orti', too, emphasizes the medicinal properties of tobacco. The plant could be used as spittle to stultify burrowing parasites such as the *ubi ch'a'k,* the "chigger," so they could be removed. The "chewing" (*k'oy*) and application of the quid as a poultice is still done in Peten, Guatemala, as a way to extract "beef worms,"

or *colmoyotes.* The Ch'orti' curers also "spit the tobacco" (*t'uhb k'uhtz'* and *niri taka e k'uhtz'*), occasionally as "large quids" (*chohk k'oy k'uhtz'*), or they could simply "blow it as a diffuse spray or smoke" (*huht k'uhtz'*), a practice also found among the Lacandon, who wafted tobacco fumes over sacred objects (Thompson 1970:112; Tozzer 1907:142–143). The spray could, it seems, be used for divinatory purposes (*uyarar u k'uhtz'*), as could the large-scale ingestion of tobacco in doses that might, with other plants and mixed with lime, induce trancelike states. Among the early Colonial Yucatec Maya and the related Lacandon, tobacco was usually consumed in pipes or as cigars, a delicious treat linked to the sniffing of fragrant flowers (Tozzer 1907:142–143; 1941:106 n. 484). It is likely that tobacco was also ingested through the skin, either as an unguent rubbed over the body or as a balm to the lips (Bye 2001:235). According to Eric Thompson (1970:120–121), these ointments had talismanic properties and shielded the wearer from evil spirits. This raises the possibility that some of the body pigments used by earlier Maya, such as those of the Classic period, were intended both for purposes of display and as epidermal stimuli to achieve desired mental states.

Ch'orti' also includes terms for various kinds of douches, both vaginal and rectal. These use a root meaning to "stuff" or "fill," or anything designed to increase weight or size (*bu'ht'*). The sexual connotations are fairly close to the surface, in that the "filling" can also apply to the insertion of penis into vagina. This act of "filling" could stretch supplies of valuable cacao by adding ground maize (*bu'ht' e kakaw*) or filling out soap with vegetable matter (*bu'ht e xa'bun*). In addition, it could be used to douche the vagina (*bu'ht' ha' unak*) or rectum (*bu'ht' ha' uut uta'* (all Ch'orti' entries from Wisdom n.d.). Long ago, Erland Nordenskiöld (1930:189) noted that Native Americans from North America to Peru employed two kinds of enemas, one a simple bone tube, the other a nozzle with a leather, bladder, or rubber bulb (Wilbert 1987:46–47). Often, the process involved two people, one on all fours, prepared to receive the clyster, and another to blow the liquid, usually laced with tobacco, alcohol, and other inebriants, into the rectum. From ethnographic sources in South America, Johannes Wilbert (1987:48) observes that usually it is young men who participate in enema rituals; in turn, the enema is often accompanied by other forms of ingestion such as drinking or by regurgitation caused by emetics.

The absence of food and the excess of drink were subject to comment in all ethnographic and historic sources among the Maya. Again, Ch'orti' has numerous terms for "hunger," mostly based on the ancient Common Ch'olan root of *wi'n* (Kaufman and Norman 1984:135). Some will die of hunger (*chamaih umen e wi'nar*); others, like animals, will be compelled to starve (*wi'nes*). The Ch'orti' obviously understand that a "thin, delicate, anemic state" will result from starvation (*hay*), a condition that can and should be induced for religious fasts (*hayitz k'in*). Similar terms abound in languages like Colonial Tzendal: *vinal*, "hunger," or *vinaltic*, "time of hunger," and *ghay*, "thin," and *ghayal vinic*, "lean man" (J. Robertson n.d.), and in the San Francisco dictionary of Colonial Yukatek: *naual, nautal*, "becoming thin, feeble" (Michelon 1976:255). If there could be hungry people, there could certainly be those who ate too much. These were the "fat" people," *ghupem* or *cambacub* in Colonial Tzendal (J. Robertson n.d.). The Ch'orti' and other Maya also commented on excessive drinking and the drunkenness, dizziness, whirling, even insanity that might result from it (Ch'orti': *kar* or *sutuk*; San Francisco dictionary of Yukatek: *Num calan tuban uinicil ti*, "very drunk"; Colonial Tzotzil: *yakyak*, "drunk," and *jyail-chi'*, "drunkard" [Laughlin 1988, 2:387]; Tzeltal: *yacubel*, "drunk" [J. Robertson n.d.]; Ch'olti': *cal-el*, "drunkenness" [Ringle n.d.]; note the cognates *kar* and *calan*). Some of the same roots in Ch'olti', especially *yac*, can also mean "strong tobacco, wine, or powders," and, by extension, be used to label the pungent *zorillo*, "skunk" (Ringle n.d.).

Not all of these instances of want and excess came from random or extraneous events. The Maya also fasted as part of their religious life. The root for "fast," *ch'ab* in current phonological spelling, is widespread in lowland Mayan languages. Colonial Tzendal refers to *chabaghon*, "to fast," or a "type of fast," *chabal-quin*, which uses the word *quin*, "day," for extended periods of penitence (J. Robertson n.d.). Similarly, present-day ritual language among the Ch'ol takes *ch'a(h)b* to be both "fast" and "penance" (Josserand and Hopkins 1996), and the same range of meanings occurs in the Motul I dictionary of Colonial Yukatek (Acuña 1984, 1:150r; Barrera Vásquez 1980:120) and in Colonial Tzotzil, along with a related term, "abandon corn," *'iktay 'ixim*, a heavy penalty indeed for the Maya (Laughlin 1988, 2:393). Colonial Yukatek related these acts more broadly to submission (*num ocol ku*) as parts of episodic festivals of penitence known as *zukin*, possibly derived from *zuhuy*, "pure, untouched, virginal," and *k'in*, "day" (Michelon 1976:265). Yukatek also uses *ch'ab* to mean "to create" or "to make from nothing," from which one infers that the acts of self-denial and the fruitful results from them were linked conceptually (Barrera Vásquez 1980:120).

Necessarily, those who ate or drank too much or too little passed in and out of a state of "health." Being "healthy" or "sick" for ethnographic and Colonial Maya is a state that can be equally explored in lexical sources. For some reason, perhaps because of intense clerical interest in medicine, the Yukatek Mayan dictionaries of the Colonial period are especially voluble in their descriptions of disease and well-being. For example, medical volumes known as "Books of the Jew," probably in reference to Hispanic reliance on Jewish doctors and medical knowledge, occur in various guises throughout Yucatan (Barrera and Barrera Vásquez 1983), as do other medical documents based on mergers of European humoral medicine, astrology, and indigenous practices (Bricker and Miram 2002). The early San Francisco dictionary focuses on several themes. A "sweet heart," *ci ol*, is to be "content," "secure," "tranquil," and "healthy," as is a "straight" or "right" one, *toh yol* (Michelon 1976:60, 343). To be sick, however, entailed a root related to "death," perhaps in fateful expectation of what often happened to those who were ill. *Cimil* means "to die" or "death" but could also signify "sickness," as in *cimil in cah* or *kohanen*, "I am sick" (Michelon 1976:196). The fatalistic tone tinges expressions for those "carrying the sick with hammocks" (*koch chetah*) or for "the act of forcing food and drink down the throats of those too ill to open their mouths" (*cuch luktah;* Michelon 1976:72, 196). The sick were not always stoic: they could "moan" and "complain" (*acan*), although, with good fortune, they might also escape death when their "fever broke" (*chal;* Michelon 1976:2, 82–83). Colonial Tzendal contains a cognate word for "moan," which is *ahacanegh,* "to complain of sickness" (J. Robertson n.d.), a clue that the word was relatively common in lowland Mayan languages.

Other Mayan languages present similar sentiments, if not always with the same terms. To be "healthy" in present-day Ch'orti', *inputz,* is almost an aesthetic condition: if pertaining to the "body," the word connotes well-being, if to the "face," then beauty (Wisdom n.d.). "Sickness" uses another root, *mok,* and generally is of the body (*ubah*), of the stomach or belly (*unak*), or of the heart (*ki'ir*); Colonial Ch'olti' had a similar expression, *muac* or *muhac* (Ringle n.d.), as well as a word for "strong, healthy person," *tzatzal uinic* (Ringle n.d.; also as Common Ch'olan **tzatz,* "hard, strong"; Kaufman and Norman 1984:133). Both among the Ch'orti' and among most indigenous groups in Mesoamerica there is little understanding that illness or death simply happens. Every death is, in a sense, unnatural and requires an explanation in human or supernatural malice (Guiteras Holmes 1965:124–126; McGee 1990:106; Vogt 1976:23). For this reason, the Ch'orti' of the 1930s still spoke of a death god, Ah Chamer, who inflicted sickness, and the *Popol Vuh* makes clear the connection between human disease and gods like Pus Demon and Flying Scab (Christenson 2000:73). The Ch'orti' say that a sick person has been "seized," *chukur,* a verb stem that appears among the Classic Maya as a martial act in which a warrior grabs and ropes another. The implication that diseases fought like warriors imparts a purposive, sentient quality to ailments. By using a special curse in Ch'orti', *mokresnib,* one "sends a sickness back" to the enemy who caused the affliction in the first place (*suti e mok umen e ba'x;* Wisdom n.d.). Vitality itself can cause disease: *k'ek',* "strength, vitality, health," so multiplies in the bloodstream of vigorous people that it inflicts sickness on those nearby, particularly children or the weak. "Curing," *tz'a'ak,* usually with herbs, maneuvers the ill person back to a "right, exact, correct" or "well, cured, satisfactory" condition (*tz'a'akar* and *tz'a'akat,* respectively; Wisdom n.d.). Maya rulers apparently had strong vital essences, at least to judge by the *k'uh* substance issuing from their hands in Classic imagery (D. Stuart 1988a). As a consequence, it may be that they were regarded as perilous to the weak and mild.

INGESTION AND INGESTIBLES: CLASSIC EVIDENCE

For the Classic Maya, the passage of ingestibles in and out of the body involved tobacco, many foodstuffs, and liquids of various sorts. The usual food regime, depending on social status, might have mirrored the one documented for most inhabitants of early Colonial Yucatan, namely, "two liquid meals a day and one solid one," the first two taken as gruel or maize drinks, and the second as more substantive fare (S. Coe 1994:135). The emphasis on liquids, as will be especially clear later in this chapter, may reflect an overall dehydrating milieu in the tropical lowlands (as archaeologists in the field, we consume many liters of water a day). Liquids may also allow a certain degree of logistical flexibility, in that large quantities of fluids can be prepared more easily and in greater volume than labor-intensive foodstuffs. Each meal might have been prepared on a different kind of hearth, some consisting of the three stones famed in the Maya area, but also flat slabs or naked hearths that had no mediating stones between cooking vessel and fire (S. Coe 1994:167). Nonetheless, the actual process of cooking, of making slaughtered flesh into edible food, makes virtually no appearance in Classic imagery (see Vialles 1994:127). Was this devalued work? Did cooking offer little distinction to its practitioners? Or was this production thought to be sensitive and easily disrupted or impaired by the viewer's gaze? The androcentric nature of Classic Maya imagery suggests that such food preparation, usually women's labor, did not merit attention, although receiving such foods did. The presence of maize drinks is by now well known in the literature on the Classic period (Fig. 3.1; MacLeod and Reents-Budet 1994; D. Stuart 1989a): *ul* (atole of new maize, seldom available because of the inherent limitations of growth cycles), *pa ulil* (perhaps an atole of new maize mixed with shredded tortilla), *sak ha'* (according to historic sources, a ceremonial drink), and a variety of cacao decoctions, including what may be fermented ones (*cal-kakaw*, possibly "drunk [inebriating] cacao"). The presence of glyphs spelling *ul* on particular bowls (e.g., K2358) suggests that the term simply meant "*atole*" in general; that bowls held a variety of substances, despite the labeling; or that certain dishes were reserved for temporally restricted use, almost as a kind of seasonal decor. Most such vessels, and those with glyphic texts specifying recipes, could only be appreciated at close distance. Because of their small size, the glyphs can only have involved a small number of readers, in acts of enjoyment that coupled sipping with a form of literate "consumption." Meat preparations occur as well, including, if correctly translated, *sak chij we'*, "white/'artificial' venison food" (Zender 2000:1044), along with evidence of fish and, in a hunting scene, small rodents and an armadillo (K1373). Was *sak chij we'* a kind of domesticated meat? In Yukatek Mayan, *sak* signifies "a thing made with human artifice" (Barrera Vásquez 1980:709), suggesting the possibility of flesh from tame or at least partly controlled deer. Nonetheless, clear signs of domestication are not present in animal bone from the Classic period (K. Emery et al. 2000:546).

The variety of food and drink, especially on the elite table, is clear. In a comparative context, this is what was important to, among others, Roman elites, who monopolized few foods yet still had greater variety, quality, and quantity of foods than did the low-ranking people; they were also more likely to introduce or promote culinary innovations (Garnsey 1999:127). Nonetheless, in texts, imagery, and ritual practice, the Classic Maya largely reduced that variety to a basic duality of the two exemplary foodstuffs: either tamales and water or water-based chocolate beverages (S. Coe 1994: 145–152; Love 1989; Taube 1989b). The former was relatively easy to prepare and obtain, although tamales were generally not so transportable or durable as tortillas. The latter was a sumptuary item that played a large role in the tributary economy of the Classic period. The Bonampak murals show that the tribute par excellence included cotton mantles, feathers, shells, but, above all, bundles of cacao beans tabulated in groups of 8,000 grains (see Chapter 7). The soft and sweet flesh of the cacao pod probably delighted Maya palates as well; such fruit in anthropomorphic form is depicted and mentioned on a stone vessel in the collection of Dumbarton Oaks (M. Coe 1975:pl. 2). An aesthetic fascination with cacao drinks is reflected in later terminology, to the extent that Colonial Tzotzil even had a word for the sound of chocolate while it frothed and bubbled, *chojet* (Laughlin 1988, 2:622). The process of spuming cacao took place by pouring the chocolate drink back and forth from one cylinder to another. Another Maya vessel, now in the Princeton Art Museum, shows this being done by a woman just before it is consumed by a male deity (M. Coe 1973:92; S. Coe 1994:142). Several large cylinder vessels with wide, painted rim bands have been recovered in excavations at Piedras Negras, Guatemala. Such banded ornaments, frequent on Maya cylinders, may have marked how much to fill the vessel before attempting to froth a drink.

As an elemental dyad, tamales and water or chocolate, bread and drink, and drink and bread were apparently conceived by the Classic Maya in mythological terms (Fig. 3.2). An unprovenanced vessel published by Justin Kerr shows a veritable ethnoclassification of animals bringing one or the other as tribute to a central Maya deity (K3413, K1992; see also Taube 2001). Toward the bottom of the scene, two monkey scribes recorded these gifts in a book, indicating that this was one of the primary roles of scribes, to record levies of goods by means of purely numerical notations. The fact that tamales in Classic imagery tended to be hot, especially if dribbled with succulent flavorings (e.g., Reents-Budet 1994:fig. 4.11), and water or chocolate tended to be cold intimates a larger system of hot-cold balance in Maya understandings of human well-being. Health may have resulted from prudent and, above all, balanced consumption. Again, however, food preparation very seldom surfaces in

INGESTION 109

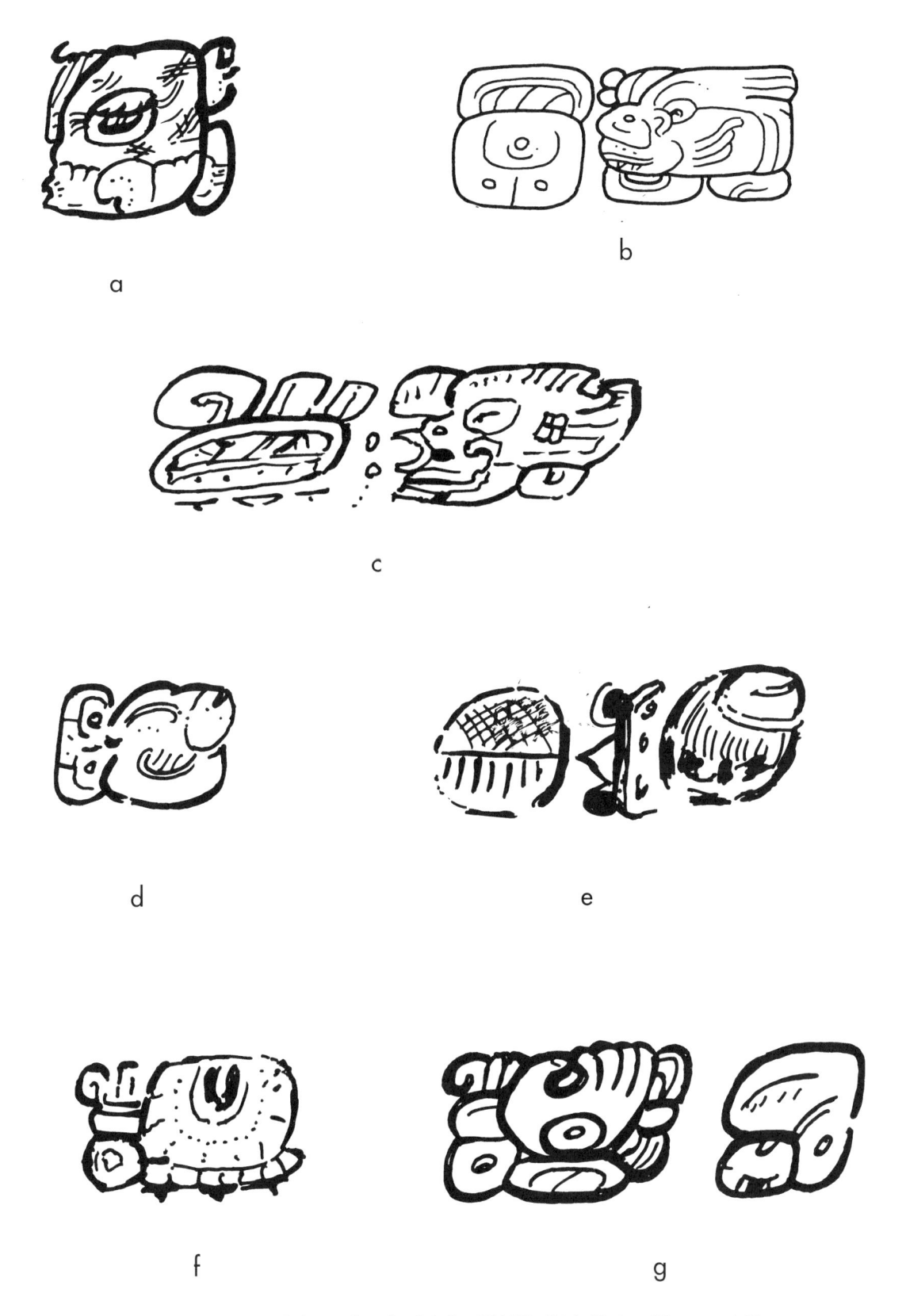

Fig. 3.1. Drinks and foods: (a) *kakaw*, "chocolate" (after K1398); (b) *kal kakaw*, "fermented (?) chocolate" (Piedras Negras Panel 3:02–P2); (c) "Naranjo" *kakaw* (after K6813); (d) *ul*, "atole" (after K2730); (e) Vessel MN16318 in Tikal National Park (after photographs from Takeshi Inomata); (f) *sak ha'*, "white water" (after Hellmuth 1987:fig. 411); and (g) *sak chihil we'*, "white deer food" (after Zender 2000:fig. 10).

Maya imagery. An unusual image of a woman grinding maize dough takes place in a supernatural, courtly scene where the Sun God converses with the K'awiil deity, a being sometimes associated with maize (Fig. 3.3; K631). David Freidel, Linda Schele, and Karl Taube have written at length about the primordial, three-stoned hearths linked to the remote, mythic past (Freidel et al. 1993:65–67; Taube 1998b). Nonetheless, these have less to do with food preparation than with acts of house renewal writ large. A few figurines, such as one from Lubaantun, portray a woman grinding corn with mano and metate (see also painted vessel, Hammond 1975:fig. 116c), with a baby on her back, in what must have been a conventional allusion to the duties of women (T. Joyce 1933). Several figurines show that such food could be sold by women vendors, some with tumplines, tamales, and a dog—perhaps for the meat dish (Fig. 3.4). This is among the clearest visual references to market activity in the Classic Maya world and is perhaps a hint of some striving toward economic autonomy by women.

The dyad of bread and drink is emphasized by glyphs recording acts of consumption (Fig. 3.5; Houston and D. Stuart 2001:fig. 3.4). These signs include a stylized human face whose mouth is stuffed with the glyph for "water" or "liquid" (*ha'*) or with the tamale or maize bread known to Classic Maya as *waaj* (Fig. 3.5a, b). It is probable that the signs spell *uk'*, "drink," and *we'*, "eat," although the phonetic evidence is stronger for the first reading than the second. There are other signs for consumption in the glyphic signary, but not all are completely clear in their meaning. One shows a face smoking a cigar (Fig. 3.5c). This head usually takes a nominalizing suffix to indicate "smoker," perhaps an obscure reference to curing practices or, at least, claims to them by elites. A few supernaturals, such as one portrayed as a peccary, are called "fire-eaters"; indeed, for unknown reasons, peccaries often breathe fire (Fig. 3.5d; e.g., K7525). Other glyphs contain mouths with "earth" signs (Fig. 3.5e), apparently read as [sa] (from the common word for *atole*?). Early Classic forms of the Maize God have signs near the mouth that recall a [sa] syllable, *sa* also being a term for a drink of maize dough (Taube 1992b). Yet another sign represents a gruesome play on the theme of consumption: it exhibits a jaguar with the glyph for

Fig. 3.2. Animals bringing food tribute (after K3413).

"person," *winik,* in his mouth, doubtless in reference to man-eating felines; a similar sign for "person" also occurs in the mouth of a bat, perhaps a vampire bat (Fig. 3.5f, g; Simon Martin, personal communication, 2003), and in the mouth of a vulture, a beast of carrion (Fig. 3.5h). In a few places, particularly in Yucatan and Campeche, the two primary glyphs for consumption, those for drinking and eating, pair up (e.g., García Campillo 1998:299; see Fig. 3.5i).

In the Postclassic Dresden Codex, scholars have long understood—without, however, any real grip on its reading—that the signs for consumption roughly concur with propitious times. This correlation led J. Eric Thompson to interpret the glyphs as "abundance of maize" (1972:41). It seems more likely that the general meaning was "eat/drink," probably in the sense of "feast" or "mealtime," a good augury in comparison to "drought" and "famine," *k'intunya'abil.* Paired signs in Mayan script usually cue meaning, as in the dyads of "wind-water" or "day-night." Despite the divergent values of their components (*ha'/ik'* and *k'in/ak'ab*), both pairs read *tz'ak.* There is thus no direct reason to think that the paired glyphs for "consumption" record either *uk'* or *we'.* One of the most explicit links between this sign pair and food is an imitation *comal,* supported on three stone balls, of which one contains the sign pair for "feast" (Robicsek and Hales 1981:fig. 62b). The *comal,* which also has the features of a burner for offering, is painted with the image of a jaguar on a stylized plate, along with a sign cluster, 1 K'an 1 Yax, that may relate to agricultural cycles and their abundance (Fig. 3.6; see Chapter 1). A predator is hardly human food, and the overall scene hints at supernatural consumption and the simulation of, or contrast with, human dining. Coveted foods, such as venison, had, strangely enough, little rhetorical salience in Classic texts and imagery. As mentioned before, there is also among the Classic Maya a decided, although not complete, rhetorical emphasis on liquids. The text mentioned above for "white deer food" is one such exception, and a few deer heads appear as paintings on the interior of plates, along with the occasional fish, always, however, fresh or recently caught, not broiled or grilled, as

Fig. 3.3. Woman grinding maize (after K631).

Fig. 3.4. Female vendor, figurine (Dieseldorff 1926:pl. 8, no. 28).

though shown flapping about on the plate (Becquelin and Baudez 1979, 1:figs. 177b, 178g, h). Did the Maya do this to preserve clarity of image? (Cooked pieces of meat, cut and stewed, are not always recognizable as to their origin.) The Postclassic Maya appear to have been more interested in meat, judging by the many ritual foods in the codices of that period (Bricker 1991). Moreover, a painted text from the Las Pinturas

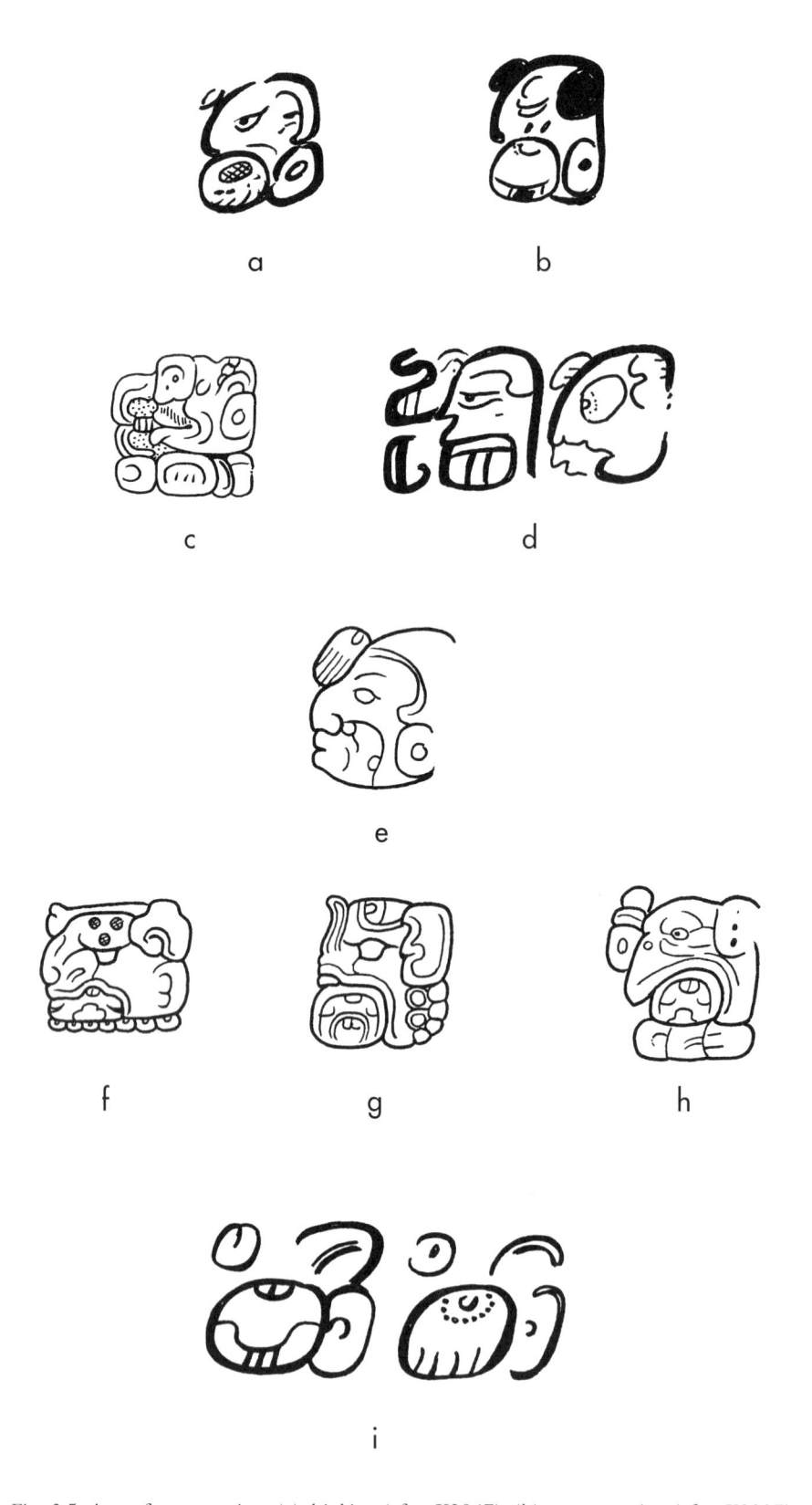

Fig. 3.5. Acts of consumption: (a) drinking (after K2067); (b) woman eating (after K8007); (c) smoker (Palenque stucco); (d) fire-eating peccary (after M. Coe 1982:fig. 6); (e) [sa] syllable (after Schele and Mathews 1979:440); (f) feline eating a human (Piedras Negras Stela 8:D4); (g) "vampire"(?) bat eating a human (after Tikal Stela 5:D7, C. Jones and Satterthwaite 1982: fig. 8a); (h) vulture eating a human (Dos Pilas Panel 7:A4, Houston 1993:fig. 5.11); and (i) "feast" or "food consumption, water consumption" (after García Campillo 1998:fig. 4a).

temple at Coba, Quintana Roo, displays, in the top row, a list of deities, from the Maize God to Itzamnaaj, and, below, offerings of fish, hearts, and venison, along with an explicit reference to an abundance of maize bread, *ox ok waaj* (Fig. 3.7; Houston 1989:fig. 19). Plausibly, this "user's" or "owner's manual" specified food offerings to particular deities.

The questions remain: What was the unit of consumption? What was the Maya concept of portions or servings, of satiety or abundance? What was their sense of when to serve foods and in what order (Goody 1982:85)? These concepts reach into the domain of table manners, a web of poses and behaviors conditioned by history and culture (Visser 1992). The number of cacao beans tabulated in bags reaches numbers (up to 40,000, multiplied when other bags were assembled) well in excess of what even a large group could consume. These quantities were storable wealth far more than raw ingredients for drink and food. If such can be trusted, representations of dishes with tamales contain immense wads of dough, three or more to a dish, to such a size that they could only be held in two hands (e.g., Reents-Budet 1994:fig. 2.20; see Fig. 3.8). A single tamale would have filled most people's stomachs; the fact that most tamales remain on the plate when people begin to drink suggests that meals began with liquids, perhaps as esophageal lubricants, and then went on to solids. No systematic study has ever been done of explicitly labeled cacao vessels *as artifacts.* Some were so

Fig. 3.6. Jaguar on plate/incense burner (after Robicsek and Hales 1981:fig. 62b).

Fig. 3.7. Painted text referring to an abundance of maize bread, Las Pinturas, Coba, Quintana Roo (Houston 1989:fig. 19).

large that they must have serviced many drinkers (K5445); others, particularly the slim ones with detailed historical scenes, tend to be small, enough for one consumer. An arbitrary sample of eleven cacao vessels in one catalogue revealed a mean of about three liters for the set, an impression at best because of variation in the ceramic thickness and broad provenance of the sample (Reents-Budet 1994:cat. 2, 4, 5, 9, 10, 11, 21, 33, 40, 48, 51). Another impression is that the amounts of food in images are singularly low for anything but a small number of people, whatever their appetites.

The consumption of tobacco powders is also attested in the Classic period, as may be the spelling *k'utz*, "tobacco," on Monument 4, a platform at Uxmal, Yucatan (I. Graham 1992:131, position B1). A transparent instance is a small codex-style flask that has, on its sides, the glyphs /*yotoot umay ahk mo'*/, "it is the home of the tobacco-powder of Turtle-Macaw," the last being the name of the owner (Fig. 3.9a). Another such reference to *may*, "tobacco power," occurs on a small flask that refers to the owner (a woman?) on one side and, on the other side, just between two handles for suspension, three plant leaves; their idiosyncratic pattern of three circles probably corresponds to Maya conventions for the tobacco plant (Fig. 3.9b; M. Coe 1973:pl. 77; see also glyph A12, in M. G. Robertson 1983:171, in connection with the name of "ancestors" or *mam*, a reference also found as an image on an Early Classic cache vessel [Schele and Mathews 1998:fig. 3.33]). The leaves of the plant are highly distinctive, with broadleaf, veins, and circular markings. Moreover, tobacco smoke can be indicated, as on a sculpted panel at Dumbarton Oaks, by the issuance of tobacco leaves through earspools, probably in analogy to puffs of breath and fragrance (Chapter 4). Another set of leaves occurs on an altar from Tikal that may have been used for the burning of tobacco and other substances in sacrifice (Fig. 3.9c). For many years, tobacco/snuff flasks have been known, rather fancifully, as "poison bottles," presumably because they held doses of venom. In fact, they have a distinctive appearance that strongly resembles snuff containers from South America (Wilbert 1987:58–59) or the gourds known to have been used for snuff and quids in the Maya region (Thompson 1970:110–112). One Early Classic example even reproduces the shape of a squash (R. E. Smith 1955:fig. 66a-7). An even more striking parallel can be seen in snuff bottles from China that display almost precisely the same dimensions and flattened form as Maya snuff containers, along with stopper and base (S. Lorin and F. Lorin 1997:pls. 1, 15, etc.).

Fig. 3.8. Plate with tamales (photograph by David Stuart of unprovenanced Late Classic vessel).

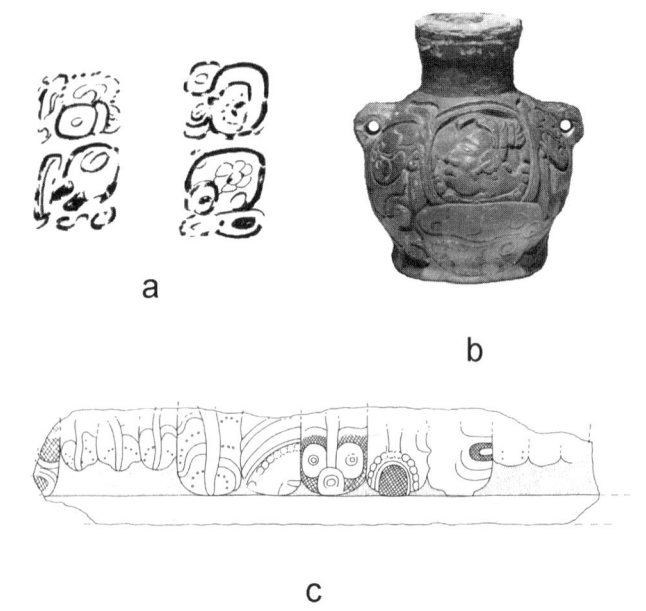

Fig. 3.9. Tobacco in Maya texts and images: (a) text on snuff flask showing ownership of the "home of his tobacco," *yotoot umay* (from unprovenanced ceramic bottle); (b) tobacco flask showing leaves of tobacco (M. Coe 1973:pl. 77); and (c) Tikal Altar 2, showing tobacco leaves (C. Jones and Satterthwaite 1982:fig. 8b, with permission of Sharon Misdea, Tikal Project, University of Pennsylvania Museum).

The Maya examples could sit on a flat surface or, as permitted by their compressed shape, be suspended around the neck (e.g., Adams 1971:fig. 63d, e; R. E. Smith 1955:fig. 12n [an example filled with copal, perhaps as an ingestible for the deceased with whom it was buried]). They had highly restricted orifices, held about 12 cm^3 of powder, and were nearly circular or at least rounded from the front yet narrow from the side. The openings are of just the right size to insert into one nostril at a time or to accommodate a small, lime-encrusted spatula. Although lacking lime residue, spatulas occur at many Maya sites (e.g., Kidder 1947:fig. 41; Taschek 1994:fig. 36a; Thompson 1970:110). One example of a "poison bottle" from Piedras Negras, Guatemala, shows peculiar iconography, a bird extracting the eye of what may be a jaguar, suggesting that there is much to the bottles that remains unexplored and unknown (Fig. 3.10). Among the Aztec, tobacco containers were a prime insignia of priests. Yukatek priests of the Late Postclassic could be termed *ah k'in may*, "tobacco priests" (Thompson 1970:111). Holders of such flasks among the Classic Maya may have been priests, too, a category that is otherwise difficult to detect in surviving texts and images. Or perhaps the owners of flasks simply wished to avail themselves easily of tobacco and its soothing or appetite-suppressing qualities. Whatever the ownership of these tobacco-related items, it seems clear that tobacco and its products deserve more attention from specialists in ancient Maya agriculture. The plant thrives on limestone and the ashy soils left by swidden agriculture, and can be cured and compacted to serve as an ideal trade item. The ubiquity of snuff bottles in the area of Copan and El Salvador may indicate a local specialization—now as then!—in tobacco and its by-products.

The ubiquity of tobacco may also explain an occasional find at many Classic cities: small, flat grinding palettes, usually of exotic stone, raised on nubbin feet and with a carefully marked groove at one end (Kidder 1947:fig. 76a). Although far distant from the Maya, the Karuk of California used flat mortars of this sort to pound tobacco stems that could then be mixed with the leaf (Harrington 1932:95–98, 217; note, however, that there is also a strong possibility for multiple metate functions, such as the grinding and preparation of pigments [Inomata 1995:figs. 8.26–8.32; Inomata and Stiver 1998]). The pounding and mixing led to a smoother smoke, since some native varieties of tobacco were of such strength as to cause fainting (Harrington 1932:195–196). The evidence from the Karuk is also impressive because of clear statements about their widespread addiction to tobacco. To quote an informant, "When some people say that the Indians do not get the tobacco habit, it is

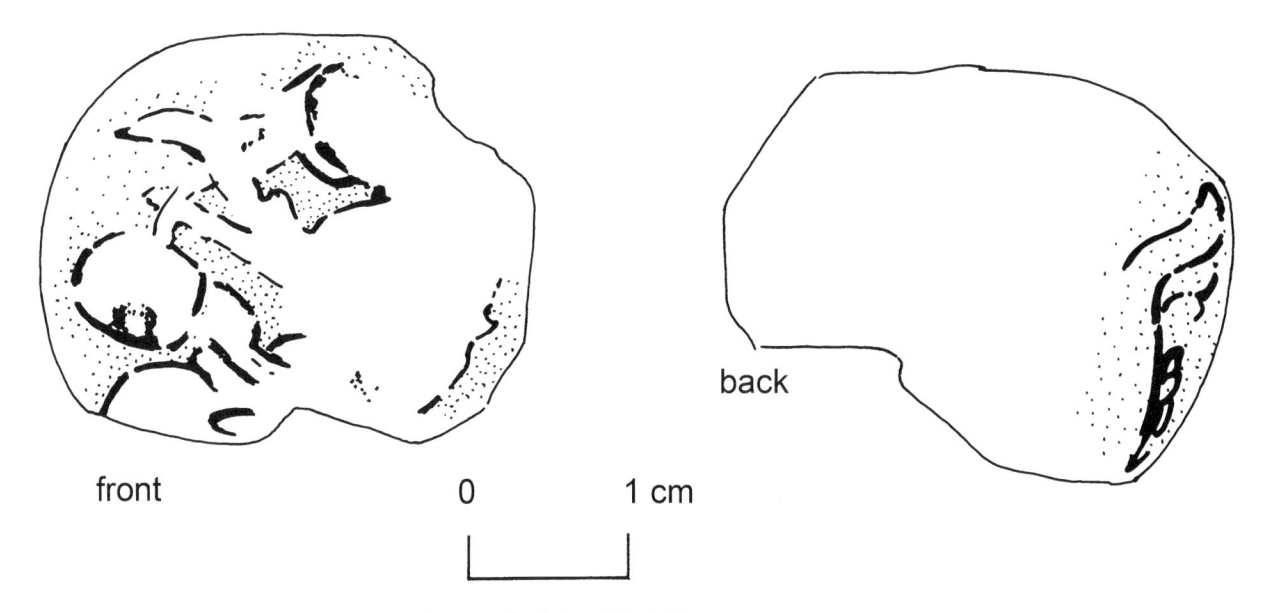

Fig. 3.10. Tobacco flask, Piedras Negras, front and back (PN52G-1-3).

not right. . . . They cannot stay without tobacco, including women when they are doctors" (Harrington 1932:216). This suggests that tobacco consumption among the Classic Maya was incremental and, with frequent ritual encouragement, extremely common. Among the Karuk, sweat lodges did double duty by being used for the smoking and curing of tobacco leaf, which then had to be stored in the house (Harrington 1932:93). An analogy to the human body, in addition to practical exigency, probably molded these practices and suggests supplementary functions to Classic Maya sweatbaths.

During the final years of the Late Classic period, the "bottles," which almost certainly held tobacco and other powders, were widely traded. Yet perhaps the contents, not the bottles, were the desired trade items, rather like mints or shortbread within fancy tins: a memory of delectable treats, kept around after the goodies had been consumed. Cigar smoking also appears in Classic imagery, either as pencil-thin elegant cigarettes, the usual accoutrements of courts, or as enormous cigars. Tobacco lashings of this sort could be smoked by many people, passed around from participant to participant, much like the gigantic, ritual cigars of the Tucano in South America (Wilbert 1987:91; such stogies make an appearance in the Madrid Codex as well, and reports exist of Classic Maya cigars excavated by Rudy Larios in Group H, Tikal [de Smet 1985:66]). In contrast, people smoking cigarettes often appear to the side, as figures not quite central to the action—the occasional flourishing of torches nearby suggests that the idea was mostly to denote nighttime and the lambent drama of flame and glowing embers, along with individual enjoyment of a good smoke, yet another pleasure of leisurely life at court (e.g., K1728). The synesthetic objective of the painters was to inject the aromas of court into the perception of the viewer.

There was some momentum toward increased velocity of consumption, as Wolfgang Schivelbusch (1993:111–116) has noted for tobacco in the West, where there was first the fussy pipe of the seventeenth century, to be cleaned and smoked at unhurried pace; then the cigar of the Napoleonic period, delivering a half-hour's smoke or more; and on to the cigarette of the late nineteenth century. This cigarette was first bought in small quantities from the neighborhood tobacconist, sucked in eight minutes or less, and eventually offered in cardboard cartons that allowed a lung-tarring rate of consumption. In much the same way, pipes are not seen in Classic imagery, but cigars and, at some later courts, cigarettes are. Cigars are sociable, and can be passed around, whereas cigarettes bespeak a higher degree of purely personal consumption. In contrast, the Maya plate and all but the narrowest and smallest cylinder vase reflect a commitment to sociable dining. Tobacco was different: perhaps the more addictive the substance, the more self-focused and greedy the consumer.

A final ingestible was alcohol. It appeared to be a slightly paradoxical substance, in that the natural breakdown of its constituents was only partly channeled by cultural acts. In contrast, food was "cooked" in Claude Lévi-Strauss's meaning of undergoing cultural transformation—if not, it would rot (Goody 1982:21–23; Lévi-Strauss 1965), although, to be sure, alcohol also required some processing, albeit, in the Maya case, with relatively little effort and time. Ethnography and history tell us that the Maya prepared a kind of mead known as *balche'*, in part concocted from the bark of the *pitarilla* tree (Tozzer 1941:92). The bark was probably used as a retardant so that the fermentation could occur at a steady rate and thus raise alcohol content (Dahlin and Litzinger 1986). Such mead drinks are shown in some Classic Maya images, as designated by signs for "honey" on the sides of vessels (Fig. 3.11a; Barrera Rubio and Taube 1987:figs. 15e, f; de Smet 1985:pl. 7b). More often the glyphs refer consistently to *chih* (not *chij*, "deer"), especially as a label on necked vessels with flaring rims (e.g., K1092; Fig. 3.11b); in contrast, the glyphic recipes for drinks seem without exception to have involved nonalcoholic liquids. The range of terms mentioned above points to pulque, the mildly alcoholic juice of the agave plant, or even sisal (**chih* in Proto-Ch'olan; John Justeson, cited in de Smet 1985:61–65; also Barrera Vásquez 1981; Kaufman and Norman 1984:118). In an influential study, submitted in 1940 as a doctoral thesis at Berkeley but published only recently, Henry Bruman presented a map of what he called the "pulque region" (2000:62). The southern and eastern borders corresponded closely to the Isthmus of Tehuantepec because, to Bruman, ethnographic data did not justify an extension of pulque into the Maya region. This merely underscores the limits of his evidence: the Pompeii-like site of Ceren, El Salvador, contains agave plants, and the glyphic data confirm the special importance of this drink over a millennium ago in northern Central America (Sheets 2002).

It is now certain that drinks were consumed by mouth and through the rectum (Barrera Rubio and Taube 1987; de Smet 1983, 1984, 1985; P. Furst and M. Coe 1977; Stross and J. Kerr 1990), probably going back to the Early Preclassic period (Taube 1998a). Several Maya images show scenes of self-insertion with clysters or enema syringes atop pulque pots. The syringe has, as expected, a tube and a bulb or a bottle gourd (*Lagenaria siceraria*) with a blowhole for the forced introduction of fluid (e.g., K1381, K1550). Nonetheless, the existence of the blowhole implies that another person had to participate (Fig. 3.12). Bundles of leaves stuffed into enema jars recall a statement by Karl Sapper (2000:24) that fermentation was assisted by rolling slightly spoiled corn in leaves and placing them in a pot for several days, with moderate heat provided from a nearby hearth. Most enema scenes are intensely sociable ones, with two or more people gathered around a vessel that supports, on its lid, a cup for drinking and a syringe for enemas (e.g., K530, K4605). The same vessel supplied liquid for both activities. The salacious undertones of enemas, perhaps inevitable given their penetrative nature, sharpen with the presence of women assisting enema insertion (K1550, K1890) and by signs of jollity and merriment, along with music by small orchestras (K1563). The same use of enemas in sexual acts can also be seen among the Moche of South America (Bourget 2001:fig. 12). Among the Maya, when supernaturals appear, such as the aged God N, comely women massage their sides, a delicate gesture that conveys considerable intimacy. Some deities strip down to loincloths, gaze into mirrors, and anoint their bodies with salves while painted ladies fan them in coquettish gestures (K530; M. Coe 1975:pl. 11). The stripping and fanning, as well as the presence of a cave or a rocky, enclosed space, hint at sweatbathing, erotic dalliance, and gushing or streaming fluids of all sorts. The body is penetrated; it effuses.

Mark Child's excavations of sweatbaths at Piedras Negras, Guatemala, reveal ample space for such activities; possible organic residues on the floor; and ancillary buildings containing small, secluded rooms with sleeping benches (personal communications, 1999, 2000; Fig. 3.13). In another Classic scene (Reents-Budet 1994:fig. 2.27c), also of supernaturals, a grim goddess of midwifery and healing induces a scribal god to vomit (Fig. 3.14). His companion deity (not shown here), one of accounting and numbers, seems to await his turn. A young goddess buttresses and massages the head of the scribal god while, in the full image, two other females sit behind,

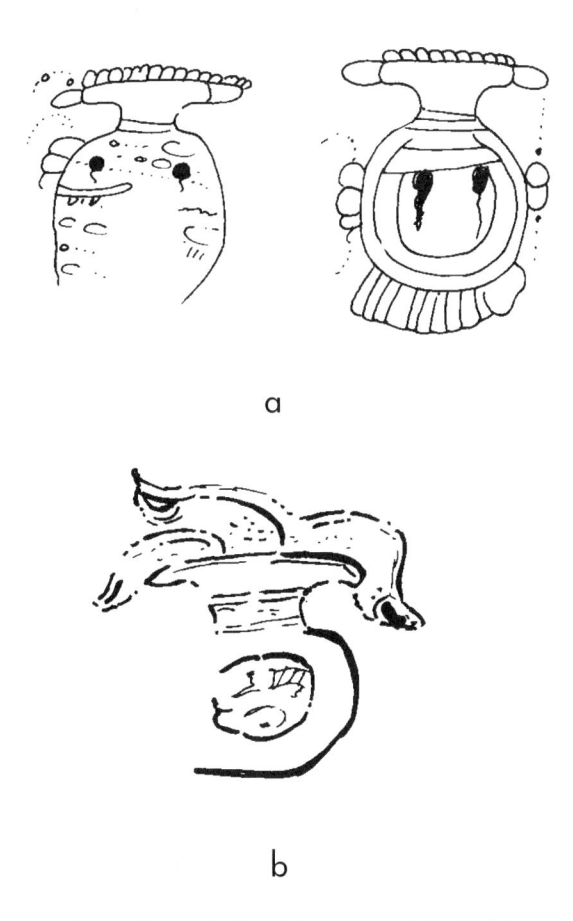

Fig. 3.11. Jars for alcoholic drinks: (a) mead (*balche'*) jars (Barrera Rubio and Taube 1987:fig. 15f); and (b) pulque (*chih*) jar (after K1092).

Fig. 3.12. Enema insertion by female (after K1550).

perched on a bench above various foods and drinks. The combination of drink, food, vomit, enemas, sweatbathing, and sex inspires some bewilderment, but it may be that the Classic Maya did not see these as fully separate things: some acts concerned healing, some pleasure, some a rough and thorough purging or cleansing. All restored balance to the body, in part by taking it to extremes and bringing it back as though by recalibration to an unstable midpoint. It may also be that the root for "douches" in Ch'orti', *bu'ht'*, occurs once in the Classic texts, on the Palenque Palace Tablet (N11) as a transitive verb, *u but'-uw*, "he/she/it fills it" (M. G. Robertson 1985b:fig. 258). The context is some kind of mortuary event, so this may refer to indigenous embalming, especially of the abdomen, the first area of the body to be tended by ancient undertakers, since, without removal, the viscera and organs putrefy quickly. Such "stuffing" is also known for shrunken heads worn by warriors (e.g., K767). Often, cotton or kapok padding extrudes from the mouth, and these may have been the same materials employed by Classic Maya undertakers, perhaps the very same elderly women involved in curing and healing.

The nature of Maya "medicine" needs comment here. For example, most vessels designed to hold chocolate drinks display a variety of *way*, or companion spirits. Most appear to be ghastly and, to judge from their gruesome names, redolent of disease (Grube and Nahm 1994; Houston and D. Stuart 1989). One *way*, a cat of some sort (*hix*), clutches an enema syringe (Fig. 3.15a). On one pot he lies on his back, just about to introduce a clyster. Every now and then, depending on the scene, he vomits. A flower or vegetal necklace like a Hawaiian lei contributed to the festive atmosphere (Fig. 3.15c; see K1563, K5538). Another *way* is labeled Akan, meaning "moan" (Fig. 3.15b). He is a god associated with bees and fermenting drink, probably a mead brewed from honey (Amy Willats, personal communication, 1991; also Grube 2001a; K6508). One lord appears to impersonate him in a standing sculpture at Tonina (Peter Mathews, personal communication, 1985; also see Mathews 1983:22). Not surprisingly, Akan—the "little death" of sex, inebriation, or, perhaps, the moans of the dying—occurs in historic sources as the "god of wine" (Barrera Vásquez 1980:5; Grube 2001a:295).

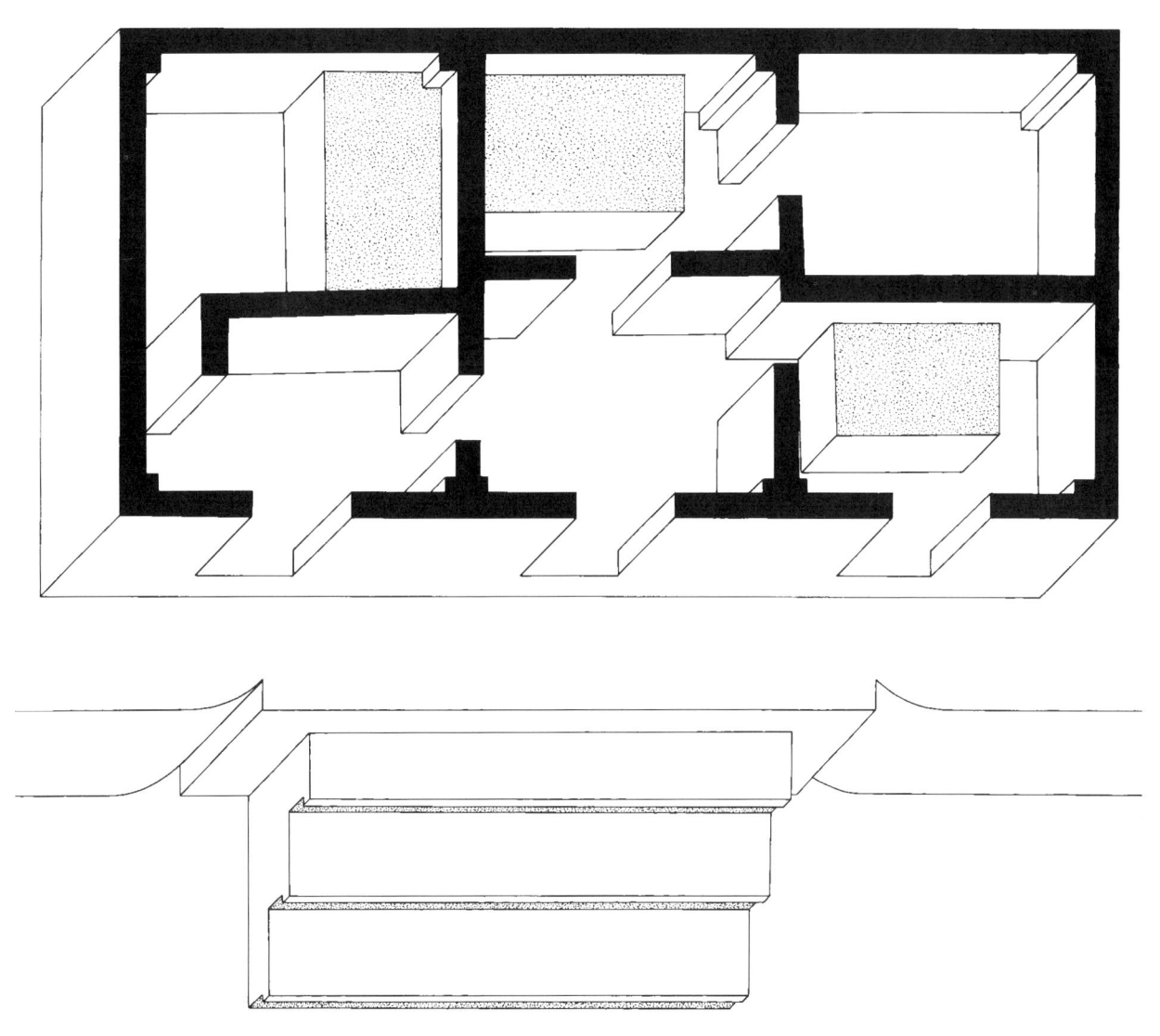

Fig. 3.13. Plan of building near sweatbath, Piedras Negras, Guatemala; building ca. 10 m long (courtesy of Mark Child, Yale University).

The explanation for this conjuncture that drink is associated with unattractive and dangerous beings may lie in the clinical and apotropaic practices of the Maya. Intoxication and related acts laid the path to well-being and, it should not be forgotten, altered mental states. The experience was not always pleasant, presumably: in Ch'orti', the more stinking and unsavory the remedy, the more likely to be efficacious (*ink'o' tz'ak*, "any stinking remedy"; Wisdom n.d.). Finally, there is one brewing deity known as Mok Chiih, apparently "disease pulque," whether as cure or instigator of disease (or both) is uncertain (Grube and Nahm 1994:707–708; n.b.: The original translation by Grube and Nahm of *mok chih*, "knot mouth" in Yukatek Mayan, involves the wrong language; in the inscriptions, the term for "mouth" was *ti'*). For the Classic Maya, as with many other people, the distinction between "food" or "ingestibles" and "medicine" was at best flexible (Mintz 1996:60–62). In Europe, valuable "spices," which we now add for reasons of pleasure, were once regarded as medicines (Dalby 2000a:16–17).

Drunkenness was permitted in Late Postclassic Maya society, often during important celebrations, as in most Maya communities today (e.g., Vogt 1976:34–38). The so-called realistic paintings at Tetitla, Teotihuacan, Mexico, almost certainly from

Fig. 3.14. Vomiting god (after Reents-Budet 1994:fig. 2.27c).

an enclave decorated in part by literate Maya painters, emphasize the connection between drink, drunkenness, and Maya-style imagery, as though this enjoyment were an "ethnic attribute" of peoples that lived far distant from Teotihuacan (Fig. 3.15d, e; Foncerrada de Molina 1980:figs. 14–22). In the Classic period, the determination of who drinks what and when recognized and confirmed hierarchy. Yet scenes of inebriation are quite rare at this time (e.g., K1092), and even images of drinking are uncommon in other parts of Mesoamerica (see the mural *Los bebedores,* "The Drinkers," of Cholula, Mexico, in Marquina 1971; Rodríguez Cabrera 2003:34–35). The chaotic effects of a drunken population can be imagined and must have been tightly controlled. The effects of alcohol were accelerated through ingestion by enemas, which allowed the rapid absorption of alcohol into the bloodstream. Today, for example, the French pharmacopoeia often calls for suppositories rather than the pills preferred by North Americans, although with the claim that this is done, not for speed of absorption, but to avoid stomach upsets (DeBoer et al. 1982). Sweatbathing, too, heightened the effect of drink by inducing greater blood flow throughout the body.

The public consumption of alcohol, either by the mouth or the rectum, is attested in two places. The first is a set of stone altars at Copan, Honduras, that were involved in the consumption of *chih,* or pulque. One monument in the set, dating from the time of the last secure ruler of the city, Yax Pasaj, refers to *yuk'ij chih,* "his drinking of pulque" (Fig. 3.16a). It is likely that the top surface of the altar

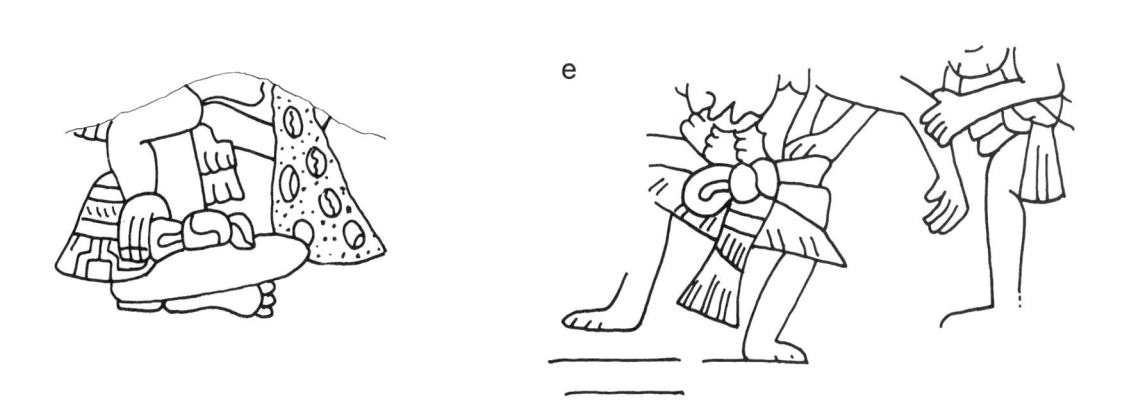

Fig. 3.15. Enema syringes, jars, and drunkenness: (a) feline with syringe (after K7525); (b) Akan with syringe (after K927); (c) enema jar with festive collar (K5538); and (d, e) scenes of drunkenness at Teotihuacan (after Foncerrada de Molina 1980:fig. 16, fig. 23).

once held vessels with this drink, or perhaps libations were poured over the stone. Another altar from Copan is just as explicit, but with an added twist (Fig. 3.16b). The relevant portion of the text refers to an act of god impersonation, an important ritual in Maya practice in which lords and rulers dressed as deities and, according to indigenous thought, assimilated their supernatural essence (Chapter 8; Houston and D. Stuart 1996). The name of the deity is none other than a variant of Akan, the god of drink. The second example comes from an enigmatic building at San Diego, Yucatan (Barrera Rubio and Taube 1987; Mayer 1984:pls. 143–149). For what seems to have been a public building—only a few panels remain at the site, just near Structure I—the scenes are surprising and homoerotic: they document the preparation of enema juice, the transport of liquid by tumpline (see also backracks with enema jars, Mayer 1984:pl. 161), and the insertion of clysters, along with a barrage of whirling, dazed bodies, two sitting or kneeling in a stunned state with hair over their faces. One figure looms over another, penis partly erect, as though ready for oblivious sex (Fig. 3.17; Mayer 1984:pl. 146). These scenes may relate to homosocial and homoerotic activities within a young men's house and contrast with heterosocial and heterosexual enemas involving older men, with women acting as the penetrators, the inserters of enemas. It is interesting for this reason that the feline *way* linked to enemas was *ch'ok*, "young." Moreover, the owners of many chocolate pots were known as *chak ch'ok*, "red" or "great youth" or even "very young person," or *keleem*, another term for "youth" (e.g., K2704, K3025, K3026, K5062, K5390, K5847, K7716). A strong possibility exists that such vessels were used in age-grade rituals, perhaps those involving initiation and feasting.

STRANGE FRUIT

Humans ingest, but, to the Classic Maya, so did deities and the dead. Texts and imagery point to shared foodstuffs, such as drink and food. Other scenes hint that supernaturals consumed things that were unappetizing to living humans and that their food differed categorically from that of other beings. (The foregoing has had little to report, regrettably, on what the Classic Maya did *not* eat, on what was not regarded as food, although, like many peoples around the world and, indeed, Maya today, they presumably avoided predators, carrion eaters, and meats that spoiled quickly [Bober 1999:2; Ikram 1995:33]). One category consisted of repellent foods, especially those associated with beings of death and darkness. Such creatures—

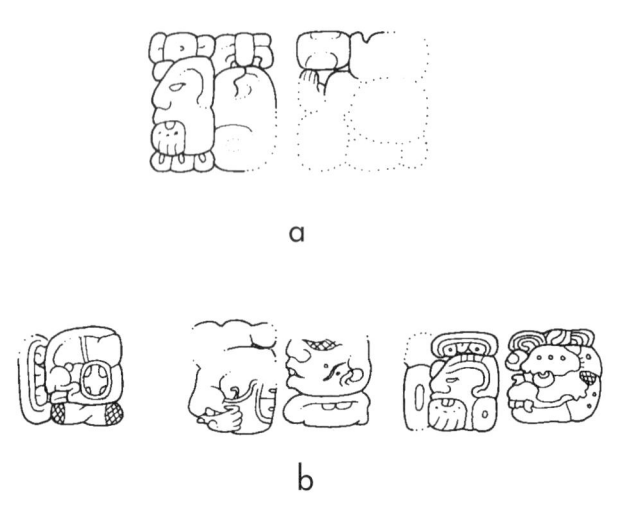

Fig. 3.16. Pulque rituals at Copan: (a) undesignated altar (after field drawing by David Stuart); and (b) Altar U (after field drawing by Linda Schele).

Fig. 3.17. Drunken, homoerotic scene from San Diego relief (photograph by Karl Taube).

apparently not subject to heartburn—relished a hearty offering of human hands, feet, skulls, and eyeballs arranged neatly into bowls, in short, all the offal and scrapings of the butcher's abattoir (e.g., K1080; Fig. 3.18). Other deities consumed hearts, with venous and arterial attachments shown in the form of three curls (Robicsek and Hales 1984:fig. 4). Hummingbird deities craved flowers and nectar (Culbert 1993:fig. 84). Still, the most succulent flesh for gods was probably human. A vessel in the Museum of Fine Arts, Boston (K1377), although perhaps overpainted, shows an agnathous god feasting on the heart of a sacrificed youth (rather like a tamale, the human heart consists of meaty innards surrounded by "doughy" fat and pericardium). Another bowl (K4992) displays a person being macerated in a drinking vessel for consumption by monkeys. An Early Classic text from Yaxchilan, Chiapas, brings such godly consumption into the political sphere. It refers to a war captive, evidently the subordinate of a ruler of Calakmul, who was unlucky enough to become the "eating" (*u-we'-iiy*?) of two patron gods of Yaxchilan, one a version of the Storm God (O' Chaak), the other the Jaguar God of the Underworld (Fig. 3.19; Yaxchilan Lintel 35:C5–D8, I. Graham 1979:79). Two references to *k'ux*, "chewing, biting," occur in circumstances relating to war captives, but whether as food for patron gods or as provender for cannibals is hard to say. The first text comes from Tonina Fragment 1, which records that a captive was "chewed" or "bitten," *k'ux-j-iiy* (Fig. 3.20a; Becquelin and Baudez 1982, 2:fig. 180; Geo. Stuart 1987:29). The second text appears at Naranjo, but in a monument that originally came from Caracol (Simon Martin, personal communication, 2000); thus *k'u(h)x-aj sak-chuween*(?), "White Monkey is bitten," occurred under the supervision of a king from Calakmul (Fig. 3.20b; Naranjo Hieroglyphic Stairway 2, Step VI:L2, I. Graham 1978:109). The meaning is partly about torture but, from the evidence of *k'ux*, also about man-food, an example of so-called exocannibalism, or the eating of those outside one's group (Lindenbaum 2004:478). The most exquisite food for deities may well have been human hearts, of the sort depicted at Chichen Itza (Fig. 3.21a) and on a plate in front of the Sun God in the Dresden Codex (Fig. 3.21b). The number seven probably stipulates the desired quantities, although only three such hearts (note the venal and arterial connections on the tops) are shown; another Postclassic text, from Coba, specifies "thirteen hearts" (see Fig. 3.7, position D3). An altar for the consumption of food by deities occurs on the eastern part of the Copan valley, where the text refers to the "food" of the Sun God (Fig. 3.21c). Surrounding this altar was a larger number of tiny metates, as though in allusion to food preparation. If, as seems possible, the tamale was linked conceptually to the human heart, then this organ or its symbolic substitutes may well have been the offering on the altar.

Then there are the "dead," to use an inapt term, since the deceased did not lack needs or the force to satisfy those cravings. The clearest evidence of such "food consumption" comes from burials. At the site of Altar de Sacrificios, not a few burials contain inverted bowls, sometimes drilled with "kill holes" (Fig. 3.22). Perhaps these symbolized the proverbial "finished feast" or inversionary concepts of consumption in the afterworld, where food was not-food (see above; M. Coe 1988; A. L. Smith 1972:figs. 42–43). Alternatively, they held offerings that had been consumed during mortuary repasts. There may well have been the kind of shift witnessed in ancient Egypt, in which the necessity of placing actual food shifted to various "magical" stratagems for provisioning the dead (W. Emery 1962:2). Other patterns come from a wide variety of sites, from Caracol, Belize, to Seibal, Guatemala, and elsewhere (Ruz Lluillier 1968:180). At these centers, mortuary furniture typically consisted of dishes—presumably for serving tamales—and drinking vessels. These last probably contained chocolate beverages or, at least, were said to be used for such drinks (A. Chase 1994:fig. 13.1; MacLeod and Reents-Budet 1994). It is possible that the Maya understood, as did the ancient Egyptians, that honey was a first-rate preservative because bacteria cannot endure high sugar content (Ikram 1995:170). Such residue, along with salt, another obvious preservative, may yet be found in some dishes from Classic tombs (A. Andrews 1983).

Fig. 3.18. Food of evil beings (after photograph by David Stuart).

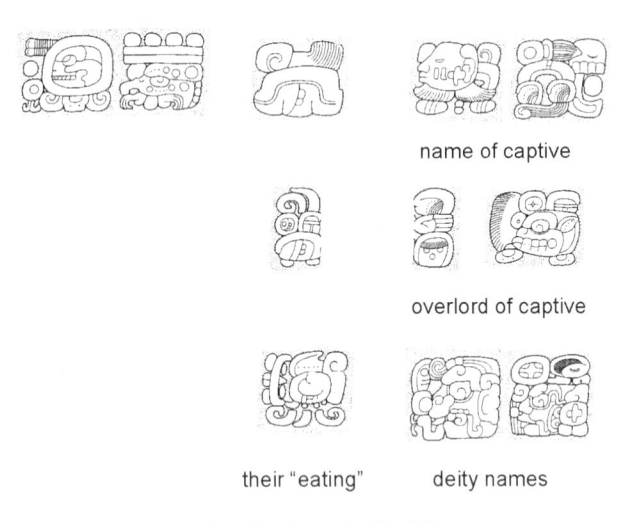

Fig. 3.19. Eating of captive by gods, Yaxchilan Lintel 35:C5–D8 (I. Graham 1979:79).

their "eating"   deity names
name of captive
overlord of captive

The impression one gets of Maya serving vessels and drink containers in Classic-era burials is that they fell into two general categories, although statistical proof of this is lacking. The first included a very limited inventory of one or two plates or bowls and a corresponding number of drinking vessels. There are many burials that do not have even these (Houston et al. 2003). Then, in a distinct category, were burials with large numbers of vessels, far in excess of the number required by a single person. These burials, usually royal or elite ones, suggest a meal, not for one, but for many—here are portions beyond those consumed by the living (see above and A. L. Smith 1972:figs. 48 and 49). Another possibility is that the assortment conveys a sense of culinary richness, boundless royal appetite, and diverse recipes enjoyed at court. Recall that, for most Maya, getting by was, according to some sources, a habitual condition, not free access to a surfeit of food (e.g., Storey 1999:178). Did the Maya farmer live, physically and psychologically, within a "famine of living" (created by want) and a "time of suspicion" (compelled by uncertain etiology of contagious disease), such as Piero Camporesi (1996:86–89) envisions for peasant Italy? The osteological evidence from Maya skeletons would seem to be ambiguous about this question. Some physical anthropologists point to many

INGESTION   125

episodes of nutritive stress, of persistent or at least episodic shortages of food, as in Classical Antiquity (Garnsey 1999:34); others point to solid nutrition, depending on region. A collection of burial vessels, none clearly with food or drink, cluster within a hole in a mythological scene containing old gods and luscious maidens (K1485). The trope of old men with drink and voluptuous ladies may have played the same role as in enema scenes: the very embodiment of license and randiness, to the extent that one pot shows an old man as a "drinking snake," . . . *uk'-kaan,* entwined around a naked woman (K2067). Among the Aztec, the elderly could drink all they wished, and the same may have held true for the Classic Maya.

A final "food" for gods and the "dead" was altogether more intangible. This would have been smoke issuing from incense burners—solid substances such as paper, blood, copal, and rubber transformed into wreaths of smoke floating skyward

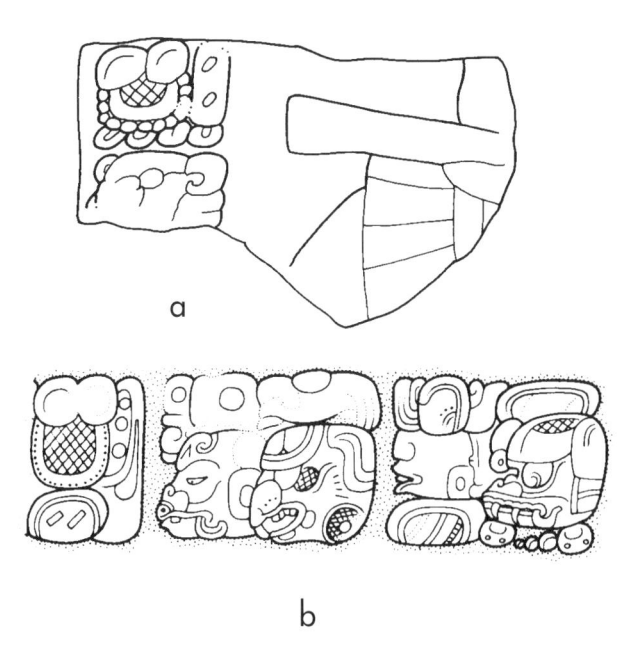

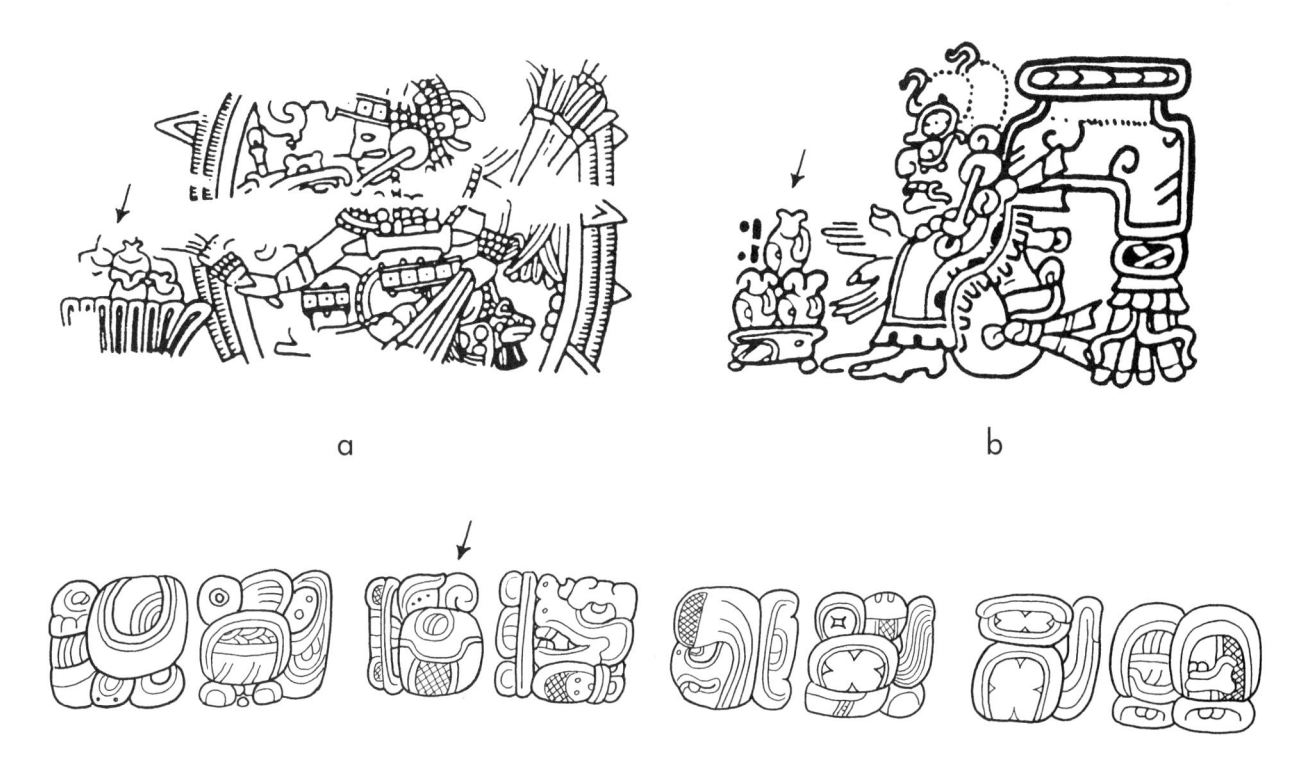

Fig. 3.20. *K'ux,* "biting," of captives: (a) Tonina Fragment 1 (after Becquelin and Baudez 1982, 2:fig. 180); and (b) Naranjo Hieroglyphic Stairway 2, Step VI:L2 (I. Graham 1978:109).

Fig. 3.21. Consumption by the Sun God of human hearts and other foods: (a) Toltec container of hearts, lintel from the Upper Temple of the Jaguars, Chichen Itza; (b) Dresden Codex, p. 26b (Thompson 1972); and (c) Altar G'', Copan, Honduras (after drawing by Barbara Fash).

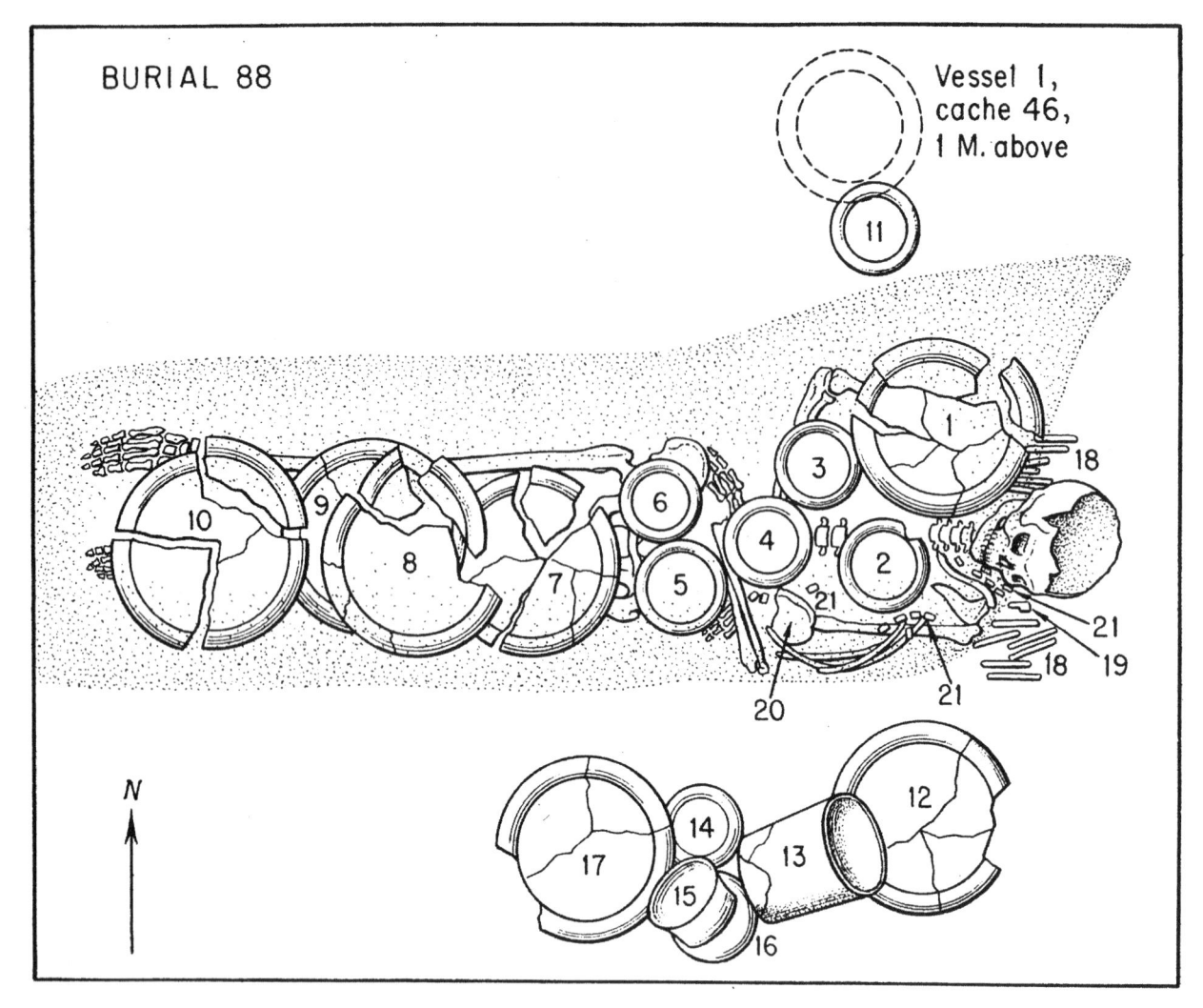

Fig. 3.22. Burial 88, Altar de Sacrificios (A. L. Smith 1972:fig. 45a).

(Fig. 3.23; Rice 1999; Taube 2004a). Incense was seen in the *Popol Vuh* as a substitute for the hearts craved by gods, and, in fact, most Mayan languages employ the same words for "blood" and "tree sap," the raw material of incense (Christenson 2003:133). Fires dedicated to particular deities were frequently mentioned at important dates, such as the completion of calendrical periods (Grube 2000:96–100). Similar practices occur among the contemporary Lacandon, who burn "food" (incense) offerings to deities in *läk-il k'uh*, "god pots," each of which bears the face of a deity (McGee 1990:49). Many stone supports for incense burners at the site of Palenque, especially on terraces around the Temple of the Cross, served as mortuary monuments to members of the court.

When complete and readable, the texts on the supports uniformly refer to death and burial (e.g., Easby and Scott 1970:pl. 175; Schele and Mathews 1979:pls. 281, 282, and probably 283). Similarly, the incense burners that teem in other Maya cities may well have been used, along with music and fragrance, to "feed" gods and, secondarily, to attract their sacralizing presence by providing nourishment for them.

Reciprocally, this scent can be understood as the breath emanation of deities. An incense burner from Tikal shows an old god—the same one that corresponds to the syllable [ye]—"blowing" incense out of his mouth onto a human head, perhaps as a means of infusing the object with life (Fig. 3.24a; Culbert 1993:fig. 14). This figure, apparently

Fig. 3.23. Incense burner with sacrificial heart, El Cayo Altar 1 (after drawing by Peter Mathews).

accepting a "sacrifice," is better understood as part of a creative act that relates to scenes of supernatural artists holding up freshly sculpted heads (Fig. 3.24b, c). Another Early Classic censer depicts the monkey artisan holding such a head in his hands, "breathing" on it in a comparable act of vitalization (M. Miller and Martin 2004:pl. 66). In the *Popol Vuh*, the original creator is called Tz'aqol B'itol ("framer, shaper"), the latter term explicitly referring to someone who models "pottery from clay, or a sculpture from carved stone" (Christenson 2003:60 n. 13). Rather than a god of death or sacrifice, the deity on the Tikal censer is more likely to be an aged creator being.

Eva Hunt (1977:89) and John Monaghan (2000:37) have described Mesoamerican religion as "phagiohierarchical," meaning that it thought about things eating other things, not just as a mere food chain of plants to animals, animals to humans, and humans to gods, but in symmetrical consumption, with humans eating the Maize God within *waaj* and the spiritual force within other foods (Monaghan 2000:37). The expectation was threefold: that such consumption *would* take place, that all beings *must* participate as part of the same condominium, and that these primordial arrangements or "covenants" *might be* deferred by supplying proxy foods to those who want to eat you (Monaghan 2000:38). The sacrifice of captives thus offered a kind of food. The captive represented the proxy flesh of the sacrificer's own body; smoke from incense burners provided delicious scents to gods, who may, perhaps, have just been satisfied before returning for seconds.

FEASTING

Glyphs for eating and drinking raise several issues. First, the actual act of consumption represents an exceptional image in Maya iconography, with twinges of markedness or vulgarity. Among the only known scenes of drinking are those involving a dwarf (Fig. 3.25; K1453) or other beings that appear to be supernatural (K1381, K4377). In enema consumption, users are almost always well and truly smashed. Paradoxically, this accords with the ample evidence that the Classic Maya conformed to "court societies," in which, among other features, etiquette and personal style were hyperrefined and behavior closely monitored for bumptiousness and *lèse-majesté* (Inomata and Houston 2001): gross acts of consumption may have been carefully hedged and seen negatively (see Walens 1981). Second, images from the Classic period do not indicate the presence of redistributive or reciprocal feasts but rather of Dietler's "diacritical" ones. Food and drink occur mostly as tokens of bounty. To a notable extent, the ruler, usually shown on his throne, receives food but does not offer it to others. There is, at least in the Classic Maya evidence, little hint

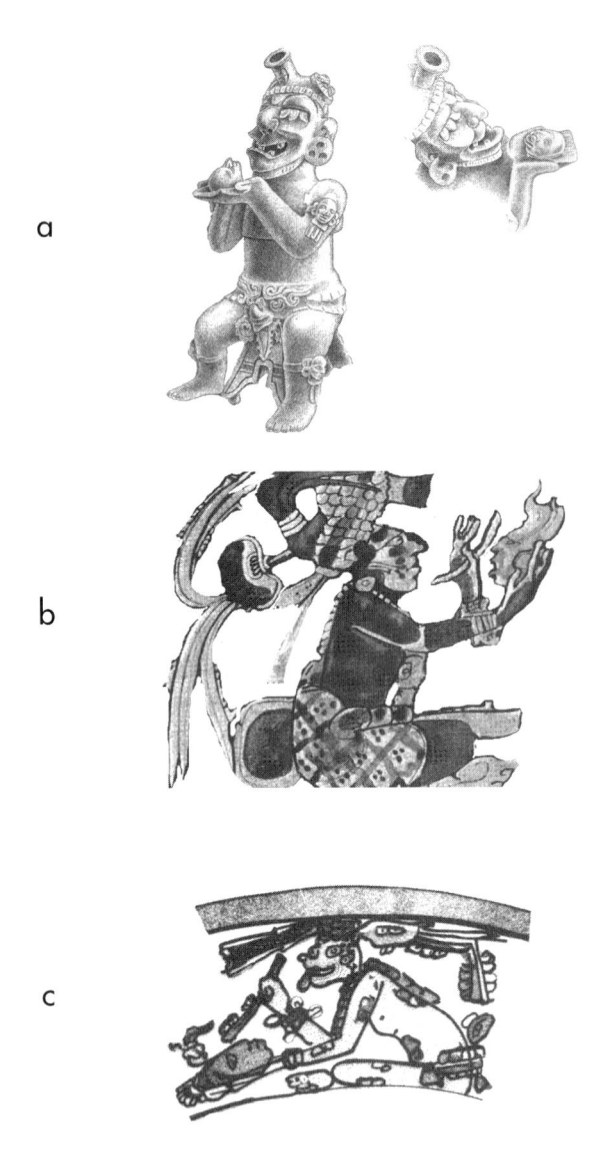

Fig. 3.24. Creator gods: (a) incense burner from Tikal (Culbert 1993:fig.14, used with permission of Sharon Misdea, Tikal Project, University of Pennsylvania Museum); and (b, c) supernatural sculptors on unprovenanced vessels (drawings by D. Peck, in M. Coe 1977:figs. 6, 7).

Fig. 3.25. Dwarf drinking from bowl (after K1453).

of redistribution or anything but unidirectional flow of comestibles into the court. The focus is on what is available to the king, not to his underlings.

The concept of "feasting" among the Classic Maya merits more thought. By now, it has become a commonplace among scholars that the Maya practiced formal commensality, by which, extending Michael Dietler's definition, we take to mean ingestion that involved relatively large numbers of people outside the immediate domestic unit and sets of formal behaviors beyond the scope and scale of ordinary repasts. Specifically, most scholars see

evidence for redistributive or Dietler's "patron-role" feasts, in that such repasts would have been expected as ways of gratifying retainers and subjects or as a means of recruiting labor for civic works (Reents-Budet 2000). In fact, the slipped and burnished surfaces of most serving vessels probably existed for aesthetic reasons, to glisten by reflecting light, and for practical ones, to provide a better preparatory coat for fine painting and to ease the task of removing organic materials that might cling to rougher pots. Vessels could have been cleaned quickly and recycled at once back into food service.

One of the best illustrations of feasting comes from Piedras Negras Panel 3, which shows a group of subsidiary lords known as *sajal* seated in front of a seated ruler on his throne and high-ranking members of his court, including his heir, known as the *ch'ok yokib ajaw* (Fig. 3.26). The feast must have been so central to the dynasty that they chose to remember it some twenty years later. The image on the panel records one lord holding a cylindrical vessel, probably for chocolate, and the principal text above refers to the act of drinking (*uk'ni*) by the ruler. The event took place at night (*yik'in*), but only after a long set of rituals, including dance, that revolved around the anniversary of the ruler's succession. The Mixtec and Aztec data point to such feasts as sumptuous arenas for competitive hospitality (Hodge 1996:26, 28; Pohl 1998:201–204). Diego de Landa, our authoritative source on early Colonial Yucatan, noted with disapproval the lavish banquets that nearly bankrupted Maya hosts. He also remarked on the acutely distributive aspects of these parties, not only of food but of woven cloth mantles and ceramic vessels (Tozzer 1941:92). The obligation to reciprocate was pervasive and transcended even the death of guests: children and heirs would in turn need to prepare compensatory feasts. Nonreciprocal celebrations were those involving marriage and ancestral commemoration, which incurred no such burdens (Tozzer 1941:92).

By applying these notions to the Classic period, scholars can achieve credible explanations for a variety of archaeological features. A pot with dynastic texts might have been transferred to another royal center by means of the largesse described by Landa (Houston et al. 1992). This would account for the widespread distribution of certain particularly valued vessels from the central Peten, Guatemala, to the Pasión River region in the south (Adams 1971; Valdés 1997; see also Ball 1993). Their surfaces depicted scenes in palaces from nonlocal courts, yet this did not seem to diminish their worth as a trade item in any way, despite the historical specificity of the imagery. Similarly, John Fox (1996) has examined the inventory of broken vessels near ballcourts in Honduras and suggested that they show the linkage of ballplaying and formal meals as a communal activity—the ubiquity of serving vessels would seem to confirm this supposition. And then there are a series of striking deposits from Tikal to Piedras Negras and Arroyo de Piedra to Buenavista del Cayo and Lagartero (S. Ekholm 1979) that consist of an unusual concentration of finely made vessels and exotics that might be the vestiges of extravagant blowouts, perhaps involving the ostentatious destruction of goods in drunken feasts. The removal of such goods from the political economy requires some explanation, and a competitive or redistributive feast is as good as any.

The problem with each of these explanations is that they can be reworked to support alternative views. Formal commensality, or consumption involving more than a household, may or may not have led to the movement of fine ceramics and other preciosities. One can imagine tributary mechanisms, trade and mercantile behavior, war booty, and alliance gifts as equally credible explanations. The ballcourt middens described by Fox come from fairly limited excavations, and it is unclear whether these deposits were of the same date as other uses of the ballcourts (cf. J. G. Fox 1994:

Fig. 3.26. Feasting scene, Piedras Negras Panel 3 (photograph by David Stuart).

181–183). The wholesale destruction and interment of goods recalls Diego de Landa's report on the purifications taking place in the New Year (Tozzer 1941:151–152): houses were swept and objects removed and replaced, alongside periods of fasting and sexual abstinence. We need to introduce caution about supposed instances of "feasting" and request higher standards of proof. No one can deny that many kinds of feasts took place in Classic Maya life. Demonstrating the presence of actual cases is more difficult. The Classic Maya appear, as ever, to have stressed royal needs and royal satiety, not what others received from royalty. Ingestion implies the production of basic foodstuffs, their preparation, even the cleaning of plates and utensils. But such activities do not take center stage: ingestion is the thing, and, indeed, ingestion by the ruler (Goody 1982:37).

FASTING

A final matter fails to appear in most discussions of formal commensality. This would be its polar opposite: the *ayuno* in Spanish, the "fast," often just as conspicuous and controlled by protocol as the feast itself. Diego de Landa makes it clear that many celebrations linked to the calendar involved both a form of abnegation and cleansing as well as subsequent feasting (Tozzer 1941:103, 152, 153). The body was covered with soot during fasting, and its coloring was then adjusted and brightened for the feast. In this way, variable internal states disclosed themselves on what Terence Turner (1980) called the "social skin," the body surface as boundary and as expressive frame (Preamble, this volume). The *Popol Vuh* mentions that "fasting" itself referred mostly to avoidance of maize, the basic foodstuff (Christenson 2003:222, 287–288). In Colonial Ch'olti', fasting was understood as a time of misery and pain, but also as a "cleansing of the mouth" (*pocti*). It often coincided with sexual abstinence as well. Some fasts were inadvertent, coming from drought and famine. Marc Zender (personal communication, 2002) points out that a unique instance of such terms may come from an incised stingray spine excavated by Ricardo Armijo at the site of Comalcalco, Tabasco

(Fig. 3.27a). The text pairs, in a still-opaque way, the terms *k'intuun*, "drought," and *wi'nail*, "hunger, famine" (Martin et al. 2002, 2:49), a term much like the *k'intunyabil* expression detected by Eric Thompson (1972:150) in the Dresden Codex (Fig. 3.27b).

There is arresting evidence that fasts were a central preoccupation of the Classic Maya, just as they played a pivotal role in later periods. The crucial glyph is one that reads [CH'AHB], an obvious parallel to the ethnographic and historic terms for "fast," and perhaps to a K'iche'an expression for penitence and, ultimately, to acts of creation and renewal (Fig. 3.28; Allen Christenson, personal communication, 2003). As mentioned before, one of its meanings in Yukatek had also to do with "creation" and "making anew." When combined with *aka'b* in the inscriptions, this expression is one that David Stuart prefers to view as a term involving powers of procreation and renewal. At least one context in which it appears relates to the parents of royal offspring. Here it may well refer to a term for "creation" and such procreative forces. Other settings are noteworthy for their connection to war captives. A text from the Palace at Palenque tells us:

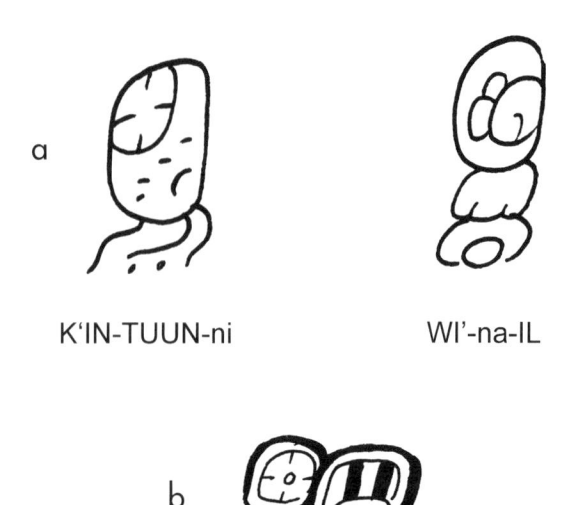

a K'IN-TUUN-ni   WI'-na-IL

b K'IN-TUUN-HAAB-IL

Fig. 3.27. Glyphs for "drought" and "famine": (a) Comalcalco incised stingray spine (after drawing by Marc Zender, in Martin et al. 2002, 2:49); and (b) Dresden Codex, p. 72c (after Thompson 1972).

ilij aba ach'ahb a(w)ak'abil (Schele and Mathews 1979:142). The register is unusual for glyphic rhetoric, in that there are second-person references: "seeing yourself, your *ch'a(h)b*, your darkness," followed by a euphemistic expression for the local, victorious king.

The dress of the figure near the text is eye-catching, for it consists of torn and perforated cloth. Mayanists observed some time ago that this costume usually adorns captives who have been placed in front of their conquerors (Chapter 6). Not a few of these captives are emaciated, as in a celebrated wretch with accentuated ribs and bony legs on Piedras Negras Stela 8 (D. Stuart and I. Graham 2003:44): if pathos has an image, this is it (Fig. 3.29). Such deprivation would also have "softened" captives, rendering them docile and breaking down their will to escape or rebel. Although there is no consensus for want of further lexical entries, it may be that the well-known expression *nawaj*, used in describing captives and, at Piedras Negras, a young female, derives from the root mentioned before for "becoming thin," *naual*. (Another possibility is that it relates to a Ch'olti' term for "shave," "adorn," or "beautify,"

Fig. 3.28. *Ch'ahb* glyph, Yaxchilan Lintel 24:C1 (I. Graham and von Euw 1977:53).

naual; Ringle n.d.) Both captives and royal females may have become thin through preparatory fasting. Could there have been some link to blood and bloodletting, either from the veins by sacrificial acts or from the onset of menstruation? It is highly probable that this clothing is the dress of penitence and abnegation. As attire, it reflects and expresses fasting in its purest meaning of self-denial, perhaps by means of "anti-cuisines" used to dull hunger and destroy pleasure, as among the hermits of late Medieval Italy (Camporesi 1994:65). In martial settings, *ch'ahb* had two senses, the punishment of captives but also, in the Palenque panel, a belief that captives represented a kind of penitence and renewal by proxy—the Palenque lord sees in the person of the captive that his own penance, self-denial, and phagiohierarchy have been deferred. There is suggestive evidence that Maya sacrifice involved elaborate concepts of substitution, or *k'ex*, a dismembered bird or human replacing temporarily the debts and duties owed by the sacrificer (Taube 1994a:669–674). Ultimately, those payments needed to be discharged in full, either by bloodletting or by death. For a small moment, however, war captives such as the one at Palenque lifted and delayed those heavy debts: they suffered so that another did not, experienced forced hunger on behalf of those who wanted to avoid voluntary, self-willed hunger (Mintz 1996:4–5). As an aside, we should add that a few captives, including a mythological one in the Dresden Codex, are described in negating terms—they have "no fast or penitence, no darkness." This hints at categorical differences in the existential state of captives, so very different from those who do possess such attributes. Have their procreative powers been nullified or removed through the "social death" of enslavement?

Many scholars comment that feasts accompanied "life-crisis" rituals. So, too, with Classic Maya fasts, along with evidence for other forms of bodily discipline. Stela 3 from Caracol (Fig. 3.30; Beetz and Satterthwaite 1981:fig.4) informs us that the heir, one Sak Baahwitzil, experiences his *yax ch'ahb*, "first fast" (with an intransitivizing or antipassive suffix), at little more than five years of age—clearly, part of a long passage to adulthood. This event is also discussed in Chapter 2 as a rite involved in acts of dynastic origin and the inception of time. The iconographic correlate of this ritual occurs on Dos Pilas Panel 19 (Houston 1993:fig. 4-19) where the royal parents preside over what appears to be the first bloodletting of the dynastic heir. Another figure, someone known as Sakjal Hix, "Cat-becoming-white," kneels to assist the heir with a stingray spine. Droplets of blood spurt into a bowl that contains folded paper. From other evidence, this paper would have been burned and the smoke used as a means of "feeding" supernatural beings. The youth had been introduced to the rigors of royal obligation.

CLASSIC MAYA INGESTION

The Classic Maya paid heavy attention to matters of ingestion and, at times, the purging and flushing of bowels. This is scarcely surprising: without consumption there can be no living. But the Maya embedded these basic necessities in a world where body concepts played a central role, both of supplying that body with a surfeit of ingestibles and of removing them by deliberate acts of purging and self-denial—arguably all involved in adjustments of mental states and in making someone, at root, feel better, despite a painful passage through acts of cleansing and evacuation. Disciplined eating, drinking, fasting, and bloodletting alternated with acts of wild excess, for reasons that remain unclear and even inexplicable, pending further decipherment.

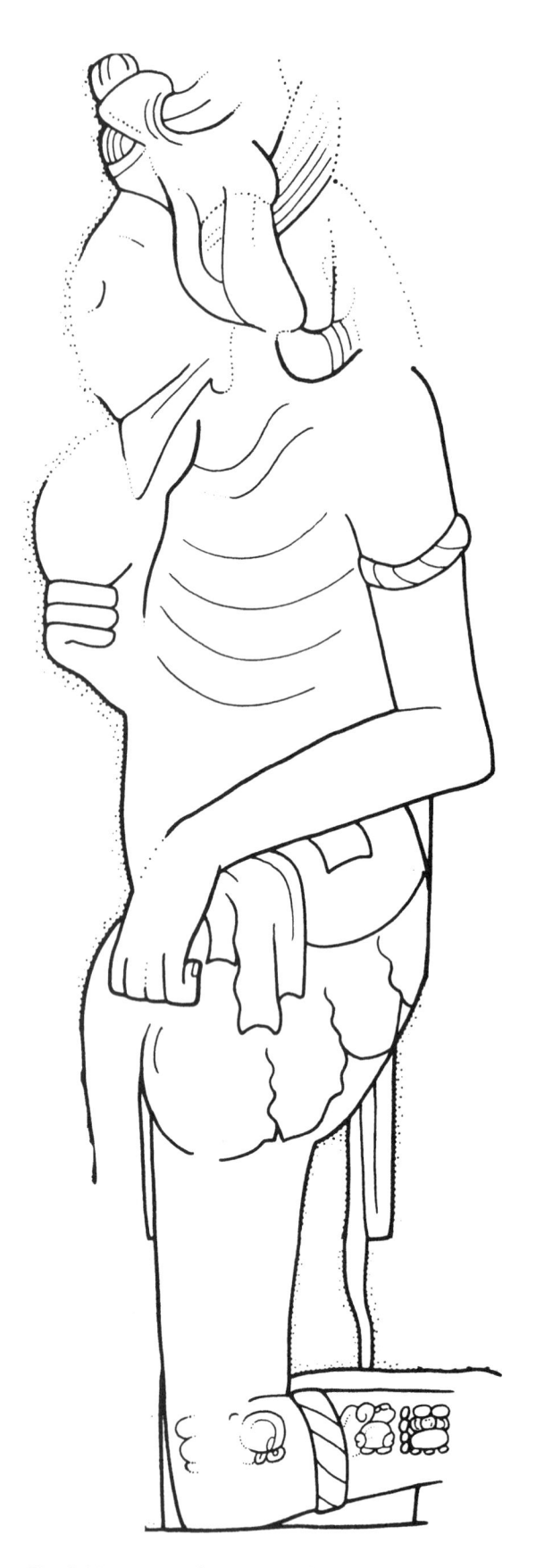

Fig. 3.29. Emaciated captive, Piedras Negras Stela 8 (drawing by David Stuart).

Fig. 3.30. Glyphic text for "first fast" or "penance," Caracol Stela 3:A19–B20 (after Beetz and Satterthwaite 1981:fig. 4).

The social role of eating, a traditional concern in anthropology (Richards 1951), is everywhere in the imagery, inherent in the public placement of sculptures, and facilitated by the creation of palatial spaces for commensal acts. Complex and multidimensional in reality, feasting was reduced in Classic Maya imagery to the appetites of the royal body and, contrary to anthropological expectation, to foods and goods flowing outward to loyal subjects. In the final analysis, the question of whether to share or to withhold, in what quantity and with what motive, existed within a wider cultural understanding of what the body, especially a royal one, craved and needed.

CHAPTER FOUR ◂▸

Senses

Sight, taste, touch, hearing, and smell are not the usual concern of archaeologists. After all, the senses do not leave vestiges that can readily be accessed. Far more approachable are the ways in which imagery and writing encode or activate the senses. Such signs and devices reveal ancient categories and beliefs about the interaction of the body and the external world. They allow us to engage the past in ways that go beyond words and abstraction; they take us into the realm of sensory experience, into a feature of the body that has been understood in the West, from Plato on, as a suspect and morally ambivalent part of our animal nature (Stoller 1997:5–6; Synnott 1991:62–63). This chapter takes up the senses by focusing on smell, hearing, sight, touch, and taste as these categories of experience were perceived by the Classic Maya.

Octavio Paz's poem, presented at the beginning of the book, had it just right: among the Maya, the senses were linked in a near-synesthetic fashion, with stimulus in one modality—sight—triggering perception in others—hearing, smell, touch, and taste. Or, among Nahuatl speakers, synesthesia could pass from sound to sight, as in the Aztec notion of the creation or invocation of colors by song (Hays-Gilpin and J. Hill 1999; Hosler 1994:242). By means of graphic devices such as speech, scent, and sight scrolls, the Classic Maya communicated the presence, nature, and semantic content of sight, smell, hearing, touch, and taste to an extent unparalleled in most other parts of the ancient world. The visual conveyance of sense suggests that it was understood to be projective, meaning that the body did not receive passively but actively reached out to see, smell, taste, touch, and hear, as though by tendrils extending from the body. Moreover, the binocular and peripheral vision that comes naturally to humans was, for the Maya, given a moral valuation that informed their view of space as an interactional field. Buildings were configured according to sensory properties that can only be understood through culturally bound ideas about sight and its creative and ratifying qualities.

THE NATURE OF THE SENSES

Smell, sight, hearing, touch, and taste can be studied from a purely physiological perspective. With smell, the olfactory epithelium receives molecules, exciting neurons that transmit electrical impulses to the brain (Takagi 1978:233). In sight, the retina receives images that are transmitted as electrical signals through the medium of receptor cones and nerves. From there they travel to the striate and extrastriate cortices, where neural representations attach meaning to the signals (Goldstein 1999:97). If there are no physical maladies, perception takes place. Light transforms itself into "sight," spectra into "colors," binocular clues into "depth," and so on. Similarly, the physical stimulus of changes in air pressure results in the bending of cilia in the inner ear. These motions generate electrical signals that pass along auditory nerve fibers to the temporal lobe of the cortex (Goldstein 1999:325). The result is "sound," the actual experience of acoustic signals. In much the same way, taste buds and the nose interact to create "taste," and nerve signals leave the skin to induce a feeling of heat, cold, texture, and other effects of "touch." Various sectors of the brain process such visual, auditory, tactile, and gustatory flags through the formulation and testing of cognitive hypotheses (Gregory 1997:10). To put this another way, the brain attempts to answer the questions: From an infinity of possibilities, what, exactly, is the object being seen; what is the nature of the sound being heard, the flavor savored, the touch experienced? Such mind-generated assertions about reality are "representations" that do more than simply show pictures in the mind. They also annex background information that gives meaning to the perceived object, sound, taste, or touch (Gregory 1997:8). These meanings are most tenaciously and indelibly held when emotions, or memories of bodily reactions, adhere to representations of the mind. Here, as mentioned in the preamble, is Proust's madeleine, the tea-dipped crumble of cake that evokes a world of recollection.

Such meanings are what interest us here. The senses can be categorized and understood within particular cultural and historical idioms. Using an analogy from linguistics, we might call this the realm of the "meta-senses," a web of secondary reflections and graphic renderings of what the senses are and what they do. Just as perception "selects" from a large inventory of sensation, so do people invariably select and narrowly establish what the senses might be. This is how they can readily be described, even though the sensations themselves are ineffable, literally beyond full description in speech or prose. Defined partly in terms of human physical capabilities, the meta-senses inevitably involve local ideas determined by tradition and practice. Changes in ideas about the senses are, as in eighteenth- and nineteenth-century European concepts of visuality, "inseparable from a massive reorganization of knowledge and social practices that modified in myriad ways the productive, cognitive, and desiring capacities of the human subject" (Crary 1990:3). A few scholars, such as Marx Wartofsky (1981), have gone so far as to see human vision as largely a cultural artifact based on historical changes in representation. Nonetheless, this discounts the physical bases of sensation (Jay 1993:5) and denies a modified "universalist" position that we believe must play a role in any study of Maya body, being, and experience. Perception can never be isolated totally from the physiological equipment and biological universals that make it possible.

As in any culture, Western beliefs are shaped by history. Sight, for example, was not always regarded as a unidirectional flow from external world to retinal receptors (Gonzalez-Crussi 1989:100–103). In Greece at about 550 BC, light and intelligence were thought to emanate from the eye, although this notion was later rejected by Aristotle, who located such stimuli firmly in the shapes of the external world: the substance of light, likened to heat, could vibrate physically from "empty space" (Aristotle 1964; Sennett 1994:43). Even an intellectual giant like Aristotle, however, could not suppress the "emanating eye" from the public imagination, for it appeared—and continues to appear—in folk society as the *oculus fascinus,* or "evil eye" (Dundes 1981; Gifford 1958; Gonzalez-Crussi 1989:101; B. Gordon 1937; Hocart 1938; Maloney 1976a). This gaze could inflict disease and pain with a glance (Di Stasi 1981; Maloney 1976a; Siebers 1983), an idea that may have stemmed from the reflective properties of the eyeball (Jay 1993:n. 26). Francis Bacon described the "envious eye" as "an ejaculation [emission] or irradiation" from the eyeballs (Bacon 1985:83; Gonzalez-Crussi 1989:102). The injurious concept of vision, as conceived in southern Europe, can be divided into an indiscriminate emission, the *jettatura*, and one that is invited only by the fortunate and prosperous—the "envious glance" described by Bacon (Gifford 1958:14). For Bacon and others, this glance involved the "the power and act of imagination, intensive upon other bodies than the body of the imaginant" (Bacon 1985:83), and may well have accorded with Bacon's more general philosophical objective of restoring human dominion over the universe after the Fall (Collinson 1987:45). In this conceptual framework, it would not seem unusual for Johann von Goethe to state much later that "/i/f the eye were not sunny, how could we perceive light? If God's own strength lived not in us, how could we delight in Divine things?" (Arnheim 1996:81). These debates influence the visual arts. Svetlana Alpers (1983:xxv, 244) describes two different "visual cultures," one northern and especially Dutch and the other Italian, in art of the early Modern period. Southern artists focused on the *lux*, light from the eye, or "extramission," and northerners, on the *lumen*, light received by the eye, or "intromission" (see also Gombrich 1976:19–35; Lindberg 1976:3–9). To this day, many people in the United States believe in extramission (Winer and Cottrell 1996).

Hearing, too, had certain associations: it could calm or excite the emotions, cure derangement, and prompt, as in the case of the divine voice heard by Saint Augustine in a child's call, a process of spiritual self-renovation (Gonzalez-Crussi 1989:38–40). Again, these beliefs have in common the idea that perception is semantically and emotionally loaded. Something other than, or in addition to, sound waves and light and scent assails our sensory apparatus. In the late 1500s, the learned could even hope to perfect a "perspective lute" that linked colors and musical tones in synesthetic union, perhaps as part of an underlying reality that resounded with occult themes prevalent at the time (Evans 1973:190). More recently in Europe, cross-sensory perceptions were taken for granted, sight being associated inherently with touch. This logic is readily explainable: distant views had the potential for being touched if one could only draw closer (Crary 1990:19, 60).

Generally, meta-sensory views tend to adopt the notion that acts of emanation, whether of sight, smell, sound, taste, or touch, are inseparable from perception and its semantic interpretation. What is understood in scientific terms as a chain of separable processes becomes, in much of premodern thought, a sudden epiphany that bridges external worlds and internal discernment. This is the "communion-oriented notion" of sight that predominated in pre-Socratic thought of ancient Greece and later in Medieval descriptions of beatific and saintly visions (Jay 1993:39). Clarence Maloney notes that such beliefs, particularly with respect to the malevolent force of sight, occur throughout Europe, the Middle East, India, northern and eastern Africa, and Mesoamerica; for reasons that remain obscure, they seem generally absent in Siberia, Australia, and much of North and South America (1976b:xii–xiii; see also Gifford 1958, which provides thorough evidence from European and Near Eastern traditions). Our suggestion is that, broadly conceived, the reciprocal communion of external and internal worlds characterized perceptual theories among the Classic Maya. In sight, power and affective terror could be involved, especially as prompted by the gaze of rulers, but there could also be creative, positive associations. These models were expressed through codes in art and writing, and might reflect a monistic view that blurred insubstantial essences and united them with the material world (Burkhart 1989; Monaghan 1995:137). However, what will always remain elusive are individual acts of perception, forever lost, or the role of "observing subject(s)," long dead (Crary 1990:5). The sensations of the past cannot be retrieved, only their encoding in imperishable media.

SYNESTHESIA

To examine the Classic Maya evidence, we must introduce a term, or, more precisely, a modified application of a term, used in perceptual psychology. As discussed before, this is *synesthesia*, meaning the release of one sensation through another, or, in technical language, a "cross-modality experience," such as the perception of sounds that also precipitate colors, or of images that prompt the softness of feline pelage or swagged curtains (Goldstein 1999:343–344; Marks 1984:445). Physiologically, synesthesia probably occurs because two parts of the brain are implicated in certain sensations (Paulesu et al. 1995). The synesthesia we stress is different: the "cross-modality" occurs in graphic media, so that something seen by the eye as an object or sign conveys parallel sensations, or, more precisely, such signs signal the *presence* of those sensations that ordinarily can only be received by the ear or nose, the mouth or skin. The synesthesia is culturally coded, not neurologically triggered. The cunning here is that, like cartoon bubbles (which in a European context seem to have come into existence by at least the Medieval period and probably much earlier), signs and graphemes make visible that which is invisible: a good example is the humorous Japanese image of a monkey engaged, through a speech scroll, in the worship of a frog Buddha (Fig. 4.1; Jay 1993:60). The modality of sight gleans signs that are intended to carry meaning, sound, and scent.

Throughout ancient Mesoamerica, the principal means of synesthetic communication was writing. There is persuasive evidence that most script, regardless of geographical zone, was intended to be read aloud (Houston 1994; King 1994; Monaghan 1990), a point reinforced by the occasional appearance of first- or second-person references and quotative particles in Classic Mayan script (Houston and D. Stuart 1993). This was no less true of the ancient Mediterranean, where Eric Havelock and others identified the ubiquity of "recitation literacy," involving oral delivery and public performance

Fig. 4.1. Speech scrolls of monkey prelate worshiping frog Buddha, from Choju Giga scrolls, first half of twelfth century AD (after Stanley-Baker 2000:fig. 64).

(Houston 1994:30). What this means is that Mesoamerican writing was not so much an inert or passive record, but a device thought to "speak" or "sing" through vocal readings or performance. Similarly, books such as the *Popol Vuh* might be described as *ilb'al*, "instruments of sight or vision," and, as documents written in the present progressive, they unfold as though before the listener's eyes (Allen Christenson, personal communication, 2003). As a form of communication, writing was inseparably bonded to the language that it recorded. The view that script was an abstract, isolatable text was most likely unthinkable. To quote Richard Sennett on ancient Greek writing, the "reader would have thought he heard the voices of real people speaking even on the page, and to revise a written text was like interrupting someone talking" (1994:43). When looking at inscriptions in the plaza of Maya cities, indigenous spectators probably responded as cultural adepts in synesthetic decoding. They operated in cross-sensory modes, auditory as much as visual.

Maya peoples also had the means to record sight, in what might be described as a meta-sensory manner. That is, the act of "seeing" truly absorbed them, at least to judge from the available evidence. In contrast, the processes of "hearing," "smelling," "touching," and "tasting," as opposed to their results, interested them far less, or, based on modern Tzotzil evidence, they were encompassed by "sight" as the general expression for total physical apprehension (Vogt 1976:61–83). Great subtleties may exist here. As we shall see, the Classic Maya regarded sound, odor, sight, taste, and touch in highly concrete ways, as tangible yet invisible phenomena. For the Maya mind, the substance of the senses was neither empty nor ethereal; rather, it invested vitality and meaning in the spaces it traversed and occupied.

Our sources on the Classic Maya need to be supplemented by broader evidence from elsewhere in Mesoamerica, especially those rich sources on senses that come to us from the Early Colonial period. From the Nahuatl-speaking peoples of Central Mexico, we learn that all the senses were equated with the act of knowledgeable perception, leading in turn to judgment. That is, the act of direct perception, higher-order cognition, and the decisions that result from these were indistinguishable. Rather like the *oculus fascinus*, the eye illuminated and directed, serving in Nahua belief as "our total leader" (López Austin 1988, 1:176–177), in itself a suggestion of an underlying hierarchy of the senses. The cross-cultural preeminence of sight may have a physical basis, since it commandeers far more nerve endings than does the cochlear apparatus of the ear (Jay 1993:6); sight also extends farther than hearing, gathering more information than is possible through the other senses (E. Hall 1982:43). The focus on the sensory organs had another dimension. Each organ—the pupil, the lips, the tongue, the fingers, the ears—apparently possessed an individual consciousness. To an unspecified extent, they were believed to have their own capacity for "decision, will, and creative action" (López Austin 1988, 1:176). How these were organized into a gestalt remains uncertain, if, in fact, a gestalt or unity was even present in conceptual terms. For Alfredo López Austin, the overall housing for sensory and vitalistic centers was a body that reflected the universe and in turn projected its functions on the universal whole (López Austin 1988, 1:180). The evidence we present in Chapter 5 suggests that the center of the body, the "heart" that "felt," provided at least some degree of centralized organization. That same "heart" functioned, much like López Austin's gestalt, as a model for terrestrial centrality.

The earliest hints of Mesoamerican concern with the senses appears in a set of three icons linked repeatedly in the Olmec period, a time of close conceptual community that corresponds roughly to the later years of the Early Formative and much of the Middle Formative (ca. 900–500 BC). A vessel from Tlapacoya, Mexico, links the head of a particular deity with a human hand, an eye with lids, and an ear (Fig. 4.2a). The opacity of much Olmec iconography makes this complex of signs difficult to interpret, but there is a good chance that it embodies the senses of touch, sight, and hearing (David Joralemon, personal communication, 1995). The very quality of Olmec jade, long known to scholars as the most tactile and hand-responsive of any Mesoamerican objects, contributed to that effect. When polished, this precious stone is highly resonant, and undoubtedly the jade belt celts used by both the Olmec and the later Classic Maya served a sound-making function. During both the Middle and Late Formative periods (ca. 900–100 BC), signs came into existence that represent bodily exhalations, including breath and speech (Fig. 4.2b–e). The most developed example appears on Chalcatzingo Monument 1, a Middle Formative Olmec carving portraying an elaborate series of scrolls issuing from the mouth of a zoomorphic cave (Fig. 4.2b). The entire scene contains cloud motifs, falling rain, and growing maize, indicating that these mouth scrolls are probably not sound but breath-like emanations of water-filled clouds or mist (see C. Gay 1971:fig. 11). Along with denoting breath, a scroll issuing from the mouth serves as a basic Mesoamerican convention for denoting speech or song. The first unambiguous example appears in a Middle Formative Olmec mural from Oxtotitlan Cave, Guerrero, which portrays a speech scroll with an individual wearing a serpent mask (Fig. 4.2c). In the Maya region, the earliest known speech scroll appears on Kaminaljuyu Stela 9, a monument probably dating to ca. 500 BC from highland Guatemala (L. Parsons 1986:16). The figure stands upon a crocodile with an upturned, segmented tail, quite probably the earliest documented depiction of the earth crocodile (a model of the terrestrial world) in ancient Mesoamerica (Chapter 5). The head of the man is raised in supplication, and his nakedness suggests that we are looking at a captive (Fig. 4.2d). The mouth blows cloud or smokelike volutes from a cross-sectioned conch, a basic symbol of wind throughout Mesoamerica (Taube 2002a). What attracts our interest is that sound, an invisible force, is rendered as though it were visible and substantial, much in the manner of smoke, or as clouds pregnant with rain.

LATER WORDS

Terms used by later Maya and other Mesoamerican peoples reveal meanings that describe and envelop the senses.

Smell

The words for "smell" are varied in Mayan languages. Ch'olti' has *boc* and *utzi*, the latter, oddly enough, also being a word for "kiss" (Ringle n.d.). This is clearly the same as the reconstructed term in Common Ch'olan, **uhtz'i*, along with Tzendal *utziy* and Ch'orti' *uhutz'*, "to smell," the last being linked in the dictionaries to words for incense and flowers (Kaufman and Norman 1984:135; J. Robertson n.d.; Wisdom n.d.). In Yukatek there are expressions relating specifically to "bad smells," *tzih*, as though these were categorically different from good ones (Michelon 1976:369). In Colonial Tzotzil it appears that "to smell" meant "to attempt, to test," usually in preparation for eating (Laughlin 1988, 1:128).

Sight

The terms for "sight" are pan-Mayan and universally involve the root *il*, a word going back to the remote beginnings of Mayan language (Kaufman and Norman 1984:121).

Hearing

Ch'olan languages take their word for "hear" from *ub'-i*, a word that is obviously cognate with Tzendal *abiy* and Tzotzil *a'i'*, "hear," and *a'iabil*, "hearing" (Kaufman and Norman 1984:135; Laughlin 1988, 2:405; J. Robertson n.d.). Things that are loud are "strong," *ip*, in Colonial Tzotzil, and to be quiet is to be "calm" or "withdrawn," *ch'an chi* (Laughlin 1988, 1:147, 196). Other descriptions relate sounds to musical instruments, as in Yukatek *ch'eh*, which can apply to the human voice and to a trumpet (Barrera Vásquez 1980:129).

TASTE AND TOUCH

Later words from Colonial and modern Mayan languages establish connections between "touching" and "playing an instrument" (Ch'olti', *tala*; Ringle n.d.), along with, in Colonial Tzotzil, a subordination of "taste" to "hearing" (Laughlin 1988, 2:518). Another root is Colonial Tzendal *pic*, which

Fig. 4.2. Representations concerning the senses in Formative Mesoamerica: (a) incised ceramic vessel, Tlapacoya (after L. Parsons 1980:41); (b) zoomorphic cave expelling breath, detail of Chalcatzingo Monument 1 (after C. Gay 1971:fig. 2a); (c) Olmec figure with speech scroll, Oxtotitlan Cave (after Grove 1970:fig. 19); (d) figure with speech scroll standing atop crocodile, Kaminaljuyu Stela 9; and (e) severed head with speech scroll, Mound J, Monte Albán (image inverted for comparison; after Scott 1978:J-112).

also has the meaning of "intelligent action" or "to use a thing" (J. Robertson n.d.; see also Colonial Tzotzil *pik* in Laughlin 1988, 2:519). This root is certainly cognate with Ch'orti' *pihch'*, "feeling, sense of touch," as in "to feel one's pulse," *pihch'i upixan uk'ab*, or "to grope" or "touching he walks along," *pihch'mah axanah* (Wisdom n.d.). Tzendal also records *mach*, "to touch with hands," a verb that may relate to the Classic Maya concept of "birth" in the expression "touching earth" with the hands, perhaps in reference to the fact that, in traditional birthing practices, Maya babies fell out of the uterine channel while their mothers stood (Chapter 1; Lounsbury 1980:113–114). Ch'orti' in particular makes very clear the relation of various senses, as in the phrases *ahk'u uyak' taka*, "to put tongue to, to taste," and also *ahk'u u-ni' taka*, "to sniff," both implying "give" (*ahk'*) but also tentative action or testing, *ehta uk'ihnar*, "to test to determine if hot" (Wisdom n.d.). In much the same way, a common term for "ferment," *xuk'*, also applied to the scent or taste of juices processed in that way (Wisdom n.d.). That smell, not entirely pleasant, could just as easily describe maize beer or urine. Other acts of tentative tasting are also based on the root *ehta*: thus *ha'hta*, "to sip water, to taste water" or *we'hta*, "to taste food" (Wisdom n.d.; also Kaufman and Norman 1984:120, **eht-ä* in Common Ch'olan).

CLASSIC MAYA SMELL

Smell figured strongly in ancient Mesoamerican thought and was closely joined to notions of courtly life. Among the Aztec, fragrant flowers spread "gladness and joy"; lords surrounded themselves with flowers and would give blossoms to their subordinates along with other presents (Berdan and Anawalt 1997:228–229; Durán 1971:238). A well-known image in Classic Maya art shows a nobleman sniffing a bouquet (Reents-Budet 1994:52). Was this emphasis on *one* smell, a fixation on one odor, in reaction to the many that must have pervaded Maya cities? The same held true in Medieval or Early Modern France, where the stinking entrails of criminals and smells of the charnel house lingered near stalls of food (Corbin 1986:24–31, 48–56; Vialles 1994:15). Not surprisingly, the act of "searching for a community" in Colonial Yukatek was "to smell it like a dog," *boboc ni u cah*, perhaps because of its stench (Michelon 1976:31). Dirt required a vigorous response: the act of cleansing or "sweeping" could be used, as among the Tzotzil Maya, to clean a house but also to banish the evil eye or remove anger, exhaustion, or fear. In Tzotzil ritual speech, dancing was also compared to sweeping, perhaps because of its ability to purify and renew a community (Laughlin 1975:235).

On a Classic Maya polychrome vessel, an anthropomorphic hummingbird sits near baskets filled, not with tasty human food, such as tamales, but with bundled flowers, wrapped neatly into garlands or into small bouquets that could be grasped by the hand (Culbert 1993:fig. 84). A few buildings associated with accession, such as House E at Palenque, Mexico, display numerous flowery emblems, and the building was likely considered in synesthetic fashion to exude a heady, exquisite aroma (see M. G. Robertson 1985a:fig. 29). Flowery designs occur on many Late Classic vessels, lending pleasant associations and sensual richness to the daily courtly life of Classic Maya elite (e.g., Reents-Budet 1994:17–19, 61, 83, 159; Robicsek and Hales 1981:206–209). Even the jade ornament of the lords resembled to a striking degree the botanical structures of flowers (D. Stuart 1992a).

Along with speech scrolls, bead or flowerlike signs for breath also appear in Formative Olmec and Maya art (Fig. 4.3). Among the Maya and in Central Mexico, this convention continues into the Late Postclassic period (AD 1250–1521), a temporal span of some two thousand years. Rather than issuing as a stream from the mouth, the breath element hovers before the nose, occasionally in pairs that correspond to each nostril. In many instances, this device is a bead, and in the Dresden Codex, the old god Itzamnaaj displays an earspool bead identical to the breath sign before his face (Fig. 4.3d). The long jade bead assemblages appearing in the nostrils of serpents, crocodiles, and other creatures are surely not allusions to Classic-period zoomorphic fashion, but rather constitute—as Michael Coe (1988) observed for jade beads in general—the physical representations of precious breath. Most of these beads are of floral form. At times, the bead or floral tokens mark some refined quality of royal and godly breath or allude to exalted status. On Monument 65 from Kaminaljuyu, Guatemala, only the three presiding rulers display this element before their faces, in striking contrast to the abject prisoners who flank their thrones (see L. Parsons 1986:fig. 149). We see comparable patterns in Classic Maya imagery, where animals like deer have split, snakelike breath or no breath at all (M. Coe 1973:82). Other creatures, such as frogs, fish, and turtles, display water scrolls as their breath, in contrast to the sinuous exhalations of air-breathing beings (Fig. 4.4). This convention occurs as early as Izapa Stela 1, which depicts a pair of fish with water volutes in front of their faces (Fig. 4.4a). This convention clearly relates to the two minimally contrasting Maya syllables [bu] and [mu]; these bilabials are distinguished by little more than, in the case of [bu], two small dots within the volute (Fig. 4.4e, f). Sinister deities, such as death gods, exude sacrificial, sometimes blood-spotted paper as breath, perhaps as a sign of impermanence, or, as in a sculpture from the Cotzumalguapa civilization of piedmont Guatemala, the speech of skeletons is crooked and angular like bones (Fig. 4.5; K521, K771, K791, K1644, K1652). Other sculptures from that area, such as Monument 1, Finca San Cristóbal, show conversation as intertwined, roping speech scrolls (Chinchilla Mazariegos 2003:fig. 37). They may invert the usual senses by having, not eyes, but snake emanations that issue from the mouth (Yadeun 1993:116). These scenes indicate that not all soul breath was alike. Indeed, the breath of death gods may itself have induced illness to those unfortunate enough to smell such miasma (Chapter 3). In both Olmec and Maya art, paired beads appear in front of the nostrils, and it seems that Early Classic Maya elite often wore a pair of beads strung through the pierced septum. Even in these physical instances, the nasal elements allude to breath and thus can be portrayed with profile serpent faces and scrolls. Here the swirls and serpent faces both imply the material presence of breath and the ephemeral and supernatural quality of the jewelry. A recent find from Temple XIX at Palenque underscores the importance of precious, animating breath: a small hole was drilled in front of a figure on a roof pillar, cinnabar was placed within it, and the hole was filled with a polished cap of limestone, which was invisible to those looking at the sculpture. A similar hole occurs on a panel recently excavated in Palenque Temple XXI (M. Miller and Martin 2004:pl. 129). In Temple XIX it is only the ruler who bears this special breath "bead" in contrast to other figures in the scene. At an earlier date, only the rulers on Kaminaljuyu Monument 65 have such emanations, suggesting great antiquity for this concept (Houston and Taube 2000:266; L. Parsons 1986:fig. 149).

An ancient burial practice in Alta Verapaz, a location deep within the Maya region, provides striking support for the identification of beads with breath. According to the sixteenth-century Dominican Fray Bartolomé de las Casas, the northern Poqom Maya captured the breath soul of a dead ruler in a stone jewel, probably jade:

> When it appears then that some lord is dying, they had ready a precious stone which they placed at his mouth when he appeared to expire, in which they believe that they took the spirit, and on expiring, they very lightly rubbed his face with it. It takes the breath, soul or spirit; to make the ceremony and keep the said stone was a principal office, and no one had it but a person of the most principal of the pueblo or of the house of the king . . . (Miles 1957:749)

In Mesoamerica, the living soul is widely identified with breath, and at death both expire (J. Furst 1995:160–172; López Austin 1988, 1:232–236; Thompson 1950:73; see Strother 2000:58, 60, for comparative evidence from Africa). William Hanks (1990:86) describes this concept among the contemporary Yucatec Maya: "One's breath and animacy are one's *-iik'*, 'wind'

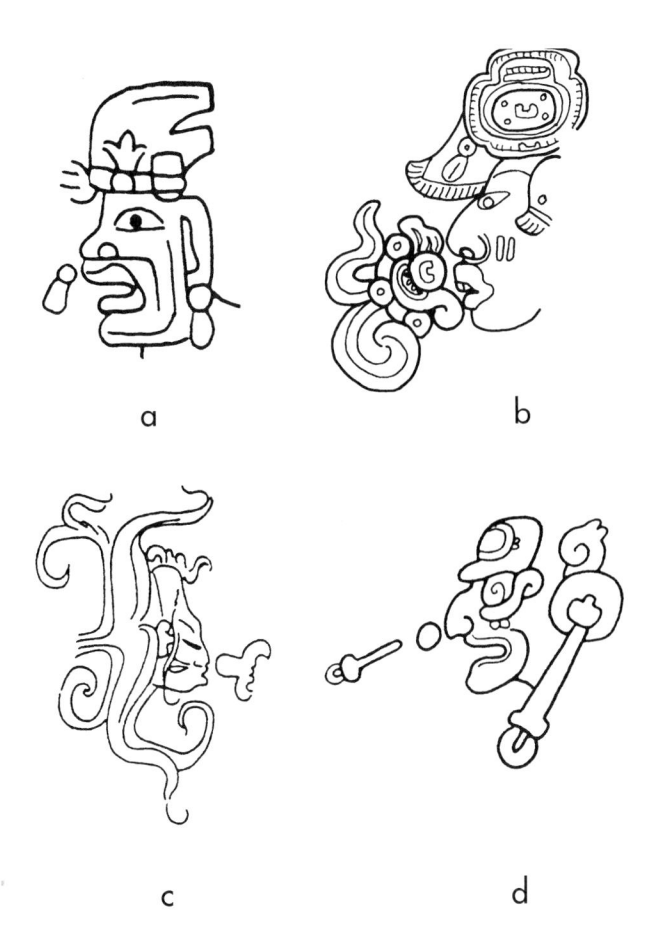

Fig. 4.3. "Nose beads" or exhalations from Olmec to Late Post-classic Maya: (a) Olmec figure with nose beads, detail of Stela 19, La Venta; (b) Late Preclassic Maya deity with breath element, detail of Diker Bowl (after M. Coe 1973:26–27); (c) unprovenanced Late Classic vessel; and (d) Itzamnaaj with breath beads, Dresden Codex, p. 9b.

..." In one Aztec chant recorded by Bernardino de Sahagún, the supernatural origin of a child is described by the acts of breathing and drilling, much as if the child were fashioned like a precious jewel (López Austin 1988, 1:208). Jill Furst (1995:42–47, 54–55) notes that the Aztec related the breath soul to the heart, which was encapsulated in a precious green stone placed in the mouth of the corpse at cremation. As in the Poqom burial rite, the bead remaining after bodily incineration preserved the breath soul of the deceased. If Classic Maya jade beads are usually in floral form, expressing sweet fragrance, then the breath element before the nose alludes to the olfactory quality of the breath soul: dulcet air that contrasts with the stench of death and decay. In K'iche', *uxilab* signifies "breath, soul, smell" (Edmonson 1965:139). The long, upwardly spiraling form commonly projecting from the nasal area is the embodiment of breath, making the entire face into a flower (e.g., Tikal Stela 16 and Quirigua Monument 26). Clearly enough, breath is the perfume emitted from this face (Fig. 4.6a). In much the same way, breath from earspools can be shown as tobacco leaves, probably an emanation of sacred smoke, or as precious feathers, as at Tonina, Mexico (Fig. 4.6b, c; compare with a Hopi example, Fig. 4.6d).

Classic Maya texts provide strong support for the identification of the breath soul with flowers. Glyphs reveal that one common death expression refers to the expiration (*k'a'-*) of a floral form that incorporates the glyph for "white," or *sak*, as well as the stylized form of the Ajaw day sign (Fig. 4.7a). The Ajaw glyph appears on flowers, and in Central Mexico, the equivalent day name is Flower. In view of the *sak* sign, the flower glyph in these death expressions may refer to the fragrant white plumeria (*Plumeria alba*), known as *sak nikte'* in Yukatek (Barrera Vásquez 1980:712). In Maya thought, the plumeria and other flowers relate to wind, the means by which scent is carried. One source in Colonial Yukatek links the day name Ik', meaning "wind," or *ik'*, to winds and the plumeria (Thompson 1950:73). The *ik'* sign, denoting "wind," typically occurs with the floral sign in the death expression, leading Tatiana Proskouriakoff (1963:163) to surmise that it concerns the termination of breath and, by extension, life. We have noted elsewhere (David Stuart cited in Freidel et al. 1993:440) that Colonial Tzotzil uses *ch'ay ik'* to record the death of an individual. One Late Classic death expression containing the phrase *k'a'-ay-i/ u-*, "white flower," *-ik'-u-tis*, "it is finished his flower breath, his flatulence," contrasts two body exhalations, one sweet smelling and oral, the other foul and anal; one a property of the celestial soul, the other linked to the underworld (Fig. 4.7f). Signs for "excrement" or "earth" also issue from the nose and mouth of 1 Ajaw, one of the Hero Twins, perhaps a sign that, in accord with the later myths in the *Popol Vuh*, he has passed through death and

Fig. 4.4. Watery breath: (a) fish, Izapa Stela 1 (after Norman 1973:pl. 1); (b) directional Xook variant (after Hellmuth 1987:fig. 277); (c) God-N turtle (after K1892); (d) toad (after Schele and Mathews 1979:pl. 412); (e) [bu] syllable (after M. G. Robertson 1983:pl. 170); and (f) [mu] syllable, Dos Pilas Stela 8:H14 (after drawing by Ian Graham).

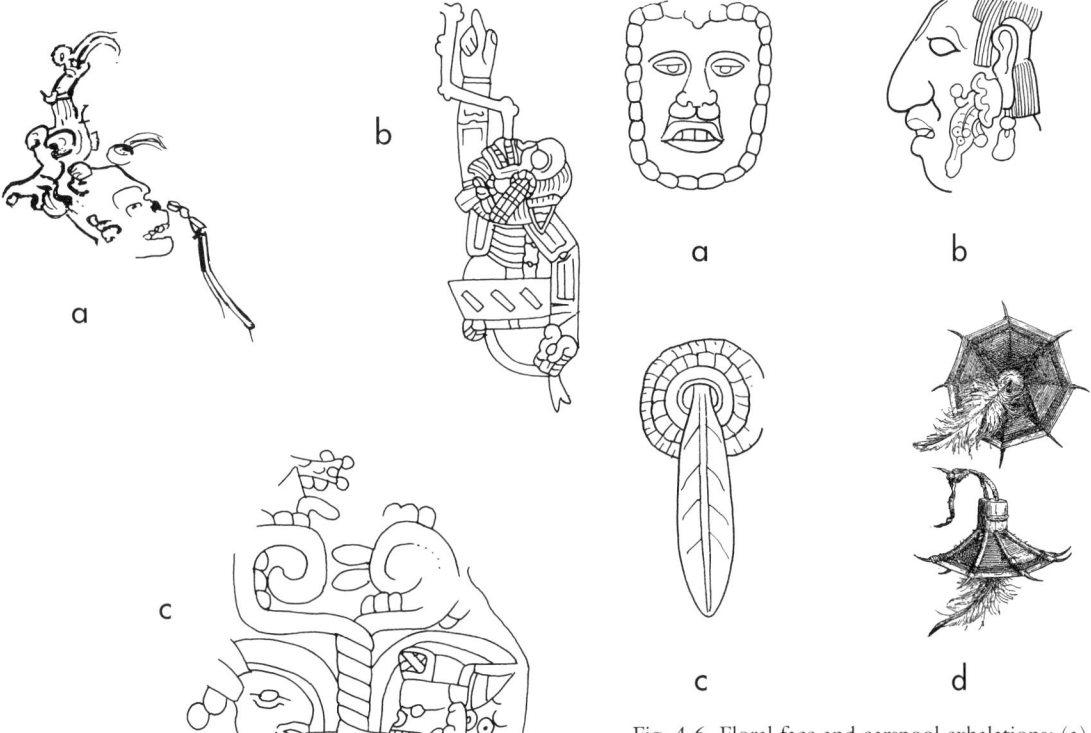

Fig. 4.5. Speech and breath of death gods, along with depiction of conversation: (a) death deity with centipede headdress (after K791); (b) Bilbao Monument 3 (drawing courtesy of Dr. Oswaldo Chinchilla Mazariegos, Museo Popol Vuh); and (c) Finca San Cristóbal Monument 1 (drawing courtesy of Dr. Oswaldo Chinchilla Mazariegos, Museo Popol Vuh).

Fig. 4.6. Floral face and earspool exhalations: (a) face of lord on Quirigua Monument 26 (after Sharer 1990:fig. 47); (b) tobacco earspool, Dumbarton Oaks Palenque-style tablet (after drawing by Linda Schele); (c) earspool with feather exhalation from unnumbered Tonina stela (after Yadeun 1993:86); and (d) Hopi earspool with feather exhalation (Hough 1919:fig. 43).

thus exhales the stench of decomposition (K512, K1202). Not surprisingly, a common epithet for the Death God in Yucatan was *kisin*, "flatulence."

The scribal palace known as the House of the Bacabs at Copan, Honduras, portrays profile centipede heads emitting the white Ajaw flower sign as breath from their nostrils (Fig. 4.7a). A Late Classic Maya shell plaque portrays a skull expelling the floral breath soul out of the mouth (Fig. 4.7b). Skeletal or corpse heads in Classic texts sometimes show the same exhalation, although with *ik'* wind signs rather than the white flower element (Fig. 4.7c). A probable Late Formative carving from Monte Albán may portray an earlier Zapotec version of the breath scroll issuing out of a lifeless severed head, here with the breath marked with flowers and beads (Fig. 4.2e). Was this the very moment of expiration?

The *ik'* sign—so intimately tied to scent as well as wind—is of great antiquity in the Maya area. The first known example of this device appears on a Late Preclassic monument from Kaminaljuyu, probably from near the time of Christ (Fig. 4.8a). The scene portrays a profile deity face with a prominent *ik'* sign as the mouth, along with an exuberant exhalation. Symmetrical breath volutes issue out of the mouth, quite like the series of breath scrolls appearing on Chalcatzingo Monument 1 from Morelos, Mexico (Fig. 4.2b). One of the most striking traits of Late Classic Río Bec– and Chenes-style temples from Campeche and Quintana Roo, Mexico, are the great serpent doorways with inverted *ik'* signs as the mouth and huge breath scrolls to either side (Fig. 4.9; Gendrop 1983:figs. 67h, j–m, 80e). In Maya art, the *ik'* sign frequently appears inverted, with no

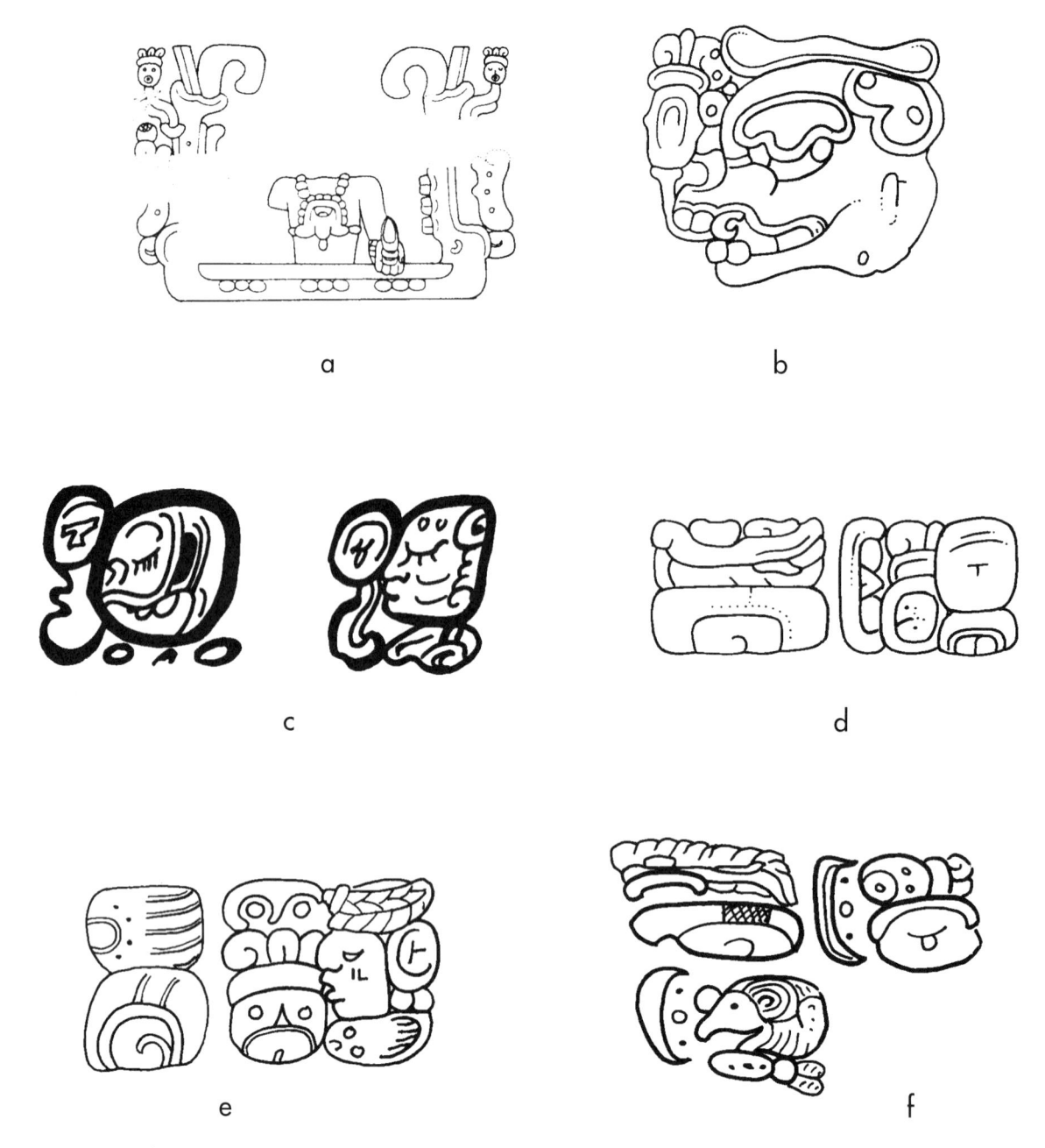

Fig. 4.7. The floral Ajaw sign and other breath elements appearing in Classic Maya death expressions: (a) scribe within centipede maw with floral Ajaw expelled as breath (after Fash 1989:fig. 41); (b) shell carving of skull exhaling floral breath element; (c) glyphs showing wind-sign exhalations (after Reents-Budet 1994:figs. 4.17, 4.26); (d) death expression, Yaxchilan Lintel 27 (after Graham and von Euw 1977:59); (e) death expression (after Schele and Mathews 1979:nos. 397–398); and (f) death-related couplet on incised alabaster bowl (after J. Kerr 1994:594).

apparent change in meaning. Paul Gendrop (1983:98) compares these Late Classic serpent doorways to Chalcatzingo Monument 1, the Olmec zoomorphic cave with the breath scrolls (Fig. 4.2b). There is also the Aztec temple dedicated to the wind god Ehecatl Quetzalcoatl, whose round temple was in the form of a giant serpent mask (Pollock 1936:6–9). Maya elites also displayed the *ik'* element within the mouth, in the form of upper incisors cut to represent the wind sign in silhouette (Houston and Taube 2000:fig. 5b). Along with the *ik'*-shaped incisors, the teeth of such elites were also inlaid with jade. Utterances emitted from such mouths were probably imbued with qualities of preciousness and purity or, in the case of polished hematite, with a reflective sheen that expressed the aesthetics of speech or served as talismanic protection for the mouth—a purification filter as it were. The jeweled nose bars and labret or lip plug worn by nobles of Late Postclassic Central Mexico may also have been material references to lordly breath and speech (Houston and Cummins 1998).

The Classic Maya Sun God frequently displays incisors in the form of the *ik'* sign, which is appropriate, considering the basic Mesoamerican identification of the sun with flowers. For the ancient Maya, the solar *k'in* sign is simply a four-petaled flower (Thompson 1950:142), a trope that goes back to Olmec times in Mesoamerica (e.g., Brockington 1967:fig. 28; Joralemon 1971:fig. 83). In Classic Maya art, flowers are commonly related to the *ik'* sign and wind. The west façade of House E at Palenque displays not only an elaborate series of hovering flowers but also three prominent *ik'* sign windows (M. G. Robertson 1985a:fig. 29). We have mentioned the common use of flowers to represent breath. The aroma of flowers is often represented by a symmetrical pair of outwardly turning elements (Fig. 4.8c–f). The same convention also appears hovering over the mouths of alcoholic vessels, here alluding to the pungent fermented beverages contained within (e.g., Madrid Codex, p. 50a; de Smet 1985:pls. 5, 18, 21). Images of Early Classic date show that pairs of nose beads represent the same device and refer to precious and perfumed floral breath. For one Early Classic jade mask from Calakmul, the outwardly spiraling breath elements appear as white shell flanking a pair of red nose beads (Fig. 4.8b). The mask also portrays sinuous white shell elements curling from the corners of the mouth. Often found in the mouth of the sun deity and other Maya gods, these elements are probably also a form of the aromatic signs issuing from flowers, in this case markers of fragrant breath. In Late Classic Maya art, the sweet scent of flowers can appear sinuous and ethereal, much like speech scrolls or smoke (Fig. 4.8d, e). However, the pairs of emanations can also be stiff, resembling L-shaped elements placed back to back (Fig. 4.8f). What this version creates is the form found on filed Classic Maya incisors and the *ik'* sign. In addition, profile representations of flowers typically evoke the shape of the *ik'* wind symbol.

The identification of wind and the breath soul with jade jewels, flowers, and even the occasional green quetzal plume may explain some burial practices of elite Maya. We have mentioned jade beads in the mouth, a custom documented by many excavations of Maya burials (Ruz Lluillier 1965:459). But what of the jade mosaic masks and masses of jade in such interments? It is quite possible that these objects served to capture and store the breath soul of deceased rulers. In addition, hovering jewels and flowers appear in the tomb murals of Tikal Burial 48 and Río Azul Tomb 1, both from northern Guatemala, as well as on the Sarcophagus Lid of Pakal at Palenque, Mexico (W. Coe 1990:fig. 175; G. Hall 1989:fig. 37; Schele and M. Miller 1986:pl. 111). A Postclassic Mixtec representation of the floral tomb symbolism appears on page 14 of the Codex Bodley (Fig. 4.10a). In this scene, the bundled remains of the famous king Lord 8 Deer is in a tomb chamber marked with flowers. The flowers display the same symmetrical pairs of fragrance volutes found with ancient Maya floral representations. In the Codex Bodley, the floral emanations also occur as the personal name of a particular Mixtec noblewoman (Fig. 4.10b, c). In view of the prominent, fragrant scrolls, she might best be named Lady 1 Grass Aromatic Flower.

The floral devices appearing in Mesoamerican tombs are not simply to counter the filth and foulness of death but to ensure the vitality of the deceased king and to devise a paradisiacal container for his remains. Francisco de Fuentes y Guzmán describes the funeral preparations of the royal corpse among the southern Poqom Maya: "They bathed it and purified it with decoctions of aromatic herbs and flowers. . . . They dress him afterwards in rich and figured clothes, in the style that he wore in life, with the same insignia which he wore reigning" (Miles 1957:749). In these funeral preparations, the sweet-smelling flowers and other plants negate the reality of death and reinforce the continued presence of the king. Fuentes y Guzmán (Miles

Fig. 4.8. Signs denoting wind, breath, and aroma in ancient Maya art: (a) deity expelling breath from mouth in form of *ik'* sign, detail of Late Preclassic Kaminaljuyu monument, Museo Popol Vuh; (b) schematic drawing of Early Classic jade mosaic mask, Calakmul; note spiral nasal elements and forms curling out of corners of mouth (after Schmidt et al. 1998:no. 141); (c) Early Classic flower with aroma elements in form of paired spirals (after Hellmuth 1988:fig. 4.2); (d) Late Classic jade and floral sign with aromatic scrolls, detail of Creation Tablet, Palenque (after J. Porter 1994:fig. 3); (e) quatrefoil flower with aromatic scrolls, detail of Late Classic vase (after Reents-Budet 1994:17); and (f) quatrefoil flower with pairs of aromatic signs forming *ik'* signs, House E, Palenque (after M. G. Robertson 1985a:fig. 42).

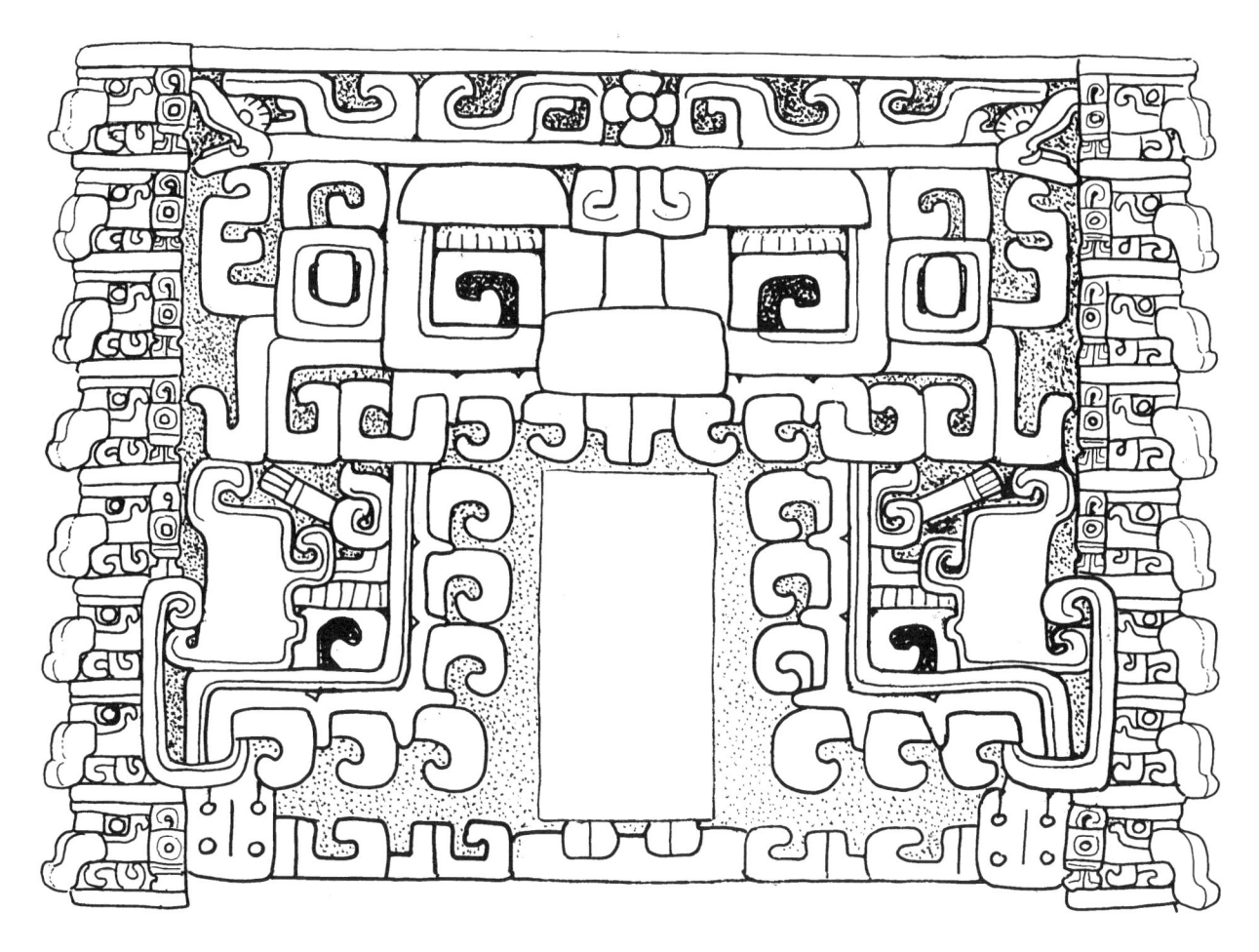

Fig. 4.9. Building façade with "breath" emanating from doorway (after Gendrop 1983:fig. 80e).

1957:749) notes that, following burial, the dead king received copal and flowers. Throughout Mesoamerica, the dead are "fed" with fragrance, whether it be in the form of incense, flowers, or the aroma of cooked food. For both ancient and contemporary Maya, "incense burners are the kitchen hearths of the gods and ancestors" (Taube 1998b:446; see also Chapter 3). At times, Maya censers appear as flowers, as though the pungent incense were the floral perfume of the burning urn (e.g., Taube 1998b:fig. 10a, b). In addition, one kind of censer lid from Early Classic highland Guatemala features a central smoke funnel in the form of an open, petaled blossom (Berlo 1984:pls. 222–226). Among the Aztec, the souls of dead warriors became birds and butterflies that sucked the nectar of flowers (Sahagún 1950–1982, bk. 3:49). Just as the breath soul conveys sweet smells in life, the dead dine on the perfume of flowers and other fragrances.

In Maya art, flowers usually display a four-lobed rim and thereby resemble the Mesoamerican cave sign, first known for Middle Preclassic Chalcatzingo but continuing into early Colonial times. In Classic Maya art, the lobed cave displays flowers at the corners, strikingly like the plants growing on the exterior of the Olmec Chalcatzingo cave image (Fig. 4.2b). The similarity may derive from the natural phenomena of caves that "breathe," a peculiar property activated by local atmospheric effects that cause air to stream in and out of such openings (Chapter 8). Much like wind emerging from caves, flowers thus exude aroma, not by inhalation but by an act of exhalation of their own. The symmetrical spirals of breath exhaled by the Chalcatzingo Monument 1 cave are

Fig. 4.10. Mixtec representations of aromatic flowers in the Codex Bodley: (a) mortuary bundle of Lord 8 Deer in crypt marked with fragrant flowers, Codex Bodley, p. 14; and (b, c) Lady 1 Grass Aromatic Flower, Codex Bodley, pp. 11–12.

mirrored by the Classic and Postclassic representations of flowers emitting outwardly spiraling volutes of fragrance. However, the similarity of Classic Maya flowers to caves or passageways may be based on a more profound belief—that of a supernatural Flower World, a concept of paradise that is well documented among Uto-Aztecan speaking peoples of Mesoamerica and the Greater Southwest (Hays-Gilpin and J. Hill 1999; J. Hill 1992). One imagines that the emphasis on flowers in such a desirable abode probably also involved the bright and varied colors of floral vegetation, thus promoting an aesthetic of bright and diverse tinctures. In Early Classic Teotihuacan, effigy censer lids portray the metamorphosis of dead warriors into fiery butterflies, here surrounded by flowers and brilliant mirrors (Taube 2000). The identification of deceased Classic Maya nobles with flowers and the Sun God suggests that an equivalent concept operated among the ancient Maya. The floating flowers and jewels found in Maya tombs allude to this supernatural floral realm. At Late Classic Palenque, these elements float on the Sarcophagus Lid of Pakal and on the Tablets of the Cross, the Foliated Cross, and the Sun (M. G. Robertson 1991). In these scenes, Kan Bahlam stands with his dead father, Pakal, in a transcendental realm of flowers, precious birds, and jewels.

Classic and Postclassic effigy censers of honored ancestors and gods reveal that copal or other smoke represented the breath and speech of supernatural beings. The effigy lid placed atop the "live," burning urn usually has an aperture passing from the interior through the open mouth (e.g., Culbert 1993:fig. 14). Smoke issuing from the effigy censer mouth forms a pungent exhalation from the supernatural being. As mentioned before, on floral censer lids from highland Guatemala a face occupies the center of the flower, with the smoke spreading out as fragrant breath (Berlo 1984:pl. 224). In the Teotitlan del Camino region of northern Oaxaca, Late Postclassic censer lids known as *xantiles* portray Xochipilli, the "flower prince" god of music and palace folk (Fig. 4.11a). The large and elaborate necklace worn by the figure is in the form of a flower, causing the smoke "breath" issuing forth to be the aroma of the flower. In the Codex Borgia, an identical form of Xochipilli, complete with the same butterfly mouth, appears as the patron of the day Ozomatli, or Monkey. Clearly, the butterfly is another expression of the sweet soul (Fig. 4.11b; J. Furst 1995:25, 31). The precious breath from his mouth takes the shape of a floral jade assemblage, precisely the same breath element noted in Olmec and Maya art. The Ozomatli scene also features a fishing youth with a breath element in the form of a long strand of jade tipped by a flower (Fig. 4.11c). The corresponding Ozomatli scene in the Codex Vaticanus B portrays a similar floral strand of jade beads coming out of the mouth of Xochipilli (Fig. 4.11d).

One youthful Maya god appears to be the Wind God and the personification of breath soul. (A duck-billed wind deity may have been associated specifically with rain borne by wind, perhaps a reflection on the migratory patterns of such birds;

SENSES 151

as in Central Mexico, this deity combines features of a monkey with a duck [Fig. 4.12; Matos Moctezuma and Solís Olguín 2002:423–424, pls. 100, 102].) Appearing as the head variant of the number three and patron of the month Mak, he is also the deity known as God H in the Postclassic codices (Taube 1992b:56–60). In both Classic inscriptions and the Postclassic codices, he has a prominent *ik'* wind sign on his cheek and a flower or bead on his brow (Fig. 4.13). The Diker Bowl, so named after the collector who owned it, shows a young god with a prominent flower headdress and a bead atop his brow, making it likely that this is an early form of the same being (Fig. 4.3b). His function as the personification of the number three recalls the fact that, in some Mayan languages, including Yukatek and Mopan, forms of the term for

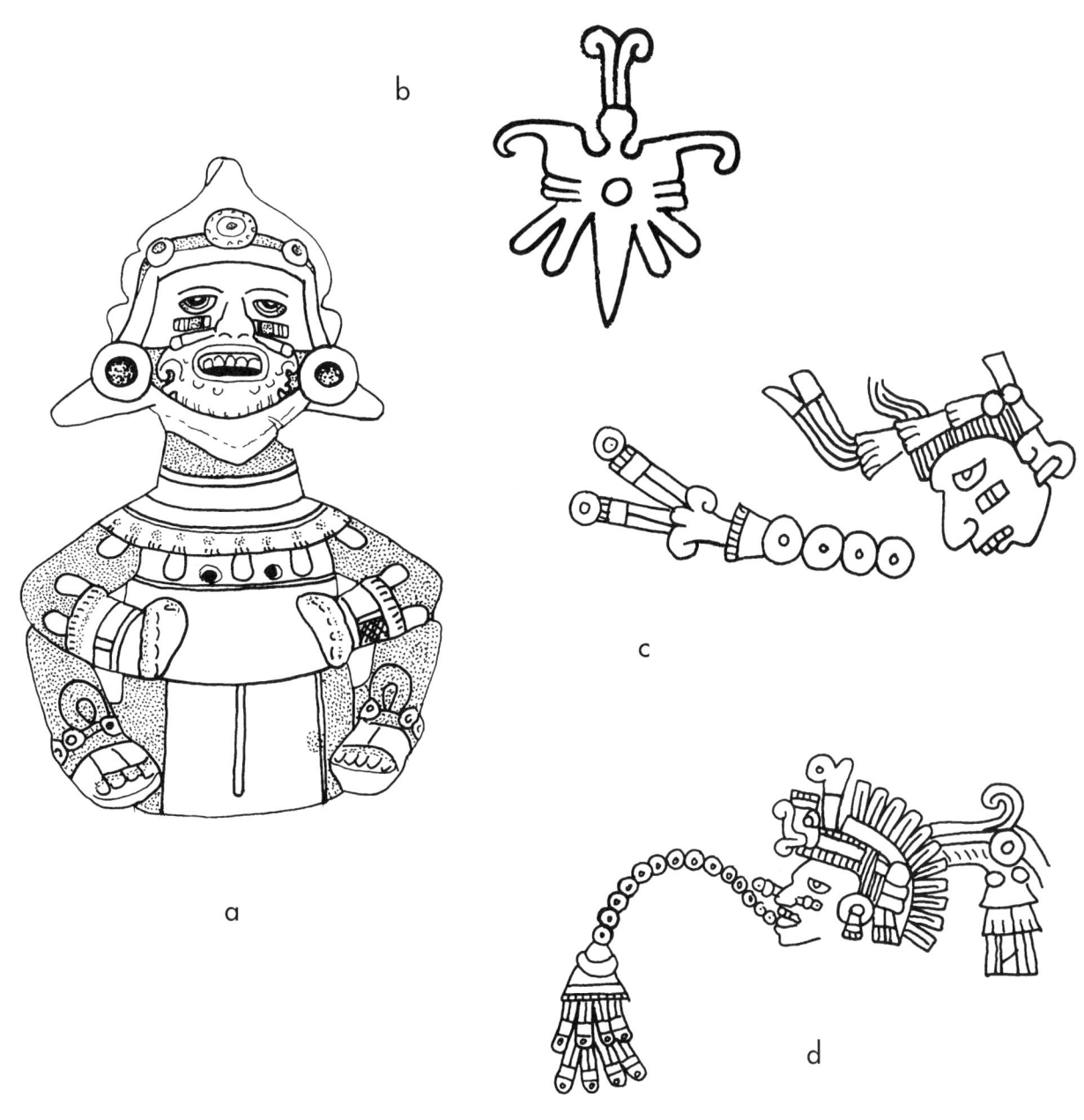

Fig. 4.11. Late Postclassic representations of Xochipilli: (a) polychrome *xantil*, or incense burner, from Teotitlan del Camino, Oaxaca (after Bowditch 1904:pl XLII); (b) butterfly from Codex Borgia, p. 36; (c) fishing youth with flower and jade breath element, Codex Borgia, p. 13; and (d) Xochipilli as patron of day Ozomatli, Codex Vaticanus B, p. 32.

"three," *ox,* also signify "breath." In one Late Classic example of the white-flower death expression, this god substitutes directly for the *ik'* sign (Fig. 4.7e). Noting the strong identification of God H with flowers, Andrea Stone (1995b) compares this being to Xochipilli, the Aztec god of music and dance. Just as the Maya god expresses fragrant scent, Xochipilli signifies "sweet music." Page 67 of the Madrid Codex portrays God H striking a drum and shaking a rattle, and on Dresden Codex page 34c, his name glyph appears in a text concerning Chaak playing a drum atop a mountain. As with wind, breath, and aroma, music is ethereal and incorporeal; possibly for this reason, Classic Maya musical instruments often display *ik'* wind signs (Fash 1989:fig. 48; Schele and Mathews 1998:pl. 11). An Early Classic incised vessel features a complex scene filled with floating flowers and music, here represented by two pairs of tasseled rattles and a drum marked by a prominent *ik'* sign (Hellmuth 1988:fig. 4.1). Moreover, the thin jade belt celts of Classic Maya royal costume are frequently marked with *ik'* signs (e.g., Caracol Stelae 5, 6). The tinkling sounds created by the clusters of belt celts evoke the breath soul not only by the *ik'* wind signs but by the material itself: precious jade (Chapter 8).

Constance Classen raises the possibility that some tropical peoples, such as those of the Amazonian Basin, privileged smell because of limited visibility in their environment (1990:731). Smells could be vividly experienced in such a milieu, but it was in the cold Andes that sound and sight achieved greater salience. The Classic Maya discussed in this book manifestly occupied a warm zone, with a few exceptions such as Tonina, Chiapas. At the risk of making a deterministic argument, we suspect the focus on flowers and pungent smells derived in part from the redolent air in and around the tropical forest, a world where smells invaded the nostrils long before the eyes perceived objects at a distance.

Fig. 4.12. Wind God combining attributes of a monkey and a duck, from burial in Structure 9, Becan, Campeche (after Campaña and Boucher 2002:68).

Fig. 4.13. Classic forms of God H, the Maya wind god: (a) God H as patron of month Mak (from Taube 1992b:fig. 28e); (b) Copan 9N-8 bench (after drawing by Anne Dowd); and (c) Palenque Palace Tablet:A1–B2 (after M. G. Robertson 1985b:pl. 263).

CLASSIC MAYA SOUND AND HEARING

Elsewhere we have discussed the nature of sound and speech in Mesoamerica, particularly with respect to the perceived heat of lordly utterances (Chapter 7). Speech is the oratorical privilege of the lord and appears to underpin his titles: Nahuatl *tlahtoāni*, the term for "lord" among the Aztec, comes from a word meaning "to speak, to issue proclamations and commands" (Karttunen 1992:266); *ajaw*, "lord" in most Mayan languages, may derive from **aj-aw*, "he of the shout, shouter" or "proclaimer" (Houston and D. Stuart 1996:295); and in Colonial Tzotzil, a Mayan language, *k'opoj*, "speak," is the same as "become a lord" (Laughlin 1988, 2:569). Oddly enough, the most common term for "word" or "speech" in Ch'olan and Yukatekan languages, *t'an*, is not yet found in the Classic Maya sources—a disembodied speech scroll found in texts at sites like Naranjo, Guatemala, may record the word, but there is not enough evidence to prove the reading. Lordly speech is hot and solar, a trope that stems from the sunlike associations of rulers (Houston and Cummins 1998). This also means, presumably, that such sounds can be felt as well as heard. In the Maya area, where powerful lightning storms are common, the reverberations of thunder percuss wildly, a quality that can readily be appreciated with such instruments as trumpets and drums. In Yukatek Mayan, the verb *'u'uyik* signifies not only "hearing," but all other senses apart from sight (Hanks 1990:88). In many Mayan languages, "to hear" means "to understand, to comprehend," as it does today in Ch'orti' (Wisdom n.d.). Speech scrolls ensure that, through graphic means, sound can be seen as something concrete and imperishable, in deliberate subversion of the intrinsically ephemeral nature of speech.

In Mesoamerica, speech occurs in varying settings, including myths of creation and human origin. One of the earliest explicit discussions of speech scrolls appears in a posthumously published report by Hermann Beyer (1955:33–34). Thanks to the foundation he laid, there is much that can be said about scrolls. In some texts, such as the mythogenic Codex Vindobonensis of Mixtec provenance (52 obverse), speech marks an attribute of humanity at the beginning of time: such orations relate to the founding and making of all things (Anders et al. 1992:81). Speech also figures prominently in the creation account of the K'iche' Maya *Popol Vuh*, in which genesis results from a dialogue between the creator deities (Christenson 2000:40–41). In addition, the multiple attempts at creating people ensured that gods could be nourished through compliant human speech and prayer (Christenson 2000:49, 128–134). In the Aztec Codex Boturini, the patron god Huitzilopochtli speaks from an oracular cave when the Aztec leave their primordial home of Aztlan (Boone 1991:125).

There seems little doubt that speech resembles breath and wind in the Central Mexican sources: devastating gusts, not linked to lips but shattering a tree, occur in the Codex Telleriano-Remensis as tokens of "great winds breaking the trees" (Fig. 4.14a). The same spotted scrolls emanate from human lips in the Codex Historia Tolteca-Chichimeca, a manuscript of early post-Conquest date (Fig. 4.14b). Speech scrolls formed of lines of dots appear in Late Postclassic Mixtec codices, including the Codex Bodley, as well as in Late Classic Maya vessel scenes (Fig. 4.14c). Moreover, Late Classic Maya vessel scenes often portray speech scrolls as a series of dots in a single curving line, quite probably also an allusion to breath and wind. In Colonial Yukatek, *yik'al* signifies "breath"; *yik'al kuxtal*, "vital spirits"; and *yik'al t'an*, "wind or sound from one who speaks"—all these terms deriving from the root *ik'*, or "wind," in addition to the meaning of being "rich," perhaps in the sense of "precious things" (Barrera Vásquez 1980:977). The connection between the *ik'* sign and speech scrolls is made explicit on a pot showing a palace retainer in the act of talking (Fig. 4.14e). The resemblance is clear between the first glyph in this image and a sign for speech in a dedication verb on a Maya pot (cf. Fig. 4.14e, f).

The speech scrolls of Mesoamerica can communicate the content and property of vocalizations. In the art of ancient Teotihuacan (ca. AD 250–650), large and elaborate sound scrolls are qualified with series of elements lining the sides or in the volutes. Among the more usual signs are flowers, the breath soul in ancient Mesoamerica (A. Miller 1973:99–101, 134–345, 170). Precious jewels, another metaphor for the breath soul, also appear in Teotihuacan speech or song scrolls (A. Miller 1973:fig. 317). The beaded elements lining Teotihuacan, Zapotec, Cotzumalguapa, and Maya speech or song volutes are probably also references to schematic flowers or beads (Figs. 4.2e, 4.5b, c). One Early Classic Maya monument, Lacanha Stela 1, portrays a Teotihuacan-style figure with speech, not as a volute, but as a series of strung beads issuing from the mouth (Proskouriakoff 1950:44b). The later Aztec also related oral expression to both flowers and jade. Miguel León Portilla (1963:75) observes that the Nahuatl phrase *in xōchitl in cuīcatl*, or "flower and song," denoted poetry. These poems are filled with allusions to flowers and precious jewels: "And now I sing! So let there be flowers! So let there be songs! I drill my songs as though they were jades. I smelt them as gold. I mount these songs of mine as though they were jades" (Bierhorst 1985:207). There is frequent mention of birds, and according to John Bierhorst (1985:19), such texts conjured the souls of dead warriors residing in their floral solar paradise. Louise Burkhart (1992:89) describes this celestial paradise as a garden filled with brilliance and beauty: "The garden is a shimmering place filled with divine fire; the light of the sun reflects from the petals of flowers and the iridescent feathers of birds; human beings—the souls of the dead or the ritually transformed living—are themselves flowers, birds, and shimmering gems." Birds will roost again in Chapter 7, where they are seen to be the principal messengers of contact between humans and supernaturals. For the moment, note that images of bird-filled flowery trees from Chichen Itza, Yucatan, are explicitly named as the abode of the *mam*, or "ancestors."

The Aztec Florentine Codex provides explicit evidence that royal oratory was identified with a spirit in the form of precious jewels: "only as precious things do the spirit, the words of our lords come forth. For they are the words of rulers; for they are considered as precious green stones, as round, reed-like precious turquoises" (Sahagún 1950–1982, bk. 6:99). The term used for this spiritual force, *ihīyōtzin*, is the *ihīyōtl* breath spirit discussed by López Austin (1988, 1:232–235). Although López Austin stresses the negative aspect of breath or wind expelled at death, the passage in the Florentine Codex indicates that the *ihīyōtl* has a precious nature consistent with the widespread identification of breath with jade and flowers.

The flowery and precious attributes of the breath soul and the afterlife are strongly linked to rulers and gods, the figures most likely to appear in elite art. According to Tlaxcalan belief in Central Mexico, the souls of nobles and lords became precious stones, clouds, and birds of rich plumage, while those of commoners became lowly creatures that reeked of urine (Mendieta 1980:970). Burkhart (1992:84) notes that in early Colonial Aztec thought, angels were regarded as "nobles,"

Fig. 4.14. Representations of wind and speech scrolls in ancient Mesoamerica: (a) Aztec representation of tree-destroying winds, Codex Telleriano-Remensis, fol. 46v; (b) figure with dotted speech scrolls, Codex Historia Tolteca-Chichimeca, p. 2; (c) Mixtec figure with dotted speech scroll, Codex Bodley, p. 28; (d) Late Classic Maya warrior with dotted speech scroll, detail of Late Classic Maya vessel (after J. Kerr 1992:421); (e) seated figure with speech scroll, from Late Classic Maya vessel (after J. Kerr 1990:297); and (f) dedicatory glyph with *ik'* breath element, Late Classic Maya vase (after Reents-Budet 1994:fig. 4.22).

or *pīpiltin*. The celestial flowery paradise savored by Aztec warrior souls was not the common fate of the dead, who traveled to the dingy, foul-smelling underworld realm of Mictlan (Sahagún 1997:177–178). Similarly, Colonial Yukatek referred to the underworld Death God as *kisin,* a term derived from the word for "flatulence," or *kis* (Barrera Vásquez 1980:321). One Late Classic vessel portrays a noxious skeletal insect with breath marked with the sign for "darkness," and another shows the Death God with a stench scroll marked with eyeballs (M. Coe 1973:99, 134). It remains to be seen whether there was a widespread basic qualitative difference between the souls of commoners and kings in ancient Mesoamerica. But it does seem certain that regal speech was often compared to finer qualities of the breath soul. The so-called Zip monster, a snouted being with rectilinear nose, is in all likelihood the image of solar breath, something hot and strong (Fig. 4.15). It can emanate from mortuary bundles in tombs, as on Piedras Negras Stela 40 (Fig. 4.15a), from noses (Fig. 4.15b, c), and from earspools (Fig. 4.15d).

Just as speech was closely related to flowers and jade, so, too, was hearing. The large earspool assemblages represented in Classic Maya art are typically flowers with projecting breath elements. In addition, jade examples of Maya earspools are often carefully carved in the form of open, petaled flowers (Schmidt et al. 1998:nos. 141, 146, 155, 157, 159–160). The jade flower earspools expressed the refined and omniscient nature of elite hearing, or perhaps served to symbolically enrich or purify the sounds penetrating the regal head. In the same manner, death gods or the deceased have earspools exuding the breath souls of the dead (Fig. 4.16) or a peculiar assortment of human body parts (Fig. 4.17). An explicit linkage of "hearing" to earspools occurs on a jade example from the tomb of Pakal the Great at Palenque: [u-b'u-ji-ya], *ub' j iiy,* "it was heard" (Fig. 4.18; Houston and Cummins 1998). The Maya also, from an early date, likened earspools to a sign for "road" and vice versa, perhaps because the ear permits access to the body. Unfortunately, there are no known spellings of common terms for "ear," such as *chikin* in Ch'orti,' although the word for "nose," *ni',* is represented by a human face sporting untrimmed nose hairs. The long chains of earspools worn in elite Maya costume, such as those hanging from the headdress of the lord Siyaj Kan K'awiil on Tikal Stela 31, probably underline the unique hearing capabilities of kings, as do the stacked headdresses and associated earspools in some Early Classic images, such as Corozal Stela 1, Guatemala (Clancy 1999:fig. 46; see also Chapter 7). In the Classic Maya courtly life, speech was transmitted and hearing received through flowers and jade. An Early Classic façade mask from Acanceh, Yucatan, has a mutilated mouth and nose, an expected pattern given its ubiquity elsewhere, but also hacked-out earspools, as though such acts of enforced "deafness" marked rituals of termination (Chapter 2; see also a Late Classic example on an unprovenanced throne, in M. Miller and Martin 2004:pl. 1). The act of hearing may occur on Resbalon Hieroglyphic Stairway 1 (Block 22), a complex and disordered sculpture from Quintana Roo, Mexico. It displays an ear receiving a looped scroll.

Not surprisingly, there was a strong distinction between mere sound and songs of beauty and praise. One Late Classic shell carving portrays a musician grasping a pair of rattles while singing, the sound delineated by a long, beaded scroll swirling out of his mouth (Fig. 4.19a). Speech scrolls per se occur on a distinctive word sign, or logograph, consisting of a youthful head, mouth open, exuding a speech scroll that ends in a flower. Contextually, as at Bonampak, Mexico, and on a ceramic vessel, this word sign functions as a title that accompanies musicians, often those shaking rattles (Fig. 4.19b, c). A clue to its reading may be found in its subfixed sign, [ma], and in a fully phonetic version from the Early Classic period that appears to describe the owner of a conch trumpet: both hieroglyphic spellings indicate that the reading is [K'ΛYOOM-ma] or [k'a-yo-ma], "singer" (Fig. 4.19d, e; note also the logographic alternate, Fig. 4.19f). At Bonampak, in Chiapas, Mexico, this is a title of subsidiary figures at court, but an interesting detail emerges from an example at Tikal, Guatemala (Fig. 4.19d). This title clearly refers to a Late Classic ruler of the city, suggesting that singing counted as an important accomplishment

SENSES 157

Fig. 4.15. Hot breath: (a) Piedras Negras Stela 40 (drawing by David Stuart); (b) jade plaque in British Museum (after Schele and M. Miller 1986:pl. 34); (c) Quirigua Stela D, E4 (after Maudslay 1889–1902, 2:pl. 26; and (d) earspool with emanation, Yaxchilan Lintel 25 (after I. Graham and von Euw 1977:55).

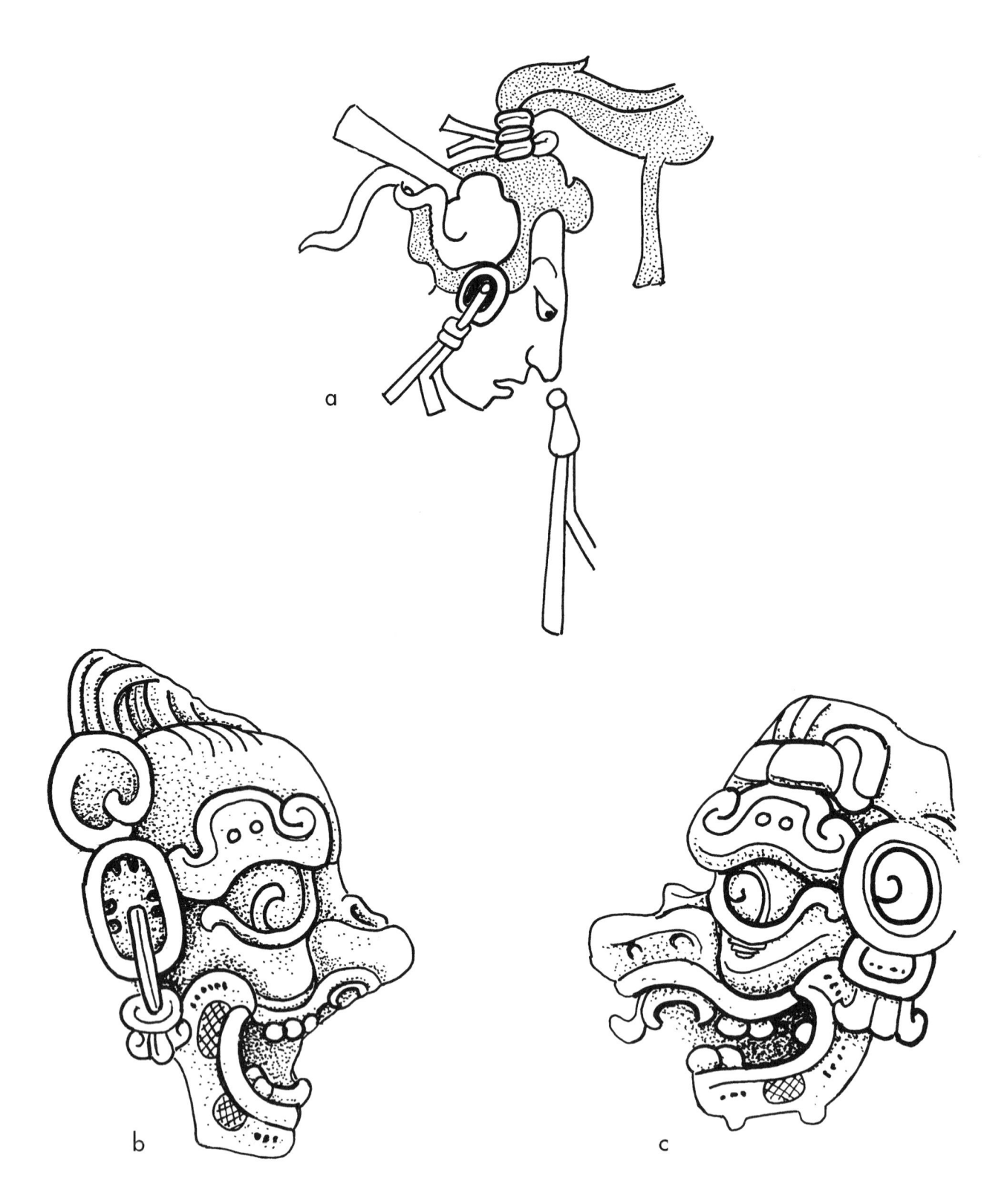

Fig. 4.16. Deathly exhalations from earspools: (a) Late Classic polychrome vessel (after K688); (b) stucco figure, Tonina (after Yadeun 1992:24); and (c) stucco figure, Tonina (after Yadeun 1992:81).

SENSES

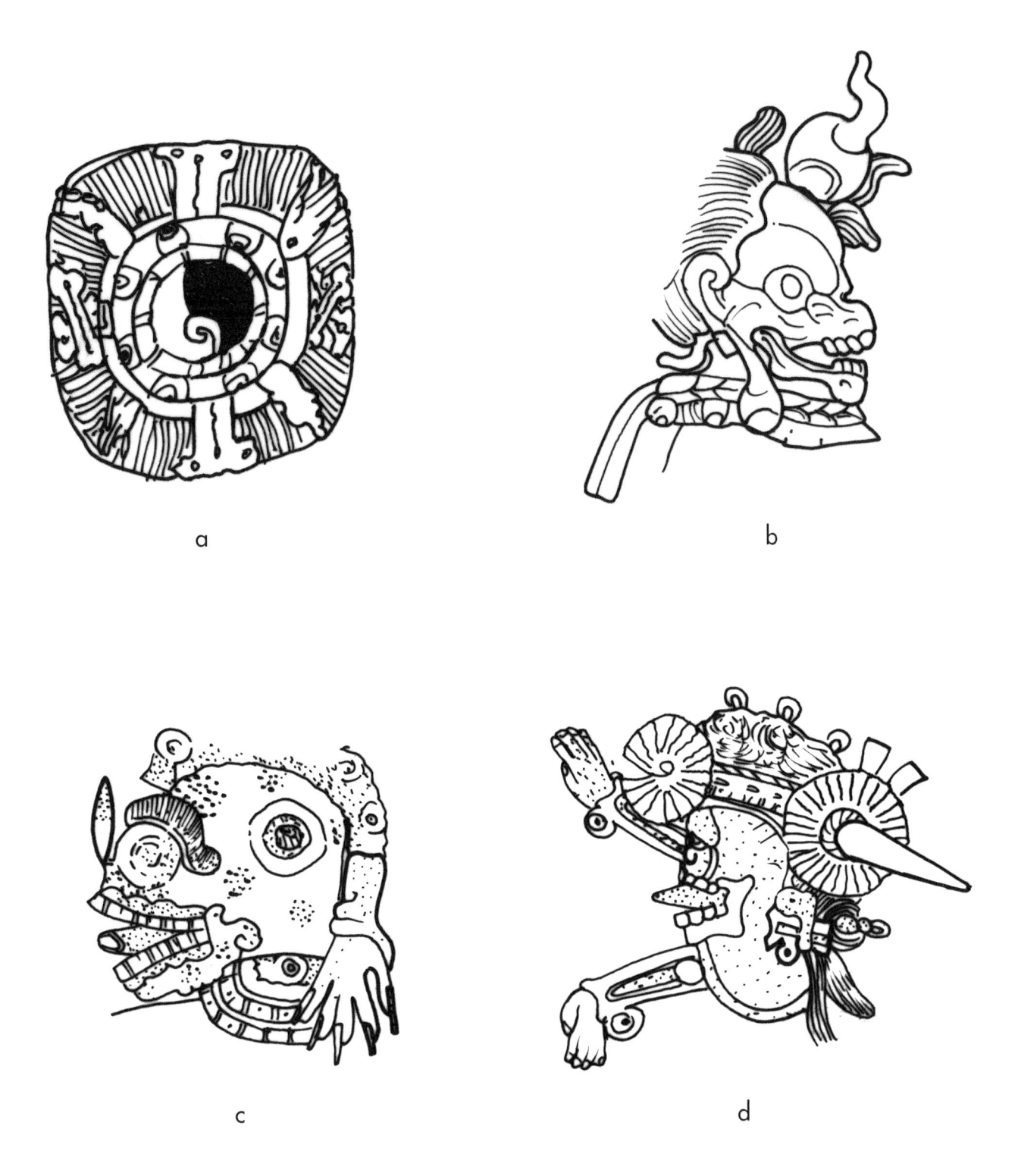

Fig. 4.17. Body parts in place of earspools: (a) parasol with body parts (after K3924); (b) Death God with eyeball threaded through earlobe (after Yadeun 1993:108); (c) Death God with hand inserted into earlobe, Codex Borgia, p. 56; and (d) Death God with bone piercing earlobe, Codex Borbonicus, p. 10.

u-bu-ji

Fig. 4.18. Jade earspool from Pakal's tomb, Temple of the Inscriptions, Palenque (drawing from photographs in Corpus of Maya Hieroglyphic Inscriptions, Peabody Museum).

of royalty. The songlike nature of such scrolls is emphasized by an Early Classic bird from Tikal with exactly the same looped line coming from the mouth (Culbert 1993:fig. 31a).

Among the Aztec, sound scrolls designating song could be marked with a complex motif formed of a contiguous series of rectangles containing paired scrolls and other decorative elements. The design goes all the way back to Olmec times (Fig. 4.20a). In the Codex Borbonicus, the music god, Xochipilli, emits a large and elaborate form of this scroll, here marked with a prominent jeweled flower sign (Fig. 4.20b). The same element appears in the Codex Mendoza toponym for Cuīcatlān, or "place of song" (Fig. 4.20c). In the Códice de Santa María Asunción, a schematic form of this song scroll appears several times for the surname Cihuicuicatl, or "female song." Aside from song volutes, the ornamented-rectangles motif also appears in representations of scribes and sculptors (Fig. 4.20d–f). In terms of both form and specific elements within the sign, this motif is strikingly similar to Maya skybands (Nicholson 1955; Seler 1904a). Eduard Seler (1904a:207–208) established that one of the most prominent elements in the Aztec skyband, a pair of diagonal scrolls, also appears in a sixteenth-century Aztec census for the name Pedro Ylhuj (Fig. 4.20d). According to Seler, the sign stands for *ilhuitl*, meaning "day" or "festival," but this gives little explanation for its occurrences and similarity to the Maya skyband. It is far more likely that the sign refers to *ilhuicatl*, the Aztec term for "sky" (see Karttunen 1992:104). This Aztec skyband indicates that in Postclassic Central Mexico, artistically produced works— whether they were songs, paintings, or sculpture— were considered to have celestial qualities, probably relating them both to creation and the Flower World.

Aside from bearing flowers and other qualifying elements, speech scrolls can also contain hieroglyphic texts. Murals from the Tepantitla compound at Teotihuacan reproduce speech scrolls along with adjectival hieroglyphic descriptions of

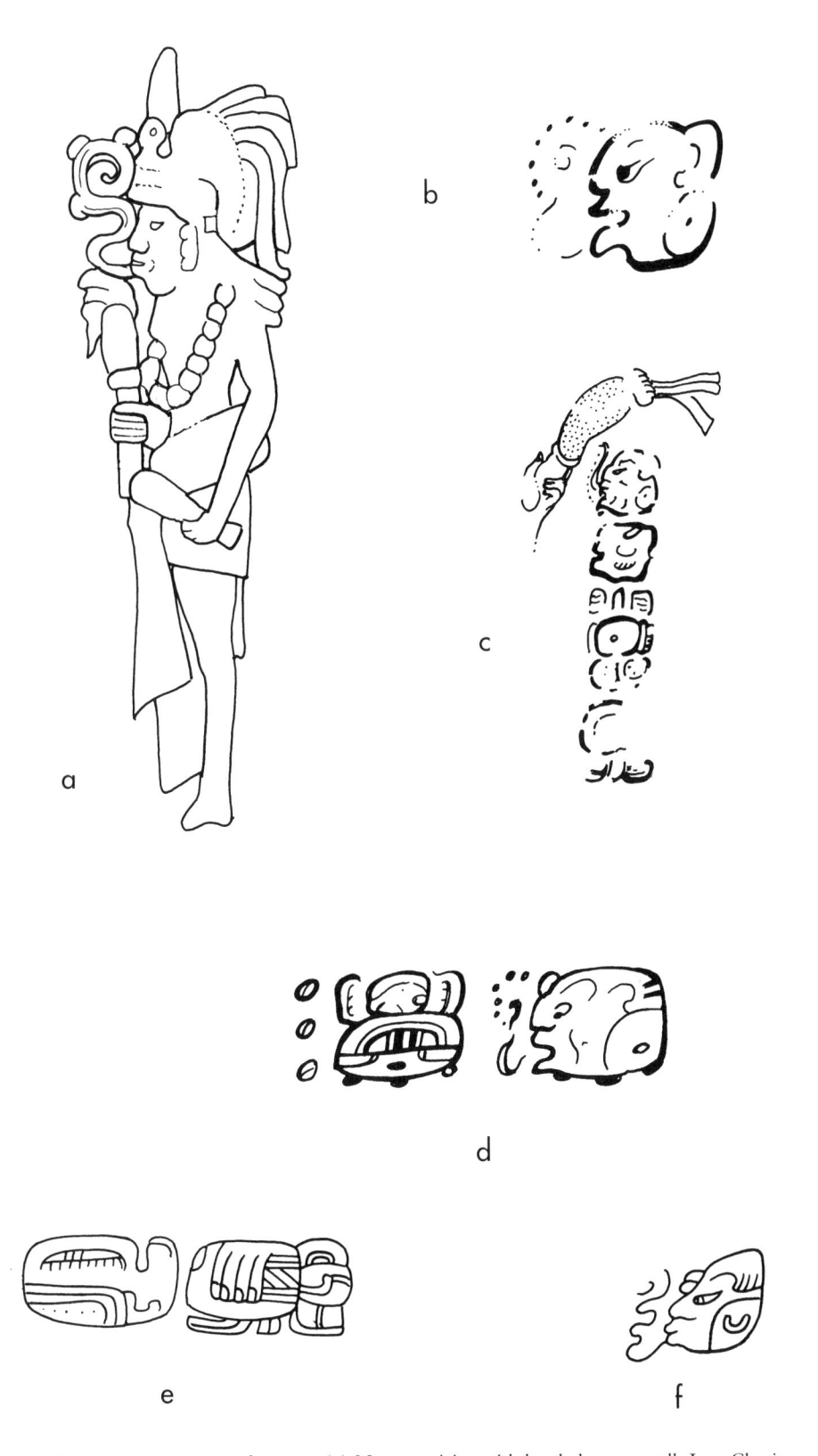

Fig. 4.19. Classic Maya signs for song: (a) Maya musician with beaded song scroll, Late Classic carved shell; (b) singer glyph, Bonampak murals, Room 1; (c) Late Classic ceramic vessel text with singer glyph (after de Smet 1985:pl. 16a); (d) Ruler B as a singer, ceramic text from Burial 196, Tikal (after Culbert 1993:fig. 184); (e) phonetic spelling of "singer," Early Classic conch trumpet (after Schele and M. Miller 1986:309); and (f) logographic sign for "singer," Early Classic conch trumpet (after Schele and M. Miller 1986:309).

162   THE MEMORY OF BONES

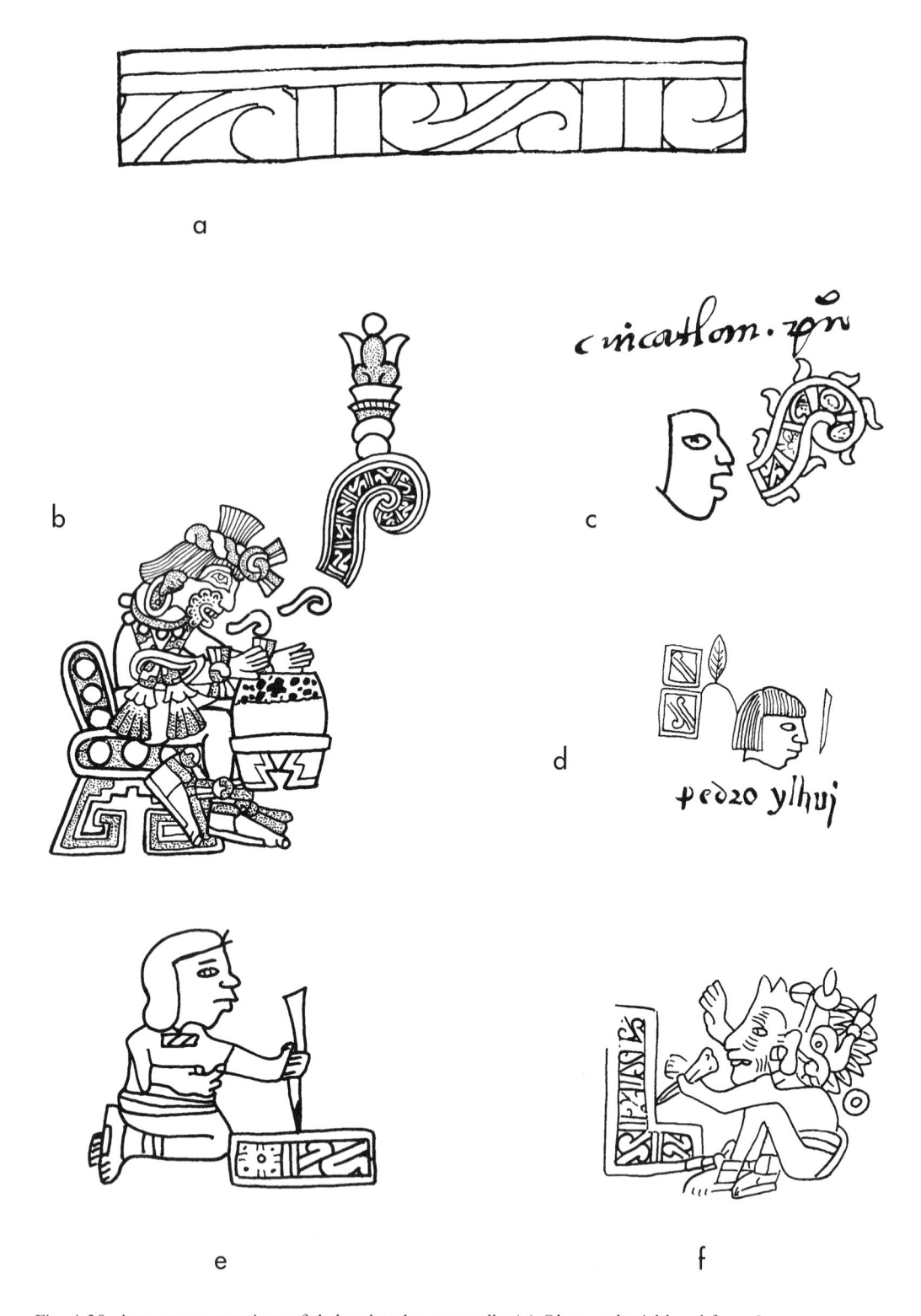

Fig. 4.20. Aztec representations of skyband and song scrolls: (a) Olmec celestial band from San Lorenzo, Mexico (after Cruz Lara Silva and Guevara Muñoz 2002:fig. 36); (b) Xochipilli with elaborate song scroll marked with jeweled flower, Codex Borbonicus, p. 4; (c) celestial song scroll marking Cuīcatlān, or "place of song," Codex Mendoza, p. 43r; (d) skyband accompanying name Pedro Ylhuj, Humboldt Fragment VIII; (e) woman painter, Codex Telleriano-Remensis, p. 30r; and (f) old man of creator couple as a sculptor, petroglyph from Coatlán, Morelos (after Guil'liem Arroyo 1998:50).

what is being said. In one place, a "knot-bird" game is being mentioned, elsewhere a "kick-resounding-bone" game, and even a "centipede" game, the latter accompanied by a line of linked figures. A Teotihuacan-style mirror back displays a relatively long hieroglyphic text ending with a speech scroll, quite probably serving as a quotative particle for the previous portion of the text (Fig. 4.21). The affixation of texts to speech scrolls is not limited to Teotihuacan. Javier Urcid (1991) notes that speech scrolls with hieroglyphic signs also appear on Zapotec monuments. Late Classic Maya vessel scenes contain abundant examples of speech scrolls connected to often quite lengthy hieroglyphic texts, like the curving line connecting to the texts of modern cartoon bubbles (Fig. 4.22). The convention of placing texts with speech scrolls continued in Postclassic Mesoamerica. John Pohl (personal communication, 1999) notes an instance in the Codex Nuttall where one figure emits a sound scroll containing the date 7 Flower (Fig. 4.22c). In this instance, the day name Flower is strikingly similar to the jeweled flower on an Aztec Xochipilli song scroll. This is by no means coincidental, as the god 7 Flower is none other than the Mixtec equivalent of Xochipilli, the god of music (J. Furst 1978:164). In other words, the Mixtec sound scroll can be song, personified by the god name 7 Flower. Some of the most complex instances of texts linked to speech scrolls occur in the Codex Xolotl, an early Colonial manuscript from the vicinity of Texcoco, in the eastern Valley of Mexico. In one scene, a speech scroll text of a prisoner contains no less that ten glyphic signs (Fig. 4.22d).

Speech scrolls are relatively common in Classic Maya art. In one image, set in a ballcourt, the artist showed echo effects in architectural spaces through the expedient of stray speech scrolls detached from human lips (Fig. 4.23a). The convoluted, tightly bent, and modulated quality of these scrolls may denote echoing intensity of sound. Pure, resonant sounds occur as thunderous reverberations from the mouth of the rain and lightning god, Chaak, or from other deities (Fig. 4.23b; note the similarity to birth clefts—see below). The undulating or jagged lines seem to denote powerful, rumbling sound. A similar convention also occurs in Mixtec codices. The face of the Mixtec rain and lighting god emanates undulating lines as a probable reference to thunder (Fig. 4.23c). The same motif often appears with the chevron band, which is the Mixtec war sign, probably to denote the din of battle. There is a possibility that parallel lines near or on Classic Maya drums represent such resounding noise (Fig. 4.24).

Speech scrolls, although often faint and easily undetected, loop about in whiplash motions in Late Classic Maya art. This may indicate the modulated tone or oscillating volume expected in rhetoric. Truly, the glyphs talk: in most cases the speech scrolls loop from open mouths to glyphic captions. One vessel scene specifies the reciprocal etiquette of such speech, so that those holding or giving objects speak while those receiving do not (J. Kerr 1997:754). The analytic implications of an emphasis on spaces filled with speech are that archaeologists need to pay more attention to the acoustics of buildings, especially palaces (Chapter 8). For example, most visitors to Maya sites comment anecdotally on whisper effects or the astonishing distances that sound can travel over plazas and up or down staircases. Nonetheless, to date, there has been little systematic study of such properties. It is improbable that the Maya were unaware of such qualities and that, as master builders, they failed to manipulate the interplay of sound and speech. Moreover, such "spaces" were not hollow or vacant, as we might understand them from an occidental perspective, but were substantively, if intermittently, filled with rhetoric and song.

CLASSIC MAYA SIGHT

Sight was often represented in Mesoamerican sources. In the Codex Mendoza, an early Colonial account of Aztec conquest and tribute, a priest gazes at stars shown as a celestial canopy of eyeballs; but his gaze, too, consists of a projected eyeball connected to his orbits by a dotted line (Fig. 4.25a). Elsewhere in the Codex Mendoza such dots indicate connections between elements

Fig. 4.21. Teotihuacan glyphs appearing on a mirror back (after E. Benson and Joralemon 1980:36).

that are not contiguous and also convey movement of persons and objects. It is likely that the eyeball and dotted line denote distant gazing, such as at stars or events removed from the immediate area of an individual. Lines of dots also appear in the Codex Xolotl, where they are used to connect a series of eyeballs pointed to another scene (Fig. 4.25c). In one telling scene, one of a pair of figures within a ballcourt observes four traveling individuals, while his companion is shown below leaving the ballcourt to greet the approaching group (Fig. 4.25c). The speech shared between them concerns the name of the gazing figure back at the ballcourt. The first glimpse of the Spaniards' caravels in 1518 occasioned a scene in the Codex en Cruz in which a native traveler or merchant looks at the bearded conquistadors in their moon-shaped boat on the water (Fig. 4.25b). As in the

SENSES 165

Fig. 4.22. Mesoamerican texts with speech scrolls: (a) Late Classic Maya vessel (after Robicsek and Hales 1981:53); (b) Zapotec text from Lápida de Matatlan (after Urcid 1991); (c) Mixtec image of a song scroll with name of the deity 7 Flower, Codex Nuttall, p. 20; and (d) Aztec rendering of speech and its contents, Codex Xolotl, pl. 8.

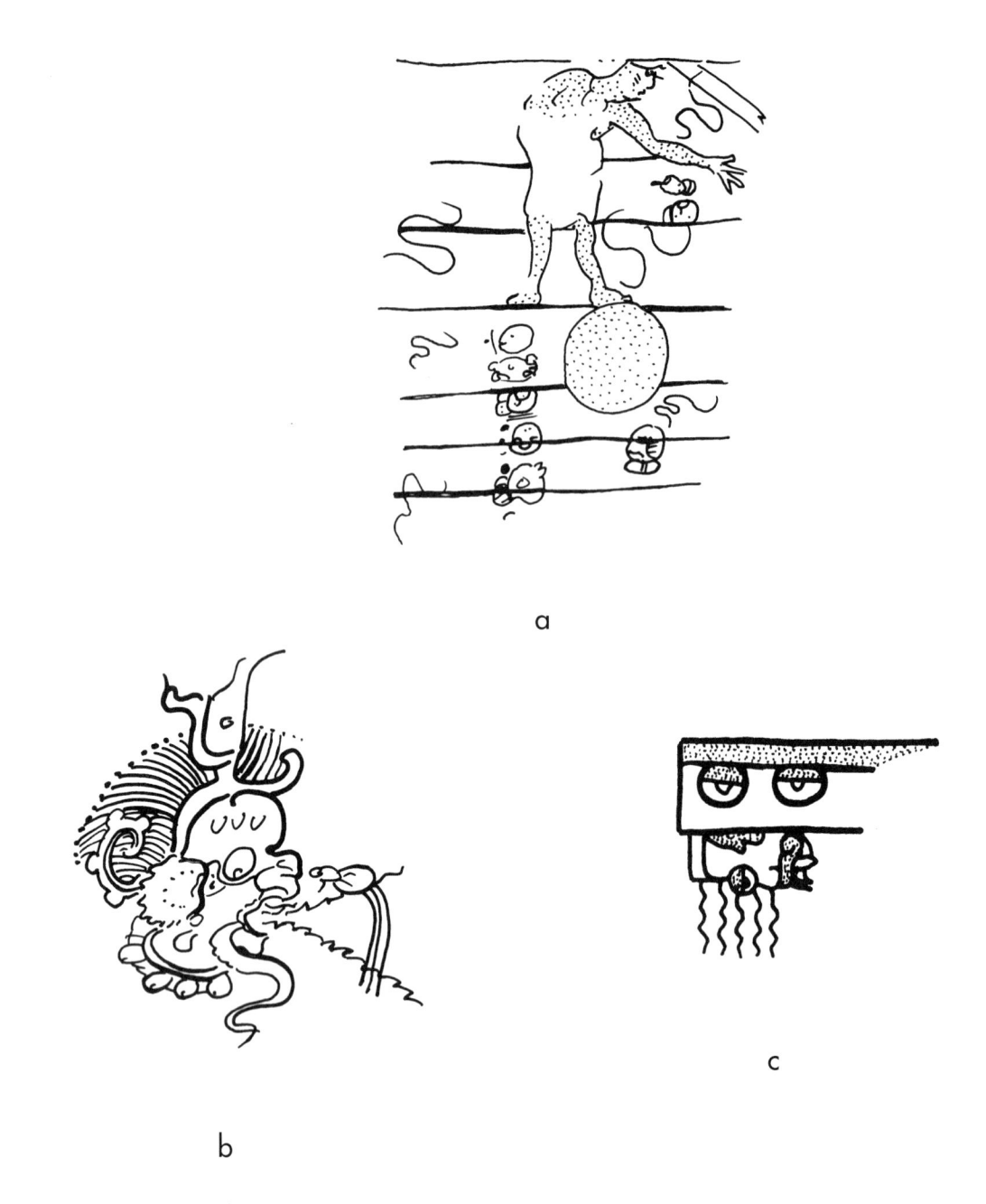

Fig. 4.23. Symbols for echoes and vibrant sounds: (a) Late Classic Maya ballcourt scene (after Reents-Budet 1994:266); (b) Chaak roaring (after J. Kerr 1990:285); and (c) Mixtec hieroglyph with sound symbols flanking "war chevron," Codex Selden, p. 7.

case of the Codex Xolotl, the repeated eyeballs probably denote distance; the Aztec figure was undoubtedly observing a ship at sea, not on nearby land.

The Classic Maya showed eyeballs as well, often with grim attention to anatomical details. Extruded eyeballs, still dangling on the optical stalks, issue from the orbits of animals and supernaturals (Fig. 4.26). A lintel from the site of Sayil, Mexico, portrays a supernatural being calmly holding its extruded eyes in both hands (Fig. 4.26a). Until the stalk is severed, the eye can still receive optical input, a property the Maya seem to have been aware of, since the animals are often engaged in other activities. A more important feature of eyesight in Classic thought, however, concerns the projective nature of sight. An incised resist vessel of Late Classic date displays a scene in which virtually

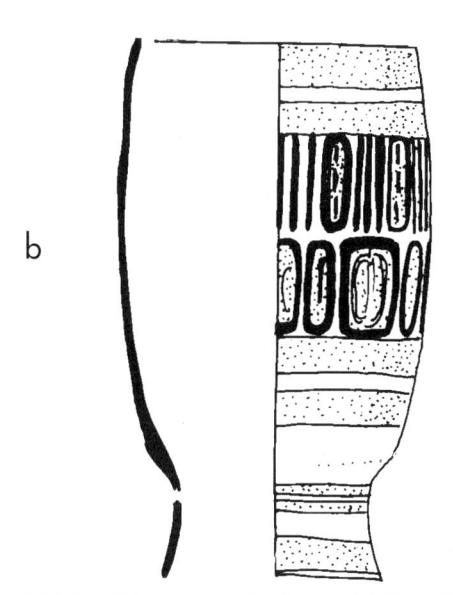

Fig. 4.24. Possible notation for drums: (a) Early Classic vessel (after Hellmuth 1988:fig. 4.2); and (b) Uaxactun (after R. E. Smith 1955:fig. 41b).

every eye has been excised to create an effect of glowing orbits that catch the viewer's gaze, including objects such as rattles and scepters (K3844). Another scene, showing a newborn, recumbent Maize God, contains a hieroglyphic caption: [a-si-ya/i-chi] or *a-siy-a?-ich,* "he who is born from liquid or secretion" (Houston and Taube 2000:fig. 17). Below is a disembodied head emitting vegetal motifs, and from its eye issues the V-shaped cleft associated with birth in Mesoamerica. Precisely the same icon lies underneath the feet of a Maya lord on an unprovenanced stela from the Usumacinta drainage of Guatemala and Mexico (Anonymous 1998:fig. 215). This may demonstrate either that the "secretion-birth" scene refers to an actual place-name, or that the lord on the stela was being likened to the Maize God, a common conceit in Classic Maya art; alternatively, such images show that the ruler was locally born (see Calakmul's Structure IV-B lintel, with a lord above a cleft place-name with mythological associations, R. Carrasco 1996:50).

What is crucial here is that the eye is *procreative*. It not only receives images from the outer world, but positively affects and changes that world through the power of sight—in short, it behaves as an "emanating eye" that establishes communion between internal will and external result. For example, among the Yukatek Maya, ethnography tells us that sight had an "agentive quality" through "willful act[s]," a property notably missing from the act of hearing (Hanks 1990:89), although scent and projective sound would seem to possess this quality (signs much like birth clefts occur on glyphs for drums, and such markings also flow from flowers and the mouths of gods [see above]). The K'iche'an *Popol Vuh* describes the first people of the present creation to be all-seeing, and consequently all-knowing: "Thus their knowledge became full. Their vision passed beyond the trees and rocks, beyond the lakes and the seas, beyond the mountains and the valleys" (Christenson 2000:131). Fearful of this godly power, the creator deities diminished their vision: "They were blinded like breath upon the face of a mirror" (Christenson 2000:134).

The *Popol Vuh* stresses the penetrating power of sight. In ancient Mesoamerican thought, vision was so related to light that eyeballs were used as signs of reflective brilliance. Nicholas Saunders (1988) notes that, at night, the eyes of jaguars shine with a mirrorlike brightness, and in this regard it should be noted that three of the four original humans in the *Popol Vuh* are named "jaguar": "Balam Quitze, Balam Acab . . . and Iqui Balam" (Christenson 2000:131). On the walls of Palenque House C,

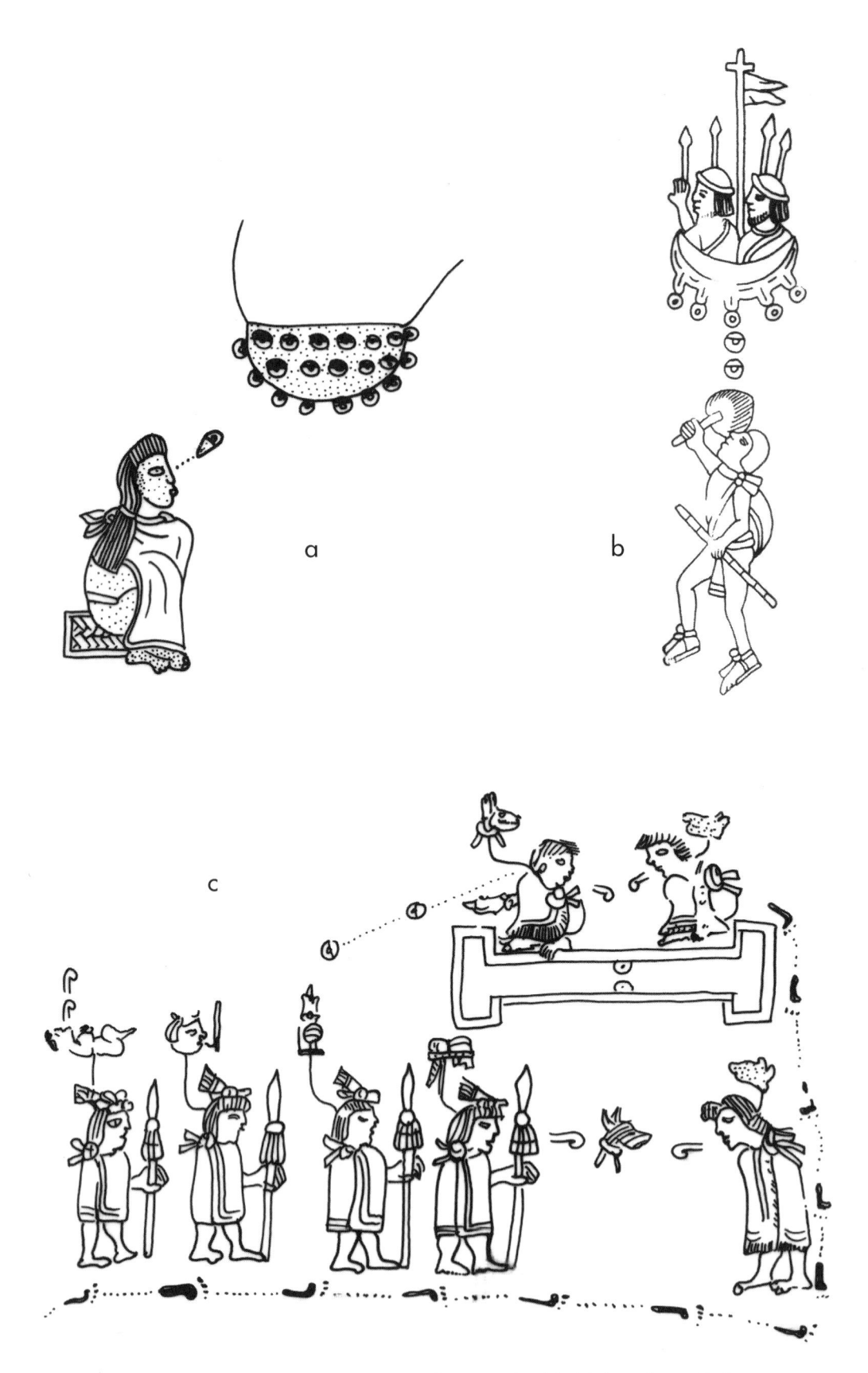

Fig. 4.25. Aztec conventions for representing long-distance sight: (a) sighting of stars, Codex Mendoza, 63r; (b) first sighting of Spaniards in boat by Aztec messenger (Codex en Cruz); and (c) sighting of visitors, Codex Xolotl, pl. 9.

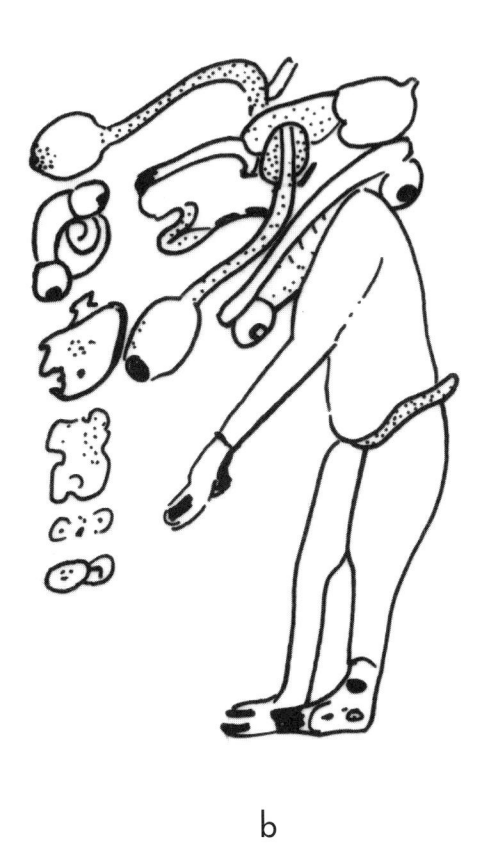

Fig. 4.26. Extruded eyeballs in Classic Maya art: (a) supernatural being, Sayil (after Pollock 1980:fig. 255a); (b) deer as companion spirit, named with doubled eyeball glyph (after J. Kerr 1994:112); and (c) mammal holding vessel (after J. Kerr 1989:83).

from the Late Classic period, flowers contain eyeballs, as though underscoring the projective force of scent (Houston and Taube 2000:fig. 5i; see also Brockington 1967:fig. 28, for an example from the Olmec period).

The sun, the most elemental and powerful source of radiant light, is widely identified with eyes in Mesoamerica. The ancient Maya term for the jaguar sun god, K'inich Ajaw, means "Sunlike Lord," and there are instances where solar *k'in* signs appear in place of eyes (e.g., Altar of Stela D, Copan). In the Dresden Codex eclipse pages, projecting eyeballs portray solar rays (Houston and Taube 2000:fig. 18). In one instance, a pair of eyes serves as the butt ends of barbed darts. This corresponds to a common Aztec means of representing the current sun Nahui Ollin, or 4 Motion, in which a pointed barb projects above a central eye. Quite frequently, dart points rim Aztec solar images, including the famed Calendar Stone. Seler (1904b:384–385) also notes that in Postclassic Mesoamerica, the rays of light emitted by the first appearance of Venus as morning star were believed to be deadly darts. In Postclassic Mesoamerica, both Venus and stars were often rendered as eyes, in many cases rimmed with pointed darts (Houston and Taube 2000:fig. 18).

The Classic Maya appear to have assigned the emanating power of vision to portraits as well. These were conceived as physical, essentially charged extensions of the person being represented. When mutilated, either by antagonists or through ritual "killing," it was usually the eyes that were effaced or hacked, presumably because of the forces thought to radiate from them (Houston and D. Stuart 1998:88). It is just possible that the Maya observed a ceremony much like the Buddhist "opening of the eyes," which activated, enlivened, and empowered sculptures (Gombrich 1966). The inscription of Stela 3 from Machaquila, Guatemala, ends in an impersonal expression: *ila-aj / k'al-tuun / na-ho-tuun*, "it is seen / wrapped [dedicated] stone / fifth stone" (I. Graham 1967:fig. 49; also Machaquila Stela 7: *il-b'a*, "see body/self/image," I. Graham 1967:fig.57; D. Stuart 1996: 157). In another publication (Houston and D. Stuart 1998), we argued that this refers to the first reading of the text, but it may also suggest that the sight of the monument, probably by the ruler himself, vitalizes and consecrates it to service as a royal representation. Tellingly, the dead are shown throughout Mesoamerican art with closed eyes (Fig. 4.7c).

The eyes of Classic Maya deities fall generally into two categories. One set is clearly human, marking youthful or female gods such as the Hero Twins, the Moon Goddess, or the Maize God (Taube 1992b:figs. 19, 28, 30). The other set of gods has eyes with square outlines and inset designs of varying shape. Such characterize the Sun God and various deities with elderly features or strikingly inhuman visages (Taube 1992b:figs. 4, 12, 22). The differences between the two kinds of eyes raise interesting questions about what the Maya intended. If sight was transmissive and procreative, such distinctions might have signaled that one group had a particular kind of sight, perhaps as original or creator gods, and that the other did not.

The pupils of "square-eyed" gods in Classic Maya art also form two major categories. One type, commonly found with the Sun God, the aged creator Itzamnaaj, and his avian aspect, displays a crossed-eye pupil (Fig. 4.27b). The pair of curving lines delineating the pupil is identical to the mirror sign used to designate hard, reflective surfaces, such as stone mirrors or polished celts (Fig. 4.27a); most likely, it derived from a Late Preclassic form of L-shaped eyes. The same reflective sign can also appear on the brow of the sun deity and other gods (Fig. 4.27b). The other type of eye is a swirl or spiral, and it seems to correspond to gods of the dark and watery underworld (Fig. 4.27c). Thus the nocturnal aspect of the Sun God, the Jaguar God of the Underworld, displays these pupils, in sharp contrast to the diurnal form of the sun deity. In Mesoamerica, eyes are widely identified with mirrors (Saunders 1988; Taube 1992b:181–182), and along with the pupil marking, the spiral element also appears on the surfaces of mirrors, although it is often worn by death and underworld beings, including the Moan Owl and the deathly God of Completion (Fig. 4.27d). The differing eyes denote two qualities of reflective light, one a bright gleam from hard, shiny surfaces, and the other, more muted and opaque. Along with the Jaguar God of the Underworld, the piscine god known as G1 also displays swirling eyes, and it is likely that this eye form derives from bodies of water, widely identified with the underworld in Maya thought (Fig. 4.27c). Thus Early Classic images of flowing water often display swirls identical to the eyes of aquatic and underworld beings (Fig. 4.27e). A similar convention appears in the Early Classic art of Teotihuacan, where falling drops, streams, and even the ocean display eyes, probably to denote the reflective, shining quality of liquid (Fig. 4.27f).

Maya writing abounds in glyphs for sight. This sign includes affixes necessitated by grammar, but also a principal or "main sign" that shows an eyeball from which the pupil exudes two lines, very similar to the pairs of lines denoting scent and sound (Fig. 4.28a). In a rather macabre fashion,

Fig. 4.27. Comparison of deity eyes and reflective surfaces in Classic Maya art: (a) "mirror" sign (after Schele and J. Miller 1983:fig. 3a); (b) head of the Sun God, stucco head, Palenque (after Schele and J. Miller 1983:fig. 3f); (c) mask of G1 (after Taube 1992b:fig. 9a); (d) God of Completion with spiral mirror in headdress, Copan (after Taube 1992b:fig. 55f); (e) water emblem, Río Azul Tomb 1 (after G. Hall 1987:fig. 37); and (f) youth fishing for shells, mural from Tetitla compound, Teotihuacan (after A. Miller 1973:fig. 277).

death gods in the Dresden Codex display seeing eyes on their bodies, and even eyes as a form of speech or breath (for eye emanating from the mouth, see Dresden Codex, pp. 8a, 10a, 11a, 15a, c). In the case of the vision sign, the lines begin within the eye, often as a U-shaped cleft around the pupil. The similarity of this form to birth verbs and birthing expressions shows again that the Classic Maya perceived a fundamental linkage between sight and birth, both equally projective from the body. This sign is read *il* or *ila*, a Classic Maya expression meaning "see" (Fig. 4.28b). The same sign occurs in the so-called Glyph D of the lunar series in the Classic calendar (Thompson 1950:fig. 36). This, the first appearance of the new moon, involves the concept of "holy sight" or "the god sees," quite like the heliacal rising of Venus as the morning star. In fact, the Aztec Florentine Codex compares the heliacal appearance of the morning star to the shining moon: "it burst forth completely, took its place in full light, became brilliant, and shone white. Like the moon's rays, so did it shine" (Sahagún 1950–1982, bk. 7:11–12). Another variant of the Maya lunar sign, read *hul* or *ul*, "to arrive," consists of a moon glyph with an eye inside. Present evidence does not allow us to establish the exact meaning of this complex of signs, although it does suggest a strong association between sight and physical manifestation, in this case of the crescent moon.

As a verb, the glyph for "to see," *ila-aj* or *y-ila-ji*, is found throughout the corpus of Classic and particularly Late Classic inscriptions (ca. AD 600–850; Houston and Taube 2000:figs. 20, 21). Two kinds of contexts exist. One features the verb in initial position, as the first element in a phrase meaning "it is seen." Typically, these expressions specify location of the event, as in a reference to a mortuary pyramid on a panel from the area of Cancuen, Guatemala ("at *ho janahb wits*," perhaps

Fig. 4.28. Maya glyphs and icons for "see": (a) Postclassic Dresden Codex, p. 12b, with Death God and sighted eyeballs; and (b) La Corona (?) panel (after drawing by I. Graham).

the Maya Flower World), and in many texts from the wall paintings of Naj Tunich, Guatemala ("at *mo'pan*"). The physical mooring of sight clearly conferred materiality to that action. The second context is that of a secondary verb—namely, positioned after an initial phrase containing an initial verb (see Ixtutz Stela 4:A5–B5). The individual who "sees" is always someone of high status, an overlord or crucial visitor. Such statements indicate that the act of seeing and, implicitly, the physical presence of the overlord or visitor held singular importance for the Classic Maya, just as it does for some Maya groups today (Vogt 1993:205). Such presences imply that sight discharged a witnessing or authorizing function in Classic society. In a moral and perhaps a legal sense, the events being seen achieved validity not only because they took place, but because others used sight to participate in them, as "co-creators" of a signal event. It is probably relevant that, in most Mayan languages, to see something is also to discern and understand; thus, the act of perception is regarded as physiological, but equally cognitive, intellectual, and, in the case of shamans, at once visionary and spiritually omniscient (Hanks 1990:88; Vogt 1993:187, 205).

SIGHT AND MORAL VALUATION

The notion of perceptual and interactional fields embracing bodies and actions leads to a final piece of evidence, a set of glyphs that refer explicitly to visual fields during the Classic period and how they might differ from one another. What is a broadly held perceptual region for later Maya becomes, for the Classic lords, a field of vision and witness that appears to have been crucial in validating ritual. It served almost as a notarial presence that made actions more concrete through shared experience and participation. Such witnesses were not passive, but, through eyesight, were active celebrants in the events before them, somewhat analogous to the Nahuatl concept of *ixco* (nahuatl.ifrance.com/nahuatl/nahuatl.page.html). The phrase in question is the *y-ichnal* expression, usually spelled [yi-chi-NAL] (Fig. 4.29), which is certainly cognate with Yukatekan *y-iknal*, an inalienably possessed noun that requires a possessor (D. Stuart 1997:10). William Hanks has done a penetrating analysis of the *-iknal* expression among modern Yukatekan speakers. From him we learn that the *-iknal* can be one of two things: either a habitual place or home, and thus anchored in space, or a corporeal field of interaction, a region that is a "mobile field of action related to an agent the way one's shadow or perceptual field is" (Hanks 1990:91). There is some hieroglyphic evidence that the Classic Maya intended the latter meaning, albeit in a narrower sense. Among modern Yucatec Maya, the *-iknal* is closely "linked to bodily activity of a speaker" and within the body's line of view (Hanks 1990:92). The *-iknal* field generally lies in front, although it may include peripheral fields that can be accessed by head movement (Hanks 1990:91, 93). Although predicated on sight, it is not, in James Gibson's terms, a "visual field" that relies only on eyesight from a fixed vantage or a hypothetical, perspectival frame (1979:285–286). Rather, it lies closer to a "visual world" that is "ecologically intertwined with the other senses" and that reaches out to projected "depth shapes" (Gibson 1979:206–207; Jay 1993:4). This understanding contemplates vision not from a single vantage but in terms of the totality of objects within view, each as a participant in that world. In Gibson's view, such *-ichnal* represents an event that can be understood and classified in relation to its creation of space/time, its nesting within other events, and the possibilities afforded for other suitable responses (1979:100–102).

What is so intriguing is the appearance of this term in Classic inscriptions (Fig. 4.29b). Without exception, the entity to whom an *-ichnal* belongs is either a ruler or a deity—lords appear singly, whereas gods occur in pairs toward the eastern Maya lowlands and as triplets or quadruplets in the western Maya region. Chronologically, the expression is restricted to the middle years of the Late Classic, with scattered examples all the way into the Terminal Classic period (ca. AD 800); the largest number (n=10) involve the act of "receiving" regalia or a ritual (n=5) that may entail "dressing" or "adornment." The date of such references possibly demonstrates the increasing importance of

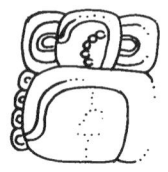

Fig. 4.29. The *y-ichnal* expression: (a) Aguateca Stela 1:D6 (after I. Graham 1967:fig. 3); and (b) El Peru stela fragment (after drawing by I. Graham).

consensus, collective acts, and nonregal influence in political and ritual life of the time (Houston and D. Stuart 1998). The visual field always embraces another person and someone else's action. Evidence from sites in the Petexbatun area of northern Guatemala emphasizes that the *-ichnal* shifts: the same deities will associate their *-ichnal* with different place-names, demonstrating that the perceptual field is not, at least at first, rooted in a particular location (cf. I. Graham 1996:59; D. Stuart and Houston 1994:fig. 5). Moreover, when the Classic Maya regarded individual perception, at least in their glyphic texts, it was not simply as a vista or a bracing view of architecture, but as a reciprocal, heavily social context involving other people or beings. In truth, this was "communion-oriented" vision, an "ecological event" of a very special sort. With gods in particular, the *-ichnal* would have been extended, presumably, by the field of view of multiple participants.

In addition, Hanks observes that, among the Yucatec Maya, the *-ichnal* tends to contain areas that are "up" and to the "right" (1990:91). Among the Classic Maya, this perceptual field is preferably "down," especially as it encompasses lower-ranking persons. For example, Stela 2 from Aguateca, Guatemala, situates the perceptual field with respect to a humbled captive writhing under the ruler's feet, and the same seems to be true on other monuments of deities floating above lords, looking "down" through the space of their *-ichnal* (I. Graham 1967:fig. 5). In glyphic inscriptions, no captive or inferior lord ever possesses or experiences an *-ichnal*. We should also emphasize the moral valuation of orientation: "up" being good, "down" less good, and right preferable to left (Palka 2002). There are delicate tensions that result from relative position in Maya art (Houston 1998).

How are we to relate this to movement and perception in Classic Maya buildings? The meaning of a place comes not only from architectural setting, usually vertically disposed, but also from the fact that something is being done and that several people are involved in undertaking or supervising such an action. In this view of place, architecture becomes, not surprisingly, a prop—even if a grand one—for reciprocal, socially meshed behavior that has the formulaic repetition of ritual. Expansive fields, issuing from the few bodies accorded *-ichnal* in Classic Maya rhetoric, impart meanings to architectonic spaces; sight lines through windows or along the edges of walls seem to have been less important than is sometimes asserted (e.g., Hartung 1980:74). Nonetheless, it would be an overstatement to disengage entirely the mobile *-ichnal* from the settings where they played such a large role in royal and ritual life. The closed courtyards in Maya palaces that emphasize the sweep of peripheral vision; the fixed thrones and benches where rulers sat; or the stairways where lords surveyed tribute, captives, and musicians served, in a sense, to tether and bind the *-ichnal* to focal spots on the axes that configured Maya buildings. For architectural settings, the Classic Maya may well have conceived of the *-ichnal* in Hanks's first sense, that of a habitual place. To put this in Gibson's language, such settings were designed to stage and control the *-ichnal* as a recurrent ecological event in the distinctive hierarchical sense intended by the Classic Maya.

TASTE AND TOUCH

The senses of taste and touch are left for last because the evidence for them is relatively weak. Physiologically, taste is a means of distinguishing harmful and indigestible things from those that are not. Bad-tasting things are often difficult to metabolize, although thresholds for tolerating certain tastes may shift, including proclivities for "hot" foods like chiles (Coren et al. 1999:210; Zellner 1991). Touch is regarded by some experts as the principal sensation of sex, a key component of tool-making, and a way of avoiding temperature extremes; not surprisingly, the most sensitive areas of the body are the face, hands, and bottoms of the feet (Coren et al. 1999:227, fig. 8.13).

Both tongue and touch discerned things that were "cold" (Ch'olti': *ziz;* Ch'orti': *sis*), often in the extended meaning of "numb" or as applied to refreshing tart flavors like lime or lemon. And there were things that were "hot." Ch'olti' had *tican* or *quinquin*, the former relating to things heated by humans, the second to natural warmth, a term derived from an emphatic repetition of the word for "sun" (**tikäw*, Kaufman and Norman 1984:132; also Ringle n.d.; Wisdom n.d.). Ch'orti', too, uses *ink'ihn*, "warm, angry, agitated, excited," and also perceives such fiery heat as a potentially dangerous property that can sicken by "warming the blood," *ink'ihn uch'ich'er* (Wisdom n.d.). An internal inflammation was likened to "fire," *k'ahk'ir* (Wisdom n.d.). Constance Classen has gone so far as to characterize the present-day Tzotzil Maya as primarily stressing a "thermal" system of hot and cold balances (1993:122–126). The emphasis on sweatbaths at many Maya cities suggests a similar concern among the Classic Maya (Houston and Evans 2001), but there was surely much more to the Classic Maya sensorium beyond solar heat and its absorption by humans.

Tastes could be "sour" or "acidy" (Ch'orti': *su't*, from an earlier term for "return" or "stomach reflux," **sut;* Kaufman and Norman 1984:131), closely related to the perception of "bitterness" or "gall" (Ch'orti': *ch'ah;* Colonial Tzotzil: *ch'a;* Common Ch'olan: **ch'ah*) or "sourness" in the stomach" (Ch'orti': *pah;* Kaufman and Norman 1984:118; Laughlin 1988, 2:517–518; Wisdom n.d.). "Bitterness" was linked in Colonial Tzotzil to the odor of incense, and "flavor" itself to the "delicious, fragrant wind" or, perhaps, "essence," *muil'ik'*, showing a clear understanding of how the senses were experientially linked (Laughlin 1988, 2:517). Something without taste was "sterile," "flat," "diluted," "unsweetened" (Ch'orti': *pax*), as in the tasteless part of a banana, *upaxir e kene'* or soil that will not grow, *pax e rum* (Wisdom n.d.). "Sweet" was, in most lowland languages, *chi'* or *ki'*.

The other principal attributes concerned whether something was "hard" or "soft." This often related to consumable plants, so that maize or beans could be "hard" or "ripe" (Ch'olti': *tzatz;* Ch'orti': *intzatz nar* [maize cob] or *intzatz bu'ur* [beans] and *nehpah;* Wisdom n.d.; also Common Ch'olan: **nejep'*, "half-ripe," "old-man"; Kaufman and Norman 1984:126). A tough, gristly thing, like cartilage, artery, or muscle, was *chich*. Softer, more flexible, tender things, like the impotent penis, a nipple, the inner part of the lips, are *k'un* or *pak* in Ch'orti', **k'un* or **pak,* "bend over," in Common Ch'olan (Kaufman and Norman 1984:124, 128). The first word is more likely to refer to flesh, and the second, to woody things. As for the skin, it could be irritated (*inxe'k',* "pierce," in Common Ch'olan; Kaufman and Norman 1984:136) or massaged with the palm of the hand (*lahba*), a term that turns up in Classic words for "drum," *lajab'* (Chapter 8).

The frustrating problem with such rich terminology is that very little of it can be found in the Classic sources. The adjective *ch'aj* appears to label the contents of a container that may have held tobacco snuff or *atole* (Chapter 3; M. Coe 1973:75; Grube 1990b:fig. 6), and the word for incense itself, *ch'aaj,* and, possibly, the person who deploys it, *ch'ajoom,* occur widely in the Classic corpus of texts, including one small vessel that takes on the role of incense holder, *u ch'ok ch'ajoom* (M. Coe 1973:137). Yet we cannot find any of the other terms for flavor, as much as they are connoted by mouth-watering displays of tamales streaked with sauce or vessels brimming with pulque or by the texts on such vessels. Was the reaction to the very experience of flavor far less important than its formal production, recitation of contents, and display? In this we see no evidence of gastronomic commentary among the Classic Maya, none of the specialized haute cuisine that came into existence with Jean-François Vatel in seventeenth-century France (Trubek 2000:145).

As for "touch," this sense must be inferred by textual cues in Maya imagery. Maya vessels that show textile designs—a vast majority of them, in fact—connote coverings that impart a distinctive "feel" to the viewer. The same holds true for feline pelage, which would have been "soft" and, like the textiles, intensely valuable: such simulacra connote high value and make the objects thus adorned choice and deluxe. From their pottery and their sculptures, it would seem that the Classic Maya did not esteem rough, unpolished surfaces—that tactile experience was best left for those wretches lugging water from reservoirs, wells, and rivers. The fleshiness of plump women and well-fed lords figured in some local traditions of imagery, but not in all. One set of nearly contemporary pots, probably from the area of Lake Peten Itza in northern Guatemala, exulted in the fatness of its lords, their bellies draped out over concealed waistlines. This plumpness invites the touch to poke and "feel" its softness. In the same way, the god markings on deities project a notion of "hardness" along with "shininess," of inhuman flesh that has an adamantine strength and no give. Similarly, Maya jades gave a slippery feel that must have appealed to them, along with a delight in strong surface color, very much in contrast to earlier Olmec fascination with translucence and filtered light.

The social and erotic nature of touch was clear in Early Modern Europe, where the desire and need to sense with the hands or skin struck many with deep ambivalence, something wished for at some basic level of comfort yet also perceived as polluting or contaminating (Harvey 2003:12–13). Several scholars suggest that ideas about "tactility," the nature and meaning of social touch, changed over time, as in the shift from the midwife's use of hands to the cold, obstetrical instruments of the modern doctor (Keller 2003:80). Classic Maya tactility is equally revealing: rulers were never touched, and they stood or sat apart. Only captives, lecherous couples, drunkards, or children invaded the space around another person. Captors on the field of battle express the same revulsion of touch by grasping the hair, not the body, of their captive.

SECRECY AND THE UNSENSED

Any discussion of the senses needs to examine things that are not disclosed and cannot be sensed yet are known to exist. As a concept, "secrecy" implies deliberate concealment, a withholding from those who wish to know. It takes considerable energy to maintain secrets and a self-conscious evaluation of others' need to access that information (Kelly 2002:3). Secrets do not exist in isolation. They are secrets kept *from* someone, even from other groups within a particular community (Brandt 1980:132–135). In a pioneering study of these matters, Georg Simmel suggested that secrets had a triadic or three-part quality. Two people were needed to share a secret and to keep it from, at a minimum, another person, for three in total

(Simmel 1992:383–455). To Simmel, the choice of whether to talk or not to talk was necessarily an individual one, even if such a breach might be condemned by society as a whole (Kippenberg and Stroumsa 1995:xiii, xxiv).

Practically, secrets are better preserved through oral transmission. By their very permanence and transparency, written records lead, at least potentially, to damaging cases of "leakage" (Brandt 1980:134). In many mystical traditions, concealment implies a set of truths that can only be revealed to initiates. To announce secrets indiscriminately would be irresponsible, even reprehensible. Yet the urge to discover secrets, a knowledge at once forbidden and coveted, can be strong—indeed, it is in the very advertising that a secret exists that those holding secrets acquire authority and distinction (Urban 2001:5, 214). The key is to let people know that secrets exist, but not to reveal them. In much the same way, if this kind of learning is possessed by marginal and disenfranchised people, then it can be seen as threatening or destabilizing. The likelihood is that it will be censured and repressed (Lattas 1998:289). Several scholars have argued that the expansion of magic and sorcery in late Classical Antiquity resulted from a growing sense of "private life" and an increasing feeling of disempowerment (P. Brown 1970; P. Long 2001:47, 70–71; Veyne 1987:33–49). Could it be that this is why the use of caves, inherently dark, intimate, and difficult of access, grew so markedly among the Classic Maya?

Colonial Tzotzil refers to secrets by the metaphor of "burying," as in *muktal k'op,* a "buried word" (Laughlin 1988, 1:451). Colonial Yukatek uses a similar expression, *mukbail,* "secret thing," and perceives such concealment as, apparently, a good act, since *ah bal uts* is someone who can, until the proper occasion arises, modestly conceal good intentions by hiding them behind something else (Acuña 1984, 1:5v). Tzendal, too, refers to *mukul,* "secrets," as "things kept in the heart," *otani,* and Ch'orti', as "images, portents, or signs," *ma cheker,* that "cannot be seen," that are "secret" (J. Robertson n.d.; Wisdom n.d.). Its close relative, Ch'olti', describes "secrets" as things revealed in stories, *tzolo,* the narrative being understood as the repository of hidden things (Ringle n.d.). The afflictions of "blindness," "deafness," and "muteness," are partly related: in Ch'orti, *ma cheker uut* means "no images of the face," and this and other maladies are regarded as grave losses, *satba'ar uti',* "mouth gets lost," or *satba'ar u chikin,* "ear gets lost," in which the relevant body part comes to represent the handicap (Wisdom n.d.). Other terms include Ch'olti' *coc,* "deaf," and *mem,* "mute," which respectively derive from Common Ch'olan **kohk* and a word that may be related to Yukatek *memel,* "imperfect thing" (Barrera Vásquez 1980:520; Kaufman and Norman 1984:123; Ringle n.d.).

Classic Maya buildings are as much about exclusion as inclusion. They are places where sacred objects reside, seldom seen and only under special conditions by advantaged people, and palaces are where the wealthy live, engaging in domestic activities and dynastic celebrations that were known to exist but were attended, perhaps, by few. An ethnographic account of the Ch'orti' Maya by Charles Wisdom states that the gods dwell in darkness (Wisdom 1940:431). In Classic society, there may have been secret things and behaviors that were absolute, unsuspected by most, and relative, meaning that they could be heard from afar, or that there was a sacred effigy known to exist in an unapproachable temple up high, or that there were rooms occupied exclusively by members of certain societies, perhaps organized by age grade. This is exemplified by the small "god houses" carved in stone at Copan, each of which could be covered in part with small curtains (Fig. 4.30). In such cases, it was important to accentuate exclusivity by making others aware of their exclusion. Access to those mysteries involved privilege and initiation into the mysteries in a process of being setting apart. Hieroglyphic texts among people of limited literacy can be divulged by those willing to read aloud. But, until that time, they stand mute.

CLASSIC MAYA SENSES

As cultures differ in many ways, so does their conception of the senses. The senses attain central importance because they channel how we regard the world and they explain how the world is influenced by creative, willful projections from the eyes and mouth, as well as from and to the ears, hand, and tongue. The meta-sensory expressions that are described in this study may have reached their most overt and elaborate expression in Maya civilization of the Late Classic period, but their roots penetrated deeper in time, and ethnographic parallels suggest a continued presence to this day. The acts of perception and cognition were near instantaneous and thus indistinguishable, hence their perceived fusion into a single event. Similarly, regardless of society, binocular and peripheral vision oriented the body in space. But meanings and social position consistently intervened: within Mesoamerica in general, and the Classic Maya region in particular, peripheral vision acquired moral and hierarchical significance; the perfume of flowers enchanted the socially privileged; sound and hearing related to heated oratory; and "empty" or unsensed, veiled spaces flickered and filled with lambent meaning. Such effects were communicated through ingenious synesthetic codes that were visual, graphic, and permanent. Of all the senses, those of taste and touch remain the least understood, mostly because the Maya did not bother to expound on their properties.

Mesoamerican and Maya signs for sound, smell, and sight are notably similar and typically feature gently outcurving pairs of volutes. These

Fig. 4.30. Curtained deity house, Copan (after Freidel et al. 1993:fig. 4:4).

senses significantly overlap in ancient Mesoamerican thought. Thus the sound of speech or song would be metaphorically expressed through beautiful aromatic flowers or shining jade. Sound and scents appear to have been especially integrated and related closely to concepts of the soul and the afterlife. In all of this there is strong evidence that the Classic Maya adopted a "projective" or "extramissive" model of the senses. The body reached out to experience the world, not the reverse. The sinuous curves denoting the senses in ancient Maya writing and art are also one of the most striking characteristics of the Classic Maya style, and they are seen in portrayals of human bodies and facial features as well as in cloth, feathers, and other elements of costume. Michael Coe (1973:91) notes the sinuous nature of ancient Maya art: "Like the practitioners of Art Nouveau around 1900, the finest Classic Maya artists were obsessed with the 'whiplash line.'" For the Classic Maya, such curving lines were particularly "sensual," as they replicated the forms used to portray qualities of sight, sound, and scent. As a visual embodiment of sensual communication, Classic Maya art evokes qualities attributed to the senses. There seems also to have been a privileged position accorded to fragrant smell, whose presence evoked the "good life" in this world and the next. These and all sensory experiences must be understood, not as ordinary and everyday, but as singular episodes that stand out from others: Maya texts and imagery do not exalt the mundane but the exceptional. That is why they were thought worthy of record. Although idealized and conventionalized, such representations were treated as though they were the most real of the real—they were moments of authentic experience in its most distilled, self-conscious form.

Left to the very end is the topic of the distorted senses: of the drunkenness described elsewhere in this book, of the visions summoned by acts of conjuring (*tzahk*) and discerned in clouds of incense, and of the things—frightening apparitions—"seen" in dark caves. Drawing on work by a number of scholars, from David Lewis-Williams (2002) to Gerardo Reichel-Dolmatoff (1978a), William and Anita Haviland (1995) have detected "entoptic" images in Maya evidence, which are the neurologically encoded forms, often geometric in shape, that characterize the dark zones of rock art from Paleolithic France to South Africa. In other words, these would be the leavings of senses deranged by hallucinogens, sleep or food deprivation, or even blood loss. They are, to Lewis-Williams (2002:124–126), an "intensified trajectory" of consciousness that involves all five senses and lies outside the normal drift into sleep. There is a certain appeal to this "universalist" explanation for Maya designs, but it falters on two points: we cannot know, beyond speculation, the circumstances behind the creation of these shapes, nor is it clear that we benefit from comparing the occupants of royal Maya courts, as the Havilands do, to hypothetical shamans from remote prehistory or those living within very different societies. Nonetheless, we can be certain that the Maya understood the mental effects of inebriation, denial of light and abrogation of the senses within caves or darkened chambers, bloodletting, and, finally, fasting, which provided so many visions of holy bliss to the "fasting virgins" of Medieval Europe and later (Christian 1981:68–69; Vandereycken and van Deth 1994: 29). But is it reasonable to expect the Maya to "see" or experience their deities only through physical adjustments of this sort? That explanation rings of modern skepticism. It may well be that faith and the believing senses detected a supernatural world that was, to the Classic Maya, both "natural" and pervasive. Spirits existed *materially* all around them, relict in stone and fully perceptible to human senses.

CHAPTER FIVE ◂▸

Emotions

Can we ever access and understand the ancient Maya expressions of rage, love, mourning, and exultation? The vagaries of history and culture make that question difficult to answer. Yet we believe that empathy and analysis allow us to understand emotions in very different times and places (R. Rosaldo 1984:192–193; Spiro 1986:282). The problem is in weighing what is legitimately and plainly clear to all against the differences prompted by culture and history. At the nub of this chapter are categories of feeling—anger, love, shame, grief, and happiness, among others. Each is freely recognizable to any observer, regardless of background. At the same time, they are inherently elusive because of the slightly different meanings they convey. After all, even when placed in particular categories, emotions are always prompted by particular circumstances and social settings. To some people, such as those in Europe before Aristotle, it was not ever clear that the "emotions," *pathe* in his coinage, belonged in the same category: many feelings responded to pleasure and need, others to pain and avoidance—how could they share anything at all (W. Harris 2001:402; McLemee 2003:A14–A15; Rosenwein 2002:836)? It is also true that we are at a double disadvantage as scholars of a remote time. Unlike ethnographers, who have living informants to clarify obscure points, the emotions represented by the Classic Maya are accessible only through representations of passions or, if from literate traditions, of stylized emotions thought suitable for written display. There are many filters here, some quite cloudy. Those filters get even more smudged when we consider the problem of relating expressions, such as the texts and images under study here, to *experience,* which is impossibly distant, taking place as chemical and perceptual processes within a single person's brain (Dilthey 1976:175). This is where we must speak of "intersubjectivity," a bond of empathy, of shared understandings, that allows us to feel as others feel. Distinguishing between "experience" and "*an* experience," Wilhelm Dilthey (1976:210) defined the first as mere existence, the second as a distinct episode, lush and personally transformative. By the process of recording in stone and other imperishable media, the Classic Maya stressed a set of singular experiences over the unremarked monotony of daily life.

But there are advantages to evidence left by the Maya. Their representations of the human body are, for the ancient Americas, unusually expressive, with a degree of verisimilitude or "naturalism" that is deceptively transparent to our Western gaze (Fig. 5.1). As a label, naturalism suggests an unstudied, near-photographic directness between the human subject and the object (or "portrait") that depicts it (Brilliant 1991:7–8). Nonetheless, Classic Maya imagery is conventionalized, and, as explained in Chapter 2, our customary distinction between image and original collapses into shared identities and presences, involving effigies that both represent and *are* the things they portray. Attention to details of body and clothing probably did not arise from quite the same doctrine of shared identities, since these concepts pervade other, more schematic representational styles in Mesoamerica. But they do indicate a choice or strategy of depiction that emphasizes the recording of minute details, including faces and bodies in torment, lust, and grief. Maya imagery stressed close observation of an external world in all its subtle variety. These images provide sufficient raw material for understanding how certain passions were selected for display and what was meant by them.

EMOTION, SENTIMENT, AND AFFECT

The ethological or behavioral study of emotion goes back in its modern form to the time of Charles Darwin, who saw feelings and their outward manifestations as signals of human intention and as salves or facilitators of social interaction (Darwin 1998; Ekman 1980). Darwin's larger goal was to draw parallels between human and animal expression and, by implication, to discern universals in primary emotional states, an effort categorically disclaimed by some (Barrett 1993; Birdwhistell 1970:29–30; Ortony and T. Turner 1990) and strongly defended by others (Ekman et al. 1987). A later investigator, Alfred Radcliffe-Brown, focused on "sentiments," a series of linked feelings organized without conscious intent into systems for regulating conduct (1964:234–237). His advance was in suggesting that emotions varied by society, and that they conformed systematically to the needs and impositions of social structure: "The sentiments in question are not innate but are developed in the individual by the action of the society upon him" (Radcliffe-Brown 1964:234). The personality and culture school of American anthropology, typified by the works of Ruth Benedict, built on these observations in ways unforeseen by (and probably unappealing to) Radcliffe-Brown. For Benedict and her colleagues, emotions operated in particular cultures as attributes of "national character" or "cultural configurations" (Benedict 1959:51–53; see also Daun 1996:111–134). Useful as cross-cultural comparison, these views could just as easily—and often did—descend into caricature and stereotype, such as the image of the amorous Italian or the depressive Swede.

Since then, two principal ideas about emotions have emerged. The first asserts that anger, love,

Fig. 5.1. "Naturalism" in Classic imagery, detail of bench, Temple XIX, Palenque; note details of cloth (drawing by David Stuart).

shame, joy, and other passions are largely physiological and basic to human nature, without any necessary influence from culture or society. To claim the opposite is, in one notable riposte, little more than "rubbish" (Leach 1981:32). This physiological or biological approach has been described as "universalist" or "positivist" (C. Lutz and White 1986:406). It views emotions as the result of chemical and electrochemical interactions between brain structures introduced at different moments in the evolutionary career of human beings (Damasio 1999:280–281). In its less extreme form, this approach regards the emotions as internal feelings with a natural origin, yet, following Radcliffe-Brown, may also acknowledge the role of overt "sentiments," which invoke norms and appear ideally in certain well-established contexts (C. Lutz and White 1986:409, 410). William Reddy has described this theory, which he endorses, as one in which emotions are "largely (but not entirely) learned," the emphasis being on two things: the fact that there is often "deep goal relevance and mental control" to emotions, and the proviso of being "not entirely" learned (2001:xi, 32). As such, the emotions spring from an "open genetic program" that is subject to modification and adjustment during the lifetime of an individual (Mayr 1974:652; see also Darwin 1998:386; Konner 1982:150–151, 207). A mind-body dualism—the mind assembling the "sentiments," the body experiencing the "emotions"—is implicit in these descriptions. To these ideas comes a firm objection from Michelle Rosaldo, who argues persuasively "that feeling is forever given shape through thought and that thought is laden with emotional meaning . . . [feelings] are *embodied* thoughts, thoughts steeped with the apprehension that 'I am involved'" (1984:143; emphasis in original).

The second perspective, very much in agreement with Rosaldo's, interprets the emotions as social constructions, or at least as an "ethos" of culturally arranged feelings (Bateson 1958:32; C. Lutz 1988). Feelings come into play according to particular situations or scenarios involving specified audiences. In its more extreme form, this perspective of "ethos" might be described as "constructionist," in that it accords little if any weight to the possibility of universal emotional attributes (Reddy 1997:329). Rather, all is "constructed" by people influenced by culture and history. An intermediate view contends that emotion and sentiment are physical experiences that nevertheless take place in social settings (Kövecses and Palmer 1999:253). This approach, which we endorse readily, allows universalist and constructionist models to be reconciled by seeing them as complementary descriptions of linked phenomena (Hinton 1999:9–10). Another means of bridging internal states and external perceptions is by using the term *affect,* defined by Niko Besnier as "the subjective states that observers ascribe to a person on the basis of the person's conduct" (1990:421). Affect is inherently a social understanding, collectively held but credited to another human being through an act of individual empathy: to see someone cry is to feel vicarious distress, having cried ourselves at some point in our career as human beings.

Ancient images can neither document ethnographic subtleties nor resolve difficult issues in cross-cultural psychology. However, they can reveal what was thought compelling enough for permanent record. Through such displays, long-deceased informants highlight concepts of importance to them, at great convenience to those who no longer have access to this information. The art historian Ernst Gombrich (1996:121, 123) has described displays of emotion or "expression" in terms of "pictographic" modes designed to facilitate nonverbal communication. Contexts help determine the meaning of certain gestures and allow a gesture of the hand or the look on a face to engage and move the viewer. Of necessity, the entire process relies on conventional images understood by artist and spectator alike—this conventionalization helps communicate the meaning of an expression (Montagu 1994:105–106). Another art historian, David Freedberg, has similarly focused on the intentions behind images, which require "a public trained to respond in particular ways to particular scenes" (1989:169). Robert Levy (1973:324–325; 1984:218–219; see also Besnier 1993:80) points usefully to the variable visibility or prominence of affect, with consequences for visual displays of it. Some emotions, those best described as *hypercognated,* can be elaborately labeled and articulated in particular societies; other, *hypocognated* emotions are muted, ignored, or, in his words, "underschematized." Note that "hypocognated" does not mean the same thing as unexpressed. The latter, although not immediately visible, could still have been discussed and analyzed—or felt. Unfortunately, it is impossible to reconstruct precisely how images might have been received (Iser 1978), even in the most abundantly documented instances from the historical past (Meskell 2000:737). Any presumed empathy is potentially misleading, since the "trained public" mentioned by Freedberg is long gone, and contextual clues are no longer as obvious as they once were. But, by their very selection, these displays of emotion represent hypercognated affect and, as such, penetrate to the core of culturally prominent feelings. They are our key to the ancient Maya "heart."

MAYA EMOTIONS IN LATER SOURCES

The anthropology of emotion among the Maya, both ancient and modern, is still underdeveloped. Much of it, particularly anger, relates to the heart (e.g., R. Hill and Fischer 1999; Laughlin 1988, 2:577–597), perhaps for the universalist reason that strong emotion triggers a rapid heartbeat. But the "heart" does not seem to have been so much an organ as the place of desire (Chapter 1). For example, the actual muscle and attached blood vessels, the "material heart" or *corazón material,* was known as *puczical* in Ch'olti'; *puksík'al* in Yukatek; *pucsikal* in Acalan, a Colonial form of Chontal; and *ki'* in Ch'orti', with "heart pain" being a "bite" of that organ, *k'ux ki'* (Barrera Vásquez 1980:673; Ringle n.d.; J. Robertson n.d.; Smailus 1975:164). These terms are not clearly present in the hieroglyphs, although physical hearts do occur in imagery. The heart that "feels" and "motivates" is known generally by other roots. In Yukatek it is *ol—ohl* in the Classic inscriptions—the locus of will, intent, and reason, although that notion is sometimes extended to the physical organ, too (Barrera Vásquez 1980:604, 673). The Classic Maya do not speak of "sin," a particular preoccupation of Colonial priests, but there is, in Tzendal, *otanil mulil,* "sin of the heart" (J. Robertson n.d.). In all cases, *otan* probably bears a close connection to the glyph read as *ohl-tahn,* "heart-chest." This is also reflected in Colonial Tzotzil, a language closely related to Tzendal, which has *'olal* or *'olil* for "heart" as well as "unquiet thing," and *'olontonil,* "heart, mind," which only drops the /l/ in modern Tzotzil *'o'onil* (Kaufman 1972:113; Laughlin 1988, 1:154, 2:405).

The *-ton* in Colonial Tzotzil is plainly the same word as *tan* or *tahn,* "chest," in the other languages (Chapter 1). This means that all of the dictionary entries above, from *otan* in Tzendal to *'olonton* in Colonial Tzotzil, rest on the same set of meanings, all linking will, human impulse, and emotion to the upper torso, a generalized center of the body. Clues from the Classic period confirm the etymology: *yohl-tahnil,* "his heart/mind," perhaps in the sense of "existence" or "sentience," occurs in connection with a royal birth at Palenque, as though this were the individual state achieved at delivery (Fig. 5.2; Palace Tablet, C7, M. G. Robertson 1985b:fig. 258). Even the more stylized forms of the Classic glyph for "chest," *tahn,* represent the solar plexus with dots for the belly button and two nipples. In hieroglyphic writing, this body sector supplied a body term, a spatial orientation, to mean "within" or "in the middle." The *ohl* seems to have disappeared from some languages of highland Guatemala and Chiapas, replaced by the Spanish word for "soul," *ánima.* Examples of this are Jacaltec *ánma* and Mam *-aní:m* (L. Campbell 1988:223). Still, it appears certain that the human body could only "feel" or process emotions by means of something outside the heart: this conduit was, evidently, the "ear," so that "to feel" or "to perceive" in Common Ch'olan was **ub-i,* with a joint meaning of "to hear" (Kaufman and Norman 1984:135; see also Tzendal *abi,* "to understand, enjoy, hear, feel" [J. Robertson n.d.], a term that is related to Colonial Tzotzil, *'a'i,* again with the consonant replaced by a glottal stop [Laughlin 1988, 1:127]).

What of the emotions themselves? Of the positive, there are several terms for physical desire, such

Fig. 5.2. *Yohl tahnil*, Palenque Palace Tablet, C7 (after M. G. Robertson 1985b:fig. 258).

as Common Ch'olan **yah*, "desire, love" (Kaufman and Norman 1984:137), often in the sense of urgent, almost covetous need, as in Colonial Tzotzil *k'up*, Acalan *kupan*, or Ch'orti' *t'un*, "appetite, craving, lust" (Laughlin 1988, 1:238; Smailus 1975:154; Wisdom n.d.). Acalan also has the root *yahin*, "love," and Tzendal uses *yal cotan*, "fall in love," and *yacub yotan*, "become passionate with love" (Smailus 1975:177). There is an inkling from Yukatek that this concept is akin to "pain," something strong, an emotion that shivers throughout the body (Barrera Vásquez 1980:958). This is spelled out in Ch'olti', which directly connects such passion with "to torment," *yalauel* (Ringle n.d.). Ch'ol, too, employs the word "bite, pain" as part of an expression for "love," *k'uxbintel* (Josserand and Hopkins 1988, 2:17).

Visceral sensations contrast with states of less physical love or generalized happiness—or at least we suspect so, despite the eerie resemblance to Christian notions of physical and pure love. St. Augustine in his "Handbook" and Bishop Latimer in his sermons both wrote eloquently about the distinction between carnal love or "animal affection" and the "charitable love" that defined good works. Such theological ideas must have influenced the clerics who recorded Mayan languages in the Colonial period. Nonetheless, not all of this was introduced. Tzendal employs a term for "flower" or "blossom," *nich*, as part of these expressions, including *nichim yotan*, "flowery his heart," which means "happy" (J. Robertson n.d.); the same term for "flower" may be found in Ch'ol (Josserand and Hopkins 1988, 2:24), and, on Tortuguero Monument 6, it occurs in Classic times as a way of describing offspring. That state is brought about by a more sentimental love, occasionally used in later Christian liturgy among the Maya as a way of describing God's "mightier power of love" (Augustine 1996, Chapter XXXI:118): thus Ch'olti has *chohben*, "to love," or *chohbia*, "love," as does its living relative, Ch'orti', *chohbe*, "love, desire, esteem," from which comes, in Ch'olti, the state of "being gladdened," *chichael*, much like Acalan *ch'ach'an*, "to be content" (Smailus 1975:139). In Yukatek, this is the condition of having a "straight" or "right heart," the *toj ol* (Barrera Vásquez 1980:802); here, as mentioned in Chapter 1, the Maya privilege the right over the left. At such moments, people "laugh," **tze'* in Common Ch'olan, *tze'nal* in Ch'ol, or "mock," such as Colonial Tzotzil *tze'* (Josserand and Hopkins 1988, 2:33; Kaufman and Norman 1984:13; Laughlin 1988, 1:172), or their "hearts laughing," Tzendal *tse'el (y)o'tan*. And those who walk together as companions by definition exhibit "friendship," Tzendal *ghoyil* (J. Robertson n.d.).

Negative emotions are common, too. "Fear" in Common Ch'olan can be reconstructed as **bahk'ut* (Kaufman and Norman 1984:116) and also occurs as *bakat* in Acalan (Smailus 1975:129); *bacat* in Ch'olti' (Ringle n.d.); and *ba'k'ta'ar*, "timidity, lack of aggressiveness,'" in Ch'orti' (Wisdom n.d.). The more ancient term, from Common Mayan **xi'w*, also appears in Mayan lowland languages (Kaufman and Norman 1984:116). Tzendal contains *xivon*, "to fear, place in shadow," but also with the sense of deferring fearfully to those of higher station, *xiavanon*, "honor, revere" (J. Robertson n.d.). It is possible that the glyphic syllable [xi], which shows a human skull with dots, relates in some way to this concept (Fig. 5.3), as does the broadly disseminated term "Xibalba" for the underworld (Kaufman and Norman 1984:136).

The fearful heart can also be "lazy" and without vigor (*k'oy* in Ch'orti'), rather like shapeless dough, the same word being reconstructible in Common Ch'olan (Kaufman and Norman 1984:124). Or the

EMOTIONS

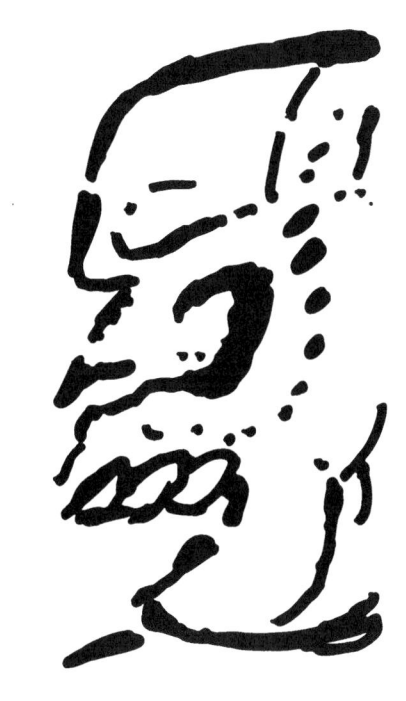

Fig. 5.3. The [xi] syllable (after A. Stone 1995a:fig. 8.18).

heart can be full of self-regard (Ch'orti': *sa'ran*, "boastful, vain") that, in related terminology, Colonial Tzotzil couples with states of confusion or mistrust, probably as a moralizing gloss on self-delusion (Laughlin 1988, 1:293). The enraged, choleric person shows *loquil loquil* in Ch'olti', the duplication indicating a high level of intensity and the terms themselves linked to words for "exit" (*loq*) and "thunder forth," as when someone loses control and their rage emerges from the heart (Ringle n.d.). Colonial Tzotzil similarly has *loklon 'olonton*, "seethe with anger" (Laughlin 1988, 1:247). In Ch'olti', rage possesses an intensifying color, "red," and an unpropitious direction, the "south," *nool*. In the same language, the angry person is "bitter" or "sour," *chaic*, and may experience "rage" or be exiled to "places of rage," *illi* and *illib*, respectively (Ringle n.d.). In Tzendal, he or she "chews" again and again, grinding teeth in the utmost anger, *xax ghuy ghuy* (J. Robertson n.d.; cf. Laughlin 1988, 1:218, 301). From such imbalances, it seems, come only trouble and "sin," *mul* in virtually all lowland languages, where it may have the sense of being "drowned" or "covered," as in Tzendal *mul*, a root found with words meaning "to submerge under water" and "covered in filth" (J. Robertson n.d.). These states are "ugly" (*colal* in Tzendal), and lead to "bad" or "inhuman" people, the *te'te' vinic*, an enigmatic term that appears to relate to the "very wooden people," perhaps in reference to earlier, less successful creations of humanity mentioned in the *Popol Vuh* (Christenson 2000:49–52). These were beings without real hearts and minds, perhaps in much the same way as the cruel, who do not exercise proper judgment.

CLASSIC MAYA AFFECT

The key hieroglyph "emotion" is a variant of the tamale glyph, ordinarily read as *waaj* (Love 1989; Geo. Stuart 1987:44–45; Taube 1989b). Not surprisingly, just as the "heart" served as the food par excellence of the gods, the sign seems also to have been read *ohl*, "heart, within," in many texts of the Classic Maya (Fig. 5.4). The reading became clear to scholars in the late 1980s, when it was noticed that the glyph often had clues to its initial vowel (the syllable [yo]) and other indications of its final consonant (the syllable [la]). Findings about spellings of long vowels or internal /h/ in the mid-1990s, along with new understandings of cognate forms, made it clear that the glyph could only read *ohl*, or *y-ohl* when possessed in the third person, "his, hers, its, theirs." These spellings were confirmed when completely syllabic variants were found, each of which specified exactly the sounds within the word.

Fig. 5.4. The *ohl* sign, anthropomorphic version, Palenque Tablet of the 96 Glyphs:H3 (after drawing by Linda Schele).

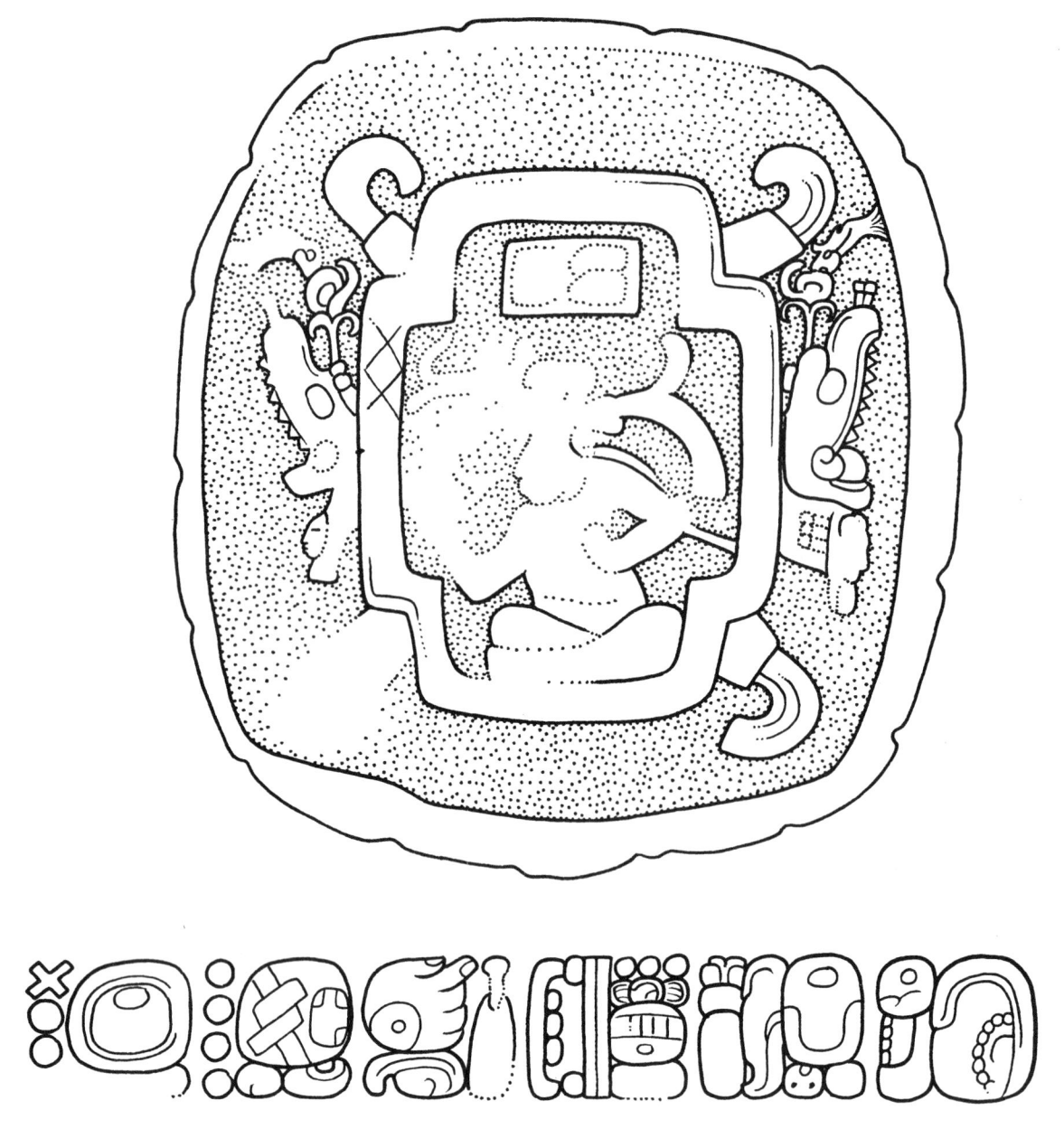

Fig. 5.5. El Peru altar (after drawing by Ian Graham).

The contexts for this sign begin with the locational sense of "inside" and "heartlike," as in an expression found by Stephen Houston and others at the site of El Peru (Fig. 5.5; see also Freidel et al. 1993:fig. 4:27): there a ruler "finishes his fifty-two years *tu-yohl ahk*," "within the turtle's heart." This event took place on an important date that evokes the beginning of things, 2 Imix (the day name that commences the Maya sequence of 20 days), and 4 Pop (the first month of the 365-day calendar). Mention of fifty-two years is hardly coincidental, as that is the merging date of both calendars and, perhaps, an average lifetime for most Classic Maya. The expression reveals that the Maya regarded the world as a floating turtle, within which humans sat, as shown in the image atop the altar displaying the text from El Peru. A similar scene occurs about the time of Christ on a stela from Izapa, Mexico (Fig. 5.6; Norman 1973:pl. 16). Such metaphors, which accord with other terrestrial ones, including a crocodile bearing emblems of time, occur frequently in Maya sculpture, even into the Postclassic period

EMOTIONS 187

Fig. 5.6. Izapa Stela 8, photograph and drawing (Norman 1973:pl. 16).

Fig. 5.7. Top of altar, Art Institute of Chicago (C37396.1971.895).

Fig. 5.8. Tonina Monument 69 (I. Graham and Mathews 1996:103).

and beyond (Taube 1988a:figs. 2a, 3–5; 1989a). The interplay of time and space is intensely inscribed on such objects: peripheries consist of hieroglyphs relating narratives or sequences of concluded time that pass around the margins of the turtle shell, which floats within, at once eternal and hedged by time. In other such images, as on an altar at the Art Institute of Chicago (Fig. 5.7), a deceased person has, twenty-six years after his death, become enshrined within such a cavity, his chest emblazoned with a mat for sitting and his right hand holding the head of the god K'awiil, a deity that, once taken, becomes an emblem of ancestors. Another apparent hole, on an altar from Tonina (Monument 69; Fig. 5.8), explicitly marks the surface on which the deceased sits as the body of a crocodile, another model for the terrestrial plane.

A second setting for the *ohl* sign relates to supernatural beings. The Classic Maya could refer to such beings individually, by name or title, and collectively, as in the epithet *kanal k'uh kabal k'uh,* "celestial gods, earthly gods," or the rather dizzying *1 pih k'uh,* "the eight thousand celestial gods, earthly gods"—the very ability to remember them must have constituted a rare and exclusive feat (Fig. 5.9). Another honorific used the *ohl* sign, in *ohlVs k'uh* (Fig. 5.10). The meaning of this is still unclear. The *-Vs* ending (again, the *V* simply means a variable or unknown vowel) implies that what comes before is a verb that is made into a noun by adding this suffix. If so, the expression might mean "the desiring gods," those who crave. It is still unclear why an inscription from Copan Stela B uses *mih-yohl,* "none are the hearts" of the earthly gods, the celestial gods (Fash 1991:fig. 17). Are the gods literally "heartless," or do they want for their distinctive food (see Chapter 3)? Strangely, this condition or state appears to coincide with a particular date in the Maya Long Count, 9.15.0.0.0; it also characterizes another inscription of this date at Copan on Altar S.

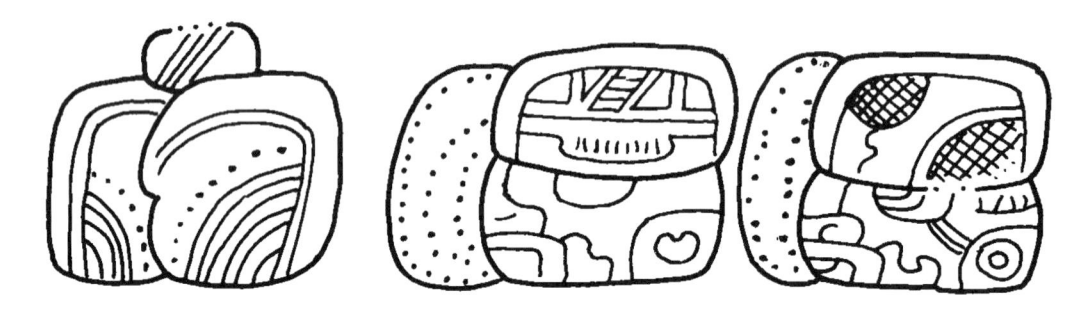

Fig. 5.9. Collective terms for gods, Tikal Stela 31:B13–B14 (after C. Jones and Satterthwaite 1982:fig. 52b).

Fig. 5.10. *OhlVs k'uh* (after Palenque Palace Tablet:E14–F14; M. G. Robertson 1985b:pl. 258).

Perhaps the most transparent examples of "desire" and "wishing" in the texts, and a certain reference to states of the heart, appear in a highly unusual scene from Palenque (Fig. 5.11). The setting is a disastrously jumbled array of stucco glyphs and figures that had crumbled off the interior surface of Temple 18 (Ringle 1996). This image presents what may have been a highly emotive scene, assembling a ruler and his grandsons, perhaps as part of an elaborate negotiation of power sharing or inheritance. Most of the grandsons are relatively young, as shown by their *ch'ok*, "youth," titles. One sequence, carefully reconstructed from piecing together fallen stuccos, reads *tz'akbu-aj awajawil matajaw*, "your lordships are assembled, *mat* Lord," presumably in reference to the heirs brought before the king, the *mat* Lord himself. Then, a central caption records *timaj awohl atz'ak'bu-ij* . . . , "your heart is *tim*-ed (by means of) your assembling of . . ." Another place in which the *tim* verb is used is on the West Tablet of the Temple of the Inscriptions, Palenque, where three passages in succession refer to *tim*. This is always recorded in reference to possessed terms for "heart," *ohl*, in the first case that of the Palenque gods, known generally as *k'uh*. *Tim* is not an especially common word, but it has two possible cognates in Yukatek. The first is *chimil ol*, "become irritated" (Barrera Vásquez 1980:100). The correspondence of /ch/ to /t/ is well documented in Yukatek and Ch'olan languages, so that, for example, Yukatek *chi'*, "mouth," ties to Ch'olan *ti'*. This means that *tim* is plausibly related to *chim*. The other possibility is a Yukatek expression *tem ol*, "satisfaction" or even "placation" (Barrera Vásquez 1980:783–784), but whether this has a secure relation to *tim* is not clear. The linguistic correspondence, if it exists, would be irregular (John Robertson, personal communication, 2003). What is certain is that the *tim* verb must indicate some state of the heart and its various agitations, good or bad.

But these glyphic references to emotion and stylized affect are limited. Of the full range of possible effusions, only a very small number make an appearance, a clear signal that, in Robert Levy's classification, the Classic Maya "hypercognated" emotions within their texts. The same is true for imagery, which presents only a few categories of obvious affect, most of which are identifiable to modern viewers with relatively little difficulty. The more usual image shows stolid warriors or expressionless queens and rulers. Even figures in dance appear to perform in barely perceptible motion,

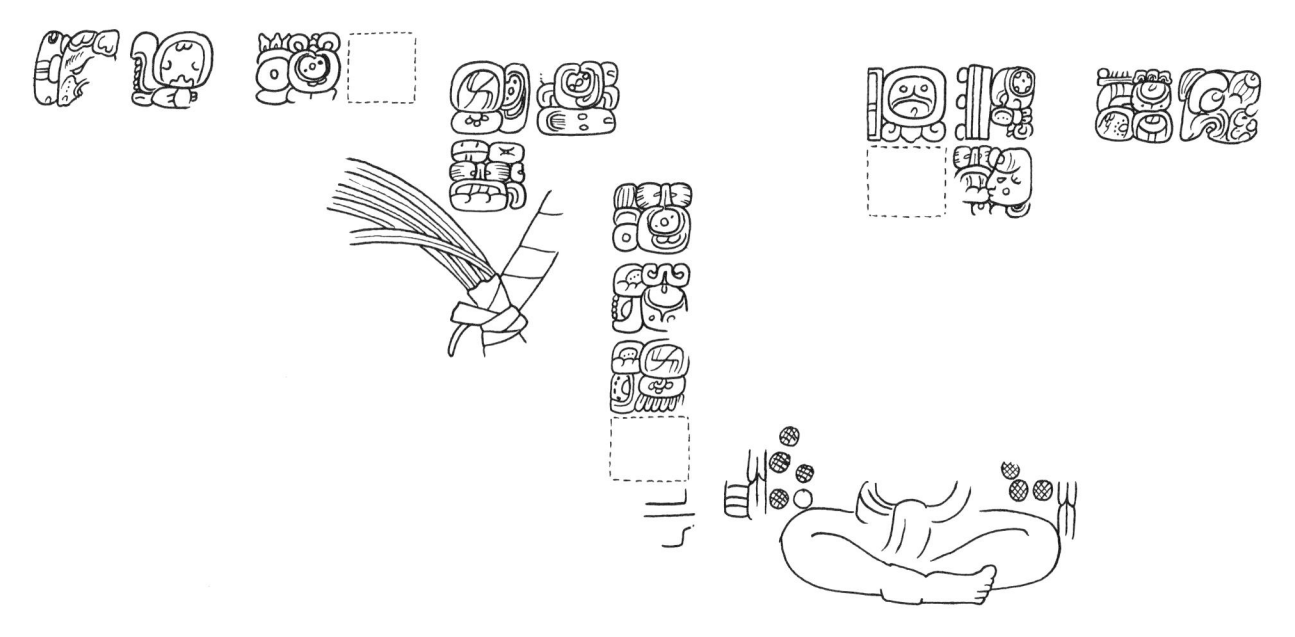

Fig. 5.11. Scene from Temple 18, Palenque (composite of drawings by Linda Schele, with information from Blom and La Farge [1926–1927, 1:fig. 135] and Ruz Lluillier [1958:fig. 18]).

with legs slightly bent, one foot lifted (Chapter 8; Grube 1992:fig. 16). At the same time, there existed a rich gestural language, with hands in various positions of animated gesticulation. As explained in Chapter 1, these signals might have been a rich mine (and mime) of affect, but the system underlying this language has proved strikingly resistant to interpretation (Ancona-Ha et al. 2000:1083; V. Miller 1983). Given the right "trained public" or appropriate contextual understanding, certain poses of the hand might well have elicited emotion, yet viewers will not easily understand the cues, and the effect is now lost to present-day spectators. Instead, the overriding impression one gathers of Classic imagery is of calculated restraint, decorous movement, and economy of expression—of bodily practices that were at once improvised and highly regulated (Appadurai 1990:92; Spinden 1913:31). These traits are fully consistent with the rigid etiquette and finely tuned social encounters that characterized court societies of the Classic Maya (Inomata and Houston 2001). Overt, bald emotion would seem to have been negatively valued by those making and commissioning these images.

The exceptions are all the more noteworthy for their rarity. The kinds of affect openly emphasized in Classic Maya imagery tend to fall into five categories, with little direct evidence that the Maya even recorded them as similar in organization and expression: (1) the terror and depression of captives; (2) drunken abandon or delirium; (3) lust; (4) grief and mourning; and (5) humor that prompts laughter through ridicule. The accompanying glyphs provide no "emotion words" for such scenes, but the imagery clearly represents bundles of emotion states (Tarlow 2000:716). The first category is by far the most abundant, in that captives represent a central theme in Classic Maya imagery. For them and for other minor figures, Maya artists reserved their most experimental and fluid depictions of the human body. By the seventh and eighth centuries AD, as at the sites of Yaxchilan and Bonampak, Chiapas, they succeeded in drenching some scenes with clear signs of their distress, including hands clenched in mouths, pitiable glances to their captors, and slumped resignation (Chapter 6; M. Miller 1999:153, 157). Representations of emotion, like the senses (Chapter 4), have histories that reflect changing views as well as firmly rooted continuities. An important shift in the representational resources of the Maya during the Late Classic period (AD 600–850) was a heightened transparency of emotions—aside from their contorted and deliberately uncomfortable body positions, captives in the Early Classic period typically register the same facial expressions as their tormentors.

Panel 15, a recently discovered monument from Piedras Negras, Guatemala, that dates to AD 706, illustrates the change (Fig. 5.12). The bodies of the captors—the ruler (Ruler 2), and two lieutenants—are shown in stiff vertical poses, eyes looking directly ahead and mouths closed. In contrast, the captives stroke their bodies, their mouths open, perhaps as cues for cries of pain or entreaty. Other related images indicate despair by the act of looking down (K5451). The format on Panel 15 (captives, ruler, two lieutenants with distinctive staffs and headdresses), begun in the reign of Ruler 2's father, Yo'nalahk (Panel 4, AD 658), achieved its most elaborate development on the front of Stela 12 (AD 795), which displays the same contrast between impassive victors and affect-laden images of the defeated. The exhibition of affect takes its meaning from this very contrast: the successful warriors exercise tight control over their self-presentation; the vanquished do not and thereby accentuate their humiliation and drastically reduced status. Maya depictions of captives vividly underscore the absence of self-restraint, in that hair is disheveled and arms are akimbo, again with evidence of acute physical discomfort, as in the anticipatory scene of garroting with ropes and sticks that is shown in Figure 5.13 (this action was evidently known as *hatza* or *biti* in Colonial-era Ch'olti', a language with strong connections to Mayan script). In some respects, captives are treated almost as bound game, and, indeed, the glyphic verb for "to capture" or "to seize" (*chuhkaj*) applies both to people and animals. Chapter 6, on dishonor, will show that pain and terror also played a strong role in Classic imagery, with figures screaming so forcefully that their jaws verge toward dislocation (Schele 1997:pls. 13, 14). Similarly, the glee of those inflicting pain marks the joyous, immoderate dance of death gods holding child sacrifices (K2213).

Maya imagery of the Classic period gives little evidence of compassion. Indeed, there are more than subtle hints of a pervasive iconography of odium and a culture of scarcely moderated aggression. Other royal courts provided antagonists and, as in Renaissance Italy, offered "a process in which [men] assimilated themselves to the group through provoking hereditary enemies" (Muir 1993:280). But the quarrels were directed outward: hatred targeting lowly people from the same community fails to appear in Classic Maya evidence, nor do the sources show that such humble subjects were involved to a noteworthy extent in quarrels between dynasties. Still, the likelihood is strong that more than a few were engaged in such vendettas, whatever their cause, and that emotions were crucial in showing the necessity of odium, the logic of joint strategy, and the need to get people motivated through various kinds of exhortations (Goodwin et al. 2001:6). The failure to excite such emotions will lead to the decline of collective identity (Goodwin et al. 2001:21).

Scenes of drunken abandon are far less common, but their most dramatic expression occurs in a monumental setting, at the Yucatec site of San Diego (Barrera Rubio and Taube 1987; Mayer 1984:pls. 143–149). The occasion is the ingestion of alcoholic drinks in enema rituals (Chapter 3). The figures are violently agitated and off balance, their hair unkempt and their faces occasionally obscured: clearly, as with captives, they are people no longer concerned with appearances and self-projection. A similar scene occurs on an unprovenanced vessel (Fig. 5.14; K1092; Reents-Budet 1994:fig. 3.14) that shows the consumption of agave brews by youths (*ch'ok*), perhaps in the men's houses attested ethnographically and archaeologically for the Maya (Tozzer 1941:124; Webster 1989:22). The age of the drinkers differs with custom in other parts of Mesoamerica, where drinking in small, nonintoxicating quantities by the elderly was acceptable, but draconian penalties awaited those who chose to ignore such injunctions (S. Coe 1994:84–87). Among the Aztec, hortatory tales moralize the excessive consumption of alcohol, which led, ineluctably it would seem, to material loss, exile, and other forms of punishment.

Lust in Classic Maya imagery can be recognized in several scenes. One typically shows an elderly man, chapfallen, scoliotic, and creased with wrinkles, fondling the breasts of a young woman or tending to a harem of beauties (Fig. 5.15; K4485; see also M. Miller 1999:fig. 139; Taube 1989c:367). There is some sense or hint that such scenes are seen as ludicrous or beyond the pale, the behavior of bad royalty as exemplified by the anticourts in some scenes on Maya pottery. Another discloses acts of bestiality between women and spider monkeys or, bizarrely enough, a woman and an insect, as on a well-known vessel from Uaxactun (Fig. 5.16). A smoking figure nearby tells us, by this convention, that the lewd fumblings are taking place at night. Other tableaux highlight women exposing themselves for sex with brocket deer. One woman touches her breast and strokes the lower jaw of a deer while the animal—the painter linking consumption to sex—chews on sweet plants (K2794). Some of the scenes are almost certainly representations of dances and doubtless the impersonations of supernaturals (Taube 1989c:371). A unique, recently excavated altar from Tonina, Chiapas, exhibits a scene of coupling, again with a female bearing prominently displayed breasts (Chapter 6, Fig. 6.4).

For a society that found the display of genitalia repugnant or distasteful—outsized, slightly tumescent genitalia occur mostly on captives and animals—these images must be understood as "marked," in the sense of out-of-the-ordinary, contrary to usual practice, and deserving of special notice. Moreover, the identity of some of the participants is patently supernatural, given their distinctive clothing and other attributes. Constructions of sexuality are as culturally informed here as elsewhere (Clarke 1998:7–18), and such images may be best explained, not as prurient erotica, but as comments on illicit, disapproved, or abnormal behavior, distinguished from everyday human acts by exceptional settings. The few Classic Maya images of sexual acts, including a painting apparently of an ejaculating member and another of autoeroticism, occur in the "dark zone"

Fig. 5.12. Piedras Negras Panel 15 (drawing by Stephen Houston).

of the Naj Tunich cave (Fig. 5.17), whose texts refer to pilgrimage visits and visions of supernatural paths or companion spirits (*il-bi, il-way*), hardly the stuff of commonplace behavior (A. Stone 1995a:figs. 8-17, 8-18, 8-20). The unique three-quarter view of the masturbator underscores the out-of-the-ordinary quality of the scene. One scene on a Late Classic vessel combines licentiousness with drunkenness and enema use, possibly in a sweatbath or the antechamber of such a building (Fig. 5.18; M. Coe 1978:pl. 11). Young women fan and massage old deities, all in attendance on Chaak, the storm god. As social commentary, such images may epitomize subtle and subversive

Fig. 5.13. Tonina stucco relief, showing three captives with sticks and ropes for garroting (after drawing in the Corpus of Maya Hieroglyphic Inscriptions Project, Peabody Museum, Harvard University).

parables of unrestrained rulers, again, as illustrations of "anti-courts" that inverted appropriate behavior. Strangely, many such anti-courts appear to be governed by a deity, God L, who is closely associated with trading. Did such figures, who engaged in economic practices beyond any one community, embody morally unscrupulous figures, as likely to cheat as to arrange fair bargains? The anxiety that underscored trade between figures jockeying for advantage may have been an issue here. Another, almost humorous expression of lust may be in what are called "full-figure" glyphs, the raucously interacting signs that occur at a number of different sites, often in pairs (e.g., Maudslay

Fig. 5.14. Drunken scene (K1092, copyright Justin Kerr).

1889–1902, 2:pls. 14, 15). Is there a possibility that joined signs were regarded metaphorically as forms of copulation?

The rarest affects are those of grief and mourning, so far found only on a few painted or incised vessels (Fig. 5.19; Schele and Mathews 1998:fig. 3.27). Now in Berlin, one is of Early Classic date and unknown provenance, but likely to be from northern Guatemala because of its textual allusion to the area of Lake Peten Itza. Although highly complex, the tableau presents an unmistakable scene of grief and mourning, again, however, in supernatural circumstances. The body is that of the Maize God, and his mourners are other maize deities (the metaphoric remnants of a crop or seed stored for another year?). It is likely that they are the corn maidens of the sort well attested in the American Southwest and among the Q'anjob'al of Guatemala (Benedict 1935:20–21; E. Parsons 1939:172; Peñalosa 1995:137); in our view, the notion that corn deities were ungendered or of mixed gender is incorrect (cf. R. Joyce 1996:182; Looper 2002:173). The Maize God's wrapped body lies atop a throne, and his solar, fiery soul rises above the bier. To either side the maidens weep, conceal their face, or raise their hand to their forehead in a Classic Maya gesture for death and lamentation, a pose also shown by dying Maize Gods on incised bones from Tikal, Guatemala. Once more, the affect makes its appearance in a "marked" or supernatural context. By Late Classic times, this scene had been stripped of most affect and signs of mourning, showing rather the dressing of the Maize God in the process of departing on a "journey," in Maya parlance a metaphor for death (*ochbil*; Robicsek and Hales 1981:fig. 82). Still, even in such scenes a few females look downward in apparent despair (Fig. 5.20). They gnaw their fingertips, contemplate the departed's jewelry, and wring their hands, but generally without the copious weeping of earlier times (Robicsek and Hales 1981:fig. 82). A Hero Twin, 1 Ajaw, his mouth

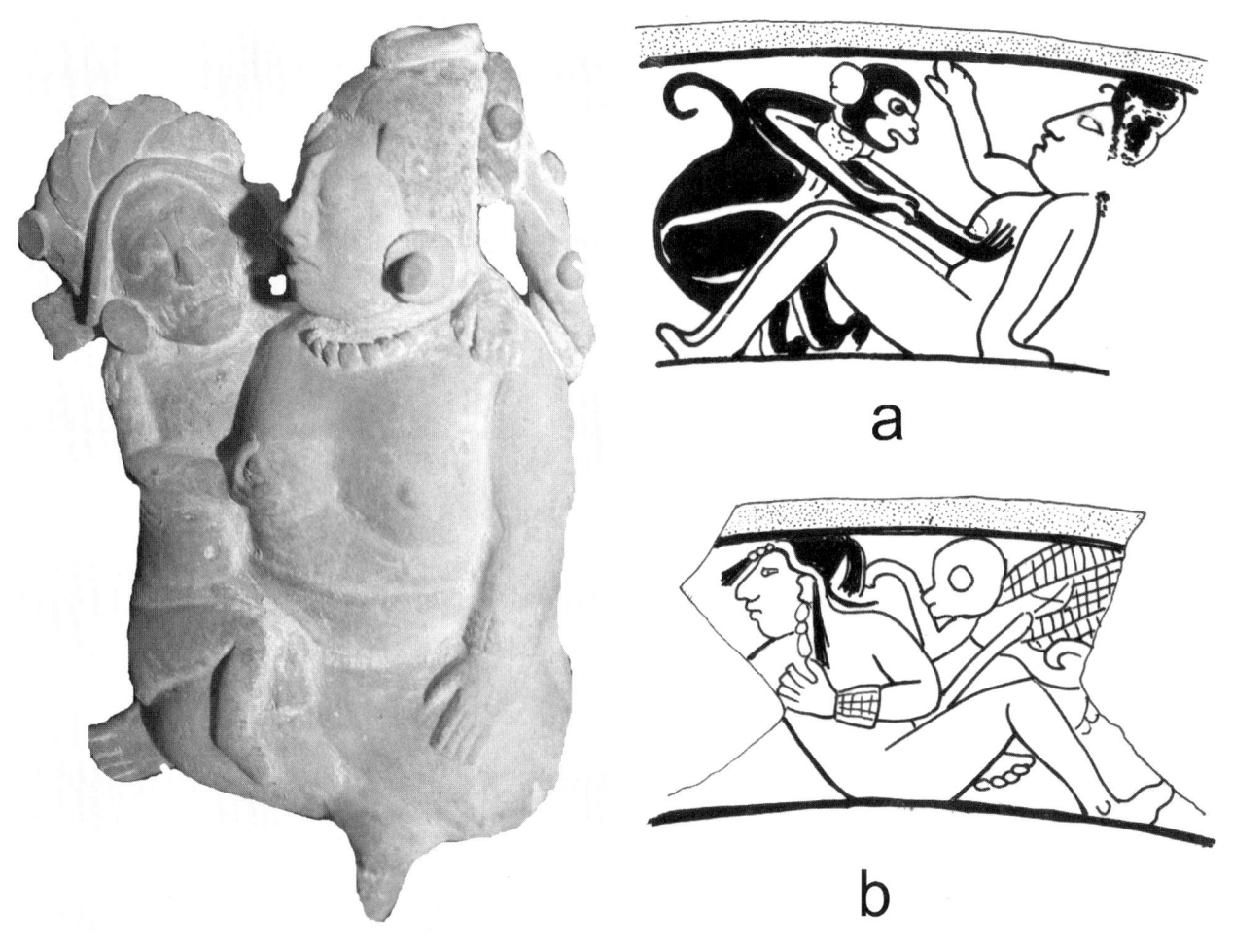

Fig. 5.15. A lecherous old god with a young goddess (photograph by David Stuart of unprovenanced Late Classic figurine).

Fig. 5.16. Scenes of cross-species lovemaking (after R. E. Smith 1955:fig. 2g).

emitting a scroll for excrement or fertilizer, has a seed bag around his neck, rather like the seed bags illustrated in Colonial sources on Aztec farming (Sahagún 1950–1982, 3:f. 30v). But what is worth noting here is the gendered quality of overt mourning, which is seen by Classic Maya, apparently, as a womanly activity. Moreover, the mourning resembles the weeping and bemoaning of intimates (T. Lutz 1999:198–201). In contrast to the Early Classic image, tears, the ejection of fluids, thought in some cultures to be inauspicious, have disappeared (T. Lutz 1999:211). The Late Classic period is a dry-eyed time, it seems.

An extraordinary codex-style vessel scene (K6979) that illustrates the death of the Maize God records a systematic set of contrasts between opposed states of emotion, all expressed by women (Fig. 5.21; M. Miller and Martin 2004:fig. 15). The first contrast is that between a live woman and a dead one, the first shown as a voluptuous maiden, with an earspool doing duty as a hair cinch. She sits on the right of the Maize God, in a position of honor and principal interaction. Across from her is a deceased maiden, with signs of death (the so-called percentage sign), an extruded eyeball in counterposition to the earspool on the other female, and banded eyes. Another series of contrasting pairs occurs on the other side of the vessel. One maiden displays the attributes of life; she raises a jade jewel and appears to be singing. A death figure—the same female as on the other side of the vessel?—exposes her breasts directly to the viewer, wrings her hair, and looks downward. The body is twisted to the side. Both are responses to death.

Fig. 5.17. A scene of autoeroticism, Naj Tunich cave, Guatemala (after A. Stone 1995a:fig. 8.20).

One involves decorous and solemn accompaniment through prayer and song, the other wild grief and release. In between the singing and wild-eyed maidens are the Hero Twins, also in opposed pairs: 1 Ajaw carries the water gourd and maize sack of the Maize God, and "Xbalanque" (his Classic-era name is not yet deciphered) exhibits a death collar.

Humor that induces laughter, the risible spell of the grotesque, cannot be left outside our treatment of emotion and affect (Taube 1989c). Outright laughter does not obviously appear in Classic imagery. Rather, the Maya use the ridiculous; the graceless dance of the co-essence, or *way;* and the absurd, distended faces of clownish gods and their impersonators to trigger a reaction in the viewer. As in ancient Mesopotamia, Egypt, Medieval Europe, and Japan, animals parody people as farcical counterfeits of humans (Camille 1992:figs. 12, 17; Houlihan 1996; Meskell and R. Joyce 2003:fig. 6.4). Dwarfs must have been figures of fun, a striking contrast to elegant deities such as the Maize God or court personages. They also served as key courtiers who held mirrors for the lord (Schele 1997:pls. 14, 15). A few statues in wood would have preserved that role in palace furnishings, in the form of carved dwarfs that would have held or propped up removable mirrors (Campaña and Boucher 2002:65). A particularly fine Early Classic example is almost regal in appearance and comportment, although his achondroplastic features reveal him to be a dwarf (G. Ekholm 1964). The same can be said for the stone statue of a scribe discovered in Structure 9N-82 at Copan (Schele and M. Miller 1986:pl. 46). Widely identified as a "monkey," the figure is surely a dwarf. Dwarfs filled a variety of functions at Classic Maya courts, serving as scribes and bearers of sacred regalia and incense (presupposing a priestly role), as well as being sources of amusement (cf. M. Miller and Martin 2004:pl. 11; and for examples of copal incense, see Coggins and Ladd 1992:figs. 9.1, 9.3, 9.4; and Lounsbury 1973:fig. 10). As fixtures at court, they could be memorialized and made permanent by being incorporated as imagery into royal thrones (M. Miller and Martin 2004:pl. 7).

The ridiculous personage walks with too much leg extension; bends his neck; and presents a face with too prognathous a nose, too bulging a forehead, and too much unruly facial hair, and short figures are interspersed with tall ones. A vase from the area of Chama, Guatemala, now in the University of Pennsylvania Museum, brings together these traits in a ludicrous manner to the amusement of a long-departed audience (Fig. 5.22; M. Coe 1978:pl. 9). Just as amusing to the Classic Maya were rabbits (Fig. 5.23): one pot shows them multiplying as rabbits tend to do, spilling out in a riot of ears and tufted fur (K2026); another shows a rabbit in the guise of a trickster, stealing clothing from a deity and then hiding behind another god, the personification of the sun (K1398). Rabbits also accompany Moon Goddesses, who cradle or present them as they would children, perhaps as emblems of fertility (K5166). For some reason,

EMOTIONS 197

Fig. 5.18. Orgiastic scene, possibly in sweatbath (M. Coe 1978:pl. 11, photograph copyright Justin Kerr).

Fig. 5.19. Mourning scene on Early Classic vessel (after rollout photograph by Justin Kerr).

Fig. 5.20. Grieving and anxious goddesses (after Robicsek and Hales 1981:fig. 82).

Fig. 5.21. Contrast of mourning styles (K6979, copyright Justin Kerr).

probably unrelated to humor, the Classic Maya identified rabbits with scribes. One bunny is shown writing in a book (M. Coe 1978:pl. 2), another holds an inkwell and is shown being daubed by a simian scribe (K1491), and a final scene displays him being held aloft by a female sprouting numbered plants associated with accounting (K3462). Was this because rabbit fur served as fine material for brushes? Or was it because the rabbit was a wily trickster for the Classic Maya, an inflection of humor that was sure to undermine the pomposity of the court?

CLASSIC MAYA EMOTIONS

For the Classic Maya, affect was seldom shown or emphasized. Its appearance was highly marked, and those who displayed it were likely to be in extraordinary settings. Comparisons with what appears to be a stolid ideal of comportment are overt and covert: overt in the case of calculated contrasts between victorious warriors and kings and their captives; covert in the frantic displays associated with drunkenness, lust of the elderly, and grief, in which viewers (members of a "trained public") served as witnesses, involved as spectators but otherwise detached from such lush exhibitions of affect. In visual terms, the Classic Maya unquestionably found an ideal in unexpressed emotion and rigid self-control, insofar as they associated these properties with the principal illustrations of their lords and members of royal courts. Open expressions of emotion in unusual, often supernatural contexts point to the opposite: a lack of control and a wildness of appearance and bodily position that is remarkable for its rarity in the corpus of Classic Maya imagery. The bestial associations of the emotions—note the monkeys in lovemaking or

Fig. 5.22. Comical figures (M. Coe 1978:pl. 9, photograph copyright Justin Kerr).

captives as trussed prey—recall the K'iche' Maya epic, the *Popol Vuh,* which linked such creatures with prior, unsuccessful stages of humanity, banished for being unworthy simulacra of the real thing (Christenson 2000:49; D. Tedlock 1996:3). Not surprisingly, a very "cruel" person in Tzendal or Colonial Tzotzil was essentially a person of "wood," of unfeeling, inflexible material. In Classic Maya imagery, monkeys are exceptional by being shown in the act of urination or defecation, an act presumably expressing their lack of control—and also, as we can attest, linking them to a form of self-defense and enraged response by spider monkeys in the forest.

Robert Levy's discussion of hypercognated and hypocognated affect has bearing here. By their very appearance in painting and sculpture, affect, fear and despair, drunkenness, lustful abandon, and grief must have been subject to comment and dissection. In a word, they were hypercognated by the Classic Maya. But the absence of such affect must also have been hypercognated as part of an idealized mode of self-constraint and concealment of emotion behind stylized gesture. Morally, both modern and ancient Maya countenance misbehavior in isolated ritual contexts, in which humor defines and ridicules the deviant so as to underline that which is normative (Bricker 1973:151; Taube 1989c:352). The contemplation of affect is thus evaluative and contrastive with the decorum prized by the elite in Classic Maya kingdoms. A similar concern may explain the negative and morally

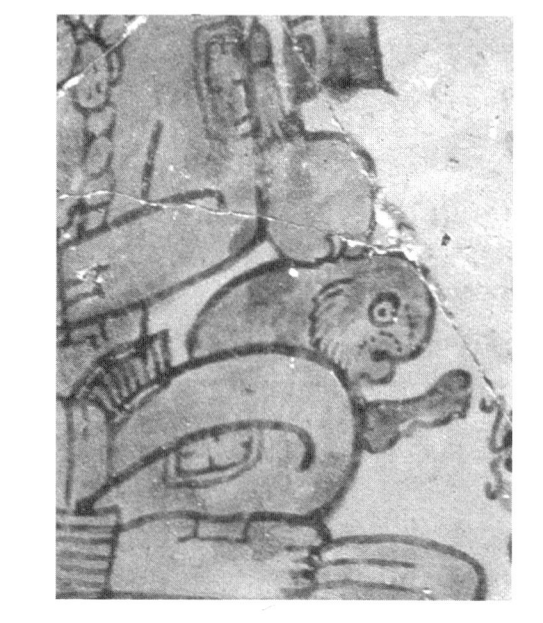

Fig. 5.23. Rabbits: (a) "many rabbits" (K2026); and (b) trickster rabbit with the Sun God (K1398, photographs copyright Justin Kerr).

dangerous value assigned to wild forests and uncultivated natural spaces (Hanks 1990:306; A. Stone 1995a:15–20; Taube 2003a): these landscapes manifestly do not lie under human control. By analogy, the openly affective have, for the ancient Maya, reverted to an undomesticated or predomesticated—almost inhuman—state, as figures of ridicule, fun, contempt, fear, and anomaly.

Speech styles in nonegalitarian, cephalous societies tend to use an elite pose of affective flatness, whereas the low-ranking may counter with "highly demonstrative" displays (Besnier 1990: 435–436).

Among the Wolof of Senegal, "laconic, bland, [and] unelaborated" are adjectives that best characterize "noble speech," used by aristocrats who in turn value "restraint, self-control, and *sangfroid*" (Irvine 1985:575–576; 1990:131, 133). Similar patterns occur among the Fulani of West Africa, for whom a lack of emotional expression signals and undergirds the communications directed by nobles to their former slaves (Riesman 1983). Courtly societies in Java likewise linked emotive, "angry" speech to lower registers of discourse; the "polite" levels associated with people of high status expressed tranquillity and orderly behavior (Irvine 1990:129), a pattern that strongly recalls the cool-headed reserve prized by Egyptians of the Middle Kingdom, who valued the "silent one" above the "heated one" (Meskell 2002:190).

These examples utterly violate conventional understandings of "pre-Modern" emotion (Rosenwein 2002:821–836). Lucien Lévy-Bruhl (1966), for example, saw "primitives" as emotionally open and unrestrained, just as historians have understood, incorrectly, that people of the Middle Ages in Europe lacked "general emotional control" (Stearns and Stearns 1986:25) or were nearly incapacitated by "severe, even psychotic anxiety" (Clark 1983:69) and relied on a "conspicuous show of . . . emotion" (M. Becker 1988:xi). In court societies, even those of millennia ago, it is more likely that the emotional etiquette of appropriate displays was tightly monitored, a point made controversially by Norbert Elias in his work on the "civilizing process" (1994:445, discussed in Rosenwein 2002:827) and more persuasively by Edward Muir in his studies of Italian nobles, who learned during the Renaissance to curtail vendettas by adherence to courtly decorum (Muir 1993, 1994). For the Classic Maya, vendettas and the obligations of honor or the compulsions of anger were probably channeled against those outside the kingdom, in instances where, it seems, no legal mechanism existed to resolve disputes beyond the influence of shadowy alliances and the machinations of the two overweening polities, centered on Calakmul, Campeche, and Tikal, Guatemala (Gallant 2000; Martin and Grube 2000:20–21).

In these cases the "truth" of an emotion—whether it is honestly and deeply felt, an external state congruent with an internal one—is irrelevant to particular moments of personal interaction (Besnier 1990:423). The intensified exhibition of affect in Late Classic imagery may reflect a growing concern with social differentiation in unequal encounters between members of burgeoning courts and assertive nobles. Yet their representations do not promote the forthright expression of the passions, which lie distant from us, in images at once remote and empathetically near.

CHAPTER SIX ◂▸

Dishonor

Some societies place heavy emphasis on honor and personal prestige, to the extent that they have been described as *timocracies,* a label taken from the Greek *timē,* "honor, worth, value," and *kratia,* "power," with the added sense of "rule by" (Sykes 1976:12–14). Commonly perceived by anthropologists who work in the circum-Mediterranean region, these societies, or at least traces of them, can also be detected in Mesoamerica, where a sharp sense of personal value ("pride"), especially among men, played a marked role in face-to-face interaction. The Aztec in particular accorded high importance to deeds of valor and would remove insignia of martial achievement when a warrior performed poorly (Hassig 1988:42). In timocracies, personal value requires acknowledgment by others; if impugned, that same sense of honor leads potentially to conflict, sometimes carried over many generations (Pitt-Rivers 1966:23–24).

Nonetheless, timocracies are not so much pure societal types as persistent orientations or dispositions that guide individual action and then ripple into wider spheres of interaction. In timocratic behavior, the humiliation of one person affects the honor of kin and allies, who in turn would need to respond in order to maintain collective honor (Bourdieu 1966:211); after all, pride can be a brittle projection that must be maintained through constant vigilance. One is not, from comparative ethnographic evidence, "born a man," but is so created through acts of assertiveness, endurance, procreation, and provisioning, often within a milieu of intense competition or even danger (Gilmore 1990:222–224). Acts of assertion, of aggressive self-projection, extend to a finely tuned rhetoric of self-regard (Herzfeld 1985:11, 16, 233). In this light, enduring antagonisms between certain Maya kingdoms—Tikal and Calakmul, Piedras Negras and Yaxchilan, Tonina and Palenque—existed in part because of long-term, strategic collisions (Martin and Grube 2000), but also, one presumes, because of accumulated grievances between timocratic networks Hieroglyphic texts, as on Piedras Negras Stela 12, record durable memories of alliance with long-standing friends as well as vengeance against hereditary enemies. Stela 12 in particular shows a series of captives, taken from the kingdom of Pomona, Mexico, probably in reprisal against a conflict centuries before, when Piedras Negras suffered at the hands of Pomona. The earlier "defeat" is also registered on the stela, an unusual instance of moral justification and claims to a legitimate vendetta.

Odium may have been politicized, but it was no less intensely felt or sustained for being channeled and conditioned by larger dynastic strategies. At some point, those strategies may themselves have resulted from, or been intensified by, the obligations of vendetta. These functioned as their "alibis for aggression" (P. Gay 1993:35). The story of the Late Classic Maya (ca. AD 600–850) was one of increasing conflict, perhaps brought on by demographic increase and border tensions (Webster 2002:223–228). To judge from the rawness of imagery, it was also conflict that heightened the degree of emotional intensity between antagonists.

The existence of pride and honor also presupposes their opposites, shame and humiliation. Maya lexical sources, such as the Santo Domingo dictionary of Colonial Tzotzil, characterize these concepts as inherently social understandings, an honored person being someone who inspires belief, respect, even fear from others—the honored one is raised up, made large, and suffused with fragrant, pleasing odors in a state that is closely linked to a notion of "exchange" or "substitution," *k'ex*; in the reversed condition, a shamed person wishes only "to run away," having changed a preferred state for another, less desirable one (Laughlin 1988, 1:231; 2:407; see also Ringle n.d. for comparable Ch'olti' entries and J. Robertson n.d. for Colonial Tzeltal ones). The connection of "honor" to "obedience" is also attested in Colonial Yukatek, which further shows that there was a thin line between meriting "respect" and becoming "arrogant" (Barrera Vásquez 1980:860; Michelon 1976:368–369). "Vengeance" was thought in Colonial Tzotzil to involve "hot" states that necessitated "doubling back" (*pak*) on another or, in Colonial Yukatek, to *ch'a toh*, "to take [make] something straight or right" in the sense of rectification or restitution (Andrews Heath de Zapata 1978:213; Laughlin 1988, 1:278; Michelon 1976:104).

In the available representations from the Classic period there are no more shamed or dishonored persons than elite captives, most of whom were taken in raiding or combat. After battle, captives were stripped of jewelry and badges of rank or office (with a few notable exceptions; see below) and, when put on display, compressed into poses of extreme discomfort. Yet captives also awakened a sense of contradiction. Victors wished to humiliate prisoners *and* to accentuate the status of their trophies. According to surviving imagery, captives were beaten and ground under toe and heel (some faces are nearly pulped, with eyes swollen shut), yet they also received the dignity of personal names, titles, and, in a few cases, badges of rank: Monument 122 from Tonina pictures K'an Joy Chitam of Palenque with the "jester god" jewel and cloth headband (*sak huun*) of lordship (Fig. 6.1). The irony of the "mighty thrown low" must have resonated with knowledgeable observers, who received subtle messages about the fate confronting *all* Maya warriors. Read this way, scenes of triumph implicitly admonished those who were unprepared for battle and its uncertain outcome. They served as a *memento mori* or *contemplus mundi* for people who needed to think more deeply about what might affect them personally (Ariès 1981: 218–219). Maya testimonials to prowess in war operated more as memorials to defended honor and exhortations to future conduct than as crude "propagandistic" boasting about the past (cf. Marcus 1992).

Another discrepancy lies in the ways captives were set apart from each other yet also lumped into broad categories. Captives could be shown at the very moment of defeat, with a warrior grabbing

Fig. 6.1. Monument 122, Tonina (photograph provided by Mary Miller, Yale University).

their forearm or hair (if tangled and disorderly, the hair implied direct passage from battle or the misery of captivity [e.g., K6416]; see also Assyrian practices of hair grabbing [Cifarelli 1998]). Yet those same captives also took a slot, especially in or near the Usumacinta drainage, within larger, rather impersonal tabulations. By means of a relatively common title, so-and-so was absorbed into his victor's identity as, say, "Captive 5," a mere step or "coup" along the martial career of a successful warrior (D. Stuart 1985). After "21" captives, the Maya apparently felt it pointless to continue the count. The scene of capture, historically unique yet stylized according to fixed canons, focused on the singularity of captives and the valor and dexterity of those who vanquished them. In contrast, the title tallied captives in a perfunctory manner, much like a shorthand for personal glory. The concentration of such titles in smaller sites—none are known at Tikal or Calakmul—hints that timocratic impulses played a heavier role in royal courts with smaller forces of warriors and more-engaged involvement of rulers in messy scuffles. In discussing Medieval Iceland, William Miller suggests much the same: that there is a divide between what he calls the "epic" and "romantic societies," the first having only "the thinnest notion of the state" among "near equals . . . [or] players in the game of honor"; the second shifting to honors conferred by superiors (1993:84). Classic Maya societies oscillated back and forth along that divide.

The ambiguity of captives is underscored by the fact that one deity associated with rulership, 1 Ajaw, occasionally appears as a victim of battle. Tikal Altar 10 pictures different versions of 1 Ajaw with long, disheveled hair; arms tied behind the back; face looking downward in dejection or upward in appeal (Fig. 6.2; C. Jones and Satterthwaite 1982:fig. 34a, b). His identifying marks, a headband and spots, are all in place. Tonina, too, presents images of captives, often with full display of genitals, in the guise of 1 Ajaw (Monument 33, in I. Graham and Mathews 1996:80). Ordinarily, as in the Pasión region of Guatemala, lords conflate their identities with 1 Ajaw by marking their bodies with larger circles that also serve, on the sides of monuments, as cartouches for glyphs (e.g., Arroyo de Piedra Stela 6 and Tamarindito Stela 5, Houston 1993:figs. 3.4, 3.5)—the stela almost becomes a simulacrum of royal skin (see Chapters 1 and 2). But, at Tonina, it is captives who bear such circles, including some that contain their names (e.g., Tonina Monument 84, in I. Graham and Mathews 1996:114, figs.

Fig. 6.2. Sides of Tikal Altar 10 (after C. Jones and Satterthwaite 1982:fig. 34b, used with permission of Sharon Misdea, Tikal Project, University of Pennsylvania Museum).

3–5; see also an unprovenanced Terminal Classic scene of warfare, K503). The kings who enslave or kill such figures exemplify moral ambiguity and, in a sense, embody evil, for in a variety of Colonial sources, it is the lords of death who kill 1 Ajaw.

In the K'iche' epic, the *Popol Vuh*, 1 Ajaw is a figure of acute paradox. He enters the underworld, suffers death, and is then miraculously reborn. In Classic imagery, his very blotches, circles on face and across his body, are markers of death (the settling of noncirculating blood? [J. Furst 1995: 40–41]). As an exemplar for kings and captives, he embodies themes of defeat but also of resurgence, recycling, and mythic charter (Christenson 2000: 103–122; M. Coe 1973:12–13). One vessel shows 1 Ajaw as a supplicant captive of an important deity, God D, with another supernatural standing on his body (M. Coe 1982:33). Two ballcourt markers, from Copan and La Esperanza respectively, emphasize his role as a loser in the Maya ballgame (Kowalski 1989:figs. 1, 4). A ruler who, like 1 Ajaw, employs cunning in adversity hopes for rebirth and triumph; a captive depicted as 1 Ajaw is more equivocal emotionally and morally in that he elicits both disgust and sympathy, the former as a defeated enemy, the latter as a worthy foe who might yet prevail. We also see clues that the historical conflicts were mythologized, as, at Quirigua, in the supposed "self-decapitation" of a losing lord from Copan (D. Stuart 1992b:176) and, at Naranjo, in the way in which captives were burned like primordial, mythic victims (Martin and Grube 2000:82).

Elsewhere in the world, evidence exists for a relationship of fictive, quasi-parental ties between captives and victors. Susan Rasmussen identifies the key properties of such relations as the denial of jural adulthood to slaves but also, by implication, a long-term bond that may involve eventual inheritance from the owner (1999:75, 85, 98; also see Hoskins 1996:5). To James Watson (1980), certain systems of servility and bodily control were "open" in that they had the capacity to absorb enslaved people as quasi-kin. Watson further claimed that "open" systems were more likely to characterize societies that valued labor over widely available land. In contrast, "closed" systems, such as many in Asia, attached greater worth to land and thus treated "slaves" as chattel (J. Watson 1980). If valid, this theory would predict a changing status for Classic Maya slaves, from those in "open," kinlike systems during the Early Classic, when land was abundant, to "closed" ones during the Late Classic, when land became cramped with dense settlement. Another perspective would stress the importance of rank, as in the head-hunting societies of Southeast Asia. In places where rank was important, the head of a nobleman was taken, often in revenge killing, but females or children were more likely to be enslaved, adopted, or held for ransom (Hoskins 1996:13). It is likely that, for the Classic Maya, the identity of the head mattered—not any old skull would do.

In many respects, the war captive was placed, as a human being, in a nearly impossible position. As Igor Kopytoff (1982:222) argues, something had to be done to such figures betwixt and between: first, the captive had to be dehumanized and stripped of social status; but, second, he or she had to be "resocialized" or "rehumanized" so as to slip as a subordinate into the waiting society: the *Popol Vuh* gives evidence that "slaves" were labeled with kinship terms such as "sons" and "daughters" (Christenson 2003:248). Notably, the exceptions to this process were, in Africa and elsewhere, precisely those captives dispatched quickly as sacrifices (Kopytoff 1982:222; Patterson 1982). Unfortunately, the Classic Maya are notably silent on the subject of "open" and "closed" systems. Captives may well have been kept around or subjugated for long periods of time—K'an Joy Chitam is a prime example—but fictive kinship between warrior and captive has yet to be documented. It is noteworthy that, among the Huron of North America, war captives could be labeled as "kin" and also subjected to death by torture (Heidenreich 1978:386)—Watson and Kopytoff's formulations may not capture the subtle and paradoxical meanings in the Maya evidence.

Based on present evidence, there were three sorts of captives: (1) those of royal rank, albeit stripped of royal epithets such as the "holy," *k'uhul*, or "sunlike," *k'inich* (e.g., Tonina Monument 122), and all but the most direct clues to rank (headbands with jewels of office); (2) those who carried names and were probably of noble status; and (3) unidentified figures (although perhaps recognizable to those intended to see the images), shown as little more than gruesome, anguished props. These captives may have been of the lowest status, hardly worth mentioning by scribes and sculptors. (Conceivably, they were the ones who served as slave labor in Maya cities, but this is nearly impossible to prove.) The Aztec, too, valued captives differentially. The Wastek, for example, a Mayan-speaking people, were regarded as the most contemptible, easily defeated prey, and those from Nahua-speaking Huexotzinco, among the most difficult to take and thus praiseworthy (Hassig 1988:39–40; Sahagún 1950–1982, bk. 8:77). It is likely that, like all features of the Maya world, the treatment and presentation of captives had a history: the earliest depictions of captives displayed them at moments of entreaty, hair wild and undisciplined (Fig. 6.3; Adams 1999:fig. 3-33). Not a few occur on earspools, as though designed to flood the wearer's ears with the gratifying cries of supplicants (G. Stuart 1987:17)—as pointed out in Chapter 4, earspools among the Maya underscored heightened powers of hearing and discernment. The distorted, often angular postures of captives—a domain in which Maya sculptors and painters could experiment with the human form in ways inconceivable for the stiff displays of royalty—have been thoroughly discussed by others, especially by Mary Miller, as have the various forms of mutilation, ranging from the truncation of digits to the burning of torsos, and from the slicing of fingers to acts of decapitation or disembowelment (D. Chase and A. Chase 1998:309; M. Coe 1973:77; Dillon 1982; Dillon et al. 1985:33–38; Johnston 2001; M. Miller 2001:217–218; Schele and M. Miller 1986:215–220, 228). Most of these brutalities, or at least the representations of them, date to the Late Classic period, when captives were treated as so many commodified goods to be rendered as tributary obligations to overlords (e.g., Schele and M. Miller 1986:pl. 86, especially the expression *u baak ti yajaw*, "his captives for his lord").

A central theme in acts of personal dishonor is that of the unwilling flesh: of bodies that were debased, dehumanized, and stripped of all but the

Fig. 6.3. Río Azul captive (after Adams 1999:fig. 3.33).

will to express pain. Even after death, their bodies and body parts belonged to others—their shame was total. Three escalating modes can be observed by which the Classic Maya created the dishonored body. The first involved an ambiguous mix of features: the loss of volition in sexual acts, a form of aggressive eroticism or erotic aggression, often homoerotic, that denied any consent to the subordinate partner. From a slightly different point of view, it regarded the subordinate as someone who had lost control over his sexuality (M. Miller 2001:218). Some would argue that the captive has become feminized and that for this reason female attributes were assigned to the weak and vulnerable (W. Miller 1993:55; Trexler 1995:1). The inverse might be equally valid: the central wish was to express vulnerability, and women provided the readiest template for this property. The Aztec provide evidence for both points of view, for men being forced to dress shamefully like women, thus provoking war, and for bellicose women who, although valiant, typically lose (Klein 1994:113–115; see discussion below of the *Rabinal Achi*). Whether these sexual acts actually took place probably mattered far less than the comprehensive debasement of the captive. The second mode was a systematic categorization of captives as so much animal flesh, mere meat and body parts, to be hunted, cut, and dressed or prepared like animals, especially deer, a succulent and much-esteemed prey. Unlike most humans, captives exposed their genitals, unmindful, like animals, of what appear to have been Classic Maya strictures against such display. As with the Aztec, there is more than a suggestion here of ritualized cannibalism. The consumption of human flesh played a smaller role, however, than the intent to dishonor and, perhaps, to acquire properties from, and spiritual control over, the captive through ingestion of his remains (López Austin 1988, 1:382–383; Ortiz de Montellano 1978). The third mode achieved the ultimate form of dehumanization in that captives had become, figuratively and perhaps literally, manure to fertilize the victor's soil and provide building materials for the enemy's city.

EROTIC DEGRADATION

The act of rape, usually understood as the sexual violation of an unwilling partner by a male, is itself a category of multiple interpretations. To some, such as Susan Brownmiller (1975) and Andrea Dworkin (1989; also MacKinnon and Dworkin 1997), rape is not so much about sex as the wish to dominate and control, perhaps as the natural proclivity of human males toward "pathologized . . . [and] toxic" heterosexuality (Friedman 2001:225). Or, according to another controversial discussion, rape arises from evolutionary pressures that cause males, whether human or scorpionfly, to overcome female "choosiness" by acts of forcible insemination (Friedman 2001:221; Thornhill and Palmer 2000:238–240; cf. Fausto-Sterling 1992, 1995). An added layer of meaning is that, in some societies, such as those of ancient Greece and Rome, rape undermined status, the conception of heirs, and the protection of freeborn people from "debasement" (Latin: *stuprum*; Clarke 1998:279). It thus represented a crime inflicted less against the individual than against the community and consequently merited severe retribution (Omitowoju 2002:17; Rousselle 1989:311–314). Nevertheless, in Classical Greece, rape did not seem to have been regarded as a serious transgression when it involved females of "marginal status"; the consent of such women was barely at issue (Omitowoju 2002:13, 17; for examples from Colonial America, see D'Emilio and Freedman 2002:156). Yet, among the ethnohistoric Maya, there appears to have been an acute contempt for the act itself, regardless of the victim's and the transgressor's social identities. In early Colonial Yucatan, even high-ranking rapists of "virgins" were killed by stoning (Tozzer 1941:32, 231), and "rape" was described in Colonial Tzotzil as "struggling angrily" (Laughlin 1988, 1:176), highlighting a lack of consent. Colonial Yukatek also stressed "breaking," "ridiculing," or "loss of purity" as the central descriptives of this act (Barrera Vásquez 1980:42, 614, 719). The lone depiction of Aztec rape, in the Codex Boturini, contrasts slightly with Maya practice (see below) in that it connects acts of martial prowess with sexual violation (Codex Boturini, last page; see also Klein 1994:139).

The question is, which system of valuation applied to the Classic Maya? One that assigned greater weight to the relative status of victims? Or a perception that rape and, as emphasized here, sexual aggression were altogether bad? The male rape of women, however sanitized, is rarely shown by the Classic Maya. There is no comparable body of literature and imagery to that of rape in Classical Antiquity (e.g., Wolfthal 1999). The site of Tonina, Chiapas, is virtually unique for its scene on a carved altar that shows a woman, breasts dislodged from her *huipil* garment, coupling with a man, whose hand she grabs (Fig. 6.4). The event is dated by a Calendar Round position. Although most of the text is irretrievably eroded, the date points to a high probability that this was a historical act and, judging from the open location of the altar, one that was performed in full view of others. There is a great deal in the sculpture that is puzzling—her resistance with a handheld weapon and the grasping of the male's hair—yet it seems to represent a scene in which a captive woman—note the name glyphs along her thigh, much like other captives at Tonina—has been compelled into performing sexual acts, resisting and yielding at the same time. The exposed breasts, for example, represent a key erogenous zone in Classic Maya imagery (Chapter 1). A related scene, carved out of a shell, shows a woman with her arm around a lover, the Maize God, his hands touching her breast (Fig. 6.5). Another sculpture from Tonina (Monument 99) exhibits a woman with loose hair, arms bound behind her back, and the ripped or perforated clothing associated with Classic Maya captives (Schele and M. Miller 1986:212, 226); the verb *k'ahlaj*, also with a date, describes her "binding," presumably with ropes (I. Graham and Mathews 1996:122). Two unprovenanced objects, one a conch trumpet, the other a ceramic vessel (K5451), show what may be rape. The conch, which is very likely, if authentic, to have been retouched by a restorer, shows a bare-chested, bound women, legs splayed to the side. Its erotic theme is underlined by a male captive nearby forcibly fellating a standing, unbound male (Sotheby's 1994:#117). The other tableau appears to display bleeding women being assaulted by warriors from distant parts, some holding their travel packs and parasols; one woman appeals to the warrior by clutching his parasol handle, which passes close to where his genitals should be.

The vessel scene is in part or perhaps completely mythological, but the images from Tonina suggest a localized form of warfare—or at least its emphasis in imagery—that targeted royal women as part of a martial strategy, rather like a Maya "Rape of the Sabines." Female captives of high rank attest

Fig. 6.4. Rape scene (?), Tonina (drawing by Lucia Henderson, Corpus of Maya Hieroglyphic Inscriptions, Peabody Museum, Harvard).

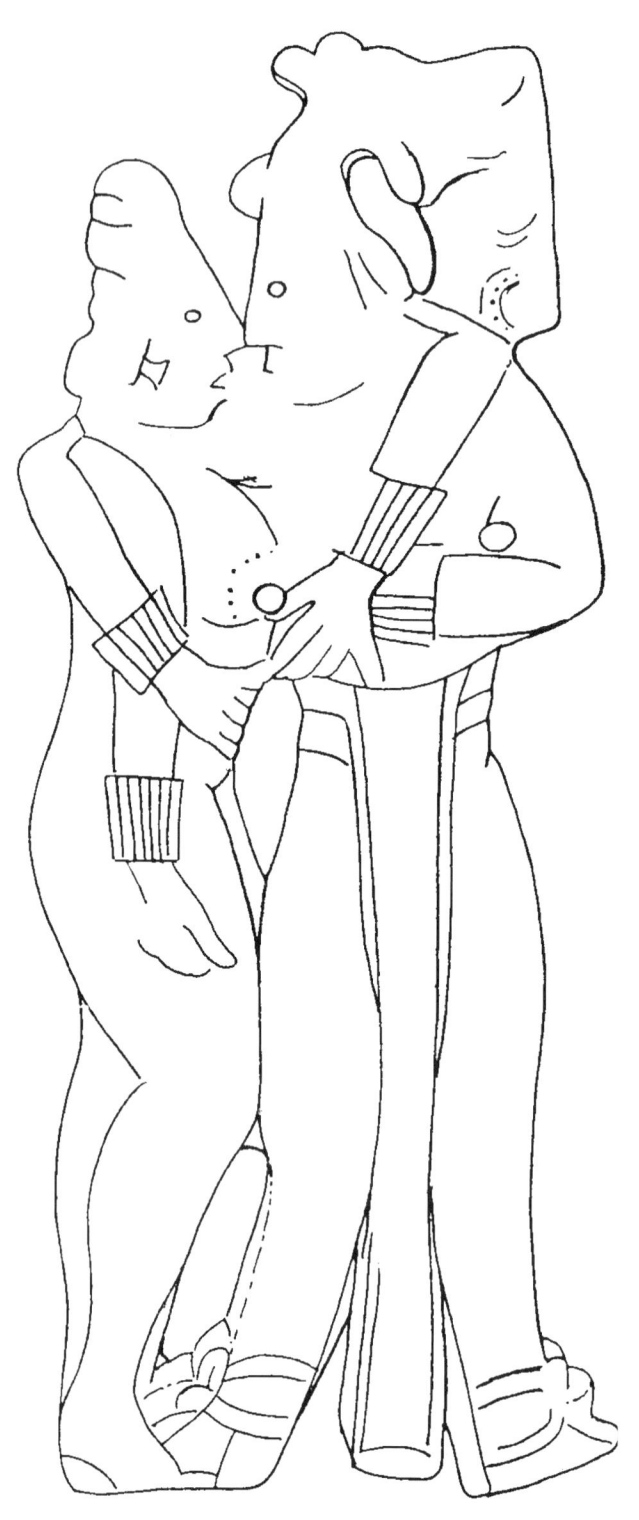

Fig. 6.5. Lovemaking on carved shell (unprovenanced object drawn by Karl Taube).

to a more intrusive form of warfare than the apprehension of warriors in jungle skirmishes. Plausibly, most such females were closeted in palaces. Their capture by Tonina implies an encroachment of the most lacerating sort: into the royal seraglios of enemy cities. The resulting damage deliberately affected the dynasty at its core, in its capacity for physical reproduction and the husbanding of elite bloodlines. It would also throw doubt on its ability to protect women, the ultimate duty of what William Miller describes as a more "Mediterranean" form of timocratic disposition, one that focuses on the morality or sexuality of female relatives as opposed to an "Icelandic" pattern that trafficked in personal insult, challenge, and riposte (1993:118–119; see also Brandes 1980:76–77, 87–91). Still, the evidence from Tonina consists of two images out of many dozens of male captives. Even within the city, such scenes are an anomaly within an anomaly.

Violence and sex play a more general role in the treatment of male captives, a point often made to us by Mary Miller in conversations over the years (e.g., M. Miller n.d.). To understand this pattern, however, requires some discussion of homosexuality or same-sex practices in the pre-Modern world. As part of an article on changing attitudes in Europe, David Halperin (2000:92) declares that "homosexuality" was not a self-evident category but, rather, a creation of nineteenth-century forensic medicine (Halperin [2000:109] dates its origin precisely to 1869; see also Bray 1995:114; Foucault 1976:59; Williams 1999:6–7; and see Jordan 1997:161, 164, for an earlier date, well back in the Middle Ages). Halperin distinguishes four kinds of "prehomosexual [i.e., pre-nineteenth-century] categories of male sex and gender deviance": (1) "effeminacy," an excessive indulgence in sexual pleasure, including lovemaking between men and women; (2) "pederasty" or "active sodomy," the penetration of a subordinate male by a superior one—to Halperin this category involves "hierarchy, not mutuality" and typifies the behavior of prison inmates who do not ordinarily regard themselves as homosexuals (Brandes 1980:95–96; Halperin 2000:96; Trexler 1995:29; Williams 1999:7, 51); (3) "friendship or male love,"
a virtuous affection between male equals (Halperin 2000:100)—a form of homosociality that is fairly common in Maya imagery; and (4) "passivity or inversion," ranging from a penetration in which the recipient takes pleasure, surrendering willingly to another man, to someone dressing in women's clothes (Halperin 2000:103, 109; also Karras and Boyd 1996:108–109). John Clarke, who has devoted much time to understanding the erotic images of Pompeii and elsewhere, agrees that terms such as *homosexuality* do not apply to the variety of encounters and orientations in ancient Rome (1998:14). As a result, he disputes John Boswell's well-known claim that "gay" people, "as we understand them today," existed from the Roman period through the Middle Ages and beyond (Clarke 1998:8; also Bray 1995:8–9; cf. Boswell 1980, but see a partial retraction in Boswell 1990).

It is not our intention to argue for or against the evolving nature of same-sex desire, although, in reaction to Halperin and Clarke, we doubt that post-nineteenth-century experience differed fundamentally from the urges and affections of earlier times. A divergence of understanding, self-perception, and representation is not the same as a difference of feeling and experience. Halperin himself admits, with provisos, that "aspects of sexual life . . . persist through time" (2000:88). However, we can focus on the role of the eroticized body in tableaux of masculine domination.

With regard to Halperin's four categories, rage, aggression, submission, and violence are more likely to characterize "pederasty" or "active sodomy," which he sees as a physical engagement between socially unequal partners—even the Psalms recall, "And he struck his enemies in the behind . . . giving them eternal shame," the worst punishment being, as a male, to suffer violation as a "woman" (Trexler 1995:19, 20). Such "pederasty," although it would not have been so labeled, characterized many sexual milieu, such as that of early Renaissance Florence, where male encounters took place within a framework of "age difference and a rigid distinction in sexual roles"; in fact, Florence was so well known for these practices that "to sodomize" was described in contemporary Germany as *florenzen* and a "sodomite" as a *Florenzer* (Rocke 1996:3, 88).

At this point, the later information from the Maya would seem to conflict with the earlier, implying a historical shift or at least a variable transparency in available evidence. Colonial sources of Mayan languages consistently express a negative view of male-to-male sex and of effeminacy. Yukatek documents refer unambiguously to "sodomy" as an act punished by death (Tozzer 1941:124–125 n. 576)—the *u topob u yit uinicobe*, "carnal acts with people's anuses" (Restall 1997:145; translation slightly emended here)—and a more-or-less contemporary dictionary of Tzendal refers to *xichoc mulil*, "sin against nature" (J. Robertson n.d.). Similarly, Colonial Tzotzil labels one who engages in such acts as *jkobel-xinch'ok*, "male prostitute who suffers," clearly distinguishing between passive and active participants, one taking pleasure, the other not (Laughlin 1988, 1:221). There are also clues from Colonial Yukatek of Halperin's state of "effeminacy," the *ch'upal ol*, "young-womanly heart" (Michelon 1976:111). Nonetheless, most of these documents were compiled by Spanish clerics. For reasons of sixteenth- and seventeenth-century Catholic theology, their entries on such matters would probably ooze with abhorrence (Jordan 1997:163–164; R. Joyce 2000b:278). Anecdotal evidence from modern Yukatek communities points to a different perspective, one in which male-to-male encounters are seen mostly as simple release, without connotations for permanent sexual identity (see also R. Joyce 2000b:278). In general, the display of phalli and erotic clowning, as on Telantunich Monument 3, hints at regional differences in Classic Maya eroticism, with more open exhibitions in northern Yucatan than in other parts of the Maya lowlands (Fig. 6.6a; E. W. Andrews 1939:pl. 1e). A figure from Cumpich, a site on the border between Campeche and Yucatan, Mexico, shows a personage much like those from Telantunich, with a snake around the neck (reflecting a distinctive dance?) and enlarged testicles (Fig. 6.6c; Bernal 1969:pl. 91). Other, similarly well-endowed figures occur in Pustunich, Campeche (E. W. Andrews IV 1941: figs. 44, 45).

Classic images clarify Maya sexuality and, at the same time, inject further ambiguities. In the first

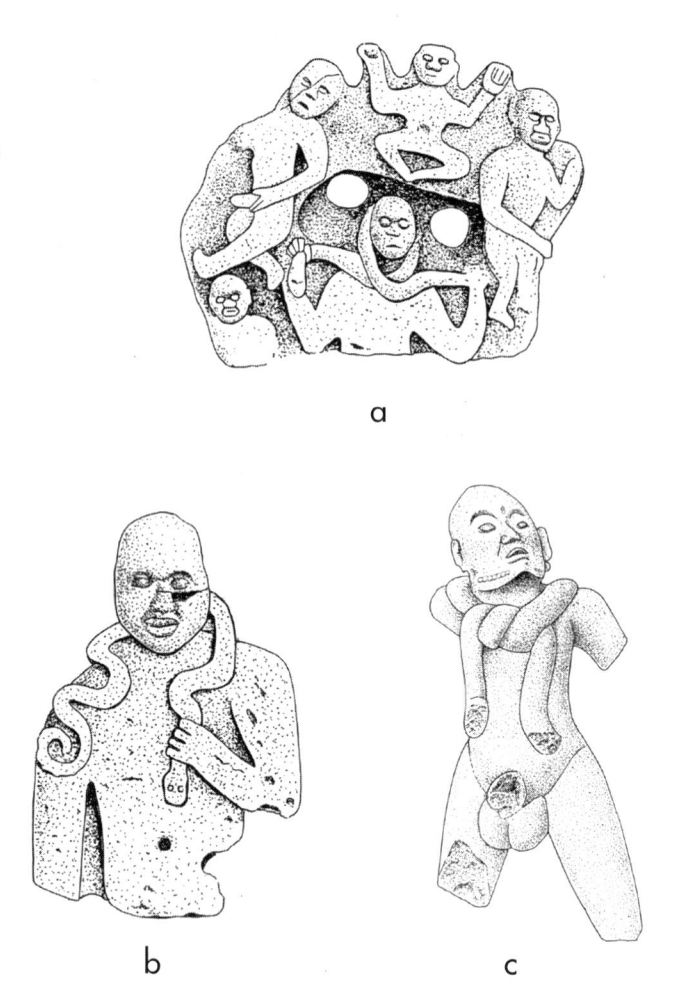

Fig. 6.6. Penises and clowning in northern Yucatan: (a) Telantunich Monument 3 (after E. W. Andrews 1939:pl. 1e); (b) figure from Kabah, Yucatan (Taube 1989c:fig. 24.16a); and (c) Cumpich sculpture (after Bernal 1969:pl. 91).

place, captives are often shown as sexualized beings, not just with exposed genitals, a feature seldom seen with other lords, but with tumescent penises and enlarged testicles, a theme that goes back to Olmec times, as in Chalcatzingo Relief 2, from Morelos, Mexico (Fig. 6.7a), and, from a Classic Maya context, in Drawing 1 from the Actun Ch'on cave (Fig. 6.7b; A. Stone 1995a:63). Rosemary Joyce (2000b:270) argues that such depictions emphasize the beauty of the male body in a form of "aesthetic delight" for male audiences, perhaps those gathered in young men's houses. It may be that the male body was regarded as "beautiful" (Chapter 1), and, indeed, some homoerotic activity (Halperin's "friendship" or "male" love) may have characterized the young men's houses that appear to have existed in Classic Maya cities. The Aztec had such places, *tēlpōchcalli*, "house[s] of youth," where boys enrolled between the ages of ten and fifteen and left when they married (Calnek 1988a; Karttunen 1992:221). Young men were enlisted in a variety of activities, some ritual, such as dancing and signing; some agricultural, including the preparation of land and digging of canals; and the outright martial, fighting in mock battles that trained them for more serious conflicts (Brumfiel 2001:293–295).

Evidence for such places and practices exists among the last independent Maya, the Itza of Peten, Guatemala (G. Jones 1998:333). The reports from that time evoke the work of Gilbert Herdt and others, who have studied life-cycle homosexuality between men and youthful initiates in New Guinea (e.g., Herdt 1984). The Ara dictionary of Colonial Tzotzil hints at these practices,

too, with terms such as *antz*, "female"; *antzil*, "effeminate thing"; *antzil vinic*, "beardless person"; and *antzil mulil*, "sin against nature," apparently also in the sense of lesbian enjoyment (J. Robertson n.d.). In the Classic period, there is one scene from graffiti at the site of Kinal, Peten, Guatemala, that shows a "Maize God Person," Jun-?-Winik, as a youth, bending over and receiving attentions from an older, bearded figure (Fig. 6.8a; I. Graham 1967:fig. 26). A linked image shows what appears to be intercrural (between-thigh) lovemaking, an older male to the left penetrating a younger male to the right (Fig. 6.8b). These present striking parallels to Greek intercourse between a dominant, older man, the *erastes*, and a younger, often demure protégé, the *eromenos* (Dover 1989:98). Peter Brown (1988:29–30) provides a comparable view from Late Antiquity, when such practices smacked generally of immaturity, nothing more. Commenting on peoples closer to the Maya, Cecelia Klein (2001:225) observes that Nahua speakers thought poorly of the chaotic sexuality that characterizes unmarried males; marriage was the felicitous state that controlled such impulses. This pattern recalls that of early Renaissance Florence, where young men were thought to cavort sexually in an unrestrained and irresponsible manner (Rocke 1996:113). This was not the crime, however; the crime was to continue in such behavior past youth.

In other respects, however, Joyce's claim is potentially misleading. As in the Classical world, displays of phalli in Maya society transmitted many meanings, including fertility and good luck (Johns 1982:62–64). The same must be said for the phallic waterspouts from sites in northern Yucatan (e.g., Amrhein 2002:fig. 8), which clearly equate semen with procreative fluids such as seasonal water. It may be an anachronism to see the male phallus exclusively in terms of sexual pleasure or as a "celebration of male sexuality and male beauty for exclusively male audiences" (R. Joyce 2000b: 270). The stone phalli from Yucatan are difficult to study (Joyce: "most out of original context" [2000b:fig. 15.5]) because they have often been shifted from their primary setting. We cannot know who saw them and who did not. One doorjamb

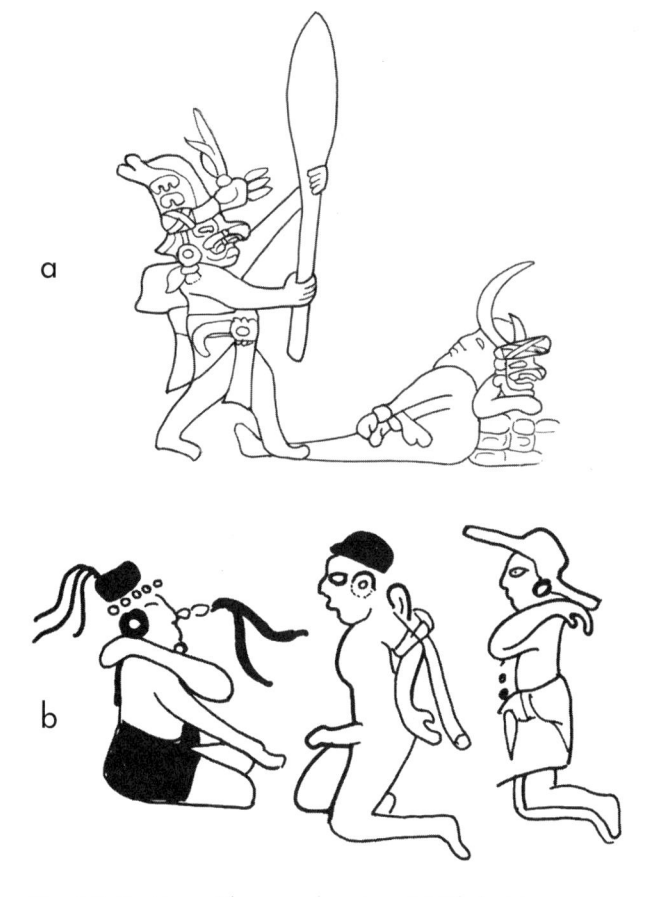

Fig. 6.7. Captives with aroused penises: (a) Chalcatzingo Relief 2, Morelos, Mexico (after Gay 1971:figs. 17, 19); and (b) Drawing 1 from the Actun Ch'on cave (after A. Stone 1995a:63).

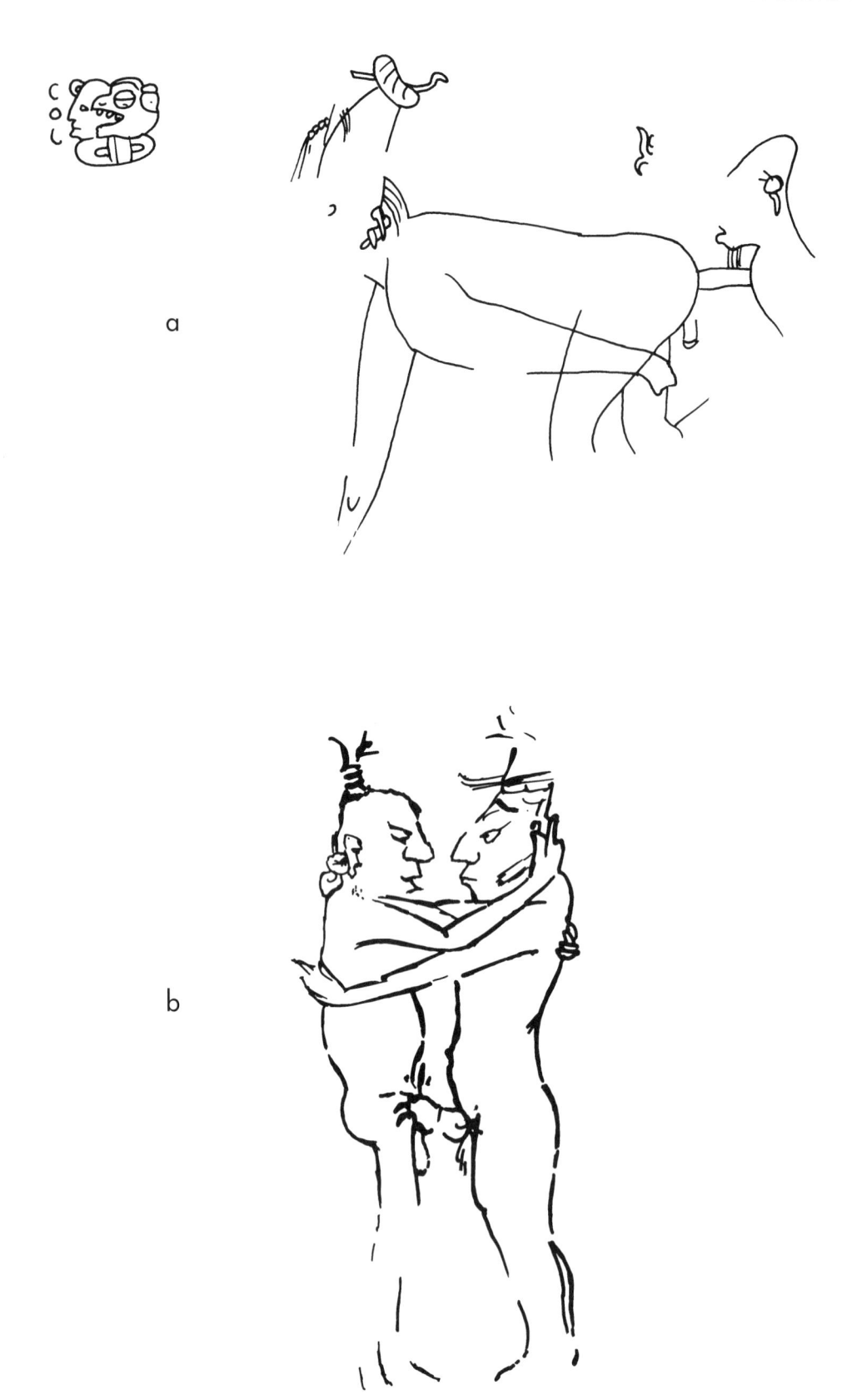

Fig. 6.8. Older male with younger male: (a) Kinal graffiti (after I. Graham 1967:fig. 26); and (b) homosexual lovemaking, Naj Tunich Drawing 18 (after A. Stone 1995a:fig. 8.18).

from Xcochkax, Campeche, shows a dancing skeleton with a dangling penis, putrid vapors spilling from its gut (Michelet et al. 2000:fig. 2.22c). It is doubtful that this image was "beautiful" to anyone. Moreover, among the Classic Maya, there is little evidence for what Eva Keuls calls "genital narcissism," a focus on aggressive display of phalli that she discerns, rather tendentiously, in ancient Athens (1993:67; Keuls goes so far as to denounce that society for its thoroughgoing misogyny). Rather, and in contrast to the timocratic systems of, say, Andalusian Spain, the phallus is a highly ambiguous organ (cf. Brandes 1980:92–94).

In Classic Maya imagery, animals such as jaguars and monkeys flourish penis and testicles (Fig. 6.9a)—a sign of animal nature that would seem to imply an indifference to physical modesty. (Or were monkey testicles so prominent because humans would see them from below!) Assyrian modes of displaying nude captives are similar. In the *Gilgamesh Epic*, to be human is to put on clothing and acquire possessions (Cifarelli 1998). Could this also have been an attribute attached to the naked poor or those of low status in Maya society? Similarly, a stela from Dos Caobas, Chiapas, a site not far from Yaxchilan, emphasizes the large procreative organs of a captive, distending lazily from the groin onto the floor, the testicles traced with great detailing of wrinkles and imperfections of the skin (Fig. 6.9b; Tovalín et al. 1998:figs. 3, 6). This pattern can also be seen on Uxmal Stela 14: its two captives are placed within a hole, stylized as gaping centipede jaws, and disposed in such a way as to feature their outsized genitals (Fig. 6.9c; I. Graham 1992:108). The tumescent penis of captives occurs in a graffito from Tikal (Fig. 6.10a; Orrego Corzo and Larios Villalta 1983:lám. 23) and in a mural painting from Mulchic, Yucatan, which shows a captive hung by the neck from a tree, his left hand clutching an engorged penis in a possible side effect of strangulation, a parallel to the scene of autostrangulation from San Diego, Yucatan (Fig. 6.10b; Barrera Rubio 1980:fig. 1; Barrera Rubio and Taube 1987:fig. 17). Other hung captives appear as figurines, and, at Tonina, Chiapas, such figures suffered the garrote, choked of breath at the whim of their captors (Chapter 6; Schele 1997:pls.

25–26). Most of the captives featured on a carving in bedrock from Calakmul assign disproportionate emphasis to their privates. In some cases, the penis is nearly as long and stiff as the thigh. One of the earliest images of naked captives, from Monument 65 at Kaminaljuyu, prefigures this proportion almost exactly (Fig. 6.11; L. Parsons 1986:149), as does a captive etched into bedrock near the entrance to the cave at Loltun, Yucatan. The most grotesque example of all is the figure with massive penis on the East Court, east side, of the Palace at Palenque (M. G. Robertson 1985b:fig. 290). A full erection appears on a stray piece from Oxkintok, Yucatan, although, unfortunately, it is impossible to say what its original setting might have been (Pollock 1980:fig. 541a).

The phalli are clearly not intended as beautiful emblems that trigger admiration—they are decidedly "ugly," being displayed by the defeated, a theme also present among the Moche (Donnan and McClelland 1999:figs. 3.36, 3.38, 3.52, 4.2, 4.6, 4.7, 4.100). Unfortunately, the evidence that Joyce musters is misconstrued. The phallus that occurs in the name of a deity (R. Joyce 2000b:fig. 15.8) is not well understood in this godly name, so we cannot interpret its use. There is no secure evidence that the glyph was designed to exalt the beauty of the male member. At Chichen Itza, the mythological context of a penis in a backrack is opaque, and the object in question appears in a noncentral position. The penis is not an object of veneration or contemplation. Several spines passing through the skin of the penis suggest prior painful acts of insertion, perhaps as part of rites of passage to adulthood or, secondarily, as sexual aids for vaginal stimulation (cf. R. Joyce 2000b:fig. 15.4; cf. two similar slashes on the penis of the captive at Palenque, M. G. Robertson 1985:fig. 290). There seems little doubt, particularly with the murals from San Bartolo, Guatemala, that deities let blood from the penis as painful, instigative acts of creation.

In all of these images, captives, like animals, demonstrate a signal lack of control, an inability to cover their privates, and a wanton exposure of erections to public view. Not coincidentally, most of the creatures shown in Maya imagery to evacuate their

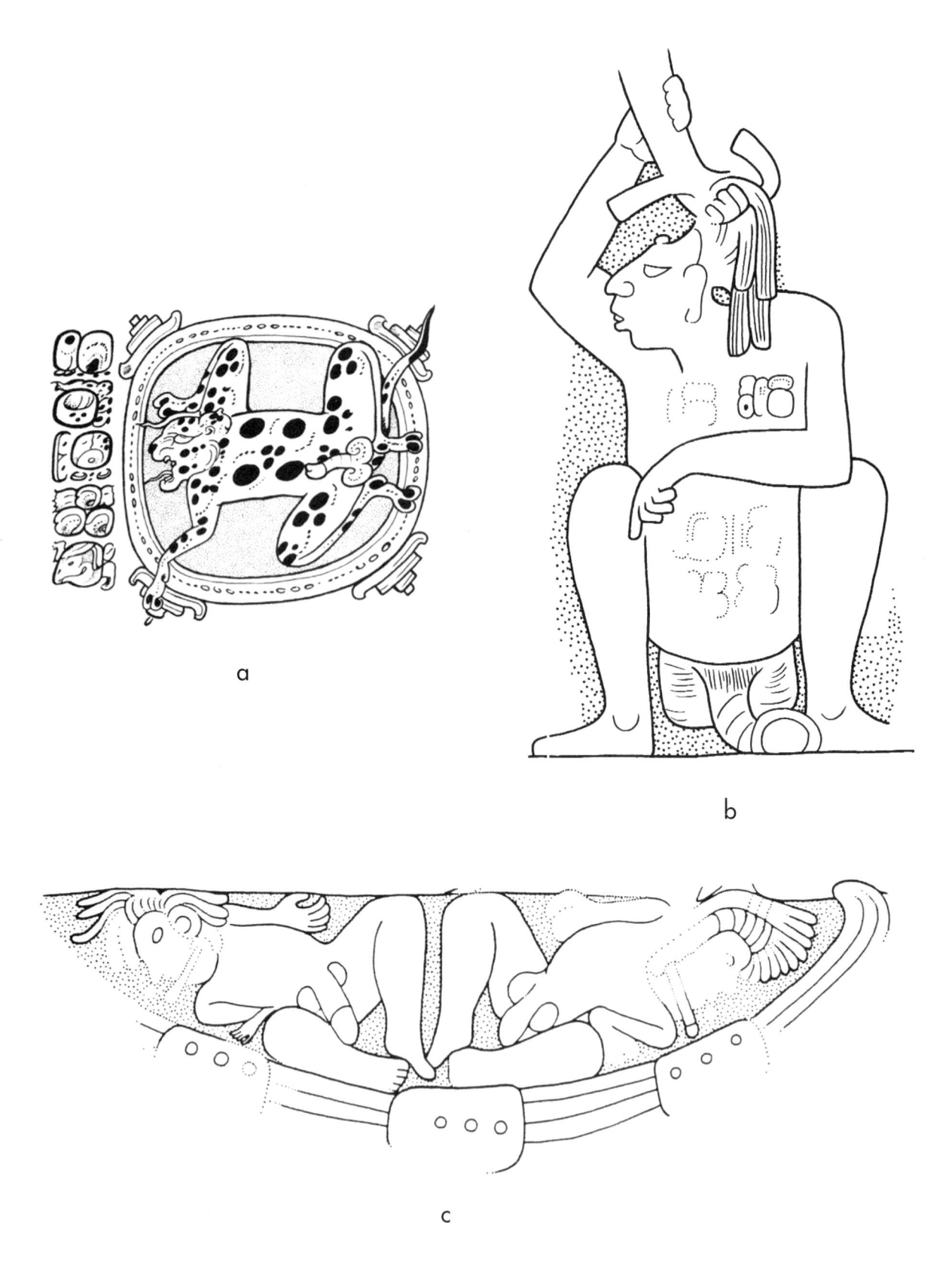

Fig. 6.9. Penises: (a) jaguar *way*, vessel in the Museum of Fine Arts, Boston (after K771); (b) captive from stela in region of Yaxchilan (after Tovalín et al. 1998:fig. 3); and (c) captives on Uxmal Stela 14 (I. Graham 1992:108).

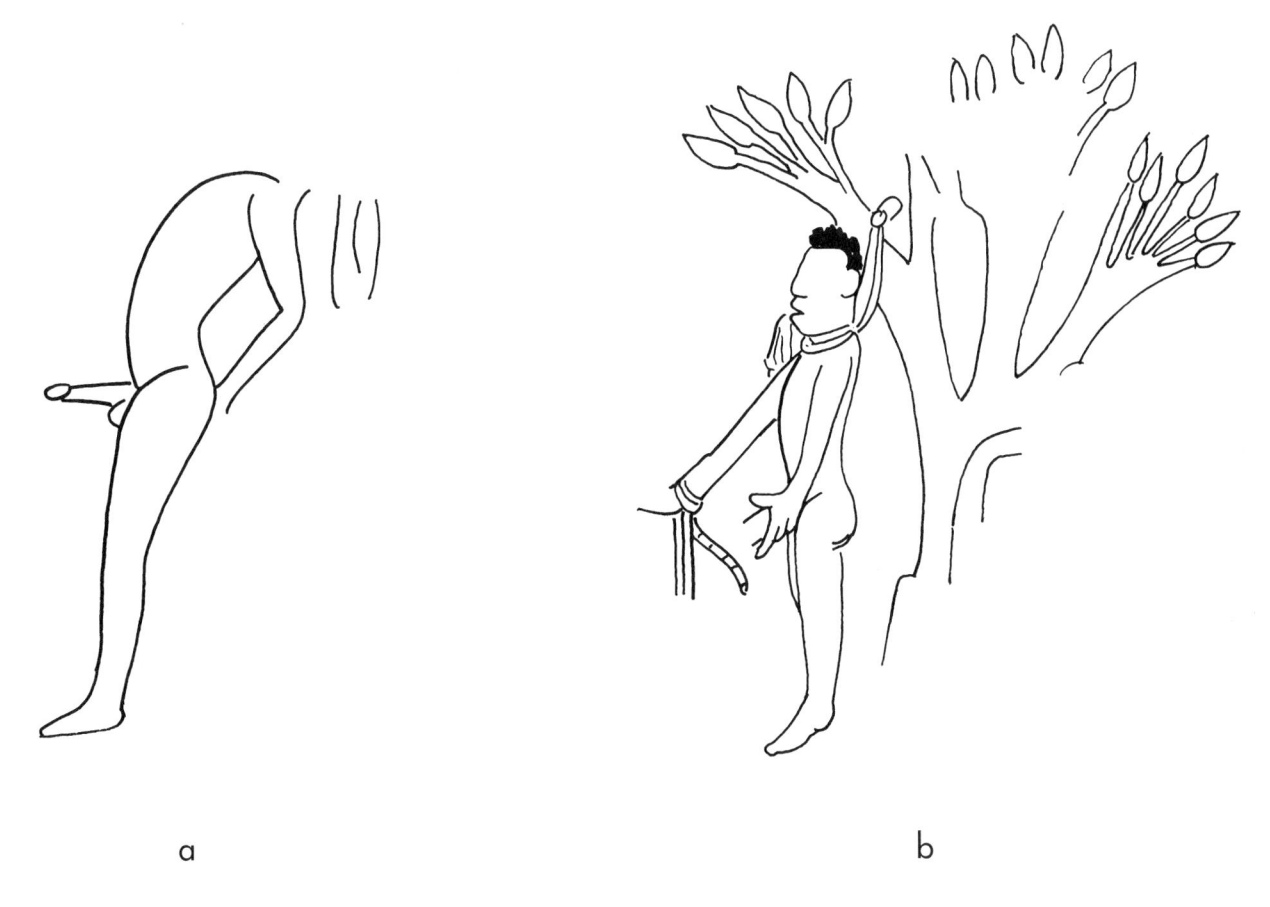

Fig. 6.10. Erections and captives: (a) graffito from Tikal (Orrego Corzo and Larios Villalta 1983:lám. 23); and (b) captive hung from tree, Mulchic, Yucatan (Barrera Rubio 1980:fig. 1).

bowels or gush urine are animals, with the exception of some death gods (the oozings of decomposition?), what may be a captive impersonating a rodent (K728), and a poorly understood picture of a deity (A. Stone 1995a:fig. 6-15). By no reading can these be regarded as beautiful or aesthetically pleasing sights: here is a culturally specific anatomy of disgust and dishonor, not lust and delight, especially with respect to the genitals (W. Miller 1997:17, 82, 101–108). Their accentuation in images of captives may further suggest a desire to control their reproduction or to curtail it (Gelya Frank, personal communication, 2002). Tellingly, no ruler in the corpus of Maya images appears in this manner, excepting the unique image on the conch mentioned before, which combines forced sex from both male and female captives. When examples of elite genital bloodletting are shown, the privates are almost always concealed, as on La Pasadita Lintel 2 or Yaxchilan Lintel 17 (Schele and M. Miller 1986:pls. 64, 70, 76). Quite simply, Maya rulers did not make a habit of exhibiting their penises.

Examples of uncontrolled behavior extend to even more subtle images. In many scenes of capture and subsequent acts of display and humiliation, captives reach up to touch the groins of their captors. One mythic representation, with God N taking a supernatural captive, has him grasping the hair of his victim at the same time that the captive reaches over for his groin (Fig. 6.12a; Orrego Corzo and Larios Villalta 1983:lám. 8). At Yaxchilan, Mexico, a prominent captive, widely recorded in the monuments of the captor, also clutches clothing near the midsection of the king (Lintel 45; I. Graham 1979:45). Joyce sees this same image only in terms of an "aesthetic delight in the male body," eventually to be combined in her argument with "male sexuality and male beauty" embodied in the "erect penis" (R. Joyce 2000b:

Fig. 6.11. Captive and lord on Monument 65, Kaminaljuyu (after L. Parsons 1986:149).

267, 270). In the doorjambs of the Codz Poop, Kabah, Yucatan, a captive's hand disappears beneath the loincloth of his captor, and his other hand touches the spear, perhaps a proxy for the captor's penis and another marker of aggression (Fig. 6.12b; Pollock 1980:fig. 372); a far earlier parallel may be found on the Early Classic Xultun Stela 12 (von Euw 1978:39). In one enigmatic image, two intertwined captives on Monument 83 from Tonina paw at each other, partly in agony, partly in what may be homoerotic groping. They have become insensate to the expectations of rank and courtly poise; they are degraded, almost bestial in their indifference to appearance (I. Graham and Mathews 1996:113; see also San Diego, in Barrera Rubio and Taube 1987:fig. 6, and K728). Another possibility is that they wrangle in a form of compulsory, gladiatorial conflict (see below). (Note that one female touches the blade—a surrogate penis?—of a warrior [Fig. 6.13].)

In none of these scenes do the victors openly solicit homoerotic gestures, nor is there any shadow of affection, as between Alexander and the Persian Boy: this is the iconography of loathing and the assertive imputation of weakness. Even the clowns from Telantunich, Yucatan, are intended to be amusing in a buffoonish way, not attractive. By contrast, the victor has a physical carriage—such as that expressed in images of Naram-Sîn in Mesopotamia—that emotes masculine potency, vigor, and authority (I. Winter 1996:11, 15, 21). The victors can take what they want, when they want, with perfect regulation of the "docile body" that may be "subjected, used, transformed" but not, against Michel Foucault (1995:136), "improved." At a much later date, the great K'iche'an drama *Rabinal Achi* contrasts the courageous, noble captive Cawek with a sexually ambiguous slave, *mun*, portrayed by a man wearing a bearded mask but women's clothing (D. Tedlock

2003:figs. 4, 19). In this performance, the figure is referred to as "man slave, woman slave" (D. Tedlock 2003:109–112). One possible inference is that these images express a moral gloss on the appetites of enemies, in an earlier version of the repugnance felt by Yukatek Maya and others for the supposed "nefarious vices" (*vicio nefando*) of the Itza (G. Jones 1998:211, 333). The Aztec went on at length in early Colonial sources about the lewdness, weakness to temptation, and vile habits of the Wastek, a Mayan-speaking people on the coast of Veracruz (Sahagún 1950–1982, bk. 10:193). In much the same manner, many ancient peoples associated male homosexuality with "others" from whom those practices crept in to infiltrate local society: The Greeks understood that homosexuality came from the Persians; Medieval Europeans blamed the Arabs; Hebrews, the Egyptians and Canaanites; the Tudor English, whomever they were at war with at the moment; and the Tokugawa Japanese identified male-to-male sex as a Chinese "teaching" but, much like the Greeks, did not see it in such a negative fashion (Leupp 1995:12–13). By their nature, then, many antagonists coveted acts of passive and pleasurable penetration; that is why they disgusted; that is what they were meant to do as weaklings. From this it would seem that certain homosexual acts were regarded unfavorably in official imagery of the Classic Maya except in rare instances of drunken excess (see Chapters 3 and 5). Halperin's "passivity" and "inversion" were what other disagreeable people did, especially in rival kingdoms nearby. In this, the Maya of the Classic period were quite different from the Zhou, Han, and later Chinese, who stated in one proverb that "a beautiful lad can ruin an older head," a warning directed at high officials who might be swayed by favorites: the advice had force not because homoerotic bonds were rare, but because they were relatively common (Hinsch 1990:31, 35–36).

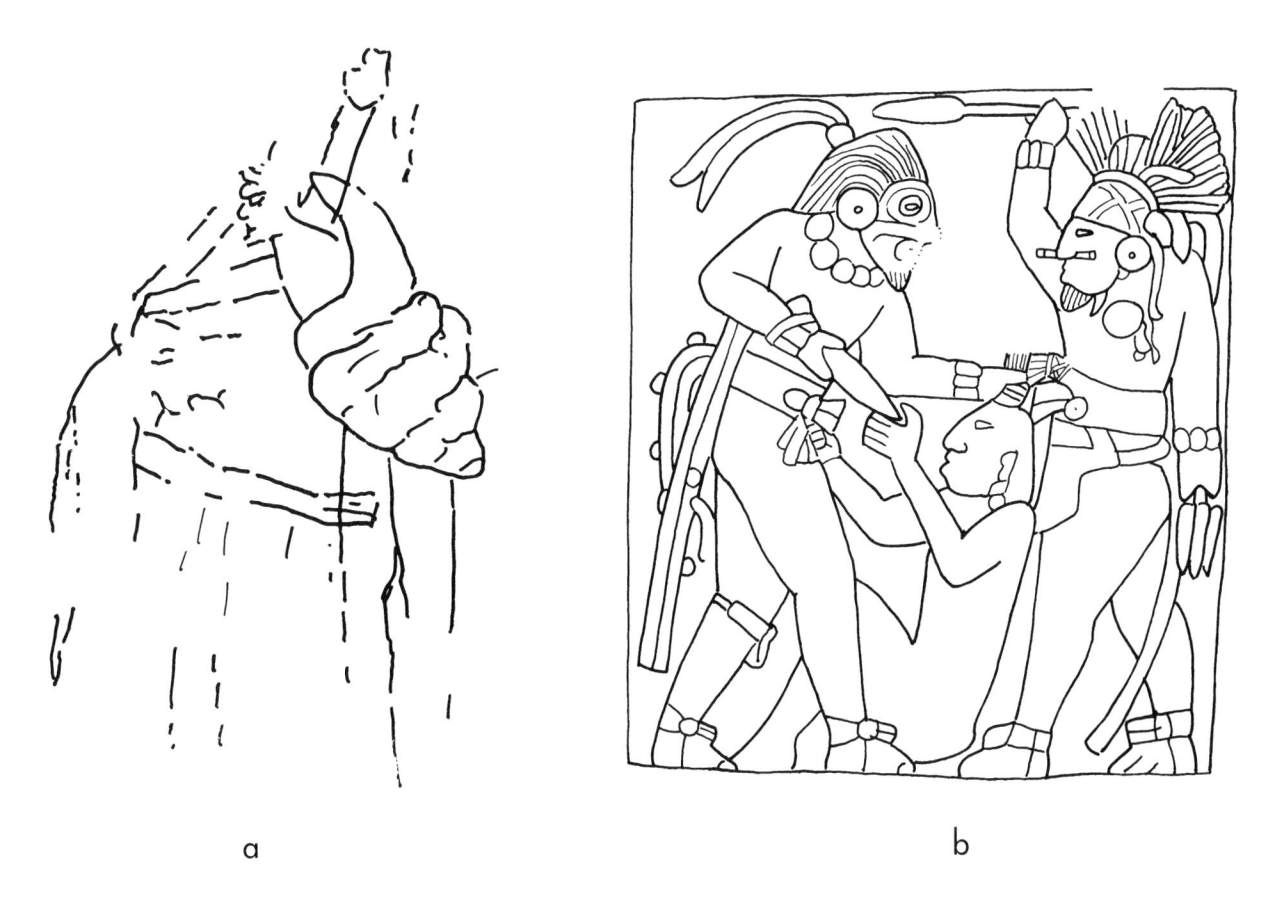

a   b

Fig. 6.12. Sexual gestures from captives: (a) captive and God N, Tikal graffito (Orrego Corzo and Larios Villalta 1983:lám. 8); and (b) captive on doorjamb of Codz Poop, Kabah, Yucatan (after Pollock 1980:fig. 372).

Fig. 6.13. Female touching the blade (surrogate penis?) of warrior (after K5451).

A second inference is that the captive was so much unwilling flesh, to be done with as the captor wished. In this sense, there is more than a glimmer of Halperin's "pederasty" or "active sodomy," an enforcement of one will over another. A revealing piece of comparative evidence comes from a painted Athenian vessel on which a young man holds his penis and shouts, "I am Eurymedon," in a battle against the Persians, and runs toward a bent-over Persian, who exclaims, "I stand bent over," while presenting his behind to the Greek (Dover 1989:105; Kilmer 2002:135–138; Trexler 1995:fig. 1). A central discrepancy with Maya imagery, however, is the generalized identity of these figures, whereas the Maya emphasized very particular acts of capture. The imposed will may also account for evidence of gladiatorial contests between Maya, perhaps involving captives goaded on by their owners (K7749): they fight without animosity, only the determination to survive—in a subtle way the very act of wrestling evokes the sweatiness of erotic contact. Some captives depicted in graffiti at Tikal (Fig. 6.14a; Orrego Corzo and Larios Villalta 1983:lám. 17) and on Stela 24 at Xultun (Fig. 6.14b; von Euw and I. Graham 1984:84) have had their lips tied shut with cloth passing through holes in the lips—indeed, as is mentioned as a threat in the *Rabinal Achi:* "Would that I could just bind / his lower lip / to his upper lip" (D. Tedlock 2003:89, 309). The result is that they have been deprived of speech, a key human attribute, as an extreme example of bodily control and volitional deprivation. In much the same way, the behavior of Classic Maya captives alludes once again to Halperin's category of "passivity."

But this is crucial: whether such acts took place or not is almost irrelevant to the assertion of absolute dominance in an eroticized domain, much like the strong evidence of symbolic homoerotic violence visited on the enemies of the Tumucua in Florida (Trexler 1995:68). This is stark aggression couched in the idiom of sexuality, not sexuality per se. Joyce sees pleasure, but when dealing with captives, the Maya in fact stressed pain, humiliation, and antipathy. Yet we must concede one point: it is possible for the hated to be beautiful as well. Certain images emit rich and ambivalent meanings—that is what makes the scenes poignant and intoxicating to the viewer, somewhat like the poet Heinrich Heine's oxymorons of "sweet cruelty," the "voluptuousness of revenge," and "cruel tenderness" (P. Gay 1993:7). For example, the "Songs of Dzitbalché" from Colonial Yucatan contain paeans to the comeliness of male sacrifices, particularly the handsome messengers sent to communicate with deities (Sigal 2000:131–133). As mentioned before, Mary Miller has often commented on the artful and noncanonical experimentation in human form afforded by the bodies of captives. The beauty of the male captive is clearly emphasized on an incised image from Tikal that shows a captive with jade beads woven into his hair (Fig. 6.15). But we should remember: those who are killing victims hear from the spectators, "Do not

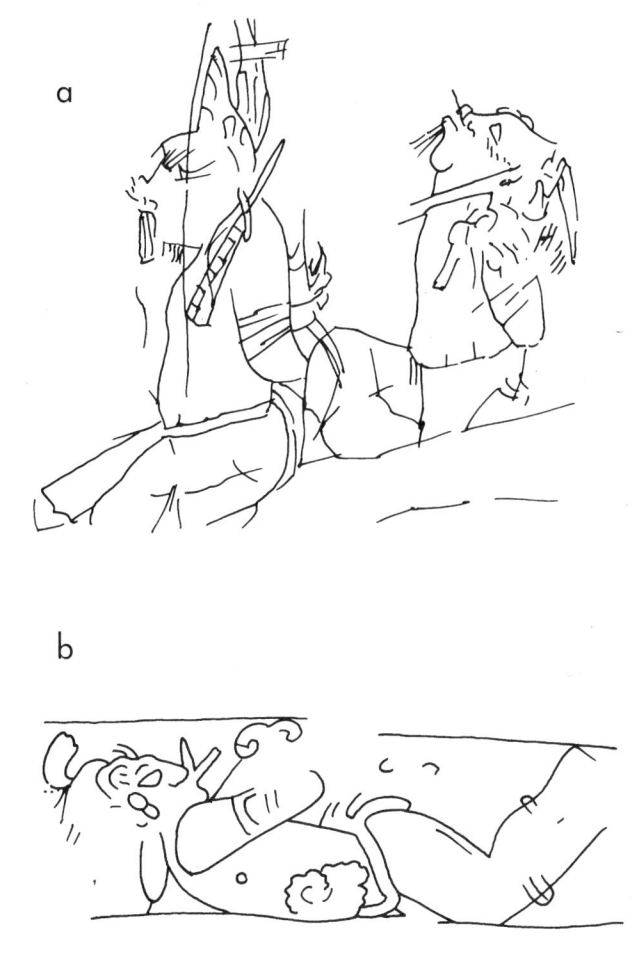

Fig. 6.14. Captives with lashed lips: (a) graffito from Tikal (Orrego Corzo and Larios Villalta 1983:lám. 17); and (b) Stela 24, Xultun (von Euw and Graham 1984:84).

wound him to the depths of his flesh, for he should suffer little by little" (Sigal 2000:137).

MEAT

In escalating rhetoric, the Classic Maya went from the degradation of captives to outright dehumanization: the captive diminished from unwilling person to unwilling flesh (Taube 1988b), rather like the Assyrian strategy of comparing adversaries with animals (Cifarelli 1998). At this point, the captives equated to the deer that Maya lords hunted and consumed, at least to judge from the high proportion of deer bones in palace middens, perhaps items of food brought as tribute (Pohl 1994). In Classic Maya imagery, scenes of deer hunting abound. The usual weapons were spears and atlatl; loving attention was paid to leaping movements

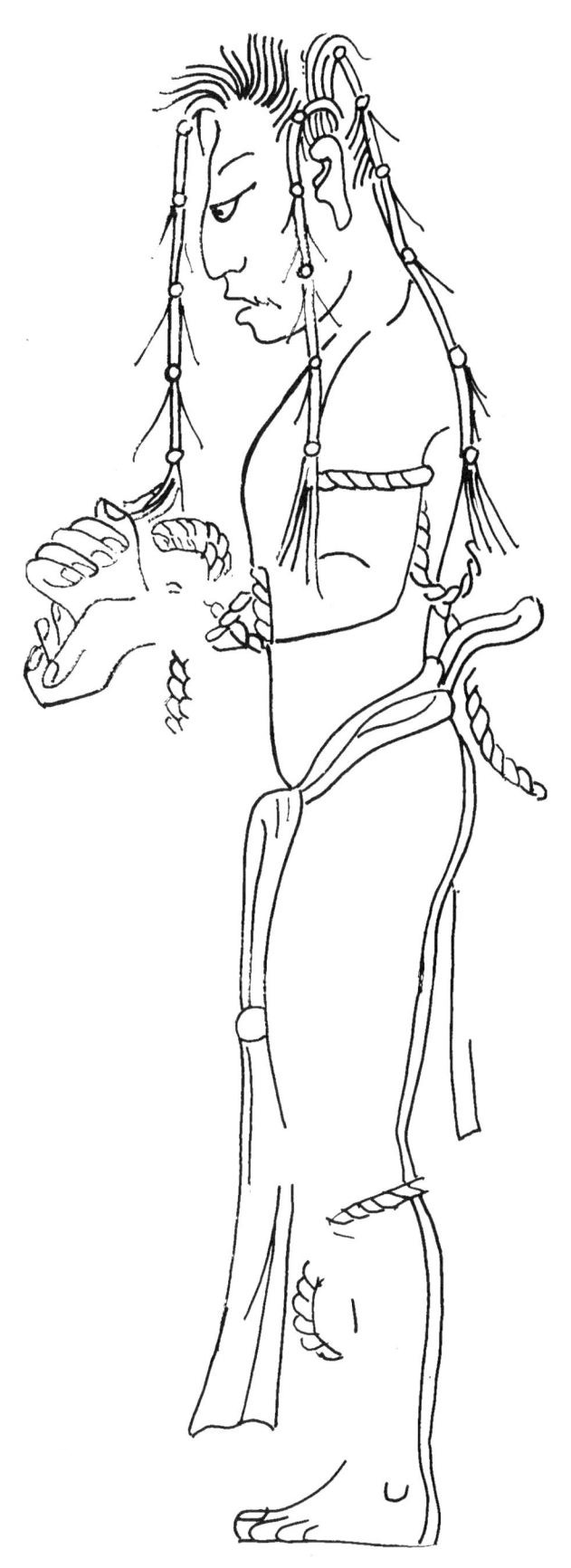

Fig. 6.15. A beautified captive (after W. Coe 1967:128).

and, eventually, the lolling tongue of the exhausted prey, its genitals in full view (K1788, K6420). Drums and especially conches were used to disorient the deer and coordinate the movements of hunters (K771, K2785, K3055). When caught, often by a spear through the neck, the deer was cut up into distinct parts, a tidy package of skin, guts, and head, all lashed by tumpline to be carried back for cooking. Not a few scenes focus on this final act and the satisfactory image of a cut, cleansed, and prepared deer (Fig. 6.16; K1116, K1373, K2995, K8553). As anthropomorphic creatures, sometimes depicted with clothing or ornaments, the deer appears also to have been regarded as lascivious. He cuckolds a sleeping older deity with a beautiful spouse (-*atan*), who willingly offers her body to the deer (K1182, K2794, K1339; see also Chapter 1). This dissolute quality—an editorial comment on the many sexual partners of male deer and their propensity to raid females from other groups?—may explain the frequent occurrence of signs for filth and excrement (the "*caban*" scroll) on their ears. The contradiction is evident: attractive, tasty beasts that, as voluptuaries, appear morally *dis*tasteful.

At some juncture, the deer-as-animal merges closely with the captive-as-deer, both as prey and as ritual food. Moche imagery from the coast of South America is replete with similar conceptual fusions (Donnan and McClelland 1999:135). The most overt merger among the Maya appears on an unprovenanced vessel showing warriors with conches, apparently doing a hunting or victory dance (Fig. 6.17; K1082); drums, flutes, and rattles complete the orchestration. The camouflage worn by hunters, dark spots to blend with forest greenery, is also used by warriors. Between the dancing figures are butchered or bleeding captives, including body parts (heads, haunches) cut up and lashed like venison. Comparable hunting scenes exhibit the same acts of cutting and reduction of the body into delectable parts (K1373). Excavations at San Lorenzo, Mexico, attest to strong evidence of cannibalism in earlier Olmec contexts (M. Coe and Diehl 1980, 1:390). Grant Jones expresses deep skepticism about later accounts of Itza Maya ritual cannibalism—"they chopped up their bodies and tossed them into pots, having separate female Indian cooks for this"—and describes this as a spurious "rhetoric of depravity" that justified Spanish incursions into the last Maya kingdom (1998:329–332).

Yet there is increasing physical evidence in other martial polities, such as those of the Moche in Plaza 3A of the Huaca de la Luna, that captives were regarded as flesh to be cut up, body parts to be inserted in other captives, and repositories of blood to be poured into offering vessels (Bourget 2001:95–96; Donnan and McClelland 1999:fig. 4.85); other Moche information confirms repeated mistreatment of captives prior to death (Verano 2001:118–121). The Anasazi Southwest supplies credible evidence of such behaviors as well (C. Turner and J. Turner 1999; White 1992). Several figures of *way*, including a jaguar and a human on the celebrated bowl in the Popol Vuh Museum, show the fleshy, muscular parts of the limbs removed, as though part of a customary butchering process (e.g., Robicsek and Hales 1981:fig. 88). This practice of butchering continued into the Early Postclassic at Chichen Itza, Yucatan, and Tula, Hidalgo (Diehl 1983:pl. 18; Seler 1902–1923, 5:figs. 237–239). The Maya perspective, however, doubtless involved something other than caloric intake, as has been unpersuasively suggested for Aztec cannibalism (Harner 1977).

Fig. 6.16. Butchering of deer after hunt (K1373, copyright Justin Kerr).

Fig. 6.17. Butchering of captives (K1082, copyright Justin Kerr).

Instead, it transgressed the captive's volition by another, more dramatic step. The victim's very fabric, the soul force inhering in human remains, no longer belonged to him and his kin, but was disposed of, as a ritual cache or foodstuff, according to the will of the captor, rather like Renato Rosaldo's information on the ferocious emotions involved in Ilongot headhunting (1980:140; for examples of fetishized body parts, see Sharp 2000:294–295) or the corpses of Libyans castrated by Egyptians (Trexler 1995:17–18). The Classic term for "captive," *b'aak*, literally means "bone," the core constituent of the body and the most salient feature of starving captives (see Chapter 3). It also carries a striking similarity to a lowland Mayan term for "meat and the privates," *b'ak'*, the sole phonemic difference being the glottalization of the final consonant and, perhaps, vowel length—was there an ancient perception of semantic affinity between the terms (e.g., Barrera Vásquez 1980:29; Ringle n.d.: Ch'olti' *bacat*)? Maya imagery often shows shrunken heads, hair astray, faces inverted, and even complete bodies worn as a human ornament (e.g., K1080, K1206; Yaxchilan Lintel 9, I. Graham and von Euw 1977:29): again, whether these were real or clever props matters little beyond the fact that such things were employed as elements of dress.

The supreme spectacle would have been the Classic version of a skull rack, an arbor of heads in varied stages of decomposition, within which existed the dread *way*, or companion spirits, of the wild and undomesticated forest (Fig. 6.18a, b; K3924; Taube 2003; also at Tonina, Yadeun 1993:108–115). Nonetheless, in all these examples, human body parts are not to be taken lightly (so to speak), in that the more usual consumers of human hands, eyeballs, bones, and other gristle were those same *way* (Chapter 3). The Maya skull rack is likely to have existed at Tonina: the back of the rack, of modeled stucco showing *way*, would have been visible through an armature, now disappeared, whose only vestiges are a series of holes for wooden supports.

The infliction of pain recalls a Maya figurine that shows a captive wearing a deer headdress hunched over and bound to a sacrificial scaffold (Taube 1988b). A similar scene, from a vessel in the collection of Dumbarton Oaks (Fig. 6.19; K2781), encapsulates this image within a larger one in which white-painted celebrants are about to torch the back of the captive—similar burnings occur in a variety of other contexts in Maya art, in practices that must have triggered almost unimaginable torment, far beyond any possible empathy from, or understanding on the part of, the audience (Martin and Grube 2000:82; Scarry 1985; Schele and M. Miller 1986:pls. 94, 228; Taube 1988b). Many victims of social trauma find small places of refuge; torture violates that place and disables it (Kleinman and Kleinman 1994:717). The predicament of inflicted pain is that the body labors to avoid it but cannot. Moreover, pain is such that it is heightened

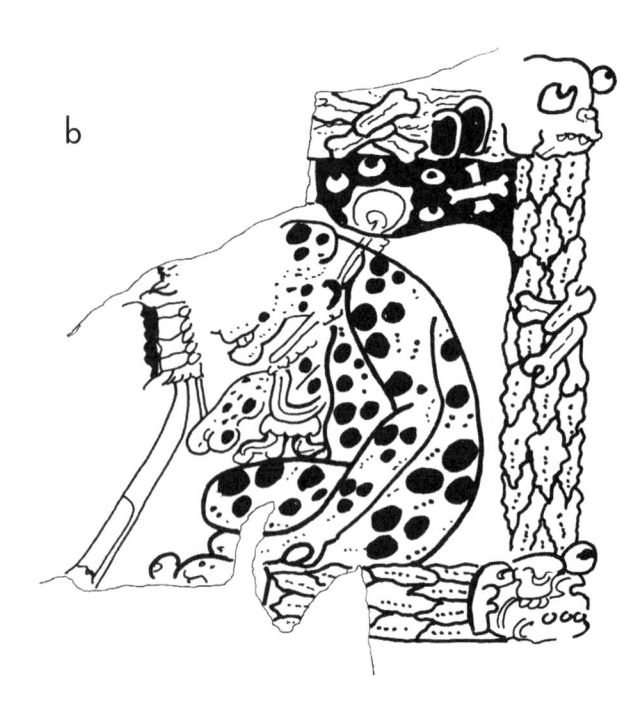

Fig. 6.18. Skull racks and arbors: (a) *way* seated within an arbor house (after K3924); and (b) jaguar *way* with arbor house (after drawing by Jodi Hansen).

by multiple assaults to which the body cannot adjust or adapt (Coren et al. 1999:245).

A productive, nonsensational approach is to provide a context for pain and suffering in Classic Maya rhetoric. Within Christian belief, torture could be seen judicially as a means of extracting truth by bypassing the obdurate human will—there was, as Lisa Silverman suggests, a linkage of suffering with "spiritual perfection and ultimate meaning," just as, in the eighteenth century, that same suffering became associated with "physical corruption and [thus] meaningless" (2001:10). For the Maya, pain may have been seen as both provocation and test; the pain of captives remained the one locus of self-expression—namely, whether to scream or not, whether to control the flesh driven beyond endurance. In a warrior ethos, as is well attested among the Huron and other North American groups, the silent endurance linked with suffering in the anthropological literature would have been a sign, not of weakness, but of strength (Fig. 6.20; Heidenreich 1978:fig. 4; cf. Kleinman et al. 1996:xiv–xv). Again, contrary to the literature, there is in the Classic Maya experience a "voyeurism" of a didactive, even empathetic sort. To see is to behold what may eventually happen to the viewer. There is nothing particularly "safe" about it (cf. Kleinman et al. 1996:xvii; Kleinman and Kleinman 1996:1); we are witnessing, in this landscape of pain, a mode of active torture and passive torment that must have been taught and considered (Kleinman and Kleinman 1996:2). From the victor's perspective, captives were not "victims" but figures of suspense, failures waiting to happen or to be forestalled in the final moments of testing—here is where the timocratic orientation returns to the fore, as the challenging may result in personal glory or everlasting shame. In the standard repertoire of images, the captive, alas, meets the low expectations of the victors: the gutted captive tied to a stake projects his tongue and howls; the captive shows no reserve but clutches his upper arms in the Maya gesture of subordination; he will grovel and eat earth—all are images well documented in the Classic Maya corpus (Fig. 6.21a, b; M. Coe 1973:pl. 33; I. Graham and von Euw

Fig. 6.19. Scaffold sacrifice (K2781; M. Coe 1975:26–27, pl. 16).

1977:33, 41; Orrego Corzo and Larios Villalta 1983:lám. 8b; Schele 1997:13–14). Again, like Assyrian reliefs (Cifarelli 1998), it is the victor, or the dancer gutting the captive, who will participate in these tests without the slightest emotion. In the final analysis, he, not the captive, possesses the truly disciplined body (see Chapter 5). His manliness rests on a fettered and controlled sexuality that contrasts with the less manly, undisciplined displays of war captives (Gutmann 1997:386, 398). At the same time, with these images, Classic Maya elites found a sexualized frame for showing, above all, submission, which is among the most central preoccupations of timocratic orientations (Brandes 1980:27).

EARTH

The final disgrace of the captive is for him to be less than a person, less than an animal: he has now become fertilizing earth or parts of the built environment—the first to provide food for the victor, the second to support his feet. A large number of Maya stelae exhibit toponymic registers, that is, areas beneath the feet of lords with "earth" signs or thin bands, representing a surface perhaps, and, underneath further still, the distorted bodies of captives (Aguateca Stela 7, I. Graham 1967:fig. 17; Dos Pilas Stelae 5, 14, Houston 1993:figs. 3-12, 3-24; Xultun Stelae 14, 21, 22). If the registers are absent, then the lords or ladies may stand directly on captives who are surrounded by signs for stone (Naranjo Stelae 29, 30, I. Graham 1978:77, 79). In a Classic convention that is probably meant to show comic grotesquerie, some of the captives violate the norms of facial display by presenting themselves *en face* to the viewer, rather like lame extras staring into a movie camera or, perhaps more empathetically, as figures who attract the viewer's gaze by means of direct address (Naranjo Stela 33,

Fig. 6.20. Torture among the Huron (after Heidenreich 1978:fig. 4).

I. Graham 1978:87; Xultun Stelae 4, 5, 8, von Euw 1978:19, 23, 31)—in all such displays the viewer is the arbitral figure, necessary for the image to "complete" itself and to achieve its full function as a confirming witness of personal honor (W. Miller 1993:59). The same facial view occurs in the enigmatic scenes of sexual license in the deep, dark zone of the Naj Tunich cave, another indication of the highly marked nature of those images (cf. R. Joyce [2000b:fig. 15.7 and p. 273], who herself admits that "these images are remarkable" while suggesting that they exemplify "sexualization of the Classic Maya male body" and that they "stand firmly within the canons of Classic Maya art").

Fig. 6.21. Gutting: (a) victim on scaffold (after M. Coe 1973:pl. 33); and (b) victim tied to stake (after Orrego Corzo and Larios Villalta 1983:lám. 8b).

It is unlikely to be a coincidence that the most common expression for royal agency in Maya texts, read *u-chab'-j-iiy,* almost certainly involves a perceived equivalence between royal or palace work and the manuring and cultivation of fields (Laughlin 1988, 1:184–185)—the labor of peasants who must have been broadly recognized, although seldom celebrated, as the mainstays of daily life and the purveyors of maize, the Maya domesticate of distinction. The *Rabinal Achi* also specifically equates conquest with a kind of cultivation: "*I* was working the soil / *I* was resetting the boundaries of the land" (D. Tedlock 2003; in one monument, Dos Pilas Stela 14, the themes of captive and "cultivation" are nicely integrated by the inclusion of the *u-chab-j-iiy* expression in the toponymic register, just above the figure and name of the captive; Fig. 6.22). The supposition is that the most appropriate repository for captives is one that fructifies the land of the victorious enemy. Certain rocky outcrops, as at Tikal and Calakmul, display captives; at Calakmul they are plump and ungainly (Fig. 6.23; W. Coe 1967:84; corpulence was also used by the Maya to denote the bloating that accompanied putrescence, e.g., K2286, K2716; the extruded belly button in such figures, the *sitz' chamay*(?), may come from the pressure of internal gases). In the tropics, heat, insects, and birds would soon strip such captives of flesh and leave a gruesome residue to be picked for bones that might be inserted into caches (D. Chase and A. Chase 1998; for parallel instances of sarcoaprophagy, see Verano 1986). The captives highlighted on the east side of the East Court of Palenque Palace look as though they may well have been hewn from irregular bedrock before being removed to their final setting (M. G. Robertson 1985b:figs. 289, 290). An expression from Dos Pilas Hieroglyphic Stairway 2 (east, Block 3: E2–H1) may describe this ritual as *witz-aj u jolil nahb'-aj u-k'ik'el*(?), roughly, "hills are their heads, pools are their blood (?)." The occasional skull caches at sites like Altar de Sacrificios and Uaxactun, Guatemala, may involve such rituals,

Fig. 6.22. Dos Pilas Stela 14 (Houston 1993:fig. 3.24).

Fig. 6.23. "Captive rock," Calakmul (after field drawing by Ian Graham).

though the blood, however, is long since gone (A. L. Smith 1950:93; 1972:211). The captive's body has now gone beyond a homoerotic agent, a fleshy counterpart to the succulent meat of deer, to become a fertilizer that provides food and sustenance for the victor and the fabric of royal spaces in the conqueror's city. Degradation is complete.

CONCLUSION

The dishonor of captives has been presented so far as a pattern of escalating humiliation—a set of actions that became accentuated in an atmosphere of increased antipathy during the Late Classic period—but it is not at all clear that most captives were treated this way. The imagery and texts of the Classic Maya emphasize a theatrical role for captives that ridicules enemies and exhorts retainers and dynasts alike to acts of valor. Yet, some captives may well have evaded this cycle by achieving utilitarian and sentimental value as members of households and families through gestures of grace and conciliation: they were no longer "objectified," in the sense of barely or nonanimate flesh, but preserved as people—over the long term they were allowed to keep their "subjectivities" or partial assertions of self-identity (Sharp 2000:290). The few known instances of captive kings spotlight their subordinate position yet typically with some modicum of dignity. Such rulers could be dishonored, perhaps, but at the cost of endangering the very institution that undergirded Maya polities: in a comparable case from early Modern Europe, François I of France was treated by the Spaniards, after his defeat and capture at the Battle of Pavia, with the deference due a *roi très chrétien*, to the extent that his attendance at mass took place "amidst a pomp normally reserved for Spanish monarchs" (Knecht 1994:225–227, 239–246). On a more practical level, rulers served a useful role as hostages in the power plays of Classic conflict. However, these exceptions were nearly invisible: the exemplary captive was bruised, tortured, eaten, mulched into soil, dishonored. The shame of the Maya war captive was, their captors avowed, now and forever.

◀▶ CHAPTER SEVEN

Words on Wings

Barring various pathologies, all human beings employ a vocal apparatus and use the sounds it produces to communicate. There are universals to be found here, more than a hint of the pan-human (Pinker 2001). Yet, there are also three widely held tenets of anthropology: (1) that people around the world categorize speech in different ways, depending on performer, audience, and intention; (2) what those categories mean will vary, depending on individuals and local understandings; and (3) if such categories are embedded in society and within that web of meanings we call "culture," then they stand a good chance of changing through time, not only as evolving practices but as shifting ideas about what they might mean and how they might be construed in hierarchical societies. A result of this is that ideas and their representations have a history. Those ideas can be inspected by examining the ways in which they were expressed in texts, imagery, and residual evidence from descendant peoples, many of whom continue to live in Central America and Mexico. This chapter examines the embodied shape of fleeting communications, in this case envisioned as the bird messengers of deities. Here, too, as expressed in earlier chapters, is abundant testimony to the indistinct membrane between the material and the nonmaterial, the volitional and nonvolitional, the animate and the inanimate.

MAYA NOTIONS OF FORMAL SPEECH

Later evidence of Colonial and post-Colonial date provides a useful entrée into such concepts. The methodological question is whether these valuations and characterizations of speech result from our views or reflect some detectable and persistent grooves of thinking. For example, in 1974, Gary Gossen presented a classification of speech types taken from statements by his informants in the Tzotzil Maya community of Chamula, Chiapas (1974:46–55). Some twenty-five years later, he disavowed these ethnocategorizations of Maya discourse as "naive" and favored the foregrounding of a "Kansan from Oz," namely, Gossen himself (1999:xviii–xx, 27–28). So which Gossen is correct? The answer is less a prima facie one than a matter of utilitarian appraisal: Are there enduring, coherently organized ideas apparent in dictionary evidence?

The *Great Tzotzil Dictionary of Santo Domingo Zinacantán* (Laughlin 1988, 2:550–552) records a wide selection of Colonial-period terms for speech, including labels for "gossip intended to arouse discord"; swearing of oaths; speaking abusively; speaking at length, coldly, or elegantly—often in lordly fashion—or with barbs, wit, and restraint. Brian Stross sees these categorizations as being, in theory, part of an "open" system with numerous possibilities depending on setting, yet, somewhat alarmingly, with "little consistency among informants"; the one common feature appears to be a distinction between "recent speech" and "ancient" or "traditional speech" (1989:218, 220). In Tzotzil Maya, there may be ritual speech or deceitful speech, but above all, as Evon Vogt reminds us, it must be effective discourse: *k'op*, for example, means "word" or "language" but also "dispute," pointing to a need for intermediaries who can "say the correct things at the right time" (1993:204–205). Colonial Tzendal, a related language, appears to have prized talk that was to the point; a negative value attached to those who spoke with little economy or twisted and "doubled" words (J. Robertson n.d.). Unlike inconsequent mumbling or jabbering, speech of this more formal sort obeyed rules of decorum. In Ch'ol ritual language, for example, "to speak to candles" (*sub nichim*) was to address supernaturals or ancestors, and "to pray" or "to summon" involved a term for "call" or, in Tzeltal, spoken nearby, a "greeting from the heart" (*pat 'o'tan;* Josserand and Hopkins 1996). Supernaturals ingested such words like food, along with other "tasty" offerings, including flowers, rum, music, candles, tobacco leaves, and fireworks (Gossen 1974:161). The *Popol Vuh* explains this, too: "For it is with words that we [the gods] are sustained" (Christenson 2000:47).

In lowland Mayan languages, the more common terms for "words" and "talk" or "speech" include *t'an*, which implies two-way communication and, in Colonial Yukatek, sexual intercourse, and the more transparent *ik'ti'* (*ycti*), "breath-mouth," in Ch'olti' (Ringle n.d.). According to modern understanding, breath sucks oxygen into the lungs and, in reverse direction, removes carbon dioxide. In contrast, and as explained in Chapter 4, the ancient Maya believed that vitalizing forces resided in the breath and other exhalations, including "flatulence," the onomatopoeic *tis* in Mayan. Logically, then, the Classic Maya would affirm that speech discharged or included part of the speaker's essence. It consisted of not just empty words but potent emanations, sometimes of an especially fiery nature. In Colonial Tzotzil, this is how one might describe the fierce gust emitted by kings (*k'ak'al ik';* Laughlin 1988, 2:558). In Tzendal, not surprisingly, terms for "curing" involved *wuchiy*, "blowing like dust" or the steaming from "hot food," as if emanating grit, thrust, and heat or perhaps the curative smoke of tobacco (*Vuchiy*, "*curar con palabras*," and "*soplar como polvo, comida caliente*"; J. Robertson n.d.; Wilbert 1987).

The material nature of speech is amply attested in the many "speech scrolls" that exist in Maya imagery (Chapter 4; Houston and Taube 2000:273–281). These are looping scrolls that snap from lips and connect with texts nearby or slither about as disjointed echoes in one ballcourt scene. There are several dozen examples of these from the Late Classic period. The Classic Maya used them in a highly selective fashion. Most occur only on vessels from Peten, Guatemala. On some pots (K2914), only one person, a lowly servant, has one, whereas higher-status figures nearby do not. Is he whispering an aside to the reader, in commentary on the splendid scene around him? Relatively few deities, goddesses, or supernaturals are ever shown with speech scrolls (but see K732, K1560). When they so appear, the chat appears to be very one-sided, perhaps because of intensely hierarchical relations; only one party addresses the other at a time (e.g., K1196). As we shall see, this is the nature of the bird messengers, who call out but may not necessarily listen.

A departure from this is the famed Rabbit Pot from the area of Naranjo, Guatemala, in which God L entreats the Sun God, who responds in turn, within glyphs peppered with first-person references (Fig. 7.1). These references enrich the ordinary third-person expressions of most Mayan glyphic texts by injecting instances of multiple points of view, including first- and second-person pronouns, such as *ni-*, "I, my"; *a(w)-*, "you, your";

and *ka-*, "we, our" (Bricker 1986:89–91; Houston and D. Stuart 1993). Nonetheless, their use was extremely rare, and the Maya deployed them only in special circumstances in which they attempted to break the existential field between the viewer or reader and those who were depicted or referenced (Chapter 2). In such contexts, the observers' aloofness from an image or an inscription was obliterated; by forthright invitation, they were encouraged to enter the time and space of prior events. Another device was the use of quotative statements. These recorded speech acts and then, by using the expression "say," *-al-*, identified who said what and to whom. Most such statements occur between supernaturals. The references also contain a hierarchical twist in that the "speakers" tend to be supplicants: higher-ranking personages listen but may not always deign to talk, an important clue to sociolinguistic behavior of courtly Maya. They allude to kinds of speech that have no direct witness and exist in a category of proverbial, almost timeless oration. In contrast, Nikolai Grube (1998) describes other statements (*cheen*, perhaps "thus says so-and-so") of particular artists and, in one case, a ruler. Presumably, these statements were presented within a less suppositional or proverbial frame. Chapter 4 introduced many other examples of speech scrolls and tabulated their adjectival properties: dotted or dashed lines may have indicated stuttering or interrupted, segmented talk or possibly some localized convention that underscored the ephemeral nature of speech; this convention also appears in a few scenes with human protagonists (K3469). To a striking extent, goddesses or noble ladies rarely have any such scrolls, whether dashed or continuous (Fig. 7.2; see K7727 for an exception). Palace discourse of a formal sort may not have countenanced an overt role for female participants, although one can well imagine that their voices were heard, rather strongly, behind the palatial curtain.

Unfortunately, it is difficult to find a single explicit reference to a category of formal speech in Maya hieroglyphs. Several pieces of evidence were introduced in Chapter 4, including a dedicatory verb on Maya ceramics containing the skull of a death god, from which threads a skein of wind, so identified by the "wind," or *ik'*, signs at its end or the glyphs for courtly singers at Bonampak and Tikal. Did the Maya distinguish carefully between "song" and "eloquent spoken word," or did courtly address veer between lyrical, full-throated vocalization and something closer to cadenced speech? In Nahuatl, the language of the Aztec, *xochitia*, "to utter witticisms and bon mots; to make people laugh" (Karttunen 1992:328) comes from a root meaning "flower." This word implied an aesthetic judgment, for the reason that the Aztec (and the Classic Maya) were much concerned with floral metaphors. Similarly, Classic Maya notions of "song" may have reflected multiple genres of speech, including lofty oration and other feats of eloquence. For example, modern Yukatek discourse is divided into genres that range from "song" to "prayer" and "ritual greetings" to "conversation" (Burns 1983:24). The fact that the Classic Maya god of wind was also a deity connected with song—connected explicitly at Copan (9N-8 Bench) and Palenque (the Palace Tablet) with the shaking of rattles—suggests a close bond between the breath of speech and Classic music making (Taube 2004a:74). However, formal utterances tend to take the shape of dialogue, of antiphonal responses or questions and answers in which several people perform. A Classic Maya vessel (K2697) excavated by Juan Pedro Laporte at Tikal shows at least two figures speaking simultaneously, at least to judge from their speech scrolls (see also K625, K4996). Very likely, there were moments that had real conversation; others, only unilateral harangues.

BIRDS AS MESSENGERS

One term for "message" or "tidings" was deciphered long ago by Yurii Knorosov as part of his stunning proof for syllabic phoneticism in Mayan writing (Fig. 7.3). This is the term *mut*, [mu-ti] in hieroglyphs, which, according to his hypothesis, corresponded both to a word for "bird" and another for "tidings" (Kelley 1976:181). J. Eric S. Thompson had very different ideas about this word, which occurs frequently in the Postclassic Dresden Codex. For him, images of birds represented "diseases" (Thompson 1958:301); for another

Fig. 7.1. Speech on the Regal Rabbit Pot (K1398, copyright Justin Kerr).

scholar of the time, Thomas Barthel, these creatures were sacrificial birds (1955:18). *Mut* for "bird" is widely documented in lowland Mayan languages, with the key distinction being that, in the Classic period, it contained a long vowel, thus being read *muut*. In this it differed from an expression for "knot of plaited hair," *mut*, which formed the place-name of Tikal, Guatemala. This second word does not have a long vowel and must have entailed an entirely different origin.

The sense of "tidings" or "news" and "fame" that Knorosov inferred came from an early dictionary of Colonial Yukatek, the Motul I (Acuña 1984, 2:314). Parenthetically, another term in the Dresden Codex, *chich*, also communicated the idea of "controlling, strong word," as in the cries of war captains and the themes of preachers or any fast-moving object (Barrera Vásquez 1980:93–94); a glottalized term, *ch'ich'*, was the term for "bird." It is striking that one of these pages from the Dresden refers to a "hummingbird" (*tz'unu*n*) as the *chich*, "word," not *ch'ich'*, "bird," of a deity. The question is whether the term was simply a homophone for "bird," *muut*, or a metaphor of some sort or perhaps even a rare example of punning. The central claim here is that the meaning was both metaphorical and literal in that it visualized messages or tidings as winged creatures.

The claim is not unreasonable or unexpected. Consider the winged boots of Hermes, which were described in Greek poetry as the "lovely sandals" that "carried [the god] over the liquid sea or endless

Fig. 7.2. Woman with speech scroll (after K7727).

Fig. 7.3. *Muut* spelling in the Dresden Codex, p. 18b.

earth as messenger" (Vermeule 1979:65). Emily Vermeule suggests that such boots probably derived from Hittite antecedents and were thus drawn from exceedingly ancient ideas. The wings would also have assisted the deceased, who might, on occasion, have worn facsimiles of winged boots in the hopes of traveling smoothly over the unknowable paths that lie beyond the grave. In the "trecena" (thirteen-day "week" of the sacred calendar) pages of the Aztec documents known as the Codex Borbonicus, Codex Borgia, Codex Tudela, and the Aubin Tonalamatl, different gods associate with different birds, the quetzal, for example, with the voracious Earth God, Tlalteuctli (Kendall 1992). In these scenes, each deity speaks, probably in declarations linked with the appearance of the birds, their messengers (Fig. 7.4; López Austin 2002:fig. 26). Closer to the Classic Maya, the K'iche' wrote of bird messengers in their epic, the *Popol Vuh:* "These messengers were the owls—Arrow Owl, One Leg Owl, Macaw Owl, and Skull Owl—for so the messengers of Xibalba were called" (Christenson 2000:75). Similar birds abound as messengers in the highly esoteric document in Yukatek Maya, the *Ritual of the Bacabs* (Roys 1965:7–8), and Colonial Tzendal likens the calling or luring of birds to legal acts of "summoning" (*Ihc mut,* "reclamar aves," and *Icoghibal mut,* "reclamo"; J. Robertson n.d., in evidence from the Ara dictionary). Such messengers did not operate casually but embodied high and terrible portents. They were, in a word, oracles that pierced the membrane between different worlds, underworld and "aboveworld," divine and human. The cross-cultural linkage of birds or winged deities with messages does not require much of a stretch. Birds, much like messengers, move with swift resolve. They dart through the air like speech scrolls but communicate beyond the normal projection of human lungs. Some birds, such as those on an Early Classic vessel from Tikal, Guatemala, are even shown with speech or song scrolls (Culbert 1993:fig.31a, Burial 48). And perhaps they even served as vehicles of inspiration: a figurine from Jaina, Campeche, shows a weaving woman accompanied by a "bird"—her creative inspiration?—perched on the loom (M. Miller and Martin 2004:pl. 53). Among the ancient and contemporary Maya, birds are similarly placed on the ends of weaving pins (Agrinier 1970:fig. 72.7).

Seen in this light, the birds of the Dresden Codex can be understood as messengers or embodied messages, much as Knorosov suggested close to half a century ago. Thus, "the death god is the message/messenger of Sak Ixik," possibly the Moon Goddess (Dresden Codex, p. 18b; Fig. 7.5). Many of the birds are loud, screechy ones, from macaws to owls. The important point is that the message is almost inseparable from the messenger. Such winged messengers make sense of many Maya images from the Preclassic to the Postclassic. In the recently discovered murals of San Bartolo, Guatemala, William Saturno has found Preclassic images of birds as a central motif (Fig. 7.6; William Saturno, personal communication, 2002). Postclassic contexts some thirteen hundred years later often show descending winged deities on the façades of their temples, usually just above portals or central doorways, in themselves liminal zones between different kinds of spaces. (Note that the "falling" is not the same as a more acrobatic pose in which the Maize God's legs extend into the air and his body appears with serpent or reptilian markings: see Fig. 1.48; snakes are occasionally depicted in this position, as on a palma bearing a Mayan text [Easby and Scott 1970:pl. 154], and Houston has personally seen tropical vipers with pinned heads lift their entire bodies into the air.) A celestial place of origin accords with Classic Mayan expressions for "heaven" or "sky-born" deities (*siyaj kan*). One example, from Tulum Structure 16, is especially noteworthy, for it displays a descending bird deity, usually mislabeled a "diving god" because of the plunging, acrobatic orientation of its body, a position linked iconographically with World Trees and other pivots of space and time (Fig. 7.7b; A. Miller 1982:pl. 37). As one of us (Taube) has pointed out, this is clearly the Maize God, as indicated by details of his headdress (Taube 1992b:41). In his hands the god clutches a human heart, the quintessential food for deities. Three such hearts are piled in a bowl drawn in the Paris Codex, and a painted text from the Las Pinturas building at Coba provides an explicit instruction manual that stipulates how many hearts—in this case thirteen—are to be offered to

Fig. 7.4. Codex Borbonicus, excerpt from p. 6.

particular deities (Chapter 3, Fig. 3.7; Houston 1989:fig. 19). Whether the Maize God at Tulum brings the gift of human hearts or consumes them is somewhat unclear.

Another image, from a rare Postclassic stela that comes from the site of Mayapan, shows two deities within what appears to be a structure or temple (Fig. 7.8a; Martin and Grube 2000:228). Floating just above is a bird messenger who accompanies a date, as though to serve as an oracle of that period issuing from a building. It is also an emblem of the twenty-year, or *k'atun*, cycle: among the Aztec the birds correlated with days; among the Maya, with lengthier cycles, for thirteen *k'atun*s in total. The format of this scene is heavily codexlike and suggests that the origin for the image comes from a manuscript, not another sculpture. The same kind of image also occurs on a Terminal Classic or early Postclassic stela from Flores, Guatemala, where a figure descends in the company of two quetzal birds. Perhaps the largest assemblage of oracle or augural birds occurs in the Paris Codex, where pages 2–11 show a systematic correlation between *k'atun*s, particular birds—some with deity heads—and gods (Fig. 7.8b): the Maize God with a hummingbird, his usual companion and alter ego; an *'o* bird with the Sun God; a parrot with God N; a vulture (apparently) with Chaak. Again, these tidings or omens revealed the properties of particular *k'atun*s (Love 1994:18–20, 43), and they may also help explain the diversity of messenger birds in the San Bartolo murals uncovered by Saturno and drawn by Hurst. Related images may be found at Classic sites, such as Oxkintok, where a series of stelae show the storm god, Chaak, in an upper register and birds below, one a vulture–Old God carrying a codex (a set of tidings?). This figure, on Stela 9, appears to receive an offering bowl as well, perhaps an enticement for the message or payment for its delivery (Fig. 7.9a, b; Pollock 1980:figs. 545a, f, 547). The complex of images from Oxkintok hints at a central local practice of formalized communications between ruler and Chaak, perhaps expressing local anxieties about rain for agriculture or tempests from the north or east. The same can be seen in the small temples with inscriptions in the southern part of Chichen

Fig. 7.5. Moon Goddess with "bird", Dresden Codex, p. 18b.

Itza, Mexico, where "houses," especially in the Temple of the Four Lintels, were labeled both as the homes of gods and as their "nests" or "dwellings," *-otoot*. In Figure 7.10, note the small bird head issuing from the nest, rather like a small tropical oriole.

To summarize the points so far: The Preclassic and more certainly the Postclassic Maya recognized birds as messengers. Avian couriers also played a large role in other areas, as in Oaxaca, where bird images appear within temple models (Marcus and Flannery 1996:fig. 211). Some birds are easily identifiable by species; others combined wings and

Fig. 7.6. Mural fragment, San Bartolo Structure 1 (courtesy of William Saturno, Director, San Bartolo Project; rendering by Heather Hurst, Yale University).

tail feathers with marks that identify certain gods. The birds come from somewhere else; they carry—they are—portents. The challenge is to determine whether these concepts apply to the Classic Maya as well and, if so, what they might say more generally about the nature of messages and their transmitters. Both goals come within reach by considering two sets of evidence and the arguments relating to them: first, gods as messengers in bird form; and, second, human messengers who overlap in meaning with avian ones.

Turning to the first point, we observe that one of the most conspicuous birds of a composite sort—that is, a creature not linked to a natural species—is the Principal Bird Deity, studied long ago by Lawrence Bardawil and subsequently by many others (Bardawil 1976; Cortez 1986; Taube 1987). There seems little doubt that this is a birdlike avatar of the major deity known as Itzamnaaj (Fig. 7.11a). The head belongs to the god, the wings and body to a bird. One vessel shows Itzamnaaj in the process of transforming into the bird, a long, graceful tail issuing from his rump and wings appearing under his arm (Fig. 7.11c; see also Anton 1970:fig. 245). Itzamnaaj remains an enigmatic figure. He is prominent, perhaps a kind of Classic Maya overgod. This role appears to be fleshed out in an unprovenanced text from the Early Classic period. The back of this deity mask shows that Itzamnaaj presided in some way over the mysterious events taking place at 3114 BC. These are the so-called creation events, which do not securely have anything to do with creation per se (cf. Freidel et al. 1993:75); they relate to hearths, but by no clear reading do they refer to cosmic genesis. But there is solid evidence that the Principal Bird Deity is related in some manner to a

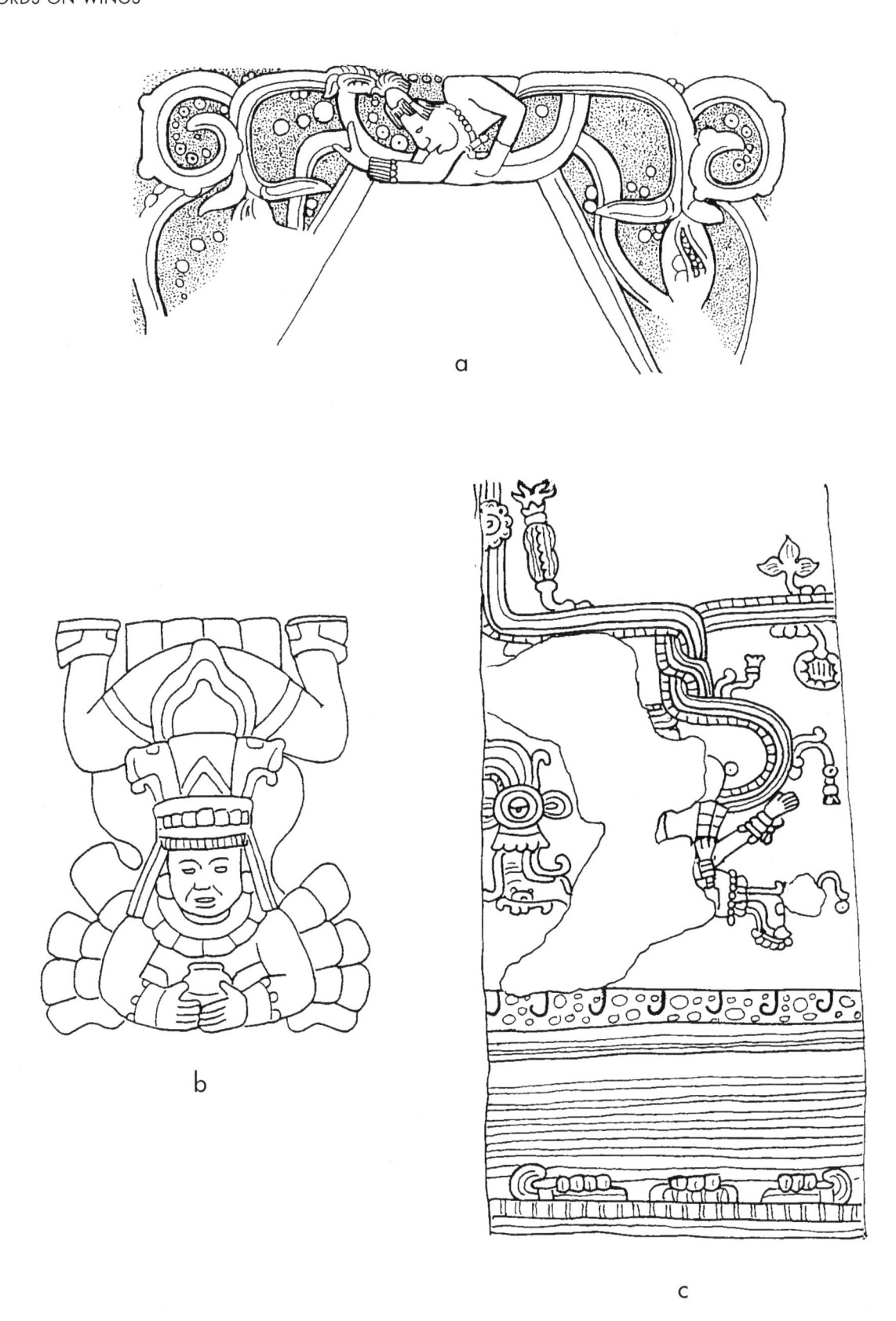

Fig. 7.7. "Diving" gods: (a) Maize God in falling pose, "enclosed corridor," Palace, Palenque (after Maudslay 1889–1902, 4:pl. 45a); (b) Tulum Structure 16, exterior (after A. Miller 1982:pl. 37); and (c) Tulum Structure 16, Mural 6 (after A. Miller 1982:pl. 40).

Fig. 7.8. *K'atun* birds: (a) Mayapan Stela 1 (after Martin and Grube 2000:228); and (b) Paris Codex, p. 6.

personage in the K'iche'an *Popol Vuh* known as Vuqub Caquix: both are blowgunned out of a tree by a Hero Twin, a theme that extends from the Classic period back into imagery of the Preclassic Maya.

Several texts refer explicitly to the Principal Bird Deity and specify his relation to Itzamnaaj. It is sometimes suggested that this bird was called "Itzam Yeh" (Freidel et al. 1993:70), but this reading is based on a misconstruction of a single text; the more likely reading of those glyphs is simply Itzamnaaj, in which the final element is *naaj*, perhaps a term for "earspool." But there is another, extended variation of this name. An inscription and image from Lintel 3, Xcalumkin, shows, on its underside, the Principal Bird Deity (Fig. 7.12a; I. Graham and von Euw 1992:160). The text on the front of the lintel, although eroded, refers, apparently, to Muut Itzamnaaj, or "Bird Itzamnaaj."

Another text from Xcalumkin, Column 3, again records a "Bird Itzamnaaj" after an expression that refers to deity impersonation (Fig. 7.12b; I. Graham and von Euw 1992:175, A6; Houston and D. Stuart 1996). Presumably someone at Xcalumkin visibly manifested this composite bird. The two signs are elegantly conflated in a full-figure text from Tonina, a site at some distance from Xcalumkin (Fig. 7.12c). The Principal Bird Deity, with the indisputable head of Itzamnaaj, is followed by the syllabic sign [ti], almost certainly as a phonetic component to the "bird," or *muut*, spelling. Given the information presented thus far, it appears plausible, then, that these birds are both the messages from a crucial deity and a birdlike communicative facet of its identity. They are words made visible, oracles fluttering into human apprehension. Another hint of the Principal Bird Deity's role appears on a vessel where he serves as an

WORDS ON WINGS 237

Fig. 7.9. Birds from Oxkintok, Yucatan: (a) Stela 9 (after photograph from Corpus of Maya Hieroglyphic Inscriptions, Peabody Museum, Harvard University); and (b) Stela 21 (Pollock 1980:fig. 547).

Fig. 7.10. Temple as "bird house" at Chichen Itza, Yucatan (drawing by Stephen Houston).

attendant, clutching a blowgun or something like a "beadle's rod," in service to the Lord of the Animals, one of the Hero Twins, whose skin is marked by feline pelage (Fig. 7.13; Taube 2003a).

The contexts of the texts about Itzamnaaj are not always clear, but Classic-period iconography depicts the Principal Bird Deity at the culmination of accession ceremonies. An engraved bone of uncertain provenance shows the act of coronation in which a Principal Bird Deity headdress is held aloft, presumably to be placed on the head of the youthful god seated within a sky-rimmed alcove (Fig. 7.14a). The Principal Bird Deity itself looks on, having alighted on the coronation structure, a position he also occupies on accession monuments at Piedras Negras, Guatemala. Not a few Maya buildings, including the well-preserved Rosalila structure excavated by Ricardo Agurcia at Copan, show the very top façade of the building as a Principal Bird Deity in the act of landing or descending (Fash 1991:fig. 52). The same occurs on a Terminal Classic vessel with stuccoed surface from Chichen Itza, where the Principal Bird Deity hovers over a palace scene in which a mirror and two figures play a central role (Fig. 7.14b). The wing feathers face upward, signaling an act of whooshing descent and, eventually, perching. The majority of headdresses worn by Maya rulers are in themselves such descending and landing birds—the feathers face outward; the principal wing supports, often shown as serpents, are evident; and the rulers look out from beneath the godly visage of these birds (Fig. 7.15). Interpreting this imagery poses problems, but it seems safe to say that the Maya saw oracular or messenger birds around them, on the façades of buildings, which sustain monstrous birds, and on the heads of rulers whose mouths, because of their position within the open beaks of oracular birds, speak divinely inspired truths to the assembled. The semantic interpenetration of "building" and "body" was deliberate. Occasionally, rulers will display stacked heads of such deity birds, yet this may be better read as the ruler embodying multiple voices, all speaking at once or alternately through his vocal organs. By the same token, if temples were the homes of such oracles, and their doors were, as throughout the Maya region, known as "mouths," then temples themselves spoke of things to come and of things commanded.

A fair number of such avian deities exist, including ones from the Classic period. It is tempting to see them as messages related to agriculture. Other deities range from an Early Classic eroded image of a bird-god (Fig. 7.16a; Uaxactun Stela 3, I. Graham 1986:137) to a veritable flock of bird-gods on several Terminal Classic stelae from Uxmal, Yucatan (Fig. 7.16b; Uxmal Stelae 2 and 3, I. Graham 1992:87, 89). Of course, some scenes of birds, as on Xelha Structure 86, Ichmac Structure 1, or the Temple of the Warriors at Chichen Itza, are simply collections of birds, sometimes hovering over mountains: almost certainly they refer to paradisical locations resounding with the cries of birds (Fig. 7.17; Taube 2004a). Several texts from the so-called Old Castillo at Chichen Itza explicitly describe these afterlife realms as ones that pertain to the "ancestors," or *mam* (*u-baah u-nikte u mam*, "images of the flowers of the ancestors"). Nonetheless, avian deities are not limited to Maya civilization. Sculptures from the Cotzumalguapa civilization of the Guatemalan piedmont swoop down to retrieve or consume body parts after ballgames (Fig. 7.18; Greene 1972:pls. 188, 192, 200). The sense that offerings were used to feed deities is pronounced. One winged deity, a death

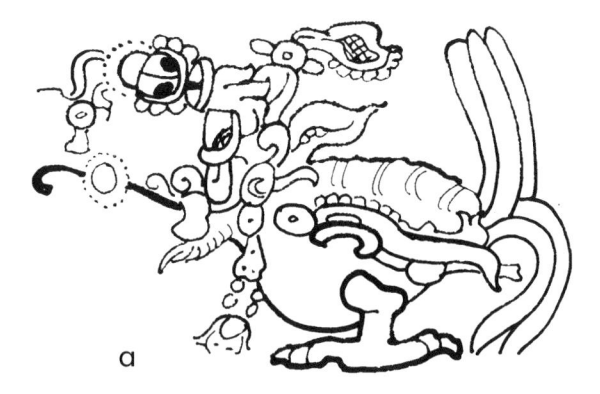

Fig. 7.11. The Principal Bird Deity: (a) full bird form (after photograph by David Stuart of K5227); (b) Xunantunich (after Anton 1970:fig. 245); and (c) Itzamnaaj transforms into bird (after Hellmuth 1987:fig. 578).

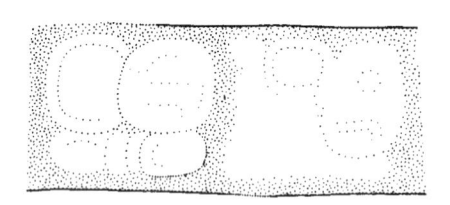

Fig. 7.12. Principal Bird Deity from Xcalumkin, Campeche: (a) Lintel 3 (I. Graham and von Euw 1992:160); (b) Column 3 (I. Graham and von Euw 1992:175, A6); and (c) unnumbered Tonina panel (drawing by David Stuart).

Fig. 7.13. Lord of Animals with birdlike Itzamnaaj (drawing by Karl Taube after unprovenanced Late Classic vessel).

god on Bilbao Monument 13, serves as an animated day sign that functioned as an augury or personal name (Fig. 7.19).

A final bird-god deserves mention because of his widespread appearance in Mayan texts. He was called the "sky-god" by Proskouriakoff and appears in royal names both at Yaxchilan and at Altar de Sacrificios, and as a bird-god, *muut,* at Palenque (Fig. 7.20a, b; J. Graham 1972:fig. 35; M. G. Robertson 1985b:fig. 259, position C7). At Altar de Sacrificios he is shown with a full body—that of a bird—along with a distinctive jawless face. The full text may be read "the deity who spears in the sky," as part of his name includes a hand holding a spear-thrower. The other text, from Yaxchilan, shows a sequence of full-figure glyphs. The body of the deity appears first, in nonavian form, but the glyphs that follow detail his nature: [mu-ti], or *muut,* "bird." It is unclear which deities could take a birdlike form, or whether only some supernaturals were regarded as messengers.

The second topic is that of birds and humans as "messengers" or "emissaries." The information presented so far suggests strongly that messages from gods—oracles—were conceived indigenously as birds of a composite nature, composed of the head and speaking parts of deities, but with wings and tails for flying. It is likely that these messages would be controlled in some way or restricted in application to certain messages, with personal visions distinguished rigorously from those issuing out of rulers' mouths or those of their representatives. It was for precisely this reason that individual revelations came under increasing scrutiny in Renaissance Spain—they came to be seen as dangerous breaches of hierarchical order (Christian 1981:151). One unprovenanced object, known as the Sáenz Throne after its first owner, shows a pair of royal personages (Fig. 7.21). (Another individual may well have sat to the side, but that part of the throne is missing.) In between them is a deity labeled by specialists as the "Pax god" because his face occurs in inscriptions as the patron of the month Pax. He has no lower jaw, yet he does have, on the throne, a set of wings, and he appears to be conversing with the central male figure in this tableau. The wings alone would signal that he is a messenger of some sort. The text makes this even clearer: the event, although partly obscured, is linked to a supernatural location known as the "six-sky-place," followed by the head glyph for the little winged god in attendance on the king; the god's folded arms denote subordinate status. The sign that comes thereafter consists of three syllables, [ye-be-ta], which spells *yebeet,* "his messenger," a term descended from Common Mayan *abaaty* and cognate with a large set of terms meaning "servant" or "worker" (Kaufman and Norman 1984:119). The name that possesses the winged god and describes him as "his messenger" is none other than Itzamnaaj, who is probably impersonated by the central figure in the throne. The winged supernatural will also, in all likelihood, be the omen, the embodied message of Itzamnaaj. Yet other supernatural messengers, such as God N on an unprovenanced vessel, cannot yet be explained (e.g., K4143).

The notion of "bird messengers" is not restricted to supernatural settings. A key context is on an unprovenanced vessel that shows a central act of the Classic period: the rendering of tribute by a

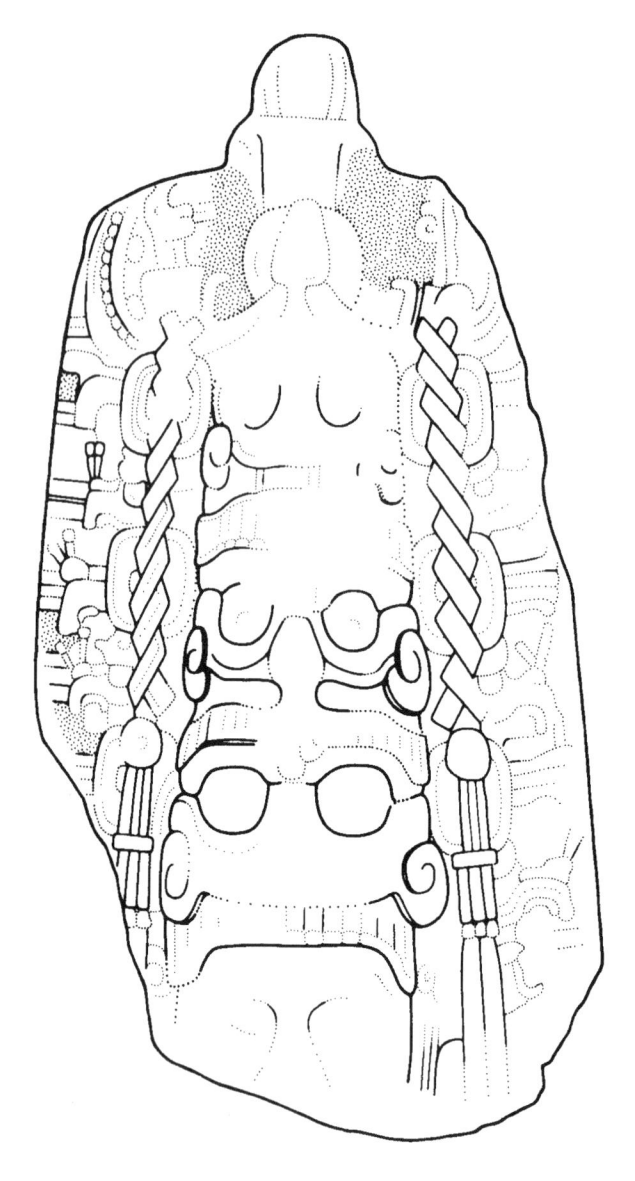

Fig. 7.15. Headdress with multiple birds, Tonina Monument 32 (I. Graham and Mathews 1996:79).

Fig. 7.14. Principal Bird Deity as witness to coronation: (a) engraved bone (after slide in possession of Michael Coe); and (b) scene from bowl found in the Cenote of Chichen Itza, Yucatan (after Ediger 1971, unnumbered plate).

lord from Calakmul to a ruler of Tikal (Fig. 7.22). The celebrated antagonism between these two cities, elegantly fleshed out by Simon Martin and Nikolai Grube (2000), represents a dynastic pivot around which many other polities swung. Other parts of the vessel show that the tribute consisted in part of chocolate beans. These precious items were customarily bundled in groups of 8,000. One such bundle from the murals of Bonampak tabulates a total of 40,000 beans, with other bundles behind multiplying that number considerably. The tribute pot from the Tikal area records a text that relates closely to messengers. First comes a reference to

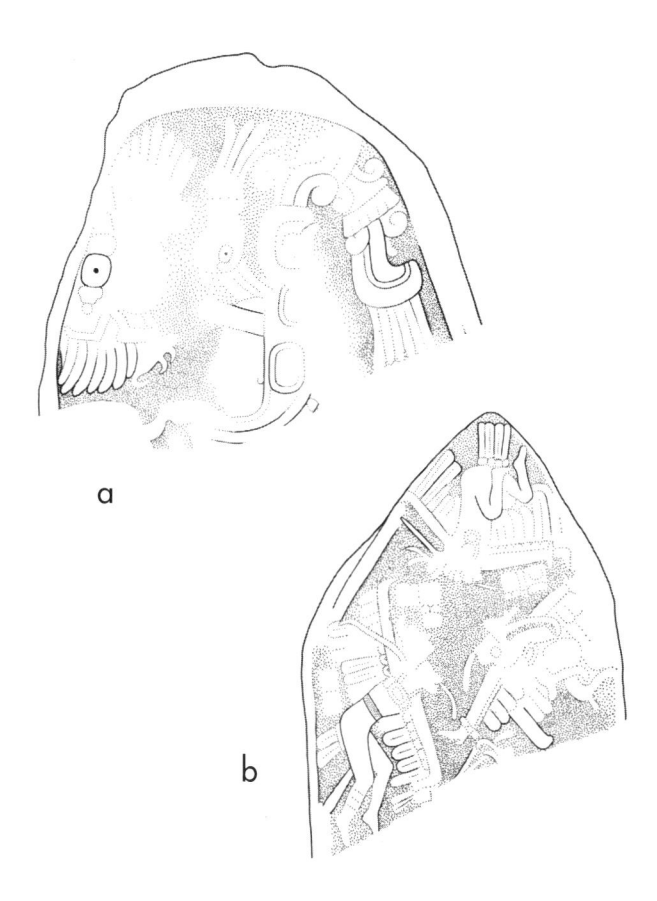

Fig. 7.16. Messenger birds: (a) Uaxactun Stela 3 (I. Graham 1986:137); and (b) Uxmal Stela 2 (I. Graham 1992:87).

Fig. 7.17. Xelha painting with birds over mountains (after Navarijo Ornelas 2001:fig. 6).

the "self" or image of the tributary lord, an individual named, probably, "K'ahk' Hix," or "Fire-cat." Just afterward he is further identified by a familiar expression, [mu-ti], spelling *muut*, "bird" or "tidings." The same association of "bird," *muut*, with human messengers occurs as part of the titles of courtiers depicted within holelike cartouches on the Sarcophagus Lid at Palenque (M. G. Robertson 1983:fig. 99). Another tributary scene, on a vessel from the area of Lake Peten Itza, uses the same term in a historical setting (Fig. 7.23): cloth tribute is mentioned (*yubte'*, a kind of textile held by a courtier to viewer's left), then a positional expression, *k'eblaj muut*, meaning that "the bird" or "messenger" "inclines" or "leans over," probably as a mark of deference to the figure on the throne and an explicit reference to the gestural or "body" language that occurs in most scenes from Classic Maya courts (cf. Yukatek [Barrera Vásquez 1980:393], *k'eb-ba*, "*irse ladeando por mal asentado*," and Ch'orti' [Wisdom n.d.] *k'e'b*, "deflation, a flattening out"; K1728). The same term appears slightly later in this caption, when it says that this individual is the "payment" or "debt" (*u-tojil*) of another *muut*, who happens to carry the *sajal* title that is borne by subordinate lords in some areas of the Classic Maya world. The notion that human beings could be as much tribute or payment as cloth or bundled chocolate beans is increasingly evident in Maya texts and imagery. Piedras Negras Stela 12 confirms that captives could be assembled by subsidiary lords and given as tribute to an overlord, in this case the final ruler of Piedras Negras; one text, now in the Los Angeles County Museum of Art, reports on the seizure of these captives on the field of battle. Piedras Negras Stela 12 then shows the end of their long journey from the battlefield to the feet of the regional sovereign (Greene et al. 1972:pl. 24).

What is important here is that "bird messengers" were not only supernatural or oracular but flesh-and-blood emissaries from tributary courts. The text from the Tikal area stresses this theme (Fig. 7.22). After the glyphs for "bird, tidings" (*muut*), it states [ye-be-ta], *y-ebeet*, or "messenger," followed by the name of a contemporary ruler of Calakmul. The spelling of *yebeet* changes through time as the language of the inscriptions experienced vowel shortening. This is documented

Fig. 7.18. Bilbao Monument 1 (drawing courtesy of Oswaldo Chinchilla).

in a stucco text from the so-called Caana pyramid at Caracol, most likely the royal palace of that center (Fig. 7.24). This text reads [ye-be-te-pa-pa-ma-li], or *y-ebet papamil*, "the messenger of *papamil*," *papamil* being a cryptic title mentioned on another late text at Caracol (Altar 12:Z4) and on a stela from Naranjo (Stela 33:X3–U4, Grube 1994:fig. 9.18). Almost certainly it was used by people from a site other than Caracol.

The place in which these various concepts are brought together is in the Bonampak murals. That mural program has many enigmas, but one of them concerns the nature of the ceremonies displayed in Room 1. In her doctoral thesis on the subject, Mary Miller emphasized that the room is, above all, a visual narrative of heir designation, as underscored by the presence of a child in the arms of a courtier and the main text that runs as a band around the center of the room—that text does indeed appear to mention accession, although not of any person documented elsewhere in the murals (1986:149). When Miller, Taube, Gene Ware, and Houston returned to Bonampak in the mid-1990s to accumulate new evidence, thinking about the "heir" began to change. First, when seen within the broken viewing angles of Room 1, the child appeared to diminish in centrality, being stuck over in a corner near a throne. Second, the text that was supposed to mention the heir designation did not use the *ch'ok*, "green, immature," expression associated with youths. Finally, infrared images revealed the presence of several tribute bundles under the throne, including the text mentioned before, along with lashed *Spondylus* shells, another common item of tribute. As a result, the entire thrust of the iconography in Room 1 shifted away from rites of enthronement or accession to overt, almost ostentatious, displays of accumulated wealth.

A decisive component of the Room 1 scenes is a set of nobles dressed in a distinctive outfit (Fig. 7.25a; D. Stuart 1998): they wear white cotton mantles with elaborate embroidered or woven selvages; around their necks are strung *Spondylus* shells. Many of them have quetzal feathers or green-tinted bird plumage in their headdresses. Such figures, although rare, occur in the imagery of other sites. At Yaxchilan, on Stela 4 and Stela 7,

Fig. 7.19. Death God as bird, Bilbao Monument 13 (drawing courtesy of Oswaldo Chinchilla).

they kneel at the feet of the penultimate king of that site, Shield Jaguar II, and receive a flowing blessing of spirit matter, perhaps emanating from royal blood (Fig. 7.25b; Tate 1992:pls. 86, 89). On a vessel excavated from a royal tomb at Tikal (Burial 116), the same kind of lords, perhaps in their earliest known appearance in Maya imagery, approach a throne (Fig. 7.25c; Culbert 1993:fig. 68a). Some kneel, others stand, and two in particular seem to have detached their feathers, jewelry, and, in the background, their cloaks, and offer them to the enthroned personage. When such figures occur to the left, the Maya understanding was evidently that the lords to the right were local, and that the person to the left a more exalted but non-local overlord.

Seen in this light, there is compelling testimony that lords in this uniform—the consistency of its elements permits the term—were tributary lords bringing the most coveted items to court: quetzal feathers, cotton mantles, *Spondylus* shells, and, at Bonampak, chocolate beans. The template of such messengers may go back to the time when the San Bartolo murals were devised, since they also show a messenger with large jade beads bound to his elaborately woven cloak. Similar items of tribute occur

Fig. 7.20. Bird-god: (a) Altar de Sacrificios Stela 12 (after J. Graham 1972:fig. 35); and (b) Yaxchilan bench (after field drawing by Ian Graham).

Fig. 7.21. Saenz Throne, detail with winged god (field drawings by E. von Euw).

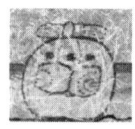

Fig. 7.22. Polychrome vessel showing lord of Tikal receiving tribute from Calakmul (K5453, copyright Justin Kerr).

in the Temple of the Chac Mool, on a mural fragment displaying quetzal feathers attached to selvages, cotton mantles, and heaps of broken rough jadeite in bowls (Fig. 7.26; Taube 1994b:fig. 18a; also Lothrop 1952:fig. 41). Another such lord, whose image has just been excavated at Palenque, is supporting the headdress of the king. A few of these subsidiary figures, including another character identifiable in the reign of the final ruler of Piedras Negras, resemble the favorites, or *mignons,* at royal courts in Europe (Elliott and Brockliss 1999). These figures result structurally from court systems. They were raised with, or intimate with, the king; availed themselves of royal largesse; and could be, in the worst case, figures much loathed by factions around the ruler. In court intrigue, they could be sacrificed figuratively as penance for failed royal policies, but they also afforded a richer emotional

k'eblaj muut u-tojil

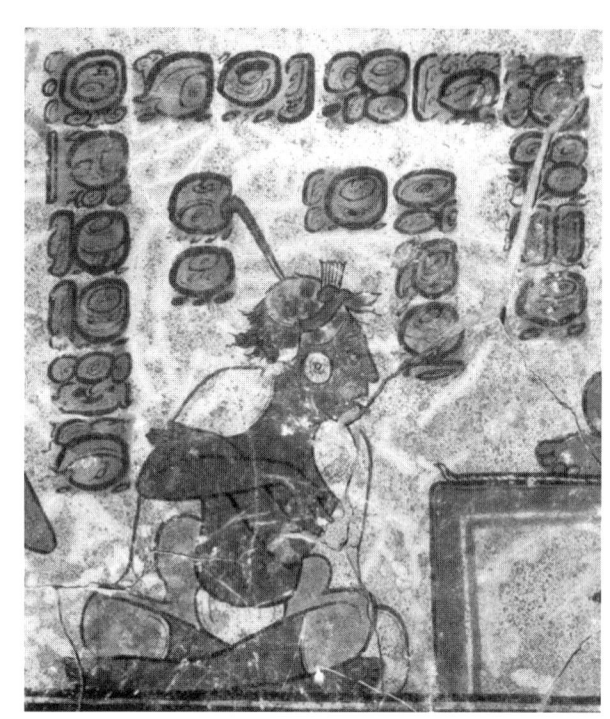

Fig. 7.23. Details from pot with tributary scene (K1728, copyright Justin Kerr).

life to monarchs. They were friends to those who, by their nature, had few disinterested companions.

Quite literally, then, the figures at Bonampak and elsewhere can be understood as walking tribute bundles. In stripping off their raiment, they cede their dress to the overlord, remove overt marks of social status by peeling off clothing, and are left in little more than loincloths before the sovereign, who closely monitors and hoards the gifts he reaps. Scholars have long known that, at Bonampak, the dancers who also dominate Room 1 perform a "quetzal" or "feather dance" (Grube 1992; Houston 1985). This was performed by important youths at court and accompanied by assembled mummers and musicians. Given the overriding theme of tribute in Room 1, it now seems probable that they *embodied* tribute: they dance as bobbing quetzal plumes, precious objects made animate in the same way that the lords above embody the tribute bundles that are commonly depicted in Maya imagery of the Classic period. Messengers both carry and are messages; these particular kinds of messengers both transport and are the precious objects craved by the court. The Classic Maya are known to have held the view that objects possessed vitalizing essences. This existential doctrine is reflected in the numerous animated depictions of rocks, buildings, and sundry other articles. It also reflects a worldview that can, with minimal effort, contemplate courtly drama in which bundles walk and feathers dance. This theme comes back full circle with a set of images from Altun Ha, Belize, and Kaminaljuyu, Guatemala, of winged maize deities offering tribute, perhaps as a supernatural expression of courtly practice (Fig. 7.27; Pendergast 1979:fig. 34a, b).

A final point can be inferred. For mysterious reasons, many of the tributary lords do not have painted captions in the Bonampak murals (Fig. 7.28a). Ware and Houston have looked closely for these texts, at all spectral wavelengths, to little avail. This feature led Miller to argue in her

Fig. 7.24. Messenger glyph from stucco text at Caracol (after Grube 1994:fig. 9.18).

Fig. 7.25. Tributary lords: (a) Bonampak Room 1, Structure 1 (reconstruction by Heather Hurst [and in some cases, "with Leonard Ashby"], copyright the Bonampak Documentation Project); (b) Yaxchilan Stela 7 (drawing by Ian Graham, in Tate 1992:pl. 89); and (c) vessel from Tikal Burial 116 (Culbert 1993:fig. 68a, used with permission of Sharon Misdea, Tikal Project, University of Pennsylvania Museum).

doctoral thesis that the paintings were essentially unfinished. She was undoubtedly correct, but for a proviso: recent imaging proves that the murals themselves exhibit a very high degree of finish, even down to almost microscopic details. The few named tributary lords occur on the eastern wall of Room 1 (Fig. 7.28b). The texts are difficult to read, yet infrared imaging shows one sequence clearly: [ye-be-ta-CHAK-HA-a?-AJAW-wa], *yebeet chak-ha ajaw*, "he is the messenger of the Red or Great Water Lord," probably a site in the vicinity of Bonampak. (By this time, the language of Bonampak had shifted from T12 as [AJ] to ['a], and thus the reference is most likely to "water.") This text brings the argument full circle, for it fails to mention any personal name for the tributary lord. It simply says that he is a messenger of a high-ranking individual, an *ajaw*, who is patently not present. The result of such clues is the demotion of the Room 1 personages from important local courtiers to nearly anonymous, unremarkable emissaries from sites presumably under Bonampak's control. This in itself displays a strange degree of reticence and mutual suspicion. The tribute bearers—if in fact the murals reflect geopolitical reality rather than wishful thinking—did not want to risk their actual physical presence at the sovereign's court but rather sent relatively disposable figures. Whether the Maya had "amnesty days" like the Aztec, who extended unrestricted passage to enemies attending coronations or temple dedications, remains unclear. Such "amnesties" may have been used in ceremonies at Seibal, Guatemala, where foreign lords of high rank attended the close of an important calendrical cycle (J. Graham 1990:33).

An even more disquieting possibility, not yet provable, is that the scenes shown in the murals relate, not to Bonampak, but to events centered on its overlord, the nearby site of Yaxchilan. In the principal throne scene in Room 1, we cannot identify the leading personage, nor can we do so in Room 3. There is a chance that he was, in fact, the king of Yaxchilan and that the scene took place at his capital. In the war tableaux of Room 2, the glyphic texts are explicit in naming Bonampak lords, but whether these actions merely harvested captives

Fig. 7.26. Tribute in the form of a feathery backrack and other materials, Temple of the Chac Mool, Chichen Itza, Yucatan (Taube 1994b:fig. 18a).

Fig. 7.27. Avian Maize God with tribute, Kaminaljuyu, Guatemala (after Kidder et al. 1946:fig. 205f).

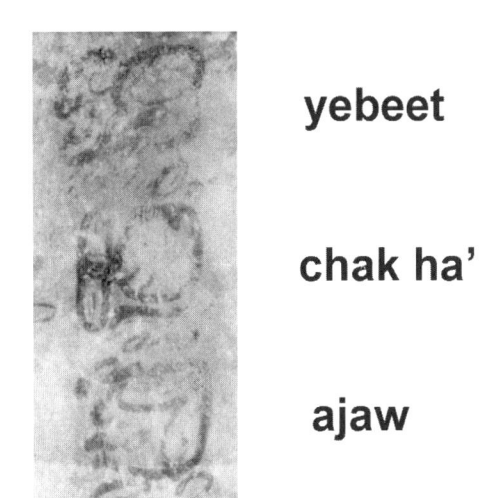

yebeet

chak ha'

ajaw

Fig. 7.28. Names of messengers, Bonampak, Chiapas, Mexico: (a) blank caption, Room 3 (reconstruction by Heather Hurst [and in some cases, "with Leonard Ashby"], copyright the Bonampak Documentation Project); and (b) caption, eastern wall, Room 1 ([infrared photography by David Wooddell], copyright the Bonampak Documentation Project).

for the overlord, in events perhaps not taking place at Bonampak, remains unclear. The local holy lord of Bonampak, a person we call Chan Muwaan, may well have been the "Duke of Wellington" of the Yaxchilan hegemony, with his role in battle made central to, and exalted in, the murals but the captives given eventually to their due repository, Yaxchilan. Moreover, the carved lintels that cover and define the doorways of the murals building are labeled as the work of a sculptor from Yaxchilan. The possibilities remain good that the murals themselves could not easily have been commissioned by a relatively small site like Bonampak. Future work needs to reexamine the spatial frame delineated in the paintings and decide whether its tableaux occurred in part at the far larger and more imposing regional power of Yaxchilan. The Bonampak murals

Fig. 7.29. Index finger extended as a sign of authoritative speech: (a) unprovenanced Olmec plaque; (b) image from the San Bartolo murals (rendering by Heather Hurst, courtesy of William Saturno, San Bartolo Project); (c) speech in the Dresden Codex, p. 9b; (d) Mixtec Lienzo of Zacatepec I, detail (after M. Smith 1973:fig. 88); and (e) Florentine Codex, Book 12, folio 21v.

are that rarity, a collaborative production between different holy lords of the Classic period, with subtly cross-talking agenda worked out in the fabric of the paintings and the building that contains them. Some of its ambiguities may derive not from interpretive poverty on our part but from the paintings' diverse sources of patronage.

WINGED WORDS

Unlike the sturdy stones left by the Classic Maya, speech and messages were ephemeral. That the Maya and other Mesoamerican peoples highlighted some kinds of speech as more important, more authoritative, than others is made evident by a convention in which an extended index finger secured emphasis (Fig. 7.29). The use of apparent metaphors such as "birds" successfully captured an impermanent quality and the long-distance, swift movement of these communications.

Yet "metaphor" may not be the right word to describe the use of *muut*, "bird." There is no literary allusion at work but, instead, a literal concept of heaven-sent annunciations or inspirations by birdlike beings. To Maya thinking, this was the medium by which gods made their wishes and meanings known—presumably the messengers were summoned in some manner, perhaps by burnt offerings often depicted in Maya imagery, but the bird messages appear to have been unidirectional. The birdlike messengers were embodiments of cognitive creativity. From the information in this chapter, we can also understand a wide variety of forms in Classic Maya texts and imagery, from headdresses in which rulers speak as oracles to buildings that proclaim celestial tidings (or serve as oracular temples), and from key figures in Maya iconography, such as the Principal Bird Deity, to rich manifestations, in both godly and courtly form, of formal messengers. The presence of oracles, so well attested in ancient Mexico (Pohl 1994:118–120), hints at their ubiquity among the Classic Maya. Woven into these pronouncements is a related set of dynastic uses and tributary behaviors in which those who give do not necessarily want to meet or to fall under the physical control of those who receive. Instead, they offer human versions of the tributary exotics that undergirded prestige at Maya courts.

CHAPTER EIGHT ◀▶

Dance, Music, Masking

The Classic Maya danced, made music, and costumed themselves. These acts passed quickly but left indelible traces in more permanent records. They also helped form an aesthetic of dynamic, integrated performance that filtered into other forms of creative expression. People who participated as dancers, musicians, or audience might remember such vibrant performances to varying degrees. But there were also those who saw such displays reenacted in commemorative images and texts. As explained in earlier chapters, the Classic Maya perceived vital energies in sculpture, painting, and glyphs according to a distinctive metaphysic of representation. For the knowledgeable viewer and reader, a dancing figure, whether on a stela or in a figurine, danced always and forever. Musicians blared, rattled, sang, thumped, and whistled away heedless to the erosions of time. There was thus a first layer of synesthesia, by which a reference summoned recollections of either this performance or similar ones, and a second layer in which the actual performer, in a blurring of time and setting, continued in perpetual, inexhaustible dance, attended by inaudible sounds and swift bursts of color. The audience might change, but the dancer or musician did not.

Several categories of performance have been defined and studied by anthropologists. In an everyday sense, most human interaction is, loosely speaking, a kind of "performance" in that it draws on prior habitual acts (Goffman 1959; Herzfeld 1985:16, 18). When transmitting messages to others—through movement or sound that expresses a particular thought or feeling—this behavior usually conforms to expected ways of doing things. That is how the "performer" makes sure that his "audience" understands, be it through a stylized grimace, a hand signal, a shrug, a smile, or a compact gesture of desire (Chapter 1; de Jorio 2000:79–91; Kendon 1997:109, 118–120). A more narrow notion of performance, which applies to this chapter, focuses on "markedness," the exceptional, set-apart quality of such acts. Markedness is established behaviorally by an elevated stage or special location; special costuming; or, as Richard Bauman notes, a reliance on discrete times, places, scripts, and public coordination, this last being important because it allows an audience to assemble (1992:46; Beeman 1993:378). Other relevant categories include "spectacle," an extravagant public entertainment (Houston 2002b); "festival," a successive set of performances or spectacles; and structured movement or "dance" (Kaeppler 1985:92–93), often accompanied by music as propulsive accompaniment, counterpoint, or explanation through song and oratory. Alfred Gell (1985:202–203) notes that most "dances" in ethnographic contexts, as among the Umeda in Papua New Guinea, accord with a similar pattern of stylized movement that detaches it from the world of "nondance." At the same time, those motions contain meanings and inspirations referring back to the world of unmarked movement and speech.

Such performances have three further properties: the sensorium is meant to be fully engaged by sound, sight, and dynamic movement, even though the audiences' attention often wanders, perhaps by competing concurrent displays; there is likely to be an aesthetic evaluation of the performance's success or efficacy, despite the expectation that performers and audience always hope for the best (B. Tedlock 1980:32); and a gradient exists between, say, a British stage actor's drive toward superficial plausibility masking cold artifice underneath, a "method actor's" need for merger of identity between performer and character, and a trancelike state by which another being or force displaces the performer (Kaeppler 1985:92). Nonetheless, even the most sacred performances contain elements of artifice and submergent identity, bald theatricality and mysticism, and the sense that some performers, no matter how earnest, prove eventually to be less skilled than others. In studies of dance, many anthropologists propose that such performances link to broader directives, such as social catharsis; ways of educating, commenting, scolding, or praising; competing (as between variously recruited performers and the groups they represent); and, according to Victor Turner (1974), the forging of transcendent bonds within a community (Spencer 1985:3, 8, 11, 15, 21, 27). If a performance does not perform a social role, it is hardly worth doing.

The problem with abstract understandings of function is that they do not adequately reflect the momentum, meaning, and shifting character of Mesoamerican performance. As a category, *dance* is a term that may not be as accurate as Adrienne Kaeppler's "structured movement systems," which includes many forms of stylized motion and gesture (1985:92). But "dance" certainly sounds more euphonious and reflects the distinct nature of such actions among the peoples of ancient Mesoamerica (Taube 2001:305). There were many varieties of dance in the broader neighborhood of the ancient Maya, as among the Mixtec and other peoples (Fig. 8.1): ones of courtship or casual liaison, dramatizations of historical events, dances related to hunting or warfare, and, most amusing of all, those depicting clowning or social parody that both pierced and amused; these took shape in the foolery of performers posing as "older men" pawing "young women" or of "monkeys," eerily human yet also bestial, cavorting against all decorum in the midst of solemnity (Bricker 1981:130; Taube 1989c:367–377).

Some dances, especially among the Aztec, could only be performed by certain age grades, genders, or persons of certain social status. The performance itself sharpened those boundaries. Other dances conjured gods through rites of impersonation. By analogy with Zuni dances of the American Southwest, the Maya and other peoples nearby may have distinguished between public dances and "sacred" ones seen by small groups of initiates (B. Tedlock 1980:13). In all cases, such performances were, one presumes, enjoyed by participants and audience. But the dances were also

Fig. 8.1. Mixtec dance (after Codex Selden, p. 7).

regarded as "work," a form of duty or obligation requiring diligent attention to correct execution of detail (Frisbie 1980:308; Monaghan 2000:24). Throughout Mesoamerica, dances were also understood as forms of offering, a kind of "food" or enticement by pleasing performance to supernaturals and a means of facilitating prayer and petitions by "awakening" such beings (Colby and Colby 1981:51; Ichon 1973:230–231; Monaghan 2000:32). Awakening these deities was not always a good thing: in the K'iche'an *Popol Vuh,* the pounding ballplay of the Hero Twins drew the attention and ire of maleficent underworld gods (Christenson 2000:99, 119). Whether by drums or other instruments, music also aroused deities, paced and guided the rhythm of dancers, induced trance through repetition, mimicked bird or animal calls, and glutted the sensorium by giving sound to visual displays (Fig. 8.2).

Fig. 8.2. Maya dancer with sacred bundle, Atitlan, Guatemala (photograph by Allen Christenson).

THE EVIDENCE OF LATER WORDS

The Spanish clerics who recorded descriptions of dance, music, and masking tended to emphasize terms for music, but not the other two categories of dance and masking. The reason is clear: music could be molded easily to the needs of Catholic liturgy, whereas dance and masking could not. They were practices to be tolerated or ignored rather than encouraged. This attitude comes to the surface when the Colonial lexicographers referred to long lists of "forbidden" or "prohibited dances" (*bailes vedados*). According to the San Francisco dictionary of Colonial Yukatek, these included the *max okot* (monkey dance), the *boyal che* (protection/shade tree?), the *kaymam* (singing opossum/clown), the *tankinam* (within-sun shaking?), the *tzool* (line), the *bulam* (stranger/foreigner shaking), and the *naual* (old dances of women [Michelon 1976:35]). Another was the *tum teleech* of Yucatan, which may have involved captive sacrifice (Uchmany de la Peña 1967). One Colonial document refers explicitly to an audience of fifteen thousand people for the "more than one thousand" kinds of dances, a few of which were erotic, involving the *ach,* "penis," and *pel,* "vulva" (Acuña 1978:19, 30–32). In lowland Mayan languages, most words for "dance" are closely cognate, thus Yukatek has *okot,* Colonial Tzendal *acot,* Ch'olti' *acut,* Ch'orti' *ak'ut,* and Colonial Tzotzil *'ak'ot*—in all cases, despite the spellings, with a glottalized /k'/ but with a varying initial vowel, /o/ clearly being an innovation from the more ancient form that began with /a/ (Laughlin 1988, 2:380; Michelon 1976:273). The supernatural overtones of the dance were never far from the surface. Colonial Yukatek records an expression *okot ba,* literally, "dance-self," meaning "pray" or "advocate" (Acuña 1984, 2:348–349). There were special places to dance (Colonial Tzotzil: *'ak'otajeb;* Ch'orti': *ak'utal*), as well as leaders or specialists who helped with choreography and rehearsals: Yukatek *ah yum ak'ot,* "the one [who is] the dance-master," or, in Ch'orti', the one who "teaches to dance," *ah ak'tesyah* (Laughlin 1988, 1:134; Wisdom n.d.). Much like the Aztec, who had their *cuicacalli,* "house of song," the early Colonial Maya had locations for performance, rehearsal, and storage of costumes, respectively the *popol na, popol na tzublal,* or *nicteil na* (flowery house), described explicitly as the house of a "municipal council" (*cabildo*), a gloss suggesting official or corporate sponsorship.

The dictionaries hint that there was a pronounced aesthetic of dance and a set of desired sounds. Colonial Tzendal has "to clap palms with delight when dancing" (*pac pone zcahb*), and Colonial Yukatek overtly established a connection between dance and making oneself "handsome," "elegant," or "gallant" (*tzublal;* Barrera Vásquez 1980:865). The dance should make certain sounds (*culuc*), a "deep thundering," almost like drums fashioned from tree trunks (Michelon 1976:74). Colonial Tzendal employs the same root to mean "great clamor or racket" of the sort produced by split wooden drums (*culinte;* J. Robertson n.d.). The word *pom,* probably onomatopoeic in origin, corresponded to much the same or perhaps to the idea that dances were, like *pom,* "incense," a favored "food" of deities. The movements themselves appear to have simulated the motions of animals, whether the shuffling of a worm, the scurrying of crabs (**hop;* Kaufman and Norman 1984:120), or the jump of a feline (Ch'orti' *uhopir e churur,* "spring of a tigrillo"; Wisdom n.d.), or they could describe human trembling and shaking (Colonial Yukatek *-am;* see above), perhaps of dancers serried into lines. A few references allude to the use of props, such as reeds or canes (Colonial Yukatek *hech;* Michelon 1976:133). It may not be a coincidence that one of the major figures of Classic Maya dance was the Maize God, whose elegant swaying, much like the lively movement of corn leaves, translated well into the undulations of a human body (Taube 1985). Such mimetic dances are of the type that Alfred Gell (1985:202–203) saw as referring back to the nondance world. Bishop de Landa reports on many such mimetic performances in early Colonial Yucatan (Tozzer 1941:179).

The words for "music" and "music making" reveal more because of their variety and richness. "Music" and "song" are not clearly distinguished semantically in Colonial Yukatek (*kay* or *cici kay,* the latter meaning "well done," "very sweet," or "slowly done"; Michelon 1976:55). Or it could be vulgar and ribald, the *coco kay* sung by lovers or otherwise impassioned people. The "singer" and "musician" used the same label, *ahkay* or *kayom,* the latter a word attested in Classic texts (Chapter 4) and in other Colonial languages, such as Tzendal (*cayom*). It seems clear that dancers were expected to use portable instruments like rattles or other *juguetes,* "playthings" (*zooktah, zot;* Barrera Vásquez 1980:738). Historical narratives in Colonial Yukatek could be related by such performance (*ukay lay be;* Michelon 1976:186), as could public declarations or oratory (*cayogh* in Tzendal; J. Robertson n.d.). These and other performances were appraised aesthetically: *tax u cal* or *tzublal u cal,* "even his/her voice [throat], "fine his/her voice [throat]" (Michelon 1976:372). The bad singer or musician sounded like a blatting trumpet (*ch'ech;* Michelon 1976:105). More complex orchestrations, of the sort called for in European liturgy, appear in terms for "arrange or organize voices," *cetcunah cal* (Michelon 1976:54). In other parts of Mesoamerica, high, wailing, or plaintive speech or song was used in awakening or supplicating deities (Monaghan 2000:32). This may explain references to falsetto or treble voices in Colonial Yukatek, such as *bekech cun a cal,* "thin your voice," like a soprano or even a bird (Chapter 7; Michelon 1976:27), although such sounds were also used in European traditions of liturgical chant through the medium of boys' choirs.

Colonial Yukatek had words for "drums" (*pax*) that were apparently extended to describe many other instruments, even "guitars" or "organs," all in the sense of things touched, strummed, or struck, but not blown (Michelon 1976:288). In Ch'orti', the various ways of hitting drums (*tun* or, with deer hide, *k'eweer tun*) were labeled in conscientious detail: one could "tap lightly" (*t'oht'i*), "beat repeatedly" (*leb tu'n*)—a play of flickering fingers that also related to the flute (*xu'r*)—"stroke with the dexterity of the tortilla maker" (*lahb*), and "pound with progressive force" (*kut* or *ha'tz';* Wisdom n.d.). Trumpets or horns were likened to the buffets of natural wind (*hom* or *hum*) or the crying of a human voice (*auatez*) and classified by material, whether of bone (*bac*), gourd (*box*), or clay (*lac* in Yukatek; Michelon 1976:147). Here, too, there is probable evidence of onomatopoeia, as in the Yukatek words *xob* (blow) and *xuxub* (whistle hiss), which clearly derives from the buzzing of wasps, *xux* (Michelon 1976:407). The same term occurs in Colonial Tzendal (*xuxob*) and Ch'orti' (*xuxoh*), along with other sounds that take their inspiration from nature, such as *chinchin* for the noise made by shaking gourd rattles and *huht* for "blowing a flute" (Wisdom n.d.), a word whose pronunciation recalls a sudden exhalation. It is possible that different pitches of whistle were indicated by the same attempt to simulate natural sounds, as in the Tzendal term for another whistle, the *vilil*, or the flute, *viyet* (J. Robertson n.d.). Among present-day Tzotzil of Zinacantán, Chiapas, Mexico, gourds are half filled with salt water and maize kernels and blown to summon lost souls; when played back to Zinacantecos on a tape recorder, the sound evokes deep emotion, suggesting that the affective impact of sounds varied greatly (Vogt 1977:232, 241). Drumming itself has been said by some researchers to target the central nervous system and result in unusual behavior (Neher 1962:159). Finally, there were, in Yukatek, labels for the rattles used by dancers, perhaps as items attached to clothing (*ch'eh oc*, "foot with penetrating sound"; Acuña 1978:39).

With "masks," the clerics again become circumspect. Almost all such terms in the Maya lowlands reflect the same root, *koh* (*k'oh*). Colonial Yukatek uses the root for "representative," "image," *kohbail* or *winbail*, the latter documented in Classic texts (Chapter 2), or in words for "to mask oneself," *kohbezah ba*. Our lone source on Ch'olti', aside from a few scattered words in historical documents, gives us *choh* (*ch'oh*; Ringle n.d.). In Tzendal, a term of uncertain etymology, *ghtancatib*, refers to "masks of the sort used in sacrifices" (J. Robertson n.d.). Robert Laughlin notes that this word may come from a root relating to "plaster," perhaps for "plastered masks" (1988, 1:308). In Colonial Tzotzil, a closely related language, there is *k'oj*, meaning "to chisel" or "to carve," and *koj te'*, a "wooden [carved] mask" often used by an *homarrache*, a "clown" or "buffoon" (Laughlin 1988, 1:233).

What of the audience? The available glosses are strangely ambivalent, as though the audience saw but also "spied" by standing apart from the performance. Ch'orti' has several words reserved for "those who witness or observe festivals," *ch'uhksan* (Wisdom n.d.). The term also applies to those attending "wakes," or *velorios*. There, naturally, the "apartness" from the dead was thoroughgoing (Wisdom n.d.). The root *ch'uhk* is certainly related to one in Colonial Yukatek, *ch'uk*, "to spy" (Barrera Vásquez 1980:143), with a related use in a phrase for "eavesdropping" (*ch'uk t'an*); these in turn link to a root reconstructible in Common Ch'olan, **ch'uk* (Kaufman and Norman 1984:119). If these terms convey the general understanding of what spectators do, aside from the extremely limited, quasi-legal sense of "witnessing" discussed in Chapter 4, they must thereby point to an imporous membrane or at least a carefully defined distance between audience and performers. Sources from Colonial Yucatan refer to impermanent scaffolds, *pepem che'*, "butterfly tree/wood," that were designed to support an audience or the officials presiding over them; the same term applied to temporary scaffolds for constructing and plastering buildings (Acuña 1978:38).

CLASSIC PERFORMANCE AND MASQUERADE

Classic Maya images began to "move" when Michael Coe and Elizabeth Benson (1966:16) noticed that figures with lifted feet, bent knees, and extended arms represented dancers (Fig. 8.3). George Kubler broadened that identification by seeing similar motions in many different settings, including the dancers of the Bonampak murals (1969:13, 17, 25; Freidel et al. 1993:257–292). This work was amplified by Nikolai Grube's invaluable discovery that a relatively common expression, hitherto read in a variety of ways (e.g., Houston 1985), recorded the Ch'olan term for "dance," *ak'ot* (Grube 1992). The mincing step seems to have been described in one instance, from the Dumbarton Oaks Palenque-style panel, as *te(h)k'aj*, "is stepping on" (Kaufman and Norman 1984:132; Schele and M. Miller 1986:fig. VII.3), perhaps contrasting with another step in which both heels were lifted, a form of jumping seen in some stelae at Motul de San José, Guatemala, and in Temple 16, Copan, where the dynastic founder adopts a plié position. In all such cases, the dance was highly contained, however, with minimal movement of the body despite the large variety of dances named in the glyphic texts. Another type of farcical dance parodied such delicate, contained movement with wild shuffling of feet and leaning torsos.

Since the publication of Grube's paper, a bridge has been built between the dances of the Classic period and the abundantly documented dances of the historic and modern periods. The *Popol Vuh,* for example, is replete with many different dances, often simulating animals or involving props like stilts; the expertise of the dancer shined especially when he knew as many dances as possible (M. Coe 1973:44). The difficulty, however, has been to get past the basic understanding that the Classic Maya danced and devised platforms ("plazas") and spaces for that purpose (Fig. 8.4). More to the point, when did the Classic Maya dance, who danced, and why did they dance? Was there a fixed canon, a choreography, a playlist of songs and oratory, and to what extent did they allow for improvisation? How did preparations take place, the backstage activities that figure so prominently in ritual drama of the American Southwest (Frisbie 1980:315)? What were the breaks and ruptures, the moments of silence? In all of this, archaeologists can achieve momentary connection with the past by blowing a Classic whistle or fingering a

Fig. 8.3. Dancers in Late Classic imagery: (a) monkey with sash (after K505); and (b) Kan Bahlam as dancer on tablet of Temple XIV, Palenque (after drawing by Linda Schele).

flute, but the sequences of notes and their unison with other instruments cannot be reconstructed in the absence of notation. What is clear is that dancers and even singers coordinated movement with music they themselves performed, as in a peculiar rasp used by Opossum dancers on a Late Classic vessel (Taube 1989c:fig. 24.1). The aesthetics of such sound seemed to have been one of loudness, high pitch, and clarity of tone, at least to judge from Colonial accounts (Donahue n.d.a; Stevenson 1976:91).

Music is, therefore, the most difficult to fathom and for that reason the best to tackle first. It has been known since the 1980s, thanks to the work of Mary Miller (1988:327), that when assembled into larger groups, Maya musicians appear in fixed sequences (Fig. 8.5): first are the rattlers, who, at Bonampak, were called "singers," with the proviso that this may have been extended to "musicians" (Houston 2002); then come flautists playing the *amay,* a later term unfortunately not found in the glyphs; they are followed by drummers using the booming floor drums (*culinte,* perhaps, to use a preferable term to the Nahuatl *teponaztli*) and people knocking deer antlers against turtle carapaces; these are attended in turn by musicians puffing through great trumpets and hammering, perhaps, handheld wooden drums. (At Bonampak, the effort of expelling air is shown by the strenuously rounded cheeks of trumpeters.) The elaborate ends of these trumpets, most of which were surely made of gourds, indicate that the instruments were tended on the vine to achieve a desired shape (K1453, K3814). This would result, presumably, in varying tones according to the idiosyncratic shape of a plant. In one case, mastic or other pliable materials

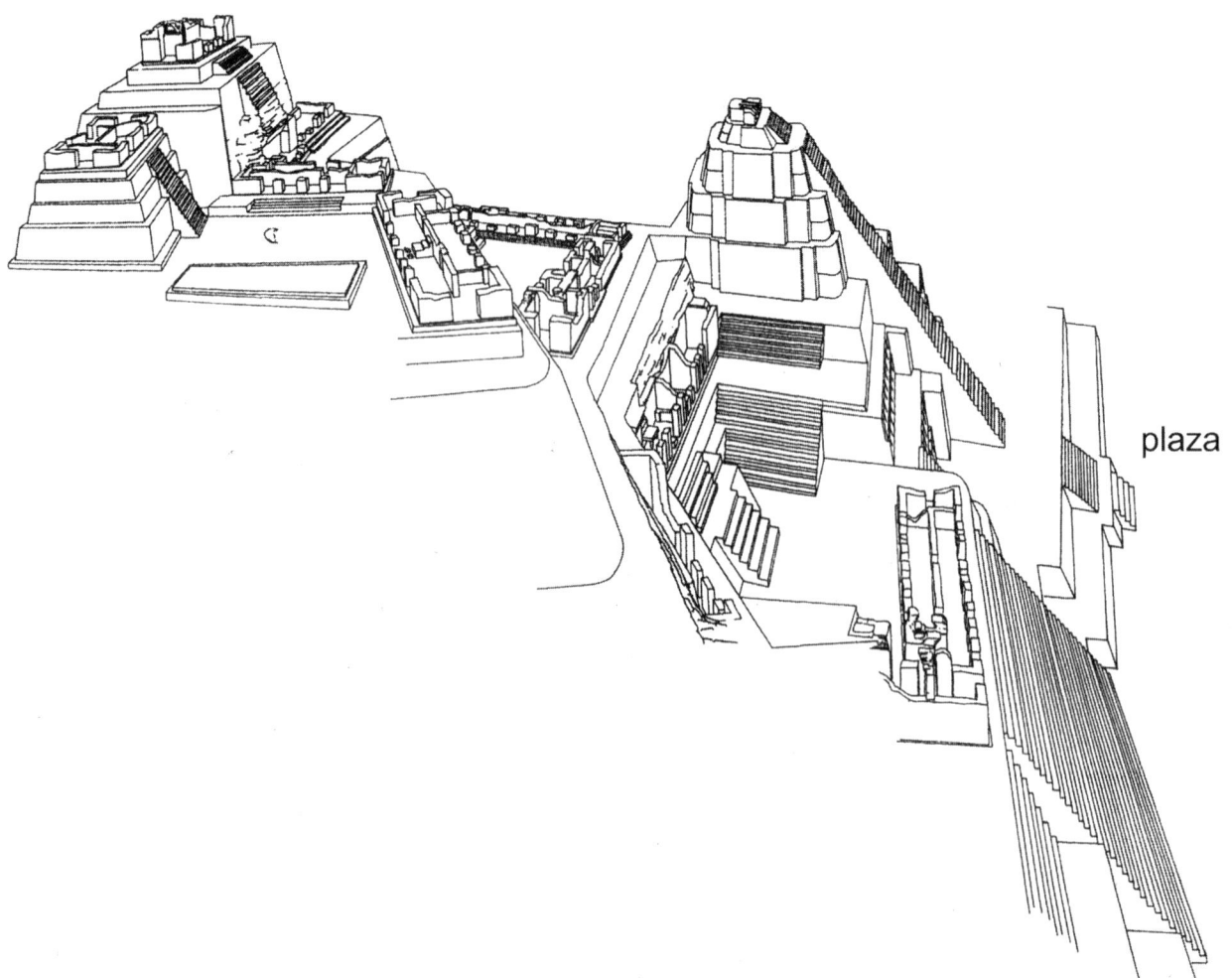

Fig. 8.4. Plaza of Piedras Negras (drawing by Heather Hurst, Piedras Negras Project, Stephen Houston, codirector).

may have been applied to the end of the horn to adjust tone. One trumpet, regrettably not fully exposed by the painter, has a string-and-stick attachment that suggests a sliding effect like a trombone (Fig. 8.6; K1453). A few trumpets incised as graffiti at Tikal, Guatemala, have tufts at their far end (Trik and Kampen 1983:fig. 58c). Expelled air would contribute to the overall display by agitating such feathers or strings, as would the flapping banners that appear to have existed at many Classic cities (e.g., Trik and Kampen 1983:figs. 48e, 58c, 64c, d). Another strong possibility is that such feathers themselves represented puffs of breath (Chapter 4).

The striking feature of Miller's find is that the same arrangement of instruments occurs far away, in Las Higueras, Veracruz (Fig. 8.7; Machado 2002:fig. 16), also with rattles, then drums, followed by trumpets, which, as among the Maya, are often in groups of three (for three-note chording, as in some flutes from Classic sites[?] see K4120, K6294, K6984). This particular assembly of musicians, which could be abbreviated from the full sequence at will, rather like a chamber ensemble from a full orchestra, suggests a musicological understanding that the crisper, more treble instruments should be positioned close to the audience, and the deeper instruments, like the drum and triple trumpeters, disposed to the back, rather like a Western orchestra with violins in front and tympani and double basses at back. In rare cases where musicians were identified, as on K3814, they are youths, perhaps fulfilling a form of page duty at court. The acoustics must have been clearly understood, because the same scene shows the youths directing the cones of their trumpets into the alley of a ballcourt. By practice and tradition, Maya architecture must have permitted particular sonic effects, reverberation in some cases, heightened boom or resonance in others. Vladimir Horowitz was said to have inserted a tack into the place on the stage at Carnegie Hall where his grand piano produced the finest tone. It is likely that musicians at Maya courts understood their stages just as well. The notion of certain fixed combinations of instruments occurs in Chiapas, Mexico, where drums and flutes are seen as natural companions, and the *Popol Vuh* uses a sequence of instruments and voice

Fig. 8.5. Sequence of musicians on polychrome vessel (M. Coe 1973:76).

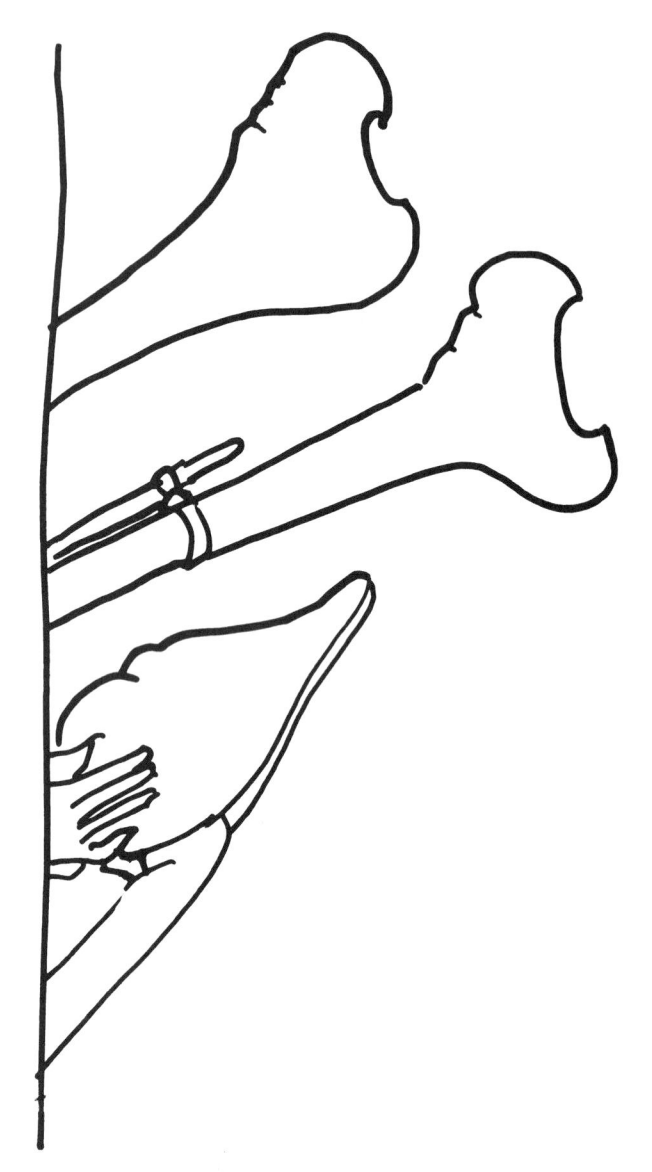

Fig. 8.6. Trumpet with unusual attachment (after K1453).

Fig. 8.7. Fragment of mural from Las Higueras, Veracruz (after Machado 2002:fig. 16).

in close resemblance to the pattern at Bonampak and Las Higueras: song, flute, drum (Christenson 2000:93; Vogt 1977:239). Fragmented paintings from Tajín, Mexico, hint at further combinations, as yet undocumented in the Maya region, including conch players marching in front of men holding long rattle staffs (Brüggemann et al. 1992:157). Details of these paintings make it clear that the occupants of Tajín, perhaps the Mayan-speaking Wastek, used gourdlike trumpets, too.

A subset of orchestras consists of traveling ones, which are never shown playing but were apparently intended to accompany a lord on a journey. To judge from their style, most such images come from vessels found in Alta Verapaz, Guatemala. The length of the journey appears to be recorded in day notation on one cylinder (K594), the famed Ratinlixul vase (Fig. 8.8; G. Gordon and Mason 1925–1934:pl 52): thus, Akbal, Ik', and Imix, all in reverse of expected order. Such a disposition of day signs may spell out the traveling time from origin point. The lord, often accompanied by a dog, has been interpreted by many—on plausible grounds, given the mortuary associations of canines—as a deceased personage en route to the underworld (M. Coe 1973:13). Contrary to a prevalent interpretation first made by Eric Thompson (1970:137), there seems little need to interpret the principal traveler in his hammock as a merchant. After all, where are the goods to be traded? Nor is the dog necessarily a sign of death, as such animals would be effective in detecting ambush or other dangers of travel during Classic times, or even in finding game needed by empty stomachs on long journeys. Rather, we are probably looking at state visits, in which a lord required, when not moving, a barrage of music to announce his approach. The "journey vessels" emphasize trumpets, drums (usually carried on some lackey's back), flutes, conches, and some rattles. These scenes open up to a larger world of "arrival from" (*tali* in Classic Ch'olti'an) and "arrival to" (*huli* in the same language; MacLeod 1990:339–340), in which processional movement could not have been choreographed as much as any dance within a fixed location (Fig. 8.9). If there were fresh or new arrivals, as in a royal bride to her new home or a lord visiting another court to "witness," there were also returns involving the verb *pakxi,* "to return" (MacLeod and A. Stone 1995:178). Some features of dance, including deity impersonation, also play a role in arrivals, as in an event recorded on Naranjo Stela 24 (I. Graham and von Euw 1975:64). A lady from Dos Pilas, Guatemala, evidently marries into the local dynasty, thus rejuvenating it. Her arrival at the site is reported by using a glyph associated with the age of current moons, a sign that diffused from a strictly astronomical meaning to one that likened celestial movement to royal processions. Some years later, she (or the sculptors of Naranjo) inscribes a reference to her impersonation of the Moon Goddess (Naranjo Stela 24:E4). We will return to such impersonations later in this chapter. The elevated roads within Maya cities, known in glyphs as *sak bih,* "road, path," allowed formal movement within sites but also replicated arrivals and departures of deities and their impersonators, thus weaving through cities internally by means of ritualized "journeys." One such road, that between Yaxuna and Coba, Mexico, has a panel that contains an explicit reference to the causeway (Fig. 8.10; Villa Rojas 1934).

The drums of the Classic Maya are among the most varied in their shape and manufacture. One category was cradled within the crook of an arm and consisted of a thin, flaring cylinder at the bottom that widened into a bowl covered with lashed skin (Fig. 8.11a). At Piedras Negras, the Maya labeled these as *lajab,* "things for striking with the hands," and, according to nametags that declare possession, they seem to have belonged to royalty (Fig. 8.11b). Such portable drums can be relatively small but go

day signs

Fig. 8.8. Vessel from Ratinlixul (K594).

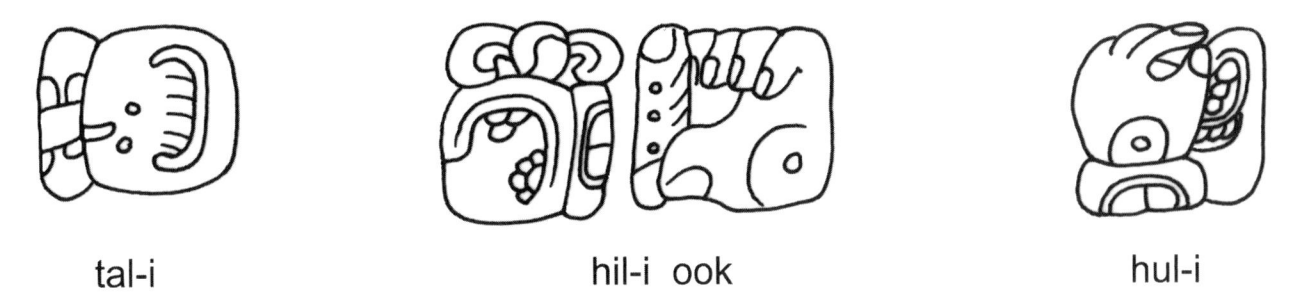

tal-i   hil-i ook   hul-i

Fig. 8.9. Verbs: (a) *tal-i,* "arrival from"; (b) *hil-i ook,* "to rest feet"; and (c) *hul-i,* " arrival to," all from Copan Altar Q (after drawing by Barbara Fash).

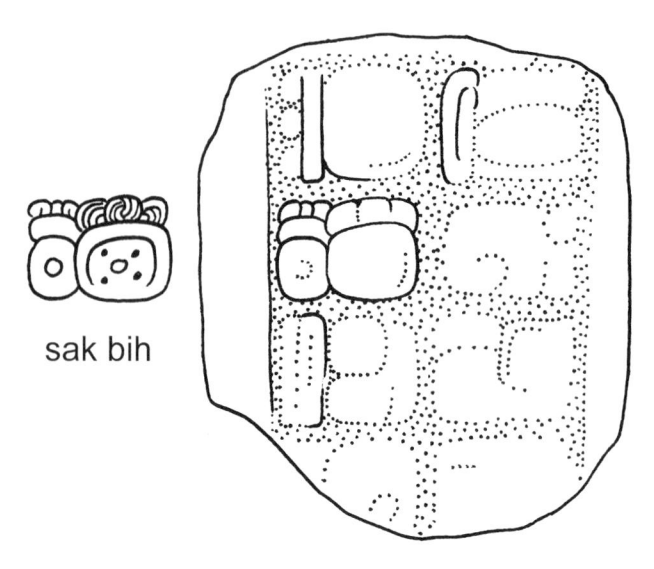

Fig. 8.10. Panel from causeway in Coba/Yaxuna, Mexico (after photograph in Corpus of Maya Hieroglyphic Inscriptions Project, Harvard University).

all the way to hand drums over 30 cm high or more, each presumably having a different tone depending on the volume of the resonating chamber and the tautness of the drum head. Surviving examples, of which a fair number occur in caves, are of clay and date to the Late Classic period. Others, with cleft bottoms, closely resemble gourds (Fig. 8.11c). This suggests that these plants, carefully grown to the desired shape, were the primordial material for such drums (e.g., K1549). This may also explain why so few occur in the Early Classic period; if they were made of gourds, they would have long since decomposed. Another possibility is that not a few drums were improvised alterations of ceramic vessels. A number of images show drums with skin heads of jaguar or feline pelt and carved wooden supports (e.g., K3247, K3332; Kelley 1976:135). In one example, the "drum" carries exactly the same marks as a local pot, the chevron band associated with ceramics from Chama, Guatemala (Fig. 8.12; K3332). If so, this would expand the number of potential musical instruments from archaeological sites, as virtually every cylinder could have been used as a drum. The wooden support would have magnified resonance by creating a removable and perishable sound chamber beneath the vessel. A final kind of drum is an Early Classic worked conch from Uaxactun, Guatemala: it has cuts in the shape of an H, much like those of later wooden drums (Kidder 1947:fig. 48).

The portable drums were matched by ones that stood on the floor. In the Bonampak murals, one such drum appears to come well up to chest level (see also K206). Very few of these resemble the split drum used today in highland Guatemala and Chiapas; rather, they are much closer to the Aztec standing drum, the *huehuetl* (Matos Moctezuma and Solís Olguín 2002:pl. 156). The split drums are struck by sticks with rubber knobs on their tips, and their general absence in the Classic Maya corpus hints at a late introduction from Mexico (proposals that the Pax month sign resembles a split drum are not entirely persuasive because of the opaque origins of that sign [cf. Kelley 1976:fig. 49]). On the other hand, the standing floor drum, whose sound must have carried over considerable distances, was played tabla- or conga-style, with flickering movements of the hand and fingers. The repetitive sound of North American powwow drums probably does not resemble the delicate play of fingers shown in the Bonampak murals (Fig. 8.13a). Unlike the smaller drums, including those with jaguar or feline hide, the great drums must have been anchored in place as part of larger ensembles. In highland Guatemala today, drums emit "voices," not sound, and are encouraged with tots of alcohol to give them "strength" (Allen Christenson, personal communication, 2003). A similar kind of exuberant bellow is shown explicitly as speech scrolls coming from the drums in the Postclassic murals of Santa Rita, Belize (Fig. 8.13b; Gann 1900:pl. 31). A final variety of large drum appears in representations at Copan, Honduras, and Ek' Balam, Mexico (Baudez 1994:fig. 73; Vargas de la Peña and Castillo Borges 1999:fig. 3). The "drum" from Copan is a stone facsimile of an instrument that, in cross section, looks like an inverted trapezoid, narrow surface on the bottom, its wide "playing" surface on the top (Fig. 8.14a). The same kind of drum appears in a mural from Ek' Balam in which musicians and singers perform (Fig. 8.14b). There are glyphs on the drum that cannot be read. Presumably, they named the object.

DANCE, MUSIC, MASKING 263

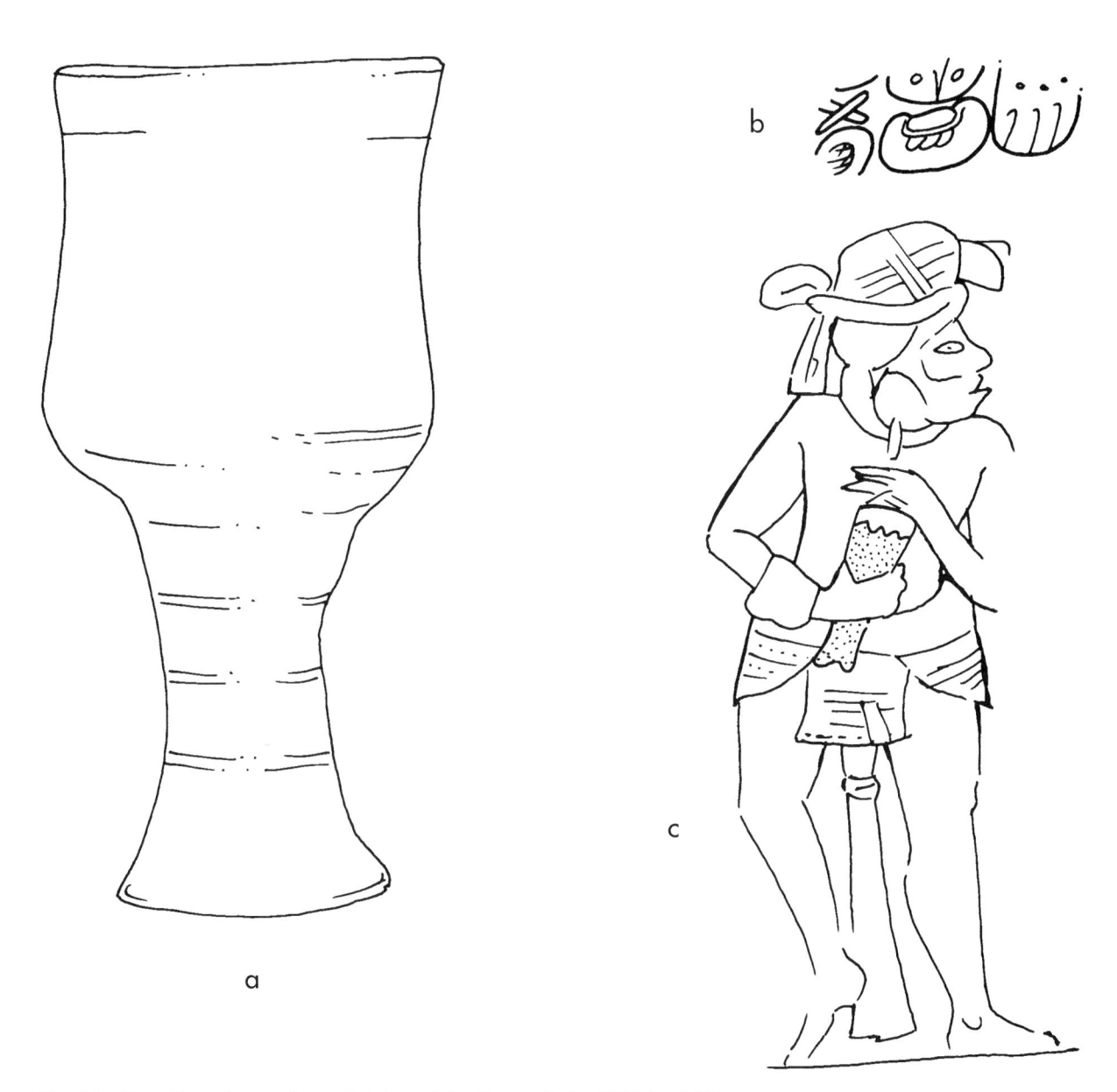

Fig. 8.11. Portable underarm drums: (a) drum (after Reents-Budet 1994:fig. 3.18); (b) text on drum from Piedras Negras (after Holley 1983:fig. 69w); and (c) drum with bottom cleft (after K1549).

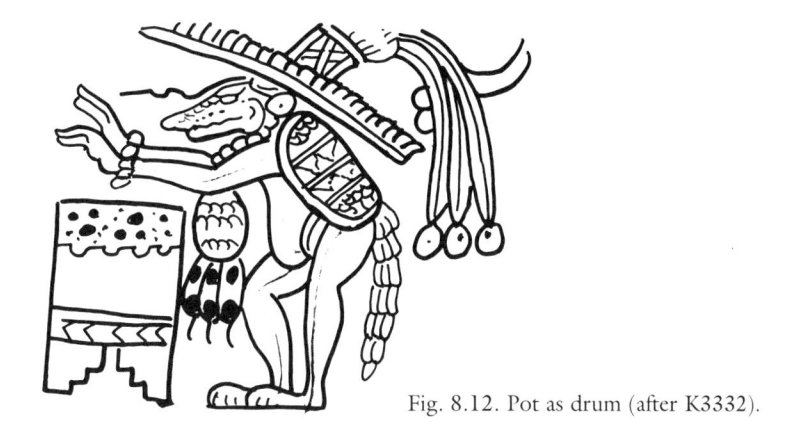

Fig. 8.12. Pot as drum (after K3332).

Other instruments abound in Classic imagery. Conch shells clearly correlated with hunting and with hunting deities, serving as a means of disorienting prey and coordinating a kill (K531, K1882, K2785, K4336). One conch shell, briefly on display in a European museum, goes so far as to record a date for "he spears deer," *u juluw chij* (Fig. 8.15a). Another pot shows the tidily dressed guts and skin of a deer perched on top of the conch that helped confuse and entrap him (Fig. 8.15b; K1901). With these instruments, one hand—the left with humans—was inserted into the conch to modulate tone, a method of play also seen in Veracruz. In other actual conches that have survived from the Classic period, finger holes (probably known as *ti'*, "mouths," by analogy with Ch'orti' usage) occur, along with personal names for the conch: one identifies the conch with a particular deity, as though it issued the voice of that very god (M. Coe 1982:pl. 63). Other terms include *huub'*, "marine shell trumpet" (Barrera Vásquez 1980:238; Schele and M. Miller 1986:pl. 59a), from which emerges a serpent head, perhaps as an embodiment of its voice. At Copan, a supernatural band also plays in the four corners of a sign for "cave" or "place of emergence" (Fig. 8.16; Baudez 1994:fig. 72). The chances are good that these figures represent deities of wind, song, and music, an identification consistent with the fact that the Maya conceived of four winds and that many winds were thought throughout Mesoamerica to issue from caves (MacLeod and Puleston 1978). A trumpet of incised and drilled conch doubles as the face of a *way*, or companion spirit (Schele and M.

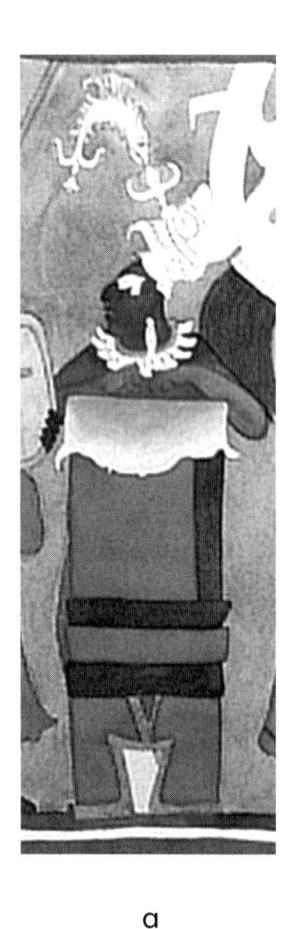

Fig. 8.13. Drumming: (a) play of hands on drum at Bonampak (reconstruction by Heather Hurst [and in some cases, "with Leonard Ashby"], copyright the Bonampak Documentation Project); and (b) "singing drum" from Santa Rita, Belize (after Gann 1900:pl. 31).

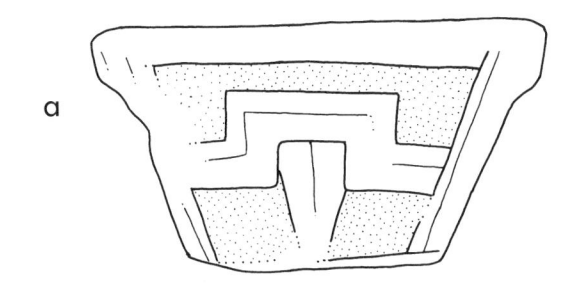

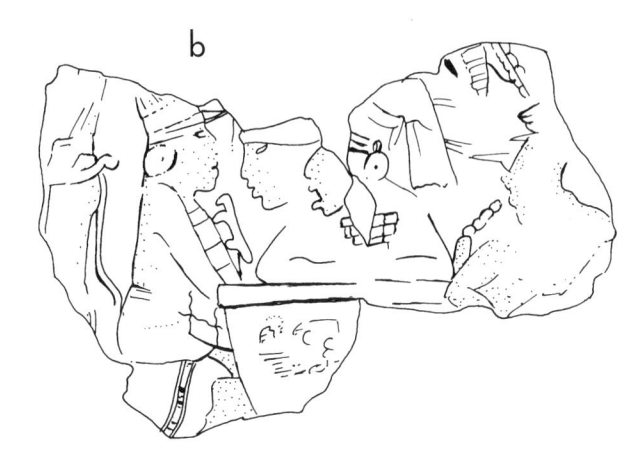

Fig. 8.14. Trapezoidal drums: (a) Copan (after Baudez 1994:fig. 73); and (b) Ek' Balam (after Vargas de la Peña and Castillo Borges 1999:fig. 3).

Miller 1986:pl. 121). Perhaps the voice of the trumpet related to soul loss and soul capture, as Evon Vogt mentions for certain musical instruments in Zinacantán (Vogt 1977:232, 241).

The connection of deities with song and music is strengthened by an evident association with the most robust noisemakers of all, the many Chaak, or storm gods, who perform at a supernatural party on one vessel (Fig. 8.17; M. Coe 1978:pl. 11). On that vessel also occur the turtle carapace and deer-antler rasp found in other images (Fig. 8.18a; e.g., K3040). The rasping noises probably filled the sonic spaces between rattles and drums and could be achieved with other instruments, too, including a gourd with what appear to be dark, jagged inserts that were rubbed with a thin stick (Fig. 8.18b). There may even have been a friction drum attached by string to a resonating chamber (K5233), perhaps used to reproduce a jaguar cry (Donahue n.d.b).

A few dextrous musicians played two instruments at a time, often flutes and drums or rattles

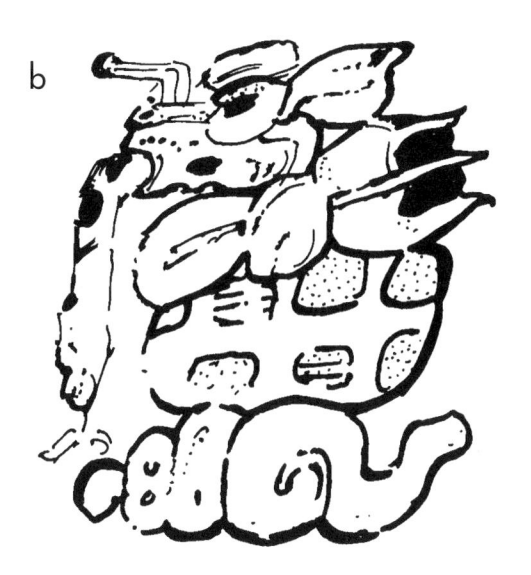

Fig. 8.15. Deer hunting with conches: (a) *u juluw chij*, "he spears deer," glyphs incised on conch (after drawing by Nikolai Grube of unprovenanced conch); and (b) hunted deer, with wrapped flesh and conch (after K1901).

Fig. 8.16. Band of musicians (wind gods?) in flowery cave, Copan Sculpture 131 (after Baudez 1994:fig. 72).

Fig. 8.17. Chaak musicians (M. Coe 1978:pl. 11, photograph copyright Justin Kerr).

and flutes, shaken in vigorous, opposed motions (K1982). The rattles themselves, clearly of gourds, appear with various slits, including some that resemble the glyphic syllable [xa] (pronounced "sha"). This sound may have reproduced the swishing of a rattle. The slits enhanced the noise of seeds or pebbles inside by allowing sound to escape what was otherwise a closed chamber. As for the feathers that sprout from such rattles, it is likely that they represent breath and wind (Chapter 4). For inexplicable reasons, whistles are common at some sites, infrequent at others, with one of the largest assemblages occurring at Piedras Negras, Guatemala. Their ubiquity—most deposits turn up fragments—suggests a broad dispersion of music making, perhaps as part of communal celebrations or casual entertainment. There is no reason to think that all Classic cities were equally musical, in much the same way that, to an unusual extent compared to other parts of the United States, Mormon communities in Utah prize and develop such skill for reasons of religious observance and family fun.

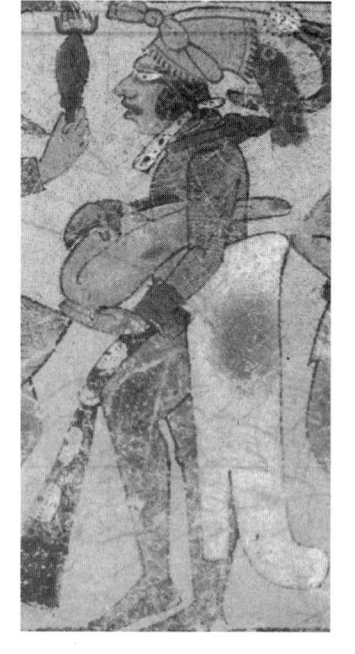

a

b

Fig. 8.18. Rasp instruments: (a) antler and turtle carapace (K3040); (b) gourd rasp with stick (K1549).

As Charles Golden has pointed out to us, most whistles at Piedras Negras can only be played by holding the object to the face, and thus the molded figurine, be it of a bird, an animal, or some deity, fronts and, in a sense, replaces the human face behind. In this way, the figurines "walked" and "sang" when manipulated by a performer. Finally, there were clinking celts of schist or greenstone or the rattle of oliva shells, all of which produced rhythmic sounds when worn on belts by dancers, noblemen, and royalty (Fig. 8.19). The fact that many such celts refer to ancestors evokes the "voice" of the conch, each clang of the celts (perhaps calibrated carefully for pitch or tone, as in Chinese jade chimes) summoning forth the voices of ancients. The exotic nature of these materials, seashells and Motagua River jade, paralleled the existential remoteness of ancestral song. Celts also occur on jaguar-pelt thrones, and the cross-ties are certain between such thrones, the ancestors they may represent, and the costuming of a dancer's midsection with identical, perhaps even the same, elements.

Dance is more firmly attested and described than music making. In fact, many stelae at Maya sites can now be understood to represent dancers. Here, much like the Chaak as music makers, the supple, primordial dancer was the Maize God, who also performed as an acrobat, the epitome of beauty in motion, dripping with jade jewels and bearing, as his duty, the patron animals of particular sites (Fig. 8.20; K4386; also M. Coe 1978:pl. 14). The elaborate, mountainlike backrack of the dancing Maize God recalls an expression in Colonial Yukatek, *ah cuch vitz,* "a certain representation of the Indians" during dance or performance (Acuña 1978:45). In grotesque counterpoint, dwarfs dance, too, almost in replication of courtship dances (see below).

As depicted in Maya imagery and as commemorated in texts, Classic dances fell into decided categories, with the shared feature that most did not involve many performers; even the ambitious murals, which deploy dozens of figures, concentrate on relatively few dancers, three youths in the Room 1 mural and ten figures in the Room 3

Fig. 8.19. Oliva shells, celts, and jaguar pelt around belt: (a) Copan Stela 8 (after drawing by Barbara Fash); and (b) Dos Pilas Stela 15.

Fig. 8.20. Maize God (after K1560).

mural, most being labeled as "youths," *ch'ok*. The mural in Room 1 celebrates a dance of tributary plumage, and the one in Room 3, a dramatic glut of bloodletting or spurious bloodletting in manly stoicism. Long sticks, possibly representing snakes, pass through mock "penises"—or perhaps even real ones?—in what must have been an impressive sight to the credulous. (Similar feats of theatricality may be found in a scene where a dancer supplies the "forearms" of a jaguar throne on which the dancer "sits" [K1439], or in the concealed spaces behind stairs and dance platforms in Puuc-style buildings in the northern part of the Yucatan peninsula.) In this there is a strong disparity with Spanish accounts of eight hundred dancers in some festivals, in itself a suspiciously rounded number, given the vigesimal system of Maya counting (Tozzer 1941:94). Several dances have a burlesque quality, such as ones in which what may be a faux woman (no breasts are visible) capers with a dancer equipped with a phallic nose (Fig. 8.21; K1549). The presence of the whisk fan appears to be an erotic touch, as on an orgy scene elsewhere (M. Coe 1978:pl. 11). Other scenes are almost matrimonial,

Fig. 8.21. Erotic dance (K1549, photograph copyright Justin Kerr).

involving women being transported by men, or they concern courtship, represented by a distinctive display of bent wrists, hands open in cupped fashion, male across from female (K554, K4356; M. Coe 1973:pl. 36; see Tozzer 1941:93, 94, 128, for later mention of erotic dances). Synesthetically, these images convey sound, including, in two secure instances on ceramics from the transition between the Early Classic and Late Classic periods, jeweled flowers and disembodied song floating around the dancers. These were the very essence of numinous, beautiful places, pleasing to all the senses and plain evocations of paradise (Fig. 8.22; K4824, K5746; Taube 2002a). Another kind of performance, seen only once in the surviving images, is of what may be a puppeteer, leaning over and manipulating a small figure by means of sticks (Trik and Kampen 1983:103c).

Regrettably, there is much we do not understand about Maya dance. Most dances probably took place in the open plazas of Maya cities. Humbler undocumented versions, as part of purely domestic or household celebrations, played out in courtyards of varying size. A few correlate with solstitial events, especially those using the so-called flap-staff clutched by dancers at Yaxchilan and La Pasadita (Tate 1992:94–96). For most others, however, we know little, but they must have numbered in the dozens or more and been subject to waves of introduction, adaptation, and extinction within particular communities: the Classic Maya never simply danced, but always danced with or as something. A "knot" dance, the *kach*, makes a mark at Copan (Grube 1992:213) but nowhere else, based on current knowledge. A "sky-snake" dance—evidently, we note with relief, using a nonvenomous serpent—can be seen in a monument from the area of Yaxchilan, perhaps as part of a larger complex involving rainmaking (Fig. 8.23; Grube 1992:fig. 15). However, the sky-snake dance is hardly widespread either. There seems to have been a divide between dances that include youths, who are dressed by other males, as in Room 1 of the Bonampak murals and on a vessel that shows a very similar dressing scene (K7288)—a youth's first dance and a selection of gift bundles to mark the occasion?—and a separate set of adult dances, in which rulers are being offered clothing

Fig. 8.22. Numinous Flower World (K5746, photograph copyright Justin Kerr).

and masks by women, perhaps spouses (e.g., K6316). These scenes figured importantly in Classic visuality. They afford a glimpse into the "backstage" and a peek into the suspension of disbelief required by "performances" of supernatural entities.

It is in the realm of such supernaturals that dance involves itself with the profound enterprise of trance states and impersonations of deities. A useful way of understanding such performances is through the concept of "concurrence," otherwise described as "deity impersonation" (Houston and D. Stuart 1996:297–300; see also A. Stone 1991). The dancer is always specified, as is the deity he or, far more rarely, she "impersonates" (Fig. 8.24). The glyphic expression of this action includes a statement that an image or "self" is present (*u-b'aah*), along with a specialized suffix that usually pertains to supernaturals or the deceased (*-il*)—in one context the term for "god" (*k'uh*)—followed by a title ([a-nu]) of uncertain meaning, the names of a deity, and, finally, the names and titles of a ruler or noble. The important point is that nothing is dissembling, feigned, or concealed. There is no evident "fiction," but there is, apparently, a belief in godly immanence and transubstantiation, of specific people who become, in special moments, figures from sacred legend and the Maya pantheon.

Fig. 8.23. Snake dance on unprovenanced panel from area of Yaxchilan, Mexico (drawing by Nikolai Grube).

DANCE, MUSIC, MASKING 271

In a recent paper, Takeshi Inomata cites Thomas Gage to underscore the resilience of these beliefs into the Colonial period (Gage 1958:247; Inomata 2004): "They seem almost to believe that they have actually done what they only performed for the dance," whether it be in the benign guise of John the Baptist or the malevolent pose of Herod.

The concurrence of human and divine essence is emphasized by the iconographic counterpart to these texts. These images show costumes with what has been termed "X-ray" views (M. Coe 1978:pl. 20; Trik and Kampen 1983:fig. 20c); a narrow space is left exposed around the face of the dancer or performer to underscore their historical identity. Strangely, although one such X-ray view is known from the Olmec cave of Oxtotitlan, Guerrero (Grove 1970), many of these images on ceramic vessels tend to come from one part of the Maya lowlands, somewhere around and to the northwest of Lake Peten Itza, Guatemala: some lords dress as bloated toads holding rattles (and, as toads do today, probably making a fiendish racket during mating season); others, as horrific jaguar beings with overbites beyond any dentist's skill and composite birds with sharp bills. One vessel (K1439), now in the Art Institute of Chicago,

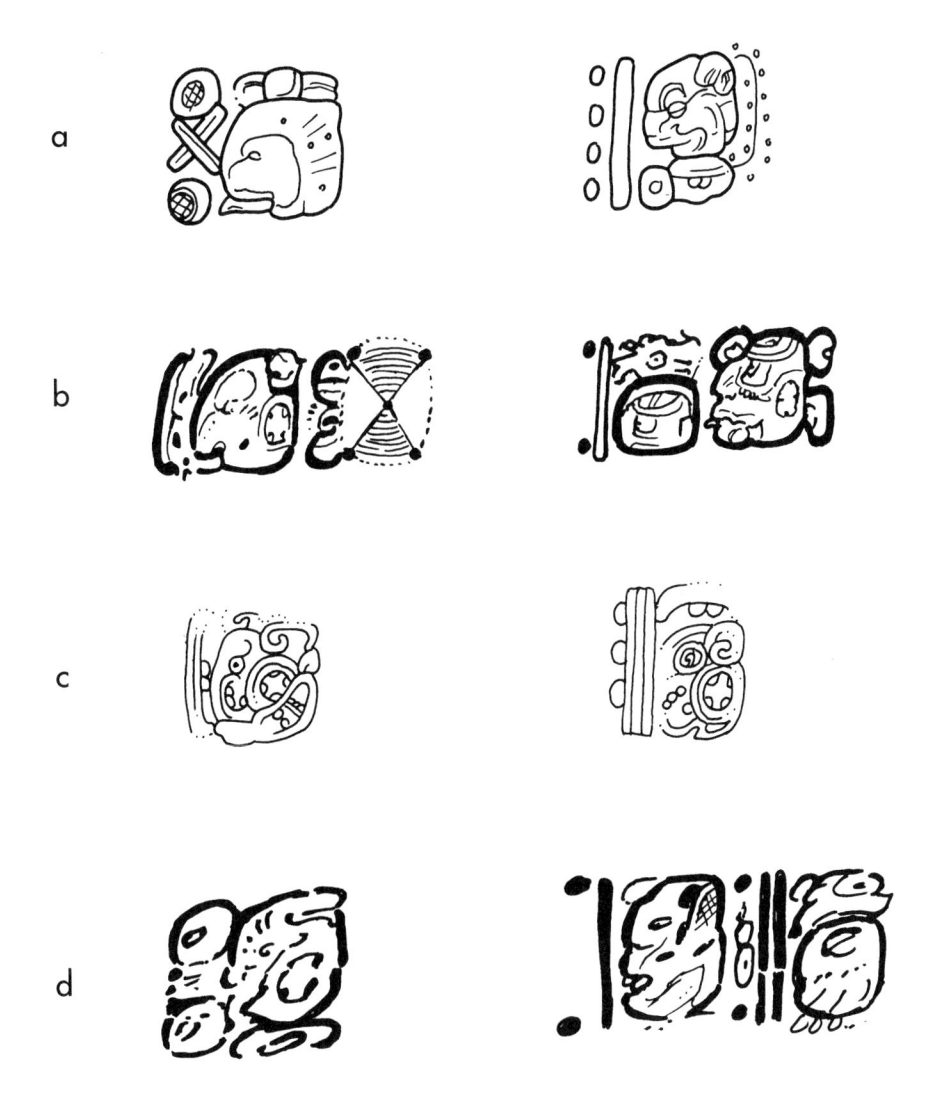

Fig. 8.24. Deity impersonation glyphs as examples of deity "concurrence": (a) 9 *yokte' k'uh* (after photograph by Justin Kerr); (b) Sun God impersonation (after K7224); (c) impersonation of deity from Teotihuacan, Xcalumkin Jam 6:A6–A7 (I. Graham and von Euw 1992:168); and (d) impersonation of deity linked to ballplaying (after K1883).

shows lords dressed as other humans (see also K4606, K6888). The texts on this vessel are difficult to read, but it may be that this represented a historical reenactment in which temporal frames blurred and later actors replicated actions of earlier ones (Schele and M. Miller 1986:pl. 92b). The historical nature of some dances is explicitly mentioned in the *Rabinal Achi* of Alta Verapaz (Akkeren 1999, 2000) and, in Classic times, on Hieroglyphic Stairway 4 of Dos Pilas. The risers of the stairway were positioned at two different times. The bottom four, the first to be put in place, commemorated a civil war between the local cadet and the progenitor dynasty at Tikal, and the top riser, a dance on what may have been the anniversary of the cadet branch's first important ruler (Houston 1993:fig. 4-11, 102, 107). The overall impression is that this dance reviewed and celebrated the events mentioned on the bottom risers. An even more general observation is that the masks thus refer to mythic, satirical, and historical settings—Dos Pilas, we presume, being an excellent example of the last.

The archaeological expression of such impersonations has been found in the form of lightweight masks fortuitously preserved, against all odds, at the site of Aguateca, Guatemala (Fig. 8.25; Inomata et al. 1998:fig. 7). The material is previously unknown, being composed of textiles soaked in clay, fashioned into the heads of deities, and then dried and painted red. The storage of such masks within the most formal buildings of the royal palace at Aguateca demonstrates their importance. Such thin masks figure prominently in a dressing scene on one ceramic vessel: the ruler has his bracelets applied, apparently a two-person job, then checks details in a polished obsidian mirror kept within a wooden box, and other dancers, already equipped with gear, hold thin sticks with masks attached to them (K6341). Were these used as a puppeteer might, placed in front of the face and then removed in sudden gestures? A vessel excavated from Tikal (K2695) shows a ruler being dressed for just such an impersonation (Fig. 8.26; see also K764, K1454, K1524). A courtier holds a mirror so that the dancer can make adjustments, and two females, both identified by the same title ([IX-'i-sa]), respectively offer a mask and a shield to the dancer, who already grasps a rattle. The dressing takes place within a building called the "house of writing (*tz'ib'alnaah*), the home of the *b'akab'*," this last being an exalted honorific. The scene evokes history in that the impersonation is of a male with highly detailed facial features that do not appear to be supernatural. As explained in Chapter 2, the Maya often placed names in headdresses. In this case, the name of the impersonated personage is similar to that of early rulers of the Tikal dynasty. Intersecting here are the highly complex onomastics, or naming practices, of the Classic Maya elite in which repeated names and all they imply of shared identity with past figures follow personal names of more restricted personal reference (Colas 2003). It does not appear to have been troubling that one could be several kinds of person at once.

Fig. 8.25. Mask of composite material, Structure M7-22, easternmost room, Aguateca, Guatemala (courtesy of Takeshi Inomata, University of Arizona).

DANCE, MUSIC, MASKING

Fig. 8.26. Ruler dressing, Mundo Perdido, Tikal (K2695, photograph copyright Justin Kerr).

Scenes of dressing, the removal of headdresses from storage, and their presentation to others are not uncommon in Classic imagery (Fig. 8.27). In fact, some of the headgear worn by Maya lords, especially of forward-swept, wrapped cloth, may have been lightweight armatures for interchangeable headdresses. The storage and presentation of headdresses are now known from many scenes (Taube 1998b:fig. 19). Even Veracruz, so closely linked to Classic Maya practices, shows a view in which such a headdress is supported on a frame (Fig. 8.27d). The well-known "incensario bases" from Palenque, often found on temple platforms in the Cross Group of that city, strongly resemble such headdresses (Taube 1998b:464). In a few scenes, such as on the south side of the bench within Temple XIX at Palenque, the headdress is stored on what may be a "last," or a cloth-draped cone, to preserve its shape and keep it upright. At Palenque, tributary nobles, all impersonating different deities, are about to offer a cloth crown or diadem to the ruler, K'inich Ahkal Mo' Nahb: the lead noble impersonates the high deity Itzamnaaj, or at least the "first" (*yax*) of his series, while the ruler himself adopts the identity of a fishy deity known as G1. In this image, the disembodied, unworn headdress almost functions as a separate participant, facing over toward the subordinates and taking second place only to the ruler himself.

In one context, probably fully mythological, the presentation of a headdress and its wrapping onto the forehead correspond to rites of accession, the acceptance of a headdress connoting the embrace of rule. Another such "cone," also displaying a headdress, appears on a polychrome vessel showing a dancer being dressed (K1454), and similar raisings of headdresses, in these instances by the wearer himself, occur in Early Classic contexts, on Tikal Stela 31 (C. Jones and Satterthwaite 1982:fig. 51c), and in the Late Classic, too, on a graffito from the same city (Trik and Kampen 1983:fig. 96c). Such acts of elevation probably formed part of the performance, perhaps as part of a mid-dance switching of roles. It seems plain, as mentioned in Chapter 1, that the Classic Maya saw headdresses as merging indissolubly with the "roof combs" of temples: the body wearing an upper façade like a pyramid, the pyramid wearing a headdress like a body (Taube 1998b). These free-floating roof combs, evidently blurring with headdresses, occur on incised bricks at Comalcalco, Tabasco (Steede 1984:P-D-79, P-D-110). In much

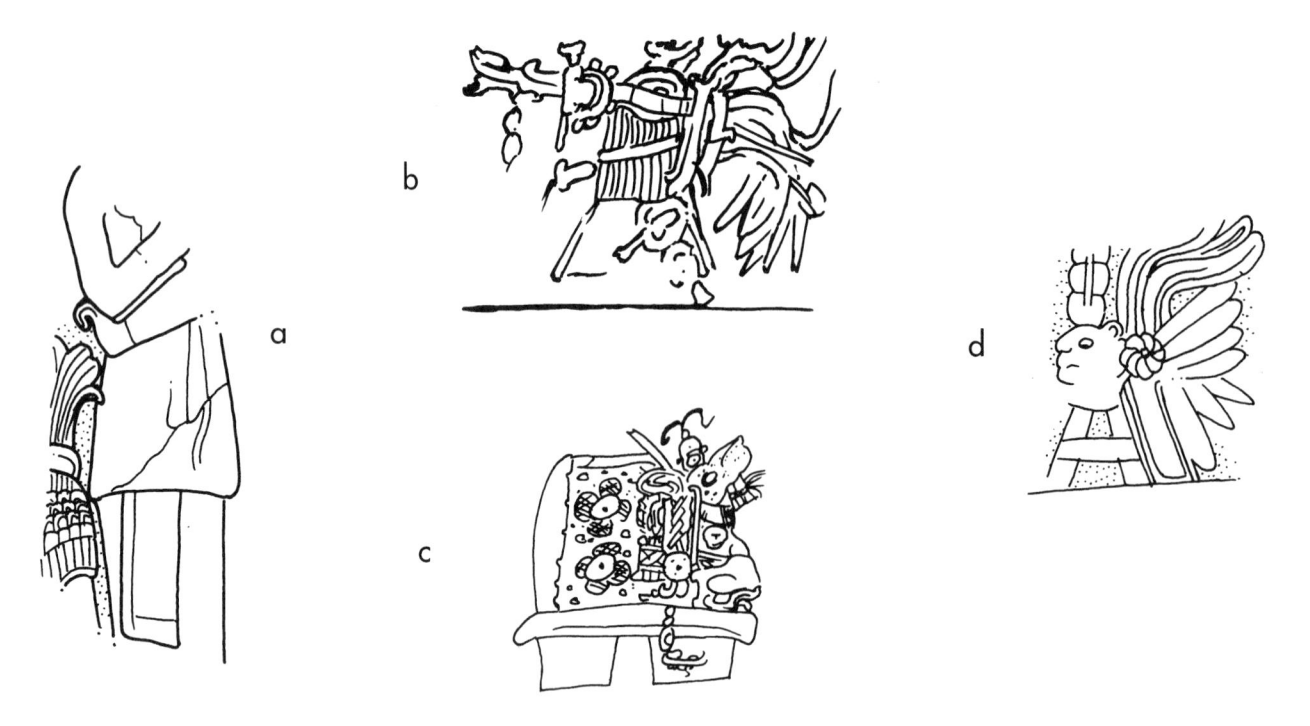

Fig. 8.27. Storage of headdresses: (a) unnumbered Tonina stela (after Yadeun 1993:95); (b) tribute scene on polychrome vessel (photograph by David Stuart of unprovenanced Late Classic vessel); (c) enthroned headdress on polychrome vessel (Taube 1998:fig. 19c); and (d) headdress on rack at El Tajín, Veracruz (after Kampen 1972:fig. 34b).

the same way, rulers wore features of thrones around their waist, including ancestral jewels, feline pelts, shiny mirrors, and prominent bulges. As mentioned before, the ruler transported his throne with him; indeed, the thrones may have been little more than such costumes at rest, waiting for their next performance (e.g., Tikal Stelae 5 and 22; Lintel 2, Temple I; Lintel 2, Temple III [C. Jones and Satterthwaite 1982:figs. 7, 33, 70, 72).

Approximately fifty separate references to "deity concurrence" occur in the Maya corpus of texts (Chapter 2; Fig. 8.24). They show a great range of supernaturals: wind gods (*ik' k'uh*); an enigmatic god or set of gods known as *9 yokte' k'uh*, a watery serpent ("concurrent" with several royal ladies); gods of incense burning; the Sun God; underworld gods who exercise dominion over (pre-Hawking) "black holes"; supernaturals connected to the Mexican site of Teotihuacan (*18 u-b'aah kan*); gods of ballplaying; Moon Goddesses; hunting gods; stony gods; fire-drilling jaguar deities; and the major god known as Itzamnaaj. It is difficult to detect any systematic patterns in this luxuriance of prancing gods. The most obvious are the wind gods, who, for the Classic Maya, operated as Atlantean figures. They were often "concurrent" with nobles who, by analogy, did not support the world so much as the royal throne and whoever sat on it. People drilling sacred fire often adopted the guise of a distinctive deity known as the Jaguar God of the Underworld.

What this evidence suggests is that, with deeper knowledge, we should be able to sort out specific motivations for "impersonation." There are hints that the motivations reflect a theory of dual action, such that actions or roles (the two are scarcely distinguishable) in one frame parallel those in another. The injection of the divine brings those frames—one human, the other supernatural—into contact and congruence; a timeless action was made timely and vested with all the sonorities of a particular court and its personalities. The more-sociological features of such impersonation are not easily contemplated. These matters are best addressed by determining who could dance, much as, among the Pueblos of the Rio Grande valley today, only certain moieties or subgroups inherit

DANCE, MUSIC, MASKING

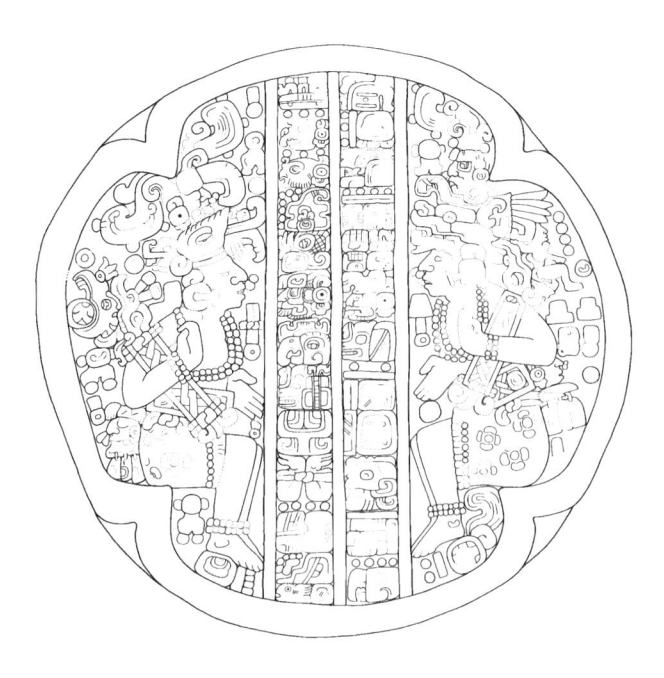

Fig. 8.28. Mot Mot Marker, Copan, Honduras (drawing courtesy of Barbara and William Fash).

the right to perform (Markman and Markman 1989:69). The Classic evidence limits participation to lords, although there must have been broader involvement, too.

CLASSIC MAYA DANCE, MUSIC, MASKING

Among Classic Maya, the nature of music was to propel dance, and the essence of song was to gloss and explain music and dance, and, at times, to evoke the experience of the good life, even paradise (Chapter 4). Stately movement in stylized ways represented the high-stepping, bent-legged ideal. Like song, that dance was flowery and beautiful. The experience would have vibrated with the paradox of transubstantiation, a paradox that brought different beings and world frames into concurrence. *Transcendence* would be precisely the wrong

Fig. 8.29. A human sacrifice (M. Coe 1973:pl. 33, drawing by D. Peck).

word to describe this experience. The spectator and performer were not taken anywhere else; they did not lose themselves in their roles. Rather, divine essences came to visit, briefly, and were made animate by human flesh and motion. A rain of flowers also assisted in communications with the dead, as on a floor marker from Copan (Fig. 8.28; Martin and Grube 2000:194). Practiced movement, especially of the feet, may have summoned these essences. Choreography was a way to replicate other frames, place them in the present, and fashion a narrative structure to shape the whole. If cadence and pacing are at the heart of any great performance, such moments of concurrence may have materialized only at the peak or crescendo of sacred theater. The smaller episodes of spectacle, the dancing, whistling, and drumming, set the stage for the time when gods descended to dance with humans. It is likely, to judge by comparative evidence from indigenous groups in North America, that songs and dances were "owned," strictly controlled, and passable to others by gift or purchase (Fletcher 1995:115–116).

In two respects, however, successful performance and "concurrence" inspired awe and even horror. What beauty can come from a dance of decapitated heads and rotting skin bespeckled with maggots and blood drops (Fig. 8.29; K2025)? The horrific scene of a corpulent sacrificer gutting a captive could not have been comely to many eyes (M. Coe 1973:pl. 33; see also masked arrow sacrifice at Tikal, Guatemala [Trik and Kampen 1983:fig. 38a]). These scenes of impersonation—we presume they are human figures under the flayed faces and bulging stomach—mirror the typical pose of the co-essences, the *way* linked with the wild component of human nature and with the deep forests and caves. In most cases, their animated movement and high-stepping ways equate to dancing, although attended by what music we can only guess: some of their movements in themselves connote aesthetic horror at unbalanced motion and overeager lunges. The beautiful and awesome can also be the dangerous and frightening. Dance, music, and masking sublimely demarcated places and times and brought exceptional events into the hum of Classic-era life.

◀▶ EPILOGUE

Body, Being, and Experience among the Classic Maya

Octavio Paz, a Mexican poet tuned in to all things Mesoamerican, wrote of *ansias afán lisonjas horas cuerpos,* "anxieties desire flatteries hours bodies," a full gazetteer of what life has to offer, a worthy record for the *lauda,* or "tombstone" (1991:88). An epilogue, too, makes a final address to the audience or, in this case, to the reader, drawing conclusions about what came before. Duplication is tedious, even in summary form. Yet it seems a necessary service to do just that at the end of a long discourse on the Classic Maya body and its multiple representations. The following is how we understand, in small measure, what it meant to be alive over twelve hundred years ago.

For us, the Classic Maya body was seen through masculine eyes, not only because that happens to be an accident of our genetic makeup. Any system of Classic "gender" as a network of perspectives becomes, we fear, nearly impossible to reconstruct as a complete system. Moreover, the rich nomenclature of the body found in Colonial and present-day Mayan languages compares unfavorably with the crimped inventory from the Classic Maya themselves. That such terminology existed cannot be doubted, but it was apparently thought beneath notice in hieroglyphic texts.

It is in the corporal body, the *baah,* that the Maya supplemented the person, the *winik.* They extended that body to all manner of forms, all physical yet not always fleshy. The multiplication of the royal body complicated and enriched the social field by establishing many presences. In sacrifice, the body itself contributed to the creation of time and space by means of events exalted at a variety of sites, but not in every instance according to an identical story. The fact that concurrent divergent narratives existed among the Classic Maya probably mattered not at all, or, perhaps, only a little. In much the same way, a deity or royal body could be in many places at once, in simultaneous if varied action, and perceived by the unrecorded bodies—those of long-deceased viewers—who flitted through this world.

The Classic Maya ate, drank, smoked, and snorted. They also flushed such substances out of their bodies and reshaped their consciousness through strong drinks. The ultimate objective was doubtless one of health and physical balance. Descriptions of such acts were restricted, however, to a dyad of draughts of water and the consumption of tamales, regardless of the assorted and valued offerings at the royal or elite table. Not all foods would have been savored today: cannibalism is allusively attested, as is the provender of human flesh to gods. Although it certainly took place, feasting or "formal commensality" is not securely documented in our evidence. Still, with feasting must have come fasting, seldom commented on by archaeologists: the self-denial and the purging that afforded the balance sought by the Maya, in activities that served as gifts of sacrifice that also led to creation and redefinition.

Of the senses much can be said, some experienced through the work of imagination as we attempt to put our bodies in Maya places: a nose today performs the same functions as a nose long ago, far in the past. Generally, for the Classic Maya, the senses were not passive but active, operating as "extramissive" forces that reached out to embrace and access the world. This form of sensation can only be understood as an empowering one, in that the body moved out from its physical frame to engage the universe around it. Bodies were clearly disposed in a hierarchical fashion. Royal and godly sight was, to people at the time, infinitely more potent and validating than nonroyal vision. Lords heard more than others. They discerned and knew things beyond most human ability. That which could be sensed directly still resided intermittently within secret and holy places, in the lairs of gods whose images sallied forth at infrequent intervals. Above all presided a lucidly structured form of synesthesia by which stone, clay, and other media were made to "emit" fragrant odors associated with elites or the stench of death, along with a variety of other triggered sensations.

The emotions were much the same, hierarchically organized according to the status of the person laughing, lusting, and grieving. The Maya body (or, more precisely, the heart) felt deeply: while doing archaeology, only the hard-hearted specialist fails to perceive the ancient pain associated with the burial of an infant or the anguish that must have been felt by sacrificial victims. That adult or parental love of children differed radically from today seems unlikely, even a moral defamation of the past (Bedaux 2000:11–12; cf. Ariès 1960). Yet the representations of passions showed the kings as people who were emotionally cold, carefully contained and reserved. In contrast, captives lost all restraint and, one presumes, their sense of dignity. The regulated, disciplined body was that of the captive who had lost autonomous will. But it was also that of the ruler who emoted little if at all as a way of demonstrating his superiority.

Without emotion, we cannot understand the Classic Maya system of honor and dishonor. By definition, victors were the honored ones; war captives, the defiled and dishonored. The Classic Maya operated on both an "Icelandic" pattern, in which the honor of men and their titles was at stake, and a "Mediterranean" one that bestowed great attention, especially at a city like Tonina, Mexico, to sexual control over women. Homoeroticism played a role in Classic Maya society, faintly attested in probable age-grade houses linked to young men and, perhaps, their older lovers. Most of all, it came into strong view in the captive's need to submit sexually, pathetically, to the victor, who appeared, by Maya representations, to have disdained the body thus offered. An escalating rhetoric of dishonor in these timocratic (honor-fixated) societies eventually adopted a notion that captives were so much meat and then, finally, dirt, a fertilizing element to fructify the crops of the victor's settlement, a building block in the architecture of conquerors.

Speech is ephemeral. Still, as shown in the chapter on the senses, the Classic Maya and other Mesoamerican peoples found ways of showing it. Some kinds of speech, however, went beyond courtly bombast and reflected heavy portents from gods. Here the messages were embodied as birds, even as avatars of the gods sending communications. Omens, divinely phrased, could also be mimicked by the royal court, as when messengers arrived as walking tribute bundles, embodied messages sent by those who preferred, for good and practical reasons, to dispatch proxies in their stead. Although enmeshed in dynastic politics, these messengers were also treated as "birds." The ancestors, too, floated as ethereal beings, apparently within a fragrant celestial realm. To conjure them, to treasure objects linked to ancestors, revealed an insistence on the sustained presence of the "dead."

The most joyous, agitated movement comes last: the dancing, music making, and masking that culminates a volume about past life, loudly and passionately lived. Again, synesthesia imparts to the knowledgeable viewer a barrage of sound and orderly music. These silent images resonate with movement and flash. Intermittently came moments of solemnity, when divine presences joined the social world of the Classic Maya through acts of "impersonation" or, better stated, "concurrence": a dancer might shuffle the feet, but concurrent with his or her body was the vital energy of a supernatural come to visit.

To paraphrase Paz, these chapters have offered, then, *a memory of other bones, a glimpse that touches, and words that burn*. This has been our glance at body, being, and experience among the Classic Maya.

Bibliography

Abbott, Elizabeth. 1999. *A History of Celibacy.* Cambridge, Mass.: Da Capo Press.
Acuña, René. 1978. *Farsas y representaciones escénicas de los mayas antiguos.* Centro de Estudios Mayas Cuaderno 15. Mexico City: Universidad Nacional Autónoma de México.
———, ed. 1984. *Calepino Maya de Motul,* by Antonio de Ciudad Real. 2 vols. Mexico City: Universidad Nacional Autónoma de México.
Adams, Richard E. W. 1971. *The Ceramics of Altar de Sacrificios.* Papers of the Peabody Museum of Archaeology and Ethnology 63(1). Cambridge, Mass.: Harvard University.
———. 1999. *Río Azul: An Ancient Maya City.* Norman: University of Oklahoma Press.
Adamson, John. 1999. Introduction: The Makings of the *Ancien-Régime* Court. In John Adamson, ed., *The Princely Courts of Europe: Ritual, Politics, and Culture under the Ancien Régime, 1500–1750,* 6–41. London: Seven Dials.
Agrinier, Pierre. 1970. *Mound 20, Mirador, Chiapas, Mexico.* Papers of the New World Archaeological Foundation No. 28. Provo, Utah: Brigham Young University.
Akkeren, Ruud W. van. 1999. Sacrifice at the Maize Tree: Rab'inal Achí in Its Historical and Symbolic Context. *Ancient Mesoamerica* 10(2):281–295.
———. 2000. El baile-drama Rab'inal Achí: Sus custodios y linajes de poder. *Mesoamérica* 21(40):1–39.
Allen, David W. 1974. *The Fear of Looking; or, Scopophilic-Exhibitionistic Conflicts.* Charlottesville: University Press of Virginia.
Alpers, Svetlana. 1983. *The Art of Describing: Dutch Art in the Seventeenth Century.* Chicago: University of Chicago Press.
Amrhein, Laura. 2002. An Iconographic and Historic Analysis of Terminal Classic Maya Phallic Imagery. Report submitted to FAMSI, www.famsi.org/reports.
Ancona-Ha, Patricia, Jorge Pérez de Lara, and Mark van Stone. 2000. Some Observations on Hand Gestures in Maya Art. In Barbara and Justin Kerr, eds., *The Maya Vase Book: A Corpus of Rollout Photographs of Maya Vases,* 6:1072–1089. New York: Kerr Associates.
Anders, Ferdinand, Maarten Jansen, and Aurora Pérez Jiménez. 1992. *Origen e historia de los reyes mixtecos: Libro explicativo del llamado Códice Vindobonensis.* Mexico City: Fondo de Cultura Económica.
Anders, Ferdinand, Maarten Jansen, and Luis Reyes García. 1993. *Los templos del cielo y de la oscuridad, Oráculas y liturgia: Libro explicativo del llamado Códice Borgia.* Mexico City: Fondo de Cultura Económica.

———. 1994. *Códice Féjerváry-Mayer: El libro de Tezcatlipoca, señor del tiempo.* Mexico City: Fondo de Cultura Económica.

Andrews, Anthony P. 1983. *Maya Salt Production and Trade.* Tucson: University of Arizona Press.

Andrews, E. Wyllys, IV. 1939. *A Group of Related Sculptures from Yucatan.* Contributions to American Archaeology and History 5(26). Washington, D.C.: Carnegie Institution of Washington.

———. 1941. Pustunich, Campeche: Some Further Related Sculptures. In César Lizardi Ramos, ed., *Los mayas antiguos: Monografías de arqueología, etnografía y lingüística mayas,* 125–135. Mexico City: El Colegio de México.

Andrews Heath de Zapata, Dorothy. 1978. *Vocabulario de Maythan.* Mérida, Mexico: Area Maya.

Anonymous. 1998. *Mexique, Terre des Dieux: Trésors de l'art précolombien Musée Rath, 8 octobre 1998–24 janvier 1999.* Geneva: Musées d'Art et d'Histoire Genève.

Anton, Ferdinand. 1970. *Art of the Maya.* London: Thames and Hudson.

———. 1997. North America: Portraits of a Great Past. In Karl Grönig, ed., *Decorated Skin: A World Survey of Body Art,* 34–51. London: Thames and Hudson.

Appadurai, Arjun. 1981. Gastro-Politics in Hindu South Asia. *American Ethnologist* 8:494–511.

———. 1990. Topographies of the Self: Praise and Emotion in Hindu India. In Catherine A. Lutz and Lila Abu-Lughod, eds., *Language and the Politics of Emotion,* 92–112. Cambridge: Cambridge University Press.

Ariès, Philippe. 1960. *L'enfant et la vie familiale sous l'Ancien Régime.* Paris: Plon.

———. 1981. *The Hour of Our Death.* New York: Alfred A. Knopf.

Aristotle. 1964. *On Sense and Sensible Objects (De Sensu): On the Soul, Parva Naturalia, On Breath.* Trans. Walter S. Hett. Cambridge, Mass.: Harvard University Press.

Arnheim, Rudolf. 1996. *The Split and the Structure: Twenty-eight Essays.* Berkeley: University of California Press.

Astuti, Rita. 1998. "It's a Boy," "It's a Girl": Reflections on Sex and Gender in Madagascar and Beyond. In Michael Lambek and Andrew Strathern, eds., *Bodies and Persons: Comparative Perspectives from Africa and Melanesia,* 29–52. Cambridge: Cambridge University Press.

Attinasi, John J. 1973. Lak T'an: A Grammar of the Chol (Mayan) Word. Ph.D. diss., Department of Anthropology, University of Chicago.

Augustine. 1996. *The Enchiridion of Faith, Hope, and Love.* Washington, D.C.: Gateway Editions.

Ayres, Glenn. 1980. A Note on Mayan Reflexives. *Journal of Mayan Linguistics* 2(1):53–59.

Bacon, Francis. 1985. *The Essays.* London: Penguin Books.

Baines, John. 1985. Color Terminology and Color Classification: Ancient Egyptian Color Terminology and Polychromy. *American Anthropologist* 87:282–297.

Ball, Joseph. 1993. Pottery, Potters, Palaces, and Polities: Some Socioeconomic and Political Implications of Late Classic Maya Ceramic Industries. In Jeremy A. Sabloff and John S. Henderson, eds., *Lowland Maya Civilization in the Eighth Century A.D.,* 243–272. Washington, D.C.: Dumbarton Oaks.

Barasch, Moshe. 1995. *Icon: Studies in the History of an Idea.* New York: New York University Press.

———. 2001. *Blindness: The History of a Mental Image in Western Thought.* London: Routledge.

Bardawil, Lawrence W. 1976. The Principal Bird Deity in Maya Art: An Iconographic Study of Form and Meaning. In Merle Greene Robertson, ed., *The Art, Iconography, and Dynastic History of Palenque: Segunda Mesa Redonda de Palenque, 1974,* 195–210. Pebble Beach, Calif.: Pre-Columbian Art Research, Robert Louis Stevenson School.

Barrera Rubio, Alfredo. 1980. Mural Paintings of the Puuc Region in Yucatán. In Merle Greene Robertson, ed., *Third Palenque Round Table, 1978, Part 2,* 173–182. Austin: University of Texas Press.

Barrera Rubio, Alfredo, and Alfredo Barrera Vásquez. 1983. *El libro del judío: Su ubicación en la tradición botánica y en la medicina tradicional yucatanense.* Xalapa, Mexico: Instituto Nacional de Investigaciones sobre Recursos Bióticos.

Barrera Rubio, Alfredo, and Carlos Peraza Lope. 2001. La pintura mural de Mayapán. In Leticia Staines Cicero, ed., *La pintura mural prehispánica en México, II, área maya: Tomo IV, estudios,* 419–446. Mexico City: Instituto de Investigaciones Estéticas, Universidad Nacional Autónoma de México.

Barrera Rubio, Alfredo, and Karl Taube. 1987. Los relieves de San Diego: Una nueva perspectiva. *Boletín de la Escuela de Ciencias Antropológicas de la Universidad de Yucatán* 16:3–18.

Barrera Vásquez, Alfredo. 1980. *Diccionario Cordemex: Maya-Español, Español-Maya.* Mérida, Mexico: Ediciones Cordemex.

———. 1981. El pulque entre los mayas. In *Estudios lingüísticos: Obras completas, Tomo II*, 71–76. Mérida, Mexico: Fondo Editorial de Yucatán.

Barrett, Karen C. 1993. The Development of Nonverbal Communication of Emotion: A Functionalist Perspective. *Journal of Nonverbal Behavior* 17:145–169.

Barthel, Thomas S. 1955. Versuch über die Inschriften von Chich'en Itza Viejo. *Baessler-Archiv* 3:5–33.

Bateson, Gregory. 1958. *Naven: A Survey of the Problems Suggested by a Composite Picture of the Culture of a New Guinea Tribe Drawn from Three Points of View*. 2nd ed. Stanford: Stanford University Press.

Battaglia, Debbora, ed. 1995. *Rhetorics of Self-Making*. Berkeley: University of California Press.

Baudez, Claude-François. 1994. *Maya Sculpture of Copán: The Iconography*. Norman: University of Oklahoma Press.

Baudrillard, Jean. 1988. *Selected Writings*. Stanford: Stanford University Press.

———. 1994. *Simulacra and Simulation*. Trans. Sheila Faria Glaser. Ann Arbor: University of Michigan Press.

Bauman, Richard. 1992. Performance. In Richard Bauman, ed., *Folkore, Cultural Performances, and Popular Entertainments: A Communications-Centered Handbook*, 41–49. New York: Oxford University Press.

Beaumont, Lesley. 2000. The Social Status and Artistic Presentation of "Adolescence in Fifth-Century Athens, Representing and Perceiving Children." In Joanna Sofaer Derevenski, ed., *Children and Material Culture*, 39–50. London: Routledge.

Beck, Brenda E. F. 1975. The Anthropology of the Body. *Current Anthropology* 16:486–487.

Becker, Anne E. 1995. *Body, Self, and Society: The View from Fiji*. Philadelphia: University of Pennsylvania Press.

Becker, Marvin B. 1988. *Civility and Society in Western Europe, 1300–1600*. Bloomington: Indiana University Press.

Becquelin, Pierre, and Claude F. Baudez. 1979. *Tonina: Une cité maya du Chiapas (Mexique), Tome I*. Mission Archéologique et Ethnologique Française au Mexique, Collection Études Mésoaméricaines 6(1). Paris: Editions Recherche sur les Civilisations.

———. 1982. *Tonina: Une cité maya du Chiapas (Mexique), Tome III*. Mission Archéologique et Ethnologique Française au Mexique, Collection Études Mésoaméricaines 6(3). Paris: Editions Recherche sur les Civilisations.

Becquelin, Pierre, and Eric Taladoire. 1990. *Tonina: Une cité maya du Chiapas (Mexique), Tome IV*. Mission Archéologique et Ethnologique Française au Mexique, Collection Études Mésoaméricaines 6(4). Mexico City: Centre d'Études Mexicaines et Centraméricaines.

Bedaux, Jan Baptist. 2000. Introduction. In Jan Baptist Bedaux and Rudi Ekkart, eds., *Pride and Joy: Children's Portraits in the Netherlands, 1500–1700*, 10–31. Ghent: Ludion Press.

Beeman, William O. 1993. The Anthropology of Theater and Spectacle. *Annual Review of Anthropology* 22:369–393.

Beetz, Carl P., and Linton Satterthwaite. 1981. *The Monuments and Inscriptions of Caracol, Belize*. University Museum Monograph 45. Philadelphia: University of Pennsylvania.

Bell, Lanny. 1985. Luxor Temple and the Cult of the Royal *Ka*. *Journal of Near Eastern Studies* 44(4):251–294.

Belting, Hans. 1994. *Likeness and Presence: A History of the Image before the Era of Art*. Chicago: University of Chicago Press.

Benavides C., Antonio, and Nikolai Grube. 2002. Dos monolitos tempranos de Jaina, Campeche, México. *Mexicon* 24(5):95–97.

Benedict, Ruth. 1935. *Zuni Mythology*. New York: Columbia University Press.

———. 1959. *Patterns of Culture*. Boston: Houghton Mifflin.

Bennett, Jonathan. 1996. Spinoza's Metaphysics. In Don Garrett, ed., *The Cambridge Companion to Spinoza*, 61–88. Cambridge: Cambridge University Press.

Benson, Elizabeth P. 1976. Ritual Cloth and Palenque Kings. In Merle Greene Robertson, ed., *The Art, Iconography, and Dynastic History of Palenque*, 45–58. Pebble Beach, Calif.: Pre-Columbian Art Research, Robert Louis Stevenson School.

Benson, Elizabeth P., and Beatriz de la Fuente, eds. 1996. *Olmec Art of Ancient Mexico*. Washington, D.C.: National Gallery of Art.

Benson, Elizabeth P., and Peter David Joralemon. 1980. *Pre-Columbian Art from Mesoamerica and Ecuador*. Coral Gables, Fla.: Lowe Art Museum, University of Miami.

Benson, Susan. 2000. Inscriptions of the Self: Reflections on Tattooing and Piercing in Contemporary Euro-America. In Jane Caplan, ed., *Written on the Body: The Tattoo in European and American History*, 234–254. Princeton, N.J.: Princeton University Press.

Benthall, Jonathan, and Ted Polhemus. 1975. *The Body as a Medium of Expression*. London: Allen Lane.

Benthien, Claudia. 2004. *Skin: On the Cultural between Self and the World*. New York: Columbia University Press.

Berdan, Frances F., and Patricia R. Anawalt. 1997. *The Essential Codex Mendoza*. Berkeley: University of California Press.

Berlo, Janet C. 1984. *Teotihuacan Art Abroad: A Study of Metropolitan Style and Provincial Transformation in Incensario Workshops*. BAR 180. Oxford: British Archaeological Reports.

Bernal, Ignacio. 1969. *100 Great Masterpieces of the Mexican National Museum of Anthropology*. New York: Harry N. Abrams.

Besnier, Niko. 1990. Language and Affect. *Annual Review of Anthropology* 19:419–451.

———. 1993. Literacy and Feelings: The Encoding of Affect in Nukulaelae Letters. In Brian Street, ed., *Cross-Cultural Approaches to Literacy*, 62–86. Cambridge: Cambridge University Press.

Beyer, Hermann. 1955 [1917]. La procesión de los señores, decoración del primer teocalli de piedra en México-Tenochtitlán. *El México Antiguo* 8:1–42.

Bierhorst, John. 1985. *Cantares Mexicanos: Songs of the Aztecs*. Stanford: Stanford University Press.

Birdwhistell, Ray L. 1970. *Kinesics and Context*. Philadelphia: University of Pennsylvania Press.

Blier, Suzanne Preston. 1995. *African Vodun: Art, Psychology, and Power*. Chicago: University of Chicago Press.

———. 1998. *The Royal Arts of Africa: The Majesty of Form*. New York: Harry N. Abrams.

Bloch, Maurice. 1985. The Ritual of the Royal Bath in Madagascar: The Dissolution of Death, Birth, and Fertility into Authority. In David Cannadine and Simon Price, eds., *Rituals of Royalty: Power and Ceremonial in Traditional Society*, 271–297. Cambridge: Cambridge University Press.

Blom, Frans, and Oliver La Farge. 1926–1927. *Tribes and Temples: A Record of the Expedition to Middle America Conducted by The Tulane University of Louisiana in 1925*. 2 vols. Middle American Research Series, Publication 1. New Orleans: Tulane University.

Bober, Phyllis Pray. 1999. *Art, Culture, and Cuisine: Ancient and Medieval Gastronomy*. Chicago: University of Chicago Press.

Boone, Elizabeth H. 1989. *Incarnations of the Supernatural: The Image of Huitzilopochtli in Mexico and Europe*. Philadelphia: American Philosophical Society.

———. 1991. Migration Histories as Ritual Performance. In Davíd Carrasco, ed., *To Change Place: Aztec Ceremonial Landscapes*, 121–151. Niwot: University Press of Colorado.

Boswell, John. 1980. *Christianity, Social Tolerance, and Homosexuality*. Chicago: University of Chicago Press.

———. 1990. Concepts, Experiences, and Sexuality. *Differences* 2(1):67–87.

Bourdieu, Pierre. 1966. The Sentiment of Honour in Kabyle Society. In John G. Peristiany, ed., *Honour and Shame: The Values of Mediterranean Society*, 191–241. Chicago: University of Chicago Press.

———. 1990. *The Logic of Practice*. Stanford: Stanford University Press.

———. 2001. *Masculine Domination*. Stanford: Stanford University Press.

Bourget, Steve. 2001. Rituals of Sacrifice: Its Practice at Huaca de la Luna and Its Representation in Moche Iconography. In Joanne Pillsbury, ed., *Moche Art and Archaeology in Ancient Peru*, 88–109. Studies in the History of Art 63. Washington, D.C.: Center for Advanced Study in the Visual Arts, National Gallery.

Bowditch, Charles P., ed. 1904. *Mexican and Central American Antiquities, Calendar Systems, and History*. Bulletin 28. Washington, D.C.: Bureau of American Ethnology.

Boyer, Pascal. 2001. *Religion Explained*. New York: Basic Books.

Brandes, Stanley. 1980. *Metaphors of Masculinity: Sex and Status in Andalusian Folklore*. Philadelphia: University of Pennsylvania Press.

Brandt, Elizabeth A. 1980. On Secrecy and the Control of Knowledge: Taos Pueblo. In Stanton Tefft, ed., *Secrecy: A Cross-Cultural Perspective*, 123–146. New York: Human Sciences Press.

Bray, Alan. 1995. *Homosexuality in Renaissance England*. New York: Columbia University Press.

Braziel, Jana Evans, and Kathleen LeBesco. 2001. *Bodies Out of Bounds: Fatness and Transgression*. Berkeley: University of California Press.

Bricker, Victoria R. 1973. *Ritual Humor in Highland Chiapas*. Austin: University of Texas Press.

———. 1981. *The Indian Christ, the Indian King: The Historical Substrate of Maya Myth and Ritual*. Austin: University of Texas Press.

———. 1986. *A Grammar of Mayan Hieroglyphs*. Middle American Research Institute Publication 56. New Orleans: Tulane University.

———. 1991. Faunal Offerings in the Dresden Codex. In Virginia M. Fields, ed., Merle Greene Robertson, gen. ed., *Sixth Palenque Round Table, 1986*, 285–292. Norman: University of Oklahoma Press.

Bricker, Victoria R., and Hela-Maria Miram, trans. 2002. *An Encounter of Two Worlds: The Book of Chilam Balam of Kaua*. Middle American Research Institute Publication 68. New Orleans: Tulane University.

Brillat-Savarin, Jean-Anthelme. 1971. *The Physiology of Taste: or, Meditations on Transcendental Gastronomy*. Trans. Mary F. K. Fisher. New York: Alfred A. Knopf.

Brilliant, Richard. 1991. *Portraiture*. Cambridge, Mass.: Harvard University Press.

Brockington, Donald L. 1967. *The Ceramic History of Santa Rosa, Chiapas, Mexico*. Papers of the New World Archaeological Foundation No. 23. Provo, Utah: Brigham Young University.

Brown, Elizabeth A. R. 1981. Death and the Human Body in the Later Middle Ages: The Legislation of Boniface VIII on the Division of the Corpse. *Viator* 12:221–270.

Brown, Peter. 1970. Sorcery, Demons, and the Rise of Christianity from Late Antiquity into the Middle Ages. In Mary Douglas, ed., *Witchcraft: Confessions and Accusations*, 17–45. London: Tavistock.

———. 1988. *The Body and Society: Men, Women, and Sexual Renunciation in Early Christianity*. New York: Columbia University Press.

Brownmiller, Susan. 1975. *Against Our Will*. New York: Simon and Schuster.

Brüggemann, Jürgen, Sara Ladrón de Guevara, and Juan Sánchez Bonilla. 1992. *Tajín*. Mexico City: El Equilibrista.

Bruman, Henry J. 2000. *Alcohol in Ancient Mexico*. Salt Lake City: University of Utah Press.

Brumfiel, Elizabeth M. 2001. Aztec Hearts and Minds: Religion and the State in the Aztec Empire. In Susan E. Alcock, Terence N. D'Altroy, Kathleen D. Morrison, and Carla M. Sinopoli, eds., *Empires: Perspectives from Archaeology and History*, 283–310. Cambridge: Cambridge University Press.

Burguière, André. 1982. The Fate of the History of *Mentalités* in the *Annales*. *Comparative Studies in Society and History* 24(3):424–437.

Burkhart, Louise. 1989. *The Slippery Earth: Nahua-Christian Moral Dialogue in Sixteenth-Century Mexico*. Tucson: University of Arizona Press.

———. 1992. Flowery Heaven: The Aesthetic of Paradise in Nahuatl Devotional Literature. *Res: Anthropology and Aesthetics* 21:88–109.

Burns, Allan F. 1983. *An Epoch of Miracles: Oral Literature of the Yucatec Maya*. Austin: University of Texas Press.

Butler, Judith. 1990. *Gender Trouble: Feminism and the Subversion of Identity*. New York: Routledge.

———. 1993. *Bodies That Matter: On the Discursive Limits of "Sex."* New York: Routledge.

Bye, Robert A. 2001. Tobacco. In Davíd Carrasco, ed., *Oxford Encyclopedia of Mesoamerican Cultures*, 3:235–236. New York: Oxford University Press.

Calnek, Edward E. 1988a. The Calmecac and the Telpochcalli in Pre-Conquest Tenochtitlan. In Jorge Klor de Alva, Henry B. Nicholson, and Eloise Quiñones Keber, eds., *The Work of Bernardino de Sahagún*, 169–177. Albany: Institute for Mesoamerican Studies, State University of New York at Albany.

———. 1988b. *Highland Chiapas before the Spanish Conquest*. Papers of the New World Archaeological Foundation No. 55. Provo, Utah: Brigham Young University.

Camille, Michael. 1992. *Image on the Edge: The Margins of Medieval Art*. London: Reaktion Books.

———. 1996. Simulacrum. In Robert S. Nelson and Richard Shiff, eds., *Critical Terms for Art History*, 31–44. Chicago: University of Chicago Press.

Campaña, Luz Evelia, and Sylviane Boucher. 2002. Nuevas imágenes de Becán, Campeche. *Arqueología Mexicana* 10(56):64–69.

Campbell, John. 1994. *Past, Space, and Self*. Cambridge, Mass.: MIT Press.

Campbell, Lyle. 1984. The Implications of Mayan Historical Linguistics for Glyphic Research. In John S. Justeson and Lyle Campbell, eds., *Phoneticism in Mayan Hieroglyphic Writing*, 1–16. Publication No. 9. Albany: Institute for Mesoamerican Studies, State University of New York at Albany.

———. 1988. *The Linguistics of Southeast Chiapas, Mexico*. Papers of the New World Archaeological Foundation No. 50. Provo, Utah: Brigham Young University.

Camporesi, Piero. 1990. *Exotic Brew: The Art of Living in the Age of Enlightenment*. Cambridge: Polity Press.

———. 1994. *The Anatomy of the Senses: Natural Symbols in Medieval and Early Modern Italy*. Cambridge: Polity Press.

———. 1996. *Bread of Dreams: Food and Fantasy in Early Modern Europe*. Chicago: University of Chicago Press.

Carlino, Andrea. 1999. *Books of the Body: Anatomical Ritual and Renaissance Learning*. Chicago: University of Chicago Press.

Carlsen, Robert T. S., and Martin Prechtel. 1991. The Flowering of the Dead: An Interpretation of Highland Maya Culture. *Man*, n.s. 26(1):23–42.

Carlson, Ruth, and Francis Eachus. 1977. El mundo espiritual de los kekchíes. In Helen L. Neuenswander and Dean E. Arnold, eds., *Estudios cognitivos del sur de Mesoamérica*, 33–61. Dallas: Museum of the Summer Institute of Linguistics.

Carrasco, Ramón. 1996. Calakmul, Campeche: Arqueología de una superpotencia. *Arqueología Mexicana* 3:46–51.

———. 1999. Tumbas reales de Calakmul: Ritos funerarios y estructura de poder. *Arqueología Mexicana* 7:28–31.

Carrithers, Michael, Steven Collins, Steven Lukes, eds. 1985. *The Category of the Person: Anthropology, Philosophy, History*. Cambridge: Cambridge University Press.

Caso, Alfonso. 1967. *Los calendarios prehispánicos*. Mexico City: Universidad Nacional Autónoma de México.

Chase, Arlen F. 1994. A Contextual Approach to the Ceramics of Caracol, Belize. In Diane Z. Chase and Arlen F. Chase, eds., *Studies in the Archaeology of Caracol, Belize*, 157–182. Pre-Columbian Art Research Institute Monograph 7. San Francisco: Pre-Columbian Art Research Institute.

Chase, Arlen F., and Diane Z. Chase. 2001. The Royal Court of Caracol, Belize: Its Palaces and People. In Takeshi Inomata and Stephen D. Houston, eds., *Royal Courts of the Ancient Maya*, Vol. 2, *Data and Case-Studies*, 102–137. Boulder, Colo.: Westview Press.

Chase, Diane Z., and Arlen F. Chase. 1998. The Architectural Context of Caches, Burials, and Other Ritual Activities for the Classic Period Maya (as Reflected at Caracol, Belize). In Stephen D. Houston, ed., *Function and Meaning in Classic Maya Architecture*, 299–332. Washington, D.C.: Dumbarton Oaks.

Chinchilla Mazariegos, Oswaldo. 2003. A Corpus of Cotzumalhuapa-Style Sculpture, Guatemala. Report submitted to the Foundation for the Advancement of Mesoamerican Studies, Inc., www.famsi.org/reports.

Christenson, Allen J. 2000. *Popol Vuh: The Mythic Sections—Tales of the First Beginnings from the Ancient K'iche'-Maya*. Ancient Texts and Mormon Studies 2. Provo, Utah: Foundation for Ancient Research and Mormon Studies.

———. 2001. *Art and Society in a Highland Maya Community: The Altarpiece of Santiago Atitlán*. Austin: University of Texas Press.

———. 2003. *Popol Vuh*. London: Allen Bell.

Christian, William A., Jr., 1981. *Apparitions in Late Medieval and Renaissance Spain*. Princeton, N.J.: Princeton University Press.

Cifarelli, Megan. 1998. Gesture and Alterity in the Art of Ashurnasirpal II of Assyria. *The Art Bulletin* 80(2):210–228.

Clancy, Flora S. 1999. *Sculpture in the Ancient Maya Plaza: The Early Classic Period*. Albuquerque: University of New Mexico Press.

Clark, Stuart. 1983. French Historians and Early Modern Popular Culture. *Past and Present* 100:62–99.

Clarke, John R. 1998. *Looking at Lovemaking: Constructions of Sexuality in Roman Art, 100 B.C.- A.D. 250*. Berkeley: University of California Press.

Classen, Constance. 1990. Sweet Colors, Fragrant Songs: Sensory Models of the Andes and the Amazon. *American Ethnologist* 17(4):722–735.

———. 1993a. *Inca Cosmology and the Human Body*. Salt Lake City: University of Utah Press.

———. 1993b. *Worlds of Sense: Exploring the Senses in History and across Cultures*. London: Routledge.

Classen, Constance, David Howes, and Anthony Synnott. 1994. *Aroma: The Cultural History of Smell*. London: Routledge.

Clastres, Pierre. 1974. *La Société contre l'État*. Paris: Les Editions de Minuit.

Clendinnen, Inga. 1991. *Aztecs: An Interpretation*. Cambridge: Cambridge University Press.

Coe, Michael D. 1966. *An Early Stone Pectoral from Southeastern Mexico*. Studies in Pre-Columbian Art and Archaeology 1. Washington, D.C.: Dumbarton Oaks.

———. 1973. *The Maya Scribe and His World*. New York: Grolier Club.

———. 1975. *Classic Maya Pottery at Dumbarton Oaks*. Washington, D.C.: Dumbarton Oaks.

———. 1977. Supernatural Patrons of Maya Scribes and Artists. In Norman Hammond, ed., *Social Process in Maya Prehistory: Studies in Honour of Sir Eric Thompson*, 327–347. London: Academic Press.

———. 1978. *Lords of the Underworld: Masterpieces of Classic Maya Ceramics*. Princeton, N.J.: Art Museum, Princeton University.

———. 1982. *Old Gods and Young Heroes: The Pearlman Collection of Maya Ceramics*. Jerusalem: The Israel Museum.

———. 1988. The Ideology of the Maya Tomb. In Elizabeth P. Benson and Gillett Griffin, eds., *Maya Iconography*, 222–235. Princeton, N.J.: Princeton University Press.

———. 1989. Hero Twins: Myth and Image. In Justin Kerr, ed., *The Maya Vase Book*, 1:161–184. New York: Kerr Associates.

———. 2003. Another Look at the Maya Ballgame. In Davide Domenici, Carolina Orisini, and Sofia Venturoli, eds., *Il sacro e il paesaggio nell'America indigena*, 197–204. Bologna: CULEB.

Coe, Michael D., and Elizabeth P. Benson. 1966. *Three Maya Relief Panels at Dumbarton Oaks*. Studies in Pre-Columbian Art and Archaeology 2. Washington, D.C.: Dumbarton Oaks.

Coe, Michael D., and Richard A. Diehl. 1980. *In the Land of the Olmec*. Vol. 1, *The Archaeology of San Lorenzo Tenochtitlán*. Austin: University of Texas Press.

Coe, Michael D., and Justin Kerr. 1997. *The Art of the Maya Scribe*. London: Thames and Hudson.

Coe, Michael D., and Mark van Stone. 2001. *Reading the Maya Glyphs*. London: Thames and Hudson.

Coe, Sophie D. 1994. *America's First Cuisines*. Austin: University of Texas Press.

Coe, William R. 1967. *Tikal: A Handbook of the Ancient Maya Ruins*. Philadelphia: University Museum, University of Pennsylvania.

———. 1990 *Excavations in the Great Plaza, North Terrace, and North Acropolis of Tikal*. Tikal Report No. 14, Vol. 5. Philadelphia: University Museum, University of Pennsylvania.

Coggins, Clemency Chase, and John M. Ladd. 1992. Copan and Rubber Offerings. In Clemency Chase Coggins, ed., *Artifacts from the Cenote of Sacrifice, Chichen Itza, Yucatan*, 344–357. Memoirs of the Peabody Museum of Archaeology and Ethnology 10(3). Cambridge, Mass.: Harvard University.

Cohen, Anthony P. 1994. *Self Consciousness: An Alternative Anthropology of Identity*. London: Routledge.

Colas, Pierre Robert. 2003. K'inich and King: Naming Self and Person among Classic Maya Rulers. *Ancient Mesoamerica* 14(2):269–283.

———. 2004. *Sinn und Bedeutung klassischer Maya-Personennamen: Typologische Analyse von Anthroponymphrasen in den Hieroglypheninschirften der klassischen Maya-Kultur als Beitrag zur allgemeinen Onomastik*. Acta Mesoamericana 15. Markt Schwaben: Verlag Anton Saurwein.

Colby, Benjamin N., and Lore M. Colby. 1981. *The Daykeeper: The Life and Discourse of an Ixil Diviner*. Cambridge, Mass.: Harvard University Press.

Collinson, Diane. 1987. *Fifty Major Philosophers: A Reference Guide*. London: Routledge.

Cooley, Charles Horton. 1964. *Human Nature and Social Order*. New York: Schocken.

Corbin, Alain. 1986. *The Foul and the Fragrant: Odor and the French Social Imagination*. Cambridge, Mass.: Harvard University Press.

Coren, Stanley. 1993. *The Left-Hander Syndrome: The Causes and Consequences of Left-Handedness*. New York: Vintage.

Coren, Stanley, Lawrence M. Ward, and James T. Enns. 1999. *Sensation and Perception*. 5th ed. Fort Worth: Harcourt College Publishers.

Corin, Ellen. 1998. Refiguring the Person: The Dynamics of Affects and Symbols in an African Spirit Possession Cult. In Michael Lambek and Andrew Strathern, eds., *Bodies and Persons: Comparative Perspectives from Africa and Melanesia*, 80–102. Cambridge: Cambridge University Press.

Corson, Christopher R. 1976. *Maya Anthropomorphic Figurines from Jaina Island, Campeche*. Ramona, Calif.: Ballena Press.

Cortez, Constance. 1986. *The Principal Bird Deity in Late Preclassic and Early Classic Maya Art*. M.A. thesis, Department of Art History, University of Texas at Austin.

Coto, Thomás de. 1983. *Vocabulario de la lengua cakchiquel u (el) guatemalteca, nuevamente hecho y recopilado con summo estudio, travajo y erudición*. Mexico City: Universidad Nacional Autónoma de México.

Counihan, Carole M. 1999. *The Anthropology of Food and Body: Gender, Meaning, and Power*. London: Routledge.

Covarrubias, Miguel. 1957. *Indian Art of Mexico and Central America*. New York: Alfred A. Knopf.

Crapanzano, Vincent. 1982. The Self, the Third, and Desire. In Benjamin Lee, ed., *Psychosocial Theories of the Self*, 179–206. New York: Plenum Press.

Crary, Jonathan. 1990. *Techniques of the Observer: On Vision and Modernity in the Nineteenth Century.* Cambridge, Mass.: MIT Press.

Crocker, J. Christopher. 1979. Selves and Alters among the Eastern Bororo. In David Maybury-Lewis, ed., *Dialectical Societies: The Gê and Bororo of Central Brazil,* 249–300. Cambridge, Mass.: Harvard University Press.

Cruz Lara Silva, Adriana, and María Guevara Muñoz. 2002. *La restauración de la cerámica olmeca de San Lorenzo Tenochtitlán, Veracruz: Teoría y práctica.* Mexico City: Universidad Nacional Autónoma de México.

Csordas, Thomas. 1994. Introduction: The Body as Representation and Being-in-the-World. In Thomas J. Csordas, ed., *Embodiment and Experience: The Existential Ground of Culture and Self,* 1–24. Cambridge: Cambridge University Press.

Culbert, T. Patrick 1993. *The Ceramics of Tikal: Vessels from the Burials, Caches, and Problematical Deposits.* Tikal Report No. 25, Part A. Philadelphia: University Museum, University of Pennsylvania.

Dahlin, Bruce H., and William J. Litzinger. 1986. Old Bottle, New Wine: The Function of Chultuns in the Maya Lowlands. *American Antiquity* 51(4):721–736.

Dalby, Andrew. 1996. *Siren Feasts: A History of Food and Gastronomy in Greece.* London: Routledge.

———. 2000a. *Dangerous Tastes: The Story of Spices.* Berkeley: University of California Press.

———. 2000b. *Empire of Pleasures: Luxury and Indulgence in the Roman World.* London: Routledge.

Damasio, A. 1999. *The Feeling of What Happens: Body and Emotion in the Making of Consciousness.* San Diego: Harcourt.

Danziger, Eve. 1996. Parts and Their Counterparts: Spatial and Social Relationships in Mopan Maya. *Journal of the Royal Anthropological Institute* 2:67–82.

Darwin, Charles. 1998. *The Expression of the Emotions in Man and Animals.* New York: Oxford University Press.

Daun, Åke. 1996. *Swedish Mentality.* University Park: Pennsylvania State Press.

Davidson, James. 1997. *Courtesans and Fishcakes: The Consuming Passions of Classical Athens.* New York: St. Martin's Press.

Davis, Richard H. 1997. *Lives of Indian Images.* Princeton, N.J.: Princeton University Press.

DeBoer, A. G., F. Moolenaar, L. G. J. de Leede, and D. D. Breimer. 1982. Rectal Drug Administration: Clinical Pharmacokinetic Considerations. *Clinical Pharmacokinetics* 7:285–311.

de Jorio, Andrea. 2000. *Gesture in Naples and Gesture in Classical Antiquity.* Trans. Adam Kendon. Bloomington: Indiana University Press.

De la Fuente, Beatriz. 1996. Homocentrism in Olmec Monumental Art. In Elizabeth P. Benson and Beatriz de la Fuente, eds., *Olmec Art of Ancient Mexico,* 41–50. Washington, D.C.: National Gallery of Art, Washington.

Deleuze, Gilles. 1990. *The Logic of Sense.* Ed. Constance V. Boundas. New York: Columbia University Press.

D'Emilio, John, and Estelle B. Freedman. 2002. Family Life and the Regulation of Deviance. In Kim M. Phillips and Barry Reay, eds., *Sexualities in History: A Reader,* 141–165. New York: Routledge.

de Smet, Peter A. G. M. 1983. A Multidisciplinary Overview of Intoxicating Enema Rituals in the Western Hemisphere. *Journal of Ethnopharmacology* 9:129–166.

———. 1984. A Multidisciplinary Overview of Intoxicating Snuff Rituals in the Western Hemisphere. *Journal of Ethnopharmacology* 13:3–49.

———. 1985. *Ritual Enemas and Snuffs in the Americas.* Amsterdam: Centrum voor Studie en Documentatie van Latijns Amerika.

de Vries, Lyckle. 1991. The Changing Face of Realism. In David Freedberg and Jan de Vries, eds., *Art in History, History in Art: Studies in Seventeenth-Century Dutch Culture,* 209–244. Santa Monica: Getty Center for the History of Art and the Humanities.

Diehl, Richard A. 1983. *Tula: The Toltec Capital of Ancient Mexico.* London and New York: Thames and Hudson.

Dieseldorff, Erwin P. 1926. *Kunst und Religion der Mayavölker im alten und heutigen Mittelamerika.* Berlin: Julius Springer.

Dietler, Michael. 2001. Theorizing the Feast: Rituals of Consumption, Commensal Politics, and Power in African Contexts. In Michael Dietler and Brian Hayden, eds., *Feasts: Archaeological and Ethnographic Perspectives on Food, Politics, and Power,* 65–114. Washington, D.C.: Smithsonian Institution Press.

Dietler, Michael, and Brian Hayden. 2001. Digesting the Feast—Good to Eat, Good to Drink, Good to

Think: An Introduction. In Michael Dietler and Brian Hayden, eds., *Feasts: Archaeological and Ethnographic Perspectives on Food, Politics, and Power,* 1–20. Washington, D.C.: Smithsonian Institution Press.

Dietler, Michael, and Ingrid Herbich. 2001. Feasts and Labor Mobilization: Dissecting a Fundamental Economic Practice. In Michael Dietler and Brian Hayden, eds., *Feasts: Archaeological and Ethnographic Perspectives on Food, Politics, and Power,* 240–264. Washington, D.C.: Smithsonian Institution Press.

Dillon, Brian D. 1982. Bound Prisoners in Maya Art. *Journal of New World Archaeology* 5(1):24–50.

Dillon, Brian D., Lynda Brunker, and Kevin O. Pope. 1985. Ancient Maya Autoamputation? A Possible Case from Salinas de los Nueve Cerros, Guatemala. *Journal of New World Archaeology* 5(4):24–38.

Dilthey, Wilhelm. 1976. *Selected Writings.* Cambridge: Cambridge University Press.

Di Stasi, Lawrence. 1981. *Mal Occhio: The Underside of Vision.* San Francisco: North Point Press.

Doepke, Frederick C. 1996. *The Kinds of Things: A Theory of Personal Identity Based on Transcendental Argument.* Chicago: Open Court.

Donahue, John A. n.d.a. An Analysis of Music-Related Terms across the Mayan Languages. Unpublished manuscript in possession of authors.

———. n.d.b. Applying Experimental Archaeology to Ethnomusicology: Re-creating an Ancient Maya Friction Drum through Various Lines of Evidence. Unpublished manuscript in possession of authors.

Donnan, Christopher B., and Donna McClelland. 1999. *Moche Fineline Painting: Its Evolution and Its Artists.* Los Angeles: Fowler Museum of Cultural History, University of California at Los Angeles.

Douglas, Mary. 1973. *Natural Symbols: Explorations in Cosmology.* New York: Vintage.

Dover, Kenneth J. 1989. *Greek Homosexuality.* Cambridge, Mass.: Harvard University Press.

Dreyfus, Hubert L., and Paul Rabinow. 1982. *Michel Foucault: Beyond Structuralism and Hermeneutics.* Chicago: University of Chicago Press.

Dundes, Allan. 1981. *The Evil Eye: A Folklore Casebook.* New York: Garland.

Dupont, Florence. 1989. The Emperor-God's Other Body. In Michel Fehrer, with Ramona Naddaff and Nadia Tazi, eds., *Fragments for a History of the Human Body,* 396–419. New York: Zone.

Durán, Diego. 1971. *Book of the Gods and Rites and the Ancient Calendar.* Trans. Fernando Horcasitas and Doris Heyden. Norman: University of Oklahoma Press.

Dworkin, Andrea. 1989. *Letters from a War Zone: Writings, 1976–1989.* New York: E. P. Dutton.

Easby, Elizabeth K., and John F. Scott. 1970. *Before Cortés: Sculpture of Middle America, A Centennial Exhibition at the Metropolitan Museum of Art, from September 30, 1970, through January 3, 1971.* New York: Metropolitan Museum of Art.

Eberl, Markus, and Victoria R. Bricker. 2004. *Unwinding the Rubber Ball: The Glyphic Expression nahb' as a Numeral Classifier for "Handspan."* Research Reports on Ancient Maya Writing 55. Barnardsville, N.C.: Center for Maya Research.

Ediger, Donald. 1971. *The Well of Sacrifice.* Garden City, N.J.: Doubleday.

Edmonson, Munro S. 1965. *Quiche-English Dictionary.* Middle American Research Institute 30. New Orleans: Tulane University.

Ekholm, Gordon F. 1964. *A Maya Sculpture in Wood.* New York: Museum of Primitive Art.

Ekholm, Susanna M. 1979. The Significance of an Extraordinary Maya Ceremonial Refuse Deposit at Lagartero, Chiapas. *Proceedings of the International Congress of Americanists* (42nd session, Paris, 1976) 8:147–159.

Ekman, Paul. 1980. *The Face of Man: Universal Expression in a New Guinea Village.* New York: Garland.

Ekman, Paul, W. V. Friesen, M. O'Sullivan, A. Chan, I. Diacoyanni Tarlatzis, K. Heider, R. Krause, W. A. LeCompte, T. Pitcarin, P. E. Ricci-Bitt, K. R. Scherer, M. Tomita, and A. Tzavaras. 1987. Universals and Cultural Differences in the Judgments of Facial Expressions of Emotion. *Journal of Personality and Social Psychology* 53:712–717.

Eliade, Mircea. 1959. *The Sacred and the Profane: The Nature of Religion.* New York: Harcourt Brace.

Elliott, John H., and Laurence W. B. Brockliss, eds. 1999. *The World of the Favourite.* New Haven: Yale University Press.

Emery, Kitty F., Lori E. Wright, and Henry Schwarcz. 2000. Isotopic Analysis of Ancient Deer Bone: Biotic Stability in Collapse Period Maya Land-use. *Journal of Archaeological Science* 27:537–550.

Emery, Walter B. 1962. *A Funerary Repast in an Egyptian Tomb of the Archaic Period.* Leiden: Nederlands Instituut Voor Het Nabije Oosten.

Evans, Robert J. W. 1973. *Rudolf II and His World: A Study in Intellectual History, 1576–1612.* Oxford: Clarendon Press.

Fahsen, Federico. 1988. *A New Early Classic Text from Tikal.* Research Reports on Ancient Maya Writing 17. Washington, D.C.: Center for Maya Research.

Falasca-Zamponi, Simonetta. 1997. *Fascist Spectacle: The Aesthetics of Power in Mussolini's Italy.* Berkeley: University of California Press.

Falk, Pasi. 1994. *The Consuming Body.* London: Sage.

Faris, James C. 1972. *Nuba Personal Art.* Toronto: University of Toronto Press.

Farnell, Brenda. 1999. Moving Bodies, Acting Selves. *Annual Review of Anthropology* 28:341–373.

Fash, William L. 1989. The Sculptural Content of Structure 9N-82: Content, Form, and Significance. In David Webster, ed., *The House of the Bacabs, Copan, Honduras,* 41–88. Studies in Pre-Columbian Art and Archaeology 29. Washington, D.C.: Dumbarton Oaks.

———. 1991. *Scribes, Warriors, and Kings: The City of Copán and the Ancient Maya.* London: Thames and Hudson.

Fausto-Sterling, Anne. 1992. *Myths of Gender: Biological Theories about Women and Men.* New York: Basic Books.

———. 1995. Animal Models for the Development of Human Sexuality: A Critical Evaluation. *Journal of Homosexuality* 283(4):217–236.

Feeley-Harnik, Gillian. 1985. Issues in Divine Kingship. *Annual Review of Anthropology* 14:273–313.

Finkelstein, P., and L. Mathers. 1990. Post-Traumatic Stress among Medical Students in the Anatomy Dissection Laboratory. *Clinical Anatomy* 3:219–226.

Fish, Stanley. 1989. *Doing What Comes Naturally: Change, Rhetoric, and the Practice of Theory in Literary and Legal Studies.* Durham, N.C.: Duke University Press.

Fletcher, Alice C. 1995. *Indian Story and Song from North America.* Lincoln: University of Nebraska Press.

Flynn, Tom. 1998. *The Body in Three Dimensions.* New York: Abrams.

Fogelson, Raymond D. 1982. Person, Self, and Identity: Some Anthropological Retrospects, Circumspects, and Prospects. In Benjamin Lee, ed., *Psychosocial Theories of the Self,* 67–109. New York: Plenum Press.

Fogelson, Raymond D., and Amelia B. Walker. 1980. Self and Other in Cherokee Booger Masks. *Journal of Cherokee Studies* 5:88–102.

Foncerrada de Molina, Marta. 1980. Mural Painting in Cacaxtla and Teotihuacán Cosmopolitism. In Merle Greene Robertson, ed., *Third Palenque Round Table, 1978, Part 2,* 183–198. Austin: University of Texas Press.

Foucault, Michel. 1976. *Histoire de la sexualité 1: La volonté de savoir.* Paris: Gallimard.

———. 1995. *Discipline and Punish: The Birth of the Prison.* New York: Vintage Books.

Fought, John. 1972. *Chorti (Mayan) Texts I.* Philadelphia: University of Pennsylvania Press.

Fournier, Marcel. 1994. *Marcel Mauss.* Paris: Fayard.

Fowler, Harriet I. 1996. *Ancestor Masks and Aristocratic Power in Roman Culture.* Oxford: Clarendon Press.

Fox, James A., and John S. Justeson. 1984. Polyvalence in Mayan Hieroglyphic Writing. In John S. Justeson and Lyle Campbell, eds., *Phoneticism in Maya Hieroglyphic Writing,* 17–76. Publication No. 9. Albany: Institute for Mesoamerican Studies, State University of New York at Albany.

Fox, John G. 1994. Putting the Heart Back in the Court: Ballcourts and Ritual Action in Mesoamerica (Honduras). Ph.D. diss., Department of Anthropology, Harvard University.

———. 1996. Playing with Power: Ballcourts and Political Ritual in Southern Mesoamerica. *Current Anthropology* 37(3):483–509.

Fraser, Antonia. 2002. *Marie Antoinette: The Journey.* London: Phoenix.

Frazer, James George. 1959. *The New Golden Bough.* New York: Criterion Books.

Freedberg, David. 1989. *The Power of Images: Studies in the History and Theory of Response.* Chicago: University of Chicago Press.

Freidel, David, Linda Schele, and Joy Parker. 1993. *Maya Cosmos: Three Thousand Years on the Shaman's Path.* New York: William Morrow.

Friedman, David M. 2001. *A Mind of Its Own: A Cultural History of the Penis.* New York: Free Press.

Frisbie, Charlotte J. 1980. Epilogue. In Charlotte J. Frisbie, ed., *Southwestern Indian Ritual Drama,* 307–343. Albuquerque: University of New Mexico Press.

Furst, Jill L. M. 1978. *Codex Vindobonensis Mexicanus I: A Commentary.* Albany: Institute for Mesoamerican Studies, State University of New York at Albany.

———. 1995. *The Natural History of the Soul in Ancient Mexico.* New Haven: Yale University Press.

Furst, Peter T., and Michael D. Coe. 1977. Ritual Enemas. *Natural History* 76(3):88–91.

Gage, John. 1999. *Color and Meaning: Art, Science, and Symbolism.* Berkeley: University of California Press.

Gage, Thomas. 1958. *Travels in the New World.* Edited and with an introduction by J. Eric S. Thompson. Norman: University of Oklahoma Press.

Gallant, Thomas W. 2000. Honor, Masculinity, and Ritual Knife Fighting in Nineteenth-Century Greed. *American Historical Review* 105:358–382.

Gann, Thomas W. F. 1900. *Mounds in Northern Honduras.* Bureau of American Ethnology Nineteenth Annual Report to the Secretary of the Smithsonian Institution, 1897–1898. Washington, D.C.: Government Printing Office.

García-Campillo, José Miguel. 1998. Textos augurales en las tapas de bóveda clásicas de Yucatán. In Andrés Ciudad Ruiz, Yolanda Fernández Marquínez, José Miguel García Campillo, María Josefa Iglesias Ponce de León, Alfonso Lacadena García-Gallo, and Luis T. Sanz Castro, eds., *Anatomía de una civilización: Aproximaciones interdisciplinarias a la cultura maya,* 297–322. Madrid: Sociedad Española de Estudios Mayas.

Garibay K. Angel M. 1979. *Teogonía e historia de los mexicanos: Tres opúsculos del siglo XIV.* 3rd ed. Mexico: Editorial Porrúa.

Garnsey, Peter. 1999. *Food and Society in Classical Antiquity.* Cambridge: Cambridge University Press.

Gay, Carlo T. E. 1971. *Chalcacingo.* Graz: Akademische Druck- u. Verlaganstalt.

Gay, Peter. 1993. *The Cultivation of Hatred: The Bourgeois Experience, Victoria to Freud.* New York: W. W. Norton.

Geertz, Clifford. 1973. Person, Time, and Conduct in Bali. In *The Interpretation of Cultures,* 360–411. New York: Basic Books.

Gell, Alfred. 1975. *Metamorphosis of the Cassowaries.* London: Athlone Press.

———. 1985. Style and Meaning in Umeda Dance. In Paul Spencer, ed., *Society and the Dance: The Social Anthropology of Process and Performance,* 183–205. Cambridge: Cambridge University Press.

———. 1993. *Wrapping in Images: Tattooing in Polynesia.* Oxford Studies in Social and Cultural Anthropology, Cultural Forms. Oxford: Clarendon Press.

Geller, Pamela L. 2004. Transforming Identities, Transforming Bodies: A Consideration of Pre-Columbian Maya Corporeal Beliefs and Practices. Ph.D. diss., Department of Anthropology, University of Pennsylvania.

Gendrop, Paul. 1983. *Los estilos Río Bec, Chenes y Puuc en la arquitectura maya.* Mexico City: Universidad Nacional Autónoma de México.

Gibson, James J. 1979. *The Ecological Approach to Visual Perception.* Boston: Erlbaum.

Giddens, Anthony. 1991. *Modernity and Self-Identity: Self and Society in the Late Modern Age.* Stanford: Stanford University Press.

Gifford, Edward S. 1958. *The Evil Eye: Studies in the Folklore of Vision.* New York: Macmillan.

Gillespie, Susan D. 1989. *The Aztec Kings: The Construction of Rulership in Mexica History.* Tucson: University of Arizona Press.

———. 1991. Ballgames and Boundaries. In Vernon L. Scarborough and David R. Wilcox, eds., *The Mesoamerican Ballgame,* 317–345. Tucson: University of Arizona Press.

———. 2001. Personhood, Agency, and Mortuary Ritual: A Case Study from the Ancient Maya. *Journal of Anthropological Archaeology* 20:73–112.

Gilman, Sander L. 1999. *Making the Body Beautiful: A Cultural History of Aesthetic Surgery.* Princeton, N.J.: Princeton University Press.

Gilmore, David D. 1990. *Manhood in the Making: Cultural Concepts of Masculinity.* New Haven: Yale University Press.

Goffman, Erving. 1959. *The Presentation of Self in Everyday Life.* Garden City: Doubleday Anchor.

———. 1981. *Forms of Talk.* Philadelphia: University of Pennsylvania Press.

Goldstein, E. Bruce. 1999. *Sensation and Perception.* 5th ed. Pacific Grove: Brooks/Cole.

Gombrich, Ernst H. 1966. The Consecration of a Buddhist Image. *Journal of Asian Studies* 26:23–36.

———. 1976. Light, Form, and Texture in Fifteenth-Century Painting North and South of the Alps. In Ernst H. Gombrich, ed., *The Heritage of Apelles,* 19–35. Oxford: Phaidon Press.

———. 1996. Action and Expression in Western Art. In Richard Woodfield, ed., *The Essential Gombrich: Selected Writings on Art and Culture,* 113–138. London: Phaidon.

Gonzalez-Crussi, Frank. 1989. *The Five Senses.* San Diego: Harcourt, Brace, Jovanovich.

Goodwin, Jeff, James M. Jasper, and Francesca Polletta. 2001. Introduction: Why Emotions Matter. In Jeff Goodwin, James M. Jasper, and Francesca Polletta, eds., *Passionate Politics: Emotions and Social Movements,* 1–24. Chicago: University of Chicago Press.

Goody, Jack. 1982. *Cooking, Cuisine, and Class: A Study in Comparative Sociology.* Cambridge: Cambridge University Press.

Gordon, B. L. 1937. Oculus fascinus. *Archives of Ophthalmology* 17:291–319.

Gordon, George B., and J. Alden Mason. 1925–1934. *Examples of Maya Pottery in the Museum and Other Collections.* Philadelphia: University Museum, University of Pennsylvania.

Gordon, Ian. 1996. Gombrich and the Psychology of Visual Perception. In Richard Woodfield, ed., *Gombrich on Art and Psychology,* 60–77. Manchester: Manchester University Press.

Gosden, Chris. 1999. *Anthropology and Archaeology: A Changing Relationship.* London: Routledge.

Gossen, Gary H. 1974. *Chamulas in the World of the Sun: Time and Space in a Maya Oral Tradition.* Cambridge, Mass.: Harvard University Press.

———. 1989. To Speak with a Heated Heart: Chamula Canons of Style and Good Performance. In Richard Bauman and Joel Sherzer, eds., *Explorations in the Ethnography of Speaking,* 2nd ed., 389–413. Cambridge: Cambridge University Press.

———. 1996. Maya Zapatistas Move to the Ancient Future. *American Anthropologist* 98(3):528–538.

———. 1999. *Telling Maya Tales: Tzotzil Identities in Modern Mexico.* New York: Routledge.

Graham, Ian. 1967. *Archaeological Explorations in El Peten, Guatemala.* Middle American Research Institute Publication 33. New Orleans: Tulane University.

———. 1978. *Corpus of Maya Hieroglyphic Inscriptions.* Vol. 2, Part 2, *Naranjo, Chunhuitz, Xunantunich.* Cambridge, Mass.: Peabody Museum of Archaeology and Ethnology, Harvard University.

———. 1979. *Corpus of Maya Hieroglyphic Inscriptions.* Vol. 3, Part 2, *Yaxchilan.* Cambridge, Mass.: Peabody Museum of Archaeology and Ethnology, Harvard University.

———. 1982. *Corpus of Maya Hieroglyphic Inscriptions.* Vol. 3, Part 3, *Yaxchilan.* Cambridge, Mass.: Peabody Museum of Archaeology and Ethnology, Harvard University.

———. 1986. *Corpus of Maya Hieroglyphic Inscriptions.* Vol. 5, Part 3, *Uaxactun.* Cambridge, Mass.: Peabody Museum of Archaeology and Ethnology, Harvard University.

———. 1992. *Corpus of Maya Hieroglyphic Inscriptions.* Vol. 4, Part 2, *Uxmal.* Cambridge, Mass.: Peabody Museum of Archaeology and Ethnology, Harvard University.

———. 1996. *Corpus of Maya Hieroglyphic Inscriptions.* Vol. 7, Part 1, *Seibal.* Cambridge, Mass.: Peabody Museum of Archaeology and Ethnology, Harvard University.

Graham, Ian, and Peter Mathews. 1996. *Corpus of Maya Hieroglyphic Inscriptions.* Vol. 6, Part 2, *Tonina.* Cambridge, Mass.: Peabody Museum of Archaeology and Ethnology, Harvard University.

Graham, Ian, and Eric von Euw. 1975. *Corpus of Maya Hieroglyphic Inscriptions.* Vol. 2, Part 1, *Naranjo.* Cambridge, Mass.: Peabody Museum of Archaeology and Ethnology, Harvard University.

———. 1977. *Corpus of Maya Hieroglyphic Inscriptions.* Vol. 3, Part 1, *Yaxchilan.* Cambridge, Mass.: Peabody Museum of Archaeology and Ethnology, Harvard University.

———. 1992. *Corpus of Maya Hieroglyphic Inscriptions.* Vol. 4, Part 3, *Uxmal, Xcalumkin.* Cambridge, Mass.: Peabody Museum of Archaeology and Ethnology, Harvard University.

Graham, John. A. 1972. *The Hieroglyphic Inscriptions and Monumental Art of Altar de Sacrificios.* Papers of the Peabody Museum of Archaeology and Ethnology 64(2). Cambridge, Mass.: Harvard University.

———. 1990. Monumental Sculpture and Hieroglyphic Inscriptions. In Gordon R. Willey, ed., *Excavations at Seibal, Department of Peten, Guatemala,* 1–79. Memoirs of the Peabody Museum of Archeology and Ethnology 17(1). Cambridge, Mass.: Harvard University.

Greene, Merle, Robert L. Rands, and John A. Graham. 1972. *Maya Sculpture from the Southern Lowlands, the Highlands, and Pacific Piedmont: Guatemala, Mexico, Honduras.* Berkeley, Calif.: Lederer, Street, and Zeus.

Gregory, Richard L. 1997. *Eye and Brain: The Psychology of Seeing.* 5th ed. Princeton, N.J.: Princeton University Press.

Grimm, Linda. 2000. Biface Flintknapping: Relating Material Culture and Social Practice in the Upper Paleolithic. In Joanna Sofaer Derevenski, ed., *Children and Material Culture,* 53–71. London: Routledge.

Grosz, Elizabeth. 1995. *Space, Time, and Perversion: Essays on the Politics of Bodies.* New York: Routledge.

Grove, David C. 1970. *The Olmec Paintings of Oxtotitlan Cave, Guerrero, Mexico.* Studies in Precolumbian Art and Archaeology 6. Washington, D.C.: Dumbarton Oaks.

Grube, Nikolai. 1990a. Die Errichtung von Stelen: Entifferung einer Verbhieroglyphie auf

Monumenten der Klassichen Mayakultur. In Bruno Illius and Matthias Laubscher, eds., *Circumpacifica: Festschrift für Thomas Barthel,* 189–215. Frankfurt: Peter Lang. (Republished in Stephen D. Houston, Oswaldo Chinchilla Mazariegos, and David Stuart, eds., *The Decipherment of Ancient Maya Writing,* 486–504. Norman: University of Oklahoma Press, 2001.)

———. 1990b. The Primary Standard Sequence on Chocholá-Style Ceramics. In Justin Kerr, ed., *The Maya Vase Book: A Corpus of Rollout Photographs of Maya Vases,* 2:320–330. New York: Kerr Associates.

———. 1992. Classic Maya Dance: Evidence from Hieroglyphs and Iconography. *Ancient Mesoamerica* 3:201–218.

———. 1994. Epigraphic Research at Caracol, Belize. In Diane Z. Chase and Arlen F. Chase, eds., *Studies in the Archaeology of Caracol, Belize,* 83–122. Pre-Columbian Art Research Institute Monograph 7. San Francisco: Pre-Columbian Art Research Institute.

———. 1998. Speaking through Stones: A Quotative Particle in Maya Hieroglyphic Inscriptions. In Sabine Dedenbach-Salazar Sáenz, Carmen Arrellano Hoffmann, Eva König, and Heiko Prümers, eds., *50 Years of Americanist Studies at the University of Bonn,* 543–558. Bonn: Verlag Anton Saurwein.

———. 2000. Fire Rituals in the Context of Classic Maya Initial Series. In Pierre Robert Colas, Kai Delvendahl, Marcus Kuhnert, and Annette Schubart, eds., *The Sacred and the Profane: Architecture and Identity in the Maya Lowlands,* 91–109. Acta Mesoamericana 10. Markt Schwaben: Verlag Anton Saurwein.

———. 2001a. Intoxication and Ecstasy. In Nikolai Grube, ed., *Maya: Divine Kings of the Rain Forest,* 294–295. Cologne, Germany: Könemann.

———. 2001b. Los nombres de los gobernantes mayas. *Arqueología Mexicana* 9(5):72–77.

———. 2004. Akan—the God of Drinking, Disease, and Death. In Daniel Graña Behrens, Nikolai Grube, Christian M. Prager, Frauke Sachse, Stefanie Teufel, and Elisabeth Wagner, eds., *Continuity and Change: Maya Religious Practices in Temporal Perspective, 5th European Maya Conference, University of Bonn, December 2000,* 59–76. Acta Mesoamericana 14. Markt Schwaben: Verlag Anton Saurwein.

Grube, Nikolai, and Werner Nahm. 1994. A Census of Xibalba: A Complete Inventory of *Way* Characters on Maya Ceramics. In Justin Kerr, ed., *The Maya Vase Book: A Corpus of Rollout Photographs of Maya Vases,* 4:686–715. New York: Kerr Associates.

Grube, Nikolai, and Linda Schele. n.d. *Tzuk* in the Classic Maya Inscriptions. Texas Notes on Precolumbian Art, Writing, and Culture No. 14. Unpublished manuscript in possession of authors.

Gugel, Liane. 2000. On the Great Plains. In Christian F. Feest, ed., *The Cultures of Native North Americans,* 187–237. Cologne, Germany: Könemann.

Guil'liem Arroyo, Salvador, 1998. El templo calendárico de México-Tlaltelolco. *Arqueología Mexicana* 34:46–53.

Guiteras Holmes, Calixta. 1965. *Los peligros del alma: Visión del mundo de un tzotzil.* Mexico City: Fondo de Cultura Económica.

Guterman, Lila. 2001. Do You Smell What I Hear? Neuroscientists Discover Crosstalk among the Senses. *The Chronicle of Higher Education,* December 14, A17–A18.

Guthke, Karl S. 1999. *The Gender of Death: A Cultural History in Art and Literature.* Cambridge: Cambridge University Press.

Guthrie, Stewart Elliott. 1995. *Faces in the Clouds: A New Theory of Religion.* Oxford: Oxford University Press.

Gutmann, Matthew C. 1997. Trafficking in Men: The Anthropology of Masculinity. *Annual Review of Anthropology* 26:385–409.

Hacking, Ian. 1999. *The Social Construction of What?* Cambridge, Mass: Harvard University Press.

Haeserijn V., Esteban. 1979. *Diccionario K'ekchi'-Español.* Guatemala: Piedra Santa.

Hall, Edward. 1982. *The Hidden Dimension.* Garden City, N.J.: Anchor Books.

Hall, Grant D. 1987. The Discovery of Tomb 23 and Results of Other Tomb Investigations at Río Azul, Season of 1985. In Richard E. W. Adams, ed., *Río Azul Reports Number 3: The 1985 Season,* 107–151. San Antonio: University of Texas at San Antonio.

———. 1989. Realm of Death: Royal Mortuary Customs and Polity Interaction in the Classic Maya Lowlands. Ph.D. diss., Department of Anthropology, Harvard University.

Hallowell, A. Irving. 1976. *Contributions to Anthropology: Selected Papers of A. Irving Hallowell.* Chicago: University of Chicago Press.

Halperin, David M. 2000. How to Do the History of Male Homosexuality. *GLQ* 6(1):87–124.

Hammond, Norman. 1975. *Lubaantun: A Classic Maya Realm*. Peabody Museum Monograph 2. Cambridge, Mass.: Harvard University.

Hanks, William F. 1990. *Referential Practice: Language and Lived Space among the Maya*. Chicago: University of Chicago Press.

———. 1993. Metalanguage and Pragmatics in Deixis. In John A. Lucy, ed., *Reflexive Language: Reported Speech and Metapragmatics,* 127–157. Cambridge: Cambridge University Press.

Hare, A. Paul, and Herbert H. Blumberg. 1988. *Dramaturgical Analysis of Social Interaction*. New York: Praeger.

Harner, Michael. 1977. The Ecological Basis for Aztec Sacrifice. *American Ethnologist* 4:117–135.

Harrington, John P. 1932. *Tobacco among the Karuk Indians of California*. Smithsonian Institution, Bureau of American Ethnology Bulletin 94. Washington, D.C.: Government Printing Office.

Harris, Grace Credys. 1989. Concepts of Individual, Self, and Person in Description and Analysis. *American Anthropologist* 91(3):599–612.

Harris, William V. 2001. *Restraining Rage: The Ideology of Anger Control in Classical Antiquity*. Cambridge, Mass.: Harvard University Press.

Harrison, Simon. 1985. Concepts of the Person in Avatip Religious Thought. *Man*, n.s. 20:115–130.

Hartung, Horst. 1980. Certain Visual Relations in the Palace at Palenque. In Merle Greene Robertson, ed., *Third Palenque Round Table, 1978, Part 2,* 77–80. Austin: University of Texas Press.

Harvey, Elizabeth D. 2003. Introduction: The "Sense of All Senses." In Elizabeth D. Harvey, ed., *Sensible Flesh: On Touch in Early Modern Culture,* 1–21. Philadelphia: University of Pennsylvania Press.

Hassig, Ross. 1988. *Aztec Warfare: Imperial Expansion and Political Control*. Norman: University of Oklahoma Press.

Haviland, John B. 1988. It's My Own Invention: A Comparative Grammatical Sketch of Colonial Tzotzil. In Robert M. Laughlin, ed., *The Great Tzotzil Dictionary of Santo Domingo Zinacantán,* Vol. 1. Smithsonian Contributions to Anthropology 31. Washington, D.C.: Smithsonian Institution Press.

Haviland, William A., and Anita de Laguna Haviland. 1995. Glimpses of the Supernatural: Altered States of Consciousness and the Graffiti of Tikal, Guatemala. *Latin American Antiquity* 6(4):295–309.

Hays-Gilpin, Kelley, and Jane H. Hill. 1999. The Flower World in Material Culture: An Iconographic Complex in the Southwest and Mesoamerica. *Journal of Anthropological Research* 55:1–37.

Heidenreich, Conrad E. 1978. Huron. In Bruce C. Trigger, ed., *Handbook of North American Indians,* Vol. 15, *Northeast,* 368–388. Washington, D.C.: Smithsonian Institution Press.

Heil, John. 1983. *Perception and Cognition*. Berkeley: University of California Press.

Hellmuth, Nicholas. 1987. *Monster und Menschen in der Maya-Kunst; Eine Ikonographie der alten Religionen Mexikos und Guatemalas*. Graz: Akademische Druck- und Verlagsanstalt.

———. 1988. Early Maya Iconography on an Incised Cylindrical Tripod. In Elizabeth P. Benson and Gillett G. Griffin, eds., *Maya Iconography,* 152–174. Princeton, N.J.: Princeton University Press.

Herdt, Gilbert, ed. 1984. *Ritualized Homosexuality in Melanesia*. Berkeley: University of California Press.

Hertz, Robert. 1973. The Pre-Eminence of the Right Hand: A Study in Religious Polarity. In Rodney Needham, ed., *Right and Left: Essays on Dual Symbolic Classification,* 3–31. Chicago: University of Chicago Press.

Herzfeld, Michael. 1985. *The Poetics of Manhood: Contest and Identity in a Cretan Mountain Village*. Princeton, N.J.: Princeton University Press.

———. 1991. *A Place in History: Social and Monumental Time in a Cretan Town*. Princeton, N.J.: Princeton University Press.

Hill, Jane H. 1992. The Flower World of Old Uto-Aztecan. *Journal of Anthropological Research* 48:117–144.

Hill, Robert M., and Edward F. Fischer. 1999. States of Heart: An Ethnohistorical Approach to Kaqchikel Maya Ethnopyschology. *Ancient Mesoamerica* 10(2):317–332.

Hinsch, Bret. 1990. *Passions of the Cut Sleeve: The Male Homosexual Tradition in China*. Berkeley: University of California Press.

Hinton, Alexander L. 1999. Introduction: Developing a Biocultural Approach to the Emotions. In Alexander L. Hinton, ed., *Biocultural Approaches to the Emotions,* 1–37. Cambridge: Cambridge University Press.

Hocart, Arthur M. 1938. The Mechanism of the Evil Eye. *Folklore* 49:155–157.

Hodge, Mary G. 1996. Political Organization of the Central Provinces. In Frances F. Berdan, Richard

E. Blanton, Elizabeth Hill Boone, Mary G. Hodge, Michael E. Smith, and Emily Umberger, authors, *Aztec Imperial Strategies,* 13–45. Washington, D.C.: Dumbarton Oaks.

Holbrook, David. 1988. *Further Studies in Philosophical Anthropology.* Aldershort: Avebury.

Holley, George R. 1983. Ceramic Change at Piedras Negras, Guatemala. Ph.D. diss., Department of Anthropology, Southern Illinois University.

Hollis, Martin. 1985. Of Masks and Men. In Michael Carrithers, Steven Collins, and Steven Lukes, eds., *The Category of the Person: Anthropology, Philosophy, History,* 217–233. Cambridge: Cambridge University Press.

Hoskins, Janet. 1996. Introduction: Headhunting as Practice and Trope. In Janet Hoskins, ed., *Headhunting and the Social Imagination in Southeast Asia,* 1–49. Stanford: Stanford University Press.

Hosler, Dorothy. 1994. *The Sounds and Color of Power: The Sacred Metallurgical Technology of Ancient West Mexico.* Cambridge, Mass.: MIT Press.

Hough, Walter. 1919. The Hopi Collection in the United States National Museum. *Proceedings of the United States National Museum* 54:235–296.

Houlihan, Patrick F. 1996. *The Animal World of the Pharaohs.* London: Thames and Hudson.

Houston, Stephen D. 1985. A Feather Dance at Bonampak, Chiapas, Mexico. *Journal du Société des Américanistes* 70:127–138.

———. 1986. *Problematic Emblem Glyphs: Examples from Altar de Sacrificios, El Chorro, Río Azul, and Xultun.* Research Reports on Ancient Maya Writing 3. Washington, D.C.: Center for Maya Research.

———. 1989. *Reading the Past: Maya Glyphs.* London: British Museum.

———. 1992. A Name Glyph for Classic Maya Dwarfs. In Justin Kerr, ed., *The Maya Vase Book: A Corpus of Rollout Photographs of Maya Vases,* 3:526–531. New York: Kerr Associates.

———. 1993. *Hieroglyphs and History at Dos Pilas: Dynastic Politics of the Classic Maya.* Austin: University of Texas Press.

———. 1994. Literacy among the Pre-Columbian Maya: A Comparative Perspective. In Elizabeth H. Boone and Walter D. Mignolo, eds., *Writing without Words: Alternative Literacies in Mesoamerica and the Andes,* 27–49. Durham, N.C.: Duke University Press.

———. 1997. How Natives Think, About the Soul, For Example (with Apologies to Sahlins). *Cambridge Archaeological Journal* 7(1):145–148.

———. 1998. Classic Maya Depictions of the Built Environment. In Stephen D. Houston, ed., *Function and Meaning in Classic Maya Architecture,* 333–372. Washington, D.C.: Dumbarton Oaks.

———. 2000. Into the Minds of Ancients: Advances in Maya Glyph Studies. *Journal of World Prehistory* 14(2):121–201.

———. 2001a. Decorous Bodies and Disordered Passions: Representations of Emotion among the Classic Maya. *World Archaeology* 33(2):206–219.

———. 2001b. Food, Feast, and Fast among the Classic Maya. Paper presented at the Opening Session, "Consumption and Embodied Material Culture: The Archaeology of Drink, Food, and Commensal Politics," organized by Michael Dietler, 66th Annual Meeting of the Society for American Archaeology, New Orleans.

———. 2001c. Words on Wings: Messages and Embassies among the Classic Maya. Paper presented at the University of Pennsylvania Maya Weekend, April 3.

———. 2002a. Cantantes y danzantes de Bonampak. *Arqueología Mexicana* 10:54–55.

———. 2002b. Impersonation, Dance, and the Problem of Spectacle among the Classic Maya. Paper presented at the Working Group Session "Spectacle, Performance, and Power in Premodern Complex Society," organized by Takeshi Inomata and Lawrence Coben, 67th Annual Meeting of the Society for American Archaeology, Denver.

———. 2004. Writing in Early Mesoamerica. In Stephen D. Houston, ed., *The First Writing: Script Invention as History and Process,* 274–309. Cambridge: Cambridge University Press.

Houston, Stephen D., and Tom Cummins. 1998. Body, Presence, and Space in Andean and Mesoamerican Rulership. Paper presented at the symposium "Ancient Palaces of the New World: Form, Function, and Meaning," Dumbarton Oaks, Washington, D.C.

Houston, Stephen D., Héctor Escobedo, Andrew Scherer, Mark Child, and James Fitzsimmons. 2003. Messages from Beyond: Classic Maya Death at Piedras Negras, Guatemala. In Andrés Ciudad, M. Josefa Iglesias, and Pilar Cagiao, eds., *La muerte en el mundo maya,* 113–143. Madrid: Sociedad Española de Estudios Mayas.

Houston, Stephen D., and Susan T. Evans. 2001. Sweat Baths. In Susan T. Evans and David Webster, eds., *The Archaeology of Mexico and Central America: An Encyclopedia*, 688–690. New York: Garland.

Houston, Stephen D., and Patricia A. McAnany. 2003. Bodies and Blood: Critiquing Social Construction in Maya Archaeology. *Journal of Anthropological Archaeology* 22:26–41.

Houston, Stephen D., John Robertson, and David Stuart. 2000. The Language of Classic Maya Inscriptions. *Current Anthropology* 41(3):321–356.

———. 2001. *Quality and Quantity in Glyphic Nouns and Adjectives*. Research Reports on Ancient Maya Writing 47. Washington, D.C.: Center for Maya Research.

Houston, Stephen D., and David. S. Stuart. 1989. *The Way Glyph: Evidence for Co-Essences among the Classic Maya*. Research Reports on Ancient Maya Writing 30. Washington, D.C.: Center for Maya Research.

———. 1992. On Maya Hieroglyphic Literacy. *Current Anthropology* 33(5):589–593.

———. 1993. Multiple Voices in Maya Writing: Evidence for First- and Second-Person References. Paper presented at the 58th Annual Meeting of the Society for American Archaeology, St. Louis.

———. 1996. Of Gods, Glyphs, and Kings: Divinity and Rulership among the Classic Maya. *Antiquity* 70:289–312.

———. 1998. The Ancient Maya Self: Personhood and Portraiture in the Classic Period. *RES: Anthropology and Aesthetics* 33:73–101.

———. 2001. Peopling the Classic Maya Court. In Takeshi Inomata and Stephen D. Houston, eds., *Royal Courts of the Ancient Maya*, 1:54–83. Boulder, Colo.: Westview Press.

Houston, Stephen D., David Stuart, and Karl A. Taube. 1989. Folk Classification of Maya Pottery. *American Anthropologist* 91(4):720–726.

———. 1992. Image and Text on the "Journey Vase." In Justin Kerr, ed., *The Maya Vase Book*, 3:498–512. New York: Kerr Associates.

Houston, Stephen D., and Karl Taube. 1987. Name Tagging in Classic Maya Script: Implications for Native Classifications of Ceramics and Jade Ornament. *Mexicon* 9(2):38–41.

———. 2000. An Archaeology of the Senses: Perception and Cultural Expression in Ancient Mesoamerica. *Cambridge Archaeological Journal* 10:261–294.

Hunt, Eva. 1977. *The Transformation of the Hummingbird: Cultural Roots of a Zinacantan Mythical Poem*. Ithaca: Cornell University Press.

Hvidtfeldt, Arild. 1958. *Teotl and *Ixiptlatli: Some Central Conceptions in Ancient Central Mexican Religion*. Copenhagen: Munksgaard.

Ichon, Alain. 1973. *La religión de los totonacas de la sierra*. Serie de Antropología Social No. 16. Mexico City: Instituto Nacional Indigenista.

Ikram, Salima. 1995. *Choice Cuts: Meat Production in Ancient Egypt*. Leuven: Peeters and Department of Oosterse Studies.

Inomata, Takeshi. 1995. Archaeological Investigations at the Fortified Center of Aguateca, El Petén, Guatemala: Implications for the Study of the Classic Maya Collapse. Ph.D. diss., Department of Anthropology, Vanderbilt University.

———. 2004. Politics and Theatricality in Maya Society. Unpublished manuscript in possession of authors.

Inomata, Takeshi, and Stephen D. Houston. 2001. Opening the Royal Maya Court. In Takeshi Inomata and Stephen D. Houston, eds., *Royal Courts of the Ancient Maya*, 1:3–23. Boulder, Colo.: Westview Press.

Inomata, Takeshi, and Laura Stiver. 1998. Floor Assemblages from Burned Structures at Aguateca, Guatemala: A Study of Classic Maya Households. *Journal of Field Archaeology* 25:431–452.

Inomata, Takeshi, Daniela Triadan, Erick Ponciano, Richard E. Terry, Harriet F. Beaubien, Estela Pinto, Shannon Coyston. 1998. Residencias de la familia real y de la élite en Aguateca, Guatemala. *Mayab* 11:23–39.

Irvine, Judith T. 1985. Status and Style in Language. *Annual Review of Anthropology* 14:557–581.

———. 1990. Registering Affect: Heteroglossia in the Linguistic Expression of Emotion. In Catherine A. Lutz and Lila Abu-Lughod, eds., *Language of the Politics of Emotion*, 126–161. Cambridge: Cambridge University Press.

Iser, Wolfgang. 1978. *The Act of Reading: A Theory of Aesthetic Response*. Baltimore: Johns Hopkins University Press.

Jameson, Kimberly, and Roy G. D'Andrade. 1997. It's Not Really Red, Green, Yellow, Blue: An Inquiry into Perceptual Color Space. In C. Larry Hardin and Luisa Maffi, eds., *Color Categories in Thought and Language*, 295–319. Cambridge: Cambridge University Press.

Jay, Martin. 1993. *Downcast Eyes: The Denigration of Vision in Twentieth-Century French Thought*. Berkeley: University of California Press.

Johns, Catherine. 1982. *Sex or Symbol? Erotic Images of Greece and Rome*. New York: Routledge.

Johnson, Mark. 1987. *The Body in the Mind: The Bodily Basis of Meaning, Imagination, and Reason.* Chicago: University of Chicago Press.

Johnston, Kevin J. 2001. Broken Fingers: Classic Maya Scribe Captures and Polity Consolidation. *Antiquity* 75:371–381.

Jones, Christopher. 1969. The Twin Pyramid Group Pattern: An Architectural Assemblage at Tikal, Guatemala. Ph.D. diss., Department of Anthropology, University of Pennsylvania.

Jones, Christopher, and Linton Satterthwaite. 1982. *Tikal Report No. 33, Part A, The Monuments and Inscriptions of Tikal: The Carved Monuments.* University Museum Monograph 44. Philadelphia: University of Pennsylvania.

Jones, Grant D. 1998. *The Conquest of the Last Maya Kingdom.* Stanford: Stanford University Press.

Joralemon, Peter David. 1971. *A Study of Olmec Iconography.* Studies in Pre-Columbian Archaeology No. 7. Washington D.C.: Dumbarton Oaks.

Jordan, Mark D. 1997. *The Invention of Sodomy in Christian Theology.* Chicago: University of Chicago Press.

Josserand, J. Kathryn, and Nicholas A. Hopkins. 1988. *Chol (Mayan) Dictionary Database.* 3 vols. Final performance report to the National Endowment for the Humanities, Grant RT-20643-86.

———. 1996. Chol Ritual Language. Report submitted to the Foundation for the Advancement of Mesoamerican Studies, Inc., www.famsi.org/reports.

Josserand, J. Kathryn, Linda Schele, and Nicholas A. Hopkins. 1985. Linguistic Data on Mayan Inscriptions: The *ti* Constructions. In Elizabeth P. Benson, ed., Merle Greene Robertson, gen. ed., *Fourth Palenque Round Table, 1980,* 87–102. San Francisco: Pre-Columbian Art Research Institute.

Joyce, Rosemary A. 1993. *Embodying Personhood in Prehispanic Costa Rica, October 15, 1993–January 16, 1994.* Wellesley: Davis Museum and Cultural Center, Wellesley College.

———. 1996. The Construction of Gender in Classic Maya Monuments. In Rita P. Wright, ed., *Gender and Archaeology: Essays in Research and Practice,* 167–195. Philadelphia: University of Pennsylvania Press.

———. 1998. Performing the Body in Pre-Hispanic Central America. *RES: Anthropology and Aesthetics* 33:147–165.

———. 2000a. *Gender and Power in Prehispanic Mesoamerica.* Austin: University of Texas Press.

———. 2000b. A Precolumbian Gaze: Male Sexuality among the Ancient Maya. In Robert A. Schmidt and Barbara L. Voss, eds., *Archaeologies of Sexuality,* 263–283. Routledge: London.

Joyce, Thomas A. 1933. The Pottery Whistle-Figurines of Lubaantun. *Journal of the Royal Anthropological Institute* 63:xv–xxv.

Justeson, John S. 1983. Mayan Hieroglyphic "Name-Tagging" on a Pair of Rectangular Jade Plaques from Xcalumkin. In Stephen D. Houston, ed., *Contributions to Maya Hieroglyphic Decipherment,* 1:40–43. New Haven: HRAFlex Books.

Justeson, John S., and Peter Mathews. 1983. The Seating of the *tun:* Further Evidence Concerning a Late Preclassic Maya Stela Cult. *American Antiquity* 48(4):586–593.

Kaeppler, Adrienne L. 1978. Dance in Anthropological Perspective. *Annual Review of Anthropology* 7:31–49.

———. 1985. Structured Movement Systems in Tonga. In Paul Spencer, ed., *Society and the Dance: The Social Anthropology of Process and Performance,* 92–118. Cambridge: Cambridge University Press.

Kamp, Kathryn. 2002. Working for a Living: Children in the Prehistoric Southwestern Pueblos. In Kathryn Kamp, ed., *Children in the Prehistoric Puebloan Southwest,* 71–89. Salt Lake City: University of Utah Press.

Kampen, Michael E. 1972. *The Sculptures of El Tajín, Veracruz, Mexico.* Gainesville: University of Florida Press.

Kantorowicz, Ernst H. 1957. *The King's Two Bodies: A Study in Medieval Political Theology.* Princeton, N.J.: Princeton University Press.

Kaplan, Jonathan. 2000. A Great Emblematic Depiction of Throned Rule and Royal Sacrifice at Late Preclassic Kaminaljuyu. *Ancient Mesoamerica* 11(2):185–198.

Karras, Ruth Mazo, and David Lorenzo Boyd. 1996. "Ut cum muliere": A Male Transvestite Prostitute in Fourteenth-Century London. In Kim M. Phillips and Barry Reay, eds., *Sexualities in History: A Reader,* 90–104. New York: Routledge.

Karttunen, Frances. 1992. *An Analytical Dictionary of Nahuatl.* Norman: University of Oklahoma Press.

Kaufman, Terrence. 1972. *El proto-tzeltal-tzotzil: Fonología comparada y diccionario reconstruido.* Centro de Estudios Mayas Cuaderno 5. Mexico City: Universidad Nacional Autónoma de México.

Kaufman, Terrence S., and William M. Norman. 1984. An Outline of Proto-Cholan Phonology, Morphology, and Vocabulary. In John S. Justeson and Lyle Campbell, eds., *Phoneticism in Mayan Hieroglyphic Writing,* 77–166. Publication No. 9. Albany: Institute for Mesoamerican Studies, State University of New York at Albany.

Keller, Eve. 2003. The Subject of Touch: Medical Authorities in Early Modern Midwifery. In Elizabeth D. Harvey, ed., *Sensible Flesh: On Touch in Early Modern Culture,* 62–80. Philadelphia: University of Pennsylvania Press.

Kelley, David H. 1976. *Deciphering the Maya Script.* Austin: University of Texas Press.

———. 1982. Costume and Name in Mesoamerica. *Visible Language* 16(1):39–48.

Kelly, Anita E. 2002. *The Psychology of Secrets.* New York: Kluwer.

Kendall, Jonathan. 1992. The Thirteen Volatiles: Representation and Symbolism. *Estudios de Cultura Náhuatl* 22:99–131.

Kendon, Adam. 1997. Gesture. *Annual Review of Anthropology* 26:109–128.

Kerr, Justin, ed. 1990. *The Maya Vase Book: A Corpus of Rollout Photographs of Maya Vases.* Vol. 2. New York: Kerr Associates.

———, ed. 1992. *The Maya Vase Book: A Corpus of Rollout Photographs of Maya Vases.* Vol. 3. New York: Kerr Associates.

———, ed. 1994. *The Maya Vase Book: A Corpus of Rollout Photographs of Maya Vases.* Vol. 4. New York: Kerr Associates.

———, ed. 1997. *The Maya Vase Book: A Corpus of Rollout Photographs of Maya Vases.* Vol. 5. New York: Kerr Associates.

Keuls, Eva C. 1993. *The Reign of the Phallus: Sexual Politics in Ancient Athens.* Berkeley: University of California Press.

Kidder, Alfred V. 1947. *The Artifacts of Uaxactun, Guatemala.* Carnegie Institution of Washington, Publication 576. Washington, D.C.: Carnegie Institution of Washington.

Kidder, Alfred V., Jesse D. Jennings, and Edwin M. Shook. 1946. *Excavations at Kaminaljuyu, Guatemala.* Carnegie Institution of Washington, Publication 561. Washington, D.C.: Carnegie Institution of Washington.

Kilmer, Martin. 2002. "Rape" in Early Red-Figure Pottery: Violence and Threat in Homo-erotic and Hetero-erotic Contexts. In Susan Deacy and Karen F. Pierce, eds., *Rape in Antiquity: Sexual Violence in the Greek and Roman Worlds,* 123–141. London: Duckworth.

King, Mark B. 1994. Hearing the Echoes of Verbal Art in Mixtec Writing. In Elizabeth H. Boone and Walter D. Mignolo, eds., *Writing without Words: Alternative Literacies in Mesoamerica and the Andes,* 102–136. Durham, N.C.: Duke University Press.

Kippenberg, Hans G., and Guy G. Stroumsa. 1995. Introduction: Secrecy and Its Benefits. In Hans G. Kippenberg and Guy G. Stroumsa, eds., *Secrecy and Concealment: Studies in the History of Mediterranean and Near Eastern Religions,* xiii–xxiv. Leiden: E. J. Brill.

Klein, Cecelia F. 1984. ¿Dioses de la lluvia o sacerdotes ofrendadores del fuego? Un estudio socio-político de algunas representaciones mexicas del dios Tláloc. *Estudios de Cultura Náhuatl* 17:33–50.

———. 1986. Masking Empire: The Material Effects of Masks in Aztec Mexico. *Art History* 9(2):135–167.

———. 1994. Fighting with Femininity: Gender and War in Aztec Mexico. In Richard C. Trexler, ed., *Gender Rhetorics: Postures of Dominance and Submission in History,* 107–146. Medieval and Renaissance Texts and Studies Vol. 113. Binghamton: Center for Medieval and Early Renaissance Studies, State University of New York at Binghamton.

———. 2001. None of the Above: Gender Ambiguity in Nahua Ideology. In Cecelia F. Klein, ed., *Gender in Pre-Hispanic America,* 183–253. Washington, D.C.: Dumbarton Oaks.

Kleinman, Arthur, Veena Das, and Margaret Lock. 1996. Introduction. *Dædalus* 125(1): xi–xx.

Kleinman, Arthur, and Joan Kleinman. 1994. How Bodies Remember: Social Memory and Bodily Experience of Criticism, Resistance, and Delegitimation Following China's Cultural Revolution. *New Literary History* 25:707–723.

———. 1996. The Appeal of Experience; The Dismay of Images: Cultural Appropriations of Suffering in Our Times. *Dædalus* 125(1):1–23.

Knecht, R. J. Francis I. 1994. *Renaissance Warrior and Patron: The Reign of Francis I.* Cambridge: Cambridge University Press.

Knowles, Susan M. 1984. A Descriptive Grammar of Chontal Maya (San Carlos Dialect). Ph.D. diss., Department of Anthropology, Tulane University, New Orleans.

Kobialka, Michal. 2003. *This Is My Body: Representational Practices in the Early Middle Ages.* Ann Arbor: University of Michigan Press.

Konner, Melvin. 1982. *The Tangled Wing: Biological Constraints on the Human Spirit.* London: Heinemann.

Kopytoff, Igor. 1982. Slavery. *Annual Review of Anthropology* 11:207–230.

Kövecses, Zoltán, and Gary B. Palmer. 1999. Language and Emotion Concepts: What Experientialists and Social Constructionists Have in Common. In Gary B. Palmer and Debra J. Occhi, eds., *Languages of Sentiment: Cultural Constructions of Emotional Substrates,* 237–262. Amsterdam: John Benjamins.

Kowalski, Jeff K. 1989. *The Mythological Identity of the Figure on the La Esperanza (Chinkultic) Ball Court Marker.* Research Reports on Ancient Maya Writing 27. Washington, D.C.: Center for Maya Research.

Kray, Christine A. 1997. Worship in Body and Spirit: Practice, Self, and Religious Sensibility in Yucatán. Ph.D. diss., Department of Anthropology, University of Pennsylvania.

Kremer, Jürgen, and Fausto Uc Flores. 1996. The Ritual Suicide of Maya Rulers. In Martha J. Macri and Jan McHargue, eds., Merle Greene Robertson, gen. ed., *Eighth Palenque Round Table, 1993,* 79–91. San Francisco: Pre-Columbian Art Research Institute.

Kris, Ernst, and Otto Kurz. 1979. *Legend, Myth, and Magic in the Image of the Artist: A Historical Experiment.* New Haven: Yale University Press.

Kubler, George A. 1969. *Studies in Classic Maya Iconography.* Connecticut Academy of Arts and Sciences Memoirs 18. New Haven: Connecticut Academy of Arts and Sciences.

Lacadena, Alfonso. 2004. Passive Voice in Classic Mayan Texts: CV[h]-C-*aj* and -*n-aj* Constructions. In Søren Wichmann, ed., *The Linguistics of Maya Writing,* 165–194. Salt Lake City: University of Utah Press.

Lacan, Jacques. 1977. *Ecrits: A Selection.* London: Tavistock.

La Fontaine, Jean S. 1985. Person and Individual: Some Anthropological Reflections. In Michael Carrithers, Steven Collins, and Steven Lukes, eds., *The Category of the Person: Anthropology, Philosophy, History,* 123–140. Cambridge: Cambridge University Press.

Laporte, Juan Pedro, and Juan Antonio Valdés. 1993. *Tikal y Uaxactún en el Preclásico.* Mexico City: Universidad Nacional Autónoma de México.

Laqueur, Thomas. 1992. *Making Sex: Body and Gender from the Greeks to Freud.* Cambridge, Mass.: Harvard University Press.

Lattas, Andrew. 1998. *Cultures of Secrecy: Reinventing Race in Bush Kaliai Cargo Cults.* Madison: University of Wisconsin Press.

Laughlin, Robert M. 1975. *The Great Tzotzil Dictionary of San Lorenzo Zinacantán.* Washington, D.C.: Smithsonian Institution.

———. 1988. *The Great Tzotzil Dictionary of Santo Domingo Zinacantán.* 3 vols. Smithsonian Contributions to Anthropology 31. Washington, D.C.: Smithsonian Institution Press.

Lavery, Brian 1989. *Nelson's Navy: The Ships, Men, and Organization, 1793–1815.* Annapolis: Naval Institute Press.

Leach, Edmund. 1981. A Poetics of Power (review of *Negara* by Clifford Geertz). *New Republic,* April 4, 30–33.

Leenhardt, Maurice. 1979. *Do Kamo: Person and Myth in the Melanesian World.* Chicago: University of Chicago Press.

Le Fort, Geneviève. 2002. El traje real entre los mayas de la época clásica. In Victòria Solanilla Demestre, ed., *Actas II, Jornadas internacionales sobre textiles precolombinos,* 27–41. Barcelona: Departament d'Art, Universitat Autònoma de Barcelona.

León Portilla, Miguel. 1963. *Visión de los vencidos.* Mexico City: Universidad Nacional Autónoma de México.

———. 1973. *Time and Reality in the Thought of the Maya.* Boston: Beacon Press.

Leupp, Gary P. 1995. *Male Colors: The Construction of Homosexuality in Tokugawa, Japan.* Berkeley: University of California Press.

Lévi-Strauss, Claude. 1965. Le triangle culinaire. *L'Arc* 26:19–29.

Levy, Robert I. 1973. *Tahitians: Mind and Experience in the Society Islands.* Chicago: University of Chicago Press.

———. 1984. Emotion, Knowing, and Culture. In Richard A. Shweder and Robert A. LeVine, eds., *Culture Theory: Essays on Mind, Self, and Emotion,* 214–237. Cambridge: Cambridge University Press.

Lévy-Bruhl, Lucien. 1966. *The Soul of the Primitive.* New York: Praeger.

Lewis-Williams, David. 2002. *The Mind in the Cave: Consciousness and the Origins of Art.* London: Thames and Hudson.

Lindberg, David C. 1976. *Theories of Vision: From Al-Kindi to Kepler.* Chicago: University of Chicago Press.

Lindenbaum, Shirley. 2004. Thinking about Cannibalism. *Annual Review of Anthropology* 33:475–498.

Lock, Margaret. 1993. Cultivating the Body: Anthropology and Epistemologies of Bodily Practice and Knowledge. *Annual Review of Anthropology* 22:133–155.

Long, Pamela. 2001. *Openness, Secrecy, Authorship: Technical Arts and the Culture of Knowledge from Antiquity to the Renaissance.* Baltimore: Johns Hopkins University Press.

Long, Richard C. E. 1925. Some Maya Time Periods. *Congrès International des Americanistes* 21(1924):574–580.

Looper, Matthew F. 2002. Women-Men (and Men-Women): Classic Maya Rulers and the Third Gender. In Traci Ardren, ed., *Ancient Maya Women*, 171–202. Walnut Creek, Calif.: Altamira Press.

López Austin, Alfredo. 1980. *Cuerpo humano e ideología: Las concepciones de los antiguos nahuas.* 2 vols. Mexico City: Universidad Nacional Autónoma de México.

———. 1988. *The Human Body and Ideology: Concepts of the Ancient Nahuas.* Trans. Thelma Ortiz de Montellano and Bernard Ortiz de Montellano. 2 vols. Austin: University of Texas Press.

———. 1993. *The Myths of the Opossum: Pathways of Mesoamerican Mythology.* Albuquerque: University of New Mexico Press.

———. 1997. *Tamoanchan, Tlalolcan: Places of Mist.* Niwot: University Press of Colorado.

———. 2002. Cosmovision, Religion and the Calendar of the Aztecs. In Eduardo Matos Moctezuma and Felipe Solís Olguín, eds., *Aztecs*, 30–37. London: Royal Academy of Arts.

Lorin, Susie, and François Lorin. 1997. *Chinese Snuff Bottles.* Winter Park, Fla.: Asiantiques.

Lothrop, Samuel K. 1952. *Metals from the Cenote of Sacrifice, Chichen Itza, Yucatan.* Memoirs of the Peabody Museum of Archaeology and Ethnology 10(2). Cambridge, Mass.: Harvard University.

Lounsbury, Floyd G. 1973. On the Derivation and Reading of the "Ben-Ich" Prefix. In Elizabeth P. Benson, ed., *Mesoamerican Writing Systems: A Conference at Dumbarton Oaks, October 30th and 31st, 1971*, 99–143. Washington D.C., Dumbarton Oaks.

———. 1980. Some Problems in the Interpretation of the Mythological Portion of the Hieroglyphic Text of the Temple of the Cross at Palenque. In Merle Greene Robertson, ed., *Third Palenque Round Table, 1978: Part 2*, 99–115. Austin: University of Texas Press.

Love, Bruce. 1989. Yucatec Sacred Breads through Time. In William F. Hanks and Don S. Rice, eds., *Word and Images in Maya Culture: Explorations in Language, Writing, and Representation*, 336–350. Salt Lake City: University of Utah Press.

———. 1994. *The Paris Codex: Handbook for a Maya Priest.* Austin: University of Texas Press.

Luckmann, Thomas. 1991. The Constitution of Human Life in Time. In John Bender and David E. Wellbery, eds., *Chronotypes: The Construction of Time*, 151–166. Stanford: Stanford University Press.

Lutz, Catherine A. 1988. *Unnatural Emotion: Everyday Sentiments on a Micronesian Atoll and Their Challenge to Western Theory.* Chicago: University of Chicago Press.

Lutz, Catherine A., and Geoffrey M. White. 1986. The Anthropology of Emotions. *Annual Review of Anthropology*, 15:405–436.

Lutz, Tom. 1999. *Crying: The Natural and Cultural History of Tears.* New York: W. W. Norton.

MacDonogh, Giles. 1987. *A Palate in Revolution: Grimod de La Reynière and the Almanac des Gourmands.* London: Robin Clark.

Machado, John L., Jr. 2002. Veracruz Mural Traditions: Las Higueras, México. Report submitted to the Foundation for the Advancement of Mesoamerican Studies, Inc., www.famsi.org/reports.

MacKinnon, Catharine A., and Andrea Dworkin, eds. 1997. *In Harm's Way: The Pornography Civil Rights Hearings.* Cambridge, Mass.: Harvard University Press.

MacLeod, Barbara. 1987. *An Epigrapher's Annotated Index to Cholan and Yucatec Verb Morphology.* University of Missouri Monographs in Anthropology, no. 9. Department of Anthropology, University of Missouri at Columbia.

———. 1990. The God N Step Set in the Primary Standard Sequence. In Justin Kerr, ed., *The Maya Vase Book: A Corpus of Rollout Photographs of Maya Vases*, 2:331–347. New York: Kerr Associates.

MacLeod, Barbara, and Dennis D. Puleston. 1978. Pathways into Darkness: The Search for the Road to Xibalba. In Merle Greene Robertson and Donnan C. Jeffers, eds., *Tercera Mesa Redonda de Palenque*, 71–78. Monterey, Calif.: Pre-Columbian Art Research Center.

MacLeod, Barbara, and Dorie Reents-Budet. 1994. The Art of Calligraphy: Image and Meaning. In *Painting the Maya Universe: Royal Ceramics of the*

Classic Period, 106–163. Durham, N.C.: Duke University Art Museum.

MacLeod, Barbara, and Andrea Stone. 1995. The Hieroglyphic Inscriptions of Naj Tunich. In Andrea Stone, *Images from the Underworld: Naj Tunich and the Tradition of Maya Cave Painting,* 155–184. Austin: University of Texas Press.

Mageo, Jeannette M. 1998. *Theorizing Self in Samoa: Emotions, Genders, and Sexualities.* Ann Arbor: University of Michigan Press.

Maloney, Clarence, ed. 1976a. *The Evil Eye.* New York: Columbia University Press.

———. 1976b. Introduction. In Clarence Maloney, ed., *The Evil Eye,* v–xvi. New York: Columbia University Press.

Marcus, Joyce. 1992. *Mesoamerican Writing Systems: Propaganda, Myth, and History in Four Ancient Civilizations.* Princeton, N.J.: Princeton University Press.

———. 1998. *Women's Ritual in Formative Oaxaca: Figurine-Making, Divination, Death, and the Ancestors.* Memoirs of the Museum of Anthropology, University of Michigan 33. Ann Arbor: Museum of Anthropology, University of Michigan.

Marcus, Joyce, and Kent V. Flannery. 1996. *Zapotec Civilization: How Urban Society Evolved in Mexico's Oaxaca Valley.* London: Thames and Hudson.

Markman, Peter T., and Roberta H. Markman. 1989. *Masks of the Spirit: Image and Metaphor in Mesoamerica.* Berkeley: University of California Press.

Marks, Lawrence. E. 1984. Synaesthesia and the Arts. In W. Ray Crozier and Antony J. Chapman, eds., *Cognitive Processes in the Perception of Art,* 427–447. Amsterdam: Elsevier.

Marquina, Ignacio. 1971. La pintura en Cholula. *Artes de México* 140:25–40.

Martí, Samuel. 1961. *Canto, danza y música precortesianos.* Mexico City: Fondo de Cultura Económica.

Martin, Simon, and Nikolai Grube. 2000. *Chronicle of the Maya Kings and Queens: Deciphering the Dynasties of the Ancient Maya.* London: Thames and Hudson.

Martin, Simon, Marc Zender, and Nikolai Grube. 2002. *Notebook for the 36th Maya Hieroglyphic Forum at Texas, II: Palenque and Its Neighbors.* Austin: Maya Workshop Foundation.

Martínez Hernández, Juan. 1929. *Diccionario de Motul.* Mérida, Mexico: Compañía Tipográfica Yucateca.

Mathews, Peter. 1979. The Glyphs on the Ear Ornaments from Tomb A-1/1. In David Pendergast, ed., *Excavations at Altun Ha, Belize, 1964–1970,* 1:79–80. Toronto: Royal Ontario Museum.

———. 1980. Notes on the Dynastic Sequence of Bonampak, Part 1. In Merle Greene Robertson, ed., *Third Palenque Round Table, 1978, Part 2,* 60–73. Austin: University of Texas Press.

———. 1982. Epigraphie. In Pierre Becquelin and Claude F. Baudez, eds., *Tonina, une cité Maya du Chiapas, Tome III,* 894–901. Paris: Mission Archéologique et Ethnologique Française au Mexique.

———. 1983. *Corpus of Maya Hieroglyphic Inscriptions.* Vol. 6, Part 1, *Tonina.* Cambridge, Mass.: Peabody Museum of Archaeology and Ethnology, Harvard University.

Matos Moctezuma, Eduardo, and Felipe Solís Olguín, eds. 2002. *Aztecs.* London: Royal Academy of Arts.

Maudslay, Alfred P. 1889–1902. *Archaeology.* 5 vols. Biologia Centrali-Americana 55–59. London: R. H. Porter and Dulau.

Mauss, Marcel. 1938. Une Catégorie de L'Esprit Humain: La Notion de Personne, Celle de 'Moi.' *Journal of the Royal Anthropological Institute* 68:263–281.

———. 1950. *Sociologie et anthropologie.* Paris: Presses Universitaires de France.

———. 1985. A Category of the Human Mind: The Notion of the Person; the Notion of Self. In Michael Carrithers, Steven Collins, Steven Lukes, eds., *The Category of the Person: Anthropology, Philosophy, History,* 1–25. Cambridge: Cambridge University Press.

———. 1990. *The Gift, Forms and Functions of Exchange in Archaic Societies.* Trans. Wilfred D. Halls. London: Routledge.

Maxwell, Judith M., and Craig A. Hanson. 1992. *Of the Manners of Speaking That the Old Ones Had: The Metaphors of Andrés de Olmos in the TULAL Manuscript (Arte para Aprender la Lengua Mexicana 1547).* Salt Lake City: University of Utah Press.

Mayer, Karl. H. 1984. *Maya Monuments: Sculptures of Unknown Provenance in Middle America.* Berlin: Verlag Karl-Friedrich von Flemming.

———. 1995. *Maya Monuments: Sculptures of Unknown Provenance.* Supplement 4. Graz: Academic Publishers.

Mayr, Ernst. 1974. Behavior Programs and Evolutionary Strategies. *American Scientist* 62:650–659.

McAnany, Patricia A. 1995. *Living with the Ancestors: Kinship and Kingship in Ancient Maya Society.* Austin: University of Texas Press.

———. 1998. Ancestors and the Classic Maya Built Environment. In Stephen D. Houston, ed., *Function and Meaning in Classic Maya Architecture,* 271–298. Washington, D.C.: Dumbarton Oaks.

McGee, R. Jon. 1990. *Life, Ritual, and Religion among the Lacandon Maya.* Belmont, Calif.: Wadsworth.

McLemee, Scott. 2003. Getting Emotional. *The Chronicle of Higher Education,* February 21, A14–A16.

Mead, George H. 1964. *Selected Writings.* Edited by Andrew J. Reck. Chicago: University of Chicago Press.

Meigs, Anna. 1988. Food as a Cultural Construction. *Food and Foodways* 2:341–357.

———. 1992. Food Rules and the Traditional Sexual Ideology. In Deane Curtin and Lisa Heldke, eds., *Cooking, Eating, Thinking: Transformative Philosophies of Food,* 109–118. Bloomington: Indiana University Press.

Mendieta, Gerónimo de. 1980. *Historia eclesiástica indiana.* Mexico City: Editorial Porrúa.

Merleau-Ponty, Maurice. 1964. *Primacy of Perception.* Evanston: Northwestern University Press.

Meskell, Lynn. 1996. The Somatization of Archaeology: Institutions, Discourses, Corporeality. *Norwegian Archaeological Review* 29(1):1–16.

———. 2000. Comment. *Current Anthropology* 41:737.

———. 2002. *Private Life in New Kingdom Egypt.* Princeton, N.J.: Princeton University Press.

———. n.d. Sketching Lifeworlds, Performing Resistance. Unpublished manuscript in possession of authors.

Meskell, Lynn, and Rosemary A. Joyce. 2003. *Embodied Lives: Figuring Ancient Maya and Egyptian Experience.* London: Routledge.

Michelet, Dominique, Pierre Becquelin, and Marie-Charlotte Arnauld. 2000. *Mayas del Puuc: Arqueología de la Región de Xculoc, Campeche.* Mexico City: Centre Français d'Études Mexicaines et Centraméricaines and el Gobierno del Estado de Campeche.

Michelon, Oscar, ed. 1976. *Bibliotheca Linguistica Americana.* Vol. 2, *Diccionario de San Francisco.* Graz: Akademische Druck- und Verlagsanstalt.

Migliore, Sam. 1997. *Mal'uocchiu: Ambiguity, Evil Eye, and the Language of Distress.* Toronto: University of Toronto Press.

Miles, Suzanne W. 1957. The Sixteenth-Century Pokom-Maya: A Documentary Analysis of Social Structure and Archaeological Setting. *Transactions of the American Philosophical Society,* n.s. 47:735–781.

———. 1965. Sculpture of the Guatemala-Chiapas Highlands and Pacific Slopes, and Associated Hieroglyphs. In Gordon R. Willey, ed., *Handbook of Middle American Indians: Archaeology of Southern Mesoamerica,* Vol. 2, Part 2, 237–275. Austin: University of Texas Press.

Miller, Arthur G. 1973. *The Mural Painting of Ancient Teotihuacan.* Washington, D.C.: Dumbarton Oaks.

———. 1982. *On the Edge of the Sea: Mural Painting at Tancah-Tulum, Quintana Roo, Mexico.* Washington, D.C.: Dumbarton Oaks.

Miller, Mary E. 1986. *The Murals of Bonampak.* Princeton, N.J.: Princeton University Press.

———. 1988. The Boys in the Bonampak Band. In Elisabeth P. Benson and Gillett Griffin, eds., *Maya Iconography,* 318–330. Princeton, N.J.: Princeton University Press.

———. 1989. The Ballgame. *Record of the Art Museum, Princeton University* 48(2):22–31.

———. 1999. *Maya Art and Architecture.* London: Thames and Hudson.

———. 2001. Life at Court: The View from Bonampak. In Takeshi Inomata and Stephen D. Houston, eds., *Royal Courts of the Ancient Maya: Data and Case Studies,* 201–222. Boulder, Colo.: Westview Press.

———. n.d. The Willfulness of Art: The Case of Bonampak. Unpublished manuscript in possession of authors.

Miller, Mary E., and Stephen D. Houston. 1987. The Classic Maya Ballgame and Its Architectural Setting: A Study of Relations between Text and Image. *RES: Anthropology and Aesthetics* 14:46–65.

Miller, Mary E., and Simon Martin. 2004. *Courtly Art of the Ancient Maya.* London: Thames and Hudson.

Miller, Mary E., and David S. Stuart. 1981. Dumbarton Oaks Relief Panel 4. *Estudios de Cultura Maya* 13:197–204.

Miller, Virginia E. 1983. A Reexamination of Maya Gestures of Submission. *Journal of Latin American Lore* 9:17–38.

———. 1985. The Dwarf Motif in Classic Maya Art. In Elizabeth P. Benson, ed., *Fourth Palenque Round Table, 1980,* 141–154. San Francisco: Pre-Columbian Art Research Institute.

Miller, William Ian. 1993. *Humiliation.* Ithaca: Cornell University Press.

———. 1997. *The Anatomy of Disgust.* Cambridge, Mass.: Harvard University Press.

Mintz, Sidney W. 1996. *Tasting Food, Tasting Freedom: Excursions into Eating, Culture, and the Past.* Boston: Beacon Press.

Mintz, Sidney W., and Christine M. Du Bois. 2002. The Anthropology of Food and Eating. *Annual Review of Anthropology* 31:99–119.

Monaghan, John. 1990. Performance and the Structure of the Mixtec Codices. *Ancient Mesoamerica* 1:133–140.

———. 1995. *The Covenants with Earth and Rain: Exchange, Sacrifice, and Revelation in Mixtec Society.* Norman: University of Oklahoma Press.

———. 1998. The Person, Destiny, and the Construction of Difference. *RES: Anthropology and Aesthetics* 33:137–146.

———. 2000. Theology and History in the Study of Mesoamerican Religions. In John D. Monaghan, ed., and Victoria R. Bricker, gen. ed., *Handbook of Middle American Indians,* Supplement 6: Ethnology, 24–49. Austin: University of Texas Press.

Montagu, Jennifer. 1994. *The Expression of the Passions: The Origin and Influence of Charles Le Brun's Conférence sur l'expression générale et particulière.* New Haven: Yale University Press.

Montejo, Victor. 1993. In the Name of the Pot, the Sun, the Broken Spear, the Rock, the Stick, the Idol, Ad Infinitum and Ad Nauseam: An Exposé of Anglo Anthropologists' Obsessions with and Invention of Mayan Gods. *Wicazo Sa Review: A Journal of Native American Studies* 9(1):12–16.

Montgomery, John. 1995. *Sculptors of the Realm: Classic Maya Artists' Signatures and Sculptural Style during the Reign of Piedras Negras Ruler 7.* Master's thesis, Department of Fine Arts, University of New Mexico.

Morley, Sylvanus G. 1920. *The Inscriptions at Copan.* Carnegie Institution of Washington, Publication 219. Washington, D.C.: Carnegie Institution of Washington.

Moser, Christopher L. 1973. *Human Decapitation in Ancient Mesoamerica.* Studies in Pre-Columbian Art and Archaeology 11. Washington, D.C.: Dumbarton Oaks.

Motolinía, Toribio de Benevente. 1950. *Motolonía's History of the Indians of New Spain.* Berkeley, Calif.: Cortés Society.

Muir, Edward. 1993. *Mad Blood Stirring: Vendetta and Factions in Friuli during the Renaissance.* Baltimore: Johns Hopkins Press.

———. 1994. The Double Binds of Manly Revenge in Renaissance Italy. In Richard C. Trexler, ed., *Gender Rhetorics: Postures of Dominance and Submission in History,* 65–82. Binghamton: Center for Medieval and Renaissance Texts and Studies, State University of New York at Binghamton.

Murray, Oswin. 1996. Hellenistic Royal Symposia. In Per Bilde, Troels Engberg-Pedersen, Lise Hannestad, and Jan Zahle, eds., *Aspects of Hellenistic Kingship,* 15–27. Aarhus, Denmark: Aarhus University Press.

Navarijo Ornelas, Lourdes. 2001. Las aves en el mundo maya prehispánico. In Leticia Staines Cicero, ed., *La pintura mural prehispánica en México, II, área maya: Tomo III, estudios,* 221–253. Mexico City: Instituto de Investigaciones Estéticas, Universidad Nacional Autónoma de México.

Necipoglu, Gülru. 1991. *Architecture, Ceremonial, and Power: The Topkapi Palace in the Fifteenth and Sixteenth Centuries.* Cambridge, Mass.: MIT Press.

Neher, Andrew. 1962. A Physiological Explanation of Unusual Behavior in Ceremonies Involving Drums. *Human Biology* 34:151–160.

Newsome, Elizabeth A. 2001. *Trees of Paradise and Pillars of the World: The Serial Stelae Cycle of "18-Rabbit–God K," King of Copan.* Austin: University of Texas Press.

———. 2003. *The "Bundle" Altars of Copán: A New Perspective on Their Meaning and Archaeological Contexts.* Ancient America 4. Washington, D.C.: Center for Ancient American Studies.

Nicholson, Henry B. 1955. The Temalacatl of Tehuacan. *El México Antiguo* 8:95–134.

———. 1971. Religion in Pre-Hispanic Central Mexico. In Gordon F. Ekholm and Ignacio Bernal, eds., Robert Wauchope, gen. ed., *Handbook of Middle American Indians: Archaeology of Northern Mesoamerica,* Vol. 10, Part 1, 395–446. Austin: University of Texas Press.

Nordenskiöld, Nils Erland Herbert von. 1930. The Use of Enema Tubes and Enema Syringes among the Indians. In Nordenskiöld, *Modifications in Indian Culture through Inventions and Loans,* 184–195. Comparative Ethnographical Studies 8. Gothenburg, Sweden: Erlanders Boktryckeri.

Norman, V. Garth. 1973. *Izapa Sculpture, Part 1: Album.* Papers of the New World Archaeological Foundation No. 30. Provo, Utah: Brigham Young University.

———. 1976. *Izapa Sculpture, Part 2: Text.* Papers of the New World Archaeological Foundation No. 30. Provo, Utah: Brigham Young University.

O'Hanlon, Michael. 1989. *Reading the Skin: Adornment, Display and Society among the Wahgi.* London: British Museum.

Omitowoju, Rosanna. 2002. Regulating Rape: Soap Operas and Self-Interest in the Athenian Courts. In Susan Deacy and Karen F. Pierce, eds., *Rape in Antiquity: Sexual Violence in the Greek and Roman Worlds,* 1–24. London: Duckworth.

O'Neill, John. 1985. *Five Bodies: The Shape of Modern Society.* Ithaca: Cornell University Press.

Orefici, Giuseppe. 1997. *I Maya di Copán: L'Atene del Centroamerica.* Milan: Skira Editore.

Orejel, Jorge L. 1990. *The Axe/Comb Glyph as ch'ak.* Research Reports on Ancient Maya Writing 31. Washington, D.C.: Center for Maya Research.

Orrego Corzo, Miguel, and Rudy Larios Villalta. 1983. *Reporte de las investigaciones arqueológicas en el grupo 5E-11, Tikal.* Guatemala City: Parque Nacional Tikal, Instituto de Antropología e Historia de Guatemala.

Ortiz de Montellano, Bernard R. 1978. Aztec Cannibalism: An Ecological Necessity? *Science* 200:611–617.

Ortner, Sherry B. 1984. Theory in Anthropology since the Sixties. *Comparative Studies in Society and History* 26:126–166.

Ortony, Andrew, and Terence J. Turner. 1990. What's Basic about Basic Emotions? *Psychological Review* 97:315–331.

Otto, Beatrice. 2001. *Fools Are Everywhere: The Court Jester around the World.* Chicago: University of Chicago Press.

Palka, Joel W. 2002. Left/Right Symbolism and the Body in Ancient Maya Iconography and Culture. *Latin American Antiquity* 13(4):419–443.

Parsons, Elsie C. 1939. *Pueblo Indian Religion.* Chicago: University of Chicago Press.

Parsons, Lee A. 1980. *Pre-Columbian Art: The Morton D. May and the St. Louis Art Museum Collections.* St. Louis: St. Louis Art Museum.

———. 1986. *The Origins of Maya Art: Monumental Stone Sculpture of Kaminaljuyu, Guatemala, and the Southern Pacific Coast.* Studies in Pre-Columbian Art and Archaeology 28. Washington, D.C.: Dumbarton Oaks.

Pastoureau, Michel. 2001. *Blue: The History of a Color.* Princeton, N.J.: Princeton University Press.

Pasztory, Esther. 1983. *Aztec Art.* New York: Abrams.

Patterson, Orlando. 1982. *Slavery and Social Death: A Comparative Study.* Cambridge, Mass.: Harvard University Press.

Paulesu, E., J. Harrison, S. Baron-Cohen, J. D. G. Watson, L. Goldstein, J. Heather, R. S. J. Frackowiak, and C. D. Frith. 1995. The Physiology of Colored Hearing. *Brain* 118:661–676.

Paz, Octavio. 1991. *The Collected Poems of Octavio Paz, 1957–1987.* Edited by Eliot Weinberger. New York: New Directions.

Peñalosa, Fernando. 1995. *Tales and Legends of Q'anjob'al Maya.* Rancho Palos Verdes, Calif.: Yax Té Press.

Pendergast, David M. 1966. The Actun Balam. *Archaeology* 19(3):154–161.

———. 1968. Four Maya Pottery Vessels from British Honduras. *American Antiquity* 33(3): 379–383.

———. 1979. *Excavations at Altun Ha, Belize, 1964–1970.* Vol. 1. Toronto: Royal Ontario Museum.

Pernet, Henry. 1992. *Ritual Masks: Deceptions and Revelations.* Columbia: University of South Carolina Press.

Pick, Daniel. 1997. Stories of the Eye. In Roy Porter, ed., *Hearing the Self: Histories from the Renaissance to the Present,* 186–199. London: Routledge.

Pinker, Steven. 2001. Talk of Genetics and Vice Versa. *Nature* 413:465–466.

Pitt-Rivers, Julian. 1966. Honour and Social Status. In John G. Peristiany, ed., *Honour and Shame: The Values of Mediterranean Society,* 19–77. Chicago: University of Chicago Press.

Pohl, John M. D. 1994. *The Politics of Symbolism in the Mixtec Codices.* Vanderbilt University Publications in Anthropology 46. Nashville, Tenn.: Vanderbilt University.

———. 1998. Themes of Drunkenness, Violence, and Factionalism in Tlaxcalan Altar Paintings. *Res: Anthropology and Aesthetics* 33:184–207.

Pollock, Harry. E. D. 1936. *Round Structures of Aboriginal Middle America.* Washington, D.C.: Carnegie Institution of Washington.

———. 1980. *The Puuc: An Architectural Survey of the Hill Country of Yucatan and Northern Campeche, Mexico.* Memoirs of the Peabody Museum of Archaeology and Ethnology 19. Cambridge, Mass.: Harvard University.

Porter, James B. 1994. The Palace Intaglios: A Composite Stairway Throne at Palenque. In Virginia M. Fields, ed., Merle Greene Robertson, gen. ed., *Seventh Palenque Round Table, 1989,* 11–18. San Francisco: Pre-Columbian Art Research Institute.

———. 1996. Celtiform Stelae: A New Olmec Sculpture Type and Its Implications for Epigraphy. In Mary Preuss, ed., *Beyond Indigenous Voices: LAILA/ALILA 11th International Symposium on Latin American Indian Literatures (1994)*, 65–72. Lancaster, Calif.: Labyrinthos.

Porter, Roy. 1997. Introduction. In Roy Porter, ed., *Rewriting the Self: Histories from the Renaissance to the Present*, 1–14. London: Routledge.

Proskouriakoff, Tatiana. 1950. *A Study of Classic Maya Sculpture*. Washington, D.C.: Carnegie Institution of Washington.

———. 1963. Historical Data in the Inscriptions of Yaxchilan. *Estudios de Cultura Maya* 3:149–167.

———. 1968. The Jog and the Jaguar Signs in Maya Writing. *American Antiquity* 33(2):247–251.

———. 1974. *Jades from the Cenote of Sacrifice, Chichen Itza, Yucatan*. Memoirs of the Peabody Museum of Archaeology and Ethnology 10(1). Cambridge, Mass.: Harvard University.

Quintal Suaste, Beatriz. 1999. Los mascarones de Acanceh. *Arqueología Mexicana* 7(37):14–17.

Quiñones Keber, Eloise. 1995. *Codex Telleriano-Remensis: Ritual, Divination, and History in a Pictorial Aztec Manuscript*. Austin: University of Texas Press.

Radcliffe-Brown, Alfred R. 1964. *The Andaman Islanders*. New York: Free Press.

Radin, Paul. 1957. *Primitive Man as Philosopher*. New York: Dover.

Rasmussen, Susan J. 1999. The Slave Narrative in Life History and Myth, and the Problems of Ethnographic Representation of the Tuareg Cultural Predicament. *Ethnohistory* 46(1):67–108.

Reddy, William M. 1997. Against Constructionism: The Historical Ethnography of Emotions. *Current Anthropology* 38:327–351.

———. 2001. *The Navigation of Feeling: A Framework for the History of Emotions*. Cambridge: Cambridge University Press.

Redfield, Robert, and Alfonso Villa Rojas. 1934. *Chan Kom: A Maya Village*. Carnegie Institution of Washington, Publication 509. Washington, D.C.: Carnegie Institution of Washington.

———. 1939. *Notes on the Ethnography of Tzeltal Communities of Chiapas*. Contributions to American Anthropology and History 28. Washington, D.C.: Carnegie Institution of Washington.

Reed, Susan A. 1998. The Politics and Poetics of Dance. *Annual Review of Anthropology* 27:503–532.

Reents-Budet, Dorie. 1994. *Painting the Maya Universe: Royal Ceramics of the Classic Period*. Durham: Duke University Press.

———. 2000. Feasting among the Classic Maya: Evidence from the Pictorial Ceramics. In Justin Kerr, ed., *The Maya Vase Book: A Corpus of Rollout Photographs of Maya Vases*, 6:1022–1037. New York: Kerr Associates.

———. 2001. Classic Maya Concepts of the Royal Court: An Analysis of Renderings on Pictorial Ceramics. In Takeshi Inomata and Stephen D. Houston, eds., *Royal Courts of the Ancient Maya*, 1:195–236. Boulder, Colo.: Westview Press.

Reichel-Dolmatoff, Gerardo. 1978a. *Beyond the Milky Way: Hallucinatory Imagery of the Tukano Indians*. Los Angeles: Latin American Center, University of California at Los Angeles.

———. 1978b. Desana Animal Categories, Food Restrictions, and the Concept of Color Energies. *Journal of Latin American Lore* 4(2):243–291.

Restall, Matthew. 1997. *The Maya World: Yucatec Culture and Society, 1550–1850*. Stanford: Stanford University Press.

Rice, Prudence M. 1999. Rethinking Classic Lowland Maya Pottery Censers. *Ancient Mesoamerica* 10(1):25–50.

Richards, Audrey I. 1951. *Land, Labour, and Diet in Northern Rhodesia: An Economic Study of the Bemba Tribe*. London: International African Institute.

Riesman, Paul. 1983. On the Irrelevance of Child Rearing Practices for the Formation of Personality. *Culture, Medicine, and Psychiatry* 7:103–129.

Ringle, William M. 1988. *Of Mice and Monkeys: The Value and Meaning of T1016, The God C Hieroglyph*. Research Reports on Ancient Maya Writing 18. Washington, D.C.: Center for Maya Research.

———. 1996. Birds of a Feather: The Fallen Stucco Inscription of Temple XVIII, Palenque, Chiapas. In Martha J. Macri and Jan McHargue, eds., *Eighth Palenque Round Table, 1993*, 45–61. San Francisco: Pre-Columbian Art Research Institute.

———. n.d. *Concordance of the Morán Dictionary of Ch'olti'*. Digital file in possession of authors.

Rivero Torres, Sonia E. 1992. *Laguna Miramar, Chiapas, Mexico: Una aproximación histórica-arqueológica de los lacandones desde el Clásico Temprano*. Tuxtla Gutiérrez, Mexico: Gobierno del Estado de Chiapas.

Robertson, John. n.d. *Maya Lexical Database*. CD in possession of authors.

Robertson, Merle Greene. 1983. *The Sculpture of Palenque.* Vol. 1, *The Temple of the Inscriptions.* Princeton, N.J.: Princeton University Press.

———. 1985a. *The Sculpture of Palenque.* Vol. 2, *The Early Buildings of the Palace.* Princeton, N.J.: Princeton University Press.

———. 1985b. *The Sculpture of Palenque.* Vol. 3, *The Late Buildings of the Palace.* Princeton, N.J.: Princeton University Press.

———. 1991. *The Sculpture of Palenque.* Vol. 4, *The Cross Group, the North Group, the Olvidado, and Other Pieces.* Princeton, N.J.: Princeton University Press.

Robicsek, Francis. 1978. *The Smoking Gods: Tobacco in Maya Art, History, and Religion.* Norman: University of Oklahoma Press.

Robicsek, Francis, and Donald M. Hales. 1981. *The Maya Book of the Dead: The Ceramic Codex.* Charlottesville: University of Virginia Art Museum.

———. 1984. Maya Heart Sacrifice, Cultural Perspective, and Surgical Technique. In Elizabeth H. Boone, ed., *Ritual Human Sacrifice in Mesoamerica,* 49–90. Washington, D.C.: Dumbarton Oaks.

Robins, Gay. 1994. *Proportion and Style in Ancient Egyptian Art.* Austin: University of Texas Press.

Rocke, Michael. 1996. *Forbidden Friendship: Homosexuality and Male Culture in Renaissance Florence.* Oxford: Oxford University Press.

Rodríguez Cabrera, Dionisio. 2003. El mural de los Bebedores de Cholula, Puebla. *Arqueología Mexicana* 10(59):32–37.

Roland, Alan. 1988. *In Search of Self in India and Japan: Toward a Cross-Cultural Psychology.* Princeton, N.J.: Princeton University Press.

Romero, Javier. 1958. *Mutilaciones dentarias prehispánicas de México y América en general.* Mexico City: Instituto Nacional de Antropología e Historia.

Rosaldo, Michelle Z. 1984. Toward an Anthropology of Self and Feeling. In Richard A. Shweder and Robert A. LeVine, eds., *Culture Theory: Essays on Mind, Self, and Emotion,* 137–157. Cambridge: Cambridge University Press.

Rosaldo, Renato. 1980. *Ilongot Headhunting, 1883–1974: A Study in Society and History.* Stanford: Stanford University Press.

———. 1984. Grief and the Headhunter's Rage: On the Cultural Force of Emotion. In Stuart Plattner and Edward Bruner, eds., *Text, Play, and Story: The Construction and Reconstruction of Self and Society,* 178–195. Washington, D.C.: American Ethnological Society.

Rosenau, Pauline Marie. 1992. *Post-Modernism and the Social Sciences: Insights, Inroads, and Intrusions.* Princeton, N.J.: Princeton University Press.

Rosenwein, Barbara H. 2002. Worrying about Emotions in History. *American Historical Review* 107:821–845.

Rousselle, Aline. 1989. Personal Status and Sexual Practice in the Roman Empire. In Michel Fehrer, ed., with Ramona Naddaff and Nadia Tazi, eds., *Fragments for a History of the Human Body, Part Three,* 300–333. New York: Zone.

Roys, Ralph L. 1933. *The Book of Chilam Balam of Chumayel.* Washington, D.C.: Carnegie Institution of Washington.

———. 1965. *Ritual of the Bacabs: A Book of Maya Incantations.* Norman: University of Oklahoma Press.

Ruiz Gallut, María Elena. 2001. Entre formas, astros y colores: Aspectos de la astronomía y la pintura mural en sitios del área maya. In Leticia Staines Cicero, ed., *La pintura mural prehispánica en México, II, área maya: Tomo III, estudios,* 283–293. Mexico City: Instituto de Investigaciones Estéticas, Universidad Nacional Autónoma de México.

Ruz Lluillier, Alberto. 1958. Exploraciones arqueológicas en Palenque: 1954. *Anales del Instituto Nacional de Antropología e Historia* 10(2):117–184.

———. 1965. Tombs and Funerary Practices in the Maya Lowlands. In Gordon R. Willey, ed., Robert Wauchope, gen. ed., *Handbook of Middle American Indians,* Vol. 2, *Archaeology of Southern Mesoamerica, Part 1,* 441–461. Austin: University of Texas Press.

———. 1968. *Costumbres funerarias de los antiguos mayas.* Mexico City: Universidad Nacional Autónoma de México.

Sabloff, Jeremy A. 1973. Continuity and Disruption during Terminal Late Classic Times at Seibal: Ceramic and Other Evidence. In T. Patrick Culbert, ed., *The Classic Maya Collapse,* 107–131. Albuquerque: University of New Mexico Press.

Sahagún, Bernardino de. 1950–1982. *The Florentine Codex: General History of the Things of New Spain.* Trans. Arthur J. O. Anderson and Charles E. Dibble. Salt Lake City: University of Utah Press.

———. 1997. *Primeros memoriales.* Trans. Thelma Sullivan. Norman: University of Oklahoma Press.

Sahlins, Marshall. 1995. *How Natives Think, About Captain Cook, For Example.* Chicago: University of Chicago Press.

Sapper, Karl. 2000. Food and Drink of the Q'eqchi' Indians. In Theodore E. Gutman, trans., Marilyn Beaudry-Corbett and Ellen T. Hardy, eds., *Early Scholars' Visits to Central America: Reports by Karl Sapper, Walter Lehmann, and Franz Termer,* 17–26. Occasional Paper 18. Los Angeles: Cotsen Institute of Archaeology, University of California at Los Angeles.

Satterthwaite, Linton. 1944. *Piedras Negras Archaeology: Architecture, Part IV: Ballcourts.* Philadelphia: University Museum, University of Pennsylvania.

———. 1954. A Modified Interpretation of the Giant Glyph Altars at Caracol. *New World Antiquity* 1:1–3.

Saunders, Nicholas J. 1988. 'Chatoyer': Anthropological Reflections on Archaeological Mirrors. In Nicholas J. Saunders and Olivier de Montmollin, eds., *Recent Studies in Pre-Columbian Archaeology I,* 1–39. BAR 421. Oxford: British Archaeological Reports International Series.

———. 2001. The Colours of Light: Materiality and Chromatic Cultures of the Americas. In Andrew Jones and Gavin MacGregor, eds., *Colouring the Past: The Significance of Colour in Archaeological Research,* 209–226. London: Berg.

Scarry, Elaine. 1985. *The Body in Pain: The Making and Unmaking of the World.* New York: Oxford University Press.

Schele, Linda. 1982. *Maya Glyphs: The Verbs.* Austin: University of Texas Press.

———. 1985. Color on Classic Maya Architecture and Monumental Sculpture of the Southern Maya Lowlands. In Elizabeth Boone, ed., *Painted Architecture and Polychrome Monumental Sculpture in Mesoamerica,* 31–49. Washington, D.C.: Dumbarton Oaks.

———. 1997. *Hidden Faces of the Maya.* Mexico City: ALTI Publishing.

Schele, Linda, and David Freidel. 1990. *A Forest of Kings: The Untold Story of the Ancient Maya.* New York: William Morrow.

———. 1991. The Courts of Creation: Ballcourts, Ballgames, and Portals to the Maya Otherworld. In Vernon L. Scarborough and David R. Wilcox, eds., *The Mesoamerican Ballgame,* 289–315. Tucson: University of Arizona Press.

Schele, Linda, and Nikolai Grube. 1995. *Notebook for the 19th Maya Hieroglyphic Workshop at Texas.* Austin: Department of Art and Art History, College of Fine Arts, University of Texas at Austin.

Schele, Linda, and Peter Mathews. 1979. *The Bodega of Palenque, Chiapas, Mexico.* Washington, D.C.: Dumbarton Oaks.

———. 1998. *The Code of Kings: The Language of Seven Sacred Maya Temples and Tombs.* New York: Scribner.

Schele, Linda, and Jeffrey H. Miller. 1983. *The Mirror, the Rabbit, and the Bundle: Accession Expressions from the Classic Maya Inscriptions.* Studies in Pre-Columbian Art and Archaeology 25. Washington, D.C.: Dumbarton Oaks.

Schele, Linda, and Mary E. Miller. 1986. *The Blood of Kings: Dynasty and Ritual in Maya Art.* Fort Worth: Kimbell Art Museum.

Schele, Linda, and David Stuart. 1986. Apuntes sobre Copán, No. 1: El glifo te-tun como el jeroglífico para "estela." *Yaxkin* 9(2):89–93.

Scheper-Hughes, Nancy, and Margaret Lock. 1987. The Mindful Body: A Prolegomenon to Future Work in Medical Anthropology. *Medical Anthropology Quarterly* 1:6–41.

Scheper-Hughes, Nancy, and Carolyn Sargent. 1998. Introduction: The Cultural Politics of Childhood. In Nancy Scheper-Hughes and Carolyn Sargent, eds., *Small Wars: The Cultural Politics of Childhood,* 1–33. Berkeley: University of California Press.

Schildkrout, Enid. 2004. Inscribing the Body. *Annual Review of Anthropology* 33:319–344.

Schivelbusch, Wolfgang. 1993. *Tastes of Paradise: A Social History of Spices, Stimulants, and Intoxicants.* New York: Vintage Books.

Schlosser, Ann L. 1978. Classic Maya Lowland Figurine Development with Special Reference to Piedras Negras, Guatemala. Ph.D. diss., Department of Anthropology, Southern Illinois University.

Schmidt, Peter, Mercedes de la Garza, and Enrique Nalda, eds. 1998. *Maya.* New York: Rizzoli.

Schneider, Norbert. 1994. *The Art of the Portrait: Masterpieces of European Portrait Painting, 1420–1670.* Cologne, Germany: Benedikt Taschen.

Scholz, Piotr O. 2001. *Eunuchs and Castrati: A Cultural History.* Princeton, N.J.: Markus Weiner.

Schrader, Abby M. 2000. Branding the Other/Tattooing the Self: Bodily Inscription among Convicts in Russia and the Soviet Union. In Jane Caplan, ed., *Written on the Body: The Tattoo in European and American History,* 174–192. Princeton, N.J.: Princeton University Press.

Schroeder, Susan. 1991. *Chimalpahin and the Kingdoms of Chalco.* Tucson: University of Arizona Press.

Scott, John F. 1978. *Danzantes of Monte Albán*. Studies in Pre-Columbian Art and Archaeology 19. Washington, D.C.: Dumbarton Oaks.

Sedgwick, Eve K. 1985. *Between Men: English Literature and Male Homosocial Desire*. New York: Columbia University Press.

Seler, Eduard. 1902–1923. *Gesammelte Abhandlungen zur americanischen Sprach- und Alterumskunde*. Vol. 5. Berlin.

———. 1904a. The Mexican Picture Writings of Alexander von Humboldt in the Royal Library at Berlin. In Charles P. Bowditch, ed., *Mexican and Central American Antiquities, Calendar Systems, and History*, 123–229. Bulletin 28. Washington, D.C.: Bureau of American Ethnology.

———. 1904b. Venus Period in the Picture Writings of the Borgian Codex Group. In Charles P. Bowditch, ed., *Mexican and Central American Antiquities, Calendar Systems, and History*, 355–391. Bulletin 28. Washington, D.C.: Bureau of American Ethnology.

Sennett, Richard. 1994. *Flesh and Stone: The Body and the City in Western Civilization*. New York: W. W. Norton.

Sharer, Robert J. 1990. *Quirigua: A Classic Maya Center and Its Sculptures*. Durham, N.C.: Carolina Academic Press.

Sharp, Lesley A. 2000. The Commodification of the Body and Its Parts. *Annual Review of Anthropology* 29:287–328.

Sheets, Payson D., ed. 2002. *Before the Volcano Erupted: The Ancient Cerén Village in Central America*. Austin: University of Texas Press.

Sherratt, Andrew. 1995a. Alcohol and Its Alternatives: Symbol and Substance in Pre-industrial Cultures. In Jordan Goodman, Paul E. Lovejoy, and Andrew Sherratt, eds., *Consuming Habits: Drugs in History and Anthropology*, 11–46. London: Routledge.

———. 1995b. Introduction: Peculiar Substances. In Jordan Goodman, Paul E. Lovejoy, and Andrew Sherratt, eds., *Consuming Habits: Drugs in History and Anthropology*, 1–10. London: Routledge.

Shilling, Chris. 1993. *The Body and Social Theory*. London: Sage.

Shweder, Richard A., and Edmund J. Bourne. 1984. Does the Concept of the Person Vary Cross-Culturally? In Richard A. Shweder and Robert A. LeVine, eds., *Culture Theory: Essays on Mind, Self, and Emotion*, 158–199. Cambridge: Cambridge University Press.

Siebers, Tobin. 1983. *The Mirror of Medusa*. Berkeley: University of California Press.

Sigal, Pete. 2000. *From Moon Goddesses to Virgins: The Colonization of Yucatecan Maya Sexual Desire*. Austin: University of Texas Press.

Silverman, Lisa. 2001. *Tortured Subjects: Pain, Truth, and the Body in Early Modern France*. Chicago: University of Chicago Press.

Simmel, Georg. 1992. *Soziologie: Untersuchungen über die Formen der Vergesellschaftung*. Frankfurt am Main, Germany: Suhrkamp.

Singer, Milton. 1980. Signs of the Self: An Exploration in Semiotic Anthropology. *American Anthropologist* 82:485–507.

Siskind, Janet. 1973. *To Hunt in the Morning*. New York: Oxford University Press.

Smailus, Ortwin. 1975. *El Maya-Chontal de Acalan: Análisis lingüístico de un documento de los años 1610–1612*. Centro de Estudios Mayas Cuaderno 9. Mexico City: Universidad Nacional Autónoma de México.

Smith, Anthony. 1986. *The Body*. New York: Viking.

Smith, A. Ledyard. 1950. *Uaxactun, Guatemala: Excavations of 1931–1937*. Carnegie Institution of Washington, Publication 588. Washington, D.C.: Carnegie Institution of Washington.

———. 1972. *Excavations at Altar de Sacrificios: Architecture, Settlement, Burials, and Caches*. Papers of the Peabody Museum of Archaeology and Ethnology 62(2). Cambridge, Mass.: Harvard University.

Smith, Mary Elizabeth. 1973. *Picture Writing from Ancient Southern Mexico: Mixtec Place Signs and Maps*. Norman: University of Oklahoma Press.

Smith, Robert E. 1955. *Ceramic Sequence at Uaxactun, Guatemala*. Vol. 2. Middle American Research Institute Publication 20. New Orleans: Tulane University.

Smith, Roger. 1997. Self-Reflection and the Self. In Roy Porter, ed., *Rewriting the Self: Histories from the Renaissance to the Present*, 49–57. London: Routledge.

Sotheby's. 1994. *Pre-Columbian Art, New York: Tuesday, May 17, 1994*. New York: Sotheby's.

Spencer, Paul. 1985. Introduction: Interpretations of the Dance in Anthropology. In Paul Spencer, ed., *Society and the Dance: The Social Anthropology of Process and Performance*, 1–46. Cambridge: Cambridge University Press.

Spinden, Herbert J. 1913. *A Study of Maya Art: Its Subject Matter and Historical Development*.

Memoirs of the Peabody Museum of Archeology and Ethnology 6. Cambridge, Mass.: Harvard University.

Spiro, Melford E. 1986. Cultural Relativism and the Future of Anthropology. *Cultural Anthropology* 1:259–286.

———. 1993. Is the Western Concept of Self "Peculiar" within the Context of the World Cultures? *Ethos* 21:107–153.

Šprajc, Ivan. 2003. Archaeological Reconnaissance in Southeastern Campeche, Mexico: 2002 Field Season Report. Report submitted to the Foundation for the Advancement of Mesoamerican Studies, Inc., www.famsi.org/reports.

Stanley-Baker, Joan. 2000. *Japanese Art.* Rev. ed. London: Thames and Hudson.

Starr, Frederick. 1902. *Notes upon the Ethnography of Southern Mexico.* 2 vols. Davenport, Iowa: Putnam Memorial Publication Fund, Davenport Academy of Natural Sciences.

Stearns, Carol Z., and Peter N. Stearns. 1986. *Anger: The Struggle for Emotional Control in America's History.* Chicago: University of Chicago Press.

Steede, Neil. 1984. *Catálogo preliminar de los tabiques de Comalcalco: Una colección de inscripciones mayas inexplicables.* Cárdenas, Tabasco, Mexico: Centro de Investigación Precolombina.

Stefaniak, Regina. 1993. Correggio's Camera de San Paolo: An Archaeology of the Gaze. *Art History* 16:203–238.

Stein, Edward. 1992. Conclusion: The Essentials of Constructionism and the Construction of Essentialism. In Edward Stein, ed., *Forms of Desire: Sexual Orientation and the Social Constructionist Controversy,* 325–353. London: Routledge.

Steiner, Wendy. 1995. *The Scandal of Pleasure: Art in an Age of Fundamentalism.* Chicago: University of Chicago Press.

Stenzel, Werner. 1968. The Sacred Bundle in Mesoamerican Religion. In *Thirty-eighth International Congress of Americanists, Stuttgart-München, 1968,* 2:347–352.

Stevenson, Robert. 1976. *Music in Aztec and Inca Territory.* 2nd ed. Berkeley: University of California Press.

Stoller, Paul. 1997. *Sensuous Scholarship.* Philadelphia: University of Pennsylvania Press.

Stone, Andrea. 1991. Aspects of Impersonation in Classic Maya Art. In Virginia M. Fields, ed., Merle Greene Robertson, gen. ed., *Sixth Palenque Round Table, 1986,* 194–202. Norman: University of Oklahoma Press.

———. 1992. From Ritual in the Landscape to Capture in the Urban Center: The Recreation of Ritual Environments in Mesoamerica. *Journal of Ritual Studies* 6(1):109–132.

———. 1995a. *Images from the Underworld: Naj Tunich and the Tradition of Maya Cave Painting.* Austin: University of Texas Press.

———. 1995b. The *Nik* Name of the Codical God H. Paper presented at the 94th Annual Meeting of the American Anthropological Association, Washington, D.C.

Stone, Doris. 1977. *Pre-Columbian Man in Costa Rica.* Cambridge, Mass.: Peabody Museum Press, Harvard University.

Storey, Rebecca. 1999. Late Classic Nutrition and Skeletal Indicators at Copán, Honduras. In Christine D. White, ed., *Reconstructing Maya Diet,* 169–179. Salt Lake City: University of Utah Press.

Strathern, Marilyn. 1979. The Self in Self-Decoration. *Oceania* 49: 241–257.

———. 1988. *The Gender of the Gift: Problems with Women and Problems with Society in Melanesia.* Berkeley: University of California Press.

Stross, Brian. 1988. The Burden of Office: A Reading. *Mexicon* 10(6):118–121.

———. 1989. Speaking of Speaking: Tenejapa Tzeltal Metalinguistics. In Richard Bauman and Joel Sherzer, eds., *Explorations in the Ethnography of Speaking,* 213–239. 2nd ed. Cambridge: Cambridge University Press.

Stross, Brian, and Justin Kerr. 1990. Notes on the Maya Vision Quest through Enema. In Justin Kerr, ed., *The Maya Vase Book: A Corpus of Rollout Photographs of Maya Vases,* 2:348–361. New York: Kerr Associates.

Strother, Zoe S. 2000. From Performative Utterance to Performative Object: Pende Theories of Speech, Blood Sacrifice, and Power Objects. *RES: Anthropology and Aesthetics* 37:49–71.

Stuart, David. 1984. Royal Auto-Sacrifice among the Maya: A Study of Image and Meaning. *RES: Anthropology and Aesthetics* 7/8:6–20.

———. 1985. The Count of Captives Epithet in Classic Maya Writing. In Virginia M. Fields, ed., Merle Greene Robertson, gen. ed., *Fifth Palenque Round Table, 1983,* 7:97–101. San Francisco: Pre-Columbian Art Research Institute.

———. 1988a. Blood Symbolism in Maya Iconography. In Elizabeth P. Benson and Gillett G. Griffin, eds.,

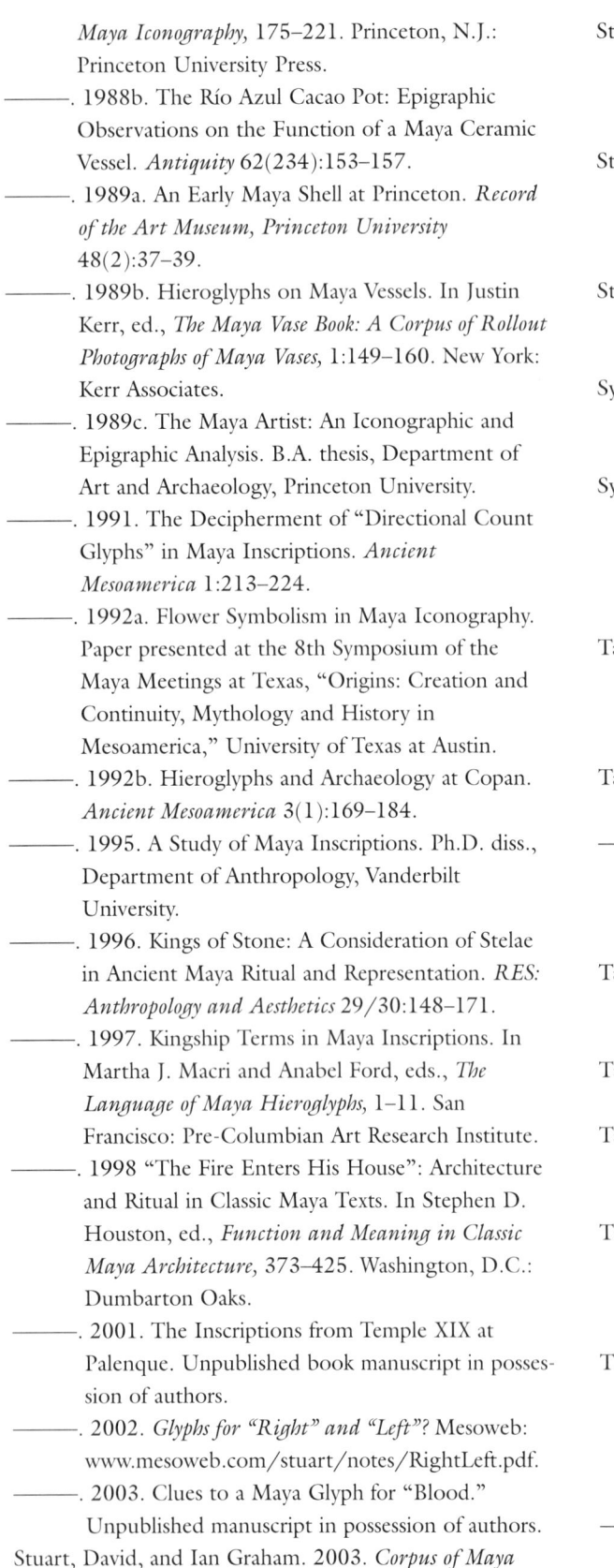

Maya Iconography, 175–221. Princeton, N.J.: Princeton University Press.

———. 1988b. The Río Azul Cacao Pot: Epigraphic Observations on the Function of a Maya Ceramic Vessel. *Antiquity* 62(234):153–157.

———. 1989a. An Early Maya Shell at Princeton. *Record of the Art Museum, Princeton University* 48(2):37–39.

———. 1989b. Hieroglyphs on Maya Vessels. In Justin Kerr, ed., *The Maya Vase Book: A Corpus of Rollout Photographs of Maya Vases,* 1:149–160. New York: Kerr Associates.

———. 1989c. The Maya Artist: An Iconographic and Epigraphic Analysis. B.A. thesis, Department of Art and Archaeology, Princeton University.

———. 1991. The Decipherment of "Directional Count Glyphs" in Maya Inscriptions. *Ancient Mesoamerica* 1:213–224.

———. 1992a. Flower Symbolism in Maya Iconography. Paper presented at the 8th Symposium of the Maya Meetings at Texas, "Origins: Creation and Continuity, Mythology and History in Mesoamerica," University of Texas at Austin.

———. 1992b. Hieroglyphs and Archaeology at Copan. *Ancient Mesoamerica* 3(1):169–184.

———. 1995. A Study of Maya Inscriptions. Ph.D. diss., Department of Anthropology, Vanderbilt University.

———. 1996. Kings of Stone: A Consideration of Stelae in Ancient Maya Ritual and Representation. *RES: Anthropology and Aesthetics* 29/30:148–171.

———. 1997. Kingship Terms in Maya Inscriptions. In Martha J. Macri and Anabel Ford, eds., *The Language of Maya Hieroglyphs,* 1–11. San Francisco: Pre-Columbian Art Research Institute.

———. 1998 "The Fire Enters His House": Architecture and Ritual in Classic Maya Texts. In Stephen D. Houston, ed., *Function and Meaning in Classic Maya Architecture,* 373–425. Washington, D.C.: Dumbarton Oaks.

———. 2001. The Inscriptions from Temple XIX at Palenque. Unpublished book manuscript in possession of authors.

———. 2002. *Glyphs for "Right" and "Left"?* Mesoweb: www.mesoweb.com/stuart/notes/RightLeft.pdf.

———. 2003. Clues to a Maya Glyph for "Blood." Unpublished manuscript in possession of authors.

Stuart, David, and Ian Graham. 2003. *Corpus of Maya Hieroglyphic Inscriptions.* Vol. 9, Part 1, *Piedras Negras.* Cambridge, Mass.: Peabody Museum, Harvard University.

Stuart, David, and Stephen Houston. 1994. *Classic Maya Place Names.* Studies in Pre-Columbian Art and Archaeology 33. Washington, D.C.: Dumbarton Oaks.

Stuart, George. 1987. *A Carved Shell from the Northeastern Maya Lowlands.* Research Reports on Ancient Maya Writing 13. Washington, D.C.: Center for Maya Research.

Stuart, George, and Gene Stuart. 1993. *Lost Kingdoms of the Maya.* Washington, D.C.: National Geographic Society.

Sykes, John B., ed. 1976. *The Concise Oxford Dictionary of Current English.* 6th ed. Oxford: Clarendon Press.

Synnott, Anthony. 1991. Puzzling Over the Senses: From Plato to Marx. In David Howes, ed., *The Varieties of Sensory Experience: A Sourcebook in the Anthropology of the Senses,* 61–76. Toronto: University of Toronto Press.

Takagi, Sadayuki F. 1978. Biophysics of Smell. In Edward Carterette and Morton P. Friedman, eds., *Handbook of Perception,* Vol. 6A, *Tasting and Smelling,* 233–243. New York: Academic Press.

Tambiah, Stanley J. 1968. The Magical Power of Words. *Man,* n.s. 3(2):175–208.

———. 1976. *World Conqueror and World Renouncer: A Study of Buddhism and Polity in Thailand against a Historical Background.* Cambridge: Cambridge University Press.

Tannenbaum, Nicola A. 1987. Tattoos: Invulnerability and Power in Shan Cosmology. *American Ethnologist* 14:693–712.

Tarlow, Sarah. 2000. Emotion in Archaeology. *Current Anthropology* 41:713–746.

Tarn, Nathaniel, and Martin Prechtel. 1990. Comiéndose la fruta: Metáforas sexuales e iniciaciones en Santiago Atitlán. *Mesoamérica* 19:73–82.

Taschek, Jennifer T. 1994. *The Artifacts of Dzibilchaltun, Yucatan, Mexico: Shell, Polish Stone, Bone, Wood, and Ceramics.* Middle American Research Institute Publication 50. New Orleans: Tulane University.

Tate, Carolyn. 1991. The Period-Ending Stelae of Yaxchilan. In Virginia M. Fields, ed., Merle Greene Robertson, gen. ed., *Sixth Palenque Round Table, 1986,* 102–109. Norman: University of Oklahoma Press.

———. 1992. *Yaxchilan: The Design of a Maya Ceremonial City.* Austin: University of Texas Press.

Taube, Karl A. 1985. The Classic Maya Maize God: A Reappraisal. In Virginia M. Fields, ed., and Merle Greene Robertson, gen. ed., *Fifth Palenque Round*

Table, 1983, 171–181. San Francisco: Pre-Columbian Art Research Institute.

———. 1987. *A Representation of the Principal Bird Deity in the Paris Codex.* Research Reports on Ancient Maya Writing 6. Washington, D.C.: Center for Maya Research.

———. 1988a. A Prehispanic Maya Katun Wheel. *Journal of Anthropological Research* 44(2):183–203.

———. 1988b. A Study of Classic Maya Scaffold Sacrifice. In Elizabeth P. Benson and Gillett G. Griffin, eds., *Maya Iconography,* 331–351. Princeton, N.J.: Princeton University Press.

———. 1989a. *Itzam Cab Ain: Caimans, Cosmology, and Calendrics in Postclassic Yucatán.* Research Report on Ancient Maya Writing 26. Washington, D.C.: Center for Maya Research.

———. 1989b. The Maize Tamale, *Wah,* in Classic Maya Epigraphy and Art. *American Antiquity* 54(1):31–51.

———. 1989c. Ritual Humor in Classic Maya Religion. In William F. Hanks and Don S. Rice, eds., *Word and Image in Maya Culture: Explorations in Language, Writing, and Representation,* 351–382. Salt Lake City: University of Utah Press.

———. 1992a. The Iconography of Mirrors at Teotihuacan. In Janet Berlo, ed., *Art, Ideology, and the City of Teotihuacan,* 169–204. Washington, D.C.: Dumbarton Oaks.

———. 1992b. *The Major Gods of Ancient Yucatan.* Studies in Pre-Columbian Art and Archaeology 32. Washington, D.C.: Dumbarton Oaks.

———. 1992c. The Temple of Quetzalcoatl and the Cult of Sacred Warfare at Teotihuacan. *RES: Anthropology and Aesthetics* 21:53–87.

———. 1994a. The Birth Vase: Natal Imagery in Ancient Maya Myth and Ritual. In Justin Kerr, ed., *The Maya Vase Book: A Corpus of Rollout Photographs of Maya Vases,* 4:650–685. New York: Kerr Associates.

———. 1994b. The Iconography of Toltec Period Chichen Itza. In Hanns J. Prem, ed., *Hidden among the Hills: Maya Archaeology of the Northwest Yucatan Peninsula,* 212–246. Acta Mesoamericana 7. Möckmühl, Germany: Verlag von Flemming.

———. 1996. The Olmec Maize God: The Face of Corn in Formative Mesoamerica. *RES: Anthropology and Aesthetics* 29/30:39–81.

———. 1998a. Enemas rituales en Mesoamérica. *Arqueología Mexicana* 6(34):38–45.

———. 1998b. The Jade Hearth: Centrality, Rulership, and the Classic Maya Temple. In Stephen D. Houston, ed., *Function and Meaning in Classic Maya Architecture,* 427–478. Washington, D.C.: Dumbarton Oaks.

———. 2000. The Turquoise Hearth: Fire, Self-Sacrifice, and the Central Mexican Cult of War. In Davíd Carrasco, Lindsay Jones, and Scott Sessions, eds., *Mesoamerica's Classic Heritage: From Teotihuacan to the Great Aztec Temple,* 269–340. Niwot: University Press of Colorado.

———. 2001. Dance. In Davíd Carrasco, ed., *Oxford Encyclopedia of Mesoamerican Cultures,* 1:305–308. New York: Oxford University Press.

———. 2002a. Flower Mountain: Concepts of Life, Beauty, and Paradise among the Classic Maya. Paper presented at the symposium "Naturaleza y sociedad en el área maya," Mérida, Yucatán.

———. 2002b. Maws of Heaven and Hell: The Symbolism of the Serpent and Centipede in Classic Maya Religion. Paper presented at the 6th Mesa Redonda de la Sociedad Española de Estudios Mayas, Santiago de Compostela.

———. 2003a. Ancient and Contemporary Maya Conceptions of the Field and Forest. In Arturo Gómez-Pompa, Michael F. Allen, Scott Fedick, and Juan J. Jiménez-Osornio, eds., *Lowland Maya Area: Three Millennia at the Human-Wildland Interface,* 461–494. New York: Haworth Press.

———. 2003b. Serpents, Flowers, and Supernatural Passageways in the Art and Ritual of Mesoamerica and the American Southwest. Manuscript in possession of the authors.

———. 2004a. Flower Mountain: Concepts of Life, Beauty, and Paradise among the Classic Maya. *RES: Anthropology and Aesthetics* 45:69–98.

———. 2004b. Structure 10L-16 and Its Early Classic Antecedents: Fire and the Evocation and Resurrection of K'inich Yax K'uk' Mo'. In Ellen E. Bell, Marcello A. Canuto, and Robert J. Sharer, eds., *Understanding Early Classic Copán,* 265–295. Philadelphia: University of Pennsylvania Museum.

Taussig, Michael. 1993. *Mimesis and Alterity: A Particular History of the Senses.* New York: Routledge.

Taylor, Dicey. 1983. Classic Maya Costume: Regional Types of Dress. Ph.D. diss., Department of the History of Art, Yale University.

Tedlock, Barbara. 1980. Songs of the Zuni Kachina Society: Composition, Rehearsal, and Performance. In Charlotte J. Frisbie, ed., *Southwestern Indian Ritual Drama,* 7–35. Albuquerque: University of New Mexico Press.

———. 1992. *Time and the Highland Maya*. 2nd ed. Albuquerque: University of New Mexico Press.

Tedlock, Dennis. 1996. *Popol Vuh: The Definitive Edition of the Mayan Book of the Dawn of Life and the Glories of Gods and Kings*. 2nd ed. New York: Simon and Schuster.

———. 2003. *Rabinal Achi: A Mayan Drama of War and Sacrifice*. Oxford: Oxford University Press.

Terwiel, Barend J. 1979. Tattooing in Thailand's History. *Journal of the Royal Asiatic Society* 2:156–166.

Thompson, J. Eric S. 1939. *Excavations at San Jose, British Honduras*. Washington, D.C.: Carnegie Institution of Washington.

———. 1946. *Tattooing and Scarification among the Maya*. Notes on Middle American Archaeology and Ethnology, Carnegie Institution of Washington, Division of Historical Research No. 63. Washington, D.C.: Carnegie Institution of Washington.

———. 1950. *Maya Hieroglyphic Writing: An Introduction*. Washington, D.C.: Carnegie Institution of Washington.

———. 1958. Symbols, Glyphs, and Divinatory Almanacs for Diseases in the Maya Dresden and Madrid Codices. *American Antiquity* 23:297–308.

———. 1962. *A Catalog of Maya Hieroglyphs*. Norman: University of Oklahoma Press.

———. 1970. *Maya History and Religion*. Norman: University of Oklahoma Press.

———. 1972. *A Commentary on the Dresden Codex: A Maya Hieroglyphic Book*. Memoirs of the American Philosophical Society Held at Philadelphia for Promoting Useful Knowledge 93. Philadelphia: American Philosophical Society.

Thornhill, Randy, and Craig T. Palmer. 2000. *A Natural History of Rape*. Cambridge, Mass.: MIT Press.

Tourney, Garfield, and D. J. Plazak. 1954. Evil Eye in Myth and Schizophrenia. *Psychiatric Quarterly* 28:478–495.

Tovalín, Alejandro, Peter L. Mathews, Armando Anaya, and Adolfo Velázquez de León. 1998. Estela 1 o de El Rey del sitio de Dos Caobas, Chiapas. *Arqueología* 20:79–96.

Townsend, Richard Fraser. 1979. *State and Cosmos in the Art of Tenochtitlan*. Studies in Pre-Columbian Art and Archaeology 20. Washington, D.C.: Dumbarton Oaks.

Tozzer, Alfred M. 1907. *A Comparative Study of the Mayas and the Lacandones*. New York: Macmillan.

———. 1941. *Landa's Relación de las cosas de Yucatan*. Papers of the Peabody Museum of Archaeology and Ethnology 18. Cambridge, Mass.: Harvard University.

Trexler, Richard C. 1995. *Sex and Conquest: Gendered Violence, Political Order, and the European Conquest of the Americas*. Ithaca: Cornell University Press.

Trik, Helen, and Michael E. Kampen. 1983. *Tikal Report No. 31: The Graffiti of Tikal*. University Museum Monograph 57. Philadelphia: University Museum, University of Pennsylvania.

Trubek, Amy B. 2000. *Haute Cuisine: How the French Invented the Culinary Profession*. Philadelphia: University of Pennsylvania.

Turner, Christy G., II, and Jacqueline Turner. 1999. *Man Corn: Cannibalism and Violence in the Prehistoric American Southwest*. Salt Lake City: University of Utah Press.

Turner, Terence S. 1980. The Social Skin. In Jeremy Cherfas and Roger Lewin, eds., *Not Work Alone: A Cross-Cultural View of Activities Superfluous to Survival*, 112–140. London: Temple Smith.

Turner, Victor. 1974. *Fields and Metaphors: Symbolic Action in Human Society*. Ithaca: Cornell University Press.

Uchmany de la Peña, Eva A. 1967. Cuatro casos de idolatría en el área maya ante el Tribunal de la Inquisición. *Estudios de Cultura Maya* 6:267–300.

Urban, Hugh B. 2001. *The Economics of Ecstasy: Tantra, Secrecy, and Power in Colonial Bengal*. Oxford: Oxford University Press.

Urcid, Javier. 1991. Una lápida zapoteca en Santiago Matatlán, Oaxaca. Unpublished manuscript in possession of authors.

Vail, Gabrielle, and Andrea Stone. 2002. Representations of Women in Postclassic and Colonial Maya Literature and Art. In Traci Ardren, ed., *Ancient Maya Women*, 203–228. Walnut Creek, Calif.: Altamira Press.

Valdés, Juan Antonio. 1997. Tamarindito: Archaeology and Regional Politics in the Petexbatun Region. *Ancient Mesoamerica* 8(2):321–335.

Vandereycken, Walter, and Ron van Deth. 1994. *From Fasting Saints to Anorexic Girls: The History of Self-Starvation*. New York: New York University Press.

Vargas de la Peña, Leticia, and Victor R. Castillo Borges. 1999. La Acrópolis de Ek' Balam, el lienzo en el que plasmaron lo mejor de su arte sus antiguos pobladores. *La Pintura Mural Prehispánica en México* 10/11:26–30.

———. 2001. Las aves en el mundo maya prehispánico. In Leticia Staines Cicero, ed., *La pintura mural pre-*

hispánica en México, II, área maya: Tomo IV, estudios, 403–418. Mexico City: Instituto de Investigaciones Estéticas, Universidad Nacional Autónoma de México.

Verano, John W. 1986. A Mass Burial of Mutilated Individuals at Pacatnamu. In Christopher B. Donnan and Guillermo A. Cock, eds., *The Pacatnamu Papers*, 1:117–138. Los Angeles: Museum of Cultural History, University of California at Los Angeles.

———. 2001. War and Death in the Moche World: Osteological Evidence and Visual Discourse. In Joanne Pillsbury, ed., *Moche Art and Archaeology in Ancient Peru*, 110–125. Studies in the History of Art 63. Washington, D.C.: Center for Advanced Study in the Visual Arts, National Gallery.

Vermeule, Emily. 1979. *Aspects of Death in Early Greek Art and Poetry*. Berkeley: University of California Press.

Veyne, Paul. 1987. The Roman Empire. In Paul Veyne, ed., Philippe Ariès and Georges Duby, gen. eds., *A History of Private Life*, Vol. 1, *From Pagan Rome to Byzantium*, 6–233. Cambridge, Mass.: Belknap Press.

Vialles, Noëlie. 1994. *Animal to Edible*. Cambridge: Cambridge University Press.

Villa Rojas, Alfonso. 1934. *The Yaxuna-Cobá Causeway*. Contributions to American Archaeology 2(9):187–208. Washington, D.C.: Carnegie Institution of Washington.

Visser, Margaret. 1992. *The Rituals of Dinner: The Origins, Evolution, Eccentricities, and Meaning of Table Manners*. New York: Penguin.

Vogt, Evon Z. 1969. *Zinacantan: A Maya Community in the Highlands of Chiapas*. Cambridge, Mass.: Harvard University Press.

———. 1976. *Tortillas for the Gods: A Symbolic Analysis of Zinacanteco Rituals*. Cambridge, Mass.: Harvard University Press.

———. 1977. On the Symbolic Meaning of Percussion in Zinacanteco Ritual. *Journal of Anthropological Research* 33:231–244.

———. 1993. *Tortillas for the Gods: A Symbolic Analysis of Zinacanteco Rituals*. Reissue. Norman: University of Oklahoma Press.

von Euw, Eric. 1978. *Corpus of Maya Hieroglyphic Inscriptions*. Vol. 5, Part 1, *Xultun*. Cambridge, Mass.: Peabody Museum of Archaeology and Ethnology, Harvard University.

von Euw, Eric, and Ian Graham 1984. *Corpus of Maya Hieroglyphic Inscriptions*. Vol. 5, Part 2, *Xultun, La Honradez, Uaxactun*. Cambridge, Mass.: Peabody Museum of Archaeology and Ethnology, Harvard University.

Walens, Stanley. 1981. *Feasting with Cannibals: An Essay on Kwakiutl Cosmology*. Princeton, N.J.: Princeton University Press.

Wartofsky, Marx W. 1981. Sight, Symbol, and Society: Toward a History of Visual Perception. *Philosophic Exchange* 3:23–38.

Watanabe, John M. 1992. *Maya Saints and Souls in a Changing World*. Austin: University of Texas Press.

Watson, Aaron, and David Keating. 1999. Architecture and Sound: An Acoustic Analysis of Megalithic Monuments in Prehistoric Britain. *Antiquity* 73:325–336.

Watson, James L. 1980. Slavery as an Institution: Open and Closed Systems. In James L. Watson, ed., *Asian and African Systems of Slavery*, 1–15. Oxford: Blackwell.

Wauchope, Robert. 1938. *Modern Maya Houses: A Study of their Archaeological Significance*. Carnegie Institution of Washington, Publication 502. Washington, D.C.: Carnegie Institution of Washington.

Webster, D. 1989. The House of the Bacabs: Its Social Context. In David Webster, ed., *The House of the Bacabs, Copan, Honduras*, 5–40. Studies in Pre-Columbian Art and Archaeology 29. Washington, D.C.: Dumbarton Oaks.

———. 2002. *The Fall of the Ancient Maya: Solving the Mystery of the Maya Collapse*. London: Thames and Hudson.

Weiss, Gail. 1999. *Body Images: Embodiment as Intercorporeality*. New York: Routledge.

Weiss, Meira. 2002. *The Chosen Body: The Politics of the Body in Israeli Society*. Stanford: Stanford University Press.

Westheim, Paul, Alberto Ruz, Pedro Armillas, Ricardo de Robina, and Alfonso Caso. 1969. *Cuarenta siglos de plástica mexicana: Arte prehispánico*. Mexico City: Editorial Herrero.

White, Tim D. 1992. *Prehistoric Cannibalism at Mancos 5Mtumr-2346*. Princeton, N.J.: Princeton University Press.

Wickett, Elizabeth 1993. The Spirit in the Body. In Katherine Young, ed., *Bodylore*, 185–202. Knoxville: University of Tennessee Press.

Wilbert, Johannes. 1987. *Tobacco and Shamanism in South America*. New Haven: Yale University Press.

Willey, Gordon R. 1972. *The Artifacts of Altar de Sacrificios*. Papers of the Peabody Museum of

Archaeology and Ethnology 64(3). Cambridge, Mass.: Harvard University.

Williams, Craig. A. 1999. *Roman Homosexuality: Ideologies of Masculinity in Classical Antiquity.* New York: Oxford University Press.

Winer, Gerald A., and Jane E. Cottrell. 1996. Does Anything Leave the Eye When We See? Extramission Beliefs of Children and Adults. *Current Directions in Psychological Science* 5(5):137–142.

Winter, Irene J. 1996. Sex, Rhetoric, and the Public Monument: The Alluring Body of Naram-Sîn of Agade. In Natalie B. Kampen, ed., *Sexuality in Ancient Art: Near East, Egypt, Greece, and Italy,* 11–26. Cambridge: Cambridge University Press.

Winter, Joseph C. 2000. Traditional Uses of Tobacco by Native Americans. In Joseph C. Winter, ed., *Tobacco Use by Native North Americans: Sacred Smoke and Silent Killer,* 9–58. Norman: University of Oklahoma Press.

Wisdom, Charles. 1940. *The Chorti Indians of Guatemala.* Chicago: University of Chicago Press.

———. n.d. *Materials on the Chorti Language.* University of Chicago Microfilm Collection of Manuscripts of Cultural Anthropology 28. Chicago.

Wittgenstein, Ludwig. 1953. *Philosophical Investigations.* New York: Macmillan.

Wolfthal, Diane. 1999. *Images of Rape: The Heroic Tradition and Its Alternatives.* Cambridge: Cambridge University Press.

Yadeun, Juan. 1992. *Toniná: El laberinto del inframundo.* Mexico City: Gobierno del Estado de Chiapas.

———. 1993. *Toniná.* Mexico City: El Equilibrista.

Yalom, Marilyn. 1997. *A History of the Breast.* New York: Ballantine Books.

Young, Allen. 1990. Moral Conflicts in a Psychiatric Hospital Treating Combat-Related Post-traumatic Stress Disorder. In George Weisz, ed., *Social Science Perspectives on Medical Ethics,* 65–82. Dordrecht, Netherlands: Kluwer Academic.

Zellner, Debra. 1991. How Foods Get to Be Liked: Some General Mechanisms and Some Special Cases. In Robert C. Boles, ed., *The Hedonics of Taste,* 199–217. Hillsdale: Lawrence Erlbaum.

Zender, Marc. 2000. A Study of Two Uaxactun-Style Tamale-Serving Vessels. In Justin Kerr, ed. *The Maya Vase Book: A Corpus of Rollout Photographs of Maya Vases,* 6:1038–1055. New York: Kerr Associates.

Index

Page numbers in italics refer to figures.

Absolute space, 5
Accession rituals: and *baah*, 67; and bundling, 83; and head, 101; and headdresses, 372; and heir, 244; and Principal Bird Deity, 238, *242*; and royal bodies, 6–7
Action: and Classic Maya body, 32–33, *34*; and portraiture, 64, *66*
Aesthetics: and body paint, 23–24; of captives, 218, *219*; of Classic Maya body, 45–48; of dance, 255; and Maize God, 45, *45*, 48; and male body, 210, 211, 215; and pole climbing, 45, *46*; and royal bodies, 45–47, *47*; and the ugly, 48, *48*
Affect, 182, 198, 199–200
Age: age-grade associations, 54, 122; aged women as dangerous, 16, 48; and ancestors, 50–51; in Classic Maya imagery, 15, 16, *16*, 48–51, *49*; and drunkenness, 191; older male with younger male, 211, *212*
Agurcia, Ricardo, 238
Ajaw, 88–89, *90*, *146*
Akan, 61, *61*, 118
Alcohol, 116–117, *117*, 119–120, 147. *See also* Drunkenness
Alpers, Svetlana, 136
Altar de los Reyes, Campeche, 95, *97*
Altar de Sacrificios, 123, *126*, 241
Altar in Tikal National Park, 93, *97*
Álvarez Bravo, Manuel, 1, 8
Ancestors, 50–51, *51*, 72, *73*, 129, 228, 267
Androsocial imagery, 53–54
Animals bringing food tribute, 108, *110*
Aristotle, 135, 180
Armijo, Ricardo, 130
Augustine, Saint, 136, 184
Autoeroticism, 191–192, *196*
Aztec warrior suits, 70
Aztecs: and breath, 143, 146; and cannibalism, 220; and captives, 206, 207; creation myths of, 91; and dances, 253, 254; and drink, 125; and drums, 262; and feasts, 129; and mortuary acts, 83, 84–85; and rape, 207; and shrunken heads, 70; and sight, 172; and skull racks, 72; and solar images, 169–170; and songs, 158, 160, 163; and speech, 153, 154, 156, 229; and synesthesia, 134; and Xochipilli, 152

Baah: compound nouns with types of objects, 67, *68*; as corporeal self, 12, 277; meaning of, 60, 61, 62, *63*, 64, 68, 72–73, 74, 81; and perceptions of personhood, 58; and reflexivity, 61; and *u-baah*, 59–60, *60*, 64, *65*, 66–67, *66*
Bacon, Francis, 135, 136
Bakab title, 62–63, *64*
Ballplay: and action, 33, *35*; and awakened deities, 254; and birds, 238, *244*; and creation myths, 93, *94*; and decapitation, 93; and feasts, 129; and interactive sculpture, 74, 76, *78*; and 1 Ajaw, 205; and sight, 164; and speech scrolls, 163, *166*
Balls, 37, *38*, 76
Banquets, 102
Barasch, Moshe, 73
Bardawil, Lawrence, 234
Barthel, Thomas, 230
Bateson, Gregory, 100–101
Baudrillard, Jean, 74
Bauman, Richard, 252
Beltin, Hans, 73
Benedict, Ruth, 181
Benson, Elizabeth, 256
Besnier, Niko, 182
Bestiality, 191, *195*
Beyer, Hermann, 153
Bierhorst, John, 154
Binding rituals, 81, 83–84
Birds: and ballplay, 238, *244*; birds over mountains, 238, *243*; as Death Gods, 238, 241, *245*; and headdresses, 238, *242*, 244–245, *248*; as messengers, 229–234, *232*, *233*, *234*, 236, *236*, *237*, 238, 241–250, 278–279; and supernaturals, 154, 231–233, *232*, *233*, 234, *234*, 235, 236, *236*, *237*, 238, *239*, *240*, 241, *243*, *245*; temple as bird house, 233, *238*
Blood: of captives, 220; and creation myths, 92–93; and day signs, 93, *94*, *95*; and fasting, 131; vitality associated with, 35
Blood scrolls, 93, *95*
Bloodletting: of captives, 27–28, *28*; and dance, 268; and fasting, 131; and founding rituals, 93, 95, *97*, 132; and penises, 213, 215; and senses, 179
Body as model for world, 5
Body as organism, 4
Body concepts: categories of, 11; central importance of, 2; in Classic Maya codified images, 1, 8, 11; comparative studies of, 4; content, network, and texture of, 3
Body in society, 4, 99

Body movement: and body theory, 5–6; and dance, 255, 256–257, *257*; and performances, 253. *See also* Dancers
Body of Christ, 6
Body or textile stamps, 24, *24*
Body ornamentation: and body theory, 5, 6; as epidermal stimuli, 105; and fasting, 130; and shrunken heads, 70, 72; and social skin, 6, 7
Body paint, 22–25, *23*, *24*
Body parts as metaphors: Cacao God, 36, *38*; and Classic Maya body, 35–36, *37*, *38*; and identity, 61–68; and Mayan languages, 36, 61
Body proportion, 14, 47
Body sensations, and body theory, 4
Body theory, 4–8
Bonampak murals, 244–250, *248*, *249*, 256, 258, 260, 262, 269
Book of Chilam Balam of Chumayel, 89
Boswell, John, 209
Breath: of caves, 149; of Death Gods, 142, 156, *158*; representations of, 139, *140*, 141–142, *143*, *144*, 145, *145*, 146, *146*, 147, *148*, *149*, 150–152, 154, 259, 266; solar breath, 156, *157*; and tobacco, 114, 143; and vitality, 228
Bricker, Victoria, 59–60, 61
Brillat-Savarin, Jean-Anthelme, 104
Brown, Peter, 211
Brownmiller, Susan, 207
Bruman, Henry, 117
Buildings: acoustics of, 3, 163, 259; and breath, 145, *149*; and circles of severance, 13–14; and flowers, 141, 147; and Principal Bird Deity, 238; and secrecy, 177; and sensory properties, 134, 163; and sight, 174–175
Bundling rituals, 81, 83, 85, *85*, *86*, 87
Burial rituals: and binding, 83; and food consumption of dead, 123–125; and incense, 125–127, *127*, *128*; and representations of breath, 142, 143, 145, *146*, 147; and royal bodies, 6–7; and scent, 147, 149
Burkhart, Louise, 154
Buttocks, 30, *31*

Cacao beans, 108, 113, 241–242, *246*
Cacao drinks, 108, *109*
Cacao God, 17, 36, *38*
Cacao vessels, 113–114
Calendar rituals, and stone binding, 81, *82*, 83–84, *83*
Calendar Stone, 170
Camporesi, Piero, 124
Cannibalism, 123, 207, 220, 278

INDEX

Cano, Agustín, 19
Captives: and ballplay, 76; beauty of, 218, *219*; biting of, 123, *125*; bloodletting of, 27–28, *28*; clothing of, 21, 131; contradictions in treatment of, 203–205; and decapitation, 22, *22*, 78, *80*, 206; dehumanization of, 219–223, *222*; and dishonor, 203, *203*, 206–207, 226; and emotions, 190, 191, *192*, *193*, 199, 206, *206*, 223; exposed genitals of, 210, *211*, 213, *214*, 215, *215*, *216*; and fasting, 130–131, *132*, 221; female captives, 42; as fertilizing earth, 223–226, *225*, *226*; and hair, 25, 203–204, 206, *206*; and headdresses, 68–69; lashed lips of, 218, *219*; pain and suffering of, 221–222, 223, *224*; rape of, 218; and scaffold sacrifice, 221, *223*, *224*; and scarification, 21–22, *21*, *22*; sexual gestures from, 215–216, *217*; and sexuality, 38, 210, *211*, 213, *214*, 215–216, *215*, *216*, *217*; and shrunken heads, 70, 72; and social distance, 37; and speech scrolls, 139, *140*; and stairways, 76; and supernaturals' eating of, 123, *124*, 127; as tribute, 243; types of, 205–206; women as, 207–209, *208*
Child, Mark, 117
Children, invisibility of, 56
Christenson, Allen, 58
Circles of severance, and part/whole relations, 13–14, *14*
Clarke, John, 209
Classen, Constance, 3, 152, 175
Classic Maya body: and action, 32–33, *34*; aesthetic of, 45–48; and body parts as metaphors, 35–36, *37*, *38*; and bones, 31, *33*; and excrement, 30, 31–32, *31*; features of, *55*, 56; and feet and legs, 30, 31, *31*, *33*; and fluids, 31–32; and hands, 30, 31, *32*; and head, 28, *29*; and internal organs, 31, 32, *34*; and masculine gaze, 51–56, 277; and measurement of space, 37–38, *38*; and overall body, 11–14, *13*; and sex and sexuality, 38–44; skin and surface, 14–28; torso, 28–30; and vitality, 33–35, *36*, *37*, 49; youth and age, 48–51
Classic Maya data, primacy of, 3
Classic Maya imagery: age in, 15, 16, *16*, 48–51, *49*; and body concepts, 1, 8, 11; and head, 68, 72
Clothing: as body adornment, 25–26; of captives, 21, 131; and dance, 270; practicality of, 26, *27*; and submissive status, 75; and tributary lords, 247, *248*
Codex Bodley, 147, 154
Codex Borbonicus, 158, 231
Codex Borgia, 93, 150, 231
Codex Boturini, 153, 207
Codex en Cruz, 164

Codex Féjerváry-Mayer, 89
Codex Historia Tolteca-Chichimeca, 154
Codex Mendoza, 70, 159, 163–164
Codex Nuttall, 163
Codex Telleriano-Remensis, 154
Codex Tudela, 231
Codex Vaticanus B, 150
Codex Vindobonensis, 153
Codex Xolotl, 164, 166
Coe, Michael, 16, 37, 141, 178, 256
Coe, Sophie, 104
Colonial sources, 11, 12, 19, 89
Comparative anthropology: and emotion, 183; and perception of human body, 57; reliability of, 2; and self, 97, 98; and speech, 227
Conch shells, 264, *265*, 267
Concurrence of essences: and deity impersonation, 270, *271*, 274, 275–276, *275*, 279; and space and time, 66, 274
Constructionism, and body theory, 4
Cooking, 107
Córdova, Juan de, 72
Corporeal fields, 78–79
Creation myths, 89, 91–93, *91*, *92*, *94*, 153, 234
Crocker, Jon, 70
Crocodile: and ballplay, 93; and creation myths, 89, 91, 92; and dynastic founding, 95, *97*; and new fire, 92–93, *93*; and speech scrolls, 139; and time, 186, *187*, 188

Dance: aesthetic of, 255, 275; and deity impersonation, 270–274, *271*; and music, 275, 276; plazas for, 257, *258*, 269; prohibition of, 254; representations of, 267, *268*, *269*; varieties of, 253–254, *253*, 256–257, 267–269, *268*, *270*
Dancers: belts of, 267, *267*; and feather dance, 247; and musical instruments, 255, 256, 258; and perceptible motion, 189–190, 256, *257*; and sacred bundles, *254*; severed heads as, *71*, 72; and synesthesia, 252, 279
Darwin, Charles, 181
Day signs: Ajaw day signs, 89, *91*; and sacrifice, 93, *94*, 95; and traveling time, 260
De las Casas, Bartolomé, 142
Death Gods: as birds, 238, 241, *245*; and body parts, 156, *159*; breath of, 142, 156, *158*; and emotions, 191; and flatulence, 145, 156; and fluids, 215; and god markings, 17
Deer hunting, 219–220, *220*, 264, *265*
Deictic markers, 38, *39*

Deity impersonation, 66, 122, 261, 270–276, *271, 272, 273, 275,* 279
Dietler, Michael, 102, 127, 128
Dilthey, Wilhelm, 180
Dishonor: and captives, 203, *203,* 206–207, 226; captives as fertilizing earth, 223–226; and dehumanization of captives, 219–223, *222;* and erotic degradation, 206, 207–219; and rape, 207, 218; themes in, 206–207, 278; and timocracies, 202
Domestication of animals, 108
Douches, 105, 118. *See also* Enemas
Dresden Codex: and birds, 232; and captives, 131; and crocodile, 92; and God C, 68; and God H, 152; and ingestion, 111, 123, 130; and representation of breath, 141; and sexuality, 43; and sight, 169, 172; and speech, 229, 230
Drought, 130, *130*
Drums: and awakened deities, 254; and dance, 255; drumming techniques, 262, *264;* notation for sound from, 163, *167;* purpose of, 256; in sequence of instruments, 258, 259, *259;* variety of, 261–262, *263, 265*
Drunkenness: and alcohol, 119–120; as distortion of senses, 178–179; emotional representation of, 190, 191, 192, *194,* 198, 199; and enemas, 127, 191, 192; and homosexuality, 217; and pulque, 120, 122, *122;* representation of, *121*
Dwarfs, 127, *128,* 196, 267
Dworkin, Andrea, 207

Egocentric space, 5, 7
Egypt, 100, 123
Elias, Norbert, 2, 201
Embalming, 118
Emblem glyphs, 95, *97*
Emetics, 106
Emotions: biological approach to, 182; and captives, 190, 191, *192, 193,* 199, 206, *206,* 223; categories of, 190, 278; cultural approach to, 181, 182; and dishonor, 190; and drunkenness, 190, 191, 192, *194,* 198, 199; elusiveness of, 180; and emotional restriction, 2, 200–201; ethological study of, 181–182; grief and mourning, 190, 194–196, *197,* 198, *198,* 199; and heart, 183, 184–185, 186, 189; and humor, 190, 196, 198, 199, *199,* 200; and hypercognated and hypocogated affect, 182–183, 189, 199; and lust, 190, 191–194, *195, 196, 197,* 198, 199, *208;* and odium, 191, 203; representations of, 180–181, *181, 185, 186, 189,* 190; and senses, 138

Enemas: administration of, 105–106, 117, 118, *118, 121,* 122, 132; and drunkenness, 127, 191; and sex, 117, 122, 125
Ethnographic Maya evidence: and alcohol, 116; and ancestors, 51; and blood, 79; and honor, 202; and ingestion, 103–107; and rape, 207; reliability of, 1; and self, 98–99; and senses, 178; and sight, 167; and speech, 227–228
Excrement: and breath, 143, 145; and Classic Maya body, 30, 31–32, *31*

Face: and *baah,* 61, 68; and Classic Maya imagery, 72; and defacement, 76, *79,* 100; glyphs of, 28, *29;* and identity, 60, 61, 76, 88
Famine, 130, *130*
Fasting, 106, 130–131, *131,* 179, 278
Feasts: and competitive hospitality, 129; diacritical feasts, 102, 103, 127; distributive aspects of, 129; meals compared to, 103; and meaning of ingestion, 102; representations of, 278; and royal bodies, 7, 127, 128–129, *129,* 130, 133
Febvre, Lucien, 2
Fish, 108
Fish, Stanley, 98
Florentine Codex, 13, 154, 172
Fluids, 31–32, 89, 91, 92, 195
Flutes, 3
Fogelson, Raymond, 99
Foucault, Michel, 6, 216
Founding of dynasties, 93, 95, *97,* 131–132, *132*
Fox, John, 129
François I (king of France), 226
Frazer, James, 6, 57
Freedberg, David, 73, 182, 183
Freidel, David, 110
Fuentes y Guzmán, Francisco de, 147, 149
Furst, Jill, 2–3, 79, 143

G1 (deity), *171,* 273
Gage, Thomas, 271
Geertz, Clifford, 99–100
Gell, Alfred, 16, 18, 253, 255
Gender, 11, 51–56, *53, 53,* 56, 277. *See also* Men; Women
Gendrop, Paul, 146
Gestalt model of human identity, 4
Gestures: and body theory, 5–6; dirt-eating gesture, 31, *32;* and emotions, 190; and hands, 31; and performances, 252
Gibson, James, 173

Gilgamesh Epic, 213
Gillespie, Susan, 93
Glyphs: and alcohol, 116; of bones, 31; and bowls, 108; for consumption, 111, *112*, 127; and emotions, 184, 185, *185*, *186*, 189, *189*; full-figure glyphs, 76, *80*; of head, 28, *29*, 72; and male genitalia, 42; and measurement, 37, *38*; and part/whole relations, 13, 64; reliability of, 2; and sight, 170, 172–173, *172*; and skin, 15; and speech scrolls, 160, 163, *164*; and vitality, 34–35, 76
God B, 17
God C, 67–68, *69*
God D, 17, 205
God H, 151–152, *153*
God houses, 177, *178*
God K, 17. *See also* K'awiil
God L, 193, 228
God markings, 16–17, *17*
God N, 17, 215, 233, 241
God of Completion, 170, *171*
Goethe, Johann von, 136
Goffman, Erving, 98, 99
Golden, Charles, 267
Gombrich, Ernst, 182
Gossen, Gary, 227
Grand narratives, 2
Great Tzotzil Dictionary of Santo Domingo Zinacantán, 228
Grief and mourning, 190, 194, *197*, 198, *198*, 199
Grube, Nikolai, 229, 242, 256, 257
Guerrero, Gonzalo, 19

Hair: and age, 49; as body surface feature, 25–26, *26*; and captives, 25, 203–204, 206, *206*; facial hair, 39; and part/whole relations, 13; pubic hair, 25, 40
Hallowell, Irving, 98
Halperin, David, 209, 210, 217, 218
Hands, 30, 31, *32*, 72, 190
Hanks, William, 78–79, 142–143, 173, 174, 175
Hatshepsut, 100
Hauberg "stela," 93, *96*
Havelock, Eric, 137
Haviland, Anita, 178, 179
Haviland, William, 178, 179
Head: and *baah*, 61, 68, 72; belt heads, *29*, 72; and body proportion, 14; and decapitation, 22, 70, 72, 93, *95*, 276; glyphs of, 28, *29*; as individual signifier, 68–72; and Maize God, 45; meaning of, 60, 61; as means of exaltation, 62, *63*; as reflexive element, 101; and skull racks, *71*, 72

Headbands: and accession rituals, 101; and bundling, 83, *84*; fastening of, 61–62, *62*; and Sun God, 87
Headdresses: and birds, 238, *242*, 244–245, *248*; and deity impersonation, 272–274, *274*; and head as individual signifier, 72; and name glyphs, 68, *70*; and Principal Bird Deity, 238; and stacked masks, 26, *27*; storage of, 273, *274*; tying of, 81
Health, state of, 106–107, 108, 277
Hearing: associations with, 136, 156, *160*; and earspools, 156, *160*, 206; and Mayan languages, 139, 153; and senses, 139, 153–163, 178; and songs of beauty and praise, 156, 158–159, *161*, *162*, 275; speech, 153–154, 156; and synesthesia, 138
Heart: and emotions, 183, 184–185, *186*, 189; as food for supernaturals, 123, *125*, 126, 188, 232–233
Hearths, 107, 110
Heine, Heinrich, 218
Herdt, Gilbert, 211
Hero Twins: and awakened deities, 254; and birds, 236, 238; and emotions, 194–195, *196*; and god markings, 17; and sight, 170
Hertz, Robert, 5, 6
Historiographic evidence: and alcohol, 116; of Classic Maya body, 11; and ingestion, 103–107; and performances, 254–256; reliability of, 1, 3; and senses, 138
Homoerotic activities, 122, *122*, 206, 210–211, 216–218, 278
Homosexuality, 209–211, *212*, 217
Homosocial imagery, 53, 122
Honor, 202–203, 278. *See also* Dishonor
Horowitz, Vladimir, 259
Hot-cold balance, 108
Houston, Stephen, 21–22, 186, 232, 244, 247
Human/supernatural relationship: and deity impersonation, 66, 122, 261, 270–276, *271*, *272*, *273*, *275*, 279; and multiple names, 70
Humor, 190, 196, 198, *199*, 200, 253
Hunger, 106
Hunt, Eva, 127

Icons, 73–74
Identity: beyond body, 76, 78; and body parts as metaphors, 61–68; complexity of, 70; extension of, 100; fusion of, 74; and head, 60, 61, 72; and shrunken heads, 72; superimposed identity, 99
Ik' wind symbol, 146–147, 151, 154
Imagery: and competitive image making, 100–101; and extended and extendible persons, 98, 100;

reliability of, 2; and self, 76–81; transcendence between image and entity, 73–74; and vitality, 72–76, 97
Incest, and royal bodies, 7
India, 74
Individuality, 98
Individuation, 57–58, 69–70
Indonesia, 100
Ingestion: and acts of consumption, 110–111, *112*; of alcohol, 116–117; and bread/drink dyad, 108, 110, *112*; and *comal*, 111, *113*; and drink, 104–105, 107–108, *109*, 110, 113, 116–120, *121*, 122, *122*, 125, 129; and drunkenness, 119–120; and emphasis on quantity, 104; and enemas, 106, 117, 132; ethnographic and historic evidence on, 103–107; excesses in, 106; and fasting, 106, 130–132; and feasts, 7, 102, 103, 127–130; and food preparation, 107–108; and food regime, 107; and liquid emphasis, 107, 111, 113; meaning of, 102; and medicine, 118–119, *121*; and nutritive stress, 124–125; social role of, 133; and state of health, 106–107; and supernaturals, 110, 117–118, *120*, 122–127, 228; and sweatbaths, 117–118, *119*; of tobacco, 105–106, 107, 114, 114–116; and units of consumption, 113–114; variety of foods, 108
Inka body concepts, 3
Inomata, Takeshi, 271
Interaction, and Maya sculptures, 74–76, *77*, *78*
Internal organs, 31
Islam, 74
Itzamnaaj, 234, 236, 238, 241, *241*, 273

Jaguar calls, 3
Jaguar God of the Underworld, 17, 85, *88*, 170, 274
Jaguar on incense burner, 111, *113*
Johnson, Mark, 5
Jones, Grant, 220
Joyce, Rosemary, 4, 52, 72, 211, 213, 215, 218, 224

Kaeppler, Adrienne, 253
K'altuun ritual, 81, *82*, 83, *83*, 85
Kantorowicz, Ernst, 6
K'awiil, 67, *69*
Kelley, David, 68
Kerr, Barbara, 9
Kerr, Justin, 9, 108
Keuls, Eva, 213
Klein, Cecelia, 211
Knorosov, Yurii, 229, 230, 232
Kopytoff, Igor, 205

Kubler, George, 256
K'uh, 79, 81

La Amelia Hieroglyphic Stairway, 76, *78*
Lacan, Jacques, 4, 5
Landa, Diego de, 3, 18, 72, 129, 130, 255
Laporte, Juan Pedro, 229
Larios, Rudy, 116
Latimer, Bishop, 184
Laughlin, Robert, 256
Leenhardt, Maurice, 70, 99
León Portilla, Miguel, 154
Lévi-Strauss, Claude, 116
Lévy-Bruhl, Lucien, 201
Levy, Robert, 182, 189, 199
Lewis-Williams, David, 178, 179
Lexical sources, and body concepts, 3
López Austin, Alfredo, 2, 79, 138, 154
Lowland hieroglyphs, 3

Madrid Codex, 68, 116, 152
Magritte, René, 73
Maize bread, 113, *113*
Maize drinks, 107–108
Maize God: and aesthetics, 45, *45*, 48; and birds, 233; and carrying heavy objects, 26, *27*; costume of, 52; and dance, 255, 267, *268*; and drink, 110; and god markings, 17; and grief, 194, 195; and human heart, 232–233; and IL mark, 18; and ingestion, 127; and lovemaking, 208, *208*; and offerings of meats, 113; and sight, 167, 170; and tribute, *249*
Malinowski, Bronislaw, 57
Maloney, Clarence, 136
Maori, 18, 19, 21
Marcus, Joyce, 25
Marriage: and arrival of new bride, 260–261; and dances, 269; and feasts, 129; and sexuality, 43–44, *44*, *45*, 211
Martin, Simon, 242
Masculine gaze: and Classic Maya body, 51–56, 277; and cooking, 107; and sexuality, 42
Masks: and dance, 270; and deity impersonation, 272, *272*, *273*, 276; and hearing, 156; and self, 99; and synesthesia, 279; types of, 256
Mathews, Peter, 24
Mauss, Marcel, 5–6, 57, 58, 98, 99
Maya calendrics, 88–89, *90*
Maya sculptures, and interaction, 74–76, *77*, *78*
Mayan languages: and aesthetics, 45; and body parts as metaphors, 36, 61; and bones, 31; consistency of,

3; and dance, 254–255; and dishonor, 203; and drink, 104–105; and emotions, 183–185; and fasting, 130; and hair, 25; and hand, 30; and head, 28, 62; and hearing, 139, 153; and homosexuality, 210, 211; and ingestion, 103–104; and K'awiil, 67; and music, 255; and overall body, 12–13; and secrecy, 177; and self, 60–61; and senses, 139, 141; and sexuality, 38–42; and skin, 14–15; and taste and touch, 175–176; and torso, 28–30; and the ugly, 48; and vitality, 33–35; and *winik*, 58; and youth and age, 48

McLeod, Barbara, 59–60
Mead, George Herbert, 4, 5, 98
Meals, 102, 103
Meat preparations, 108, 111, 113
Men: and body paint, 23; clothing of, 56; and pride, 202; and tattooing, 21; terms for, 39
Meskell, Lynn, 4
Mesoamerican sources, 3
Miller, Mary, 206, 209, 218, 244, 247–248, 258, 259
Miller, William, 204, 209
Moan Owl, 170
Monaghan, John, 58, 127
Monkey scribes, 17
Moon Goddess, 170, 196, 232, *233*, 261, 274
Morán, Francisco, 30
Muir, Edward, 201
Music: and awakened deities, 254; and breath of speech, 229; Chaak musicians, 265, *266*, 267; and dance, 275, 276; and journey vessels, 260–261, *260*, *262*; and musicians at caves, 264, *265*; musicians playing two instruments, 265–266; and performances, 253; sequence of musicians, 258, 259–260, *259*, *260*; and synesthesia, 252, 279; types of, 255, 258
Musical instruments: and hearing, 139; and *ik'* sign, 152; sequences of, 258, 259–260, *259*, *260*; sounds of, 3–4, 258–259; and touch, 139; types of, 255–256, 259, *260*, 264–267, *266*
Mut, 229–230

Narrative selves, 4
Nasal septum, piercing of, 19, *19*
Navels, 30, *32*
Nocturnal markings, 13, *14*
Nordenskiöld, Erland, 105

Ohl sign, 185–186, *187*, 188, *188*
1 Ajaw, 17, *18*, 204, *204*, 205
Optical stalk, 28, *29*
Overall body, 11–12, *13*, 64, 68

Palenque Triad, 17
Paris Codex, 233
Paz, Octavio, 1, 134, 277, 279
Peccary Skull from Tomb 1, Copan, Honduras, 81, *82*
Penises: of captives, 210, *211*, 213, *214*, 215, *215*, *216*; and clowning, 210, *210*; and sexuality, 40–41, *40*, *42*
Performances: and audiences, 256; categories of, 252; components of, 254–256; and markedness, 252; and puppeteers, 269; royal performances in deity costume, 66, 122, 261; and synesthesia, 252, 269; and trancelike state, 253, 270. *See also* Dance; Music
Pernet, Henry, 99
Personal names, 70
Plato, 73, 74, 134
Pohl, John, 163
Polished stone element, 67
Popol Vuh: and awakened deities, 254; and bird messengers, 231, 236; and captives, 205; and dances, 257; and emotions, 185, 199; and fasting, 130; and incense, 126; and music, 259–260; and 1 Ajaw, 205; and original creator, 127; and sight, 138, 167; and speech, 153, 228
Porter, James, 67
Portraiture: and Ajaw, 89, *90*; and identity, 100; and royal bodies, 8, 89, 101; and scarification, 76; and sight, 170; and *u-baah*, 64, *65*, 66, *66*
Pre-Columbian instruments, 3
Principal Bird Deity, 234, 236, 238, *239*, *240*, *241*, *242*, 251
Proskouriakoff, Tatiana, 59, 64, 143, 241
Pubic hair, 25, 41, 42, *42*
Pulque, 116–117, 120, *122*
Purifications, 130

Quetzalcoatl, 89, 91

Rabbits, 196, 198, *200*
Rabinal Achi, 225, 272
Radcliffe-Brown, Alfred, 181, 182
Radin, Paul, 98
Rape, 207–208, *208*, 218
Rasmussen, Susan, 205
Ratinlixul vase, 260, *261*
Reddy, William, 182
Reichel-Dolmatoff, Gerardo, 178
Ritual of the Bacabs, 231
Robertson, John, 9, 12
Roland, Alan, 58

Rosaldo, Michelle, 182
Rosaldo, Renato, 221
Royal spouses, 7, 43, 89
Royalty and royal bodies: and aesthetics, 45–47, *47*; and Ajaw, 89; and bloodletting, 27–28; and body theory, 4, 6–8; and breath, 147; captives as, 205, 226; and Egypt, 100; and emotions, 189, *189*, 278; and exposure of genitals, 215; and fastening of headbands, 62, *62*; and feasts, 7, 127, 128–129, *129*, 130, 133; and hearing, 156; imagining of, 7; and *k'uh*, 79, 81; and portraiture, 8, 89, 101; sanctified space around, 38, *39*; and smell, 141; and space and time, 5, 7, 78; and speech, 153; symbolic realm of, 7–8; and time, 81–89, 101; violation of, 28; and women, 52, *52*
Ruiz de Alarcón, Hernando, 79

Sáenz Throne, 241, *246*
Sahagún, Bernardino de, 143
Sapper, Karl, 117
Saturno, William, 36, 232
Saunders, Nicholas, 167
Scarification, 18, 19–22, *21*, 76
Schele, Linda, 24, 110
Schismogenesis, 100–101
Schivelbusch, Wolfgang, 116
Secrecy and the unsensed, 176–177
Sedgwick, Eve, 53
Seler, Eduard, 159–160
Self: and bodily matrix, 100; and comparative anthropology, 97, *98*; and corporeal fields, 79; dramaturgical theories of, 99–100; and ethnographic Maya evidence, 98–99; and imagery, 76–81; interior self/social person distinction, 97, 99; and intersubjectivity, 97–98; and Mayan languages, 60–61; and physical presence, 57
Self-image, 4, 5, 8
Self-sacrifice, and space and time, 89–96, 277
Semiotic communication, 100
Sennett, Richard, 138
Senses: conception of, 177–178, 278; distortion of, 178–179; and hearing, 139, 153–163; and moral valuation, 134, 173–175; nature of, 134–136, 177–179; as projective, 134; representations of, 138–139, *140*; secrecy and the unsensed, 176–177; and sight, 139, 163–173; and smell, 139, 141–152; and synesthesia, 134, 136–139, 178, 278; taste and touch, 139–141, 175–176
Sex and sexuality: abstinence in New Year, 130; and biological sex, 38–39, 51; and breasts, 42–43, 49; and captives, 38, 210, *211*, 213, *214*, 215–216, *215*, *216*, *217*; and Classic Maya body, 38–44; and dance, 268–269, *268*; and dishonor, 206, 207–219; and emotion, 190, 191–194, *195*, *196*, *197*, 198, 199, *208*; and enemas, 117, 122, 125; and female genitalia, 41, 42, *42*; ingestion compared to, 103; and male genitalia, 39–41; and marriage, 43–44, *44*, *45*; and older and younger men, 54; penises and clowning, 210, *210*; and sex act, 41–43, *43*, *44*; and touch, 175
Shrunken heads, *26*, 70, *71*
Sight: communion-oriented view of, 136; and extruded eyeballs, 166, *169*; and eyes as mirrors, 170; and glyphs, 170, 172–173, *172*; injurious concept of, 135–136; and moral valuation, 134, 173–175; projective nature of, 166–167, 169–170; recording of, 138; representations of, 163–164, 166, *168*; and senses, 134–135, 139, 163–173, 178; and synesthesia, 138; and *y-ichnal* expression, 173–175, *174*
Silverman, Lisa, 222
Simmel, Georg, 176–177
Skin: and body concepts, 12; and body paint, 22–25, *23*, *24*; of captives' genitals, 213, *214*; categorization of skin markings, 15–16; and clothing, 25–26; cutting/violation of, 27–28; and flayed faces, 21, *21*; and god markings, 16–17, *17*; and hair, 25–26, *26*; and IL mark, 17–18; rough skin, 16, *16*; and scarification, 18, 19–22, *20*, 76; and spots, 17, *18*; and tattooing, 18–22, *19*, *20*, *22*; wrinkles of aged gods and goddesses, 15, *16*, 49, 191, *195*
Skull racks, *71*, 72, 221, *222*
Smells: and burial rituals, 147, 149; and censers, 150, *151*; and nobles sniffing flowers, 3, 141; representation of, 141–143, *143*; and scent, 145, 147, *148*, 149–150, *150*, 152; and senses, 134–135, 139, 141–152, 178; and synesthesia, 138
Snuff bottles, 114–115
Social inequalities: and banquets, 102; and emotions, 200–201, 278; and homosexuality, 209; and speech, 229; and tributary lords, 247
Social skin, 6, 7
Social transactions, 103, 117
Solar symbolism, 87–89
Soul: and breath soul representations, 143, 145, *146*, 149, 150, 152, *152*, 154; butterfly as expression of, 150, *151*; and *k'uh*, 81; parts of, 79, 100; and personhood, 98
Sound. *See* Hearing

Space and time: and animate quality of day, 87–88; and body theory, 4–5; and concurrence of essences, 66, 274; and corporeal fields, 78–79; and emotions, 188; and measurement of space, 37–38; and royal bodies, 5, 7, 78; and self-sacrifice, 89–96, 277; and social distance, 37; and spatial locators, 38, *39*; time and bodies, 81–89

Speech: and birds as messengers, 229–234, *232*, *233*, *234*, 236, *236*, *237*, 238, 241–250, 278–279; and emotions, 200–201; formal speech, 227–229; index finger as sign of authoritative speech, 250, *250*; and lordly utterances, 153, 156, 200, 228; representations of, 139, *140*, 142, *145*, 147, 153–154, *155*; and song, 229

Speech scrolls: and birds, 232; and content and property of vocalizations, 154; and drums, 262, *264*; and glyphs, 160, 163, *164*; of monkey prelate worshiping frog Buddha, 137, *137*; and representation of speech, 139, *140*, *155*, 156, 163, *165*, 228, 229; and understanding, 153; and women, 229, *231*

Stefaniak, Regina, 52

Sterne, Laurence, 58

Stone, Andrea, 152

Storm God, 49, 74, *75*, 265, *266*, 267

Strathern, Marilyn, 58

Stross, Brian, 228

Stuart, David, 21, 130

Sun God: and birds, 233; and deity concurrence, 274; and food preparation, 110; and god markings, 17; and human hearts as food, 123, *125*; and *ik'* sign, 147; and rulership accoutrements, 87; and sight, 169, 170, *171*; and speech, 228, *230*

Supernaturals: and birds, 154, 231–233, *232*, *233*, 234, *234*, 235, 236, *236*, *237*, 238, *239*, *240*, 241, *243*, *245*; and blood as food, 132; breath of, 142, *145*; and captives, 123, *124*, 127; collective terms for, 188, *188*; and dance, 253, 270; and deity impersonation, 66, 122, 261, 270–276, *271*, *272*, *273*, *275*, 279; and emotions, 194, *197*, 198, *198*; and extruded eyeballs, 166, *169*; and floral realm, 150; and human hearts as food, 123, *125*, 126, 188, 232–233; and images of consumption, 127; and ingestion, 110, 117–118, *120*, 122–127, 228; and lust, 191; and music, 265; and *ohl* sign, 188; and repellant foods of evil beings, 122–123, *124*; and senses, 179; and sight, 170, *171*; smoke as food for, 125–127, *127*, *128*; speech of, 163, *166*, 228, *230*, 231

Sweatbaths, 117–118, *119*, 120, 175, 192, *197*

Symmetrical schismogenesis, 100–101

Synesthesia: and performances, 252, 269; and senses, 134, 136–139, 178, 278

Tablet of the Orator, 74, 75, *77*

Tablet of the Scribe, 74, *77*

Tamal (tamale), 104, 108, 110, 113, *114*, 123

Taste and touch, 138, 139, 141, 175–176, 178

Tattooing, 18–22, *19*, *20*, *22*

Taube, Karl, 22, 67, 110, 244

Techniques of the body, 5–6

Tezcatlipoca, 89

Thompson, Eric, 105, 111, 130, 229–230, 260

Timocracies, 202–203, 204, 209, 213, 222

Tobacco: and breath, 114, 143; and cigar smoking, 116; containers for, 114–115, *114*, *115*, 116; and enemas, 105–106; frequent consumption of, 115–116; and grinding palettes, 115; as ingestible, 105, 107, 114; medicinal uses of, 105; and snuff bottles, 114–115

Torso, 28–30, 183

Tortillas, 104, 108

Tozzer, Alfred, 21

Tribute: animals bringing food tribute, 108, *110*; cacao beans as, 108, 241–242, *246*; captives as, 243; feathery backrack as, *246*, *249*; food as, 108, *109*; and messengers, 242–244, *246*, 247, *247*, *248*, *249*, 251, 278; and tributary lords, 244–248, *248*, *249*, 273

Turner, Terence, 130

Turner, Victor, 253

Turtle, 95, *97*, 186, *187*, 188, 265

Tylor, Edward, 2–3

Urcid, Javier, 163

Vatel, Jean-François, 176

Vermeule, Emily, 231

Vitality: and breath, 228; and Classic Maya body, 33–35, *36*, *37*, 49; and floral devices, 147; and imagery, 72–76, 97; objects possessing essence of, 247, 252

Vogt, Evon, 228, 265

Vomiting god, 117, *120*

Ware, Gene, 244, 247

Wartofsky, Mark, 135

Watson, James, 205

Weiss, Gail, 8

Whisper effects, 163

Whistles, 3, 266–267

Wilbert, Johannes, 106

Wind God, 18, 150, *152*, 229, 274
Winged emissaries, 17
Winik, 11–12, *12*, 39, 58–59, *59*, 81, 277
Wisdom, Charles, 41, 177
Wittgenstein, Ludwig, 97–98
Women: and administration of enemas, 117, *118*, 122; aged women, 16, 48; and Ajaw day signs, 89, *91*; and ancestors, 50–51; and *bakab* title, 62; and bestiality, 191, *195*; and body paint, 23; as captives, 207–209, *208*; clothing of, *54*, 56; and curing and healing, 118; economic autonomy of, 110; and fasting, 131; female touching blade, 216, *218*; and food preparation, 102, 107, 110, *111*; as food vendors, 110, *111*; hair of, 25; and lack of god markings, 17; and Maize God, 208, *208*; and mourning, 195; perspective of, 54, 56; and rape, 207–208, *208*; and royal bodies, 52, *52*; and speech scrolls, 229, *231*; status of, 51–53; and tattooing, 19, 20, *20*; as template for vulnerability, 206; terms for, 39; as *winik*, 59
Writing, 137–138, 229, *231*

Y-ichnal expression, 173–175, *174*
Year bundling, 85, *86*, *88*
Yohl-tahnil (heart/mind), 183, *184*
Youth, 48, 49–50, *50*, 191, *194*, 210–211, 247, 269–270. *See also* Age

Zender, Marc, 130